# A Burning and a Shining Light

## ENGLISH SPIRITUALITY
## IN THE AGE OF WESLEY

JOHN WESLEY FIELD PREACHING
From an engraving by Fry, after a painting by Bland (1765).

# A Burning
## and a
# Shining Light

ENGLISH SPIRITUALITY IN THE
AGE OF WESLEY

*Edited by*
David Lyle Jeffrey

WILLIAM B. EERDMANS PUBLISHING COMPANY
Grand Rapids, Michigan

*For Bruce, Kirstin, and Adrienne*

**Library of Congress Cataloging-in-Publication Data**

A Burning and a shining light.

1. Spiritual life.   2. Evangelicalism — England.
   I. Jeffrey, David L., 1941-
II.  Title: English spirituality in the age of Wesley.
BV4500.B84     1986     248′.0942     86-29085

ISBN 0-8028-0234-6

# Contents

# Illustrations

# Preface

The purpose of this anthology is to provide an introduction for the general reader to some of the best of English spiritual writing in the age of the Great Evangelical Revival, from Watts to Wilberforce. It contains for the most part complete shorter texts, including devotional works by the Nonconformist pastor-writers Isaac Watts and Philip Doddridge as well as the Independent laywoman and nationally known literary figure, Elizabeth Rowe. At the other end of the ecclesiastical spectrum, high Anglicanism finds its voice in the contemplative, William Law—whose challenge to Christlike conduct stirred a complacent state church—and, in a unique way, in the charismatic poet Christopher Smart. The "Methodist" movement within the Church of England, itself indebted to both of these traditions, is exemplified in the writings of John and Charles Wesley, George Whitefield, and John Fletcher. These, in turn, provide a bridge forward to the evangelical Anglicanism represented here by John Newton and three of the most luminous laypersons to fall under his own pastoral shepherding, the poet and hymn writer, William Cowper, the feminist poet, dramatist, and educational theorist, Hannah More, and the great evangelical statesman, William Wilberforce.

Most of these men and women knew each other and worked and associated across denominational lines throughout the century. Their spiritual writings include not only sermons and tracts but also thoughtful, meditative devotional works, hymns, poetry, and pastoral letters on every aspect of the inner life from daily prayer to the most practical consequences of gospel obedience.

For almost all of these writers (even the reclusive Law), a spirituality which did not have its manifest social dimension in works of mercy was not fully Christian. The "experimental knowledge of Jesus Christ" to which they were called led them to active personal concern for the reformation of social institutions such as prisons and asylums and for the abolition of social evils such as slavery. They founded charitable societies of all sorts to minister to the poor, the infirm, the needy, the outcast and forgotten; they established clinics, orphanages, charity schools, and halfway houses for prostitutes. In this age, evangelicals were in fact the leaders in social reform, and we see in them how a deep inner experience of grace has its natural outworking in a Christlike commitment to the wounded and broken world.

Yet these were not themselves alabaster saints. From the greatest to the least, they were in fact broken vessels. Part of the encouragement we have in reading them comes in our recognition that the real worker of revival, then as now, is the Holy Spirit. As is always true of human instruments, these were "not that Light, but sent to bear witness to the Light." In that they were willing to be instruments, even in their brokenness, it may however be said of them, as it was of John the Baptist, that they became as "a burning and a shining light" to their own and subsequent generations.

The editorial principles I have followed in this volume may be briefly summarized as follows. I have maintained the original texts of all poems and hymns, usually as printed in the earliest corrected edition. I have, however, silently modernized the punctuation and spelling in some prose selections for the sake of the modern reader, and have also, though more rarely, changed awkward syntax. For the same reason I have, in some instances, exchanged now obsolete words and certain archaisms with modern equivalents, rather than create an elaborate system of philological footnotes. As far as possible, texts printed are complete units, though these are sometimes chapters from larger works; in instances where some attenuation has still seemed desirable for economy's sake, elisions are clearly marked. To aid the reader in appreciating the structure or content of some longer pieces, I have provided section headings. Standard modern editions as found in the bibliography have been consulted as a check on the original eighteenth-century texts.

The desire to explore these writings quickened while I was an undergraduate at Wheaton College in a course with Erwin Rudolph, who was at that time preparing his study of William Law, and was further sparked at Princeton in conversations with Louis A. Landa and Lawrence Lipking. Subsequently, I have profited from lively exchanges with my friend and former colleague, Leo Damrosch, and my brother Grant R. Jeffrey.

But I am indebted also to the instruction or support of many others. Among them I want especially to acknowledge the staff of the Rare Book Room in the Cambridge University Library, Mrs. Marie-Anne Orbay of the University of Ottawa Inter-Library Loan Service, and Mr. Jeremy Palin, Special Collections Librarian of Carleton University, for their patient and thoughtful assistance. Among my colleagues, Frans de Bruyn and April London also made helpful answer to what must have seemed odd inquiries.

I owe most of all to the loyal enthusiasm—and scrutiny—of my wife Katherine. Both as a church historian and as a kindly critic of my prose, she has shared in this project from beginning to end, helping to make it much better than it could otherwise have been.

# Introduction

## THE AGE OF WESLEY

*In a deep and wooded Yorkshire dale long golden beams of the late afternoon sun glide down over the western copse, slanting through massive and broken stone arches in multiple paths of shadow and light. Only the occasional call of a pheasant or whir of a woodcock breaks the stillness.*

*On the hillside up above, just beyond the crest of carefully manicured terraces and lawns, there is a sudden murmuring of voices, tinkling of teacups, and the sound of the moving of chairs. Elegantly dressed men and women rise from their garden confections and begin slowly to drift toward the very edge of the vale. They look down at last on an old ruin below—the almost breathtakingly massive remains of the once great abbey church of Rievaulx. It is like looking into another world. Nodding and exchanging comfortable words, they muse about the "gothic spirit" and admire a vista which is to them a kind of epitome of tasteful landscape.*

*Once this was a hospice in the wilderness, where on the cold flat stones of the open choir the humble abbot Aelred and his medieval brethren knelt to work out their salvation in fear and trembling, then rose to serve and love their God in the community of his faithful. Now it is part of the grounds of a luxurious estate, providing for privileged lords and ladies such an experience as their culture has bred them for, a taste of what the aestheticians of their time call the "sublime." They do not know anything about the abbot, or the spiritual life of Rievaulx. To them this is merely the occasion for a pleasant mood, an evocative relic of mysterious bygone ages of superstition and monkish darkness.*

*Behind, there is another clinking of silver and fine china as servants clear away tables from beneath the smooth stone columns of the imitation Roman temple, a fashionable adornment of this new and (the guests assure each other of this as they promenade slowly back up the terrace) more "rational" time. This is the "Augustan age" of British civilization, a gathering from other ruins of the opulence that once was Rome—Rome at its height—and an emulation of that very Roman decadence out of which the abbot's Christianity had struggled to survive, rise, and reach northward to England and Rievaulx.*

*All of these fine figures—periwigged and powdered, ruffled with lace, and impeccable in buckles, jewels, and silks—are members of the Established Church. Most consider themselves Christian as a matter of form, if nothing else. One or two like to think of themselves as Deists (or humanists), having risen above superstition altogether. All have what they like to call "polite" views of religion. None goes to church, except on occasions of state and high holiday. Yet among them, as patrons, they hold the right to appoint clergy in more than a score of*

*parish churches in various parts of England—and find it convenient thus to have*
*repositories for less successful members of their families and connections.*

### Established Authority and the "Rule of Reason"

Enlightenment England was tolerant of stark economic contrasts and
shocking political contradictions, and it cultivated genteel hypocrisy.
This was the so-called "Age of Reason," and what were considered to be
rational models from a classical past now furnished patterns for the regulation of nature and human nature alike. The goal of a great landscape
architect (such as Capability Brown, who with hundreds of men, mules,
and wagons, created the artificially symmetrical hills, lagoons, and lakes
of Blenheim Palace and other estates) was not essentially different from
that of the writer; both called their business "nature improved" or, as the
poet Alexander Pope put it, "nature methodized."[1] This was a culture as
suspicious of personal inspiration as it was evasive of candid passions; a
poet or painter in this milieu was not an "inspired" artist or a "born"
genius (*poeta nascit*), but a carefully tutored product, imitating accepted
convention (*poeta fecit*). So too in matters religious; the proper attitude, if
one was to have thoughts on the subject at all, was that of *religio fecit,*
decorum well authenticated by custom, temperate in manner, and officially sanctioned. Any claim to individual spiritual experiences, any pretense to vision, or any excess of zeal ("enthusiasm") was eschewed as
irrational and vulgar—even socially dangerous. The definition of religious extravagance was codified by the Enlightenment philosopher
John Locke, for whom any unverifiable presumption of personal revelation or divine calling was to be deplored and "any extraordinary signs"
seen as delusory. "Reason," he said, "must be our last judge and guide in
everything."[2]

In fact, reason was the ultimate guide and judge in almost nothing,
even where most laboriously invoked, to rationalize its failure. Yet the
notion that it had somehow eclipsed faith, as science eclipsed superstition,
had already helped bring about a massive decline in national religious life.
Rationalism had reinforced the moderationism of the Established
Church, which for political as well as spiritual reasons became highly
intolerant of any form of visible spirituality. After the collapse of the
Puritan Commonwealth and the restoration of the monarchy with
Charles II in 1660, the Church became effectively a department of state.
Both Puritans on the left and Catholics and Anglo-Catholics on the right
were driven out of the Church with vindictive ferocity.

First, there were laws making it effectively illegal for anyone to receive
communion except in an Anglican church. These were followed by a

political revision of the Book of Common Prayer which made loyalty to
the monarchy an article of faith and Christian obedience (1662); then
came the Act of Uniformity in the same year, making it unlawful to seek
any reform of the constitution of church or state, and requiring all clergy
to take an oath of allegiance to these terms. Nearly two thousand rectors
and vicars refused, and were ejected from their pastorates without compensation. Many eminent pastors and scholars, including Richard Baxter, Isaac Watts (father of the hymn writer), both grandfathers of the
Wesleys, and lay teachers such as John Bunyan were among those disen-
franchised, and often imprisoned, to a total of one-fifth of the English
clergy. Worse, those driven out were, as the Anglican historian J. R.
Green observes, "the most learned" of the clergy, who "from the time of
the Reformation had played the most active and popular part in the life of
the Church."[3]

Denied their churches, these people began to meet in homes. The
enraged state party immediately instituted the Conventicle Act (1664)
which "punished with fine, imprisonment and transportation [i.e., to
penal colonies abroad] all persons who met in greater numbers than five."
When the determined pastors organized groups of five and worked
around the clock to serve them, the fury of the government expressed
itself in the Five Mile Act (1665), which provided a penalty of more than
one year's salary and six months in jail for any who so much as approached within five miles of any town, borough, or parish in which they
had previously taught or preached.[4]

But the authorities were not finished. Prodded by a king and royal
party notorious for unprecedented licentiousness and corruption (John
Wesley wrote of Charles II that "Bloody Mary was a lamb, a mere dove,
in comparison of him"),[5] the Puritans, Baptists, Presbyterians, Independents, Quakers, and any Anglicans who would not swear absolute allegiance were, with Catholics, systematically excluded from the universi-
ties, denied any form of public employment, and driven out of "polite
society."

In 1685, Charles died. His son, James Stuart, declaring himself a Catholic, ascended the throne as James II. Among those most enthusiastic
about his ascent was the other notable force among active believers within
the Anglican communion, the Tory and Anglo-Catholic wing of the
Established Church. These persons were sacramentalist, committed to
the inner life of piety, and sympathetic to others of Catholic persuasion.
Though few in number, they were joined by those who simply believed
in a natural succession of monarchs in warmly welcoming the new king.
And it was not long before panic began to spread through the latitudinarian and Whig state party and its official church hierarchy. Pressure

began to mount on James, under which he finally abdicated the throne (1688), fleeing to France for his life. A Dutchman, William of Orange, was acquired to sit on the throne and to forestall what seemed the threat of revolution. In 1689, the state cause emerged on top, without any military struggle, and immediately a new purge began. The Oath of Allegiance was now directed at "Jacobites," or supporters of the ousted James. Eight bishops and four hundred clergy refused to subscribe on grounds of conscience, and on February 1, 1690, all were ejected from their parishes without compensation. Among these "nonjurors," as the new outcasts were called, were Bishop Ken, the hymn writer, and later William Law, who lost his fellowship at Cambridge because of his convictions. John Wesley's mother, Susannah Wesley, was a firm supporter of the nonjuror cause, even though it prompted her husband to separate from her for several months. The succession issue divided the nation and kept it in almost constant fear of civil war for much of the first half of the eighteenth century. But it also ensured that by the time Isaac Watts was in his first ministry and John Wesley was a boy at school, the Church of England was a spiritually flightless bird; shorn of both left and right wings, it nevertheless prided itself in having "both feet on the ground" and attempted to make its own heaven of an increasingly muddy earth.

Part of this muddiness was intellectual, and one of its expressions was a kind of philosophical humanism called Deism. It became the "enlightened" person's substitute for a scripturally based faith, and it attracted many from the nominalist middle of the Established Church. Taking some of their inspiration from the idealist rationalism of John Locke, especially in his book *The Reasonableness of Christianity* (1695), subsequent writings such as John Toland's *Christianity Not Mysterious* (1696), Thomas Woolston's *Discourses on the Miracles of Christ* (1727–29), and Matthew Tindal's *Christianity as Old as the Creation* (1730) attacked biblical prophecies, New Testament miracles, and the divinity of Jesus and were widely acclaimed within polite society as works of impressive scholarship by reasonable men.[6] For many, including Lord Shaftesbury and the Catholic-born Alexander Pope, deistic antibiblicism was a badge of intelligence and fashionable good taste.[7]

Another element of the muddiness of the time was moral, gross carnality on a scale that even today makes appalling reading for most of us. From the reign of Charles II, whose mistresses, illegitimate children, court orgies, and wholesale and predatory debauchery indeed recalled Roman times, down through the middle of the eighteenth century, the private behavior of much of upper-class English society was luridly carnal and politically corrupt. In many of its privileged devotees, such a life created all the usual diseases of dissipation, and behind the elegant veneer of official society and the brass ormolu of its politics lay much dry rot—

social, psychological, and spiritual. On great country estates, magnificent palaces in the Augustan (new Roman) style were built at fabulous cost. Here, in fresco-painted halls supported by marble columns and adorned with neoclassical art treasures, the wealthy wined, dined, caroused, and idled their lives away. Their quest for innovative entertainment produced grotesque excess: Lord Francis Dashwood (who with Benjamin Franklin revised the Book of Common Prayer for American Episcopal use), for example, presided over one of many "Hell Fire Clubs." He had underground caves and grottoes beneath his palace at West Wyckham in which he held satanic orgies by torchlight; participants attired as medieval monks debauched young girls brought in for the occasion dressed as nuns.[8]

Nor did this sort of behavior go without the tacit approval and even participation of the Established clergy. Many of them had an abundance of idle time on their hands. Lesser scions of noble families held "pluralities"—the earnings of several parishes at once without serving in any, except through hired deputies who were paid starvation wages. Better placed members of the privileged classes could expect bishoprics, at about two hundred times the salary of a parish priest, which were given out as part of the system of political patronage.[9] Few of these men were true shepherds; most were indolent and many entirely dissolute. Bishops often kept grand houses in London, in which they hosted a constant round of parties for the social elite. Hannah More, who knew many of the least worldly of these prelates, offers in a letter to one of her sisters an insight into one of the more polite gatherings of her clerical acquaintances:

> On Monday I was at a very great assembly at the Bishop of St. Asaph's. Conceive to yourself one hundred and fifty or two hundred people met together, dressed in the extremity of fashion; painted as red as bacchanals; poisoning the air with perfumes; treading on each other's gowns; making the crowd the blame; not one in ten able to get a chair; protesting they are engaged to ten other places; and lamenting the fatigue they are not obliged to endure; ten or a dozen card tables crammed with dowagers of quality, grave ecclesiastics and yellow admirals; and you have an idea of an assembly. I never go to these things when I can possibly avoid it, and stay when there as few minutes as I can.[10]

More extreme indulgence was regrettably common, as in the case of Fredrick Cornwallis, seventh son of Lord Cornwallis and archbishop of Canterbury from 1768 to 1783. After scheming, conniving, bullying, and bribing his way to the top ecclesiastical office in the land, his notoriety for orgiastic "routs and feastings"—genuine bacchanalia—became a national scandal. The virtuous Lady Huntingdon, patroness to many of the evangelical preachers represented in this volume, joined many of the latitudinarian bishops and their confederates in appealing to the archbishop to desist, but entirely without success. Finally King George III had to admonish him officially for his "vain dissipations" and threaten his recall.[11]

The practical result of the expulsion of genuine spiritual leadership from the Church and of the nearly complete corruption of its administrative hierarchy was a wholesale neglect of spiritual life at the parish level. H. C. G. Moule, bishop of Durham in the early part of our century, reflects concerning this time:

> The churches in London and the large cities continued to be all but empty. . . . Addison [the hymn writer] pronounced it to be an unquestionable truth that there was less appearance of religion in England than in any neighbouring state, whether Protestant or Catholic. And Montesquieu declared that "there was no religion in England—that the subject if mentioned in society excited nothing but laughter."[12]

When, with the rise of the evangelical movement, some of these churches began to be filled, the official hierarchy expressed predictable alarm, fueled by almost paranoid speculation concerning the possible consequences. (It is of no incidental significance for an understanding of Establishment opposition to the revival that leaders such as John and Charles Wesley, for example, were known to have sprung from a lineage deep in both Puritan and Jacobite wings of English Christianity.)

Those in authority looked for every possible weapon by which to repress any popular threat to their dominance. One of the best which lay to hand seemed to be the "rule of reason," with its classical standards of "taste" and "judgment"—in practice merely a codification of conventional habits. This they aimed at the "enthusiasm" of the new converts to evangelicalism, as though they thought themselves learned Augustan philosophers defending the state against an invasion of insane barbarians.[13] Typical was Archbishop Drummond of York, who on coming to investigate an evangelical Anglican priest at Helmsley in 1760 and listening to his sermon, accosted him afterward in the street, shouting, "if you go on preaching such stuff you will drive all your parish mad! Were you to inculcate the morality of Socrates, it would do more good than canting about the new birth."[14] "Madness" was thus the charge most often levied against any sort of serious and outspoken Christianity, and it is certain that many were locked up in insane asylums for life simply for preaching or declaring their faith openly. The unhappy fortunes of Christopher Smart (though in his case there was also some apparently genuine emotional disturbance) offer a grim insight into this type of persecution. "Reason" became at once the arch enemy of visible faith and the shibboleth of a dead religion.

THE SLEEPING CONGREGATION
Engraving by William Hogarth (1736). The satirically exposed text is Matthew 11:28.

GIN LANE
Engraving by Hogarth (1751).

## Poverty and Misrule

Within the shadow of polite society and yet untouched by the myth of
reason, London seethed with other life—the miserable existence of the
ordinary poor. From a variety of economic causes, the cities had been
growing; the capital itself more than doubled in Wesley's lifetime. Many,
coming in hope from rural poverty, looked for respectable work in vain.

Adequate housing could not be built fast enough, nor was there sufficient purchasing power among those who most needed the shelter. Deteriorated tenements in rat-infested districts were operated by slum lords and ruled by an often vicious underworld. Prostitution, gambling, "gaming" establishments offering the systematic torture of animals as entertainment, pickpocketing and more serious felonies, and a prodigious traffic in alcohol were among the most evident preoccupations of the urban poor.[15]

The disease of alcoholism was endemic. Hogarth's engraving entitled "Gin Lane" offers all too realistic a portrait of the depredation wrought upon the urban populace especially by the huge trade in spirits. It was perhaps, as W. E. H. Lecky called it, "the *master curse* of English life."[16] England had always been a beer drinking country; in 1688, with a population of slightly more than five million, the national consumption was more than twelve and a half million barrels, or about 90 gallons for every man, woman, and child. But gin was something far more serious. In 1750, the consumption of gin—poorly distilled and often virtually poisonous—was eleven million gallons. Some idea of the total debilitation wrought by this plague may be imagined in terms of simple items of record: in this same year, of 2,000 houses in the St. Giles, Holburn, district of London, 506—one quarter—were gin shops. Even in Westminster every eighth house had been turned into a gin outlet. Henry Fielding, the novelist and magistrate, reckoned in alarm that gin was "the principal sustenance (if it may be called) of 100,000 people" in London.[17]

Within the rising merchant class, loansharking, smuggling, embezzlement, stock frauds, and investment in the gin trade were among the activities which helped to reinforce and maintain social evils in all classes. The worst of these evils was the slave trade, in which abomination England became the undisputed international leader after 1713, and from which it thereafter derived fabulous wealth. This cruel degradation of human life, in which people were treated more viciously than most Western societies now tolerate treatment of animals, created a hell on earth more grotesque in its brutality than can be described here in detail. Suffice it to say that by 1750 British ships were carrying off nearly fifty thousand slaves each year to British plantations abroad with about a third of that number perishing of cruelty and starvation enroute or in their first year in the Americas. Concerning a slave ship such as the one on which John Newton served, the *Annual Register* for 1762 records this first-hand report:

> On Friday the men slaves being very sullen and unruly, having had no sustenance of any kind for forty-eight hours except a dram, we put one half of the strongest of them in irons. On Saturday and Sunday all hands, night and day, could scarce keep the ship clear, and were con-

stantly under arms. On Monday morning many of the slaves had got out of irons, and were attempting to break up the gratings; and the seamen not daring to go down the hold to clear our pumps, we were obliged, for the preservation of our lives, to kill fifty of the ringleaders and stoutest of them. It is impossible to describe the misery the poor slaves underwent, having had no fresh water for five days. Their dismal cries and shrieks, and most frightful looks, added a great deal to our misfortune; four of them were found dead, and one drowned herself in the hold.[18]

This "legitimate business" grew so rapidly within the next three decades that in the years between 1783 and 1796 alone, while William Wilberforce was rallying support in his spiritual warfare against the political and business forces which practiced it, more than eight hundred thousand slaves were transported from Africa to the New World plantations—most of them in British ships.[19] And it is unfortunate, but necessary to report, that not all of the evangelical leaders were free of involvement in this terrible traffic. George Whitefield purchased and owned slaves, as did Lady Selina, countess of Huntingdon, even as Wesley and others of their number were crying out in the name of Christ for abolition.[20]

Rome indeed. If the evangelical reformers of this period denounced various social evils in what now seem to us extreme terms, we must remember that the England of their day was for them as Rome itself was for St. Jerome or St. Augustine—a den of iniquity so vast and so rationalized in its habits and appetites that only a call to radical purity could make clarity of the confusion. Not for them the convenient dictum of Alexander Pope, "whatever is, is right."[21] Rather, they saw virtually the whole order of society, despite its reigning myths, as under a tyrannous depravity. It became central to their calling to proclaim it so, and to observe of the obviously acquiescent Establishment that the emperor had no clothes. This fearless denunciation of social mores as much as the doctrine of the new birth aroused the furious opposition they met from landed gentry and state church hierarchy alike.

When an open air preacher like George Whitefield could gather thirty thousand of the London poor for a sermon in Kensington Common, and comparable numbers at Moorfields (1742), there were of course reasons for the Establishment to fear the winds of revolution might be building for a storm. But what the Establishment could not see was that the maverick evangelist and his colleagues were only the most visible manifestations of a profoundly spiritual revolution, the scope and consequences of which would not be fully known for years to come. For all across the British Isles, in America, in every class and corner of society a more mysterious wind was beginning to blow, softly but surely.

## Revival and Reform

*Out in the beautiful English countryside, in a manor house and estate in many respects reminiscent of the one overlooking Rievaulx, it is evening, a pleasant evening, in which a formal candlelit dinner has just given way to conversation in the paneled drawing room. Someone is playing the harpsichord for the entertainment of family and guests. Several are joined in discussion, and the subject is religion. In a corner, seated at a window and listening to both, is an attractive and serious-looking young woman. Her name is Selina Shirley; she is soon to be wife to Earl Hastings, Lord Huntingdon. Since about nine years of age, she has been quietly but intensely praying for a deepening of her spiritual life, and for a good man to be her husband. Both prayers are about to be answered, but in the context of an unexpected call to tumultuous public responsibiity.*

### A Tower of Strength

The life of Lady Selina, countess of Huntingdon (1707–1791) was coextensive with the eighteenth-century revival movement and is an exemplary witness to the evident provision of the Holy Spirit for the work he was about to do. Born into one of the most eminent of English families and married into another, she was an important member of the very class which had created many of the most regrettable features of eighteenth-century society. Her own early spiritual spark was fanned into full flame by the preaching of men like George Whitefield and Benjamin Ingham and by the witness of her sister-in-law, Lady Margaret Hastings, herself converted under Ingham. She persuaded her husband to accompany her to meetings in the Fetter Lane Chapel, the Moravian meetinghouse where some of the early Methodists gathered with the Moravians for worship and teaching. She and her husband became important supporters of the chapel, and until John Wesley withdrew with some followers in 1740 in a difference of spiritual opinion with the more quietistic Moravians, she was regularly in attendance at its meetings.

From 1742, Lady Huntingdon frequently invited Charles and John Wesley as well as others among their followers to visit her home at Donnington Park and to preach to members of the aristocracy she had assembled there for that purpose. During this same period she commenced her acquaintance with Isaac Watts, who was the permanent houseguest of her friend, another noblewoman of evangelical convictions, Lady Abney. Shortly after the death of her two sons by smallpox, in 1744, she met and became fast friends also with Philip Doddridge, another clergyman of the Dissenting tradition to whom she regularly turned for spiritual counsel until Doddridge's death a few years later.

This was the period of the so-called Jacobite uprising precipitated by the landing in Scotland of the grandson of James II, Bonnie Prince Charlie. The genuine threat of revolution and of the renewed ascendancy of a Catholic monarchy led to the battle at Culloden (1745) in which the Scottish forces were defeated. But fears of Jacobite or pro-Catholic sentiments continued to be rampant. Typically anyone who seemed to command popular support was seen as a threat to the government. It was commonly reported in the press that the Wesleys and Whitefield were "Papists," even Jesuits in disguise, as the caricatures of Methodism and of Whitefield in particular by Hogarth suggest (note the tonsure under Whitefield's flying wig). It was rumored, moreover, that John Wesley hid Catholic priests in his house, and that, supplied with funds from Spain, he would join a Spanish invasion force supporting Bonnie Prince Charlie with twenty thousand men. Under this kind of pressure Wesley finally felt it necessary to publish and present a form of oath of loyalty to the king in the name of "the Societies in derision called Methodists."[22] But the opprobrium continued to attach itself to the movement, its friends, and its supporters, including Lady Huntingdon, for decades. After two generations, genuine religious convictions of any kind from Puritan to Catholic were still seen as a threat to the ruling classes: the academy of Philip Doddridge (some of whose congregation had fallen on the *English* side at Culloden) was charged with support for Catholic insurgency; Charles Wesley was accused of treason by virtue of his prayers for Prince Charles; other Methodists were threatened with imprisonment or execution. Every week Establishment pulpits denounced evangelicals of all sorts as Jesuits, seducers, and Catholic propagandists. As a result, Methodist preachers, all of whom were Anglicans and most of whom were ordained in that church, were finally forced to take refuge with the Dissenters under the dubiously titled "Toleration Act" (thus effectively becoming Dissenters in law if not by calling) in order to be safe from persecution. Eventually Lady Huntingdon herself was obliged to do the same (1772), taking with her most of her many Anglican chaplains.[23]

After her husband's death in 1746, Lady Huntingdon devoted herself utterly to support of the growing revival. She did this in a variety of ways, not least of which was the contribution of more than a hundred thousand pounds in her lifetime to support laypreachers, ordained pastors, schools, and a seminary college at Trevecca in Wales and to alleviate the suffering of the needy poor. In a time when many parishes paid an annual salary of forty pounds, this was a prodigious sum. But it is also clear that she provided for many years invaluable political protection for many of the evangelical leaders and less well known pastoral servants of the movement. This she achieved by exercising one of the rights so often abused by members of her class—purchasing advowsons and appointing evangelical clergymen to them—and by extension of another—the peer's right to appointment of private Anglican chaplains. Among the most

LADY SELINA, COUNTESS OF HUNTINGDON
(c. 1780)

## ENTHUSIASM DELINEATED

Engraving by Hogarth (1761). This satire on Methodism was dedicated to the archbishop of Canterbury. The preacher, modeled on George Whitefield, has a harlequin's robe under his surplice, and the tonsure of a Jesuit is exposed by his falling wig. His collection of puppets includes Adam and Eve, and Peter with his key pulling at Paul's hair, as well as Moses and Aaron. The text is 2 Corinthians 11:22 ("I speak as a fool"), and the thermometer which hangs in place of the usual hourglass indicates audience response, from lukewarm to convulsive fits, madness, and despair. The hymn text hanging from the lectern is "Only love to us be given," by Whitefield.

notable of those under her protection were George Whitefield, Howell Harris, John Fletcher, John Berridge, Henry Venn, William Romaine, Augustus Toplady, Martin Madan, and Thomas Haweis. But the list is long, as is that of the more than forty chapels she founded and built all over England and Wales.[24] She sent out and supported her own servant David Taylor as a Baptist preacher and was a friend of Abraham Booth, the "Particular Baptist" whose book, *The Reign of Grace,* she distributed widely. She was a constant source of support to some of the most prominent leaders of the revival, who called her "a mother in our Israel." She ran interference for them, as for some of the Dissenters, in difficulties political and ecclesiastical. She knew personally every figure represented in this volume, from Watts to Wilberforce, save the two poets, Cowper and Smart. Above all she was a prayer warrior, supporting every aspect of the work of the Spirit in her time which she could identify. Much of this, as Doddridge suggests in a letter to his wife, remained of course hidden from public view:

> Lady Huntingdon is quite a mother to the poor; she visits them and prays with them in their sickness; and they leave their children to her for a legacy when they die, and she takes care of them. I was really astonished at the traces of religion I discovered in her . . . and cannot but glorify God for her. More cheerfulness I never saw intermingled with devotion.[25]

Yet, while not herself a writer or evangelist, she was a central figure among those raised up to specific responsibility in the revival, and it is not difficult to see in retrospect how crucial was her role. As her chief biographer puts it, "wherever she was called by the providence of God she was acknowledged as 'a burning and a shining light' "[26]—the singular praise which occurs again and again in the tributes paid in that century to persons of acknowledged spiritual leadership.

### A Perfection of Weakness

It is not possible to include in these few introductory pages even a brief history of the revival.[27] Indeed, it is not possible to represent more than a few of the most significant preachers and writers in the readings which follow. A more complete collection might include, for example, the Welsh evangelist Griffith Jones, an Anglican clergyman who had begun itinerant preaching in Wales two decades before Wesley and Whitefield and who founded "circulating schools" by which he taught thousands to read the Bible in Welsh. One of his converts, Daniel Rowlands, was another important Welsh evangelist and later an assistant to Wesley. Howell Harris, whom Whitefield called "a burning and a shining light" in Wales, was another anticipator of the preaching of the Wesleys and

Whitefield; most of his spiritual writings have been neglected because they were published in Welsh. Among the best known evangelical Anglicans, John Berridge was a powerful preacher and spiritual leader, Henry Venn, Augustus ("Rock of Ages") Toplady, William Romaine, and Thomas Haweis were notable pastors, Edwin Perronet ("All Hail the Power"), Thomas Olivers ("The God of Abraham Praise"), Martin Madan, and William Williams ("Guide Me O Thou Great Jehovah") were celebrated preachers and hymn writers. Charles Simeon, who was encouraged by Newton and who from his parish church of Holy Trinity, Cambridge, did so much to direct the tide of evangelical Anglicanism forward into the next century, became a preacher of considerable power and an organizer with vision like that of Wesley and Lady Huntingdon.[28] John Cennick, who began as an assistant to Whitefield, was a saintly man and exceptional preacher who later joined the Moravian Church, becoming its principal indigenous leader in England. The Baptist writer Abraham Booth and the fine writer of Anglican meditative spirituality, James Hervey,[29] also merit consideration in a volume of this kind, yet with regret I have had to pass them over.

This was a period abundant in fruits of the spiritual life and replete with evidence that the Spirit was widely at work—before, beyond, and after the principal leaders we normally associate with the revival. In a pattern indicative of the whole period, four of these leaders who were later to be mutually associated were independently converted between Easter and Pentecost of 1735. Tavern boy Whitefield, clergyman Rowland, surveyor Cennick, and schoolteacher Harris—all of them wrestling inwardly toward salvation—were almost simultaneously raised up to a common calling.[30] Of these conversions only one came by way of contact with the Methodist movement, though all were to be leaders in it at some point.

It is also inescapable—and perhaps typical of divine irony—that many of these chosen instruments were themselves imperfect vessels. Something of this will be evident in the introductions to the individual writers which follow. But a brief look at the life of Martin Madan (1726–1790) will illustrate much.

Like Lady Huntingdon, though at a less auspicious level, Madan was a member of a noteworthy family and independently wealthy. Though proficient in Latin, Greek, and Hebrew, his principal study had been law, and he was, in his early twenties, already a practicing London lawyer with some promise. One night he was idling with some of his companions in a coffee house when the group hit upon an idea for some novel diversion. One had heard that John Wesley was preaching nearby. Madan, a noted mimic, was urged to go to hear Wesley and then to return and imitate his "manner and discourse" as a crown to the evening's entertainment. Off went Madan in pursuit of amusement, but just as he entered the hall Wesley was declaring his text, "Prepare to meet thy God!" and Madan was somewhat sobered by the force of it. He sat down and grew more sober still as the preacher exhorted his audience to repentance. When he returned later to his "midnight modern conversation" at the coffee house, he was asked whether he had "taken off the old Methodist." He replied, "No, gentlemen, but he has taken me off." From that time he left his old friends and sought means of growth for his newly awakened spiritual life.

Madan soon came to the attention of Lady Huntingdon who, with William Romaine and others, persuaded him to leave law for the ministry. He needed no salary, had full academic qualifications, and was connected to the Establishment (one brother was successively bishop of Bristol and Peterborough). Yet, as the historian Seymour succinctly put it, "in consequence of his religious sentiments, and the open avowal he made of the faith once delivered to the saints, he experienced some difficulty in obtaining orders."[31] Lady Huntingdon's influence prevailed, however, and he was eventually ordained, though he was never to receive any benefice from the Church as long as he lived. His first sermon was preached at All Hallows, Lombard Street, in London, and because of the novelty of a lawyer becoming a clergyman it was attended by a great crowd. Madan's eloquence was applauded, and this new preacher, "mighty in the Scriptures" and an evidently accomplished scion of the Establishment, by the combined force of his preaching and the advantage of his social position did much to quell "the croaking cry of prejudice" which had been expected that day.

This same Madan, as we shall see, was a timely instrument in the rescue and conversion of his cousin, the would-be legal clerk and later poet and hymn writer, William Cowper. Cowper in turn, when forced to retire for the sake of his emotional fragility to the country, went to live with the Reverend Morley Unwin and his family and was instrumental in the spiritual renewal of that household; the Unwins' son prepared for the ministry and became a chaplain to Lady Huntingdon. Madan was at the base of a number of such spiritual lineages. He became a welcome colleague of Whitefield and the Wesleys and went on to acquire a reputation for his preaching as great in his time as that of many popular evangelists today. He had an attractive personal appearance, preached without notes in a powerful, well-modulated and musical voice, and has been regarded by an authoritative historian of the revival as "a workman that needed not be ashamed of his labours, rightly dividing the word of truth."[32]

But this is also the Martin Madan who later wrote a nine-hundred-page book in defence of a biblically based "Christian polygamy" entitled *Thelypthora: or, a Treatise on Female Ruin* (1780). The subject was not, of

A MIDNIGHT MODERN CONVERSATION
Engraving by Hogarth (1732). The dissolute party takes place in St. John's Coffee House, Temple Bar, and Hogarth pointedly includes in his group Parson Cornelius Ford, a disreputable cousin of Dr. Samuel Johnson, who is seen in the corner ladling punch.

course, new in the history of the church, nor was it unique in the eighteenth century; John Wesley's brother-in-law, the Reverend Westley Hall, also held to a doctrine of polygamy. But coming from a well-known revival preacher such a controversial document could only do widespread harm, and everyone in the movement who knew about the manuscript tried to get Madan to suppress it.[33] Lady Huntingdon wrote to this effect, saying that she could send him a petition with more than three thousand signatures urging him not to publish. He replied that he would not desist if it were twice that number. His cousin and convert, William Cowper, was one among many who felt obliged to publish a refutation of the work, and a further penalty of Madan's obstinacy was that he shortly thereafter sank into almost complete oblivion.

Yet much of his positive impact remained—many converted, many strengthened, many encouraged, and many spiritual family trees established whose branches still, perhaps, continue to widen. And he has left us one further legacy which illustrates as well as anything the synergy of the revival movement: his revision and reworking of three hymns by others of his contemporaries.[34] As it stands in modern hymn books it is a cento, composed with some variations from two hymns of Charles Wesley (nos. 38 and 39 of the *Hymns of Intercession for all Mankind*) and one by John Cennick (no. 965 in the *Collection of Hymns for the . . . United Brethren*).[35] The result is one of the most magnificent of those hymns of the faith which look forward to the Second Coming:

> Lo! he comes, with clouds descending,
>   Once for favoured sinners slain:
> Thousand thousand saints attending
>   Swell the triumph of his train:
>     Hallelujah!
>   God appears, on earth to reign!
>
> Every eye shall now behold him,
>   Robed in dreadful majesty;
> Those who set at nought and sold him,
>   Pierced, and nailed him to the tree,
>     Deeply wailing,
>   Shall the true Messiah see.
>
> Every island, sea, and mountain,
>   Heaven and earth shall flee away;
> All who hate him must, confounded,
>   Hear the trump proclaim the day;
>     "Come to judgment!
>   Come to judgment, come away!"
>
> Now Redemption, long expected,
>   See in solemn pomp appear!
> All his saints, by man rejected,
>   Now shall meet him in the air:
>     Hallelujah!
>   See the day of God appear!
>
> Answer thine own Bride and Spirit;
>   Hasten, Lord, the general doom;
> The new heaven and earth to inherit
>   Take thy pining exiles home:
>     All creation
>   Travails, groans, and bids thee come!
>
> Yea, Amen! let all adore thee,
>   High on thine eternal throne:
> Saviour, take the power and glory;
>   Claim the kingdom for thine own:
>     O, come quickly,
>   Everlasting God, come down!

This great hymn, like Madan's life and like the life of many others who figure in these pages, reminds us that God is ever pouring out his Spirit upon the world by means of human vessels, and it is well that the final judgment of these vessels' worth will not be that of either contemporaries or historians.

### Fruits of the Gospel

A historical perspective nevertheless affords us some understanding of the unfolding of the eighteenth-century revival.

First of all, it makes clear that the person who now appears most eminent, John Wesley, was of course only one among many agents of the revival. He was neither the greatest preacher (that was surely Whitefield) nor its most profound spiritual writer (his meditations are easily eclipsed by those of Law, and his letters by those of Newton); he was not its greatest hymn writer (Isaac Watts and his brother Charles are only two among many who far surpass him), nor can he compare in pastoral counsel to several exemplary parish priests whom he knew (including Fletcher, Haweis, and Romaine). He was not as memorable a reformer of education and founder of schools as Doddridge, Countess Huntingdon, or Hannah More, and even his social reforms are (with less justice perhaps) often less well recognized than those of the great lay leaders who came after him like Zachary Macaulay and William Wilberforce.

But it remains true that Wesley had a hand in the development of most of these ministries, and he was, for the organization of energies in the field, a complementary force to Countess Huntingdon, the drawing room strategist. This volume is thus subtitled as it is not simply because John Wesley's long life most completely spans the age (1703–1791) and touches the lives of so many others, or because he founded a great denomination, but because history remembers the great spiritual and social renewal of the eighteenth century as a product of the movement which he, more *visibly* than anyone, organized and led from success to success. And though that visible success has tended to hide from view much of the real spiritual depth and breadth of the revival, some of which is represented in the pages which follow and which is the primary concern of this book, it would be a distortion to let these notable achievements of the early Methodists pass without comment, since they are the effective outworking of John Wesley's spirituality.

From the very first the Oxford Methodist students had been actively involved in prison ministry and charity instruction for poor children as part of their spiritual exercise.[36] When first Whitefield and then the Wesleys took to itinerant preaching, they extended their concern to orphans, the illiterate poor, and the desperate condition of inmates in mental hospitals as well. While Whitefield's Georgia orphanage seems to have been a dubious project,[37] the concern he shared with the Wesleys for improving the condition of those whom the Establishment were content to ignore was a foremost part of his evangelical witness. John Wesley, for his part, translated and edited a "Christian Library" of fifty books, mostly classics of spirituality, to provide for the education of his unschooled followers. The enormous proceeds of these works and his other publications, in turn, he entirely gave away to aid poor lay preachers and their families, charity schools, prisoners, and other missions of mercy so that he died, by deliberate design, virtually penniless.

The prison ministry alone was remarkable. Into the intolerable, vermin-ridden darkness of prisons such as London's infamous Newgate—as well as its namesake in Bristol—Methodists went to preach to inmates and their jailers and to bring food, blankets, medicine, and clothing they had collected. The conditions they met were unspeakable, with torture and starvation commonplace and jailors growing rich from the public exhibition of famous prisoners (especially just before their execution), from the gin trade, and from prostitution (often forced). The inmates might be pickpockets, murderers, or simply persons unable to pay their debts; all met with the same treatment. The lot of political prisoners was not much better. In 1759, Wesley went to a prison near Bristol to visit a company of French prisoners of the Seven Years' War:

> About eleven hundred of them, we are informed, were confined in that little place, without anything to lie on but a little dirty straw, or anything to cover them but a few foul, thin rags, either by day or night, so that they died like rotten sheep. I was much affected, and preached in the evening on (Exodus 23:9) "Thou shalt not oppress a stranger; for ye know the heart of a stranger, seeing ye were strangers in the land of Egypt." Eighteen pounds were contributed immediately, which were made up to £24 the next day. With this we bought linen and woollen cloth, which were made up into shirts, waistcoats and breeches. Some dozens of stockings were added; all which were carefully distributed, where there was the greatest want. Presently after, the Corporation of Bristol sent a large quantity of mattresses and blankets. And it was not long before contributions were set on foot at London, and in various parts of the Kingdom.[38]

Often the bishops denied Methodist preachers entrance to the prisons and asylums; as Wesley quipped caustically: "We are forbidden to go to Newgate, for fear of making them [the inmates] wicked, and to Bedlam for fear of driving them mad."[39] But they persisted wherever they could, and with remarkable results. In 1761, Wesley wrote a letter to the *London Chronicle* describing a remarkable transformation of Bristol's Newgate. It was now clean and neat, with "no fighting and brawling"; there was an unprecedented system of equitable arbitration for prisoners; drunkenness, prostitution, and abuse had been eliminated. Women prisoners had been separated from the men. Tools and materials were provided to allow for productive employment, and payment was made to prisoners from profits on goods sold. There were regular church services, Bibles had been distributed, and free medical services were available. The keeper or warden who brought all these reforms into effect was a Mr. Dagge, an early convert of the Methodists' preaching in his own prison.

Methodist preachers, many of whose names have not survived and many of whom were not ordained Anglican clergy but simply lay preachers, continued in this ministry wherever they could gain access to prisons. They gave spiritual counsel to those condemned to execution, and as Hogarth's famous engraving illustrates, they regularly accompanied them through leering mobs of spectators to the scaffold, encouraging them to repentance or to hope in their newly found justification in Christ. John Fletcher is typical of the preachers' unflagging dedication in these matters. Very ill and in convalescence in Switzerland for the tuberculosis which was soon to claim his life, he went to minister to prisoners and took the occasion to preach to "2000 people in a jail yard, where they were come to see a poor murderer two days before his execution." "I was a little abused by the Bailiff," he adds in characteristic understatement, "and [was] refused the liberty of attending the poor man to the scaffold where he was to be broken on the wheel. I hope he died penitent."[40] Apparently many did, in England and elsewhere, accompanied to their last by "despised Methodists," who often suffered the pelting of filth and other humiliations for living out their faithfulness to the gospel.

Conditions in institutions for the mentally ill—effectively another species of degrading prison—were, if anything, more despicable. To begin with, as even the fate of Christopher Smart suggests, persons could be committed indefinitely without substantive justification. Then, especially if they were too poor to afford the expense of private institutions and were clapped into the ironically named Bedlam (from Bethlehem), they could be chained till death on filthy straw mats, beset by rats at night and the prodding and jests of paying sideshow minded visitors by day. Cowper, in a compounding of ironies, used to visit Bedlam for these cruel purposes with classmates from Westminster School, and it was a regular Sunday diversion of the wealthy effete, such as the ladies depicted in the last engraving of Hogarth's series entitled "The Rake's Progress"; even notable politicians such as Bolingbroke and literary men like Johnson participated in this horrible diversion. Yet here too the Methodists and other evangelicals brought light, ministering to individuals and by their persistence both directly and indirectly through the political process they did much to mitigate the evils which were being practiced.[41] And it was the force of evangelical influence that caused charitable institutions

THE IDLE PRENTICE EXECUTED AT TYBURN

Engraving by Hogarth, Plate 11 of the "Industry and Idleness" series. Note the Methodist preacher in the cart with the prisoner, exhorting him, as Hogarth's own notes have it, "from a book of [John] Wesley's," while they move through the crowd to the gallows. The text is Proverbs 1:27, 28.

such as Magdalene House, a hospice for prostitutes and abused female children, to be founded.[42]

These then are some of the visible "fruits of the Spirit" which characterized revival in the age of Wesley. Beyond the huge crowds at Whitefield's open air sermons or the more than one hundred thousand followers of Wesley organized into societies for fellowship, study, and worship all over England, these practical outworkings of faith, and others like them, including the abolition of the slave trade, give irrefragable evidence that something miraculous was being accomplished. The revival, as historian J. R. Green has said, "changed . . . the whole tone of English society. . . . The [Anglican] Church was restored to new life and activity. Religion carried to the hearts of the people a fresh spirit of moral zeal, while it purified our literature and our manners. A new philanthropy reformed our prisons, infused clemency and wisdom into our penal laws, abolished the slave-trade, and gave the first impulse to popular education."[43] J. H. Overton, historian of the movement, summarizes its effect in a fashion which makes explicit wide experience of the "new birth":

Of the faith which enabled a man to abandon the cherished habits of a lifetime, and to go forth ready to spend and be spent in his Master's

23

**SCENE IN A MADHOUSE**

Engraving by Hogarth, Plate 8 of "The Rake's Progress." Note the religious fanatic or "enthusiast" in the inner cell (at left), imagining himself as a hermit; note also the raving figure dressed as an archbishop (extreme right).

service . . . which made the selfish man self-denying, the discontented happy, the worldling spiritually minded, the drunkard sober, the sensual chaste, the liar truthful, the thief honest, the proud humble, the godless godly, the thriftless thrifty—we can only judge by the fruits which it bore. That such fruits *were* borne is surely undeniable.[44]

What we see in the principal biographies of the period is, in effect, only the tip of an iceberg, while very little of its base is now visible. But this is just where a study of spirituality makes its contribution.

## THE SPIRITUALITY OF THE REVIVAL

Christian spirituality in the eighteenth century may be divided, like the spirituality of other periods in Western culture, into two principal traditions. The first of these, which we commonly associate with monastic or hermetical life in the Middle Ages, is the contemplative or *meditative* tradition. Early names we identify with it are St. Bernard of Clairvaux, Thomas à Kempis, and St. John of the Cross. The other tradition, vigorous in the early church and modeled in men like St. Augustine, St. Francis, the early Irish missionaries, and John Wyclif, is that of the active evangelical life, what we might call the *missionary* tradition. The first constitutes that part of the body of Christ where we often find poets, hymn writers, mystics, and intercessors in prayer; the second is the territory of prophets, preachers, and reformers of various kinds.

Typically, what we think of in connection with the age of Wesley is the second sort of spirituality, and it is in fact the most dominant tradition among those prominent in the revival. But the call to action—a mission-oriented spirituality—has almost always had its origin in a profound encounter with meditative spirituality—an emphasis on the workings of the Spirit in the inner life, on the psychology of spiritual response, and on an intimate experience of the personhood of Jesus. In this, the age of Wesley is no exception.

## The Meditative Tradition

*In yet another manor house, this one closer to London, in Stoke Newington, it is a quiet afternoon. At one end of a small but elegantly appointed library of that house, rich in leatherbound volumes of history, philosophy, classical literature, theology, and, more unusually, spirituality, there is a reading desk turned to face the leaded panes of the east windows. The desk is strewn with books. A small, frail man with striking features is bent over a large sheet of paper at one end of the desk, writing steadily. He pauses, and looks abstractedly out through the rain spattered glass toward a garden, blurry with daffodils, then lays down his quill. This is not his home. He could never have afforded a fraction of these books. Yet it has become his home, these books his colleagues, this room a hospice in which necessary seclusion has become a new vocation of prayer, meditation, and writing.*

Isaac Watts was born into a family without wealth, a family barely able to afford his schooling, and he never expected much better for himself. He had done well in classical languages, philosophy, and divinity at the academy just a few minutes' walk from the garden in Stoke Newington, only to spend two years after graduation back at home unsure of his vocation. When at last, obliged to do something, he tutored the son of a wealthy Nonconformist of this same neighborhood, he had almost abandoned his earlier hopes of proceeding into the ministry. Now, after a surprising and wonderful early success as a preacher appointed to the prestigious Mark Lane Chapel, he had suddenly been crushed by chronic sickness, becoming too ill to preach regularly, and thus even to support himself. An assistant had to be found to carry the burden, while he was kept on at the chapel almost against his wishes, seldom strong enough to come in to preach on a Sunday. The most eminent of his parishioners, Sir

Thomas Abney, Lord Mayor of London, and his wife had taken him in, and by their hospitable insistence made him a permanent houseguest.

From one point of view, the vocation of Isaac Watts was in ruins, a victim of chronic disease. Yet from another, it was just beginning to be revealed in its true character as a meditative and contemplative (rather than an active) calling. Watts's life became a life of intercession. Those he could not preach to he prayed for. And as he thought about prayer, about spiritual growth, and about enrichment of the Christian mind, he began to be concerned for the prayer life of all English Christians, of whatever denomination, and for the revival of a vital spirituality in his time. He had always been a poet; among his earliest activities as a pastor he had sought in an innovative way to modernize and enrich the hymn singing in his congregation. By 1707, the year in which both Charles Wesley and Lady Huntingdon were born, he had published a well-received volume of poetry and a volume of hymns. Now, in 1713, forced out of his pastoral ministry, he set out to write a book about prayer (selections of which are included here).

Other concerns also began to claim his attention. He began to think about the Christian education of young children and saw that it badly needed a spiritual dimension, that mere doctrinal instruction was not a proper appreciation of the work of the Spirit in young hearts; in 1715, to speak to this need, he published a volume of *Hymns for Children*. He also wanted to try to come to grips with the whole character of thinking—in the senses of both meditation and inquiry—and to define a kind of thinking which could be called truly Christian. This concern for development of the Christian mind led him to write such major intellectual contributions as his *Logick* (1725) and *The Improvement of the Mind* (1741), as well as his more accessible *Catechisms* (1730) and *Scripture History* (1732). He turned his pen also to lay theology, and with great success; his popular book, *The World to Come* (1738), still makes good reading. And he was concerned with issues of Christian maturity, as his work on the use and abuse of the emotions in spiritual life reveals. He has left us, moreover, a series of beautiful brief meditations on subjects as diverse as "Justice and Grace," "The Figure of a Cherub," and "The Saints Unknown in this World." In all of these respects he was actually charting a pattern for the revival of vital spirituality in his century.

Watts may be thought of, then, as the first (if not the foremost) English writer of the meditative tradition in the eighteenth century. He had, however, three important contemporaries in this calling, each of whom is represented in the present volume. Two are from the old Puritan, or Dissenting, tradition, like Watts himself, and were close friends. The first of these, Philip Doddridge, was a pastor and theological educator, himself a prolific writer of lay spirituality and in most respects certainly more to be associated with mission-oriented enterprise than a meditative life. But he had an evidently deep inwardness, and when Watts's poor health in his declining years would not permit him to finish an important treatise which he had long envisioned, he asked Doddridge to take up the outline and drafts of some early chapters and to bring the work to completion. This book, begun by Watts in the library of Lord and Lady Abney and finished in the study of Doddridge, was the celebrated *Rise and Progress of* ✓ *the Soul* (1745), which was destined to make a crucial spiritual intervention in many lives down to the time of William Wilberforce and beyond. Doddridge thus brought to birth one of the most important works of popular spirituality in this period, and it is in fact this work by which he himself is now remembered.

The second associate of Watts represented here fits more directly the pattern of the meditative life. Elizabeth Rowe was an exact contemporary of Watts, a member of his worship community for part of her life, and wife to the nephew of Watts's teacher. She was a poet of very wide reputation in the early eighteenth century and was courted by national literary figures, bishops, and politicians. Her religious poetry was much admired by John Wesley, who edited some of it.[45] She remained single until she was thirty-six and then, after five years of marriage, was left a widow and became a kind of spiritual recluse, retiring to a small house she had inherited from her father. After that she seldom left home. She immersed herself in spiritual writings, from Thomas à Kempis to Pascal and others of the "Messieurs de Port Royal," translated some of them, and began to compose the Christian fiction which has given her an important place in the history of women's literature. But her principal preoccupation was prayer and the inner life, something of which she recorded over many years in several hundred pages of spiritual notebooks. She left a selection of these, in her last illness, to Isaac Watts, asking that they not be published until after her death. He complied with her wishes, and her *Devout Exercises of the Heart* was published in 1737 with his commendatory introduction. This book, markedly within the traditions of continental ✓ spirituality of the late Middle Ages and seventeenth century, bears witness to an inner life much more akin to that of Julian of Norwich or Teresa d'Avila than that of Lady Selina or Hannah More. *Devout Exercises* is an intense dialogue of the soul with God. That Rowe asked for it to be withheld until her death suggests that she fully realized how far its mystical intensity was out of the range of the "polite" taste by which her earlier work had been so well received. But the book's immediate and astounding success both at home and abroad suggests also how deep a hunger there was for the kind of inner life and personal intimacy with God that it mirrored.

William Law, only slightly younger than Watts and Rowe, is the outstanding spiritual writer of the nonjuror right wing of the Anglican church, and perhaps the outstanding spiritual writer of the age. (His closest competitor for this honor is probably Fletcher.) As the introduction to his writing in this volume suggests, though he was called a "mystic," and in the best sense of that word certainly was one, his spiritual writing offers some of the most coherent and compelling exposition of Christian vocation that it is possible to find in any period. He too was a recluse, forced into retirement by nonjuring convictions which cost him his teaching fellowship at Cambridge and the possibility of ever obtaining a parish in the Established Church. But he used his years of relative solitude to produce a great legacy; two of the best and most influential of his books are represented in these pages. Law, like Rowe, drew heavily on Catholic tradition, especially its contemplative and mystical writers. But he is much more akin to Watts in his commitment to a vigorous, even insistent rationalism. Neither suffered foolishness gladly; both advocated a no-nonsense spirituality. And it was spiritual logic more than spiritual ecstasies which would speak to the evangelical leaders of the next generation.

This, then, is the group of meditative authors—two clergymen and two laypersons—who are the immediate forerunners to the evangelical revival. To their circle Christopher Smart makes later a kind of eccentric orbit; his religious poetry and hymns have a deep kinship with the more "charismatic" elements of the meditative tradition. We shall see that this group has a formative influence on the spiritual development of some of the most visible and active leaders to emerge later. Watts and Law stand out especially in this regard. Watts was a direct influence not only on Doddridge and Rowe within his own denomination but also upon Charles Wesley, Smart, Newton, More, and (via Doddridge) Wilberforce. Law's writing was foundational for the spiritual development of the Wesleys, Whitefield, and Fletcher, and he had a powerful influence on many of the other Anglican evangelicals down through the century, remaining a continuing source of challenge to the whole revival movement. It is thus that those two rejected elements of the Established Church—the Puritan and Anglo-Catholic—began at this point to reveal themselves as the very elements by which a restoration of spiritual life in the English church could become a possibility.

## The Missionary Tradition

### The Methodist Synthesis

When people from a Protestant tradition think of spiritual vocation, they usually think in terms of a call to active ministry. The scriptural model they have in mind is that afforded by the prophets, and it envisions above all else a work of preaching, teaching, and visible activism. For the Puritan tradition in the century before Wesley this was a notable pattern, and it had analogies in the experience of Anglicans like Jeremy Taylor, Lancelot Andrews, and George Herbert. When we now look back on the great evangelists of the eighteenth century, particularly Wesley and Whitefield, this is the familiar model we still see being reflected. Wesley, traveling by horseback or carriage a quarter of a million miles to preach more than forty-five thousand times in his lifetime, talked about "the world as his parish." Like the prophets of Israel he had no parish priesthood, but ranged all over the British Isles in his preaching of repentance and renewal; like the judges of Israel he organized reform. Whitefield was still more singular, perhaps, in his dedication to mass evangelism— preaching over eighteen thousand sermons to much larger audiences— but he too had projects of reform. Both were concerned, in a Pauline way, with mission outreach; each involved themselves in raising support and volunteers.

For John Wesley, as he said many times in his life, there was "no Christianity which was not social Christianity." Charles puts the point succinctly in one of his hymns for use "After Worship":

> Actions He more than words requires,
>  Actions with right intention done,
> Good works the fruit of good desires,
>  Obedience to His will alone,
> Pure hope which seeks the things above,
> Practical faith, and real love.[46]

Wesley's reservations in later life about some of the mystic writers who shaped his own spirituality need to be appreciated in the light of his rejection of the quietism of the German Moravians and his overriding concern for evangelical outreach.[47] The writers who gave him the greatest concern were not his immediate English contemporaries or the great Catholic meditative writers like Kempis, whom he always recommended to his followers, but more pronounced mystics such as Jacob Boehme and Madame Guyon (some of whose poetry was translated by Cowper). He seems especially to have feared the effect of these writers upon those whose natural disposition or circumstances might lead them into a life of withdrawal rather than of open service. To one of his correspondents he wrote:

> The Mystic writers . . . are the most artful refiners . . . that ever appeared in the Christian world, and the most bewitching. There is something like enchantment in them. When you get into them, you know not how to get out. . . . My dear friend, come not into their secret; keep in the plain, open Bible way. Aim at nothing higher, nothing

deeper, than the religion described at large in our Lord's Sermon upon the Mount, and briefly summed up by St. Paul in the 13th chapter [of the First Epistle] to the Corinthians.[48]

The meditative writers he chose to edit or translate for his followers are distinguished by their ascetic bent; he championed their spirit of self-denial and consecration as instruction or necessary preparation for the active spiritual life and witness. The specific biblical model for Wesley and many of the Methodists was that of the last of the prophets, John the Baptist—a spirituality founded in intense ascetic inwardness which nevertheless accepts a prophetically directed outward ministry, a call to repentance and renewal.

For Wesley, successful missionary outreach in fact is always built upon a foundation of rich meditative spirituality. He said to his coworkers:

> It cannot be that the people should grow in grace unless they give themselves to reading. A reading people will always be a knowing people. A people who talk much will know little. Press this upon them with your might, and you will soon see the fruit of your labours.[49]

His own education, which so largely involved absorption in spiritual writers rather than traditional theologians, provided the model. At Oxford he was much influenced by the Anglo-Catholic writings of Robert Nelson, Thomas Ken, and Nathaniel Spinckes, as well as by John Donne, Jeremy Taylor, and some of their contemporaries. These writers led him in turn to read the early fathers of the church, from both the Eastern Orthodox and Western Catholic traditions, including St. John Chrysostom, St. Basil, St. Jerome, St. Augustine, and "that man of a broken heart, Ephraim Syrus."[50] This last writer, and one called "Macarius the Egyptian"—really a Syrian disciple of Gregory of Nyssa—were of the Eastern school of Christian perfectionism, destined to have a lasting impact on Wesley's thought. While he shared with his contemporaries a complete ignorance of the great medieval spiritual writers such as Aelred of Rievaulx and St. Francis, he was, like both the Cistercians and Franciscans, drawn to an affective, emotional spirituality. Contemplation of Christ crucified and adoration of the cross were central elements of Wesley's spiritual experience. This emphasis was reinforced by the Moravians, whose hymns and teaching often stressed the physical suffering of Christ. Wesley translated some of these hymns (although often modifying their extreme intensity of focus upon the cross), the best known of which is Count Zinzendorf's "Jesus, thy Blood and Righteousness."[51]

All through the Oxford years the Wesleys and other members of the Holy Club were staunchly Anglo-Catholic in their observance of the mixed chalice, prayers for the dead, and auricular confession, and they held a eucharistic belief, as we see even in some of Charles's later hymns, which is close to transubstantiation. Among those writers whom Wesley chose to include in his Christian Library are Count Gaston Jean-Baptiste de Renty, a seventeenth-century French nobleman who founded in Paris a society for the perpetual adoration of the Blessed Sacrament, and the sixteenth-century Spanish hermit Gregory Lopez, whose mastery of the Bible and life of constant prayer were a source of lifelong admiration for Wesley. Though the emphasis in his own life's work and teaching grew to be overwhelmingly mission-oriented, he retained his interest in a deep spirituality of the inner life because he believed that without it an evangelistic enterprise would soon wither and die of exhaustion. This was the reason for his extraordinary commitment to spiritual reading among his followers, and to their development of the contemplative's ardent pursuit of a life of prayer:

> A continual desire is a continual prayer—that is, in a low sense of the word; for there is a far higher sense, such an open intercourse with God, such a close uninterrupted communion with him, as Gregory Lopez experienced, and not a few of our brethren and sisters now alive.[52]

These sentiments, expressed toward the end of Wesley's life (1771), could have been written by Catherine of Siena, St. Teresa of Avila, or Walter Hilton. If "mysticism" is essentially the soul's awareness of God, or immediate consciousness of God's presence, then "more than a touch of mysticism" undergirds the spirituality of the father of Methodism.[53] And as the *Scheme of Self-Examination Used by the First Methodists in Oxford* and Wesley's later pamphlet, *The Character of a Methodist* (1742), show, the very idea of "methodism"—a strict *religio* of discipline and duty— derives from the ascetic and meditative spirituality of the writers he most admired, even as it was prepared for in a practical way by the fierce asceticism of that remarkable woman of nonjuror sympathies, his own mother, Susannah Wesley.[54] In the hymns of Charles—always regarded by the Wesleys as an intrinsic part of their teaching and evangelizing— these elements of their spirituality are faithfully reflected.

It is thus that the gospel preached by Wesley is a complex thing *spiritually*. His call is to an active life, to evangelize and to reform society, yet he wants all those who take up the challenge to deepen themselves, acquiring the resources of a meditative inwardness; he warns against the mystics, yet highly values their experience. He deplores an excessive pretense to the "rule of reason" in his culture, yet is himself methodistic and rationalistic in much of his thought.[55]

Nowhere is this complexity more evident than in Wesley's doctrine of Christian perfection. With its roots in Eastern orthodoxy, the writings of William Law, and the "holiness" doctrine of Jeremy Taylor, and its drive to self-discipline nurtured by the ascetic traditions already mentioned, it

31

was worked out in a climate of constant tension between ambition and praxis. Was perfection an experience of growth toward something only finally realized in God's eternal presence? Or was it the result of a full experience of the presence of the Holy Spirit in the here and now? At one point John wrote to Charles an anguished letter on the subject, uncertain whether their views were consistent and wanting them both at least to be saying the same thing.[56] It is certain that the possibilities of contradiction are not worked out in John's sermons on the subject, even the specific "Christian Perfection" sermon (1741), which was published along with a twenty-eight stanza hymn on "The Promise of Sanctification" by Charles.[57] Wesley wanted in most places to deny that he was arguing for "sinless perfection," but, as Albert Outler says, he then "promptly proceeded to deny that [one] can rightly argue from the residue of sin in human life to its invincibility."[58] Which is to say that he left open the possibility for some to experience sinless perfection. Some among his followers certainly did argue for the achievement, and in certain cases Wesley himself was impressed with the evidence. But these claims proved troublesome and served to jeopardize the relationship between the Wesleys and Whitefield, among others. On April 25, 1741, Whitefield wrote:

> Dear brother Charles is more and more rash. He has lately printed some very bad hymns. Today, I talked with Brother N----. He tells me that, for three months past, he has not sinned in thought, word, or deed. He says, he is not only free from the *power,* but the very *in-being* of sin. He now asserts it is *impossible* for him to sin. I talked with three women. One said she had been perfect these twelve months; but, alas! she showed many marks of imperfection whilst I was with her. I asked her if she had any pride. She said, "No." I asked if she ever prayed for pardon, at night, for her sins and infirmities. She said, "No; for she did not commit any sin." I spoke to another woman, who said she had not sinned in thought, word, or deed, this twelve-month. I asked her, and every one of the rest, whether they ever used the Lord's Prayer. They were unwilling to answer, but afterwards said, "Yes." I asked them whether they used it for themselves, and could say, "Forgive us our trespasses." They said, "No; they used it for others only."[59]

Perhaps the fairest thing to say about "perfectionism," an ideal which was so much more clearly and unambiguously set forth by William Law, is that Wesley's doctrinal formulation never achieved the clarity of his own convictions on the subject. In this sense, it is like much else in the spirituality of John Wesley. In his *Plain Account of Christian Perfection* (1766), written to try to consolidate confused opinion on the matter, he describes his own spiritual autobiography as a progression from reading

Bishop Taylor (in 1725) to Thomas à Kempis the next year to William Law in the year or so after that. Then he says he undertook in 1729 a serious study of the Bible, concentrating (as Law had suggested) on the model of Christ himself. The sermon which he preached on New Year's Day, 1733, before the University of Oxford—entitled "The Circumcision of the Heart"—more than five years before the Aldersgate experience (which he does not even mention in this context) contains, he says, his first full statement of the doctrine.[60] Most readers today would find it a difficult, even confused statement, and it has thus been passed over here in favor of clearer examples of his exposition. But he says of this sermon, "composed first of all my writings which have been published," that it contains "the view of religion I then had, which even then I scrupled not to term *perfection*. This is the view I have of it now, without any material addition or diminution."[61]

That view is, at its best, expressed (as in Hebrews 6:1) as the goal of the perfection of love. The best summary description of Wesley's uneven attempt to make theological doctrine out of the irreducible experience of the sacrifice of self seems to be that of Albert C. Outler:

> "Perfect love," as Wesley understood it, is the conscious certainty, *in a present moment*, of the fullness of one's love for God and neighbor, as this love has been initiated and fulfilled by God's gifts of faith, hope, and love. This is not a state but a dynamic process: saving faith is its beginning; sanctification is its proper climax.[62]

If the doctrine was as difficult to express as a totally selfless love of God is difficult to offer, there was a man in that time who seemed to Wesley to be as close to a complete offering up of the whole of life upon the altar as most of us are likely ever to meet with. This man was John Fletcher, the acknowledged "saint" of the Methodist movement, a quiet, radiant Anglican vicar to the parish church of Madeley. Of his remarkable life, more follows later in this volume. But what we notice here is that Fletcher, who spent his entire life serving the same parish church, was quintessentially a pastor—as much a fixture as Wesley was a firefly. He was not part of the Oxford Methodists. He grew up in Switzerland; English was his second tongue. Yet he was deeply influenced by many of the same sources of early Christian spirituality as his Oxford friends, and was perhaps richer in the practice of the gospel in its most radical call to the imitation of Christ. He rejected itinerant ministry, believing himself called as a missionary to one place, to the people of Madeley, among whom his sanctity of life won more even than the fair clarity of his words. Fletcher was a preacher of admirable talents, but also a meditative spiritual writer whose intensive life of prayer and reflection he shared in person and on paper with his parishioners and the world at large. In few spiritual figures of any century do we find such unity between interior life and outward ministry as appears in the life and work of this remarkable man.

Among those of the active tradition in eighteenth-century spirituality none was perhaps more "outward" than George Whitefield. We might expect this from a man who could draw twenty to thirty thousand people for an outdoor sermon. Though he had begun with the Holy Club at Oxford and had been tutored in many of the same spiritual writings (he quoted Law all his life), he is perhaps the least evidently reflective in his own spirituality of all the figures represented in this volume. Prototype of the modern mass evangelist, he was first and foremost a preacher; everything else came well behind. He built no organization comparable to Wesley's, and beyond some of his sermons, journal entries, and a few letters he has left us only a small literary legacy. But as we shall see, no one aroused more wrath against the spirit of the revival than this man, and during the early years none had so large an impact for the revival upon public consciousness.

Whitefield possessed superb rhetorical skills. Atheists like Lord Bolingbroke and Lord Chesterfield, who came to hear him only to scoff and who rejected his message, nevertheless congratulated him sincerely for a mastery of Ciceronian rhetoric which they could only envy. He had dramatic training and dramatic skills, and above all an amazing sense of stage presence. As we see in some of what follows, he could control unruly crowds, even mobs like those at Moorfields, where hecklers hurled excrement and exposed themselves naked from trees in an attempt to divert the audience.

Though never on Wesley's scale, Whitefield was also committed to practical works of mercy. He regularly employed his sermons not only for a call to repentance and spiritual renewal but also as an opportunity to raise money for various missionary projects. John Newton tells a remarkable story of how Whitefield once collected six hundred pounds at a single sermon for the inhabitants of an obscure village in Germany that had been burned down—hardly the sort of cause which Londoners might normally be expected to become excited about. After the sermon, Whitefield apparently said, "We shall sing a hymn, during which those who do not choose to give their mite on this awful occasion may sneak off." No one stirred. Whitefield then descended from the pulpit, ordered all doors but one to be barred, and stood there holding the collection plate himself as the congregation squeezed past one by one.[63]

Most of Whitefield's life was directed toward his mission in Georgia; for that purpose, and for evangelistic preaching, he traveled to America seven times. On his last visit there he died within hours of his final exhortation. He is thus a superb example of an evidently mission-oriented spirituality. But although his is the kind of life we often associate with revival, what remains of his witness contains surprisingly little enduring resource for the spiritual life—less than that left by many he otherwise overshadowed. Whitefield seems, in fact, as overbalanced to the active side as William Law was to the contemplative. Yet his preaching and his activism provide a bridge to the renewal of evangelical Anglicanism in the last half of the century.

### Evangelical Anglicans

The spiritual history of the eighteenth-century revival culminates in a blossoming of lay spirituality, and it is appropriate that this volume should conclude with selections from three of its most memorable exemplars, William Cowper, Hannah More, and William Wilberforce. Significantly, the spiritual director of all three, and pastor of Cowper and Wilberforce, was John Newton, himself inspired in the early days following his conversion out of the slave trade by the preaching of George Whitefield.

John Newton's remarkable life story, first made public by the publication of a series of his letters to the Reverend Thomas Haweis, is perhaps the best-known autobiography of the revival. Recapitulated later in this book, it describes the life of someone who began well; his childhood imagination was shaped by a devout mother and the hymns of Isaac Watts. But it was not in any way a privileged life, either by fortune or education, and in this way he was set apart from many of his predecessors in this collection. Newton spent much of his boyhood and early youth at sea, in a crude, often violent way of life. He never went to Oxford or Cambridge, nor had he the superb educational advantages of one of the fine Dissenter academies. Following his conversion, he educated himself, pursuing much of his study while he worked as a tide surveyor. It was only with difficulty and with the decisive help of an influential evangelical layman, Lord Dartmouth, that he was able to get himself examined and finally ordained at the age of thirty-nine.

Thus Newton, who introduces our last group of writers and who, in the opinion of Sir George Trevelyan, became the real founder of the evangelical school in the Church of England, was at heart a layman. His influence in turn upon a remarkable group of laypersons did much to build the character of lay spirituality in the English tradition.[64] Like Fletcher, once ordained he was devoted to the pastorate, with only two churches in his lifetime. But the pastoral care he exemplified—not only in his sermons but also in his rich correspondence offering pastoral counsel—had an influence far beyond the boundaries of either parish. His letters reveal him to be a transparently honest, hearty, humorous, practical, and hardworking shepherd of his flock.

His flock included the weak as well as the strong. William Cowper notably represents Newton's patient nurturing of a person who was emotionally unstable to a degree that might have caused his complete destruction in less gentle hands, and for whom a lesser pastor would probably not have found time. From his dismal youth, Cowper was a product of the habitual emotional diseases of the upper classes of his time, some of the worst of which arose simply from indolence on a scale we would perhaps find hard to conceive. But out of his emotional fragility— in which he was sometimes up, sometimes down to the very abyss of despair—came a fine flowering of poetry and hymns of faith, and when we look at these in the light of his broken life we see how he is, as much as his pastor Newton, a trophy of "amazing grace." Against every probability, he became England's most celebrated poet in the latter years of his life.

Hannah More was also a poet. Like Newton, she came from less advantageous personal circumstances. But she too was bright, well educated (largely at her own initiative), and an extremely competitive, energetic woman. Her accomplishments are as impressive as her writing: successful young businesswoman, campaign manager to Edmund Burke when he first ran for Parliament in Bristol, then an extremely successful playwright for the London stage, she had an indomitable spirit and a contagious love for lively conversation that made her, despite her humble origins, a favorite in high society. She was a valued friend to great artists and writers such as Sir Joshua Reynolds and Dr. Samuel Johnson. She was the most colorful member of the famous Bluestockings of London—a society of women writers and thinkers. She had open access to the fashionable society of London's politicians, bishops, and wealthy merchants. Vibrant and attractive, she was always noted as a woman of great integrity, though her convictions earned her the scorn of the lascivious and the sycophantic, such as Johnson's dissolute biographer, James Boswell.[65]

More was in her late thirties when she read some of John Newton's published pastoral letters, then came to his church in London. The spiritual awakening which began to come to her during this period directed her away from writing for the stage and back to her early concern for education. She became one of England's most noted educational reformers, particularly on the subject of the education of women. In many respects she was certainly what we would call today a feminist. She saw at the center of feminine dignity a profound spiritual life and a rich education for the Christian mind. In the tradition of Watts and Wesley she recommended "dry, tough books" to women who would learn how to regenerate home life. To temper and admonish the excessive leisure of the pampered daughters of the aristocracy, she suggested great works of history and philosophy as well as spirituality; included in her list are

Locke's *Essay Concerning Human Understanding,* Butler's *Analogy of Religion,* and Watts's *Logick.*[66] The kind of spirituality she inculcated in her writing, and the spiritual motive central to all her later work, heavily emphasized the active life. More's particular mission field in her writing was the wealthy women of English aristocracy, though she reached a far wider audience. Her own practical stewardship involved the establishment, organization, and support of charity schools all over her part of England.

This emphasis on the active life is central to the evangelical Anglicans who followed Newton in the latter part of the century. Like him, they were not deeply read in ascetic or meditative spiritual writers of previous centuries, and they did not much quote the church fathers. Newton and More both knew and valued the work of William Law, but they had keen reservations about him too. More praises Law's *Serious Call,* but warns her readers away from his contemplative life:

> Few writers, except Pascal, have directed so much acuteness of reasoning, and so much pointed wit to this object [of exposing the shallowness of the age]. He not only makes the reader afraid of a worldly life on account of its sinfulness, but ashamed of it on account of its folly. Few men perhaps have had a deeper insight into the human heart, or have more skilfully probed its corruptions; yet on other points his views do not seem to be just. . . . To a fashionable woman immersed in the vanities of life, or to a busy man overwhelmed with its cares, I know no book so applicable, or likely to strike them with equal force as to the vanity of the shadows they are pursuing. But . . . I have known some excellent persons who were first led by this admirable genius to see the wants of their own hearts, and the utter insufficiency of the world to fill up the craving void, who, though they became eminent for piety and self-denial, have had their usefulness abridged, and whose minds have contracted something of a monastic severity by an unqualified perusal of Mr. Law. True Christianity does not call on us to starve our bodies but our corruptions. As the mortified Apostle of the holy and self-denying Baptist, preaching repentance because the kingdom of heaven is at hand, Mr. Law has no superior. As a preacher of salvation on scriptural grounds I would follow other guides.[67]

For More, as for Newton, salvation is worked out in the crucible of daily social life, and though More even more than her friend would shy away from the "peculiarities" of Methodism and its societies, she certainly shared his agreement with Wesley's emphasis on social reform. Though she lived the latter part of her life partly in the country, she was never in "retirement." The rural setting afforded an opportunity to write and a base from which to sortie into London in her tireless campaigns to reform education and awaken spiritual life among her contemporaries.

This impetus in the latter part of the century, which seems far removed from quiet Christianity, clearly owed much to the vital connection between revival and reform forged by the Wesleys and their followers. Among the evangelical Anglicans, this emphasis was characterized by a practical direction toward the life of ordinary lay Christians. Newton indicates this workaday application to ordinary life in many of his letters to laypeople; one of them, to a married couple in his congregation, includes the following lines:

> At the best, if a contemplative life is more quiet, an active life is more honorable and useful. We have no right to live to ourselves. I do not think our Lord blamed Martha for providing a dinner for himself and his twelve apostles, but I suppose she was too solicitous to have things set off very nicely, and perhaps lost her temper. Methinks I see her breaking in upon him, with her face red with heat and passion, to huff her sister. This was her fault. Had she sent the dinner in quietly, and with a smiling face, I believe he would not have rebuked her for being busy in the kitchen, while he was in the parlour. We like to have our own will; but submission to his is the great point. Religion does not consist in doing great things, for which few of us have frequent opportunities, but in doing the little necessary things of daily occurrence with a cheerful spirit, *as to the Lord*.[68]

Yet there were some whose opportunities allowed them to do great things, and one of the most eminent evangelical Anglican laypersons of any period, of course, was Newton's friend and parishioner William Wilberforce. That Newton, having been in his youth corrupted by the slave trade, should now be a source of pastoral encouragement to the likeable and hardworking young member of Parliament who more than anyone was to bring about an end to this abomination, now seems a perfection of divine logic.

Wilberforce, influenced in his conversion by Philip Doddridge's *Rise and Progress,* well illustrates the affection and respect evangelical Anglicans felt toward the Independents and Puritans, but he followed no particular theological controversy of his time with interest.[69] He was simply a person of the "new birth" who found himself in a political arena where practical opportunities for translation of the gospel were many. He had a distinct sense of calling, a vocation of spiritual life in the active world, and it placed him at the leadership of the abolition movement. Yet, as his writings declare, he was also an exemplary Christian of the inner life and built his life of active service upon the basis which he describes in his literary work of spiritual reflection, *Real Christianity*. For many decades this work was considered to be a kind of manifesto of evangelical Christianity. In his life's work of reform and organization for evangelism, including some of the formative planning for British foreign missions, Wilberforce shows himself to have been deeply sustained from within in his pursuit of the "real" mission-oriented and active spirituality he championed.

Wilberforce, More, Cowper, Zachary Macaulay, remarkable Christian businessmen like John and Henry Thornton—such laypersons formed a kind of third order within the Established Church at the end of the century, helping it to apply the riches of Christian spirituality to the renewal and reform of both the church and the world. These persons were vigorous foes of nominal Christianity. And because they often possessed educated and brilliant minds, they could say to the hollow idolatry of their time, as Wilberforce did: "Dim is the light of reason, and cold and comfortless our state, while left to her unassisted guidance."[70] The great triumph of the work of the Spirit in the age of Wesley was not, as the following pages make clear, to exclude or abandon that reason their contemporaries so much abused, but to nurture it as a handmaiden to obedient Christian life. What the writings and the practical witness of these great men and women of faith reveal, from Watts to Wilberforce, is that when our reason is brought with every other gift to the foot of the cross, then it *has* reason indeed, and both individuals and society are transformed by the renewing of our minds (Romans 12:2).

An old American evangelist once wondered aloud "how can there be a deep revival in a shallow generation?" The men and women in this book have something to teach us about that—and it is clear that their answer involved neither condescension to shallowness nor imitation of it. For them, mature Christian spirituality can only grow from a mature Christian mind and such a mind can only come to be when it has first hid itself in the mind of Christ.

The history of English spirituality in the eighteenth century can be seen in one way as a movement from inner to outer life, from the narrow confines of dwindling independent churches and student Holy Clubs outward boldly into the turbulence of society and the needy world, but also from a necessary deep inwardness of personal spirituality to the pressures of active commitment to missionary enterprise at home and abroad. It can also be seen as a rich tapestry of interconnections which tie together faithful Christians of Anglo-Catholic, nonjuror, Independent Dissenter, and Established Church communities into one seamless web of spiritual ministry to their culture. This tapestry is wider as well as more intricate than these pages can show and contains many gems of spiritual patterning even the specialized historian will not be able to discern. Yet from quite another point of view, some of these—hidden lives of prayer—may have been most central of all to the grand design. In his beautiful essay entitled "The Saints Unknown in this World," Isaac Watts reminds us that:

> Out of the millions of mankind that spread over the earth in every age . . . God has been pleased to take some into his own family, has given them a heavenly nature, and made them his sons and daughters.
>
> But He has set no outward mark of glory upon them—there is nothing in their figure or in their countenance to distinguish them from the rabble of mankind. And it is fit that they should be in some measure unknown among their fellow mortals. . . .
>
> The life of the saints is hidden with Christ in God. But when Christ, who is their life, shall appear, they also shall appear with Him in glory. . . . In that day they shall stand forth before the whole creation in fair evidence; they shall shine in distinguished light, and appear vested in their own undoubted honors.

Somewhere, we may suppose, sometime before all these remarkable events of revival began, there was one—or dozens, or hundreds, but perhaps just one—person praying.

*Far from the madding crowd of London, perhaps in a little cottage somewhere in the hills of southern Wales, it is the break of a new day, and spring sunlight spills through the window and across the shoulders of someone rebuilding a fire from the cold night's embers. She is kneeling on the stones of her hearth, kneeling as she prays each morning, to ask that God by his Spirit will bring revival to her country and its people. And as she rises to commence with love and joy to serve her God in the ordinary round of a quiet life, she is singing an old hymn. Perhaps it will be this very morning that a lifelong faithfulness of intercession will begin to be gathered in the hand of the Master Weaver toward the base of his own great loom, a thread of purest gold, burning and shining, reflecting and revealing his matchless light.*

## NOTES

1. Alexander Pope, *Essay on Criticism,* in *The Poems of Alexander Pope,* ed. John Butt (London: Methuen, 1963), p. 146, l. 89.

2. See John Locke, *An Essay Concerning Human Understanding,* ed. Alexander Campbell Fraser (London: Oxford University Press, 1894), Book 4, ch. 19, "Of Enthusiasm." James Kershaw's long poem, *The Methodist* (Nottingham, 1780), succinctly expresses the general response of the Methodist movement to this bias when he writes:

> While reason boasted her superior sway,
> Had she not banish'd Gospel-truths away?
> While Science bloom'd, and lib'ral Arts improv'd,
> And fancy o'er the fields of Nature rov'd,

> While nat'ral knowledge to perfection grew,
> How few once thought of being *born anew!*

3. J. R. Green, *A Short History of the English People* (London, 1877–89), vol. 3, p. 361.

4. J. Wesley Bready, *England: Before and After Wesley* (London: Hodder & Stoughton, 1938), p. 23.

5. John Wesley, *Journal,* ed. Nehemiah Curnock (London: Epworth, 1938), entry for January 11, 1768. It should be added, however, that many of the repressive measures which characterized the regime of Charles II were to some degree forced upon him by Anglicans and Royalists desiring revenge on the Commonwealth Puritans.

6. A standard, but somewhat outdated, authority on Deism is Leslie Stephen, *The History of English Thought in the Eighteenth Century,* 2 vols. (London, 1876; rev. 1927); for a quick guide see R. N. Stromberg, *Religious Liberalism in Eighteenth-Century England* (London: Oxford University Press, 1954); John H. Overton, *The Evangelical Revival in the Eighteenth Century* (London: Longmans, 1886), still affords a useful perspective for the general reader.

7. See William E. Alderman, "Shaftesbury and the Doctrines of Moral Sense in the Eighteenth Century," *PMLA,* 46 (1931), 1087–94, and A. O. Aldridge, *Shaftesbury and the Deist Manifesto* (Philadelphia: American Philosophical Society, 1951). Their friend and fellow Deist, Lord Bolingbroke, was independent enough to permit himself to be an unequivocal admirer of Whitefield's eloquence and his "piety and excellence," finding the opposition of "the bishops and inferior orders of the clergy . . . not astonishing—there is so little goodness in them." Bolingbroke appears to have had a degree of philosophical consistency some of his fellows lacked. When visited by an Established clergyman with the improbable name of Dr. Church he asked his opinion of the book he was reading, Calvin's *Institutes.* Church is said to have replied, "Oh, my Lord, we don't think about such antiquated stuff; we teach the plain doctrines of virtue and morality, and have long laid aside those abstruse points about grace." "Look you, Doctor (said Lord Bolingbroke), you know I don't believe the Bible to be a divine revelation; but they who do can never defend it on any principles *but* the doctrine of grace. To say the truth, I have at times been almost persuaded to believe it upon this view of things; and there is one argument which has gone very far with me in behalf of its authenticity, which is, that the belief in it exists upon earth, even when committed to the care of such as you, who pretend to believe it, and yet deny the only principles on which it is defensible." See A. C. H. Seymour, *The Life and Times of Selina, Countess of Huntingdon,* 2 vols. (London: Painter, 1844), vol. 1, pp. 179–80.

8. As early as 1720 there were three "Hell Fire Clubs" in London, the most famous of which was that led by Dashwood, whose members referred to themselves as "The Monks of Medmenham Abbey." Another group at Skelton Castle was called the "Demoniacs." A sketch of the character of these clubs, and of their blasphemous and obscene publications, can be obtained from Hoxie N. Fairchild, *Religious Trends in English Poetry* (New York: Columbia University Press, 1942), vol. 2, pp. 28–49.

9. Bready, pp. 45–52. One who had time to write scurrilous novels was the Reverend Laurence Sterne, author of *Tristram Shandy.* He was attacked in print by

Whitefield (1760) as an author of an "anti-gospel," and while Whitefield's criticism is typical of the time in its vitriolic censure (which was echoed by others), his language nevertheless indicates something of the character of its object—not merely Sterne but others like him. Whitefield warns his fellow Anglican clergyman:

> The hour will come, and perhaps it is not far off, when the light of thy wit and humour shall be extinguished, and *Tristram Shandy* shall know his place and more. . . . Then wilt thou mourn thy past follies, when thou shalt no longer meet with a harlot at St. James Park, or lasciviously yield to the temptation of the flesh at Ranelagh but become a feast . . . for . . . a certain convocation of politic worms.

10. In William Roberts, *The Life of Hannah More* (London, 1872), p. 63. More was on friendly terms with a number of bishops and Established clergymen of a broad church orientation who, while certainly unwilling to be thought of as "evangelical," also protested against court immorality and social evils. Their voice, however, was muted throughout the period—to the great detriment of their pastoral work and ethical witness—because of the extent to which they and their Church were mired in the politics of the time. See Gerald R. Cragg, *The Church and The Age of Reason: 1648–1789* (London: Penguin, 1960); Norman Sykes, *From Sheldon to Secker* (Cambridge: Cambridge University Press, 1959); and Sykes's earlier work, *Church and State in England in the Eighteenth Century* (Cambridge: Historical Association Pamphlet 78, Cambridge University Press, 1934), for general background. A bishop close to More who held a middle position more effectively than most, and was a considerable support to Anglican evangelicals including John Newton, William Romaine, Thomas Scott, Richard Cecil, and Basil Wood, was Beilby Porteous. Porteous's *Lectures on the Gospel of St. Matthew*, 2 vols. (London: T. Cadell, 1802), illustrate fairly well his admixturing of evangelical sympathy and latitudinarian caution.

11. Bready reprints the king's stinging letter (p. 48).

12. Moule's introduction to Mary Seeley, *The Later Evanglical Fathers: John Thornton, John Newton, William Cowper,* 2nd ed. (London: C. J. Thynne, 1914).

13. The movement was made more vulnerable to this caricature by the outbreak of charismatic phenomena—people falling down in apparently uncontrollable convulsions and unintelligible utterances during the sermons of John Wesley in particular in 1739, and to a lesser extent later during the ministry of Whitefield. Horace Walpole, the Whig wit and political writer, thought Whitefield literally insane as late as 1750. Numerous books attacked Methodist "enthusiasm," among them Thomas Green's *A Dissertation on Enthusiasm* (1755), Bishop Lavington's *The Enthusiasm of Methodists and Papists Compared* (1749), and a scurrilous pamphlet, *The Love-Feast* (1778). Sometimes the polemic cast the movement as an epidemic of mass insanity orchestrated for political purposes, as in the case of *Enthusiasm No Novelty* (1739), in which it is the threat of a Puritan rather than the usual Catholic revolution that is imagined. William Kenrick, a hack writer and translator of Rousseau, took a similar line in his dubiously titled *On the Investigation of Truth:*

> See still th'enthusiastic band
> Cant, whine, and madden o'er the land;
> By scripture-craz'd fanatics led,
> Whitefield or Westley, at their head, . . .

> Ah! think how fatal, soon or late,
> Such crazy members to the state:
> How dang'rous to the public weal
> Blind ignorance and foolish zeal.

14. Seymour, vol. 1, p. 180. Sir William Blackstone, the noted jurist, claimed to have sampled all the preachers of note in London early in the reign of George III, during which time he "did not hear a single discourse which had more Christianity in it than the writings of Cicero." "It would," he said, "be impossible for him to discover from what he heard whether its preacher were a follower of Confucius, of Mohammed, or of Christ." See Charles J. Abbey and John H. Overton, *The English Church in the 18th Century*, 2 vols. (London: Longmans, Green, 1878), vol. 1, p. 37.

15. See Bready, pp. 145–60.

16. W. E. H. Lecky, *History of England in the Eighteenth Century*, vol. 1, p. 476, quoted in Bready, p. 145.

17. Henry Fielding, *Enquiry into the Late Increase of Robbers* (London, 1751), p. 19.

18. Quoted in Bready, p. 101.

19. Wilberforce suggested in his *Twelve Propositions* (1789) a more conservative figure of "about thirty-eight thousand" per year.

20. Arnold Dallimore, *George Whitefield: The Life and Times of the Great Evangelist of the Eighteenth Century Revival*, 2 vols. (Westchester, Ill.: Cornerstone, 1970; 1980), vol. 2, pp. 219, 368–69.

21. Alexander Pope, *Essay on Man*, in *Poems*, ed. Butt, p. 515, l. 294.

22. Seymour, vol. 1, p. 66.

23. Seymour, vol. 1, p. 69. The date given by others is 1779. John Wesley was forced to the same recourse in 1787, after his own break with the Church of England in 1784.

24. Lady Huntingdon dipped deep into her resources to do this, in one case selling her jewels in order to raise funds to build one of the chapels.

25. Seymour, vol. 1, pp. 86–87.

26. Seymour, vol. 1, p. 78.

27. Four excellent histories have already been cited: Overton, Seymour, Bready, and Dallimore, but see also Horton Davies, *Worship and Theology in England: from Watts and Wesley to Maurice, 1690–1850* (Princeton: Princeton University Press, 1961).

28. Though he was a contemporary of Wilberforce (1759–1836), Simeon did most of his writing after the turn of the century; properly speaking, Simeon stands at the beginning of the nineteenth-century history of evangelicalism. An older, but invaluable, account of his life is by William Carus, *Memoirs of the Life of Charles Simeon, M.A.* (London: Hatchard, 1847).

29. Hervey is perhaps most reluctantly omitted of all. Hervey's *Meditations and Contemplations* (1748) were widely popular and greatly appreciated by his contemporaries. They are written, however, in a florid prose more reminiscent of seventeenth-century writers like Jeremy Taylor, and though literarily interesting, are not especially original in content.

30. Dallimore, vol. 1, p. 238.

31. Seymour, vol. 1, p. 166. Madan's surprising experience in "taking off Wesley" is paralleled by that of another denizen of "Midnight Modern Conversations,"—later

the Reverend Thorpe of the Independent Church at Masborough—who was converted in the midst of a drunken attempt to mimic Whitefield's preaching, when the Bible in his hand fell open to Luke 13:3: "Except ye repent, ye shall all likewise perish." See Seymour, vol. 1, p. 149.

32. Seymour, vol. 1, p. 167.

33. This can well be imagined in the context of repeated slurs against the evangelicals such as that contained in *The Love-Feast* (1779); see n. 13 above.

34. The original version by Charles Wesley is printed by Frank Whaling, ed., *John and Charles Wesley: Selected Writings and Hymns,* in the Classics of Western Spirituality (New York: Paulist Press, 1981), p. 276.

35. This version was further expanded in the early nineteenth century by Sir Samuel Egerton Brydges (1762–1837) to nine stanzas as a *"Dies irae, dies illae."*

36. See the introduction to the Charles Wesley selections following.

37. John Berridge and others in the movement thought it at best an albatross, and perhaps something worse. See the introduction to George Whitefield following.

38. *Journal,* Oct. 15, 1759.

39. *Journal,* Feb. 22, 1750.

40. *Posthumous Pieces of the Late Reverend John William de la Fletchere* (Dublin: Robert Napper, 1802), p. 221.

41. See the introduction to Christopher Smart following. Dr. Nathaniel Cotton (1705–1788) was a significant evangelical, a friend of Doddridge, and administered the "Collegium Insanorum" at St. Albans, where he was instrumental in helping William Cowper, from 1740–1788. This private institution, it should be noted, provided an admirable model for the movement and in its time was seldom equalled for its humane and healing environment.

42. See William Dodd, *An Account of the Rise, Progress and Present State of the Magdalen Charity . . .* (London: Faden, 1766).

43. Green, *Short History of the English People,* p. 736.

44. Overton, p. 131.

45. In 1744, at the request of Lady Huntingdon, John Wesley published a *Collection of Moral and Sacred Poems from the Most Celebrated English Authors.* Among the selections included are twenty-four poems by Rowe—compared to eight from Pope, thirteen from Watts, three from George Herbert, and two extracts from Milton's *Paradise Lost.* Only the Wesley family gets more space than Rowe. See T. W. Herbert, *John Wesley as Editor and Author* (Princeton: Princeton University Press, 1940).

46. In J. Allan Kay, ed., *Wesley's Prayers and Praises* (London: Epworth, 1958), p. 86.

47. John Cennick, an early affiliate of Wesley and Whitefield, joined the Moravians in 1745, and though he took four hundred people from Whitefield's Tabernacle with him, the two men remained on good terms. Wesley, however, seems to have borne a lifelong resentment against him. See Dallimore, vol. 2, pp. 38–40, 233.

48. *Letters,* vol. 5, p. 342. Professor Frans de Bruyn has suggested to me that in his shying away from too much reliance on the inner life and in his alternative emphasis on practical fruits of the Spirit, Wesley would have seemed to many to echo latitudinarians such as Tillotson, Burnet, and Stillingfleet, who typically applied 1 Corinthians 13 in this fashion.

49. *Conference Minutes,* quoted by Philip Watson, *The Message of the Wesleys: A Reader of Instruction and Devotion* (London: Epworth, 1964), p. 183.

50. "Address to the Clergy," in *Works,* vol. 10, p. 484.

51. See below. Cf. J. T. Hatfield, "John Wesley's Translations of German Hymns," *PMLA* 11 (1896), pp. 171–99.

52. *Letters,* vol. 5, p. 283. Cf. Gordon S. Wakefield, *Methodist Devotion: the Spiritual Life in the Methodist Tradition 1791–1945* (London: Epworth, 1966), pp. 25–32.

53. J. Ernest Rattenbury, *The Evangelical Doctrine of Charles Wesley's Hymns* (London: Epworth, 1941), p. 155.

54. Susannah Wesley's strict rules for living and letters containing applications of her most rigorous model are to be found in Adam Clarke, ed., *Memoirs of the Wesley Family,* 2 vols. (London: Tegg, 1843–1844).

55. Like his mother, John Wesley was an admirer of the rationalist philosopher Locke, a fact which has considerable significance for his own theology as well as his subsequent intellectual influence on others. See Richard E. Brantley's illuminating study, *Locke, Wesley, and the Method of English Romanticism* (Gainesville: University of Florida Press, 1984), especially pp. 27–47.

56. *Letters,* vol. 4, pp. 187–88; cf. vol. 5, p. 88.

57. Reprinted by Albert C. Outler, *John Wesley* (New York: Oxford University Press, 1964), pp. 252–71.

58. Outler, p. 253.

59. *The Works of George Whitefield,* 6 vols. (London and Edinburgh, 1771), vol. 13, p. 256; this letter is dated Apr. 25, 1741; cf. p. 259, a letter to Howell Harris on the same subject, Apr. 28, 1741. Count Zinzendorf of the Moravians and his colleagues Bohler and Spangenberg were also offended by Wesley's "perfectionism," as were Harris and most of the Lady Huntingdon circle.

60. *A Plain Account of Christian Perfection,* in the edition by Whaling, p. 300.

61. Whaling, p. 301.

62. Outler, p. 31.

63. Seymour, vol. 1, p. 42.

64. He was also an early encouragement to Charles Simeon, the great leader of evangelical Anglicanism of the early nineteenth century.

65. Boswell apparently made an indecent approach to her at a party at the London residence of Bishop Shipley, with which she was "heartily disgusted"; she gave him "a sharp rebuke"—which undoubtedly was responsible for Boswell's subsequent intense dislike for her (1781). See her letter on the incident in Roberts, p. 57.

66. See the solid study by M. G. Jones, *Hannah More* (New York: Greenwood Press, 1968), p. 119.

67. Hannah More, *Strictures on the Modern System of Female Education,* 2 vols. (New York and London: Garland Reprints, 1974), vol. 2, pp. 207–8.

68. This letter, to a Mr. and Mrs. Coffin, "On Serving God in the Ordinary Duties of life," may be compared to his letter included here entitled "God's Will and Our Ambitions."

69. In a "coincidence" typical of the evangelical movement, the copy of Doddridge which Wilberforce read from had been given to one of his traveling companions by young Reverend Unwin, the convert of William Cowper. The Dissenting

tradition grew much stronger again toward the end of the century, much aided by the evangelical Anglicans. Wilberforce himself, however, leaned away from a strict Calvinism and more toward a doctrine of perseverance. In a letter to his son Samuel in later life (1830), he says, ". . . you and I, who are not Calvinists, believe that even when the influence of the Holy Spirit was in the heart, that Spirit may be grieved and quenched. The good seed in the hearts of the stony ground hearers is just such an instance in point." A. M. Wilberforce, *Private Papers of William Wilberforce* (New York: Burt Franklin, 1968 [repr. of 1897 ed.]), p. 260.

70. William Wilberforce, *A Practical View of . . . Real Christianity* (London: T. Cadell, 1797), p. 24.


## SELECT BIBLIOGRAPHY

*I. Primary*

Boswell, James. *Life of Samuel Johnson*. Ed. George Birbeck Hill. 6 vols. London: Oxford University Press, 1887.

Butler, Bishop Joseph (of Bristol and Durham). *The Analogy of Religion, Natural and Revealed, to the Constitution and Course of Nature*. London, 1736.

———. *The Works*. London: J. F. Dove, 1828.

Carus, William. *Memoirs of the Life of Charles Simeon, M. A.* London: Hatchard, 1847.

Cowper, William. *The Power of Grace Illustrated: Six Letters to the Rev. John Newton*. London, 1792.

———. *Poems*. With a preface by John Newton. 2 vols. London, 1793.

———. *Memoir of the Early Life of William Cowper, Esq., Written by Himself*. London: R. Edwards, 1816.

———. *The Poems*. Ed. John D. Baird and Charles Ryskamp. Vol. 1. Oxford: Clarendon Press, 1980.

———. *The Letters and Prose Writings*. Ed. James King and Charles Ryskamp. 4 vols. Oxford: Clarendon Press, 1980–1984.

Doddridge, Philip. *The Rise and Progress of Religion in the Soul. . . .* London, 1745; New York: American Tract Society, 1812.

Fletcher, John. *An Appeal to Matter of Fact and Common Sense; or, a Rational Demonstration of Man's Corrupt and Lost Estate*. London, 1772; New York: Collord, 1835.

———. *Posthumous Pieces of the Late Rev. John William de la Fletchere, Containing his Pastoral and Familiar Epistles, together with Six Letters on the Manifestation of Christ. Collected and published by the Rev. Melvill Horne. To which is added A Letter Upon the Prophecies*. 3rd ed. Dublin: R. Napper, 1802.

———. *Collected Works of John Fletcher*. Ed. J. Benson. 8 vols. London, 1806.

Harris, Howell. *A Brief Account of the Life of Howell Harris, Esq., extracted from Papers Written by Himself. To which is added a concise collection of his letters*. Trevecka, 1791.

Haweis, Thomas. *The Communicant's Companion; or, an Evangelical Preparation for the Lord's Supper. With Meditations and Helps for Prayer*. 9th ed. Dublin: R. Napper, 1815.

Hervey, James. *Meditations and Contemplations in Two Volumes. . . . A New Edition*. London: J. Rivington, 1779.

Johnson, Samuel. *Lives of the Poets. The Works of Samuel Johnson, L.L.D.* 2 vols. New York: Dearborn, 1836.

Law, William. *A Practical Treatise upon Christian Perfection.* London: J. Richardson, 1726.

———. *The Case of Reason, and Natural Religion, Fully Stated.* London: J. Richardson, 1731.

———. *The Spirit of Prayer.* London: J. Richardson, 1749.

———. *The Works of the Rev. William Law.* 11 vols. London: J. Richardson, 1762.

———. *A Serious Call to a Devout and Holy Life.* London: J. M. Dent, 1906.

———. *Selected Mystical Writings of William Law.* Ed. Stephen Hobhouse. New York: Harper, 1948.

———. *Christian Perfection.* Ed. and Abr. Erwin Rudolph. Carol Stream, Ill.: Creation House, 1975.

More, Hannah. *Florio: A Tale, for Fine Gentlemen and Fine Ladies; and, The Bas Bleu, or Conversation: Two Poems.* London: T. Cadell, 1786.

———. *An Estimate of the Religion of the Fashionable World.* 4th ed. London: T. Cadell, 1791.

———. *Strictures on the Modern System of Female Education.* 2 vols. 2nd ed. London: T. Cadell, 1799. New York: Garland Publishing, 1974.

———. *Coelebs in Search of a Wife: Comprehending Observations on Domestic Habits and Manners, Religion and Morals.* 2 vols. London: T. Cadell and W. Davies, 1809.

———. *The Works of Hannah More.* 7 vols. London: H. Fisher, R. Fisher, and P. Jackson, 1834.

Newton, John. *Sermons in Olney.* London, 1767.

———. *Omricon's Letters.* London, 1774.

———. *Cardiphonia.* 2 vols. London, 1787.

———. *Messiah: Fifty Expository Discourses upon the Series of celebrated Scriptural Passages which form the Subject of the celebrated oratorio of Handel.* 2 vols. London, 1786.

———. *John Newton, An Autobiography and Narrative.* Ed. Josiah Bull. London: The Religious Tract Society, 1868.

Romaine, William. *A Treatise upon the Walk of Faith.* 2 vols. New York: Williams & Whiting, 1809.

Rowe, Elizabeth. *Friendship in Death, in Twenty Letters from the Dead to the Living.* London, 1728.

———. *Letters Moral and Entertaining.* London, 1733.

———. *Devout Exercises of the Heart in Meditation and Soliloquy, Prayer and Praise.* With an introduction by Rev. Isaac Watts, D.D. London, 1737; Nottingham, 1812.

Scougal, Henry. *The Life of God in the Soul of Man.* Edinburgh, 1677.

Smart, Christopher. *Jubilate Agno.* Ed. W. H. Bond. Cambridge, Mass.: Harvard University Press, 1954.

———. *Collected Poems.* Ed. Norman Callan. 2 vols. London: Routledge & Kegan Paul, 1949; rpt. 1967.

Watts, Isaac. *Poems, Chiefly of the Lyrick Kind.* London, 1715.

———. *Horae Lyricae.* London, 1731.

———. *The Improvement of the Mind.* London, 1741. Rpt. with *A Discourse on the Education of Children and Youth.* Edinburgh: Thomas Nelson, 1844.

———. *Discourses of the Love of God, and its Influence on all the Passions.* London, 1746.

————. *Logick*. 10th ed. London, 1755.

————. *The Doctrine of the Passions Explained and Improved*. 2nd ed. Coventry, 1781.

————. *The Holiness of Times, Places, and People under the Jewish and Christian Dispensations Considered and Compared*. 3rd ed. London: R. Hett and J. Blackstone, 1783.

————. *The World to Come; or, Discourses on the Joys and Sorrows of Departed Souls at Death, and the Glory or Terror of the Resurrection*. Oxford: Bartlett, Newman, and Bartlett, 1816.

————. *The Hymns of Isaac Watts*. Ed. S. L. Bishop. Glasgow: Faith Press, 1962.

Wesley, Charles. *Journals of Charles Wesley*. Ed. John Telford. London: Epworth Press, 1900.

————, and John Wesley. *Poetical Works*. Ed. G. Osborn. 13 vols. London: Wesleyan Methodist Conference Office, 1868–1872.

————, and John Wesley. *John and Charles Wesley: Selected Writings and Hymns*. Classics of Western Spirituality. Ed. Frank Whaling. New York: Paulist Press, 1981.

Wesley, John. *A Christian Library. Consisting of Extracts from and Abridgements of the Choicest Pieces of Practical Divinity, Which Has Been Published in the English Tongue*. 50 vols. Bristol, 1749–1755.

————. *Standard Sermons*. Ed. E. H. Sugden. 2 vols. London: Epworth Press, 1921.

————. *The Letters of the Rev. John Wesley, A.M.* Ed. John Telford. 8 vols. London: Epworth Press, 1931; rpt. 1960.

————. *The Journal of John Wesley*. Ed. Nehemiah Curnock. 8 vols. London: Epworth Press, 1938.

————. *Selected Letters of John Wesley*. Ed. Fredrick C. Gill. London: Epworth Press, 1956.

————. *John Wesley*. Ed. Albert Outler. New York: Oxford University Press, 1964. [an anthology of his writings]

————. *The New Birth*. Ed. Thomas C. Oden. San Francisco: Harper and Row, 1984. [an anthology of texts]

Whitefield, George. *Intercession every Christian's Duty. A Sermon Preached at the Parish Church of Great St. Helen's, Dec. 27, 1737*. London: J. Hutton, 1738.

————. *Of Justification by Christ. A Sermon Preached at the Parish Church of Saint Antholin*. London: J. Hutton, 1738.

————. *The Nature and Necessity of Self-Denial. A Sermon Preached at the Parish Church of St. Andrew, Holborn, on Sunday, Oct. 9, 1737*. London: J. Hutton, 1738.

————. *The Almost Christian. A Sermon Preached at the Parish Church of St. John Wapping*. London: J. Hutton, 1738.

————. *The Indwelling of the Spirit, the Common Privilege of all Believers. A Sermon Preached at the Parish Church of Bexly, in Kent, on Whitsunday, 1739*. London: Strahan and Hutton, 1739.

————. *Letter from the Rev. George Whitefield to the Rev. Laurence Sterne, the supposed author of a book entitled "The Life and Opinions of Tristram Shandy, Gentleman."* London, 1760.

————. *The Works of George Whitefield*. 6 vols. London and Edinburgh, 1771.

————. *Journals (1737–1741), to which is Prefixed his autobiographical A Short Account of God's Dealing with George Whitefield (1746) and A Further Account (1747)*. Ed. William Wale. 1905. Gainesville: Scholar's Facsimiles and Reprints, 1969.

_____. *Letters of George Whitefield for the Period 1734–1742*. Rpt. from the 1771 ed. of Whitefield's *Works*. London: Banner of Truth Trust, 1976.

Wilberforce, William. *A Practical View of the Prevailing Religious System of Professed Christians in the Higher and Middle Classes of this Country contrasted with Real Christianity*. London: T. Cadell, 1797.

_____. *Private Papers of William Wilberforce*. Comp. A. M. Wilberforce. New York: Burt Franklin, 1968.


*II. Secondary*


Abbey, Charles J., and J. H. Overton. *The English Church in the 18th Century*. 2 vols. London: Longmans, Green, 1878.

Ainsworth, Edward G., and Charles E. Noyes. *Christopher Smart: A Biographical and Critical Study*. Columbia: University of Missouri Press, 1943.

Balleine, G. R. *A History of the Evangelical Party in the Church of England*. London: Longmans, 1908.

Belcher, Joseph. *George Whitefield: A Biography*. New York: American Tract Society, 1857.

Beynon, Tom, ed. *Howell Harris, Reformer and Soldier*. Caernarvon: Calvinist Methodist Bookroom, 1958.

Blaydes, Sophia B. *Christopher Smart as a Poet of his Time*. The Hague: Mouton, 1966.

Bowen, Marjorie. *Wrestling Jacob: A Study of the Life of John Wesley and Some Members of the Family*. London: Religious Book Club, 1938.

Braitsford, Mabel Richmond. *A Tale of Two Brothers: John and Charles Wesley*. London: Rupert Hart-Davis, 1954

Brantley, Richard. *Locke, Wesley, and the Method of English Romanticism*. Gainesville: University of Florida Press, 1984.

Bready, J. Wesley. *England: Before and After Wesley. The Evangelical Revival and Social Reform*. London: Hodder & Stoughton, 1938.

Cecil, Lord David. *The Stricken Deer: or, The Life of Cowper*. London: Constable, 1929; 1933.

Church, Lesley F. *Knight of the Burning Heart: the Story of John Wesley*. London: Epworth Press, 1938.

Clarke, Adam, ed. *Memoirs of the Wesley Family*. 2 vols. London: Tegg, 1843–1844.

Couillard, Vernon Williams. *The Theology of John Cennick*. Nazareth, Pa.: Moravian Historical Society, 1957.

Cragg, G. R. *From Puritanism to the Age of Reason. A Study of Changes in Religious Thought within the Church of England, 1660–1700*. Cambridge: Cambridge University Press, 1950.

_____. *The Church and the Age of Reason: 1648–1784*. London: Penguin, 1960.

Dallimore, Arnold A. *George Whitefield: The Life and Times of the Great Evangelist of the Eighteenth Century Revival*. 2 vols. Westchester, Ill. Cornerstone, 1970, 1980.

Davies, R. E. *Methodism*. London: Epworth Press, 1976.

_____, and E. G. Rupp, eds. *A History of the Methodist Church in Great Britain*. Vol. 1. London: Epworth Press, 1965.

Day, Robert Adams. *Told in Letters: Epistolary Fiction Before Richardson*. Ann Arbor: University of Michigan Press, 1966.

Deacon, Malcolm. *Philip Doddridge of Northampton, 1702–51*. Northampton: Northamptonshire Libraries, 1980.

Devlin, Christopher. *Poor Kit Smart*. London: Rupert Hart-Davis, 1961.

Eayrs, George. *Wesley: Christian Philosopher and Church Founder*. London: Epworth Press, 1926.

Edwards, Brian H. *Through Many Dangers: the Story of John Newton*. Welwyn: Eurobooks, 1976.

Edwards, Maldwyn. *John Wesley and the Eighteenth Century: A Study of his Social and Political Influence*. London: George Allen and Unwin, 1933.

———. *Family Circle: A Study of the Epworth Household in Relation to John and Charles Wesley*. London: Epworth, 1946.

Fairchild, Hoxie Neale. *Religious Trends in English Poetry*. 5 vols. New York: Columbia University Press, 1942.

Fitchett, W. H. *Wesley and His Century*. Toronto: Briggs, 1906.

Flew, R. N. *The Hymns of Charles Wesley: A Study of Their Structure*. London: Epworth, 1953.

———. *The Idea of Perfection in Christian Theology*. London: Oxford University Press, 1934.

Gibbons, Thomas. *Memoirs of Isaac Watts*. London, 1780.

Gillies, John. *Memoirs of the Life of the Reverend George Whitefield, M.A.* London: E. & C. Dilly, 1772.

Grant, Patrick. *Literature of Mysticism in Western Tradition*. London: Macmillan, 1983.

Green, J. R. *History of England*. 4 vols. London: 1877–1880.

Green, Richard. *The Works of John and Charles Wesley: A Bibliography*. London: Edwin Arnold, 1961.

Green, V. H. H. *The Young Mr. Wesley: A Study of John Wesley and Oxford*. London: Edwin Arnold, 1961.

Heimert, Allan, and Perry Miller, eds. *The Great Awakening: Documents Illustrating the Crisis and its Consequences*. Indianapolis: Bobbs-Merrill, 1967.

Herbert, T. W. *John Wesley as Editor and Author*. Princeton: Princeton University Press, 1940.

Hodges, H. A. and A. M. Alchin. *A Rapture of Praise*. London: Hodder & Stoughton, 1966.

Hughes, J. A. *A Memoir of Daniel Rowland*. London: Nisbet, 1887.

Hutton, J. E. *History of the Moravian Church*. 2nd ed. London: Moravian Publication Office, 1909.

Jackson, T. *The Life of Charles Wesley*. 2 vols. London: Mason, 1841.

Jones, M. G. *Hannah More*. New York: Greenwood Press, 1968.

Jones, M. H. *The Trevecka Letters*. Caernarvon: Calvinist Methodist Bookroom, 1932.

Kirk, John. *The Mother of the Wesleys*. London: Jarrold and Sons, 1868.

Lecky, W. E. H. *A History of England in the Eighteenth Century*. London: Longmans, 1892.

Lyles, Albert M. *Methodism Mocked*. London: Epworth Press, 1960.

Manning, B. L. *The Hymns of Wesley and Watts*. London: Epworth Press, 1942.

Marshall, Madeleine Forell, and Janet Todd. *English Congregational Hymns in the Eighteenth Century*. Lexington: University of Kentucky Press, 1982.

Milner, Thomas. *The Life, Times and Correspondence of the Rev. Isaac Watts, D.D.* London, 1834.

Munk, Robert C. *John Wesley: His Puritan Heritage*. London: Epworth Press, 1966.

New, Alfred H. *The Coronet and the Cross; or, Memorials of the Right Hon. Selina, Countess of Huntingdon*. London: Partridge, 1857.

Nuttall, Geoffrey. *Calendar of the Correspondence of Philip Doddridge, D.D. (1702–1751)*. London: Her Majesty's Stationery Office, 1979.

O'Malley, Ida Beatrice. *Women in Subjection: A Study of the Lives of Englishwomen before 1832*. London: Duckworth, 1933.

Overton, John H. *The Evangelical Revival in the Eighteenth Century*. London: Longmans, Green, 1886.

Parris, J. R. *John Wesley's Doctrine of the Sacraments*. London: Epworth Press, 1963.

Piette, Maximin. *John Wesley in the Evolution of Protestantism*. New York: Sheed & Ward, 1937.

Plummer, Alfred. *The Church of England in the Eighteenth Century*. London: Methuen, 1910.

Pollock, John. *Amazing Grace: John Newton's Story*. London: Hodder & Stoughton, 1981.

Pudney, J. *John Wesley and His World*. London: Thames and Hudson, 1978.

Rattenbury, J. Ernest. *Wesley's Legacy to the World*. London: Epworth Press, 1928.

———. *The Evangelical Doctrine of Charles Wesley's Hymns*. London: Epworth Press, 1941.

———. *The Eucharistic Hymns of John and Charles Wesley*. London: Epworth Press, 1948.

Richetti, John J. *Popular Fiction Before Richardson: Narrative Patterns*. Oxford: Clarendon Press, 1969.

Roberts, William. *The Life of Hannah More, with Selections from her Correspondence*. London: Seely, Jackson and Halliday, 1872.

Rudolph, Erwin Paul. *William Law*. Boston: Twayne, 1980.

Ryle, J. C. *Christian Leaders of the Eighteenth Century*. London, 1885; rpt. Edinburgh: Banner of Truth, 1978.

Seeley, Mary. *The Later Evangelical Fathers: John Thornton, John Newton, and William Cowper*. 2nd ed. London: SPCK, 1914.

Seymour, Aaron Crossley Hobart. *The Life and Times of Selina, Countess of Huntingdon*. 2 vols. London: William Edward Painter, 1844.

Sherbo, Arthur. *Christopher Smart, Scholar of the University*. Lansing: Michigan State University Press, 1967.

Stephen, Leslie. *The History of English Thought in the Eighteenth Century*. 2 vols. London, 1876; rev. ed., 1927.

Stevenson, George J. *Memorials of the Wesley Family*. London: Partridge, 1876.

Sykes, Norman. *From Sheldon to Secker*. Cambridge: Cambridge University Press, 1959.

Thompson, E. P. *The Making of the English Working Class*. New York: Random House, 1966.

Thomas, Gilbert. *William Cowper and the Eighteenth Century*. London: Ivor Nicholson and Watson, 1935.

Todd, J. M. *John Wesley and the Catholic Church*. London: Hodder & Stoughton, 1958.

Towlson, C. W. *Moravian and Methodist*. London: Epworth Press, 1957.

Tuttle, R. G. *John Wesley, His Life and Theology*. Grand Rapids: Zondervan, 1979.

Tyerman, Luke. *The Life and Times of the Rev. John Wesley, M.A.* 3 vols. London: Hodder & Stoughton, 1870.

Wakefield, Gordon Stevens. *Methodist Devotion: The Spiritual Life in the Methodist Tradition*. London: Epworth Press, 1966.

————. *Fire of Love: The Spirituality of John Wesley*. London: Darton, Longman and Todd, 1976.

Walker, A. Keith. *William Law: His Life and Thought*. London: SPCK, 1973.

Walsh, Marcus. *The Religious Poetry of Christopher Smart*. Oxford: Carcanet Press, 1972.

Warner, Oliver. *William Wilberforce and His Times*. London: B. T. Batsford, 1962.

Watson, Philip, comp. *The Message of the Wesleys: A Reader of Instruction and Devotion*. London: Epworth, 1964.

Wearmouth, F. R. *Methodism and the Common People of the Eighteenth Century*. London: Epworth Press, 1945.

Wood, A. Skevington. *The Inextinguishable Blaze*. London: Paternoster Press, 1960.

# ISAAC WATTS
## 1674 · 1748

From an engraving by H. B. Hall and Sons, representing Watts in his early forties
(c. 1715).

INTRODUCTION

The most famous biography of Dr. Isaac Watts—though possibly the briefest—was written by Samuel Johnson, the famous eighteenth-century poet, essayist, and dictionary maker. It occurs in his *Lives of the Poets* (1779), which is actually a collection of prefaces he wrote for a large publisher's edition of famous authors. Johnson tells us, in fact, that "the poems of Dr. Watts were by my recommendation inserted in the collection."[1] This comment comes at the beginning of a testimony—by the greatest critic of the time—which is admiring, even effusive in its praise. It celebrates the life not only of a hymn-writer and preacher, but of a philosopher, teacher, student of nature and human nature alike, and, above all, a Christian personality of compelling attractiveness. Despite Johnson's own stilted awkwardness in matters of religion and his keen prejudice against Puritan and Nonconformist worship, his final praise is for the consistent witness, words and work, of Watts's whole life:

> . . . happy will be that reader whose mind is disposed, by his verses or his prose, to imitate him in all but his non-conformity, to copy his benevolence to man and his reverence to God.

Isaac Watts was born to a Dissenting family of Southampton on July 17, 1674. His father was a part-time school teacher, who, like John Bunyan, had served two terms in prison for his beliefs. His mother was a Taunton, a prominent local family descended from Huguenot stock. She brought the infant Isaac to be seen by his father for the first time (at a distance) in front of the prison where he was confined, and returned regularly until his release.

Like so many of the evangelical leaders of his time, Watts was gifted with extraordinary intellect. Eldest of nine children, he began to read at three, was learning Latin at four, and learned Greek, Hebrew, and French at what for us would be the "elementary" level of school. As Johnson puts it, "his proficiency at school was so conspicuous that a subscription was proposed for his support at the University"; that is, since he was not an Anglican, he was not eligible for entrance to Oxford or Cambridge, let alone a scholarship, so other means had to be found. Although financial sponsors presented themselves, Watts declined their offer on principle, choosing not to become an Anglican but to attend instead the Dissenter Academy of Thomas Rowe in London.[2] Like other students he had already learned to debate, to write essays, to *precis*, and to compose poetry in both Latin and English, and at the secondary level he had studied theology, ethics, and historical philosophy as well as history, language, logic, rhetoric, mathematics, physics, and geography. Now, at sixteen years of age, he was to begin his *higher* education. Rowe—who was Calvinist in theology, Lockean in philosophy, and Cartesian in physics—was to have a decisive influence on Watts, and his instruction accounts for much of Watts's later emphasis on "reasonable" faith.

In his youth, Watts had regularly attended the Above Bar Congregational Church, and occasionally visited other Nonconformist churches as well. By this means he had come under the direct and indirect influence of some of the great Puritan leaders of his day, including Joseph Caryl, Theophilus Gale, and especially John Owen. While studying at the Academy he joined Rowe's church in Basinghill Street, but after graduating and becoming tutor to the son of Sir John Hartopp, he attached himself to Sir John's local congregation. This was the famous Mark Lane Chapel in Stoke Newington, a posh residential section of London in which lived the city's wealthy Dissenter population. Two of Watts's early heroes, Caryl and Owen, had served Mark Lane as pastors, so it must have been gratifying to him to be so soon made assistant to Dr. Isaac Chauncey, the current minister. Watts prospered under Chauncey, preaching his first sermon in 1698 at the age of twenty-four. It may also have been from Chauncey that he acquired during this period a keen interest in New England (Chauncey's father had been president of Harvard from 1654 to 1671) and commenced correspondence with Cotton Mather and other American congregational leaders. Then, in 1702, Watts succeeded Chauncey as pastor of the Mark Lane Chapel.

He was a notable success. The congregation quickly grew to five hundred and had to move to a new location in Bury Street. Watts's sermons were celebrated for their depth of preparation and resulting maturity of teaching, and they were regularly accompanied by hymns he had written—always carefully selected so as to reinforce the central message of the sermon.[3]

Before the time of Watts, congregational hymn singing in both the Anglican and Nonconformist Puritan churches in England had been limited to singing actual psalms, largely owing to the widespread observance of Calvin's stern injunction against the use of music in worship for anything but the singing of psalms. But this prohibition had begun to be broken in Baptist and Independent congregations by the time Watts published his first *Hymns* (1707), so that he provided for an appetite already whetted what must have seemed a very rich banquet indeed: "Jesus shall reign where'er the sun," "When I survey the wondrous cross," "Our God our help in ages past" being but a few of the many hymns which remain in use. His subsequent volumes of religious poetry ranged from the high style of his *Horae Lyricae* (1706) to the first children's hymn book, his *Divine Songs* (1715), which, in an enlarged version, ran to more than one hundred editions by the middle of the nineteenth century.

Ironically, it is to his persistently poor physical health that we owe most of Watts's literary work. Recurrent bouts of illness had prompted the church to appoint him an assistant, Samuel Price, as early as 1703, and when in 1712 Sir Thomas and Lady Abney persuaded Watts to move a little out of the city and live with them for his health's sake, Price took over a greater proportion of the pastoral duties and preaching. Though the congregation would not let him go entirely (he offered to resign) and he still drove in to preach on Sunday as his health permitted, he now had much more time for study and writing.

Watts became, in fact, one of the most popular writers of his day. His educational works were considered standard references, and his *Improvement of the Mind* (1741) had a tremendous influence; Dr. Johnson says of it that "whoever has the care of instructing others may be charged with deficiency in his duty if this book is not recommended." His philosophical works, including his textbook on *Logick* (1725), were long in extensive popular use, as were his works of popular theology, notably *The World to Come* (1738). In recognition of his varied literary achievements the University of Edinburgh awarded him an honorary doctorate (D.D.) in 1728.

Isaac Watts appealed to men and women of his time as much, however, for his eloquent life as for his scholarly books and evangelical sermons. Johnson puts it succinctly:

> His tenderness appeared in his attention to children and to the poor. To the poor, while he lived in the family of a friend, he allowed the third part of his annual revenues, though the whole was not a hundred pounds a year; and for children he condescended to lay aside the scholar, the philosopher and the wit, to write little poems of devotion and systems of instruction adapted to their wants and capacities. . . . Every man acquainted with the common principles of human action will look with veneration on the writer who is at one time combatting Locke and at another making a catechism for children in their fourth year.

But, as Johnson went on to infer, there was no division in Watts's mind between the demands of intellectual life and the life of the Spirit. "Whatever he took in hand was by his incessant solicitude for souls converted to theology." In a time where such single-mindedness could still be accounted a virtue, not a fault, it was perhaps the highest praise his famous biographer could muster to go on to say that under Watts, philosophy became once again the "handmaiden of theology" and that in making all other motives for writing "subservient to evangelical instruction, it [was] difficult to read a page without learning, or at least wishing, to be better." This formulation—with its characteristic Johnsonian ambivalence concerning personal response—nevertheless pays Watts the only honor he would have wished his work to merit.

## NOTES

1. Samuel Johnson, "Watts," from his *Lives of the Poets,* in the *Works of Samuel Johnson, L.L.D.* (New York: Dearborn, 1836), vol. 2, p. 269. All other citations are from this edition. Cf. Boswell's *Life of Samuel Johnson,* ed. G. B. Hill (London: Oxford University Press, 1887), vol. 3, pp. 126, 370; vol. 4, p. 311.

2. See S. L. Bishop, ed., *The Hymns of Isaac Watts* (Glasgow: Faith, 1962), p. xiii.

3. Johnson dryly observes: "He did not endeavour to assist his eloquence by any gesticulations, for, as no corporeal actions have any correspondence with theological truth, he did not see how they could enforce it." Johnson, *Works,* vol. 2, p. 269.

# *from* Meditations

## *Vanity Inscribed in All Things*

TIME, LIKE a long-flowing stream, makes haste into eternity, and is forever lost and swallowed up there; and while it is hastening to its period, it sweeps away all things with it which are not immortal. There is a limit appointed by Providence to the duration of all the pleasant and desirable scenes of life to all the works of the hands of men, with all the glories and excellencies of animal nature, and all that is made of flesh and blood. Let us not dote upon anything here below, for heaven has inscribed vanity upon it. The moment is hastening when the decree of heaven shall be uttered, and Providence shall pronounce upon every glory of the earth, "Its time shall be no longer."

What is that stately building, that princely palace, which now entertains and amuses our sight with ranks of marble columns and widespreading arches, that gay edifice which enriches our imagination with a thousand royal ornaments, and a profusion of gay and glittering furniture? Time, and all its circling hours, with a swift wing, are brushing it away. Decay steals upon it insensibly, and a few years hence it shall lie in mouldering ruin and desolation! Unhappy possessor, if he has not better inheritance.

What are those fine and elegant gardens, those delightful walks, those gentle ascents, and soft declining slopes, which raise and sink the eye by turns to a thousand natural pleasures? How lovely are those sweet borders, and those growing varieties of bloom and fruit, which recall lost Paradise to mind! Those living landscapes, which regale the sense with vital fragrancy, and make glad the sight, by their refreshing verdure and entertaining flowery beauties! The scythe of time is passing over them all; they wither, they die away, they droop and vanish into dust. Their duration is short; a few months deface all their yearly glories, and within a few years, perhaps, all these rising terrace walks, these gentle verging declivities, shall lose all order and elegance, and become a rugged heap of ruins, those well-distinguished borders and lawns shall be levelled in confusion, and thrown into common earth again, for the ox and the ass to graze upon them. Unhappy man, who possesses this agreeable spot of ground, if he has no paradise more durable than this!

58

And no wonder that these labors of the hands of man should perish, when even the works of God are perishable.

What are these visible heavens, these lower skies, and this globe of earth? They are indeed the glorious workmanship of the Almighty, but they are waxing old, and waiting their period too, when the angel shall pronounce upon them that "time shall be no more." The heavens shall be folded up as a vesture, the elements of the lower world shall melt with fervent heat, and the earth and all the works thereof shall be burnt up with fire. May the unruinable world be but my portion, and the heaven of heavens my inheritance, which is built for an eternal mansion for the sons of God. These buildings shall outlive time and nature, and exist through unknown ages of felicity.

What have we mortals to be proud of in our present state, when every human glory is so fugitive and fading? Let the brightest and the best of us say to ourselves that "we are but dust and vanity."

Is my body formed upon a graceful model? Are my limbs well turned, and my complexion better colored than my neighbors? Beauty, even in perfection, is of shortest days; a few years will inform me that its bloom vanishes, its flower withers, its lustre grows dim, its duration shall be no longer, and if life be prolonged, yet the pride and glory of it is forever lost in age and wrinkles, or perhaps our vanity meets a speedier fate. Death and the grave, with a sovereign and irresistible command, summon the brightest as well as the coarsest pieces of human nature to lie down early in their cold embraces; and at last they must all mix together amongst worms and corruption. Aesop the deformed, Helena the fair, are lost and undistinguished in common earth. Nature, in its gayest bloom, is but a painted vanity.

Are my nerves well strung and vigorous? Is my activity and strength far superior to my neighbors in the day of youth? But youth has its appointed limit; age steals upon it, unstrings the nerves, and makes the force of nature languish into infirmity and feebleness. Samson and Goliath would have lost their boasted advantages of stature and their brawny limbs in the course of half a century, though the one escaped the sling of David, and the other the vengeance of his own hands in the ruin of Dagon's temple. Man, in his best estate, is a flying shadow and vanity. ✓

Even those nobler powers of human life, which seem to have something angelical in them (I mean the powers of wit and fancy, gay imagination, and capacious memory) are all subject to the same laws of decay and death. What though they can raise and animate beautiful scenes in a moment, and, in imitation of creating power, can spread bright appearances and new worlds before the senses and the souls of their friends!

What though they can entertain the better part of mankind, the refined and polite world, with high delight and rapture! These scenes of rapturous delight grow flat and old by a frequent review, and the very powers that raised them grow feeble apace. What though they can give immortal applause and fame to their possessors! It is but the immortality of an empty name, a mere succession of the breath of men; and it is a short sort of immortality too, which must die and perish when this world perishes. A poor shadow of duration indeed, while the real period of these powers is hastening every day; they languish and die as fast as animal nature, which has a large share in them, makes haste to its decay, and the time of their exercise shall shortly be no more.

In vain the aged poet or the painter would call up the muse and genius of their youth, and summon all the arts of their imagination to spread and dress out some visionary scene; in vain the elegant orator would recall the bold and masterly figures, and all those flowery images which gave ardor, grace and dignity to his younger compositions and charmed every ear. They are gone, they are fled beyond the reach of their owner's call; their time is past, they are vanished and lost beyond all hope of recovery.

The God of nature has pronounced an unpassable period upon all the powers and pleasures and glories of his mortal state. Let us then be afraid to make any of them our boast or our happiness, but point our affections to those diviner objects whose nature is everlasting. Let us seek those spiritual attainments and those new-created powers of a sanctified mind, concerning which it shall never be pronounced that "their time shall be no longer."

O may every one of us be humbly content at the call of heaven to part with all that is pleasing or magnificent here on earth; let us resign even these agreeable talents when the God of nature demands, and when the hour arrives that shall close our eyes to all visible things, and lay our fleshy structure in the dust. Let us yield up our whole selves to the hands of our Creator, who shall reserve our spirits with Himself; and while we cheerfully give up all that was mortal to the grave, we may lie down full of the joyful hope of a rising immortality. New and unknown powers and glories, brighter flames of imagination, richer scenes of wit and fancy, and diviner talents, are preparing for us when we shall awake from the dust; and the mind itself shall have all its faculties in a sublimer state of improvement. These shall make us equal, if not superior, to angels, for we are nearer akin to the Son of God than they are, and therefore we shall be made more like Him.

# The Gift of the Spirit

WHAT IS dearer to God the Father than his only Son? And what diviner blessing has He to bestow upon men than his Holy Spirit? Yet has He given his Son for us; and by the hands of his Son He confers his blessed Spirit on us: "Jesus having received of the Father the promise of the Spirit, shed it forth on men" (Acts 2:33).

How the wondrous doctrine of the blessed Trinity shines through the whole of our religion, and sheds a glory upon every part of it! Here is God the Father, a king of infinite riches and glory; He has constituted his beloved Son the high treasurer of heaven, and the Holy Spirit is the divine and inestimable treasure. What amazing doctrines of sacred love are written in our Bibles! What mysteries of mercy, what miracles of glory are these! Our boldest desires and most raised hopes durst never aim at such blessings; there is nothing in all nature that can lead us to a thought of such grace.

The Spirit was given by the Father to the Son for men, for rebellious and sinful men, to make favorites and saints of them; this was the noble gift the Son received when He ascended on high. "And he distributed it to grace his triumph" (Psalm 68:18).

Was it not a divine honor which Jesus our Lord displayed on that day when the tongues of fire sat on his twelve apostles? When He sent his ambassadors to every nation to address them in their own language, to notify his accession to the throne of heaven, and to demand subjection to his government? When He conferred power upon his envoys to reverse the laws of nature, and imitate creation—to give eyes to the blind, and to raise the dead? All this was done by the Spirit, which He sent down upon them in the days of Pentecost.

But is this Spirit given to none but his apostles and the prime ministers in his kingdom? Was that rich treasure exhausted in the first ages of the gospel, and none left for us? God forbid! Every one of his subjects has the same favor bestowed upon him, though not in the same degree; every humble and holy soul in our day, every true Christian is possessed of his Spirit, for "he that has not the Spirit of Christ is none of his" (Romans 8:9). And wherever this Spirit is, it works miracles too; it changes the sinner to a saint, it opens his blind eyes, it new-creates his nature; it raises the dead to a divine life, and teaches Egypt and Assyria, and the British Isles, to speak the language of Canaan. It is this gift of the Spirit which the Son sends down to us continually from the Father that is the original and spring of all these strange blessings.

The Father has a heart of large bounty to the poor ruined race of Adam; the Son has a hand fit to be almsgiver to the King of Glory; and the Spirit is the rich alms. This blessed Giver had enriched ten thousand souls already, and there remains enough to enrich ten thousand worlds.

The Father, what a glorious giver! The Son, what a glorious medium of communication! And the Spirit, what a glorious gift! We blush and adore while we partake of such immense favors, and gratitude is even overwhelmed with wonder.

O let our spirits rejoice in this blessed article of our religion, and may all the temptations that we meet with from men of reason, never, never baffle so sweet a faith!

## The Saints Unknown in this World

OUT OF the millions of mankind that spread over the earth in every age, the great God has been pleased to take some into his own family, has given them a heavenly and divine nature, and made them his sons and his daughters.

But He has set no outward mark of glory upon them; there is nothing in their figure or in their countenance to distinguish them from the rabble of mankind, and it is fit that they should be in some measure unknown among their fellow mortals; their character and dignity is too sacred and sublime to be made public here on earth, where the circumstances that attend them are generally so mean and despicable. Divine Wisdom has appointed the other world for the place of their discovery; there they shall appear like themselves, in state, equipage, and array becoming the children of God and heirs of heaven.

Their blessed Lord Himself, who is God's firstborn Son, was a mere stranger and unknown amongst men. He laid aside the rays of divinity and the form of a God when He came down to dwell with men, and He took upon Him the form of a servant. He wore no divine majesty on his face; no sparks of Godhead beaming from his eyes; no glaring evidence of his high dignity in all his outward appearance. Therefore the world knows us not, because it knew Him not. But He shall be known and adored when He comes in the glory of his Father, with legions of angels; and we know that when He shall appear, we shall be like Him. The life of the saints is hidden with Christ in God. But when Christ, who is their life, shall appear, they also shall appear with Him in glory (1 John 3:1,2; Colossians 3:3,4). In that day they shall stand forth before the whole creation in fair evidence; they shall shine in distinguished light, and appear vested in their own undoubted honors. But here it seems proper that there should be something of a cloud upon them, both upon the account of the people of this world, and upon their own account too, as well as in conformity to Christ Jesus their Lord.

First, upon their own account, because the present state of a Christian is a state of trial. We are not to walk by sight, as the saints above and angels do; they know they are possessed of life and blessedness, for they see God Himself near them, Christ in the midst of them, and glory all around them. Our work is to live by faith, and therefore God has not made either his love to us or his grace in us so obvious and apparent to ourselves that every Christian, even the weak and the unwatchful, should be fully assured of this salvation. He has not appointed the principle of life within us to sparkle in so divine a manner as to be always self-evident to the best of Christians, much less to the lukewarm and backslider. It is fit that it should not be too perceptibly manifest, because it is so perceptibly imperfect, that we might examine ourselves whether we are in the faith, and prove ourselves whether Christ, as a principle of life, dwell in us or not (2 Corinthians 8:5). While so many snares and sins and dangers attend us, and mingle with our spiritual life, there will be something of darkness ready to rise and obscure it, in order that we may maintain a holy jealousy and solicitude about our own state, that we may search with diligence to find whether we have a divine life or not, and be called and urged often to look inwards.

This degree of remaining darkness, and the doubtful state of a slothful Christian, are sometimes of great use to spur him onward in the race of holiness, and quicken him to aspire after the highest measures of the spiritual life, that when its acts are more vigorous, it may shine with the brightest evidence and give the soul of the believer full satisfaction and joy. It serves also to awaken the drowsy Christian to keep a holy watch over his heart and practice, lest sin and temptation make a foul inroad upon his divine life, spread still a thicker cloud over his best hopes, and break the peace of his conscience. Though the principle of grace be not always self-evident, yet we are required to give diligence to make and to keep it sure (2 Peter 1:10).

And as it was proper that every little seed of grace should not shine with self-sufficient and constant evidence on the account of the Christian himself, so, secondly, it was fit that their state and dignity should not be too obvious to those of this world, that they might neither adore nor destroy the saints. A principle of superstition might tempt some weaker souls to pay extravagant honors to the Christian if he carried heaven in his face and it were visible in his countenance that he was a son of God. On the other hand, the malicious and perverse part of mankind might imitate the rage of Satan, and attempt the sooner to destroy the saint.

This was the case of the blessed Paul. When he had wrought a miracle at Lystra, and appeared with something divine about him when he had healed the cripple by a mere word of command, the people cried out with exalted voices: "The gods are come down to us in the likeness of men"; immediately they made a Mercury of St. Paul, they turned Barnabas into Jupiter, and the priests brought oxen and garlands to the gates to perform sacrifices to them. This was the response of the superstitious Gentiles. But in several of the Jews, their malice and envy wrought a very different effect; for they urged the people into a fury, so that they stoned the blessed apostle, and drew him out of the city for dead (Acts 14).

Thus it fared with our Lord Jesus Christ Himself in the days of his flesh. For the most part He lived unknown among men; he did not cry, nor make his voice to be heard in the streets, but when He revealed Himself to them on any special occasion, the people ran into different extremes. Once, when the character of the Messiah appeared with evidence upon Him, they would have raised Him to a throne and made an earthly king of Him (John 6:15). At another time, when his holy conduct did not suit their honor, they were "filled with wrath, and led him to the brow of a hill, to cast him down headlong" (Luke 4:29). Therefore our blessed Lord did not walk through the streets, and tell the world He was the Messiah; but by degrees He let the character of his mission appear upon Him, and revealed Himself in wisdom as his disciples and the world could bear it and as the Father had appointed.

Let us imitate our blessed Lord, and copy after so divine a pattern. Let our works bear a bright and growing witness to our inward and real Christianity. This is such a gentle sort of evidence that, though it may work conviction in the hearts of spectators, yet it does not strike the sense with so glaring a light as to dazzle the weaker sort who behold it into superstitious folly; nor does it give such provocation to the envy of the malicious as if the saints had borne the sign of their high dignity in some more surprising manner in their figure or countenance.

I might add also that there is something in this sort of evidence of their saintship that carries more true honor in it than if some heavenly name had been written in their forehead, or their skin had shone like the face of Moses when he came down from the mount. It is a more sublime glory for a prince to be found among the common poor in undistinguished raiment, and by his superior conduct and shining virtues force the world to confess that he is the son of a king, than to walk through the rabble with ensigns of royalty and demand honor from them by the mere blaze of his ornaments.

# *from* On Prayer (1715)

## I. *The Grace of Prayer*

. . . THERE IS A great difference between the skill and the grace of prayer. The skill is but the outside, the shape, the carcass of our responsibility. The grace is the soul and spirit that gives it life, vigor and efficacy, that renders it acceptable to God and of real advantage to ourselves. The skill consists chiefly in a readiness of thought consistent with the various aspects of prayer, and a facility for expressing those thoughts in speaking to God. The grace consists in the inward workings of the heart and conscience toward God and our life of faith. The skill has a show and appearance of holy desires and affections, but holy affections, sincere desires, and real conversation with God belong only to the grace of prayer. The skill and the grace are often separated from each other, and it has often been found that the skill of prayer has been attained in great measure by study and practice and by the common workings of the Spirit of God communicated to some persons that have known nothing of true grace. Conversely, there may be a lively exercise of the grace of prayer in some souls who have a very small measure of skill—who hardly know how to form their thoughts and desires in a methodical or regular way, or to express those desires in tolerable language.

There are several particular graces that belong to the whole work or duty of prayer, including the following:

1. Faith or belief in the being of God, his perfect knowledge, and his gracious notice of all that we speak in prayer. The Apostle offers this instruction: "He that cometh to God must believe that He is, and that He is a rewarder of all that diligently seek Him" (Hebrews 9:6). We should endeavor to impress our minds frequently with a fresh and lively acknowledgement of God's existence (although He is invisible and unrecognized by physical presence), and of his just and merciful regard for all the actions of men, especially their spiritual affairs. In this way prayer may be a matter not of custom and ceremony, but performed with a design and hope of pleasing God and having some good at his hand. This exercise of a lively faith runs through every part of our duty, giving spirit and power to the whole act of worship.

2. Gravity, reverence, and seriousness of spirit [should also characterize our prayer]. Let a light and trivial disposition be utterly banished when we come into the presence of God. When we speak to the great

Creator, who must also be our Judge, about concerns of infinite and everlasting importance, we ought to have our souls clothed with reverence, not with those attitudes which are lawful at other seasons when we are talking with our fellow creatures about lower matters. A carelessness and vanity of mind ought never to be indulged in the least degree when we come to perform any part of divine worship, especially when we who are but dust and ashes speak unto the great and awesome God.

3. Spirituality and heavenly-mindedness should run through the whole of this responsibility of prayer. For prayer is a retreat from earth and from our fellow creatures to attend on God and hold correspondence with Him who dwells in heaven. If our thoughts are full of corn and wine and oil and the business of this life, we shall not seek so earnestly the favor and face of God as is proper to faithful worshippers. The things of the world therefore must be commanded to stand by for a season, to abide at the foot of the mount while we walk up higher to offer up our sacrifices— as Abraham did—and to meet our God. Our aims, ends and desires should grow more spiritual as we proceed in this responsibility. And although God invites us to converse with Him about many of our temporal affairs in prayer, let us nevertheless take care that the things of our souls and the eternal world always possess the chief room in our hearts. And whatever cares of this life enter into our prayers and are spread before the Lord, let us see that our aims in offering them are spiritual, so that our very desires of earthly comforts may be purified from all carnal ends and sanctified to divine purposes—to the glory of God, to the honor of the gospel and the salvation of souls.

4. Sincerity and uprightness of heart are other graces that must run through our worship in prayer. Whether we speak to God concerning his own glory, whether we give Him thanks for his abundant goodness, confess our various iniquities before Him or express our desire of mercy at his hand, still let our hearts and our lips agree. Let us not be found mockers of God, who searches the heart and examines our inward parts, and can spy hypocrisy in the darkest corner of the soul.

5. Holy watchfulness and an intent concentration of mind upon the responsibility in which we are engaged must run through every part of prayer. Our thoughts must not be allowed to wander among the things of this world or rove to the ends of the earth when we come to converse with the high and holy God. Without this holy attentiveness we shall be in danger of leaving God in the midst of our worship because of various and strong temptations arising from Satan and from our own hearts. Without this watchfulness our worship will degenerate into mere formality, and we shall find coldness and indifference creeping upon our spirits and spoiling the success of our efforts. "Watch unto prayer" is a constant direction of the great Apostle.

## II. *Prayer as Divine Correspondence*

In order to direct ourselves in the spiritual performance of this duty of prayer, we must consider it as a holy conversation maintained between earth and heaven, between the great and holy God and mean and sinful creatures such as ourselves. Now the most natural directions that I can think of for carrying on this conversation are these:

1. Possess your hearts with a most sensitive awareness of the respective characteristics of the two parties in this correspondence; that is, God and yourselves. (This directive is appropriate also to the skill of prayer, but it is most necessary in attaining the grace.) Let us consider who this glorious Being is who invites us to this fellowship with Himself—how awesome in majesty, how terrible in righteousness, how irresistible in power, how unsearchable in wisdom, how all-sufficient in blessedness, how compassionate in mercy!

Let us consider who we ourselves are who are invited to this correspondence: how vile in our original fallen nature, how guilty in our hearts and lives, how needy of every blessing, how utterly incapable of helping ourselves, and how miserable forever if we are without God! And if we have sincerely obeyed the call of his gospel and have attained to some comfortable hope of his love, let us consider how infinite are our obligations to Him, how necessary and delightful it is to enjoy our conversation with Him here, with whom it will be our happiness to dwell forever. When we feel our spirits deeply impressed with such thoughts as these, we are in the best attitude for prayer, and most likely to pray with grace in our hearts.

2. When you come before God, remember the nature of this correspondence, that it is all-spiritual; remember the dignity and privilege, the purpose and the importance of it. A sense of the high favor in being admitted to this privilege and honor will fill your souls with humble wonder and with heavenly joy such as becomes the worshipper of an infinite God. A due attention to the purpose and importance of this responsibility will fix your thoughts with the most immovable attention and strict watchfulness; it will overspread your spirit with seriousness, commanding all your inward powers to devotion and raising your desires to holy fervency.

3. Seek earnestly a state of friendship with Him with whom you converse, and labor after a good hope and assurance of that friendship. How unspeakable is the pleasure in holding conversation with so infinite, so almighty and so compassionate a friend! And how ready will all the powers of nature be to render every honor to Him while we feel and know ourselves to be recipients of his special favor, the children of his grace!

67

4. In order to obtain this friendship and promote this divine fellowship, live much upon and with Jesus the Mediator, by whose interest alone you can come near God and be brought into his company. Christ is the Way, the Truth, and the Life, and no man comes to the Father but by Him (John 14:6). Through Him both Jews and Gentiles have access unto the Father (Ephesians 2:18). Live much in dependence and trust upon Him, and live much by meditation and love with Him. When a sinner under first conviction sees with horror the awesome holiness of God, and his own guilt, how fearful he is to draw near to God in prayer! But when he first beholds Christ in his great act of mediation and his glorious all-sufficiency to save—when he first beholds this new and living way of access to God, consecrated by the blood of Christ—how cheerfully does he come before the throne of God and pour out his own soul in prayer. And how lively is his nature in the exercise of every grace suited to this responsibility, how deep his humility, how fervent his desire, how importunate his pleadings, how warm and hearty his thanksgivings! We need always to maintain within our spirits a deep sense of the evil of sin, of our desert of death, of the dreadful holiness of God and the impossibility of our conversation with Him without a Mediator, so that the name of Jesus may be ever precious to us and we may never venture into the presence of God in prepared and reverent prayer without the eye of our soul turned toward Christ our glorious Introducer.

5. Maintain always a prayerful attitude, a disposition of mind ready to converse with God. This will be one way to keep all praying graces ever ready for exercise. Visit therefore often and upon all occasions the One with whom you would obtain some immediate communion at solemn seasons of devotion. Make the work of prayer your delight, nor rest satisfied until you find pleasure in it.

Whatever advantages and opportunities you enjoy for communal prayer, do not neglect praying in secret. At least once a day constrain the business of life to give you leave to say something to God alone. When you join with others in prayer, where you are not the speaker, let your heart be kept intent and watchful, so that you may pray so much the better when you are the mouthpiece of others to God. Take frequent occasion in the midst of your duties in the world to lift up your heart to God. He is ready to hear a sudden sentence and will answer the yearnings of a holy soul toward Him in the short intervals and spaces between your daily affairs. Thus you may pray without ceasing, as the Apostle directs, and your graces may be ever lively. For if, on the other hand, you only make your addresses to God in the morning and evening and forget Him all day, your hearts will grow indifferent in worship and you will most likely pay a salutation only with your lips and knees. . . .

Thus shall you learn the perfection of beauty in this part of worship, when the skill and grace of prayer are happily joined in the secret pleasure and success of it, appearing before all in their full loveliness and attractive power. Then shall the spiritual life look like itself, divine and heavenly, and shine in all the lustre it is capable of here on earth.

# *from* Abuse of the Emotions in Spiritual Life (1746)

## I. *The Susceptibility of the Emotions to Error*

. . . THE EMOTIONS were made to be servants to reason, to be governed by the judgement and to be influenced by truth, but they were not intended to decide controversies or to determine what is truth and what error. Even the best affections, those that seem to have a strong tendency toward piety, are not always safe guides in this respect. Yet they are too often indulged, swaying the mind in its search after truth or responsibility—as in the following kinds of situations:

1. Suppose a person should be exceedingly moved by the unlimited goodness and abounding grace of God. If by this pious affection toward God and his goodness he is pursuaded to think that God is without severe vengeance for sinful and rebel creatures, and that He will not destroy such multitudes of mankind in hell as the Scripture asserts, or that their punishment shall not be so long and so terrible as God has expressly declared, here an emotional response of love and esteem for the divine goodness acts in an inordinate manner, for it diverts the eyes of the soul from his awesome holiness and his strict justice, and from recognition of the evil that is in sin. It prevents the mind from giving due attention to God's express word, and to those perfections of his divine nature and his wise and righteous government which may demand such dreadful and eternal punishment for the rebellion of a creature against the infinite dignity of its Creator and governor.

2. Suppose [on the other hand] a Christian has been powerfully impressed with the emotion of fear by the conception of God's majesty and his punishing justice, and thus he concludes that the great God will pardon no willfull sins, that He will forgive no repeated iniquities, no sins after baptism and the Lord's supper, or after vows or solemn occasions, that He will have no mercy upon apostates, even though they turn to him in repentance. This is yielding up truth to the emotion of fear, and an abuse of our appropriate dread of the majesty of God. For such an opinion runs counter to the great design of the gospel, which assures us that Christ came to save the chief of sinners, to remove the guilt of willful and repeated sins, and to provide forgiveness for some of the most profligate rebels, even for all that renounce their rebellion.

3. Some pious persons have had such an emotional zeal to honor God

that they have been led by this emotion to contrive various forms of service and ceremony, gay and costly rites, with long and painful exercises of devotion which God never appointed, and have introduced a number of them into his worship. A childish fondness to please the great God with bodily services has tempted them to forget his own divine prerogative of describing how his people should worship Him. They have been blinded with this sort of fondness for ceremony in such a degree as to lead themselves far astray from the divine simplicity of worship which the New Testament has appointed.

4. Some persons, out of a passionate desire to honor Christ and ascribe the whole train of their blessings and salvation to Him, have been tempted to think that they are to do nothing toward their own salvation but lie still and be saved without any labor or care of their own. So, they have sought no more after sanctification and holiness in themselves than they have sought to make atonement for their own sins. But this zeal has much darkness in it, and betrays them into a gross error, as though they could not ascribe their salvation sufficiently to Christ unless they fancied that He came to save them *in* their sins rather than to save them *from* sin.

5. It is possible that a person may have so high an esteem and so excessive a love for some near relation, some Christian friend, some wise and spiritual minister of the gospel, that he sees no fault in them. He imitates all their actions as though they were perfect patterns; he receives all their opinions for certain and divine truths, and believes everything which they teach as though they were infallible, without comparing it with the Bible—which is the only test of truth in matters of revealed faith. This affection of love for ministers or other Christians is certainly inappropriate when it tempts us to set up their judgements, their practices and their dictates in the place of the word of God.

6. Again, 'tis the same culpable indulgence of our emotions to sway our judgement and bias our understanding when our souls are warmed with the holy fire of love and devotion under a particular sermon and we cry out, "This is the best sermon that was ever preached. . ." Or perhaps our devout emotions flag and languish under a sermon—we sit indolent and unmoved—and then the sermon passes for a poor dry discourse, and the man that delivered it for a dull and heavy preacher. Each of these hasty and irresponsible judgements built on an emotional response is very common to Christians, and ought to be corrected.

7. I might add another instance akin to the last—that is, when our devout emotions of fear and hope, holy love and heavenly delight are raised in a place of public worship (whether of the Established Church or among the several denominations of the Protestant dissenters) and immediately we conclude, "This is the right way of worship, this is most

agreeable to the gospel, and these people are the only true church of Christ." How weak is this reasoning! And yet how many are there who have been determined both in their opinion and practice for or against a particular community of Christians or mode of worship—for their whole lifetime!—merely because of the emotional impression that one or two attendances at such a place of worship have made upon them. . . .

## II. *Common Abuses of Spiritual Emotions*

It is clear, then, that emotions were not designed to be the directing powers of the soul in the search of truth or duty, nor made to rule all within us, but intended rather to be governed by reason and understanding. In any instances where they assume a superiority over the understanding, or run before it, they are excessive and inordinate. Let us consider a few particulars:

### 1. Premature zeal

Some persons, as soon as they begin to find further light dawning upon their minds and are let into the knowledge of some doctrine or perception which they had not previously understood, immediately set their zeal to work. Their zeal is all on fire to propagate and promote this new lesson of truth before their own hearts are established in it upon solid understanding and before they have considered whether it is a doctrine of great importance or merits such a degree of zeal. How common it is among Christians, too often among ministers of the gospel, to give free rein to their emotions at the first glimpse of some pleasing opinion or some fresh discovery of what they call truth! They compensate for the weakness of the proof by the strength of their emotions, and by the pleasure they take in the opinion they have embraced. This confirms their assent too soon, and they grow deaf to arguments that are brought to oppose it. They construe every text in Scripture to support this doctrine; they bring in the prophets and apostles to maintain it. They fancy they see it in a thousand verses of their Bibles and they pronounce all that dare maintain contrary opinions heretics. Their conduct in this matter is as vehement as if every gleam of light were sufficient to determine their faith, because it happens to fire their emotions. They grow warm about it as if every opinion in spiritual life were fundamental, and every mistake deserved the severest censures. . . .

There are too many who take up most of their articles of faith initially without due examination and without sufficient argument. Their veneration for great names or their affection for a particular party has determined their opinions long before. Their passions and other prejudices have formed their schemes of doctrine to the neglect or abuse of their understanding, and yet they pronounce as positively upon truth and error as though they were infallible. Happy are those whose faith is built on better foundations!

## 2. Unrighteous indignation

Again, there are some persons who, when they begin to be convinced that such and such a practice is culpable or unlawful, their indignation is too soon awakened and rises too high. Immediately they condemn it as inconsistent with salvation. Their hatred of it grows as if it were blasphemy or idolatry. They are ready to break into stern speeches and railing accusations against all who practice it, and pronounce them apostates and sinners of the first rank. The sudden rise and warmth of their passions prevents them from considering that there are some faults and follies that a true Christian may be guilty of inadvertently or through ignorance, and that there are some sins that do not carry in them such malignity and poison as to destroy all our Christianity.

## 3. Impressionability

There have been some weak Christians who, when they have heard a sermon or read a discourse full of sublime language and mysterious darkness, and especially if the style and manner have been very moving, have been raptured and transported as if it contained the deepest and noblest truths of the spiritual life, and the highest discoveries of grace and the gospel. There may, however, be scarcely anything in it which accords properly with reason or Scripture; when well examined it proves to be mere jargon, a mixture of unintelligible and meaningless sounds with some arousing sentiments by which the emotions were fired without the benefit of knowledge or reason. And it is fortunate if, after these flashes of emotion and violent transports, such persons are not deluded into shameful iniquities. . . .

This inordinate exercise of the emotions before reason is eminently exemplified also in another weak sort of person, who is very sincere in the main but, if he reads an awful and terrible warning, or if he hears it pronounced in the pulpit with a suitable degree of authority and a proper accent, his fears are raised in an excessive manner and his soul filled with lasting sorrows and doubts. Or, if he happens to read or hear a sentence of comfort he is transported with sudden joy and rises almost to assurance of the love of God. He gives himself up to sudden bursts of emotion before he permits himself to inquire according to scriptural grounds whether this text of warnings—or the sentence offering comfort—really applies to him or not. . . .

### 4. Misplaced fervor

It is a very gross abuse of the emotions when we encourage them to rise high and grow very warm about the insignificant aspects of the spiritual life and yet are content to be cold and indifferent in matters of the highest importance. There are too many Christians whose warmest zeal is devoted to the mint, anise and cummin of Christianity (Matthew 23:23) and have few emotions awakened or engaged in the weighty things of the law or the gospel. They are furiously intent upon speculative notions and various peculiar opinions that distinguish the little parties of Christendom and crumble the church to pieces. Their fears, their hopes, their wishes, their desires, their grief and joy are all employed in party quarrels and in a strife of words. But they are thoughtless and indolent about the immediate duties of love to God and Christ, of justice to men, charity to fellow creatures and fellow Christians. A sickly imagination is thus fond of trifles and careless of solid treasures (as children have their little souls wrapped up in painted toys) while appropriate human concerns and necessary business awaken no desire, no delight in them.

Suppose one mourns to see the Church of England lose ground in the nation, or to see the assemblies of Protestant dissenters grow thin and decrease, and yet his soul is not grieved and his heart does not mourn over the atheism and profanity of the land, the drunkenness and lewdness, the growing heathenism and infidelity of the age. Or suppose a Christian triumphs to see the controversy about baptism well managed as his own opinion is bravely supported while at the same time he takes little pleasure to hear of the conversion of a sinner or that a wicked family has been brought to faith. What shall we think of such a person? Is not his religion in a childish and sickly state? Are not his emotions, even about spiritual matters, managed in a very inconsistent manner, and worthy of just and severe reproof?

### 5. Emotional pretense

There is also another kind of evil conduct of the emotions in matters of faith, and that is when they express themselves in an improper or indecent manner, and especially in such a way as is unnatural and uninstituted, foolish and ridiculous, savage and barbarous, contrary both to the dictates of reason and human nature and the Word of God. . . .

Some religious feelings are very properly expressed and manifested in the common way by which nature usually expresses inward sensations of the soul. Godly sorrow naturally vents itself in groans and tears (Psalm 6:6), holy joy sometimes by a smile of the countenance and often by the voice of sacred melody. And such expressions not only appear in the example of the royal psalmist but in the precepts of the New Testament also (Ephesians 5:18; James 5:13: "If any be merry, let him sing psalms.") Pious and earnest desires for the presence of God and his favor are signified by stretching the arm towards Him or lifting up the eyes and hands to Him (Psalm 68:31; 28:2; 121:1,2). Repentance and shame are naturally signified by downcast eyes and hands (Luke 18:13; Ezra 9:6).

Some of the stronger outward appearances and vehement tokens of inward and holy passions are indeed rather to be indulged in private than √ in public worship. But in all our behavior in this respect, let us take heed that the inward emotion is sincere and is the real spring of all the outward signs and expressions. Let us see to it that we do not indulge that practice which our Saviour so much condemns in the hypocrites of his day (Matthew 6:16). Let us make no sad faces nor put on dismal airs, nor smite the breast with the hand and disfigure our countenances merely to make the world believe that we are penitents. Nor let us make ourselves remarkable in public and mixed company by turning up our eyes to heaven to tell the world how often we pray in the midst of our secular affairs (even though secret prayer may and ought to be sometimes rising to God, and we may lift an eye to Him while we are among other people). Nor should we, in public worship, use frequent and loud groanings to persuade our neighbors that we are more deeply affected with divine things than they (even though a devout feeling will sometimes vent a groan or a sigh).

But above all, let us take heed lest we make use of these outward colors √ and forms of emotion to cover the lack of inward devotion and piety. We should always make our faith appear to the world with a natural and becoming aspect, and in a decent dress, to invite and not forbid those who behold us. Let us take care that we do not disguise our holy Christianity, nor make it look like an irrational thing by uncouth or unbecoming sounds or gestures, lest we thereby expose ourselves to the charge of hypocrisy and give up our holy profession to the ridicule and contempt of the profane world.

6. Emotions without integrity

It reflects improper management in the affairs of our spiritual life, or an abuse of devout emotions, when we content ourselves with the exercise of these inward and affectionate sensations of the mind while they have no influence on the holiness of our life. Consider, my friends, what the emotions were made for. Not merely for the conscious pleasure of human nature, but to give it vigor and power for useful actions. I have but a poor pretense to be a sincere lover of Christ if I rejoice to hear his name repeated often in a sermon and say ever so many moving things about Him in the language of the book of Canticles and yet take no care to keep his commandments, for this is the appointed way by which Christ has required his disciples to manifest their love to Him: "If ye love me, keep my commandments; then are ye my friends, if ye do whatsoever I command you" (John 14:15). In vain do I pretend to pious sorrows, in vain do I mourn for some great and grievous sin in my secret devotions or in public worship if I am spending my life among the gay follies and vanities of the world, if I run into new temptations whenever the world beckons to me, and follow every son of mirth who waves the hand of invitation.

True Christianity, where it reigns in the heart, will make itself appear in the purity of life. We should always suspect those flatteries of emotion, those sudden inward sensations of sorrow or delight, which have no power to produce the fruits of holiness in our daily life. The fruits of the Spirit are found in the life and the heart together, as they are described in Galatians 5:22: love to God and man, joy in holy things, peace of conscience and peace with all men as far as possible, long-suffering, gentleness, goodness, faith (that is, faithfulness), meekness, temperance, and particularly a crucifixion of all sinful affections. Let us never content ourselves with any exercise of lively devotions unless we feel our corrupt affections in some measure subdued thereby.

O how shameful a sight it is, and what a reproach to the profession of the gospel, to see a Christian just come from church and holy ordinances, where his devout affections have been raised and moved, immediately breaking out into vain, earthly merriment, and carried away with idle and sensual discourse! What a scandal is it to our faith to see some zealous believers coming down from their closet where they fancy they have been favored with holy raptures and enjoyed much commerse with God, where they think they have exercised repentance and love and holy desires, and yet immediately fall into a fit of rage against their servants or children for mere trifles, and express their wrath in very unchristian language and indecent behavior. This is an open contradiction to their profession, and the shop and the parlor, or perhaps the kitchen, gives the lie to the pretenses of the closet. O glorious evidence of a disciple of Christ, where all the consecrated emotions join to resist every temptation, where divine love keeps warm at the heart, where it purifies the whole behavior and exalts human life near to that of angels!

7. Emotional escapism

It must certainly be regarded as blameworthy conduct with respect to our spiritual affections when they are permitted to entrench upon other duties either to God or persons, and withhold us from the proper business of our place and station in the world. Though devout emotions should be indulged at proper seasons, yet they should not so far govern all the faculties and ingross the moments of life as to make us neglect any necessary work to which the providence of God has called us. This is the case when persons find so much sweetness in their spiritual devotions that they dwell there too many hours of the day and neglect the care of their families, the conduct of their children and servants and other necessary duties of life, and let all things run at random in their household, under the excuse of spiritual life and conversation with God (though I must confess this is so uncommon a fault in our godless and irreligious age that it may almost pass without censure).

It is the same blameworthy conduct when Christians experience a sacred and affectionate pleasure in public ordinances and they are tempted to run from sermon to sermon, from lecture to lecture . . . with a slight and careless performance of relative duties. 'Tis yet more criminal in persons of low circumstances in the world, who would spend all their time in hearing or reading good things or at some religious assemblies or conferences while they grossly and grievously neglect their common duties of providing for themselves and their children. They are ready to expect that the rich should maintain them, while they make their devout feelings an excuse for their shameful idleness and sloth. Let us remember there is a time for working as well as a time for praying or hearing; everything is beautiful in its season.

This sort of excessive and inordinate emotion appears also eminently when, out of pity to the poor or love to the public worship of God, dying persons leave vast legacies to the building of churches and hospitals and endow alms-houses liberally, while their near kindred—and perhaps their own decendents—are in a starving condition or lack the conveniences of life. He that takes no care of his nearest relatives living and dying is in that respect worse than an infidel. God does not love robbery for burnt offering, nor does He permit us to abandon our natural responsibility to our fellow creatures to show our love or zeal for our Creator in such instances as these.

## 8. Corruption of spiritual emotions

Spiritual emotion is certainly exercised in a very inordinate and criminal manner when we permit it to degenerate into carnal and vicious feelings and (as the Apostle expresses it in another place) when we "begin in the Spirit and end in the flesh." Examples of this kind are too common in the present age of Christians.

i. Zeal may turn into wrath and fury. A high veneration for the glorious truths of the gospel and a warm zeal for the defence of them has too often degenerated into malice and indignation against those who differ from us in spiritual sensibility, and often in matters which are of

77

small importance to practical godliness. Pious zeal against dangerous errors is a just and laudable thing when it carries moderation and good temper with it, and does not break out into wrath and malignity against the persons of those who are unhappily betrayed into those mistakes. But it becomes a guilty passion and hateful in the eyes of God our Saviour when it breaks all the bonds of charity and Christian love. The flaming bigot and the persecutor come in naturally at every turn for their share of this caution and reproof, as abusers of the emotions in the things of God and religion.

When we come sometimes into worshipping assemblies, where a person of burning zeal leads the worship, we find the wildfire of his own passions spreading through the whole congregation. Is it not a shameful thing to hear the preacher railing against his brethren because they differ a little from him (will not use some unscriptural modes of expression or will not admit some favorite explications of a verse of Scripture, or will not consent to practice some 'lesser' forms or rites of worship). And 'tis a matter of equal shame to see many persons who imagine themselves to be Christians of the first rank take a malicious pleasure in hearing such scurrilous reproaches and public railings against their fellow Christians, and curses denounced against them because they differ in ceremonies and phrases. And the crime is certainly the greater if these opinions or forms about which they disagree are but of small importance. This is a wretched abuse of emotions in the things of God, and yet so deceitful is the heart of man and so given up to self-flattery that perhaps both the preacher and the hearers vainly presume they are expressing a sacred love for divine truth and paying sublime service to God and their Saviour. What madness is mixed with mistaken zeal!

ii. There is another instance. . . very akin to this, and may stand next in rank. This is when we behold the vices of men with holy aversion and hatred and immediately transfer this hatred to their persons—whereas we ought to pity and pray for them. Or, when we see a fellow Christian fall into sin, and because we hate the sin, we hate the sinner too, and permit our hatred to grow into disdain and irreconcilable enmity, even if the offender has given signs of sincere repentance. This is not Christian zeal, but human corruption, and such criminal indulgence of the emotions ought to be mortified if ever we would be imitators of the holy Jesus. He hated even the least sin, but loved and saved the greatest of sinners, and delighted to receive penitents to his love.

iii. 'Tis a culpable exercise of the emotions when holy emulation degenerates into envy. At first we admire the virtues of others, we respect them highly, we imitate their conduct and aspire after the same degrees of piety and goodness. We have a holy ambition to equal them in every grace and in every virtue and, if possible, to exceed them. All this is right and worthy of praise. But when I fall short of the attainments of my neighbor and envy him on account of his superior character, when I feel an inward displeasure against my brother because his gifts or graces shine brighter than mine, then a holy emotion degenerates and becomes a lust of the flesh instead of a fruit of the Spirit.

iv. I might give another instance also of this kind. That is when love to fellow Christians begins on a spiritual basis between persons of different sexes, and there is mutual delight in each other's company and pious conversation; without great watchfulness this Christian love may be in danger of degenerating into sinful desires and corrupt passions.

v. It may be worth our notice also that there is another danger of the degeneracy of a devout emotion, when persons of a pious and cheerful spirit have taken great delight in singing the praises of God and meet together at stated seasons for this purpose, but in time this has degenerated into sheer pleasure of the ear, into a mere affection for harmony and delight in sounds well blended. This may easily happen when fine instruments of church music have been used to assist psalmody or when persons pride themselves in too nice and delicate a skill in singing, in too exquisite a taste for harmony, even though the words which they sing may be holy and spiritual.

To guard against these dangers, let Christians frequently enter into their own hearts and endeavor as far as possible to examine their spirit and conscience, to distinguish between the inward experience of piety and the mere exercise of human nature or the workings of corrupt affections, and setting a constant guard upon their hearts in this respect.

## 9. Substituting feelings for spiritual maturity

The last thing I shall instance is this: some Christians live entirely by their spiritual emotions and make these the only rules of self-inquiry concerning their character, their habitual state of soul and present frame of spirit, and concerning everything that belongs to their Christianity. Such persons have little regard to the growth of their knowledge, the improvement of their understanding in the things of God, the steady and fixed bent of their will toward spiritual life and the constant regular course of a holy life. They seem to make all their faith consist in a few warm and pious feelings. There are two sorts of persons subject to this mistake.

The first are newly awakened sinners, who feel their emotions of fear and desire excited by some convincing sermon or awesome providence, and the rich doctrines of grace suited to their case and state raises in them some hopes of heaven and sensitive stirrings of joy. This may continue for many months, and incline them to infer that they are converted from

79

sin to God. And being also in a great measure reformed in their lives, they imagine they are new creatures, and all is safe for eternity—whereas they never had a heart fixed in the love of God and in the hatred of every sin, they never became hearty and resolved Christians. And in a little time their devout passions die and all their religion vanishes because it has no root.

There are also some real converts who are but weak and live too much by their emotions. If their hope and desire and delight are but engaged and raised high in their secret devotions or in public worship then they are good Christians indeed, in a heavenly state, and they think exceedingly well of themselves. But if at any time there is a damper upon their emotions through the indisposition of their carnal nature, when they feel no great degree of natural fervor powerfully affecting their pious exercises, they are ready to pronounce against themselves. They sink into great despondency and imagine they have no true grace.

Such Christians as these live very much by sudden fits and starts of devotion, without that uniform and steady spring of faith and holiness which would render their spiritual life more even and uniform, more honorable to God and comfortable to themselves. They are always either high on the wing or lying motionless on the ground. They are ever in the heights or the depths, travelling on bright mountains with the songs of heaven on their lips or groaning and laboring through the dark valleys, and never walking onward as on an even plain toward heaven.

There is much danger lest these kinds of persons who profess belief should deceive themselves—if not in judging of the truth of their graces, then at least in their opinion of their strength or weakness, for they judge merely by their feelings. Let us watch against this danger, and remember that though the emotions are of excellent use in our spiritual life, they were never designed to stand in the place of reason and judgement, or to supply the role of an enlightened understanding, a sanctified will, and a life attended with all the fruits of holiness.

## III. *Conclusion*

I have now finished what I planned to say concerning the abuse of the emotions in the spiritual life. I shall make three observations following from this discourse, [for your further reflection].

1. Those Christians are best prepared for the useful and pious exercises of their emotions in the spiritual life who have laid the foundations in an ordered knowledge of the things of God. Let your understanding there-fore be fully persuaded of the necessity and excellence of spiritual things, of the duties you owe to God as your Maker and Governor. Let all your

reasoning powers be convinced of the evil of sin, of the holiness and justice of God, of the danger of eternal death, of the relief and hope that is held forth in the gospel of Christ, of the necessity of faith and holiness to eternal happiness. And amidst all the workings of devout feelings, maintain a constant exercise of your reason and judgement. The Scripture itself was not given us to make the use of our reason needless, but to assist its operations and to render it more successful in our inquiries into the things of our everlasting welfare. Knowledge and feeling should go hand in hand in all the affairs of the spiritual life. The more we know of God and the things of the higher world, the stronger spring we shall have for our holy emotions and the more secure our guard against any excesses and irregularities in the exercise of them.

2. As it is the business of a preacher to assist the devout emotions, so also it is part of his job to guard his hearers against the abuse of them.

We have granted and maintained that it is the business of every sacred orator to raise the affections of men toward the things of God. Let him therefore manage his divine arguments in such a manner as to awaken the fears, hopes, desires, penitent sorrows and pious joys of the whole assembly in a sublime degree—but in order to secure them from excesses and irregularities of every kind, let him lay the foundations of their faith in clear ideas of divine things, and in a just and proper explication of the holy Scriptures.

When he has a mind to lead his hearers into any particular spiritual perceptions which he firmly believes to be true, and which he supposes useful to their edification, let him not begin with their emotions and address himself to them in the first place. He must not artfully manipulate those warm and natural feelings before he has set these doctrines and perceptions of his in a fair and convincing light before the eye of their understanding and their reasoning faculties. The emotions are neither the guides to truth nor the judges of it, nor must the preacher set them to their spritely and fervent work until he has informed the mind by clear explication and sincere argument. The sun in the heavens gives us a fair example in this case: his light comes before his heat. The dawn of the morning grows up by degrees and so introduces the fervors of noon. So let the preacher diffuse his light over the assembly before he kindles their warm emotions. Let him convince their reason and judgement of the truth of every article of faith which he persuades them to believe. Let him show the duty and the necessity of every part of holiness which he prescribes for their practice. Let him imitate that noble pattern of divine oratory, Apollos at Ephesus, who was an eloquent man and mighty in the Scriptures. He was fervent in Spirit and could raise the emotions of those that heard him yet he was willing to kindle the flame of his own oratory by the light

81

of his own understanding, and when he himself had learned the way of God more perfectly, he mightily convinced the Jews by divine argument and "showed them by the Scriptures that Jesus was the Christ" (Acts 18:24,25,28). Then there was a proper way made for his subsequent zeal and fervor to display themselves.

3. Finally, if the emotions are of such eminent service in the spiritual life and yet are in danger of unruly excesses, how much need have we to beg earnestly at the throne of grace that they may be all sanctified? It is only the sanctifying influence of the blessed Spirit that can excite them in an ordinate degree and can give them proper limits and regulations. 'Tis nothing but divine grace can raise them to a due height on all just occasions and yet preserve them from any improper conduct and unhappy effects.

In this sinful state of corrupt nature we are averse to the things of God. Our passions are intensely directed toward material things but are hardly moved by the most important discoveries of faith. 'Tis God alone who can correct and change this corrupt bias, and turn them to Himself. They are so ready to take a wrong turn and sometimes to make serious mischief even in matters of faith that God alone can keep them constant in their right situation and course. They are living wheels of strong and powerful movement in human nature, but they make wretched work if they are not put in motion by a regular and happy mainspring. They are glorious and noble instruments of the spiritual life when under good conduct but they are ungovernable and mischievous energies when they go astray—and they are also too prone to wander from their proper place and duty. Let it therefore be the matter of our daily prayer that we may be sanctified throughout in body, soul and spirit, and that every faculty of our nature may lend its proper aid to the kingdom of grace within us, till we are trained up by the piety of this present state and made fit for the unknown exercises of a sublimer sort of devotion in the kingdom of glory.

# Hymns, Songs, and Poems

## Come We Who Love the Lord

Come, we who love the Lord,
  And let our joys be known;
Join in a song of sweet accord,
  And thus surround the throne.

The sorrows of the mind
  Be banished from this place!
Religion never was designed
  To make our pleasures less.

Let those refuse to sing
  Who never knew our God;
But servants of the heavenly King
  Should speak their joys abroad.

The God that rules on high,
  And thunders when he please,
That rides upon the stormy sky,
  And manages the seas;

This awful God is ours,
  Our Father and our love;
He shall send down his heavenly powers,
  To carry us above.

There we shall see his face,
  And never, never sin;
And from the rivers of his grace
  Drink endless pleasures in.

Yea, and before we rise
  To that immortal state,
The thoughts of such amazing bliss
  Should constant joys create.

The men of grace have found
  Glory begun below;
Celestial fruits, on earthly ground,
  From faith and hope may grow.

The hill of Zion yields
  A thousand sacred sweets
Before we reach the heavenly fields,
  Or walk the golden streets.

Then let our songs abound,
  And every tear be dry;
We're marching through Emmanuel's ground
  To fairer worlds on high.

1709

# When I Survey the Wondrous Cross

When I survey the wondrous cross
  On which the Prince of Glory died,
My richest gain I count but loss,
  And pour contempt on all my pride.

Forbid it, Lord, that I should boast,
  Save in the death of Christ, my God:
All the vain things that charm me most,
  I sacrifice them to his blood.

See, from his head, his hands, his feet,
  Sorrow and love flow mingled down:
Did e'er such love and sorrow meet,
  Or thorns compose so rich a crown?

His dying crimson, like a robe,
  Spreads o'er his body on the tree:
Then am I dead to all the globe,
  And all the globe is dead to me.

Were the whole realm of nature mine,
  That were a present far too small:
Love so amazing, so divine,
  Demands my soul, my life, my all.

1709

# Am I a Soldier of the Cross

I COR. XVI. 13.

Am I a soldier of the cross,
  A follower of the Lamb?
And shall I fear to own his cause,—
  Or blush to speak his name?

Must I be carried to the skies
  On flowery beds of ease,
While others fought to win the prize,
  And sailed through bloody seas?

Are there no foes for me to face?
  Must I not stem the flood?
Is this vile world a friend to grace,
  To help me on to God?

Sure I must fight if I would reign;
  Increase my courage, Lord!
I'll bear the toil, endure the pain,
  Supported by thy word.

Thy saints, in all this glorious war,
  Shall conquer though they die:
They see the triumph from afar,
  And seize it with their eye.

When that illustrious day shall rise,
  And all thy armies shine
In robes of victory through the skies,
  The glory shall be thine.

1720

# Our God Our Help in Ages Past

PSALM XC.

Our God, our help in ages past,
  Our hope for years to come;
Our shelter from the stormy blast,
  And our eternal home:

Under the shadow of thy throne
  Thy saints have dwelt secure;
Sufficient is thine arm alone,
  And our defence is sure.

Before the hills in order stood,
  Or earth received her frame,
From everlasting thou art God,
  To endless years the same.

A thousand ages, in thy sight,
  Are like an evening gone;
Short as the watch that ends the night,
  Before the rising sun.

The busy tribes of flesh and blood,
  With all their lives and cares,
Are carried downwards by thy flood,
  And lost in following years.

Time, like an ever-rolling stream,
  Bears all its sons away;
They fly, forgotten, as a dream
  Dies at the opening day.

Our God, our help in ages past,
  Our hope for years to come,
Be thou our guard while troubles last,
  And our eternal home.

1719

# My God, How Endless is Thy Love

My God, how endless is thy love:
　Thy gifts are every evening new;
And morning mercies from above
　Gently distil like early dew.

Thou spread'st the curtains of the night,
　Great Guardian of my sleeping hours;
Thy sovereign word restores the light,
　And quickens all my drowsy powers.

I yield my powers to thy command;
　To thee I consecrate my days;
Perpetual blessings from thy hand
　Demand perpetual songs of praise.

1709

# Lullaby

Hush, dear child, lie still and slumber.
　Holy angels guard thy bed,
Heavenly blessings without number
　Gently falling on thy head.

Sleep, my babe; thy food and raiment,
　House and home, thy friends provide,
All without thy care and payment;
　All thy wants are well supplied.

How much better thou'rt attended
　Than the Son of God could be,
When from heaven he descended,
　And became a child like thee.

Soft and easy is thy cradle,
　Coarse and hard thy Saviour lay,
When his birthplace was a stable,
　And his softest bed was hay.

Was there nothing but a manger
　Wretched sinners could afford,
To receive the heavenly Stranger?
　Did they thus affront their Lord?

See the joyful shepherds round him,
　Telling wonders from the sky;
Where they sought him, there they found him,
　With his virgin-mother by.

1715

# Jesus Shall Reign Where'er the Sun

Jesus shall reign where'er the sun
Does his successive journeys run;
His kingdom stretch from shore to shore,
Till moons shall wax and wane no more.

Behold! the islands with their kings,
And Europe her best tribute brings;
From north to south the princes meet
To pay their homage at his feet.

There Persia, glorious to behold,
There India, shines in eastern gold;
And barbarous nations, at his word,
Submit, and bow, and own their Lord.

For him shall endless prayer be made,
And princes throng to crown his head;
His name, like sweet perfume, shall rise
With every morning sacrifice.

People and realms of every tongue
Dwell on his love with sweetest song;
And infant voices shall proclaim
Their early blessings on his name.

Blessings abound where'er he reigns;
The prisoner leaps to lose his chains;
The weary find eternal rest,
And all the sons of want are blest.

Where he displays his healing power,
Death and the curse are known no more;
In him the tribes of Adam boast
More blessings than their father lost.

Let every creature rise, and bring
Peculiar honors to our King;
Angels descend with songs again,
And earth repeat the loud Amen!

1719

# Mutual Love Stronger than Death

Not the rich world of minds above
Can pay the mighty debt of love
   I owe to Christ my God:
With pangs which none but he could feel
He brought my guilty soul from hell:
Not the first seraph's tongue can tell
   The value of his blood.

Kindly he seiz'd me in his arms,
From the false world's pernicious charms
   With force divinely sweet.
Had I ten thousand lives my own,
    At his demand,
    With cheerful hand,
I'd pay the vital treasure down
In hourly tributes at his feet.

But, Saviour, let me taste thy grace
   With every fleeting breath;
And thro' that heaven of pleasure pass
   To the cold arms of death;
Then I could lose successive souls
   Fast as the minutes fly;
So billow after billow rolls
   To kiss the shore and die.

# Desiring to Love Christ

Come, let me love: Or is thy mind
Harden'd to stone, or froze to ice?
I see the blessed Fair One bend
And stoop t' embrace me from the skies!

O! 'tis a thought would melt a rock,
And make a heart of iron move,
That those sweet lips, that heav'nly look,
Should seek and wish a mortal love!

I was a traitor doom'd to fire,
Bound to sustain eternal pains;
He flew on wings of strong desire,
Assum'd my guilt, and took my chains.

Infinite grace! Almighty charms!
Stand in amaze, ye whirling skies,
Jesus the God, with naked arms,
Hangs on a cross of love, and dies.

Did pity ever stoop so low,
Dress'd in divinity and blood?
Was ever rebel courted so
In groans of an expiring God?

Again he lives; and spreads his hands,
Hands that were nail'd to tort'ring smart;
'By these dear wounds,' says he; and stands
And prays to clasp me to his heart.

Sure I must love; or are my ears
Still deaf, nor will my passion move?
Then let me melt this heart to tears;
This heart shall yield to death or love.

# Flying Fowl, and creeping Things, praise ye the Lord

PSALM CXLVIII. 10.

### I.

Sweet flocks, whose soft enamel'd wing
Swift and gently cleaves the sky;
Whose charming notes address the spring
  With an artless harmony.
  Lovely minstrels of the field,
  Who in leafy shadows sit,
  And your wondrous structures build,
Awake your tuneful voices with the dawning light;
To nature's God your first devotions pay,
  E'er you salute the rising day,
'Tis he calls up the sun, and gives him every ray.

### II.

Serpents, who o'er the meadows slide,
And wear upon your shining back
Num'rous ranks of gaudy pride,
Which thousand mingling colours make,
  Let the fierce glances of your eyes
    Rebate their baleful fire;
  In harmless play twist and unfold
  The volumes of your scaly gold:
That rich embroidery of your gay attire,
  Proclaims your Maker kind and wise.

### III.

Insects and mites, of mean degree,
That swarm in myriads o'er the land,
Moulded by wisdom's artful hand,
And curl'd and painted with a various die;
  In your innumerable forms
  Praise him that wears th' ethereal crown,
  And bends his lofty counsels down
    To despicable worms.

# ELIZABETH SINGER ROWE
## 1674 · 1737

Engraved frontispiece to an early edition of her fiction, representing her at about age
forty (c. 1715).

INTRODUCTION

One of the best-known parishioners of Isaac Watts, Elizabeth Singer Rowe was born eldest of three daughters of Walter Singer, a Nonconformist minister, and his wife Elizabeth Portnell. Singer, a contemporary of John Bunyan, had like him been imprisoned for his Puritan convictions and had met his wife while she was visiting prisoners as an act of charity.

The Singers gave their daughter a sound education in music, drawing, poetry, and the spiritual life, and during her early years she began writing a group of poems that were published to considerable acclaim in 1696 under the pseudonym of "Philomela" (Nightingale). Patronized by Lord Weymouth, whose son, Henry Thynne, taught her French and Italian, Elizabeth came by this connection to the attention of Bishop Ken, who visited her once weekly in her parents' home in order to "cultivate her society."

Matthew Prior, the well-known poet, was evidently attracted to her person as well as her poetry. He printed her "Love and Friendship" along with his own collected poems, appending verses declaring himself to be desperately in love with her. His *amours* were, however, quite unrequited. About this same time, Elizabeth also met Isaac Watts, and the lifelong bachelor, evidently enchanted by her, wrote her an admiring verse epistle, referring to her under her *nom-de-plume* of Philomela.

In 1709, at the age of thirty-five, Elizabeth met a serious and intelligent young man named Thomas Rowe, thirteen years her junior, while on holiday in Bath. His father, too, was a Nonconformist minister, his uncle had been the teacher of Isaac Watts, and he had, like Elizabeth, acquired a superior education, especially in the classics which he had further pursued at the University of Leyden. He was also, by this time, a successful translator and poet in his own right. He and Elizabeth were married within the year and had five years together before his untimely death in 1715. (His poems were published posthumously in the collected edition of Elizabeth Rowe's work in 1739.)

Mrs. Rowe wrote an elegy on the death of her husband which "was at the time credited with almost infinite pathos,"[1] and which attracted the sincerest flattery of Alexander Pope, who seemed glad enough to imitate some of her lines in his own poems, as well as to print the elegy itself in 1720 as an appendix to the second edition of his "Eloisa and Abelard." Apparently Rowe never completely recovered from her loss, and went into a kind of spiritual retirement at Frome, where most of her later writings—primarily letters—were written. In 1728 she published *Friendship in Death, in Twenty Letters from the Dead to the Living,* an enormously successful book resembling (in some respects) C. S. Lewis's *The Great*

*Divorce.* This was followed by *Letters Moral and Entertaining* (1729–31; 1733), which she hoped would create spiritual awareness in the "careless and dissipated." The vividness of her characterization leads to some imbalance, however, and the modern reader may wonder if some of the careless and dissipated in her readership did not receive this work too much in the spirit of soap opera-like "true confessions." For all that, she was warmly recommended by Samuel Johnson for being the only contemporary writer to combine "the ornaments of romance" with "the decoration of religion." Her other major works include a long biblical poem, "The History of Joseph" (1736), written when she was much younger, and the large posthumous volume, *Devout Exercises of the Heart in Meditation and Soliloquy, Praise and Prayer,* which was revised and published at her request by Isaac Watts in 1737. Of this work, from which the selections here are excerpted, Watts writes in the preface: "Though many of her writings published in her lifetime [have] a pious and heavenly spirit . . . yet she chose to conceal the devotions of her heart till she got beyond the censure and applause of mortals. It was enough that God, whom she had loved with ardent and supreme affection, was witness to all her secret and intense breathings after Him."

For readers in our own time it may seem that Rowe's penchant for melodrama and "operatic" style run a danger of transgressing some of Watts's own injunctions concerning "abuse of the emotions." Nevertheless, her spiritual diary, penned in its artificial high diction, was heralded abroad as well as in England as a spiritually evocative outpouring of spontaneous prayer. In this, it harks back to the tradition of Dame Julian of Norwich, Margery Kempe, and Teresa d'Avila and like these earlier writings is deeply indebted and responsive to parts of Isaiah and to the Psalms. A noteworthy and recurrent theme is the covenant, experienced as a reciprocity of God's promises and the grateful correspondence of a faithful soul; it is in this light that we can understand Rowe's *Devout Exercises* as a "sacrifice of the heart."

The book went into numerous editions in Great Britain and America, while some of Rowe's other religious prose and poetry was being translated for enthusiastic readers in France and Germany. She was widely mourned at her death. Of the woman whom the German poet Klopstock called "die gottliche Rowe," Dr. Johnson was to claim that human eulogies were vain, but that such as she "were applauded by angels and numbered with the just."

# *from* Devout Exercises of the Heart (1737)

## I. *Supreme Love Toward God*

WHY, O my God, must this mortal structure put so great a separation between my soul and thee? I am surrounded with thy essence, yet I cannot perceive thee; I follow thee, and trace thy footsteps in heaven and earth, yet I cannot overtake thee. Thou art before me, and I cannot reach thee; behind me, and I perceive thee not.

O thou whom, unseen, I love, by what powerful influence dost thou attract my soul? The eye has not seen, nor has the ear heard, nor has it entered into the heart of man to conceive what thou art, and yet I love thee beyond all that my eye has seen or my ear heard—beyond all that my heart comprehends. Thou dwellest in the heights of glory, to which no human thoughts can soar, and yet thou art more near and intimate to my soul than any object. These ears have never heard thy voice, and yet I am better acquainted with thee, and can rely on thee with more confidence than on the dearest friend I have on earth.

My heart cleaves to thee, O Lord, as its only refuge, and finds in thee a secret and constant spring of consolation. I speak to thee with the utmost confidence, and think thy being my greatest happiness. The reflection on thy existence and greatness recreates my spirit and fills my heart with alacrity. My soul overflows with pleasure. I rejoice, I triumph in thy independent blessedness and absolute dominion. Reign, O my God, for ever, glorious and uncontrolled!

I, a worm of the earth, would join my assent with the infinite orders above, with all thy blazing angels who rejoice in thy kingdom and glory. . . .

I love thee. Thus far I can speak, but all the rest is unutterable, and I must leave the pleasing tale untold till I can talk in the language of immortality. Then I'll begin the transporting story which shall never come to an end, but be still and still beginning. For thy beauties, O thou fairest of ten thousand, will still be new, and shall kindle fresh ardor in my soul to all eternity. The sacred flame shall rise, nor find any limits till thy perfections are concluded.

I love thee—and O, thou that knowest all things, read the lines that love has written on my heart! What excellence but thine, in heaven or earth, could raise such aspirations of soul, such sublime and fervent affections as those I feel? What could fix my spirit but boundless perfection:

What is there else for whose sake I would despise all created glory? Why am I not at rest here among material enjoyments? Whence arise these importunate longings, these infinite desires? Why does not the complete creation satisfy, or at least delude me with a dream of happiness? Why do not the objects of sense awaken more ardent feelings than things distant and invisible? Why should I, who "say to corruption, 'Thou art my father'," aspire after union with the immense Divinity?

Ye angels of God, who behold his face, explain to me the sacred mystery; tell me how this heavenly flame began—unriddle its wondrous generation. Who has animated this mortal body with celestial fire, and given a clod of earth this divine aspiration? What could kindle it but the breath of God, which kindled up my soul! And to thee, its lovely Origin, it ascends, it breaks through all created perfection and keeps on its restless course to the first pattern of beauty.

Ye flowery varieties of the earth, and you sparkling glories of the skies, your blandishments are vain, while I pursue an excellence that casts a reproach on all your glory. I would gladly close my eyes on all the various and lovely appearances you present, and would open them on a brighter scene: I have desires which nothing visible can gratify, to which no material things are suitable. O when shall I find things more entirely agreeable to my intellectual faculties! My soul springs forward in pursuit of a distant good, whom I follow by some faint ray of light which only glimmers . . . before me. O when will it disperse the clouds and break out in full splendor on my soul?

But what will the unbroken vision of thy beauties accomplish if, even while thou art only faintly imagined, I love thee with such a sacred fervor! To what blessed heights shall my admiration rise when I shall behold thee in full perfection, when I shall see thee as thou art, exalted in majesty, and complete in beauty! How shall I triumph then in thy glory, and in the privileges of my own being! What ineffable thoughts will rise, to find myself united to the all-sufficient Divinity, by ties which the sons of men have no names to express and by an engagement that the revolution of eternal years shall not dissolve! The league of nature shall be broken, and the laws of the mingled elements be cancelled, but my relation to the Almighty God shall stand fixed and unchangeable as his own existence— "nor life, nor death, nor angels, nor principalities, nor powers, nor things present, nor things to come, shall ever separate me from his love."

Triumph, O my soul! and rejoice! Look forward beyond the period of all earthly things. Look beyond ten thousand ages of celestial blessedness. Look forward still, and take an immeasurable prospect. Press on, and leave unnumbered ages behind, ages of ineffable peace and pleasure; plunge at once into the ocean of bliss, and call eternity itself thy own.

There are no limits to the prospect of my joy. It runs parallel with the duration of the infinite Divinity. My bliss is without bounds: O when shall the full possession of it commence?

## II. *The Truth and Goodness of God*

. . . Thy promises are built upon the unchanging truth and goodness of thy nature. Thou dost not speak at random like vain men, but whatever thou hast engaged to perform is the result of eternal counsel and design. Thou has uttered nothing that thou canst see occasion to alter on a second preview. Thou canst promise nothing to thy own detriment nor be a loser by the utmost liberality. Thou art every way qualified to make good thy commitments by the fullness of thy riches and power.

Nor hast thou any necessity to flatter thy creatures, or to say kinder things to them than thou meanest to fulfil. Miserable man can bring no advantage to thee, nor has he any right to claim from thee. In what respect art thou in his debt? By what right can he demand the least of thy favors? Thy engagements are all free and unconstrained, founded on thy own generosity and not on the merits of thy creatures.

While I consider this, my expectations arise. I set no limits to my hopes, I look up with confidence and call thee my father and, with an humble faith, I claim every advantage that tender name imports. My heart confides in thee with steadfastness and alacrity; fear and distrust are inconsistent with my thoughts of the generosity of thy nature.

Every name and attribute by which thou hast revealed thyself to man confirms my faith. Thy life, thy being, is engaged. I may as well question thy existence as thy faithfulness. As sure as thou art, thou art just and true. The protestations of the most faithful friend I have cannot give me half the consolation that thy promises give me. I hear vain man with diffidence. I bid my soul beware of trusting false mortality, but I hear thy voice with joy and full assurance.

Thy words are not writ on sand, nor scattered by the fleeting winds, but shall stand in force when heaven and earth shall be no more. Eternal ages shall not diminish their efficacy, nor alter what the mouth of the Lord has spoken. I believe, I believe with the most perfect assent: I know "that thou art, and that thou art a rewarder of them that diligently seek thee." I feel the evidence, for thou hast not left thyself without a witness in my heart. . . .

## III. *Longing after the Enjoyment of God*

My God, to thee my sighs ascend; every complaint I make ends with thy name! I pause, I dwell on the sound, I speak it over again, and find that all my cares begin and end in thee. I long to behold the supreme beauty. I pant for the fair Original of all that is lovely, for beauty that is yet unknown, and for intellectual pleasures yet untasted.

My heart aspires, my wishes fly beyond the bounds of creation, and despise all that mortality can present me with. I was formed for celestial joys, and find myself capable of the entertainments of angels. Why may I not begin my heaven below, and taste, at least, of the springs of pleasure that flows from thy right hand forever?

Should I drink my fill, these fountains are still inexhaustible; millions of happy souls quench their infinite desires there, millions of happy beings gaze on thy beauty and are made partakers of thy blessedness; but thou art still undiminished. No liberality can waste the store of thy perfection, for it has flowed from eternity and runs forever fresh. And why must I perish for want?

My thirsty soul pines for the waters of life. O, who will refresh me with the pleasurable draught? How long shall I wander in this desert land, where every prospect is waste and barren! I look round me in vain, and sigh, still unsatisfied. O, who will lead me to the still waters, and make me repose in green pastures, where the weary are forever at rest? How tedious are the hours of expectation! Come, Lord . . . despatch thy commission, give me my work, and activity to perform it, and let me as a hireling fulfil my day. Lord, it is enough. . . .

> I am but a stranger and a pilgrim here
> In these wild regions, wandering and forlorn,
> Restless and sighing for my native home,
> Longing to reach my weary space of life,
> And to fulfil my task. O haste the hour
> Of joy and sweet repose! transporting hope!

Lord, here I am waiting for thy commands, attending thy pleasure. O speak and incline my ear to hear. Give me my work, let me finish it, and gain my release from this body of sin and death, this hated clog of error and guilt, corruption and vanity. O, let me drop this load, and bid these scenes of guilt a final *adieu!*

## IV. *A Covenant with God*

Incomprehensible Being! Thou who "searchest the heart, and triest the reins of the children of men," who knowest my sincerity, my thoughts are all unveiled to thee! I am surrounded with thine immensity; thou art a present, though invisible, witness of the solemn affairs I am now engaged in. I am now taking hold of thy strength that I may make peace with thee, and entering into articles of contract with the Almighty God. These are the happy days long since predicted, when "one shall say, I am the Lord's, and another shall call himself by the name of Israel, and another shall subscribe with his hand to the Lord; and I will be their God, and they shall be my sons and my daughters, saith the Lord Jehovah."

With the most thankful sincerity, I take hold of this covenant, as it is more fully manifested and explained in thy gospel by Jesus Christ; and, humbly accepting thy proposals, I bind myself to thee by a sacred and everlasting obligation. By a free and deliberate action I do here ratify the articles which were made for me in my baptism, in the name of the Father, the Son, and the Holy Spirit. I religiously devote myself to thy service, and entirely submit to thy direction. I renounce the glories and vanities of the world, and choose thee as my happiness, my supreme felicity, and everlasting portion. I make no article with thee for anything else; deny or give me what thou wilt, I will never be resentful, while my principal treasure is secure. This is my deliberate, my free and sincere determination—a determination which, by thy grace, I will never retract.

O thou, by whose power alone I shall be able to stand, "put thy fear in my heart, that I may never depart from thee." Let not the world with all its flatteries, nor death, nor hell, with all their terrors, force me to violate this sacred vow. O, let me never live to abandon thee, nor draw the impious breath that would deny thee.

And now let surrounding angels witness for me, that I solemnly devote all the powers and faculties of my soul to thy service. And when I presumptuously employ any of the advantages thou hast given me to thy dishonor, let them testify against me, and let my own words condemn me.

ELIZABETH ROWE

Thus I have subscribed to thy gracious proposals, and bound myself to be the Lord's. And now let the malice of men and the rage of devils combine against me. I can defy all their strategems, for God himself is become my friend, Jesus is my all-sufficient Saviour, and the Spirit of God, I trust, will be my Sanctifier and Comforter.

O happy day, transporting moment! The brightest period of my life! Heaven, with all its light, smiles upon me. What glorious mortal can now excite my envy? What scene to tempt my ambition could the whole creation display? Let glory call me with her external voice, let pleasure, with a softer eloquence, allure me. The world, in all its splendor, appears but a trifle, while the infinite God is my portion. He is mine by as sure a title as eternal truth can confer. The right is unquestionable; the conveyance unalterable; the mountains shall be removed and the hills be dissolved before the everlasting obligation shall be cancelled.

## V. *Confession of Sin, and Hope of Pardon*

Break, break, insensitive heart! Let confusion cover me, and darkness black as my own guilt surround me. Lord, what a monster am I become! How hateful to myself for offending thee! How much more detestable to thee, to thee against whom I have offended! Why have I provoked the God on whom my being every moment depends?—the God who out of nothing raised me to a rational and immortal nature and granted me the capacity of being happy forever; the God whose goodness has run parallel with my life, who has preserved me in a thousand dangers, and kept me even from the ruin I courted—even while I was resenting the Providence that saved me?

How often has He recovered me from eternal misery and brought me back from the very borders of hell, when there was but a dying groan, but one faint sigh, between me and everlasting perdition! When all human help failed, and my mournful friends were taking their last farewell, when every smiling hope forsook me and the horrors of death surrounded me, to God I cried, from the depths of misery and despair. I cried, and He responded, rescuing my life from destruction. He "brought me out of the miry clay, and set my feet on a rock." A thousand instances of thy goodness could I recount, and all to my own condemnation.

Could I consider thee as my enemy, I might forgive myself. But when I consider thee as my best friend, my tender father, the sustainer of my life and author of my happiness, good God, what a monstrous thing do I appear, who have sinned against thee! Could I charge thee with severity, or call thy laws rigorous and unjust, I had some excuse; but I am silenced there by the conviction of my own reason, which assents to all thy precepts as just and holy. But, to heighten my guilt, I have violated the sacred rules I approve, I have provoked the justice I fear, and offended the purity I adore.

Yet still there are greater depths to my iniquity. What gives me the utmost condemnation is that I have sinned against unbounded love and goodness. Horrid ingratitude! Here lies the emphasis of my folly and misery. The awareness of this torments me . . . as much as the dread of hell or the fear of losing heaven. Thy love and tender compassion, so recently the pleasing subjects of my thoughts, are on this account become my terror. The titles of an enemy and a judge scarce sound more painful to my ears than those of a friend and benefactor. . . . Those sacred names confound and terrify my soul because they furnish my conscience with the most exquisite reproaches. The thoughts of such goodness abused and such clemency affronted seem to me almost as insupportable as those of thy wrath and severity. O, whither shall I turn? I dare not look upward;

the sun and stars upbraid me there. If I look downward, the fields and mountains take their Creator's part, and heaven and earth conspire to remind me of my sins. Those common blessings tell me how much I am indebted to thy bounty. But, Lord, when I recall thy particular favors, I am utterly confounded. What numerous instances could I recount! Nor has my rebellion yet shut up the fountain of thy grace, for yet I breathe, and yet I live, and live to implore a pardon. Heaven is still open, and the throne of God accessible. But oh, with what confidence can I approach it; what motives can I urge but such as carry my own condemnation in them?

Shall I urge thy former pity and indulgence? This would be to plead against myself. And yet thy clemency, that clemency which I have abused, is the best argument I can bring—thy grace and clemency as revealed in Jesus, the Son of thy love, the blessed Reconciler of God and man!

O, whither has my folly reduced me? With what words shall I choose to address thee? "Pardon my iniquity, O Lord: for it is great." Surprising argument, yet this will signify thy goodness, and yield me an eternal theme to praise thee; it will add an emphasis to all my grateful songs, and tune my harp to everlasting harmony. The ransomed of the Lord shall join with me, while this glorious inheritance of thy grace excites their wonder and my unbounded gratitude. Thus shall thy glory be exalted.

O Lord God, permit a poor worthless creature to plead a little with thee. What honor will my destruction bring thee? What profit, what triumph to the Almighty will my perdition be? Mercy is thy brightest attribute; this gives thee all thy loveliness, and completes thy beauty. By names of kindness and indulgence thou hast chosen to reveal thyself to men; by titles of the most tender import thou hast made thyself known to my soul—titles which thou dost not yet disdain, but art still compassionate and ready to pardon.

But that thou hast, or wilt forgive me, O my God, aggravates my guilt. And wilt thou indeed forgive me? Wilt thou remit the gloomy score, and restore the privilege I have forfeited? Wondrous love, astonishing generosity! Let me never live to repeat my ingratitude; let me never live to break my penitent vows. Let me die ere that unhappy moment arrives.

## VI. *The Absence of God on Earth*

What is hell, what is damnation, but an exclusion from thy presence? 'Tis the loss of that which gives the regions of darkness all their horror. What is heaven, what are the satisfactions of angels, but the vision of thy glory? What but thy smiles and good pleasure are the springs of their immortal transports?

Without the light of thy countenance, what privilege is there in being alive? What canst thou thyself give me to make up the infinite loss? Could the riches, the empty glories, the insipid pleasures of the world recompence me for it? Ah, no; not all the vanities of the creation could satisfy me while I am deprived of thee. Let the ambitious, the licentious, the covetous share these trifles amongst themselves; they are no amusements for my dejected thoughts.

There was a time (but ah, that happy time is past, those blissful minutes gone) when with a modest assurance I could call thee "my father, my almighty friend, my defence, my hope, and my exceeding great reward!" But those glorious advantages are lost, those ravishing prospects withdrawn, and to my trembling soul thou dost no more appear but as a consuming fire, an inaccessible majesty, my severe judge and my omnipotent adversary. And who shall deliver me out of thy hands? Where shall I find a shelter from thy wrath? What shades can cover me from thy all-seeing eyes?

> One glance from thee, one piercing ray,
> Would kindle darkness into day,
> The veil of night is no disguise
> Nor screen from thy all-searching eyes;
> Thro' midnight shades thou find'st thy way
> As in the blazing noon of day.

"But will the Lord cast me off forever? Will He be favourable no more? Has God indeed forgotten to be gracious?" Will He shut out my prayer forever and must I never behold my Maker? Must I never meet those smiles that fill the heavenly inhabitants with unutterable joys, those smiles which enlighten the celestial region and make everlasting day above? In vain then have these wretched eyes beheld the light, in vain am I endued with reasonable faculties and immortal principles. Alas! What will they prove but everlasting curses, if I must never see the face of God?

> Is it a dream, or do I hear
> The voice that so delights my ear?
> Lo, he o'er hills his steps extends:
> And, bounding from the cliffs, descends:
> Now, like a roe, outstrips the wind,
> And leaves the panting hart behind.

"I have waited for thee as they that wait for the morning," and thy returns are more welcome than the springing daylight after the horrors of a melancholy night, more welcome than ease to the sick, than water to the thirsty, or rest to the weary traveller. How undone was I without thee! In vain, while thou wast absent, the world hath tried to entertain me; all it could offer was like jests of dying men, or like recreations to the damned. On thy favor alone my tranquility depends; deprived of that I should sigh for happiness in the midst of paradise, for "thy loving-kindness is better than life." And if a taste of thy love be thus transporting, what ecstacies shall I know when I drink my fill of the streams of bliss that flow from thy right hand forever! But

> When shall this happy day of vision be?
> When shall I make a near approach to thee?
> Be lost in love, and wrapt in ecstacy?
> Oh, when shall I behold thee all serene,
> Without this envious cloudy veil between?
> 'Tis true, the sacred elements impart
> Thy virtual presence to my faithful heart;
> But to my sense still unreveal'd thou art.
> This, though a great, is an imperfect bliss,
> To see a shadow for the God I wish:
> My soul a more exalted pitch would fly,
> And view thee in the heights of majesty!

## VII. *Banishment from God Forever*

"Depart from me, ye cursed!" Oh, let me never hear thy voice pronounce these dreadful words! With what terror would that sentence pierce my heart, while it thunders in my ears. Oh, rather command me into my primitive nothing, and with one potent word finish my existence. To be separated from thee, and cursed with immortality, who can sustain the intolerable doom?

> O dreadful state of black despair,
> To see my God remove,
> And fix my doleful station where
> I must not taste his love:—

nor view the light of thy countenance forever. Unutterable woe! There is no hell beyond it. Separation from God is the depth of misery. Blackness of darkness, and eternal night, must necessarily involve a soul excluded from thy presence. What life, what joy, what hope is to be found where thou art not? I lack words to paint my thoughts of that dismal state. Oh, let me never be destined for that dreadful experience! Rather let loose thy wrath, and in a moment reduce me into non-existence. . . .

## VIII. *Seeking after an Absent God*

Oh, let not the Lord be angry, and I, who am but dust, will speak. Why dost thou withdraw thyself, and suffer me to pursue thee in vain? If I am surrounded with thy immensity, why am I thus unaware of thee? Why do I not find thee, if thou art everywhere present? I seek thee in the temple, where thou hast often met me; there I have seen the traces of thy majesty and beauty; but those sacred visions bless my sight no more. I seek thee in my secret retirements, where I have called upon thy name, and have often heard the whispers of thy voice; that celestial conversation hath often reached and raptured my soul, but I am solaced no more with thy divine condescension. I listen, but I hear those gentle sounds no more. I pine and languish, but thou fleest me. Still I wither in thy absence, as a drooping plant for the reviving sun.

O when wilt thou scatter this melancholy darkness? When shall the shadows flee before thee? When shall the cheerful glory of thy grace dawn upon my mind at thy approach? I shall revive at thy light; my vital spirits will confess thy presence. Grief and anxiety will vanish before thee, and immortal joys surround my soul.

Where thou art present, heaven and happiness ensue; hell and damnation fills the breast where thou art absent. While God withdraws I am encompassed with darkness and despair; the sun and stars shine with an uncomfortable lustre; the faces of my friends grow tiresome; the smile of angels would fail to cheer my languishing spirit. I grow unacquainted with tranquility; peace and joy are empty sounds to me, and words without a meaning.

Tell me not of glory and pleasure—there are no such things without God. When He withdraws, what delight can these trifles afford? All that amuses mankind are but dreams of happiness, shadows and fantasies. What compensation can they make for an infinite good departed? All nature cannot repair my loss; heaven and earth would offer their treasures in vain. Not all the kingdoms of this world, nor the thrones of archangels, could give me a recompence for an absent God.

O where can my grief find redress? Whence can I draw satisfaction, when the fountain of joy seals up its streams? My sorrows are hopeless till He return. Without Him my night will never see a dawn, but extend to everlasting darkness. Contentment and joy will be eternal strangers to my breast. Had I all things within the compass of creation to delight me, his frowns would blast the whole enjoyment. Unreconciled to God, my soul would be forever at variance with itself.

Even now, while I believe thy glory hidden from me with only a passing eclipse, and while I wait for thy return as for the dawning day, my soul suffers inexpressible agonies at the delay. The minutes seem to linger and the days are lengthened into ages. But Lord, what keener anguish should I feel if I thought thy presence had totally forsaken me, if I imagined thy glory should no more arise on my soul! My spirits fail at the thought: I cannot face the dreadful apprehensions of my God forever gone. Is it not hell in its most horrid prospect, eternal darkness and the undying worm, infinite ruin and irreparable damage? Compared to this, what were all the plagues that earth could threaten or hell invent? What are disgrace, and poverty, and pain? What are all that mortals fear, real or imaginary evils? They are nothing compared to the terrors raised by the thought of losing my God.

O thou who art my boundless treasure, my infinite delight, my all, my ineffable portion, can I part with thee? I may see without light and breathe without air sooner than be blessed without my God. Happiness separate from thee is a contradiction, an impossibility (if I dare speak it) to Omnipotence itself. I feel a flame which the most glorious creation could not satisfy, an emptiness which nothing but infinite love could fill. I must find thee or weary myself in an eternal pursuit. Nothing shall divert me in the endless search, no obstacle shall frighten me back, no allurement withhold me; nothing shall flatter or relieve my impatience. My bliss, my heaven, my all depends on my success in this. Show me where thou art, O my God; conduct me into thy presence, and let my love confine me there forever.

## IX. *Inexpressible Love toward God*

Thou radiant sun, thou moon, and all ye sparkling stars, how gladly would I leave your pleasant light to see the face of God! Ye crystal streams, ye groves and flowery lawns, my innocent delights, how joyfully could I leave you to meet that blissful prospect! And you delightful faces of my friends, I would this moment quit you all to see Him whom my soul loves—so loves that I can find no words to express the unutterable ardor. Not as the miser loves his wealth, nor the ambitious his grandeur, not as the libertine loves his pleasure, or the generous man his friend: these are flat similitudes to describe such an intense passion as mine. Not as a man scorched in a fever longs for a cooling draught, not as a weary traveller wishes for soft repose: my restless desires admit of no equal comparison with these.

I love my friend; my vital breath and the light of heaven are dear to me. But should I say I love my God as I love these, I should belie the sacred flame which aspires to infinity. 'Tis thee, abstractly thee, O uncreated beauty, that I love. In thee my wishes are all terminated, in thee, as in their blissful center, all my desires meet, and there they must be eternally fixed. It is thou alone that must constitute my everlasting happiness. Were the harps of angels silent, there would be harmony for me in the whispers of thy love. Were the fields of light darkened, thy smiles would bless me with everlasting day. . . . All their beams of grace, joy and glory are derived from thee, the eternal Sun, and will merit my attention no further than they reflect thy image, or discover thy excellencies.

Even at this distance—encompassed with the shades of death, and the mists of darkness—in these cold melancholy regions, when a ray of thy love breaks in on my soul, when through the clouds I can trace but one feeble beam, even that obscures all human glory, and gives me a contempt for whatever mortality can boast. What wonder then will the open vision of thy face effect, when I shall enjoy it in so sublime a degree that the magnificence of the skies will not draw my regard, nor the conversation of angels divert my thoughts from thee? . . . Mend thy pace, old lazy Time, and shake thy heavy sands; make shorter circles, ye rolling planets. When will your destined courses be fulfilled? Thou restless sun, how long wilt thou travail the celestial road? When will thy starry walk be finished? When will the commissioned angel arrest thee in thy progress and, lifting up his hand, swear by the unutterable name "that time shall be no more"? O happy ending, my impatient soul springs forward to salute thee, and leaves the lagging days, and months, and years far behind. . . .

If I were only to reason upon this subject, I might say, What motive could earth, could hell, could heaven itself propose to tempt my soul to change its love? What could they lay in the balance against an infinite good? What could be thrown in as a stake against the favor of God? Ask the happy souls who know what the light of his countenance imports, who drink in joy and immortality from his smiles—ask then what value they set on their enjoyment. Ask them what in heaven or earth should purchase a moment's interval of their bliss. Ask some radiant seraph, midst the fervency of his rapture, at what price he values his happiness. And when these have named the purchase, earth and hell may try to balance mine. Let them spread the baits that tempt deluded men to ruin; let riches, honor, beauty, and bewitching pleasure appear in all their charms, the sensuality of the present and past ages, the Persian delicacy and the Roman pride. Let them uncover the golden mines and disclose the ruby sparkling in its bed; let them open the veins of sapphires and show the diamond glittering in its rock; let them all be thrown into the balance. Alas, their weight is too little, and too light! Let all pageantries of state be added, imperial titles and the ensigns of majesty; put in all that boundless vanity imagines, or wild ambition craves, crowns and sceptres, regal vestments and golden thrones. The scale still mounts. Throw in the world entire: 'tis insubstantial, and light as airy vanity.

Are these thy highest boasts, O deluding world? Ye ministers of darkness, have you nothing else to offer? Are these your utmost proposals? Are these a compensation for the favor of God? Alas, that boundless word has a meaning which outweighs them all: infinite delight, inconceivable joy, are expressed in it. The sight of his countenance signifies more than angels can describe or mortality imagine. And shall I quit all that an everlasting heaven means for empty shadows?

Go, ye baffled tempters, go offer your toys to madmen and fools! They all vanish under my scorn and cannot yield so much as an amusement to my aspiring thoughts. The sun, in all its spacious circuit, beholds nothing to tempt my wishes. These winding skies, in all their ample round, contain nothing equal to my desires. My ambition has far different ends, and other prospects in view. Nothing below the joys of angels can satisfy me.

Let me explore the words of life and beauty, and find a path to the dazzling recesses of the Most High. Let me drink at the fountain-head of pleasure, and derive all that I want from original and uncreated fulness and felicity.

O divine love, let me launch out into thy pleasurable depths, and be swallowed up in thee. Let me plunge at once into immortal joy, and lose myself in the infinite ocean of happiness.

Till then I pine for my celestial country, till then I murmur to the winds and streams, and tell the solitary shadows my grief. The groves are conscious of my complaints, and the moon and stars listen to my sighs. By their silent lights I talk over my heavenly concerns and give a vent to my divine affections in mortal language. Then, looking upward, I grow impatient to reach that milky way, the seat of joy and immortality:

> Come love, come life, and that bless'd day
> For which I languish, come away,
> When this dry soul these eyes shall see,
> And drink the unseal'd source of Thee.

O come, I cry, thou whom my soul loveth! I would go on, but lack expression, and vainly struggle with the unutterable thought.

Tell me, ye sons of light, who feel the force of the celestial fires, in what language do you paint their violence? Or, do the tongues of seraphs falter? Does the language of paradise lack equivalents here, and immortal eloquence fail? Surely your happiness is more perfect than all your descriptions of it. Heaven echoes to your charming notes as far as they reach, while divine love, which is your song, is infinite, and knows no limits of degree or duration.

Yet I would say, some gentle spirit come and instruct me in your art; lend me a golden harp and guide the sacred flight. Let me imitate your devout strains, let me copy out your harmony. And then

> Some of the fairest choir above
> Shall flock around my song,
> With joy, to hear the name they love
> Sound from a mortal tongue.

Blessed and immortal creatures, I long to join with you in your celestial style of adoration and love. I long to learn your ecstacies of worship and joy, in a language which mortals cannot pronounce, and to speak the divine passion of my soul in words which are now unspeakable.

## X. *Appeal to Divine Truth*

However intricate and hopeless my present distress may be to human views, why should I limit the Almighty; or why should the Holy One of Israel limit Himself? Nature and necessity are thine; thou speakest the word, and it comes to pass. No obstacle can oppose the omnipotence of thy will, nor make thy designs ineffectual.

Is thy hand at all shortened since the glorious period when thy mighty power and thy stretched-out arm formed the heavens and earth, when these spacious skies were spread at thy command and this heavy globe fixed on its airy pillars?

> The strong foundations of the earth
> Of old by thee were laid;
> Thy hands the beauteous arch of heav'n
> With wondrous skill have made.

And "these shall wax old as a garment; as a vesture shalt thou change them, and they shall be changed." But shouldest thou, like these, decay, where were the hopes of them that confide in thee? If in all generations thy perfections were not the same, what consolation could the race of men draw from the ancient records of thy wonderful works? Why are we told, "thou didst divide the sea, to make a path for thy people through the mighty waters"? That thou didst rain bread from heaven, and dissolve the flinty rock in crystal rills to give the chosen nation drink?

Thou art He that distinguished Noah in the universal flood, and preserved the floating ark amidst winds and rains and tumultuous billows.

'Twas thy protecting care that led Abraham from his kindred and his native country, and brought him safely to the promised land.

Thou didst accompany Jacob in his journey to Paden-aram and gave him bread to eat, and clothing to put on till, greatly increased in substance, he returned to his father's house. He wrestled for a blessing; he wrestled with the Almighty and prevailed.

With Joseph thou wentest down into Egypt, and didst deliver him out of all his adversities, till he forgot his sorrows and all the toil of his father's house.

Thou didst remember thy people in the Egyptian bondage and looked with pitying eyes on their affliction. After four hundred and thirty years, on the very day thou hadst promised, thou didst release and bring them out with triumphant miracles. Thy presence went with them in a pillar of a cloud by day and a protecting fire by night; thy conquering hand drove out great and potent nations and gave them entire possession of the land promised to their fathers—nor didst thou fail in the least circumstances of all the good things thou hadst promised.

What a cloud of witnesses stand on record! Joshua and Gideon, Jephtha and Samson, who, through faith, obtained the promises.

Thou didst command the ravens to feed thy holy prophet, and at the word of a prophet didst sustain the widow's family with a handful of meal.

Thou didst walk with the three Hebrews in the fiery furnace; thou wast present with Daniel in the lion's den, to deliver him because he trusted in thee. In what instance has the prayer of faith been rejected? Where were the righteous forsaken? Who can charge God without charging Him foolishly? What injustice hath been found in the Judge of all the earth? His glorious titles have stood unblemished from generation to generation, nor can any of his perfections decay or rolling years make any change in the Ancient of Days.

Are not his works clear and distinct, without a double meaning or the least deceit? Are they not such as may justly secure my confidence? Such as would satisfy me from the mouth of man, inconstant man, whose breath is in his nostrils and his foundation in the dust—unstable as water and fleeting as a shadow? And can I so slowly assent to the words of the Most High? Shall I trust impotent man, that has neither wisdom nor might to accomplish his designs, that cannot call the next breath or motion his own nor promise himself a moment in all futurity? Can I rest on these feeble props, and yet tremble and despond when I have the truthfulness of the eternal God to secure and support me?

I know He will not break *his* covenant, nor suffer his faithfulness to fail; I dare attest it in the face of earth and hell. I dare stake my all for time and eternity on this glorious truth, a truth which hell cannot blemish, nor all its malice contradict.

Exert yourselves, ye powers of darkness, bring in your evidence, collect your instances, begin from the first generations. Since the world was peopled and men began to call on the name of the Lord, when did they call in vain? When did the Holy One of Israel fail the expectations of the humble and contrite spirit? Point out in your blackest fashion the dismal period when the name of the Lord was no more a refuge to them that trusted in Him; let the annals of hell be produced, let them mark the dreadful day and distinguish it with eternal triumphs.

In vain you search, for neither heaven nor earth nor hell have ever been witness to the least deviation from his truth and justice. The Almighty shines with unblemished glory, to the confusion of hell and the consolation of those that put their trust in Him.

On thy eternal truth and honor I entirely cast myself. If I am deceived, angels and archangels are deluded too. They, like me, have no dependence beyond the divine truthfulness of their blessedness and immortality; they too hang all their hope on his goodness and immutability. If that fails, the celestial paradise vanishes and all its glories are extinct; the golden palaces sink and the seraphic thrones must totter and fall. Where are your crowns, ye spirits elect? Where are your songs and your triumphs if the truth of God can fail? A mere possibility of that would darken the fields of light and turn the voice of melody into grief and lamentation.

What pangs would rise even through all the regions of blessedness! What diffidence and fear would shake the heart of every inhabitant! What agonies surprise them all if the word of the Most High God could be cancelled! The pillars of heaven might then tremble and the everlasting mountains bow; the celestial foundations might be removed from their place and that noblest structure of the hands of God be chaos and eternal emptiness.

But forever just and true are thy ways, thou King of Saints; blessed are all they that put their trust in thee. For thou art a certain refuge in the day of distress and under the shadow of thy wings I will rejoice. "My soul shall make her boast in the Lord, and triumph in his salvation: I called on him in my distress, and he has delivered me from all my fears." Hallelujah.

XI. *Glory to God for Salvation by Jesus and his Blood*

Let me give glory to God before I die, and take shame and condemnation to myself. I ascribe my salvation to the free and absolute goodness of God, not by the strength of reason or any natural inclination to virtue but "by the grace of God I am what I am." O my Redeemer, be the victory, be the glory thine! I expect eternal life and happiness from thee, not as a debt but a free gift, a promised act of bounty. How poor would my expectations be if I only looked to be rewarded according to those works which my own vanity or the partiality of others have called good and which, if examined by divine purity, would prove but specious sins! As such I renounce them. Pardon them, gracious Lord, and I ask no more. Nor can I hope for that but through the satisfaction which has been made to divine Justice for the sins of the world.

O Jesus, my Saviour, what harmony dwells in thy name! Celestial joy, immortal life is in the sound.

> Sweet name! In thy each syllable
> A thousand bless'd Arabias dwell;
> Mountains of myrrh, and beds of spices,
> And ten thousand paradises.

Let angels set this name to their golden harps; let the redeemed of the Lord forever magnify it.

O my propitious Saviour! Where were my hope but for thee? How desperate, how undone were my circumstances? I look on myself in every view I can take with horror and contempt. I was born in a state of misery and sin, and in my best estate am altogether vanity. With the utmost advantages I can boast I shrink back, I tremble to appear before unblemished Majesty. O thou in whose name the Gentiles trust, be my refuge in that awful hour. To thee I come, my only confidence and hope. Let the blood of sprinkling, the seal of the covenant be upon me. Cleanse me from my original stain and my contracted impurity, and adorn me with the robes of thy righteousness by which alone I expect to stand justified before infinite justice and purity.

O enter not into judgement with me. For the best actions of my life cannot bear thy scrutiny. Some secret blemish has stained all my glory. My devotion to God has been mingled with levity and irreverence, my charity to man with pride and ostentation. Some latent defect has attended my best actions, and those very things which, perhaps, have been highly esteemed by men, have deserved contempt in the sight of God.

> When I survey the wond'rous cross
> On which the Prince of Glory dy'd,

My richest gain I count my loss,
And pour contempt on all my pride.

Forbid it, Lord, that I should boast,
Save in the cross of Christ my God;
All the vain things that charm me most,
I sacrifice them to thy blood.

APRIL 30, 1735

## XII. *A Review of Divine Mercy and Faithfulness*

I am now setting to my seal that God is true, and leaving this as my last testimony to the divine truthfulness. I can, from numerous experiences, assert his faithfulness, and witness to the certainty of his promises. "The word of the Lord has been tried, and he is a buckler to all those that put their trust in him."

"O come, all ye that fear the Lord, and I will tell you what He has done for my soul; I will ascribe righteousness to my Maker," and leave my record for a people yet unborn, that the generation to come may rise up and praise Him.

Into whatever distress his wise providence has brought me, I have called on the Lord, and He heard me, and delivered me from all my fears; I trusted in God and He saved me. Oh! let my experience stand a witness to them that hope in his mercy; let it be to the Lord for a praise and a glory. . . .

# WILLIAM LAW
## 1686 · 1761

No engraving, painting, or other representation of Law exists today.

## INTRODUCTION

Of all the devotional writers we may associate with eighteenth-century English spirituality, none had a more pervasive influence upon his thinking contemporaries than William Law. This is not simply because he came early in the period, or even, as Samuel Johnson somewhat ostentatiously remarked, because he wrote "the finest piece of horatory theology in any language,"[1] but because his vision of Christian perfection offered the most radical and uncompromising challenge to conventional "religious" thought in the century. He had a direct personal influence on the careers of John and Charles Wesley, George Whitefield, and John Fletcher, and his writings deeply affected John Newton and Hannah More in the next generation. Thus, the thought of the most reclusive and mystical of the spiritual leaders of the time reached out and touched the active spirituality of a whole age. Almost everyone after him was affected by, and felt it necessary to respond to, his idea of "Christian perfection."

Fourth of eight sons in a family of eleven children, Law was the child of a grocer. He seems to have had religious instruction from his parents, and given his humble origins must have shown exceptional promise for them to have undertaken what would have been a considerable effort to get him to a university. He entered Emmanuel College, Cambridge, in 1705, graduating with a B.A. in 1708; he was then ordained and elected fellow of his college in 1711. His first field of study was classics, followed by mathematics and philosophy; he wrote a thesis on the French philosopher Malebranche, taking his M.A. degree in 1712.

Law was, like the mother of John and Charles Wesley, an outspoken "nonjuror"—a supporter of the deposed Catholic monarch James II and his son, the "Old Pretender." A few allusions to this conviction in a university speech cost him his job and the suspension of his degrees in the spring of 1713. That summer he preached a sermon with similar sentiments. When the Hanoverian George I took possession of the throne in 1714, Law refused to take the oath of allegiance and abjuration, and retained his sympathy for the exiled Stewart kings even beyond the 1745 rebellion (of Bonnie Prince Charlie) unalterably until his death. Although he was for a time curate at Fotheringay, and perhaps in London as well, his Jacobite leanings prevented him from continuing as an Anglican clergyman. Law's reclusiveness, then, was at least partly forced upon him as a price for maintaining his convictions.

The first several years after 1715 are clouded. We know that Law was writing: in 1723 he attacked the cynical atheism of Mandeville's *Fable of the Bees,* and in 1726 he published his stinging criticism of the contemporary theatre, *The Absolute Unlawfulness of Stage Entertainment fully Demon-*

*strated,* the essential argument of which is succinctly recapitulated in the second chapter of his *Christian Perfection,* published in the same year.

The impact of *Christian Perfection* on a corrupt and indolent age was immediate, yet profound and lasting. For the Wesleys and Whitefield, it provided a powerful early stimulus to their own spiritual development, for Fletcher it was a lifelong influence, and for Newton and More, many years later, it was still a challenge with which to reckon. After reading it, one anonymous stranger presented Law with £1,000, allowing him to found, in 1727, a school for fourteen girls at Kings Cliffe.

In that same year, Law himself entered the family of Edward Gibbon to become tutor to his son of the same name and a "much honored friend and spiritual director of the whole family."[2] Law accompanied young Edward (later to be father to the great historian) to Cambridge to be his tutor, and during this time wrote and published his *Serious Call to a Devout and Holy Life* (1728). His own reading included John Tauler (the Dominican), Thomas à Kempis, Jan van Ruysbroeck, and other spiritual writers of the late middle ages, who, along with Jacob Boehme, had a large role to play in his own later thought. When John Wesley first visited him at the Gibbon estate in Putney (1732), he was encouraged by Law to study some of these same writers—one of whom, Kempis, Wesley subsequently translated for his *Christian Library* series (1736). Law's advice also influenced him in his decision to go to Georgia. Wesley was later to distance himself from Law, and from contemplative spirituality generally, but always referred favorably to Law in his sermons.

Law left Putney in 1737, after the death of Gibbon senior, at a time when the influence of Boehme upon him was becoming more and more profound. While early in his life he had shared with his contemporaries an emphasis on reason and rational argument—"his was the age of [Sir Isaac] Newton, whom he admired, and of Rationalism, which he studied"[3]—he had always felt the inadequacy of rationalism to create a "living sensibility of the power, life, and religion of love."[4] Now he saw in Boehme a new way to account for even the laws of nature. He became a thoroughgoing opponent of rationalism, strongly emphasizing the impotence of human reason—or at least of analytic description—and the need for an imaginative entering into the wonder of spiritual communion. Of his *Appeal to All those Who Doubt the Truths of the Gospel* (1740), in which this development is quite clear, C. S. Lewis has written:

> I . . . like it as well as any religious work I have ever read. . . . The book is saturated with delight and a sense of wonder, one of those rare works which make you say of Christianity, "Here is the very thing you like in poetry and the romance, but this time it's true."[5]

Toward the end of 1740, Law retired to Kings Cliffe, where he owned a house and where for most of the rest of his life he resided with two women—the widow of Archibald Hutchison, M.P. for Hastings, and Miss Hester Gibbon of his former household. They abided by Law's strict regimen: up at five for devotion and study, assembly for prayers at nine, devotions after the noon meal, Bible reading after tea, and church services three days a week. Law began his day by distributing the milk of four cows to poor neighbors, and always tasted the soup daily prepared for the poor to see that it was up to standard. He was keen for the education of children, writing much upon the subject, and to the girls' school already underway he and Mrs. Hutchison added a school for eighteen boys in 1745, as well as additional almshouses to shelter the destitute. The balance of Law's personal time was taken up in study (in several languages) and in his writing. But he also loved music, felt it was an important asset to devotion, and participated in teaching the young to sing.

In this way, his later life was disposed in a way consistent with his principles and secluded from the world at large. He received letters from many people affected by his books, and wrote letters of spiritual counsel, but he visited with few people of note. He never allowed his portrait to be drawn or painted. Healthy all his life, he died suddenly after catching a "chill" on April 8, 1761, at the age of seventy-five.

Law is undeniably one of the most important figures in this age of evangelical revival and certainly deserves a much wider readership today. Yet, although his language is clear and straightforward, his books are not easy reading. The contemporary reader is in fact likely to find Law disturbing, not, perhaps, for the reasons that John Wesley did—who drew back in part because (typically in his age) he clung to rationalistic models of discourse even for spiritual things—but because of Law's relentless consistency in applying spiritual principles. We may identify with someone like Johnson who, after reading the *Serious Call,* was forced to a simple candor; he says that he expected to "find it a dull book (as such books generally are), and perhaps to laugh at it" but instead found Law "quite an overmatch" for him.[6] Perhaps the real reason that, as Aldous Huxley put it, "one of the greatest masters of devotion and philosophical theology is passed over almost in silence"[7] is Law's implacable way of putting to us the question of Christ's claim upon the whole of life. The selections which follow, from his earlier works, give a representation of his high challenge to those who would own the name of Christian in any time.

NOTES

1. James Boswell, *Life of Johnson,* ed. G. Birbeck Hill (London: Oxford University Press, 1887), vol. 2, p. 122.

2. *Dictionary of National Biography* article on Law, p. 236, quoting Edward Gibbon's *Autobiography*.

3. P. Grant, *Literature of Mysticism in Western Tradition* (London: Macmillan, 1983), p. 88.

4. *The Spirit of Love,* in *The Works of the Rev. William Law* (London: J. Richardson, 1762), vol. 8, p. 3.

5. *Letters of C. S. Lewis,* ed. W. H. Lewis (London: Geoffrey Bles, 1966), p. 143. Charles Williams, in *Descent of the Dove* (London: Religious Book Club, 1939; rpt. Grand Rapids: Eerdmans, 1980), p. 195, observes further that "Law wrote in that retirement a few books which (allowing for a certain distrust of the reason provoked by the Deists) form perhaps one of the best statements of the pure Christian religion that have ever been issued."

6. Boswell, vol. 1, p. 68.

7. Grover Smith, ed., *The Letters of Aldous Huxley* (New York: Harper and Row, 1970), p. 504.

# *from* A Practical Treatise Upon Christian Perfection (1726)

The following is the fourteenth chapter of this excellent work. In the preceeding chapter, entitled "All Christians are required to imitate the Life and Example of Jesus Christ," Law has enunciated his principle of Christian perfection as the standard set for us in Jesus:

When it is said that we are to imitate the life of Christ, it is not meant that we are called to the same manner of life, or the same sort of actions, for this cannot be, but it is certain that we are called to the same spirit and character which was the spirit and character of our Blessed Saviour's life and actions. We are to be like Him in heart and mind, to act by the same rule, to look towards the same end, and to govern our lives by the same spirit. . . . I am, said the Blessed Jesus, "the way, the truth, and the life, no man cometh unto the Father but by me." Christians often hear these words, and perhaps think that they have enough fulfilled them by believing in Jesus Christ. But they should consider that when Jesus Christ says He is the way, his meaning is that his way of life is to be the way in which all Christians are to live, and that it is by living after the manner of his life that any man comes unto the Father. So that the doctrine of this passage is this, that however we may call ourselves Christians or disciples of Christ, yet we cannot come unto God the Father except by entering into that way of life which was the way of our Saviour's life.

Since Jesus came into the world to save, Law reasons, we must enter into his purpose "and make salvation the greatest business of our lives"; even if our contribution is only able to be a very poor thing—a widow's mite—it must, like that woman's giving, be all that we possess. Law's spiritual principles here are like those of the Franciscans, or Thomas à Kempis, insofar as the injunction to follow Christ is taken literally and applied to everything which the life of Jesus sets before us as a pathway. Our Lord was submissive in all to the Father's will; so also must we be. Our Lord was unrebellious in the teeth of the world's despite; so we must follow Him in that. When Jesus says, "Learn of me, for I am meek and lowly in heart," Law observes that the grammar of this injunction is imperative. "This passage," he says, "is to be considered not as a piece of good advice that would be of use to us, but as a positive command requiring a necessary duty." He concludes his chapter by inviting the reader simply to meditate on the obvious implications, and to read and reread the Gospels till the character of Jesus is stamped permanently upon our minds and hearts. It is not enough, he says, to read the Bible "so as to know what it contains; . . . [we must] fill our hearts with the spirit" of it, which spirit is nowhere so exemplified as in the life of our Savior. This, then, is the context for what follows.

# An Exhortation To Christian Perfection

WHOEVER HAS read the foregoing chapters . . . has seen that Christian perfection requires us to devote ourselves wholly unto God, to make the goals and purposes of spiritual life the goals and purposes of all our actions. He has seen, further, that it calls us to be born again of God, to live by the light of his Holy Spirit, to renounce the world and all worldly attitudes, to practise a constant, universal self-denial, to make daily war with the corruption and disorder of our nature, to prepare ourselves for divine grace by a purity and holiness of conversation, to avoid all pleasures and cares which grieve the Holy Spirit and separate Him from us, to live in a daily constant state of prayer and devotion—and as the crown of all, to imitate the life and spirit of the Holy Jesus.

## I. *The Desirability of Perfection*

It now only remains that I exhort the reader to labor after this Christian perfection. Were I to exhort anyone to the study of poetry or eloquence, to labor to be rich and great or to spend his time in mathematics or other learning, I could only produce such reasons as are fit to delude the vanity of men, who are ready to be immersed with any appearance of excellence. For if the same person were to ask me what it signified to be a poet, or eloquent, what advantage it would be to him to be a great mathematician or a great statesman, I must be forced to answer that these things would mean just as much to him as they now mean to those poets, orators, mathematicians and statesmen whose bodies have been a long while lost amongst common dust. For if one will be so thoughtful and inquisitive as to put the question to every human enjoyment and ask what real good it will bring with it, he would soon find that every success amongst the things of this life leaves us in just the same state of need and emptiness in which it found us. If someone asks why he should labor to be the best mathematician, orator or statesman, the answer is easily given: because of the fame and honor of such a distinction. But if he were to ask again why he should thirst after fame and honor, or what good they would do him, he must stay long enough for an answer. For when we are at the top of all human attainments we are still at the bottom of all human misery, and

123

have made no further advancement towards true happiness than those whom we see deprived of all these fine things. Whether a person dies before he has written poems, compiled histories or raised an estate, signifies no more than whether he died an hundred or a thousand years ago.

On the contrary, when anyone is exhorted to labor after Christian perfection, if he then asks what good it will do him, the answer is ready, that it would do him a good which eternity alone can measure, that it will deliver him from a state of vanity and misery, that it will raise him from the poor enjoyments of an animal life, that it will give him a glorious body, carry him in spite of death and the grave to live with God, be glorious among angels and heavenly beings, and be full of an infinite happiness for all eternity. . . .

This shows us how inexcusable all Christians are who are devoted to the things of this life. It is not because they lack good character or are incapable of deep reflection, but it is because they reject the first principles of common sense: they won't so much as ask what those things are which they are laboring after. . . . We must not, therefore, complain of the weakness and ignorance of our nature, or the deceitful appearances of worldly enjoyments, because the lowest level of reason, if listened to, is sufficient to discover the self-deception. If you wish, you may blindly do what the rest of the world is doing; you may follow the cry and run yourself out of breath for you know not what. But if you will but show so much sense as to ask why you should enter such a rat-race, you will need no deeper reflection than this to make you leave the broad way and let the wise and learned, the rich and great go mad by themselves. Even this much common sense will turn your eyes toward God, will separate you from all the [mere] appearances of worldly happiness, and fill you with one ambition only—eternal happiness.

1. Means and ends

When Pyrrhus, King of Epirus, told Cineas what great conquests he intended to make, and how many nations he would subdue, Cineas asked him what he would do when all this was done? He answered, we will then live at ease and enjoy ourselves and our friends. Cineas replied to this effect: "Why then, Sir, do we not *now* live at ease and enjoy ourselves? If ease and quiet be the utmost of our goals and purposes, why do we run away from it at present? What is the reason for all these battles and expeditions all over the world?"

The moral of this story is very extensive, and it carries a lesson of instruction to much the greatest part of the Christian world.

When a Christian is eager after the distinctions of this life, proposing some mighty heights to which he will raise himself, either in riches, learning, or power, if one was to ask him what he will do when he has obtained them, I suppose his answer would be that he would then retire, and devote himself to holiness and piety. May we not here justly say with Cineas, if piety and holiness are the chief end of man, if these are your ultimate goals, the upshot of all your labors, why do you not simply enter upon happiness now? Why all this wandering out of your way? Why must you go so far afield? For to devote yourself to the world, though it is your ultimate intention to retire from it to holiness and piety is like Pyrrhus's seeking of battles when he proposed to live in ease and pleasure with his friends. I believe there are very few Christians who have it not in their heads at least to be some time or other holy and virtuous and readily own that it is a happy person who dies truly humble, holy and heavenly-minded. Now this opinion—which all people hold—makes the projects and ambitions of life more mad and frantic than the battles of Pyrrhus. For one may not only say to such people, "why do you neglect the present happiness of these virtues?" but one must further add, "why are you engaged in a way of life which is quite contrary to them?" You want to be rich and great; is that because riches and greatness may make you more meek, humble and heavenly-minded? Do you aspire after the distinctions of honor, that you may more truly feel the misery and meanness of your nature, and be made more lowly in your own eyes? Do you plunge yourself into worldly cares, let your passions fix upon a great variety of objects, so that you may love God with all your heart, and raise your affections to things above? You acknowledge humility to be essential to salvation, yet make it the chief practice of your life to run away from it, to raise yourself in show and image before the world. Is not this fighting Pyrrhus's battles? Nay, is it not a much more egregious folly? For you admit that you cannot be saved without true humility, a real lowliness of temperament, and yet you are doing all that you can to keep these things out of your heart. What is there in the conduct of the maddest [tragic] hero that can equal this foolishness?

Suppose that strict sobriety was the sole end of man, the necessary condition of happiness. What would you think of those people who, knowing and believing this to be true, should still spend their time in laying in quantities of all sorts of the strongest liquors? What would you think if you saw them constantly enlarging their cellars, filling every room with decanters and competing to see who would have the largest quantities of the strongest drinks? Now this is like the folly and madness in the lives of Christians: they are as wise and reasonable as those who are always providing strong liquors in order to be strictly sober. For all the enjoyments of human life which Christians so aspire after—whether of riches, greatness, honors, and pleasures—are as much the dangers and temptations to the Christian as strong and pleasant liquors are to a person obliged to drink only water. Now if you were to ask such a person why he is continually increasing his stock of liquors when he is supposed to abstain from them all and only to drink water, he can give you as good a reason as those Christians who spare no pains to acquire riches, greatness and pleasures at the same time as their salvation depends upon their renouncing them all, and upon their cultivating heavenly-mindedness, great humility, and constant self-denial.

## 2. Priorities

Now it may be that you are not devoted to these things. You have a greater soul than to be taken with riches, equipage or the pageantry of state. You are deeply engaged in learning and sciences. You are, it may be, squaring the circle or settling the distances of the stars, or busy in the study of exotic plants. You, it may be, are comparing the ancient languages, have made deep discoveries in the change of letters, and perhaps know how to write an inscription in as obscure characters as if you had lived more than two thousand years ago. Or perhaps you are meditating upon pagan religions, collecting the history of their gods and goddesses; or you are scanning some ancient Greek or Roman poet, and making an exact anthology of their scattered remains, scraps of sentences and broken words.

You are not exposing your life in the field like a mad Alexander or Caesar, but you are again and again fighting over all their battles in your study; you are collecting the names of their generals, the number of their troops, the manner of their arms, and can give the world a more exact account of the times, places and circumstances of their battles than has yet been seen.

You will perhaps ask whether this is not a very commendable exercise, an excellent use of our time and talents. You might ask, indeed, whether people may not be very reasonably exhorted to this kind of study. It may be answered that all inquiries (however learned they are considered) that do not improve the mind in some useful knowledge, that do not make us wise in spiritual wisdom, are to be reckoned amongst our greatest vanities and follies. All speculations that will not stand this test are to be looked upon as the wanderings and impertinences of a disordered understanding.

It is a strange deficiency of thought to imagine that research is ever the better because it is taken up in Greek and Latin. Why is it not as wise and reasonable for a scholar to dwell in the kitchen and converse with cooks as to go into his study to meditate upon the Roman art of cookery and learn the variety of sauces?

A grave Doctor of Divinity would perhaps think his time very poorly employed—or that he were acting below his dignity—if he were to be an amanuensis to some modern poet. Why then does he think it suitable to the weight of his calling to have been a drudge to some ancient poet, counting his syllables for several years only to help the world read what some irreligious, wanton or epicurean poet has written?

It is certainly a much more reasonable employment to be making clothes than to spend one's time in reading or writing volumes upon Grecian or Roman fashions.

If you can show me a learning that makes man truly aware of his duty, that fills the mind with true light, that reforms the heart, that disposes it rightly toward God, that makes us more reasonable in all our actions, that inspires us with fortitude, humility, devotion, and contempt of the world, that gives us a right appreciation of the importance of spiritual life, the sanctity of morality, the littleness of everything except God, the vanity of our passions, and the misery and corrupton of our nature, I will own myself an advocate for such learning. But to think that time is well employed because it is spent in such speculations as the uneducated cannot reach, or because they are fetched from antiquity or found in Greek and Latin, is a folly that may be called as great as any in human life.

Those who think that these studies are consistent with a heart entirely devoted to God have not given enough consideration to human nature, they would do well to consult our Saviour's rebuke of Martha. Actually, she does not seem to have wandered that far from her proper business. She was not busy in the history of housewifery or inquiring into the original of the distaff. She was only taken up with her present affairs, and "cumbered about much serving." Yet our Blessed Saviour said unto her, "Martha, Martha, thou art careful and troubled about many things. But one thing is needful."

Now if scholars and theologians can show that they only pursue such studies as are serviceable to the "one thing needful," if they are busy in a philosophy and learning that has a necessary connection with the devotion of the heart to God, such learning well becomes the followers of Christ. But if they trifle in Greek and Latin, and only assist other people to follow them in the same impertinence, such learning may be reckoned amongst the corruptions of the age. For all the arguments against pride, covetousness and vanity are equally good arguments against such learning, it being the same irreligion to be devoted to any false learning as to be devoted to any other false God.

A smug satisfaction in any vain ornaments of the body, whether of clothes or paint, is no greater a mistake than a smug satisfaction in vain accomplishments of the mind.*

A person that is eager and laborious in the search and study of that which does him no good is as poor and as small a soul as the miser that is happy with his moneybags that are gathering dust. A ridiculous application of our money, time and understanding is all the same fault, whether it be found amongst the finery of fops, the hoards of misers, or the trinkets of virtuosos. It is the same false turn of mind, the same mistake in the use of things, the same ignorance of the state of mankind, and the same offence against true religion.

When we see someone brooding over bags of wealth, and laboring to die rich, we do not only accuse him of a poor smallness of mind, but we charge him with great guilt: we do not consider such a person to be in a state of faith. Let us therefore suppose that this covetous person was suddenly changed into another character, that he was grown polite and curious, that he was fond and eager after the most useless things, as long as they were ancient or scarce. Let us suppose that he is now as greedy after original paintings as he was before after money; that he will give more for a dog's head or a snuff of a candle by a good hand than ever he gave in charity all his life. Is he a wiser man or a better Christian than he was before? Has he more overcome the world, or is he more devoted to God than when his soul was locked up with his money? Alas! his heart is in the same false satisfaction, he is in the same state of ignorance, is as far from the true good, as much separated from good as he whose soul is cleaving to the dust. He lives in the same vanity, and must die in the same misery as he that lives and dies in foppery and covetousness.

## 3. Foolish choices

Here therefore I sum up my first argument for Christian perfection. I exhort you to labor after it because there is no choice of anything else for you to labor after, and there is nothing better that the reason of man can exhort you to. The whole world has nothing to offer you in its place. Choose what other way you will, and you have chosen nothing but vanity and misery; for all the different ways of the world are only different ways of deluding yourself: this only excells that as one vanity can excell another. If you want to make yourself more happy than those who pursue their own destruction, if you would show yourself wiser than fops, more reasonable than sordid misers, you must pursue that happiness and study that wisdom which leads to God, for every other pur-

*Cf. Hannah More on this subject, following.

suit, every other way of life, however polite or plausible in the opinions of the world, has a folly and stupidity in it that is equal to the folly and stupidity of fops and misers.

Take a moment, shut your eyes, and think of the silliest creature in human life; imagine something that you think is most poor and vain in the way of the world. Now you are yourself that poor and vain creature, unless you are devoted to God and laboring after Christian perfection. Unless this is your difference from the world, you ought not to be able to think of any creature more silly than yourself. For it is not any position or condition or public image that makes one person wiser or better than another. If you are a proud scholar, a worldly priest, an irreverent philosopher, a crafty politician, an ambitious statesman, your imagination cannot invent a way of life that has more vanity or folly than your own. Everyone has wisdom enough to see what a variety of fools and madmen there are in the world.

Now perhaps we cannot do better than to find out the true reason of the folly and madness of any sort of life. Ask yourself therefore wherein consists the folly of any sort of life, whatever is most condemned in your judgement. Is a drunken fox-hunter leading a foolish life? Wherein consists the folly of it? Is it because he is not getting money upon the exchange? Or because he is not wrangling at the bar? Or not waiting at court? No, the folly of it consists in this, that he is not living like a reasonable Christian; that he is not acting like a being that is born again of God, who has a salvation to work out with fear and trembling; that he is throwing away his time amongst dogs, and noise, and intemperance, which he should devote to watching and prayer and the improvement of his soul in all holy dedications. Now if this is the folly (as it most certainly is) of an intemperate fox-hunter, it shows us an equal folly in every other way of life, where the same great ends of living are neglected. Though we are shining at the bar, making a figure at court, great at the exchange, or famous in the schools of philosophy, we are yet the same despicable creatures as the intemperate fox-hunter if these states of life keep us as far from the cultivation of holiness and heavenly affections. There is nothing greater in any way of life than fox-hunting; it is all the same folly unless spiritual obedience be the beginning and end, the rule and measure of it all. For it is as noble a wisdom and shows as great a soul to die less holy and heavenly for the sake of hunting and noise as for the sake of anything that the world can give us.

If we will judge and condemn things by our attitudes and fancies, we may think some ways of life very wise, and others very foolish; we may think it glorious to be pursuing methods of fame and wealth and foolish to be killing foxes. But if we will let reason and faith show us the folly and wisdom of things, we shall easily see that all ways of life are equally small and foolish except those that perfect and exalt our souls in holiness.

No one therefore can complain of a lack of understanding in the conduct of his life, for even a small share of sense is sufficient to condemn some degrees of vanity which we see in the world; everyone is able and ready to do it. And if we are but able to condemn the vainest sort of life upon good principles, the same principles will serve to show that all sorts of life are equally vain except spiritual life. You have therefore, as I observed before, no real choice of anything to labor after instead of Christian perfection. If you can be content to be the poorest, vainest, most miserable thing upon earth, you may then neglect Christian perfection. But if you see anything in human life that you abhor and despise, if there be any person that lives as you should fear to live, you must turn your heart to God and must labor after Christian perfection, for there is nothing in nature but this that can set you above the vainest, poorest and most miserable of human creatures. You yourself are everything that you abhor and despise, everything that you can fear, and full of every folly that your mind can imagine, unless you are wholly devoted to God.

## II. *The Necessity of Perfection*

Another argument for Christian perfection is drawn from the very necessity of it.

### 1. Dedication

I have all along shown that Christian perfection consists in the right performance of our necessary duties, that it implies such holy attitudes as constitute that common piety which is necessary to salvation, and consequently is such a piety as is equally necessary to be attained by all people. But besides this, we are to consider that God alone knows what diminishments of holiness He will accept; therefore we can have no security of our salvation except by doing our utmost to deserve it.

There are different degrees of holiness which it may please God to reward, but we cannot state these different degrees ourselves. Rather, we must all labour to be as eminent as we can, and then our different achievements must be left to God. We have nothing to trust to but the sincerity of our endeavors, and our endeavors may well be thought to lack sincerity unless they are endeavors after the utmost perfection. As soon as we stop at any level of goodness, we put an end to our goodness, which is only valuable by having all the levels that we can add to it. Our highest improvement is a state of great imperfection but will be accepted by God because it is our highest achievement. But any other state of life where we are not doing all that we can to purify and perfect our souls is a state that can give us no comfort or satisfaction because so far as we are lacking in any ways of piety that are in our power, so far as we are defective in any holy disposition of which we are capable, so far we make our very salvation uncertain. For no one can have any assurance that he pleases God, or puts himself within the terms of Christian salvation except one who serves God with his whole heart, and with the utmost of his strength. For though the Christian faith be a covenant of mercy for the pardon and salvation of frail and imperfect creatures, yet we cannot say that we are within the conditions of that mercy till we do all that we can in our frail and imperfect state. So that although we are not called to such a perfection as implies a 'sinless state,' and though our imperfections will not prevent the divine mercy, yet it cannot be proved that God has any terms of favor for those who do not labor to be as perfect as they can be.

Different attainments in piety will carry different persons to heaven, yet none of us can have any satisfaction that we are going thither except by arriving at all that change of nature which is in our power. It is as necessary therefore to labor after perfection as to labor after our salvation, because we can have no satisfaction that a failure in one will not deprive us of the other. When therefore you are exhorted to Christian perfection you must remember that you are only exhorted to secure your salvation. You must remember also that you have no other rule to judge your perfection but by the sincerity and fulness of your endeavors to arrive at it.

## 2. The test: love

We may judge the measure and extent of Christian holiness from the one instance of love. This virtue is thus described: "Charity seeketh not her own, beareth all things, believeth all things, hopeth all things, endureth all things." Now this love, though it be in perfection, is yet by the apostle made so absolutely necessary to salvation that a failure in it is not to be made up by any other, even the most shining virtues. "Though I have all faith, so that I could remove mountains, though I bestow all my goods to feed the poor, though I give my body to be burned, and have not charity, it profiteth me nothing." The apostle expressly teaches us that this perfection in Christian love is so necessary to salvation that even martyrdom itself is not sufficient to atone for the lack of it. Need we now any other argument to convince us that to labor after our perfection is only to labor after our salvation? For what is here said of love must in all reason be understood of every other virtue; it must be practised in the same fulness and sincerity of heart as this love. It may also justly be affirmed that this love is so holy an attitude, and requires so many other virtues as the foundation of it, that it can only be exercised by a heart that is far advanced in holiness—that is entirely devoted to God. Our whole nature must be changed; we must have put off the old man; we must be born again of God, we must have overcome the world, we must live by faith, be full of the Spirit of Christ, in order to exercise this love.

When therefore you would know whether it is necessary to labor after Christian perfection and live wholly unto God, read over St. Paul's description of love. If you can think of any negligence of life, any defects of humility, any diminishment of devotion, any fondness of the world, any desire of riches and greatness that is consistent with the disposition there described, then you may be content with it. But if these expressions of an exalted love cannot subsist except in a soul that is devoted to God and resigned to the world, that is humble and mortified, that is full of the Spirit of Christ and a concern for eternity, then you have a plain reason for the necessity of laboring after all the perfection that you are capable of. For the apostle expressly says that without this disposition the very tongues of angels are but as sounding brass or a tinkling cymbal. Do not therefore imagine that it is only appropriate to people of a 'particular piety and turn of mind' to labor after their perfection, and that you may go to heaven with much less care. There is only one "strait gate" and one "narrow way that leadeth unto life," and there is no admission except for those who *strive* to enter into it. If you are not striving, you neglect the express condition which our Lord requires, and it is flat nonsense to think that you are striving if you are not using all your strength.

3. Spiritual effort

The apostle represents a Christian's striving for eternal life in this manner: "Know ye not that they which run in a race, run all, but one receiveth the prize? So run that ye may obtain." So, according to the apostle, he alone is in the road to salvation who is so contending for it as he that is running in a race.

Further, you can have no satisfaction that you are sincere in *any* virtue unless you are endeavoring to be perfect in *all* the instances of it. If you allow yourself any defects of love, you have no reason to think yourself sincere in any acts of love. If you indulge yourself in any instances of pride, you render all your acts of humility justly suspect because there can be no true reason for love except what is as good a reason for *all* instances of charity, nor any spiritual motivation for humility except what is as strong a motivation for all degrees of humility. So someone who allows himself any known defects of love, humility, or any other virtue, cannot be supposed to practise any instances of that virtue for the sake of truly spiritual motives. For if it was a right fear of God, a true desire of being like Christ, a hearty love for my fellow-creatures that made me give in charity, the same dispositions would make me love and forgive all my enemies and deny myself all kinds of revenge, spite and evil speaking. . . .

Too many Christians look at some instances of virtue which they practise as a sufficient atonement for their known defects in some other parts of the same virtue—not considering that this is as absurd as to think to make some apparent acts of justice compensate for other allowed instances of fraud.

A lady is perhaps satisfied with her humility because she can look at some apparent instances of it; she sometimes visits hospitals and institutions of welfare and is very familiar and condescending to the poor. Now these are very good, but then it may be that these very things are looked upon as sufficient proofs of humility—she patches and paints, and delights in all the show and ornaments of personal pride, and rests very easy with herself because she visits the hospitals. Now she should consider that she places her humility in that which is but a part, and also the smallest and most deceitful part. For the hardest, greatest and most essential part of humility is to have low opinions of ourselves, to love our own ordinariness, and to renounce all such things as gratify the pride and vanity of our nature. Humility also is much better discovered by our behavior towards our equals and superiors than towards those who are so much below us. It does no hurt to a proud heart to stoop to some low service for deprived people. Nay, there is something in it that may gratify pride, for perhaps our own greatness is never seen to more advantage than when we stoop to those we are so far below us. The lower the people are to whom we stoop, the better they show the height of our own state. So there is nothing difficult in these condescensions; they are not contradictions to pride.

The truest trial of humility is our behavior towards our equals, and those who are our superiors or inferiors in only a small degree. It is no sign of humility for a private gentleman to pay a profound reverence and show great submission to a king, nor is it any sign of humility for the same person to condescend to great familiarity with a poor person dependent upon charity. For he may act upon the same principle in both cases. It does not hurt him to show great submission to a king, because he has no thoughts of being equal to a king, and for the same reason it does not hurt him to condescend to poor people, because he never imagines that they will think themselves his equal. So it is the great inequality of condition that makes it as easy for people to condescend to those who are a great way below them as to be submissive and yielding to those who are vastly above them.

From this it appears that our most splendid acts of virtue which we may think to be sufficient to atone for our other known defects can themselves be so vain and defective as to have no worth in them. This also shows us the absolute necessity of laboring after all instances of perfection in every virtue, because if we pick and choose what parts of any virtue we will perform, we sin against all the same principles as if we neglected all parts of it. If we choose to give instead of forgiving, we choose something else instead of love.

## III. *The Double Advantage of Seeking Perfection*

A third motive to induce you to aspire after Christian perfection may be taken from the double advantage of it—in this life, and that which is to come.

### 1. Preparation for eternity

The apostle thus exhorts the Corinthians: "wherefore my beloved brethren, be ye steadfast, immovable, always abounding in the work of the Lord, forasmuch as ye know, that our labour will not be in vain in the Lord" (1 Corinthians 15:58). This is an exhortation founded upon solid reason; for what can be so wise and reasonable as to be always abounding in that work which will never be in vain? While we are pleased with ourselves, or pleased with the world, we are pleased with vanity, and our most prosperous labors of this kind are, as the preacher saith, "but vanity of vanities; all is vanity." But while we are laboring after Christian perfection we are laboring for eternity, and building to ourselves higher stations in the joys of heaven. "As one star differeth from another star in glory, so also is the resurrection of the dead": we shall surely rise to different degrees of glory, of joy and happiness in God, according to our different achievements in purity, holiness and good works.

No degrees of mortification and self-denial, no private prayers, no secret mournings, no instances of charity, no labors of love will ever be forgotten, but all treasured up to our everlasting comfort and refreshment. For though the rewards of the other life are free gifts of God, yet since he has assured us that every man shall be rewarded according to his works, it is certain that our rewards will be as different as our works have been.

Now stand still here awhile, and ask yourself whether you really believe this to be true—that the more perfect we make ourselves here, the more happy we shall be hereafter. If you do not believe this to be strictly true, you know nothing of God or religion. And if you do believe it to be true, is it possible to be awake, and not aspiring after Christian perfection?

What can you think of, what can the world show you that can make you any amends for the loss of any degree of virtue? Can any way of life make it reasonable for you to die less perfect than you might have done?

If you would now devote yourself to perfection, perhaps you must part with some friends, you must displease some relations, you must lay aside some plans, you must refrain from some pleasures, you must alter your life. Nay, perhaps you must do more than this—you must expose yourself to the hatred of friends, to the jest and ridicule of clever mockers, and to the scorn and derision of worldly men. But had you not better do and suffer all this than to die less perfect, less prepared for mansions of eternal glory? Indeed, suffering all this is suffering nothing. For why should it signify anything to you what fools and madmen think of you? And surely it can be no wrong or rash judgement to think those both fools and mad who condemn what God approves, and like that which God condemns. But if you think this too much to be done to obtain eternal glory, think, on the other hand, what can be gained instead of it.

Fancy yourself living in all the ease and pleasure that the world can give you, esteemed by your friends, undisturbed by your enemies, and gratifying all your natural inclinations. If you could stand still in such a state, you might say that you had something; but alas! every day that is added to such a life is the same thing as a day taken from it—and shows you that so much happiness is already gone. For be as happy as you will: you must see it all sinking away from you, you must feel yourself decline; you must see that your time shortens apace, you must hear of sudden deaths; you must fear sickness; you must both dread and desire old age; you must fall into the hands of death; either die in the painful bitter sorrows of a deep repentance or in sad, gloomy despair, wishing for mountains to fall upon you and seas to cover you. And is this a happiness to be chosen? Is this all that you can gain by neglecting God, by following your own desires, and not laboring after Christian perfection? Is it worth your while to separate yourself from God, to lose your share in the realms of light, to be thus 'happy'—or I may better say, to be thus miserable—even in this life? You may be so blind and foolish as not to think of these things, but it is impossible to think of them without laboring after Christian perfection. It may be you are too young, too happy, or too busy to be affected with these reflections, but let me tell you that all will be over before you are aware; your day will be spent, and leave you to such a night as that which surprised the foolish virgins. "And at midnight there was a great cry made, behold the Bridegroom cometh; go ye out to meet him" (Matthew 25:6).

The last hour will soon be with you, when you will have nothing to look for but your reward in another life, when you will stand with nothing but eternity before you, and must begin to be something that will be your state forever. I can no more reach heaven with my hands than I can describe the feelings you will have then; you will then feel emotions that you never felt before; all your thoughts and reflections will pierce your soul in a manner that you never before experienced, and you will feel the immortality of your nature by the depth and piercing vigor of your thoughts. You will then know what it is to die; you will then know that you never knew it before, that you never thought worthily of it, but that dying thoughts are as new and amazing as that state which follows them.

Let me therefore exhort you to come prepared to this time of trial, to look out for comfort whilst the day is before you, to treasure up such a fund of good and devout works as may make you able to bear that state which cannot be borne without them. Could I any way make you apprehend how dying men feel the need of a pious life, how they lament time lost, health and strength squandered away in folly, how they look at eternity, and what they think of the rewards of another life, you would soon find yourself one of those who desire to live in the highest state of piety and perfection, that by this means you may grow old in peace, and die in full hopes of eternal glory.

## 2. Spirituality here and now

Consider again, that besides the rewards of the other life, laboring after Christian perfection (or devoting yourself wholly to God) has a great reward even in this life, as it makes religion doubly pleasant to you. Whilst you are divided betwixt God and the world, you have neither the pleasures of spiritual life nor the pleasures of the world, but are always in the uneasiness of a divided state of heart. You have only so much spiritual development as serves to disquiet you, to check your enjoyments, to show you a handwriting upon the wall, to interrupt your pleasures, to reproach you with your foolishness, and to appear as a death's head at all your feasts—but not enough spiritual life to give you a taste and feeling of its proper pleasures and satisfactions. You dare not wholly neglect religion, but then you take no more than is just sufficient to keep you from being a terror to yourself and you are as loath to be *very* good as you are fearful to be *very* bad. In this you are just about as happy as the slave that dares not run away from his master, and yet always serves him against his will. Instead of having a spiritual life that is your comfort in all troubles, your religion is itself a trouble under which you want to be comforted, and those days and times hang heaviest upon your hands which leave you only to the services and duties of religion. Sunday would be very dull and tiresome, except that it is but one day in seven, and is turned into a day of dressing up and visiting, as well as divine service. You don't care to keep away from the public worship, but you are always glad when it is over. This is the state of *half*-piety: the experience of those who add religion to a worldly life. All their religion is mere yoke and burden, and is only made tolerable by occupying but little of their time.

Think of the urbane person who goes to church, but hardly knows whether he goes out of a sense of duty or to meet his friends. He marvels at those people who are profane and what pleasure they can find in *ir*religion; but he is in as great a state of wonder at those who would make every day a day of divine worship, and in fact feels, himself, no more of the pleasures of spiritual life than he does the pleasures of a profane life. As religion has everything from him except his heart, he has everything from it except its comforts. This man–about–town likes religion, because it seems an easy way of pleasing God—a decent thing, that takes up but little of his time and adds a proper 'mixture' to life. But if he were forced to take comfort in it, he would be as much at a loss as those who have lived without God in the world. When he thinks of joy, and pleasure, and happiness, he does not think at all of spirituality. He has gone through a hundred misfortunes, fallen into a variety of hardships, but never thought of making spiritual life his comfort in any of them—he makes himself quiet and happy in some other manner. He is content with his Christianity, not because he is pious but because he is not profane. He continues in the same course of religion, not because of any real good he ever found in it, but because it does him no hurt.

To such poor purposes as these do numbers of people profess Christianity. Let me, therefore, rather exhort you to a solid piety, to devote yourself wholly unto God, that entering deeply into spiritual life you may enter deeply into its comforts, that serving God with all your heart you may have the peace and pleasure of a heart that is at unity with itself. When your conscience once bears you witness that you are "steadfast, immoveable, and always abounding in the work of the Lord," you will find that your reward is already begun, and that you could not be less devout, less holy, less loving, or less humble, without lessening the most substantial pleasure that ever you felt in your life. To be content with any lower attainments in spirituality is to rob ourselves of a present happiness which nothing else can give us.

## 3. Self-deceiving excuses

You would perhaps devote yourself to perfection, but on account of this or that 'little difficulty' that lies in your way, you are not in so convenient a state for the full practice of spiritual living as you could wish. But consider that this is nonsense—because perfection consists in conquering difficulties. You could not be perfect, as the present state of trial requires, had you not those difficulties and inconveniences to struggle with. These things therefore which you would have removed, are laid in your way that you may make them so many steps to perfection and glory.

As you could not exercise your love unless you met with objects of that love, so neither could you show that you had overcome the world unless you had many worldly engagements to overcome. If all your friends and acquaintances were devout, humble, heavenly-minded, and wholly intent upon the one end of life, it would be less perfection in you to be like them. But if you are humble amongst those that delight in pride, heavenly-minded amongst the worldly, sober amongst the intemperate, devout amongst the irreligious, and laboring after perfection amongst those that despise and ridicule your labors, then are you truly devoted unto God. Consider, therefore, that you can have no difficulty but such as the world lays in your way, and that perfection is never to be had except by parting with the world. It consists in nothing else. To hold back, therefore, from setting out to be perfect until it suits with your condition in the world, is like waiting to be charitable until there are no persons needing loving attention. It is as if a man should intend to be courageous some time or other, when there is nothing left to test his courage.

Again: you perhaps turn your eyes upon the world and see all orders of people full of other cares and pleasures. You see the generality of clergy and laity, learned and unlearned, your friends and acquaintances, mostly living according to the spirit that reigns in the world. Perhaps you are then content with such a piety as you think contents great scholars and famous men, and it may be that you cannot think that God will reject the style of such numbers of Christians. Yet all this is merely amusing yourself with nothing; it is only losing yourself in vain imaginations; it is making that a 'rule' which is no rule, and cheating yourself into a false satisfaction. As you are not to be judgemental or to damn other people, so neither are you to think your own salvation secure because you are like the generality of the world.

The foolish virgins that had provided no oil for their lamps, and so were shut out of the marriage feast, were only thus far foolish—that they trusted to the assistance of those that were wise. But you are more foolish than they, for you trust to be saved by the folly of others; you imagine yourself safe in the negligence, vanity and irregularity of the world. You take confidence in the broad way because it *is* broad; you are content with yourself because you seem to be going along with the many, though God Himself has told you that narrow is the way that leads unto life, and few there be that find it.

## 4. The call to glory

Lastly, one word more and I have done. Consider what a happiness it is that you have in your power to secure a share in the glories of heaven, and make yourself one of those blessed beings that are to live with God forever. Reflect upon the glories of bright angels that shine about the throne of heaven; think upon that fulness of joy which is the state of Christ at the right hand of God, and remember that it is this same state of glory and joy that lies open for you. You are less, it may be, in worldly distinctions than many others, but as to your relation to God you have no superior upon earth. Let your condition be what it will, let your life be ever so insignificant, you may make the end and purpose of it the beginning of eternal glory. Be often therefore in these reflections, that they may fill you with a wise ambition for all that glory which God in Christ has called you to. For it is impossible to understand and feel anything of this without your heart charged with strong desires after it. The hopes and expectations of so much greatness and glory must needs awake you into earnest desires and longings after it. There are many things in human life which it would be vain for you to aspire after, but the happiness of the next, which is the sum of all happiness, is secure and safe to you against all accidents. Here no chances of misfortunes can prevent your success, neither the treachery of friends nor the malice of enemies can disappoint you; it is only your own false heart that can rob you of this happiness. Be but your own true friend, and then you have nothing to fear from your enemies. Do you but sincerely labor in the Lord, and then neither height nor depth, neither life nor death, neither man nor devils, can make your labor vain.

# *from* A Serious Call to a Devout and Holy Life (1728)

## *Spiritual Devotion*

DEVOTION IS neither private nor public prayer. Rather, prayers, whether private or public, are particular aspects or instances of devotion. Devotion signifies a life given, or devoted, to God.

He, therefore, is devout who lives no longer according to his own will or the way and spirit of the world, but to the sole will of God; he considers God in everything, serves God in everything, makes all the parts of his common life aspects of his worship by doing everything in the name of God and according to such principles as are conformable to his glory.

### I. *First Principles*

We readily acknowledge that God alone is to be the rule and measure of our prayers, that in them we are to look wholly unto Him, act wholly for Him; that we are only to pray in such a manner, for such things and such ends as are suitable to his glory.

Now let anyone but grasp the reason why he is to be thus strictly pious in his worship, and he will find the same as strong a reason to be as strictly devout in all the other parts of his life. For there is not the least shadow of a reason why we should make God the rule and measure of our worship—why we should then look wholly unto Him, and pray according to his will—but what equally proves it necessary for us to look wholly unto God and make Him the rule and measure of all the other actions of our life. For any way of life, any employment of our talents, whether of our gifts, our time, or our money, that is not strictly according to the will of God—that is not for such ends as are suitable to his glory—is as great an absurdity and failing as a prayer that is not according to the will of God. For there is no other reason why our prayers should be according to the will of God, or why they should have nothing in them but what is wise and holy and heavenly; there is no other reason for this, but that our lives might be of the same nature, full of the same wisdom, holiness and heavenly temperament, that we may live unto God in the same spirit that we pray unto Him. Were it not our strict duty to live by reason, to devote all the actions of our lives to God, were it not absolutely necessary to walk before Him in wisdom and holiness and all heavenly conversation, doing everything in his name, and for his glory, there would be no excellency or wisdom in the most heavenly prayers. Nay, such prayers would be absurdities; they would be like prayers for wings when it was no part of our duty to fly.

As surely, therefore, as there is any wisdom in praying for the Spirit of God, so sure is it that we are to make that Spirit the rule of all our actions. As sure as it is our duty to look wholly unto God in our prayers, so sure is it that it is our duty to live wholly unto God in our lives. But we can no more be said to live unto God unless we live unto Him in all the ordinary actions of our life—unless He be the rule and measure of all our ways—than we can be said to pray unto God unless our prayers look wholly unto Him. So that unreasonable and absurd ways of life, whether in labor or leisure, whether they consume our time or our money, are like unreasonable and absurd prayers, and are as truly an offence unto God.

## 1. Misplaced identity

It is for lack of knowing, or at least considering, this relationship that we see such a mixture of ridicule in the lives of many people. You see them strict about some times and places of devotion, but when the service of the church is over, they act like those who seldom or never come there. In their way of life, their manner of spending their time and money, in their cares and fears, in their pleasures and indulgences, in their labor and diversions, they are like the rest of the world. This makes the loose part of the world generally to make a joke of those that are "devout" because they see their devotion goes no further than their church-going, and that when the services are over they live no more unto God until the time of worship returns again, living rather by the same attitudes and tastes, and in as full an enjoyment of all the follies of life as other people. This is the reason that they are the jest and scorn of careless and worldly people, not because they are really devoted to God but because they appear to have no other devotion than that of occasional prayers.

A scrupulous church-goer—let us call him Julius—is very fearful of missing worship; all the congregation supposes Julius to be sick if he is not at church. But if you were to ask him why he spends the rest of his time by mere inclination or chance, why he is a companion of the silliest people in their most silly pleasure, why he is ready for every impertinent entertainment and diversion; if you were to ask him why there is no amusement too trifling to please him, why he is always at parties and receptions, why he gives himself up to an idle, gossiping conversation, why he lives in foolish friendships and fondness for particular persons who neither want nor deserve any particular kindness, why he allows himself foolish hatreds and resentments against particular persons without considering that he is to love everybody as himself; if you ask him why he never regulates his conversation, his time and fortune according to spiritual principles, Julius has no more to say for himself than the most disorderly person. For the whole tenor of Scripture lies as directly against such a life as it does against debauchery and intemperance. One who lives such a course of idleness and folly lives no more according to the religion of Jesus Christ than one who lives in gluttony and profligacy.

If someone were to tell Julius that there was no reason for so much constancy in worship, and that he might without any harm to himself neglect the service of the church as most people do, Julius would think such a person to be no Christian, and imagine that he ought to avoid his company. But if a person only tells him that he may live as the generality of the world does, that he may enjoy himself as others do, that he may spend his time and money as people of fashion do that conform to the follies and frailties of the age, gratifying his impulses and passions as most people do, Julius never suspects that person to lack a Christian spirit, or to be doing the devil's work. And yet if Julius was to read all the New Testament from the beginning to the end, he would find his course of life condemned in every page of it.

And indeed, there cannot be anything imagined more absurd in itself than wise and sublime and heavenly prayers being added to a life of vanity and folly, where neither labor nor leasure, neither time nor money, are under the direction of the wisdom and heavenly attitude of our prayers. If we were to see someone pretending to act wholly with regard to God in everything that he did—who would neither spend time nor money, nor take any labor or diversion except insofar as he could act according to strict principles of reason and piety—and yet at the same time neglected all prayers, whether public or private, would we not be amazed? And yet this is as reasonable as for any person to pretend to strictness in devotion, to be careful of observing times and places of prayer, and yet let the rest of his life, his time and labor, his talents and money, be disposed of without any regard to strict rules of piety and devotion. For it is as great an absurdity to imagine holy prayers and divine petitions without a holiness of life suitable to them as to imagine a holy and divine life without prayers. . . .

The short of the matter is this: either reason and faith prescribe principles and goals for all the ordinary actions of our life, or they do not. If they do, then it is as necessary to govern all our actions by those principles as it is necessary to worship God. For if Christian religion teaches us anything concerning eating and drinking, or spending our time and money; if it teaches us how we are to use and yet reject the world; if it teaches us what values we are to hold in ordinary life; how we are to be disposed toward all people; how we are to behave toward the sick, the poor, the old, the destitute; if it tells us whom we are to treat with a particular love, whom we are to regard with a particular esteem; if it tells us how we are to treat our enemies, and how we are to mortify and deny ourselves—then it must be a very weak person who can think these aspects of religious life are not to be observed with as much exactness as any doctrines that relate to worship.

## 2. Identity with Christ

It is very evident that there is not one command in all the Gospel for public worship; and perhaps it is a duty that is less insisted upon in Scripture than any other. The frequent attendance at it is never so much as mentioned in all the New Testament. By contrast, that religion or devotion which is to govern the ordinary actions of our life is to be found in almost every verse of Scripture. Our blessed Saviour and his apostles are wholly taken up in doctrines that relate to ordinary life. They call us to renounce the world and differ in attitude and way of life from the spirit and the way of the world—to renounce all its goods, to fear none of its evils, to reject its joys, and to have no value for its sort of happiness. We are to be as newborn babes who are born into a new state of things; to live as pilgrims in spiritual watching, in holy fear, and heavenly aspiration after another life; to take up our daily cross, to deny ourselves, to profess the blessedness of mourning; to seek the blessedness of poverty of spirit; to forsake the pride and vanity of riches; to take no thought for the morrow; to live in the profoundest state of humility, to rejoice in worldly sufferings. We are to reject the lust of the flesh, the lust of the eyes, and the pride of life; to bear injuries, to forgive and bless our enemies, and to love mankind as God does; to give up our whole hearts and affections to God and strive to enter through the straight gate into a life of eternal glory.

This is the ordinary devotion which our blessed Saviour taught in order to make it the common life of all Christians. Is it not therefore exceedingly strange that people should see so much evidence of piety in the attendance of public worship, concerning which there is not one precept of our Lord's to be found, and yet neglect these common duties of our ordinary life which are commanded in every page of the Gospel? I call these duties the devotion of our common life, because if they are to be practised they must be made parts of our everyday life; they can have no existence anywhere else.

If contempt of the world and heavenly affection is a necessary value for Christians, it is necessary that this value appear in the whole course of their lives, in their manner of using the world, because it can have no place anywhere else. If self-denial is a condition of salvation, all who would be saved must make this a part of their ordinary life. If humility is a Christian duty, then the ordinary life of a Christian is to be a constant course of humility in all its kinds. If poverty of spirit is necessary, it must be the spirit of every day of our lives. If we are to relieve the naked, the sick, and the prisoner, it must be the common charity of our lives as far as we can render ourselves able to perform it. If we are to love our enemies, we must make our everyday life a visible exercise and demonstration of that love. If contentment and thankfulness, and the patient bearing of evil are duties to God, they are the duties of every day and in every circumstance of our life. If we are to be wise and holy as the newborn sons of God, we cannot in any other way be so except by renouncing everything that is foolish and vain in every part of our everyday life. If we are to be in Christ new creatures, we must show that we are so by having new ways of living in the world. If we are to follow Christ, it must be in our common way of spending every day. . . .

But although it is thus plain that this, and this alone, is Christianity—a uniform, open and visible practice of all these virtues—yet it is as plain that there is little or nothing of this to be found even amongst the better sort of people. You see them often at church, and [they are] pleased with fine preachers. But look into their lives and you see them just the same sort of people as others who make no pretences to devotion. The difference that you find between them is only the difference of their natural personalities. They have the same taste for the world, the same worldly cares, fears and joys; they have the same turn of mind, and are equally vain in their desires. You see the same fondness for social and material standing, the same foolish friendships and groundless hatreds, the same levity of mind and trifling spirit, the same fondness for diversions, the same idle dispositions and vain ways of spending their time in visiting and conversation as the rest of the world who make no pretence to devotion.

I do not mean this comparison to apply between ostensibly good people and professed rakes, but between people of sober lives. Let us take, for instance, two modest women: let it be supposed that one of them is careful of times of devotion, and observes them through a sense of duty, and that the other has no hearty concern about it but is at church seldom or often, just as it happens. Now it is a very easy thing to see this difference between the two of them. But when you have seen this, can you find any further difference between them? Can you find that their ordinary life is of a different kind? Are not the values, customs and manners of the one of the same kind as of the other? Do they live as if they belonged to different worlds, had different views in their heads and different rules and measures of their actions? Have they not the same standards of good and evil? Are they not pleased and displeased in the same way and over the same things? Do they not live the same style of life? Does one seem to be of this world, looking at the things that are temporal and the other to be of another world, looking wholly at the things that are eternal? Does the one live in pleasure, delighting herself in show or dress, and the other live in self-denial and mortification, renouncing everything that looks like vanity, either of person, dress or carriage? Does the one pursue public diversions and trifle away her time in idle visits and corrupt conversation, and does the other study all the arts of improving her time, living in prayer and watching, and such good works as may make all her time turn to her advantage and be placed to her account at the last day? Is the one careless of expense, and glad to be able to adorn herself with every costly ornament of dress, and does the other consider her fortune as a talent given her by God, which is to be improved religiously and no more to be spent in vain and needless ornaments than it is to be buried in the earth? Where must you look to find one person of religion differing in this manner from another that has none? And yet if they do not differ in these things which are here related, can it with any sense be said that the one is a genuine Christian and the other not?

Take another instance among the men. One person—let us call him Leo*—has a great deal of good nature, has kept what they call "good company," hates everything that is false and base, is very generous and brave to his friends, but has concerned himself so little with religion that he hardly knows the difference between a Jew and a Christian.

Ernest, on the other hand, has had early impressions of religion, and buys devotional books. He can talk about all the feasts and fasts of the church, and knows the names of most men that have been eminent for piety. You never hear him swear or make a loose jest, and when he talks of religion he talks of it as a matter of ultimate concern.

Here you see that one person has religion enough, according to the way of the world, to be reckoned a pious Christian, and the other is so far

*The name suggests "lion-hearted" good nature.

from all appearance of religion that he may fairly be reckoned a heathen. And yet if you look into their everyday life, if you examine their chief and ruling values in the basic matters of life, or the central doctrines of Christianity, you will not find the least difference imaginable.

Now, to have right notions and values with respect to this world is as essential to spiritual life as to have right notions of God. And it is as possible for a person to worship a crocodile and yet be a pious man as to have his affections set upon this world and yet be a good Christian.

If you consider Leo and Ernest in this respect, you will find them exactly alike, seeking, using and enjoying all that can be got in this world in the same manner, and for the same ends. You will find that riches, prosperity, pleasures, indulgences, social position, and honor are just as much the happiness of one as of the other. And yet if Christianity has not changed a man's mind and attitude with respect to these things, what can we say that it has done for him? For if the doctrines of Christianity were practised, they would make a man as different from other people as to all worldly attitudes, sensual pleasures, and the pride of life, as a wise man is different from a simpleton; it would be as easy a thing to know a Christian by his outward habits of life as it is now difficult to find anybody who lives it. For it is notorious that Christians are now not only like other men in their frailties and infirmities—this might be in some degree excusable—but the complaint is that they are like heathens in all the main and chief articles of their lives. They enjoy the world, and live every day in the same values, the same designs, and the same indulgences as those who do not know about God or of any happiness in another life. Everybody who is capable of any reflection must have observed that this is generally the state even of devout people, whether men or women. You may see them as different from other people, so far as times and places of worship, but they are generally like the rest of the world in all other aspects of their lives—that is, they merely add Christian devotion to a heathen life. I have the authority of our blessed Saviour for this remark, where He says, "Take no thought, saying, What shall we eat? or, What shall we drink? or, Wherewithal shall we be clothed? For after all these things do the Gentiles seek" (Matthew 6:31–32). But if to be thus preoccupied even with the necessary things of this life shows that we do not yet have a Christian spirit, but are like the heathens, surely to enjoy the vanity and folly of the world as they did, to be like them in the principal values of our lives—in self-love and indulgence, in sensual pleasures and diversions, in the vanity of dress, the love of show and greatness, or any other gaudy distinctions of fortune—is a much greater sign of a heathen attitude. And, consequently, those who add devotion to such a life must be said to pray as Christians, but to live as heathens.

# The Sanctification Of Everyday Life

HAVING, IN the first chapter, stated the general nature of devotion, and shown that it implies not any form of prayer but a certain form of life that is offered to God—not at particular times or places but everywhere and in everything—I shall now descend to some particulars, and show how we are to devote our labor and employment, our time and fortunes, unto God.

## I. *All of Life Should be Regarded as Holy*

As a good Christian should consider every place as holy, because God is there, so he should look upon every part of his life as a matter of holiness, because it is to be offered unto God.

The profession of a clergyman is an holy profession, because it is a ministration in holy things, an attendance at the altar. But worldly business is to be made holy unto the Lord, by being done as a service to Him and in conformity to his divine will.

For as *all* persons and *all* things in the world belong as truly unto God as any places, things or persons that are devoted to divine service, so all things are to be used and all persons are to act in their several states and employments for the glory of God.

Men of worldly business, therefore, must not think they are at liberty to live for themselves, to sacrifice to their own whims and habits, because their employment is of a worldly nature. Rather, they must consider that, as the world and all worldly professions truly belong to God (just as persons and things do that are devoted to the altar), so it is as much the duty of those in worldly business to live wholly unto God as it is the duty of those who are devoted to divine service.

As the whole world is God's, so the whole world is to act for God. As all persons have all their powers and faculties from God, so all are obliged to act for God with all their powers and faculties.

As all things are God's, so all things are to be used and regarded as the things of God. For people to abuse things on earth and live for themselves is the same rebellion against God as for angels to abuse things in heaven because God is just the same Lord of all on earth as He is the Lord in heaven. Things may and must differ in their use, but they are all to be used according to the will of God. Men may and must differ in their employments, but they must all act for the same ends, as dutiful servants of God, in the right and spiritual performance of their various callings.

Clergymen must live wholly unto God in one particular way—that is, in the exercise of holy offices, in the ministration of prayers and sacraments, and a zealous distribution of spiritual goods. But people of other employments are, in their particular ways, as much obliged to act as the servants of God, and live wholly unto Him in their various callings. This is the only difference between clergymen and people of other callings.

## II. *The Common Business of Christians*

When it can be shown that people may be vain, covetous, sensual, worldly-minded or proud in the exercise of their worldly business, then it will be allowable for clergymen to indulge the same attitudes in their sacred profession. These attitudes are most odious and most criminal in clergymen, who besides their baptismal vow have a second time devoted themselves to God to be his servants, not in the common offices of human life but in the spiritual service of the most holy sacred things. They are therefore to keep themselves as separate and different from the common life of others as a church or an altar is to be kept separate from houses and tables of common use. Yet as all Christians are by their baptism devoted to God and have holiness as their profession, so are they all in their various callings to live as holy and heavenly persons, doing everything in their common life only in such a manner as it may be received by God as a service done to Him. For things spiritual and temporal, sacred and common, must, like men and angels, like heaven and earth, all conspire in the glory of God.

As there is but one God and Father of us all, whose glory gives light and life to everything that lives, whose presence fills all places, whose power supports all beings, whose providence rules all events; so everything that exists, whether in heaven or earth, whether thrones or principalities, men or angels, they must all, with one spirit, live wholly to the praise and glory of this one God and Father of them all. Angels as angels, in their heavenly ministrations, but men as men, women as women, bishops as bishops, priests as priests, and deacons as deacons—some with things spiritual, some with things temporal, offering to God the daily sacrifice of a reasonable life, wise actions, purity of heart, and heavenly affections.

This is the common business of all persons in this world. It is not left to any women in the world to trifle away their time in the follies and impertinences of a fashionable life, nor to any men to resign themselves to worldly cares and concerns; it is not left to the rich to gratify their passions in the indulgence and pride of life, nor to the poor to vex and torment their own hearts with the poverty of their state. Rather, men and women, rich and poor, must, with bishops and priests, walk before God in the same wise and holy spirit, in the same denial of all vain attitudes, and in the same discipline and care of their souls, not only because they have all the same rational nature, and are servants of the same God, but because they all want the same holiness to make them fit for the same happiness to which they are all called. It is therefore absolutely necessary for all Christians, whether men or women, to consider themselves as persons that are devoted to holiness and so order their common ways of life by such rules of reason and piety as may turn them into continual service unto Almighty God.

Now to make our labor or employment an acceptable service unto God, we must carry it on with the same spirit and attitude that is required in giving of alms or any work of piety. For if "whether we eat or drink, or whatsoever we do," we must "do all to the glory of God" (1 Corinthians 10:31), if "we are to use this world as if we used it not," if we are to "present our bodies a living sacrifice, holy, acceptable to God" (Romans 12:1), if "we are to live by faith, and not by sight," and "have our conversation in heaven" (2 Corinthians 5:7; Philippians 3:20), then it is necessary that the common way of our life—in every state—be made to glorify God by the same sort of disposition as makes our prayers and adorations acceptable to Him. For if we are worldly or earthly-minded in our employments, if they are carried on with vain desires and covetous attitudes only to satisfy ourselves, we can no more be said to live to the glory of God than gluttons and drunkards can be said to eat and drink to the glory of God.

As the glory of God is one and the same thing, so whatever we do which is suitable to it must be done with one and the same spirit. That same state and disposition of mind which makes our alms and devotions acceptable must also make our labor or employment a proper offering unto God. If a man labors to be rich, and pursues his business so that he may raise himself to a celebrated image and status in the world, he is no longer serving God in his employment. Rather, he is acting under other masters, and has no more title to a reward from God than one who gives alms that he may be seen or prays that he may be heard of men. For vain and earthly desires are no more allowable in our occupations than in our alms and devotions. These attitudes of worldly pride and vainglory are not only evil when they mix with our good works, but they have the same evil nature, and make us odious to God, when they enter into the common business of our employment. If it were allowable to indulge covetous or vain passions in our worldly occupations, it would then be allowable to be vainglorious in our devotions. But as our alms and devotions are not an acceptable service except when they proceed from a heart truly devoted to God, so our common employment cannot be reckoned a service to Him except when it is performed with the same attitude and piety of heart.

## III. *Letter and Spirit in Vocation*

Most of the employments of life are in their own nature lawful, and all those that are so may be made a substantial part of our duty to God if we engage in them only so far, and for such ends, as are suitable to beings who are to live above the world all the time that they live in the world. This is the only measure of our application to any worldly business; let it be what it will, where it will, it must have no more of our hands, our hearts, or our time than is consistent with a hearty, daily, careful preparation of ourselves for another life. For as all Christians have renounced this world to prepare themselves by daily devotion and universal holiness for an eternal state of quite another nature, they must look upon worldly employments as upon worldly wants and bodily infirmities, as things not to be desired but only to be endured and suffered until death and the resurrection have carried us to an eternal state of real happiness.

Now one who does not look at the things of this life as having this degree of insignificance cannot be said either to feel or believe the greatest truths of Christianity. For if he thinks anything great or important in human business can he be said to feel or believe those Scriptures which represent this life and the greatest things of life as bubbles, vapors, dreams and shadows?

If he thinks images and show and worldly glory to be any proper happiness of a Christian, how can he be said to feel or believe this doctrine, "Blessed are ye when men shall hate you, and when they shall separate you from their company, and shall reproach you, and cast out your name as evil, for the Son of Man's sake" (Luke 6:22)? For surely, if there was any real happiness in image and show and worldly glory—if these things deserved our thoughts and care—it could not be a matter of the highest joy when we are torn from them by persecutions and sufferings. If, therefore, a man will so live as to show that he feels and believes the most fundamental doctrines of Christianity, he must live above the world. This is the attitude that must enable him to do the business of life, and yet live wholly unto God, and to go through some worldly occupation with a heavenly mind. And it is as necessary that people live in their employments with this attitude as it is necessary that their employment itself be lawful.

The husbandman who tills the ground is employed in an honest business, necessary to life and very capable of being made an acceptable service unto God. But if he labors and toils not to serve any reasonable ends of life but in order to have his plough made of silver, and to have his horses harnessed in gold, the honesty of his employment is lost to him, and his labor becomes his folly.

A tradesman may justly think that it is agreeable to the will of God for him to sell such things as are innocent and useful in life, such as help both himself and others to a reasonable life, and enable them to assist those who need to be assisted. But if, instead of this, he trades only with regard to himself, without any other rule than that of his own desires; if it be his chief end in this way to grow rich, that he may live in style and self-indulgence and to be able to retire from business to idleness and luxury, his trade loses all its innocence with respect to himself, and is so far from being an acceptable service to God that it is only a more plausible course of covetousness, self-love, and ambition. For such a person turns the necessities of employment into pride and covetousness, just as the sot and epicure turn the necessities of eating and drinking into gluttony and drunkenness. Now he who is up early and late, who sweats and labors for these ends . . . lives no more to the glory of God than one who gambles and games for the same ends. For though there is a great difference between trading and gaming, yet most of that difference is lost when men begin to do business with the same desires and values, and for the same ends, that others gamble. . . .

Let us imagine one who is thus 'fervent in business'—we may call him Mr. Wheeler*—who has traded more than thirty years in the greatest city of the kingdom, constantly increasing his trade and his fortune. Every hour of the day is with him an hour of business, and though he eats and drinks very heartily, every meal seems to be in a hurry (he would say grace if only he had time). Wheeler ends every day at the tavern, but has not the time to get there till nearly nine o'clock. He is always forced to drink a good hearty glass to drive thoughts of business out of his head, and make his spirits drowsy enough for sleep. He does business all the time that he is awake, and has settled several matters even before he gets to his office. His prayers are a short utterance or two (which he never misses in stormy weather, because he always has some shipment or other at sea). Wheeler will tell you with great pleasure that he has been in this hurry for many years, and that it would have killed him long ago except

*Law's name here is *Calidus,* Latin for "hot" (i.e., fervent) in business. My change attempts to translate his point.

that it has been rule with him to get out of town every Saturday, and make Sunday also a day of quiet and good refreshment in the country.

He is now so rich that he desires to leave off his business and amuse his old age with building and furnishing a fine house in the country, except that he is afraid he should become melancholy if he was to retire. He will tell you with great gravity that it is a dangerous thing for a man that has been used to earning money ever to leave it off. If thoughts of religion happen at any time to steal into his head, Wheeler contents himself with thinking that he never was a friend of heretics and infidels, that he has always been civil to the minister of the parish, and has very often given something to the charity schools.

Now this way of life is at such a distance from all the doctrine and discipline of Christianity that no one can live in it through ignorance or frailty. Wheeler can no more imagine that he is "born again of the Spirit" (John 3:6), that he is "in Christ a new creature," that he lives here a stranger and pilgrim (1 Peter 2:11), setting his affections on things above, and laying up treasures in heaven (Colossians 3:2; Matthew 6:20): he can no more imagine this than he can think that he has been all his life an apostle working miracles and preaching the gospel.

It must also be admitted that the majority of trading people, especially in great towns, are too much like Wheeler. You see them all the week buried in business, unable to think of anything else, and then spending Sunday in idleness and refreshment, wandering into the country or in such visits and jovial meetings as make it often the worst day of the week.

Now they do not live like this because they cannot support themselves with less care and application to business; they live like this because they want to grow rich in their trades and to maintain their families in such style and finery as a reasonable Christian life has no occasion for. Take away but this ambition and then people of all trades will find themselves at leasure to live every day like Christians, to be careful of every duty of the gospel, to live in a visible course of spiritual life, and be every day strict observers both of private and public prayer.

Now the only way for people to do this is to consider their trade as something that they are obliged to devote to the glory of God, something that they are to do only in such a manner that they may make it a duty to Him. Nothing can be right in business that is not according to this principle; the apostle commands servants to be obedient to their masters "in singleness of heart, as unto Christ, not with eye-service, as men-pleasers, but as the servants of Christ, doing the will of God from the heart; with good will doing service, as unto the Lord, and not to men" (Ephesians 6:5–7; Colossians 3:22–23). . . .

## IV. *A Reasonable Service*

It is therefore absolutely certain that no Christian is to enter any further into business, nor for any other purpose than such as he can in singleness of heart offer unto God as a reasonable service. For the Son of God has redeemed us for this end only, that we should, by a life of reason and piety, live to the glory of God. This is the only rule and measure for every order and state of life. Without this rule, the most lawful employment becomes a sinful state of life.

Take this away from the life of a clergyman, and his holy profession serves only to expose him to a greater damnation. Take this away from businessmen, and their shops are but so many houses of greed and filthy lucre. Take this away from gentlemen, and the course of their life becomes a course of sensuality, pride and wantonness. Take away this rule from our tables, and all falls into gluttony and drunkenness. Take away this measure from our dress and habits, and all is turned into such paint and glitter and ridiculous ornaments as are a shame to the wearer. Take this away from the use of our fortunes, and you will find people sparing in nothing but charity. Take this away from our diversions, and you will find no sports too silly nor any entertainments too vain and corrupt to be the pleasures of Christians.

If, therefore, we desire to live unto God, it is necessary to bring our whole life under this law, to make his glory the sole rule and measure of our actions in every employment of life. For there is no other true devotion but this of living devoted to God in the common business of our lives.

People must not, therefore, content themselves with the lawfulness of their employment, but must consider whether they use them as they are to use everything—as strangers and pilgrims who are baptized into the resurrection of Jesus Christ, that are to follow Him in a wise and heavenly course of life, in the mortification of all worldly desires and in purifying and preparing their souls for the blessed enjoyment of God. For to be vain, or proud, or covetous, or ambitious in the common course of our business is as contrary to these holy aspirations of Christianity as cheating and dishonesty.

If a glutton was to say, in excuse of his gluttony, that he only eats such things as it is lawful to eat, he would make as good an excuse for himself as the greedy, covetous, ambitious tradesman who says that he only deals in lawful business. For it is required of a Christian not only to be honest, but to be of a Christian spirit and to make one's life an exercise of humility, repentance and heavenly affection. All attitudes that are contrary to these are as contrary to Christianity as cheating is contrary to honesty. Plainly, all unspiritual inclinations in trade and business are as sinful as unspiritual inclinations in eating and drinking.

Proud opinions and vain desires in our worldly employments are as truly vices and corruptions as hypocrisy in prayer or vanity in our giving. And no reason can be put forth why vanity in our giving should make us odious to God that will not also demonstrate that any other kind of pride is equally odious. One who labors and toils in a calling in order to provide himself status in the world and draw the eyes of people to the splendor of his condition is as far from the proper humility of a Christian as the person who gives in order to be recognized for his charity. For the reason that pride and vanity in our prayer and our giving renders them an unacceptable service to God is not that there is anything particular in prayers and giving that cannot prompt pride, but because pride is in no respect nor in anything appropriate for man; it destroys the piety of our prayers and alms because it destroys the piety of everything it touches, and renders every action that it governs incapable of being offered unto God.

Even if we could so divide ourselves as to be humble in some respects and proud in others, such humility would be of no service to us, because God requires us as truly to be humble in all our actions and designs as to be honest in all our actions and designs. . . . We indeed sometimes talk as if a person might be humble in some things and proud in others—humble in his dress, for example, but proud of his learning; humble in his person, but proud in his views and plans. But although such things may be said in common discourse (where few things are said according to strict truth), such a distinction cannot be maintained when we examine the nature of our actions.

It is very possible for a man who lives by cheating to be very punctual in paying for what he buys, but none assumes that he does so out of any principle of true honesty. In the same way, it is very possible for a man who is proud of his estate, ambitious in his views, or vain about his learning, to disregard his dress and outward appearance in the same manner as a truly humble man would. But to suppose that he is motivated by a true principle of spiritual humility is as absurd as to suppose that a cheat pays for what he buys out of a principle of spiritual honesty.

As, therefore, all kinds of dishonesty destroy our pretences to an honest principle of mind, so all kinds of pride destroy our pretences to a humble spirit. No one is amazed that prayers and offerings which proceed from pride and ostentation are odious to God; yet it is equally evident that pride is as pardonable there as anywhere else. If we could suppose that God rejects pride in our prayers and offerings, but bears with pride in our dress, our persons, or our estates, it would be the same thing as supposing that God condemns falsehood in some actions but allows it in others. For pride in one thing differs from pride in another about as much as the robbing of one man differs from the robbing of another. . . .

## V. *Consistency in Spiritual Life*

All these instances are only to show us the great necessity of a regular and consistent spirituality, extending itself to all the actions of our ordinary life:

—that we must eat and drink, and dress and discourse according to the sobriety of a Christian spirit, engage in no employments but those we can truly devote to God, nor pursue them any further than actually conduces to the reasonable ends of a holy, devout life;

—that we must be honest, not only on particular occasions, and in such instances as are applauded in the world, easily performed and free from danger or loss, but from such a living principle of justice as makes us love truth and integrity in all its instances and follow it through all dangers and against all opposition, knowing that the more we pay for any truth, the better is our bargain, and that our integrity becomes a pearl when we have parted with all to keep it;

—that we must be humble not only in such instances as are expected in the world or suitable to our temperament or confined to particular occasions, but in such a humility of spirit as renders us meek and lowly in the whole course of our lives, as shows itself in our dress, our person, our conversation, our enjoyment of the world, the tranquility of our minds, patience under injuries, submission to superiors, and a generous disposition toward those that are below us, and in all the outward actions of our lives;

—that we must devote not only times and places to prayer, but be everywhere in the spirit of devotion, with hearts always set toward heaven, looking up to God in all our actions, and doing everything as his servants, living in the world as in a holy temple of God, and always worshipping him with the thankfulness of our hearts, the holiness of our actions and the pious and charitable use of all his gifts, even when our lips are silent;

—that we must not only send up petitions and thoughts to heaven, but must go through all our worldly business with a heavenly spirit, as members of Christ's mystical body, so that with new hearts and new minds we may turn an earthly life into a preparation for a life of greatness and glory in the kingdom of heaven.

Now the only way to arrive at this piety of spirit is to bring all your actions under the same principles as your devotions and offerings. You know very well what it is that makes your offerings and devotions acceptable; now the same principles and the same regard to God must render everything else that you do a fit and acceptable service unto Him. . . .

# Prayer

HAVING IN the foregoing chapters shown the necessity of a devout spirit or habit of mind in every part of our common life, in the discharge of all our business, in the use of all the gifts of God, I come now to consider that part of devotion which relates to times and hours of prayer.

## I. *The Discipline of Daily Prayer*

I take it for granted that every Christian who is in health is up early in the morning, for it is much more reasonable to suppose a person up early because he is a Christian than because he is a laborer or tradesman or servant, or has business that needs attention.

We naturally conceive some abhorrence of someone who is in bed when he or she should be at labor or in the shop. We cannot find anything good to say of such a person who is such a slave to drowsiness as to neglect responsibilities for it. Let this therefore teach us to conceive how odious we must appear in the sight of heaven if we are in bed, shut up in sleep and darkness when we should be praising God, and are such slaves to drowsiness that we neglect our devotions for it. For if a person is to be blamed as a slothful drone who prefers the lazy self-indulgence of sleep than the performance of a proper share of worldly business, how much more blameworthy it is that one would rather lie folded up in a bed than be raising up his heart to God in acts of praise and adoration!

Prayer is the nearest approach to God, and the highest enjoyment of Him that we are capable of in this life. It is the noblest exercise of the soul, the most exalted use of our best faculties, and the highest imitation of the blessed inhabitants of heaven. When our hearts are full of God, sending up holy desires to the throne of grace, we are then in our highest state, we are upon the utmost heights of human greatness; we are not before kings and princes but in the presence and audience of the Lord of all the world, and can be no higher till death is swallowed up in glory.

On the other hand, sleep is the poorest, dullest refreshment of the body, and so far from being intended as an enjoyment that we are forced to receive it either in a state of insensibility or in the folly of dreams. Sleep is such a dull, stupid state of existence that even amongst mere animals we despise them most which are most drowsy.

The person, therefore, who chooses to prolong the slothful self-indulgence of sleep rather than be early at his devotions to God chooses the dullest refreshment of the body before the highest, noblest employment of the soul. He chooses that state which is a reproach to mere animals rather than that exercise which is the glory of angels.

You will perhaps say that although you rise late, you are always careful of your devotions when you are up.

It may be so. But what then? Is it commendable for you to rise late because you pray when you are up? Is it pardonable to waste great stretches of the day in bed because some time afterward you say your prayers? It is as much your duty to rise to pray as to pray when you are risen. And if you are late at your prayers you offer to God the prayers of an idle, slothful worshipper, one who rises to prayers in the way idle servants rise to their labor.

Furthermore, if you fancy that you are careful of your devotions when you are up, although it is your custom to rise late, you deceive yourself, for you cannot perform your devotions as you ought. For a person who cannot deny this drowsy self-indulgence but must pass away a good part of the morning in it is no more prepared for prayer when he is up than he is prepared for fasting, abstinence or any other self-denial. . . . For sleep thus indulged gives a softness and idleness to our whole character, and makes us unable to relish anything but what suits an idle state of mind. So a person who is a slave to this idleness is in the same attitude of mind when he is up; although he is not asleep yet he is under the effects of sleep, and everything that is idle, indulgent or sensual pleases him for the same reason that sleep pleases him. On the other hand, everything that requires care, effort or self-denial is hateful to him, for the same reason that he hates to rise. . . . The remembrance of a warm bed is in his mind all day, and he is glad when he is not one of those sitting . . . in a church.

Now you do not imagine that such a person can truly mortify that body which is thus indulged. Yet you might as well think this as that anyone can truly perform his or her devotions, or relish the joys of a spiritual life while living in such a drowsy state of indulgence. Surely no one will pretend to say that he knows and feels the true happiness of prayer who does not think it worth his while to be early at it.

It is, by definition, impossible to an epicure to be truly devout; he must renounce this habit of sensuality before he can relish the happiness of devotion. But a person who turns sleep into an idle indulgence does as much to corrupt and disorder the soul—to make it a slave to bodily appetites and keep it incapable of all devout and heavenly thoughts—as the one who turns the necessities of eating into a means of indulgence.

A person who eats and drinks to moderate excess does not feel such effects from it as those who live in notorious gluttony and intemperance.

Yet his indulgence, although not scandalous in the eyes of the world or a torment to his own conscience, is a great and constant hindrance to his growth in virtue: it gives him eyes that see not and ears that hear not, it creates a sensuality in the soul, increases the power of bodily passions, and makes him incapable of entering into the true spirit of devotion.

So it is with those who waste their time in sleep. This may not disorder their lives or wound their consciences as notorious acts of intemperance do. But, like any other more moderate sort of indulgence, it silently and by smaller degrees wears away the spirit of devotion, and sinks the soul into a state of dullness and sensuality.

If you consider devotion only as a time of so much prayer, you may perhaps perform it although you live in this daily indulgence. But if you consider it as a state of the heart, as a lively fervor of the soul deeply affected with a sense of its own misery and infirmities and desiring the Spirit of God more than all things in the world, you will find that the spirit of indulgence and the spirit of prayer cannot co-exist. Mortification of all kinds is the very life and soul of spirituality, and he that has not the minimal degree of it to enable him to be early at his prayers can have no reason to think that he has taken up his cross and is following Christ.

What conquest has he achieved over himself, what right hand has he cut off, what trials is he prepared for, what sacrifice is he ready to offer unto God, who cannot be so cruel to himself as to rise to prayer at such time as the drudging part of the world are content to rise to their labor? . . .

When you read the Scriptures you see a form of devotion that is all life, and spirit, and joy in God, that supposes our souls risen from earthly desires and bodily indulgences to prepare for another body, another world and other employments. You see Christians represented as temples of the Holy Spirit, as children of the day, as candidates for an eternal crown, as watchful virgins who have their lamps always burning in expectation of the bridegroom. But can one be thought to have this joy in God, this care of eternity, this watchful spirit, who has not zeal enough to rise to his prayers?

When you look into the writings and lives of the first Christians, you see the same spirit that you see in the Scriptures. All is reality, life and action. Watching and prayers, self-denial and mortification were the common business of their lives. But how far are you from this way of life, or rather how contrary to it if, instead of imitating their austerity and mortification, you cannot so much as renounce so pitiable a self-indulgence as to be able to rise to your prayers! If self-denials and bodily sufferings, watchings and fastings will be marks of glory at the Day of Judgement, where must we hide our heads who have slumbered away our time in sloth and softness? . . .

Here, therefore, we must fix our charge against this practice: we must blame it not as having this or that particular evil but as a general habit that extends itself through our whole spirit and supports a state of mind that is wholly wrong. It is contrary to piety not as accidental slips and mistakes in life are contrary to it but in the same way that a bad bodily habit is contrary to health.

On the other hand, if you were to rise early every morning as an instance of self-denial, as a method of renouncing self-indulgence, as a means of redeeming your time and fitting your spirit for prayer, you would find mighty advantages in the practice. This, though it seems such a small aspect of life, would in all probability be a means of great piety. It would keep constantly in your mind that softness and idleness were to be avoided, that self-denial was a part of Christianity. It would teach you to exercise power over yourself, and make you able by degrees to renounce other pleasures and states of mind that war against the soul. This one discipline would teach you to think of others: it would dispose your mind to exactness and would be very likely to bring the remaining part of the day under the disciplines of prudence and devotion.

But above all, one certain benefit from this practice you will be sure of having: it will best fit and prepare you for the reception of the Holy Spirit. When you thus begin the day in the spirit of faithfulness, renouncing sleep because you are to renounce softness and redeem your time, this disposition, as it puts your heart into a good state will also procure the assistance of the Holy Spirit. What is so planted and watered will certainly have an increase from God. You will then speak from your heart, your soul will be awake, your prayers will refresh you like meat and drink, you will feel what you say, and begin to know what saints and holy men have meant by fervent devotion.

The person thus prepared for prayer, who rises with this disposition, is in a very different state from one who has no disciplines of this kind, who rises by chance as he happens to weary of his bed or is able to sleep no longer. If such a person prays only with his mouth—if his heart feels nothing of that which he says, if his prayers are only expressions out of habit, if they are a lifeless form of words which he only repeats because they are soon said—there is nothing to be wondered at in all this. For such dispositions are the natural effect of such a [drowsy] state of life.

## II. *A Method of Daily Prayer*

Hoping, therefore, that you are now enough convinced of the necessity of rising early to your prayers, I shall proceed to lay before you a method of daily prayer. I do not take upon me to prescribe to you the use of any particular forms of prayer, but only to show you the necessity of praying at certain times and in a certain manner.

You will find here some helps, how to furnish yourself with such forms of prayer as shall be useful to you. And if you are proficient enough in the spirit of devotion that your heart is always ready to pray in its own language, in this case I press no necessity of borrowed forms.* For although I think a form of prayer very necessary and expedient for public worship, yet if anyone can find a better way of raising his heart unto God in private than by prepared forms of prayer, I have no objection to this. My design is only to assist and direct those who stand in need of assistance.

1. Forms of prayer and the spirit of prayer

This much, I believe, is certain, that most Christians ought to use forms of prayer at all the regular times of prayer. It seems right for everyone to begin with a set form of prayer and if, in the midst of his devotions, he finds his heart ready to break forth into new and higher strains of devotion, he should leave his form for awhile, and follow those fervors of his heart until once again it needs the assistance of his usual petitions. This seems to be the true liberty of private devotion; it should be under the direction of some form, but not so tied down to it that it is not free to find new expressions . . . which are sometimes more immediate and carry the soul more powerfully toward God than any expressions that were ever used before.

All people who have ever considered what passes in their own hearts must know that they are extremely changeable in regard to devotion. Sometimes our hearts are so awakened, have such strong apprehensions of the Divine Presence, are so full of deep compunction for our sins, that we cannot confess them in any language but that of tears. Sometimes the light of God's countenance shines so brightly upon us, we see so far into the invisible world, we are so affected with the wonders of the love and goodness of God that our hearts worship and adore in a language higher than that of words, and we know transports of devotion which can only be felt, but not expressed.

On the other hand, sometimes we are so sunk into our bodies, so dull and unaffected with that which concerns our souls, that our hearts are too small for our prayers. We cannot keep pace with our forms of confession, or feel half of that in our hearts which we have in our mouths. We thank and praise God with forms of words but our hearts have little or no share in them.

*Law means here the Book of Common Prayer, or other set liturgical prayers.

It is therefore very necessary to provide against this inconstancy of our hearts by having at hand such forms of prayer as may best suit us when our hearts are in their best state and may also be most likely to raise and stir them up when they are sunk into dullness. For, as words have a power of affecting our hearts on all occasions, as the same thing differently expressed has different effects upon our minds, so it is reasonable that we should make the most of language and provide ourselves with such forms of expression as are most likely to move and enliven our souls and to fill them with appropriate sentiments.

## 2. Drawing apart into a place of prayer

The first thing you ought to do when you are upon your knees is to shut your eyes and, with a short silence, let your soul place itself in the presence of God. That is, you are to use this, or some other better method, to separate yourself from all common thoughts, and make your heart as aware as you can of the divine presence.

Now if this recollection of spirit is necessary—and who can say it is not?—then how poorly must they perform their devotions who are always in a hurry, who begin in haste and hardly allow themselves time to repeat their very form with any sincerity or attention! Theirs is properly "saying prayers" rather than praying.

To proceed: if you were to accustom yourself as far as possible to pray always in the same place, if you were to reserve that place for devotion and not allow yourself to do anything common in it, if you were never to be there yourself except in times of devotion, if any little room or, possibly, any particular part of a room was thus used, this kind of consecration of it as a place holy unto God would have an effect upon your mind and dispose you to such an attitude of heart as would greatly assist your devotion. For by having a place thus sacred in your room, it would in some measure resemble a chapel or house of God. This would dispose you to be always in the spirit of devotion when you were there, and fill you with wise and holy thoughts when you were by yourself. Your own apartment would raise in your mind such feelings as you have when you stand near an altar, and you would be afraid of thinking or doing anything that was foolish near that place which is the place of prayer and holy intercourse with God.

## 3. Addressing God

When you begin your petitions, use such various expressions of the attributes of God as may make you most aware of the greatness and power of his divine nature. Begin, therefore, in words such as: "O Being of all beings, Fountain of all light and glory, gracious Father of men and angels, whose universal Spirit is everywhere present, giving life and light and joy to all angels in heaven and all creatures upon earth," etc. For these representations of the divine attributes which show us in some degree the majesty and greatness of God are an excellent means of raising our hearts into lively acts of worship and adoration. Why do you suppose most people are so deeply affected with this petition in the burial service of our church: "Yet, O Lord God most holy, O Lord most mighty, O holy and most merciful Saviour, deliver us not into the bitter pains of eternal death"? It is because the joining together of so many great expressions gives such a description of the greatness of the divine majesty as naturally affects every alert mind.

Although, therefore, prayer does not consist in fine words or studied expressions, yet as words speak to the soul and have a certain power of raising thoughts in the soul, so those words which speak of God in the highest manner—which most fully express the power and presence of God, which raise thoughts in the soul most suitable to the greatness and providence of God—are the most useful and most edifying in our prayers.

When you direct any of your petitions to our blessed Lord, let it be in some expression of this kind: "O Saviour of the world, God of God, Light of Light; Thou who art the brightness of thy Father's glory, and the express image of his Person; Thou who art the Alpha and Omega, the Beginning and End of all things; Thou who has destroyed the power of the devil, who has overcome death; Thou who art entered into the Holy of Holies, who sittest at the right hand of the Father, who art high above all thrones and principalities, who makest intercession for all the world; Thou who art the Judge of the quick and dead; Thou who wilt speedily come down in thy Father's glory to reward all men according to their works . . . be Thou my Light and my Peace," etc. For such representations, which describe so many characters of our Saviour's nature and power, are not only proper acts of adoration but will, if they are repeated with any attention, fill our hearts with the highest fervency of true devotion.

## 4. Addressing Jesus

Again, if you ask any particular grace of our blessed Lord, let it be in some manner like this: "O Holy Jesus, Son of the most High God, Thou who wast scourged at a pillar, stretched and nailed upon a cross, for the sins of the world, unite me to thy cross, and fill my soul with thy holy, humble and suffering spirit. O Fountain of mercy, Thou who didst save the thief upon the cross, save me from the guilt of a sinful life; Thou who didst cast seven devils out of Mary Magdalene, cast out of my heart all evil thoughts and wicked affections. O Giver of life, Thou who didst raise Lazarus from the dead, raise up my soul from the death and darkness of sin. Thou who didst give to thy apostles power over unclean spirits, give me power over my own heart. Thou who didst appear unto thy disciples when the doors were shut, do Thou appear unto me in the secret chamber of my heart. Thou who didst cleanse the lepers, heal the sick, and give sight to the blind, cleanse my heart, heal the disorders of my soul, and fill me with heavenly light."

Now these kind of appeals have a double advantage. First, they are proper expressions of our faith, whereby we not only show our belief in the miracles of Christ but turn them at the same time into instances of worship and adoration. Secondly, they strengthen and increase the faith of our prayers, by presenting to our minds many instances of that power and goodness which we call upon for our own assistance. For a person who appeals to Christ as one who cast out devils and raised the dead has then a powerful motive in his mind to pray earnestly and depend faithfully upon his assistance.

Again, in order to fill your prayers with excellent motives of devotion, it may be of use to you to observe this further rule: when at any time, either in reading the Scripture or any book of piety, you meet with a passage that more than ordinarily affects your mind and seems, as it were, to give your heart a new motion toward God, you should try to turn it into the form of a petition and then give it a place in your prayers. By this means you will be often improving your prayers and providing yourself with proper forms of making the desires of your heart known unto God.

### III. *Planning Our Daily Prayer*

At all the stated hours of prayer, it will be of great benefit to you to have something fixed, and something at liberty, in your devotions. You should have some fixed subject which is constantly to be the chief matter of your prayer at that particular time, and yet have liberty to add such other petitions as your condition may then require.

For instance, as the morning is to you the beginning of a new life—as God has then given you a new enjoyment of yourself and a fresh entrance into the world—it is highly proper that your first devotions should be a praise and thanksgiving to God as for a new creation, and that you should offer and devote body and soul, all that you are and all that you have to his service and glory.

Receive, therefore, every day as a resurrection from death, as a new enjoyment of life; meet every rising sun with such appreciation of God's goodness as if you had seen it and all things newly created for you alone.

163

Then, under the sense of so great a blessing, let your joyful heart praise and magnify so good and glorious a Creator.

Let, therefore, praise and thanksgiving and oblation of yourself unto God be always the fixed and certain subject of your first prayers in the morning, and then take the liberty of adding such other devotions as the accidental difference of your state or the accidental differences of your heart shall then make most needful and expedient for you. For one of the greatest benefits of private devotion consists in rightly adapting our prayers to those two conditions—the difference of our state and the difference of our hearts.

## 1. Taking account of our circumstances

By the difference of our state is meant the variance of our external circumstances or condition such as sickness, health, pains, losses, disappointments, troubles, particular mercies or judgements from God, and all sorts of kindnesses, injuries or reproaches from other people.

Now as these are great parts of our condition of life and as they make great difference in it by continually changing, so our devotion will be made doubly beneficial to us when it watches to receive and sanctify all these changes in our circumstances and turns them all into so many occasions of a more particular application to God of such thanksgiving, such resignation or such petitions as our present state more especially requires. A person who makes every change in his state a reason for presenting unto God some particular petitions suitable to that change will soon find that he has discovered an excellent means not only of praying with fervency but of living as he prays.

## 2. Taking account of our hearts

The next condition to which we are always to adapt some part of our prayers is the variance of our hearts. By this is meant the different state of the feelings of our heart, such as love, joy, peace, tranquility, dullness, dryness of spirit, anxiety, discontent, envy and ambition, dark and disconsolate thoughts, resentments, fretfulness, and a peevish disposition. Now as these moods, through the weakness of our nature, will have their succession to a greater or lesser degree, even in spiritual minds, so we should constantly make the present state of our heart the reason of some particular address to God.

If we are in the delightful calm of sweet and easy feelings of love and joy in God, we should then offer the grateful tribute of thanksgiving to God for the possession of so much happiness, thankfully owning and acknowledging Him as the bountiful giver of all.

If, on the other hand, we feel ourselves laden with heavy passions, with dullness of spirit, anxiety and uneasiness, we must then look up to God in acts of humility, confessing our unworthiness, opening our troubles to Him, beseeching Him in his good time to lessen the weight of our infirmities and to deliver us from such passions as oppose the purity and perfection of our souls. Now by thus watching and attending to the present state of our hearts, and suiting some of our petitions exactly to their wants, we shall not only be well acquainted with the disorders of our souls but also be well exercised in the method of curing them. By this prudent and wise application of our prayers, we shall get all the relief from them that is possible, and the very changeableness of our hearts will prove a means of exercising a greater variety of holy attitudes.

### 3. Maturing in personal prayer

Now by all that has here been said, you will easily perceive that persons careful of the greatest benefit of prayer ought to have a great share in the forming and composing of their devotions. As to that part of their prayers which is always fixed to one certain subject, in that they may use the help of forms composed by other persons. But in that part of their prayers which they are always to suit to the present state of their life, and the present state of their heart, there they must let the sense of their own condition help them to such kinds of petition, thanksgiving or resignation as their present state more especially requires.

Happy are they who have this business and employment upon their hands! . . .

## IV. *Stunted Spiritual Development*

It is amazing to see how eagerly people employ their talents, their sagacity, time, study, application and exercise—how all helps are called to their assistance—when anything is intended and desired in worldly matters, and how dull, negligent and unimproved they are—how little they use their talents, sagacity and abilities—to raise and increase their devotion!

Imagine a man of the world, Mr. McMammon,* a person of excellent talents and clear thinking. He is well advanced in age and has made a great reputation in business. Every part of trade and business that has fallen in his direction has had some improvement from him, and he is always contriving to carry every method of doing anything well to its greatest height. McMammon aims at the greatest perfection in everything. The

---

*Law's character is *Mundanus* (Latin "of the world"), suggesting a "worldly wise" person.

soundness and strength of his mind and his just way of thinking upon things make him intent upon removing imperfections. He can tell you all the defects and errors in all the common methods, whether of trade, building or improving land or manufactured goods. The clarity and strength of his understanding, which he is constantly improving by continual exercise in these matters—by often digesting his thoughts in writing and trying everything every way—has rendered him a great expert in most concerns of human life. Thus has McMammon gone on, increasing his knowledge and judgement as fast as his years came upon him.

The one and only thing which has not fallen under his improvement, nor received any benefit from his judicious mind, is his spiritual life. This is in just the same poor state it was when he was only six years of age, and the old man prays now in that little form of words which his mother used to hear him repeat night and morning. This McMammon, who hardly ever saw the poorest utensil or took the meanest trifle into his hand without considering how it might be made or used to better advantage, has gone all his life long praying in the same manner as when he was a child, without ever considering how much better or oftener he might pray, without considering how worthy of pursuit the spirit of devotion is, how many helps a wise and reasonable person may call to his assistance, and how necessary it is that our prayers should be enlarged, varied and suited to the particular state and condition of our lives.

If McMammon sees a book of devotion, he passes it by as he does a spelling-book, because he remembers that he learned to pray so many years ago, under his mother, when he learned to spell.

Now how poor and pitiable is the conduct of this man of sense, who has so much judgement and understanding in everything except that which is the whole wisdom of man! And how miserably do many people, more or less, imitate this conduct!

All this seems to be owing to a strange, infatuated state of negligence which keeps people from considering what the life of the spirit is. For if they did but once proceed so far as to reflect about it, or ask themselves any questions concerning it, they would soon see that the spirit of devotion was like any other sense or understanding, that it can only be improved by study, care, application, and the use of such means and helps as are necessary to make a person proficient in any art or science.

Let us imagine, further, a man of learning—a Professor Classicus— who is well versed in all the best authors of antiquity. He has read them so much that he has entered into their spirit and can very ingeniously imitate the manner of any of them. All their thoughts are his thoughts and he can express himself in their language. He is so great a friend to this improvement of the mind that if he lights on a young student he never fails to advise him concerning his studies. Classicus tells his young man that he must not think that he had done enough when he has only learned languages, but that he must be daily conversant with the best authors, read them again and again, catch their spirit by living with them, for [he says] there is no other way of becoming like them or making himself a man of taste and judgement.

How wise might Classicus have been, and how much good might he have done in the world, if he had but thought as justly of spirituality as he does of learning! He never, indeed, says anything shocking or offensive about the spiritual life because he never thinks or talks about it at all. It suffers nothing from him but neglect and disregard. The two Testaments would not have so much as a place amongst his books except that they are both available in Greek. Yet he thinks that he sufficiently shows his regard for the Holy Scriptures when he tells you that he has no other books of piety besides them.

It is very well, Professor, that you prefer the Bible to all other books of piety; no one who has any judgement will disagree thus far with your opinion. But if you will have no other book of piety besides the Bible, because it is the best, how is it that you do not content yourself with one of the best books amongst the Greeks and Romans? How is it that you are so greedy and eager after all of them? How is it that you think the knowledge of one is a necessary help to the knowledge of the other? How is it that you are so earnest, so laborious, so willing to expend your time and money to restore broken phrases and scraps of the ancients? How is it that you read so many commentators upon Cicero, Horace and Homer, and not one upon the Gospel? How is it that you love to read any book? How is it that your love of Cicero and Ovid makes you love to read an author that writes like them, and yet your esteem for the Gospel gives you no desire, nay, even prevents your reading such books as breathe the very spirit of the Gospel?

How is it that you tell your young student that he must not content himself with barely understanding his authors but must be continually reading them all, as the only means of entering into their spirit, and forming his own judgement according to them?

Why then must the Bible lie alone in your study? Is not the spirit of the saints, the piety of the holy followers of Jesus Christ, as good and necessary a means of entering into the spirit and taste of the Gospel as the reading of the ancients is of entering into the spirit of antiquity? Is not the spirit of poetry to be got only by much reading of poets and orators? And is not the spirit of devotion to be got in the same way, by frequently reading the holy thoughts and fervent expressions of devout persons? . . .

Now the reason our Professor does not think and judge thus reasonably in the matter of devotion owes to his never thinking of it in any other manner than as the repetition of a form of words. It never in his life entered his head to think of devotion as a state of the heart, as an improvable talent of the mind, as an attitude that is to grow and increase like our reason and judgement, and to be formed in us by such a regular, diligent use of proper means as are necessary to form any other wise habit of mind. And it is for lack of this understanding that he has been content all his life with the bare letter of prayer, and eagerly bent upon entering into the spirit of heathen poets and orators.

It is much to be lamented that numbers of scholars are more or less chargeable with this excessive folly—so negligent of improving their devotion, and so desirous of other poor accomplishments—as if they thought it a nobler talent to be able to write an epigram in the style of Martial* than to live and think and pray to God in the spirit of St. Augustine.

And yet, to correct this attitude and fill a man with a quite contrary spirit, there seems to be no more required than the bare belief in the truth of Christianity.

Now if you were to ask McMammon and Classicus—or any person of business or learning—whether piety is not the highest perfection of man, or true spirituality the greatest attainment in the world, they would both be forced to answer in the affirmative or else give up the truth of the Gospel. For to set any accomplishment against spiritual development or to think anything or all things in this world bears any proportion to its excellency is the same absurdity in a Christian as it would be in a philosopher to prefer a meal's meat to the greatest improvement in knowledge. For as philosophy professes purely the search and inquiry after knowledge, so Christianity supposes, intends, desires and aims at nothing else but the raising of fallen man to a divine life, to such habits of holiness and such degrees of devotion as may fit him to enter the holy citizenship of the kingdom of heaven.

He that does not believe this of Christianity may be reckoned an infidel, and he that believes this much has faith enough to give him a right judgement of the value of things, to support him in a sound mind and enable him to conquer all the temptations which the world shall lay in his way.

*A Roman writer famous for his witty epigrams, much admired among learned people in the Augustan age.

## V. *Conclusion*

To conclude this chapter, [let us recapitulate]: Devotion is nothing else but right appreciation and right affection toward God.

All practices, therefore, that heighten and improve our true appreciation of God—all ways of life that tend to nourish, raise and fix our affections upon Him—are to be reckoned as so many helps and means to fill us with devotion.

As prayer is the proper fuel of this holy flame, so we must use all our care and effort to give prayer its full power—by giving, self-denial, frequent spiritual retreats, holy readings, composing forms of prayer for ourselves or using the best we can find, adding length of time and observing set hours of prayer, and changing, improving and suiting our devotions to the condition of our lives and the state of our hearts.

Those who have most leisure would seem most especially called to a ✓ more eminent observance of these holy rules of a devout life. But they who, by the necessity of their state and not through their own choice, have but little time to be thus employed, must make the best use of what little they have. For this is the certain way of making devotion produce a devout life.

# *from* Letters

## *On Zeal and Simplicity*

To Lady Huntingdon                                    *January 10, 1754*

Madam,

I had the honor of your Ladyship's letter, and no lack of true regard for
your Ladyship or the subject has been the occasion of my delaying this
answer so long. I am in some hopes that the person who wanted my
response may, by this time, have found something better than it by being
left to God and himself, and that I have done more for him by my silence
than I should have done by my writing.*

To be always tampering with physicians upon every occasion is the
way to lose all natural soundness of health, and to be continually talking
and enquiring about the nature of ailments and powers of medicines for
the head, the heart, the spirits and nerves is the way to lose all true
judgement concerning our own sickness or health.

It is much the same with respect to our spiritual health and constitution. We do much hurt to it by running after spiritual advice on every
occasion, and wanting the help of some human prescription for every
fear, scruple or notion that starts up in our minds. This actually weakens
the true strength of our spiritual constitution which, if left to itself, would
do all that we need to have done.

If it be asked what this soundness of our spiritual constitution is, it may
be answered that it is a state or habit of such humble, total resignation of
ourselves to God as by faith and hope expects all from Him alone. This is
the health and strength of our spiritual constitution, and nothing is health
in the soul but this state. . . .

How this pious and worthy person came to think of leaving his parish,
or what scruples occasioned his doubting whether he should stay in it, I
cannot guess, and therefore can say nothing to them. I would have

*Lady Huntingdon was a kind of spiritual godmother to a number of young men of
the cloth, including, apparently, the one referred to in this letter, who had been
wondering over-loudly about reconciling his new sense of spiritual vocation with
his duties as an Anglican priest.

thought that such a change as he found wrought in himself would cause him to find that his parish and neighborhood should have everything that could render his situation agreeable to him.

The greatest danger that new converts are liable to, especially if they are young, arises from their imagining something great of their conversion, and that great things are to follow from it. Hence they are taken up too much with themselves, and the supposed designs of God upon them. They enter into reasonings and conjectures concerning what they shall become, or what extraordinary things they shall do, and so lose that simplicity of heart which should think of nothing but of dying to self, that the spirit of God might have time and place to create and form all that is missing in their inward person.

There is nothing more plain and simple than the way of spiritual life, if self is but kept out of it. All the perplexities and scruples which pious persons meet with chiefly arise from some idea they have formed of a progress they ought to make in order to be that which self wants to be. But spiritual life makes little progress until it has no schemes of its own, no thoughts or contrivances to be anything but a naked penitent, left wholly and solely in faith and hope to the divine goodness. Every contrivance for human help, from this or that, be it what it will, is at best but dropping some level from the fulness of faith and hope and dependence upon God which alone can be our way of finding Him to be the strength and God of our life.

Nothing but the life of God, opened by his Holy Spirit within us, can be the renewal of our souls, and we shall lack this renewal no longer than the time we waste seeking it in something that is not God. The faith that ascribes all to God and expects all from Him cannot be disappointed.

Nothing could hinder the centurion from having that which he asked of Christ, because his heart could thus speak: "Lord, I am not worthy that thou shouldest come under my roof; speak the word only, and my servant shall be healed" (Matthew 8:8).

He that has this sense of himself, and this faith in God is in the truth and perfection of spiritual life. If we knew the goodness of this condition we should be always content with the simplicity of it, and let everything else come and go as it would. All is well and safe so long as the heart rests all upon God alone. Your Ladyship says that this worthy person fears his zeal may be excessive, yet dreads the diminishment of it. It would be better for him not to indulge a thought about his own zeal, or to speak a word of it to anyone. For if it is a godly zeal it is no more his than it is mine, nor comes any more from him than it does from me. Therefore, when he thinks or speaks of it as his, or as something he would be glad to keep in its right state, it is giving way to delusion, both with regard to himself and the nature of true zeal. For as the wind blows where it lists, so it is with one who is driven by true zeal.

I do not wonder that [this young pastor's] audience is so much affected and increased since he had preached up the doctrine of regeneration amongst them. All other preaching passes away as a tale that is told, and indeed is nothing better until it enters into the things within man, bringing him to an awareness of the condition of his heart and its need of God's Holy Spirit therein.

How far it may be right for him to comply with their request of visiting, reading and expounding the Scripture to them, I pretend not to say, except only this much: it seems to be right to be in no anxiety about it, or use any reasoning either to persuade himself to it, or from it, or to put himself under any state rules about it, but rather leave it to be done as he finds himself inwardly stirred up to it, and able out of the abundance of his heart to perform it.

'Expounding the Scriptures' has a fine sound, but I should rather advise such persons to read only in love and simplicity of heart such Scriptures as need no expounding except one's heart turned toward God. Persons who are come to this inward conviction, that they must live and die under the power of Satan and of fallen nature unless by a fullness of faith in Christ they are born again from above, have nothing more to enquire about where or how Christ is to be found.

They have no other use to make of Scriptures except that of being refreshed and delighted with such passages as turn and stir up the heart to fullness of faith, love and resignation to the blessed guidance and operation of the Holy Spirit of God.

# PHILIP DODDRIDGE

1702 · 1751

From the engraving by W. C. Edwards, representing Doddridge as a young minister
(c. 1730).

## INTRODUCTION

In an age dominated by evangelists and spiritual writers whom we identify with Anglican (and later, Methodist) connections, Philip Doddridge stands out as a superb contribution from the Dissenting or Nonconformist side—the left bookend to Law's Anglo-Catholicism on the right, as it were, embracing and sustaining the rich library of eighteenth-century English spirituality. For if Law provided a foundational challenge for the Wesleys, Whitefield, and others in the Methodist movement, Doddridge, especially in his *Rise and Progress of Religion in the Soul,* spoke to the broad center of the evangelical revival, both as it was transpiring in the Anglican mainstream represented by Newton and Milner and as it was gathering together a fragmenting and dissipating remnant of the great Puritan communities of the preceeding century. Doddridge's personal character had a great deal to do with his accessibility; his preaching and pastoral counsel were valued by Lady Huntingdon above, perhaps, that of all others among the great Christian leaders she protected, and yet he was entirely at home with poor students and cabin boys. He was one of those rare individuals who seem to embody, almost effortlessly, the capacity to be content in any state. And although his life was short, his spirit touched the whole century. He was a friend, associate, and protegé of Isaac Watts, and his major work (the plan for which was suggested to him by Watts) was to be a key instrument in the conversion of William Wilberforce in 1785.

Doddridge was born in London on June 26, 1702. His father was a prosperous merchant of Puritan descent and his mother the daughter of John Bauman, a Lutheran pastor who had fled Prague in the persecutions of 1626 and now ran a private school in Kingston-upon-Thames. Philip was the twentieth and last child born, and seemed so lifeless on arrival that he was at first given up for dead. (Only one other of the Doddridge children lived to maturity, a sister Elizabeth.) Philip's mother commenced his education at home, with instruction in stories from the Bible which she illustrated by referring to pictures on the Dutch tiles of the hearth and chimney. He then went to a Latin grammar school run by a Dissenting minister named Stott, and subsequently, from the age of ten, attended the school founded by his maternal grandfather. During his twelfth year, Philip's father and uncle both died, and he was moved to a new school, St. Alban's, by a guardian. There was a sort of grace in this; he was taught there by the scholarly Nathaniel Wood, and the Presbyterian minister at St. Alban's, Samuel Clarke (author of *The Scripture Promises* [1750]), was like a second father to young Philip.

He began to consider further education toward the ministry, but a man named Downes lost his own property and the Doddridge business in a foolish speculative enterprise, and was himself rescued from debtors' prison only by the sale of the Doddridge family silverware. Philip was devastated, and of course forced to leave school. The Duchess of Bedford, a family friend, offered to send him to either Oxford or Cambridge, but he declined on the grounds that he did not want to desert his convictions by joining the state church. Though discouraged by at least one adviser from pursuing the ministry, Philip was invited by Samuel Clarke to come and live in his household in 1719, and not only encouraged but financially supported by him as he embarked on a course of theological study at the independent academy of John Jennings in Leicestershire. (Scholarships allowed him eventually to repay Clarke for this kindness.)

Doddridge's progress was rapid. By July 1722 he had preached his first sermon, and six months later he passed an examination before three ministers qualifying him for a "certificate of approbation." In June 1723 he took his first congregation, with one hundred fifty members, at Kibworth, for an annual stipend of £35. Almost simultaneously he had been called by a much larger and more prestigious Presbyterian congregation at Coventry, but since the offer was not unanimous he turned it down. The congregation apparently split over the issue, and he was subsequently invited (unanimously) by the new split-off church to be its first minister. He declined without hesitation, saying he would not be in opposition to the original church. Other offers came frequently over the next few years, but since many were from groups he found too narrowly legalistic, he waited until 1729, when on Christmas Day he began his ministry at Northampton, now officially as a Presbyterian. With him he brought the evangelical theological school which he had founded with the blessing of Isaac Watts earlier that year; it flourished there under his direction until the end of his life.

Doddridge was a tall, slender man of delicate features, and though extremely nearsighted, he was by all accounts vivacious, witty, and an attractive personality. Like Newton, he enjoyed his pipe while he read, and like Newton, after a number of enthusiastic romantic infatuations, he finally settled down to an extremely happy marriage. His wife was an orphan named Mercy Maris. She bore him three sons and six daughters, five of whom died in infancy. Doddridge's affection for her was open and unabashed; his letters to her even in later years display the warmth, gentleness, and humor of a lover's correspondence.[1]

His writing career began with a defense of the Dissenting churches from an attack directed at their weakening numbers and incessant internal divisions. This pamphlet (1730) was a kind of masterpiece in its kind, setting forth Doddridge's case for a united Nonconforming community based upon evangelical ministry, liberal understanding, and tolerant mutual respect. He modeled these values in his own parish ministry and was in communion with Methodists like John Wesley, George Whitefield, and Lady Huntingdon, as well as Count Zinzendorf of the Moravians and a diversity of Independent and Presbyterian leaders.[2] Early in life (1723) he had expressed himself as "moderately inclined" to Congregationalism, but in fact the whole force of his ministry was to eliminate practical distinctions between this group and the English Presbyterians. Unfortunately, because he had so many irons in the fire at once, from his schools to his vast efforts in publication, his own church suffered—declining from 342 members in 1730 to only 239 when he left twenty years later.

His schools were innovative. He was one of the first to introduce the practice of lecturing in English rather than Latin, and he adapted a system of shorthand to enable students to acquire verbatim lectures and sermons. He set up a charity school near his academy, teaching and clothing poor children of the neighboring district after the manner of his own teacher, Samuel Clarke. He had an important role in establishing a county infirmary (1743) and proposed a special society for distributing Bibles and books of devotion among the poor. He designed what may have been the first Nonconformist project for foreign missions, and in 1748 he submitted a proposal to Archbishop Herring for a pulpit exchange between the Anglican and Dissenting clergy, something he had already experimented in himself, with Whitefield and others.

Like Watts, Doddridge was a writer of hymns and versified Christian instruction for children. His hymns typically circulated in manuscript and, as was common in the Dissenter communities, would be read out line by line from the front of the church as the congregation was singing. They were published after his death by Job Orton (1755). Doddridge's major work, *The Rise and Progress* (1745), was actually planned by Isaac Watts, who revised some chapters after Doddridge himself had finished them. This work was almost instantly a classic, and had a great impact abroad, being translated into French (1754), Welsh (1788), Scots Gaelic (1811), Italian (1812), Tamil (1848), Syriac (1857), as well as Dutch, German, and Danish. In English it appeared in numerous editions in both Britain and America during the generation following Doddridge's death.

His last days were spent in Lisbon, Portugal, where on October 26, 1751, he died of tuberculosis. He had been sent there by Lady Huntingdon and other friends in a last attempt to turn back the disease, but to no avail. Something of the character of his faith is revealed in a letter to the countess from Portugal during his final illness.

I see, indeed, no hope of recovery, yet my heart rejoiceth in my God and in my Saviour; and I can call Him, under this failure of everything else, its strength and everlasting portion. I must now thank you for your heart-reviving letter to strengthen my faith, to comfort my soul, and assist me in swallowing up death in victory! God hath indeed been wonderfully good to me, but I am less than the least of his mercies, less than the least hope of his children. Adored be his grace for whatever it hath wrought by me, and blessed be you of the Lord for the strong consolations you have been the instrument of administering. . . . What a friend you will be in heaven! How glad shall I be to welcome you there, after a long and glorious course of service, to increase the lustre of your crown![3]

And no better testimonial to Doddridge exists than that of the same person to whom he wrote these words; the countess had once said of him:

His is a true catholic spirit, that wishes well to the cause of Christ in every denomination. I would that all the dissenting ministers I hear of were like-minded, less attached to all the punctilos of order, system, regularity, etc., and more determined to publish the glorious Gospel of the ever-blessed Immanuel, in season and out of season, wherever men were assembled to hear, whether in a church, a meeting-house, a field, or a barn; less desirous to convince men of the errors in the discipline of those churches who hold the great doctrines of the Reformation, and more anxiously solicitous to gather souls to Christ, the true Shiloh. This should be the one great object of those who are called to the high and honourable office of ambassadors of Christ; all others are unimportant when compared with this.[4]

The following brief excerpts from his *Rise and Progress* give a sense of the rich practicality of Doddridge's spiritual counsel.

## NOTES

1. The address in one letter (1741) is "To my trusty and well-beloved Mrs. Mercy Doddridge, the dearest of all dears, the wisest of all earthly counsellors, and of all my governors the most potent, yet the most gentle and moderate."

2. Wesley, who had been invited by Doddridge to address his students in 1745, later wrote to him for advice on establishing a syllabus of reading for young preachers and received "a very detailed reply" (June 18, 1746). See J. Wesley Bready, *England Before and After Wesley* (London: Hodder and Stoughton, 1938), p. 299.

3. Quoted in A. C. H. Seymour, *The Life and Times of Selina, Countess of Huntingdon,* 2 vols. (London: Painter, 1844), vol. 1, p. 452.

4. Ibid., vol. 1, pp. 153–54.

# *from* The Rise and Progress of Religion in the Soul (1745)

## *News Of Salvation*

MY DEAR READER, it is the great design of the Gospel and, wherever it is cordially received, the glorious effect of it, to fill the heart with feelings of love; to teach us to abhor all unnecessary rigor and severity, and to delight not in grief but in the happiness of our fellow creatures. I can hardly imagine the Christian who takes pleasure in the distress which appears even in an animal, much less in that of a human mind—especially in such distress as the thoughts of our fallen condition must give where there is any attention to their weight and urgency. I have often felt a tender regret while I have been representing these things, and I could have wished from my heart that it had not been necessary to have placed them in so severe and painful a light.

But now I am addressing myself to a part of my work which I undertake with unutterable pleasure. . . . I have been showing you that if you hitherto have lived in a state of impenitence and sin, you are condemned by God's righteous judgement, and have in yourself no spring of hope and no possibility of deliverance. But I mean not to leave you under this sad apprehension, to lie down and die in despair complaining of that cruel zeal which has "tormented you before your time" (Matthew 8:29).*

Arise, O dejected soul, prostrate in the dust before God and trembling under the terror of his righteous sentence, for I am commissioned to tell you that though "thou hast destroyed thyself, in God is thine help" (Hosea 13:9). I bring you "good tidings of great joy" (Luke 2:10), which delight my own heart while I proclaim them and will, I hope, reach and revive yours—even the tidings of salvation by the blood and righteousness of the Redeemer. And I give it to you for your greater security, in the words of a gracious and forgiving God, that "he is in Christ

---

*The early part of this book, which Doddridge allows to have been shaped mostly by Watts, is concerned with sin and the psychology of the sinner, and then with the necessity of an awareness of the condition before the possibility of doing something about it can be realized. Doddridge has emphasized the helplessness of the sinner to pull himself up by his own bootstraps.

reconciling the world unto himself, and not imputing to them their trespasses" (2 Corinthians 5:19).

This is the best news that ever was heard—the most important message which God ever sent to his creatures. Though I doubt not that, living in a Christian country, you have heard it often, perhaps a thousand and a thousand times, I will, with all simplicity and plainness repeat it to you again, and repeat it as if you had never heard it before. If you, O sinner, should for the first time feel it, then will it be as a new Gospel to you, though so familiar to your ear. . . . Nor is it absolutely impossible that some one soul at least may read these lines who has never been clearly and fully instructed in the Gospel, though his everlasting all depends on knowing and receiving it. I will therefore take care that such a one shall not have it to plead at the judgement of God that, though he lived in a Christian country, he was never plainly and faithfully taught the doctrine of salvation by Jesus Christ, "the way, the truth, and the life, by whom alone we come unto the Father" (John 14:6).

I do therefore testify unto you this day that the holy and gracious Majesty of heaven and earth, foreseeing the fatal apostacy into which the whole human race would fall, did not determine to deal in a way of strict and rigorous severity with us, so as to consign us over to universal ruin and inevitable damnation. On the contrary, He determined to enter into a treaty of peace and reconciliation, and to publish to all whom the Gospel should reach the express offers of life and glory, in a certain method which his infinite wisdom judged suitable to the purity of his nature and the honor of his government. This method was indeed a most astonishing one, which, familiar as it is to our thoughts and our tongues, I cannot recollect and mention without great amazement. He determined to send his own Son into the world, "the brightness of his glory and the express image of his person" (Hebrews 1:3), partaker of his own divine perfections and honors, to be not merely a teacher of righteousness and a messenger of grace, but also a sacrifice for the sins of men. And He would consent to saving them on no other condition but this, that He should not only labor but die in the cause.

Accordingly, at such a period of time as infinite wisdom saw most convenient, the Lord Jesus Christ appeared in human flesh; and after He had gone through incessant and long-continued fatigue, bearing all the injuries which the ingratitude and malice of men could inflict, He voluntarily "submitted himself to death, even the death of the cross" (Philippians 2:8), and having been "delivered for our offences, was raised again for our justification" (Romans 4:25). After his resurrection He continued long enough on earth to give his followers most convincing evidences of it and then "ascended into heaven in their sight" (Acts 1:9–11), and sent down his Spirit unto his apostles to enable them, in the most persuasive and authoritative manner, "to preach the Gospel." And He has given this charge to them, and to those who in every age succeed them, that it should be published "to every creature" (Mark 16:15) that all who believe in it may be saved by virtue of its abiding energy and the immutable power and grace of its divine Author, who is the "same yesterday, today and forever" (Hebrews 13:8).

This Gospel do I therefore now preach and proclaim unto you, O reader, with the sincerest desire that through divine grace it may "this very day be salvation to thy soul" (Luke 19:9). Know therefore and consider it, whoever you are, that as surely as these words are now before your eyes, so sure it is that the incarnate Son of God was "made a spectacle to the world, and to angels, and to men" (1 Corinthians 4:9). His back was torn with scourges, his head with thorns, his limbs stretched out as on a rack, and nailed to the accursed tree; and in this miserable condition He was hung by his hands and feet as an object of public infamy and contempt. Thus did He die in the midst of all the taunts and insults of his cruel enemies, who thirsted for his blood. Saddest of all, in the midst of those agonies with which He closed the most innocent, perfect, and useful life that ever was spent on earth, He had not those supports of the Spirit which [even] sinful men have often experienced when they have been suffering for the testimony of their conscience. They have often burst out into transports of joy and songs of praise while their executioners have been glutting their hellish malice and savage barbarity by making their torments artificially grievous. But the crucified Jesus cried out in the distress of his spotless and holy soul, "My God, my God, why hast thou forsaken me?" (Matthew 27:46).

Look upon your dear Redeemer! Look up to this mournful, dreadful, yet in another light delightful spectacle! And then ask your own heart, "Do I believe that Jesus suffered and died thus?" And why did He suffer and die?

Let me answer in God's own words: "He was wounded for our transgressions, he was bruised for our iniquities, and the chastisement of our peace was upon Him, that by his stripes we might be healed: it pleased the Lord to bruise him and put him to grief, when he made his soul an offering for sin; for the Lord laid on him the iniquity of us all" (Isaiah 53:5,6,10). So I may address you in the words of the apostle, "Be it known unto you therefore, that through this man is preached unto you the forgiveness of sins" (Acts 13:38), as it was his command, just after He arose from the dead, "that repentance and remission of sins should be preached in his name among all nations, beginning at Jerusalem" (Luke

24:47), the very place where his blood had so lately been shed in such a cruel manner. I testify to you, in the words of another inspired writer, that Christ was made sin, that is, a sin offering, "for us, though he knew no sin, that we might be made the righteousness of God in him" (2 Corinthians 5:21)—that is, that through the righteousness He has fulfilled and the atonement He has made we might be accepted by God as righteous, and be not only pardoned, but received into his favor.

"To you is the word of this salvation sent" (Acts 13:26) and to you, O reader, are the blessings of it even now offered by God—sincerely offered—so that, after all that I have said . . . your having broken the law of God shall not prove your ruin if you do not also reject his Gospel. It is not all those legions of sins which rise up in battle array against you that shall be able to destroy you, if unbelief does not lead them on, and final impenitence bring up the rear. I know that guilt is a timorous thing; I will therefore speak in the words of God Himself, nor can any be more comfortable: "He that believeth on the Son hath everlasting life" (John 3:36) "and he shall never come into condemnation" (John 5:24). "There is therefore now no condemnation," no kind or degree of it, "to them (to any of them) who are in Jesus Christ, who walk not after the flesh, but after the spirit" (Romans 8:1).

You have indeed been a very great sinner. . . . Nevertheless you may rejoice in the assurance that "when sin hath abounded, there shall grace much more abound," "that where sin hath reigned unto death"—where it has had its most unlimited sway and most unresisted triumph—there "shall righteousness reign to eternal life through Jesus Christ our Lord" (Romans 5:21). That righteousness, to which on believing on Him you will be entitled, shall not only break those chains by which sin is, as it were, dragging you at its chariot-wheels with a furious pace to eternal ruin, but it shall clothe you with the robes of salvation and set you on a throne of glory. There you shall live and reign forever among the princes of heaven, shall reign in immortal beauty and joy, without one remaining scar of divine displeasure upon you, without any single mark by which it could be known that you had ever been under wrath and a curse, except it be in an anthem of praise to "the Lamb that was slain, and has washed thee from thy sins in his own blood" (Revelation 1:5).

Nor is it necessary, in order for you to be released from guilt and entitled to this high and complete happiness, that before you venture to apply to Jesus you need bring any good works of your own to recommend yourself to his acceptance. It is indeed true that if your faith is sincere it will certainly produce them; but I have the authority of the word of God to tell you that if you this day sincerely believe in the name of the Son of God, you shall this day be taken under his care and be numbered among those of his sheep to whom He has graciously declared that "he will give eternal life, and that they shall never perish" (John 10:28). You have no need therefore to say, "Who shall go up into heaven, or who shall descend into the deep for me? For the word is nigh thee, in thy mouth, and in thy heart" (Romans 10:6,7,8). With this joyful message I leave you; with this faithful saying which is, indeed, "worthy of all acceptation" (1 Timothy 1:15), with this Gospel, O sinner, which is my life, and which, if you do not reject it, will be yours too.

# Growth in Grace

IF BY divine grace you have "been born again, not of corruptible seed, but of incorruptible" (1 Peter 1:2,3) even "by the word of God which liveth and abideth for ever" not only in the world and the church, but in particular souls in which it is sown, you will, "as new born babes, desire the sincere milk of the word, that you may grow thereby" (1 Peter 2:2). And though in the most advanced state of religion on earth we are but infants in comparison to what we hope to be, when, in the heavenly world, we arrive "unto a perfect man, unto the measure of the stature of the fullness of Christ" (Ephesians 4:13), yet, as we have some exercise of a sanctified reason, we ought to be diligent that we may be growing and thriving. And you, my reader, "if so be you have tasted that the Lord is gracious" (1 Peter 2:3) will, I doubt not, feel this desire. I would therefore endeavor to assist you in making the inquiry whether spiritual maturity is on the advance in your soul. First I shall warn you against some false marks of growth, and then shall endeavor to lay down others on which you may depend as more solid. In this light I would observe that you are not to measure your growth in grace only or chiefly by your advances in knowledge, or in zeal, or any other passionate impression of the mind, no, nor by the fervor of devotion alone, but by the habitual determination of the will for God, and by your prevailing disposition to obey his commands, submit to his direction, and promote the highest welfare of his cause in the earth.

It must be allowed that knowledge and affection in the spiritual life are indeed desirable. Without some degree of the former, religion cannot be rational, and it is very reasonable to believe that without some degree of the latter it cannot be sincere. Yet there may be a great deal of speculative knowledge and a great deal of rapturous affection where there is no true spirituality at all; and still more where spiritual life exists without maturity. The exercise of our rational faculties upon . . . Scripture may furnish a very wicked man with a well-digested body of orthodox theology in his head when not one single doctrine of it has ever reached his heart. An eloquent description of the sufferings of Christ, of the solemnities of judgement, of the joys of the blessed and the miseries of the damned, might move the breast even of a person who did not firmly believe them—even as we often find ourselves strongly moved by well-wrought narratives or discourses which at the same time we know to have their foundation in fiction. Natural constitution, or such accidental causes as are (some of them) too low to be here mentioned, may supply the eyes with a flood of tears . . . upon almost any occasion. And a proud impatience upon being contradicted, directly opposite as it is to the gentle spirit of Christianity, may make a man's blood boil when he hears the notions he has entertained, and especially those which he has openly and vigorously espoused, disputed and opposed. This may possibly lead him, in terms of strong indignation, to pour out his zeal and his rage before God in a fond imagination that, as the God of truth, He is the pattern of those favorite doctrines by whose fair appearances perhaps he himself is misled. And if these speculative refinements or affectionate sallies of the mind are consistent with a total absence of true religion, they are much more apparently consistent with a very low state of it. . . . I would therefore entreat you to bring your own heart to answer, as in the presence of God, such inquiries as these.

## I. *Love Toward God*

Do you find divine love, on the whole, advancing in your soul? Do you feel yourself more and more aware of the presence of God, and does that sense grow more delightful to you than it formerly was? Can you, even when your natural spirits are weak and low, and you are not in any frame of mind for the ardors and ecstacies of devotion, nevertheless find a pleasing rest, a calm repose of heart, in the thought that God is near you? That He sees the secret feelings of your soul while you are, as it were, laboring up the hill, and casting a longing eye toward Him, though you cannot say you enjoy any tangible communications from Him? Is it agreeable to you to open your heart to his inspection, to present it to Him laid bare of every disguise, and say with David, "Thou, Lord, knowest thy servant" (2 Samuel 7:20)? Do you find a growing esteem and approbation of that sacred law of God, which is the transcript of his moral perfections? Do you inwardly "esteem all his precepts concerning all things to be right" (Psalm 119:128)?* Do you discern not only the neces-

*Cf. Alexander Pope's *Essay on Man,* with its deistic resignation: "Whatever is, is right," to which this stands in sharp contrast.

sity but the reasonableness, the beauty, the pleasure of obedience, and feel a growing scorn and contempt of those things which may be offered as the price of your innocence and would tempt you to sacrifice or hazard your interest in his divine favor and friendship? Do you find an ingenuous desire to please God, not only because He is so powerful, and has so many good and evil things entirely at his command, but from a veneration of his most amiable nature and character? And do you find your heart habitually reconciled to a most humble subjection, both to his commanding and his disposing will? Do you perceive that your own will is now more ready and disposed, in every circumstance, to bear the yoke and to submit to the divine determination, whatever he appoints to be borne or forborne? Can you "in patience possess your soul" (Luke 21:19)? Can you maintain a more steady calmness and serenity when God is striking at your dearest enjoyments in this world, and acting most directly contrary to your present interests and to your natural passions and desires? If you can, it is a most certain and noble sign that grace is growing up in you to a very vigorous state.

## II. *Love Toward 'Neighbors'*

Examine also what affections you find in your heart toward those who are about you, and toward the rest of mankind in general. Do you find your heart overflowing with undissembled and unrestrained benevolence? Are you more aware than you once were of those most endearing bonds which unite all men, and especially all Christians, into one community— which make them brethren and fellow citizens? Do all unfriendly passions die and wither in your soul, while the kind, social affections grow and strengthen? And though self-love was never the reigning passion since you became a true Christian (yet as some remainders of it are still too ready to work inwardly and to show themselves, especially as sudden occasions arise) do you perceive that you are gaining ground on them? Do you think of yourself only as one of a great number, whose particular interests and concerns are of little importance when compared with those of the community, and ought by all means, on all occasions, to be sacrificed to them?

## III. *Love for Those We Find it Difficult to Love*

Reflect especially on the disposition of your mind toward those whom an unsanctified heart might be ready to imagine it had some just excuse for excluding out of the list of those it loves, and from whom you are ready to feel some secret alienation or aversion. How does your mind stand affected toward those who differ from you in their religious feelings and practices? I do not say that Christian charity will require you to think every error harmless. . . . But to hate persons because we think they are mistaken, and to aggravate every difference in judgement or practice into a fatal and damnable error that destroys all Christian communion and love, is a symptom generally much worse than the evil it condemns. Do you love the image of Christ in a person who thinks himself obliged in conscience to profess and worship in a manner different from yourself? More than this, can you love and honor that which is truly amiable and excellent in those in whom much is defective—in those in whom there is a mixture of bigotry and narrowness of spirit, which may lead them perhaps to slight or even to censure you? Can you love them as the disciples and servants of Christ, who, though a mistaken zeal, may be ready to "cast out your name as evil" (Luke 6:22) and to warn others against you as a dangerous person? This is none of the least triumphs of charity, nor any despicable evidence of an advance of the spiritual life.

## IV. *Bearing Injuries*

And in this regard, reflect further: how can you bear injuries? . . . Does everything of this kind hurry and ruffle you, and set you to imagining how you may get even or, at least, how you may disgrace and expose the person who has done you the wrong? Or can you stand the shock calmly, and easily divert your mind to other objects . . . , pitying and praying for those who are assaulting you? This is a Christlike attitude indeed, and He will own it as such, and own you as one of his soldiers and heroes, especially if you rise so far that instead of being "overcome of evil," you "overcome evil with good" (Romans 12:21). Watch over your spirit and over your tongue when injuries are offered, and see whether you are ready to meditate upon them, to make them worse in your own mind, to complain of them to others, and to lay on all the load of blame that you in justice can. Or are you ready to put the kindest construction upon the offence, to excuse it as far as reason will allow, and (where, after all this, it [still] wears a black and odious aspect) to forgive it, heartily to forgive it, even before any submission is made or pardon asked? Further, in token of the sincerity of that forgiveness, do you contrive a means of some benefit or other toward the injurious person, to teach him a better spirit?

## V. *Bearing with Things Outside our Control*

Examine further, with regard to other evils and calamities of life, and even with regard to its uncertainties, how you can bear them. Do you find your soul is in this respect gathering strength? Have you fewer foreboding fears and disquieting alarms than you once had, as to what may happen in life? Can you trust the wisdom and goodness of God to order your affairs for you, with more confidence and cheerfulness than formerly? Do you find yourself able to unite your thoughts more in surveying present circumstances, that you can understand your immediate duty though you know not what God will next appoint or call you to? And when you feel the smart of affliction, do you make a lesser matter of it? Can you transfer your heart more easily to heavenly and divine objects, without an anxious concern about whether this or that burden be removed, so that it may but be sanctified to promote your communion with God and your ripeness for glory?

## VI. *Humility*

Examine also whether you advance in humility. This is a silent but most excellent grace, and those who are most eminent in it are dearest to God and most fit for the communications of his presence to them. Do you feel your mind more emptied of proud and haughty imaginations, not prone so much to look back upon past services performed as forward to those which are yet before you, and inward upon the remaining imperfections of your heart? Do you more sensitively observe your daily failures and miscarriages and find yourself disposed to mourn before the Lord over things that once passed with you as slight matters but which, when you come to survey them in the presence of God, you find them not wholly involuntary or free from guilt? Do you feel in your breast a deeper appreciation of the infinite majesty of the blessed God and of the glory of his perfections so that you perceive yourself, as it were, annihilated in his presence, shrinking into "less than nothing and vanity" (Isaiah 40:17)? If this be your spirit, God will look upon you with peculiar favor, and will visit you more and more with the distinguishing blessings of his grace.

But there is another great branch and effect of Christian humility, which it would be an unpardonable negligence to omit. Let me therefore further inquire, are you more frequently renewing your application— your sincere, steady, determined application—to the righteousness and blood of Christ in awareness of how unworthy you are to appear before God other than in Him? And do the remaining corruptions of your heart humble you before Him, though the disorders of your life are in a great measure cured? Are you more earnest to obtain the quickening influences of the Holy Spirit? And have you such a sense of your own weakness as to engage you to depend, in all the duties you perform, upon the communications of his grace to "help your infirmities" (Romans 8:26)? Can you, at the close of your most spiritual, exemplary, and useful days, blush before God for the deficiencies of them, while others may perhaps be ready to admire and extol your conduct? And while you give the glory of all that has been right to Him from whom the strength and grace has been derived, are you coming to the blood of sprinkling to free you from the guilt which mingles itself even with the best of your services? Do you learn to receive the bounties of Providence, not only with thankfulness, as coming from God, but with a mixture of shame and confusion too, under a consciousness that you do not deserve them, and are continually forfeiting them? And do you justify Providence in your afflictions and disappointments, even while many are flourishing around you full in the bloom of prosperity, whose offenses have been more visible at least, and more notorious than yours?

## VII. *Zeal in Service*

Do you also advance in zeal and activity for the service of God and the happiness of mankind? Does your love show itself solid and sincere by a continual flow of good works from it? Can you view the sorrows of others with tender compassion, and with projects and plans for what you may do to relieve them? Do you feel in your breast that you are more frequently "devising liberal things" (Isaiah 32:8) and ready to waive your own advantage or pleasure that you may accomplish them? Do you find your imagination teeming, as it were, with conceptions and schemes for the advancement of the cause and interest of Christ in the world, for the propagation of his Gospel, and for the happiness of your fellow creatures? And do you not only pray but act for this, act in such a manner as to show that you pray in earnest, and feel a readiness to do what little you can in this cause—even though others who might, if they pleased, very conveniently do a vast amount more, will do nothing?

## VIII. *Affection for Things Above*

And [finally] reflect once more how your affections stand with regard to this world and the other. Are you more deeply and practically convinced of the vanity of these things "which are seen, and are temporal" (2 Corinthians 4:18)? Do you perceive your expectations from them and your attachments to them diminishing? You are willing to stay in this world as long as your Father pleases, and this is right and well. But do you find your bonds so loosened to it that you are willing, heartily willing, to leave it at the shortest warning, so that if God should see fit to summon you away all of a sudden—even in the midst of your enjoyments, pursuits, expectations and hopes—you would cordially consent to that remove without saying, "Lord, let me stay a little while longer, to enjoy this or that agreeable entertainment, to finish this or that scheme"? Can you think, with a habitual calmness and hearty approbation (if such be the divine pleasure) of waking no more when you lie down on your bed, or returning home no more when you go out of your house? And yet on the other hand, however great the burdens of life are, do you find a willingness to bear them, in submission to the will of your heavenly Father, though it should be to many future years, and though they should be years of far greater affliction than you have ever yet seen? Can you say calmly and steadily, if not with such overflowings of tender affection as you could desire, "Behold thy servant, thy child, is in thy hand; do with me as seemeth good in thy sight" (cf. 2 Samuel 15:26). My will is melted into thine, to be lifted up or laid down, to be carried out or brought in, to be here or there, in this or that circumstance just as thou pleasest, and as shall best suit with thy great extensive plan, which it is impossible that I, or all the angels in heaven, should mend.

These, if I understand matters aright, are some of the most substantial evidences of growth and establishment in the spiritual life. Search after them, bless God for them, so far as you discover them in yourself, and study to advance in them daily, under the influences of divine grace, to which I heartily recommend you, and to which I entreat you frequently to recommend yourself.

## A Christian Prayer for Growth in Grace

"O THOU EVER blessed Fountain of natural and spiritual life! I thank thee that I live, and know the exercises and pleasures of a religious life. I bless thee that thou hast infused into me thine own vital breath, though I was once 'dead in trespasses and sins' (Ephesians 2:1), so that I am become, in a sense peculiar to thine own children, 'a living soul'. But it is my earnest desire that I may not only live but grow, 'grow in grace and in the knowledge of my Lord and Saviour Jesus Christ' (2 Peter 3:18) upon an acquaintance with whom my progress so evidently depends. In this view, I humbly entreat thee that thou wilt form my mind . . . that I may not misjudge grace, nor measure my advances in it by those things which are merely the effects of nature, and possibly its corrupt effects!

"May I be seeking after an increase of divine love to thee, my God and Father in Christ, of unreserved resignation to thy wise and holy will, and of extensive benevolence to my fellow creatures! May I grow in patience and fortitude of soul, in humility and zeal, in spirituality and a heavenly disposition of mind, and in a concern 'that, whether present or absent, I may be accepted of the Lord' (2 Corinthians 5:9)—that whether I live or die, it may be for thy glory. In a word, as thou knowest I hunger and thirst after righteousness, make me whatever thou wouldst delight to see me! Draw on my soul, by the gentle influences of thy gracious Spirit, every trace and every feature which thine eye, O heavenly Father, may survey with pleasure, and which thou mayest acknowledge as thine own image.

"I am aware, O Lord, I have not as yet attained. Yea, my soul is utterly confounded to think how far I am from being already perfect. But this one thing (after the great example of thine apostle) I would endeavor to do: 'forgetting the things which are behind, I would press forward to those which are before'. O that thou wouldst feed my soul by thy word and Spirit! Having been, as I humbly hope and trust, regenerated by it, 'being born again, not of corruptible seed, but of incorruptible, even by thy word, which liveth and abideth for ever' (1 Peter 1:23), 'as a newborn babe, I desire the sincere milk of the word, that I may grow thereby' (1 Peter 2:2)? And may 'my profitting appear unto all men' (1 Timothy 4:15), till at length 'I come unto a perfect man, unto the measure of the stature of the fullness of Christ' (Ephesians 4:13) and after having enjoyed the pleasure of those that flourish eminently in thy courts below, be fixed in paradise above! I ask and hope it through our Lord and Saviour Jesus Christ—to whom be glory, both now and for ever! Amen."

## Grateful Joy

I WOULD NOW suppose my reader to find, on an examination of his spiritual life, that he is growing in grace. And if you desire that this growth may at once be acknowledged and promoted, let me call your soul to that more affectionate exercise of love toward God and joy in Him—which suits, and strengthens and exalts the character of the advanced Christian, and which I beseech you to regard not only as your privilege but as your duty also. Love is the most sublime, generous principle of all true and acceptable obedience. And with love, when so wisely and happily fixed, when so certainly returned, joy, proportional joy, must naturally be connected. It may justly grieve one that enters into the spirit of Christianity to see how low a life even the generality of sincere Christians commonly live in this respect. "Rejoice then in the Lord, ye righteous, and give thanks at the remembrance of his holiness" (Psalm 97:12), and of all those other perfections and glories which are included in that majestic, that wonderful, that delightful name, the Lord thy God! Spend not your sacred moments merely in confession or in petition, though each must have their daily share; but give a part, a considerable part, to the celestial and angelic work of praise. Yea, labor to carry about with you continually a heart overflowing with such an attitude, warmed and enflamed with love.

Are there not continually rays enough diffused from the great Father of light and love to enkindle it in our hearts? Come, my Christian friend and brother, come and survey with me the goodness of our heavenly Father. And oh, that He would give me such a sense of it that I might represent it in a suitable manner that "while I am musing, the fire may burn" in my own heart (Psalm 39:3) and be communicated to yours! And oh, that it might pass, with the lines I write, from soul to soul, awakening in the breast of every Christian that reads them, sentiments more worthy of the children of God and the heirs of glory, who are to spend an eternity in those very sacred exercises to which I am now endeavoring to excite you.

Have you not reason to adopt the words of David and say, "How many are thy gracious thoughts unto me, O Lord! How great is the sum of them! When I would count them, they are more in number than the sand" (Psalm 138:17,18). You indeed know where to begin the survey, for the favors of God to you began with your own life. Commemorate it therefore with a grateful heart, that the eyes which "saw your substance, being yet imperfect" beheld you with a friendly care "when you were made in secret" and have watched over you ever since—and that the hand which "drew the plan of your members when as yet there was none of them" (Psalm 139:15,16) not only fashioned them at first but from that time has been concerned in "keeping all your bones, so that none of them is broken" (Psalm 34:20); indeed, it is to this you owe your life.

Look back upon the path you have trod, from the day that God brought you out of the womb, and say whether you do not, as it were, see all the road thick set with the marks and memorials of the divine goodness. Recollect the places where you have lived, and the persons with whom you have most intimately conversed, and call to mind the mercies you have received in those places, and from those persons, as the instruments of God's divine care and goodness. Recollect the difficulties and dangers with which you have been surrounded, and reflect attentively on what God has done to defend you from them, or to carry you through them. Think how often there has been but a step between you and death, and how suddenly God has sometimes interposed to set you in safety, even before you apprehended your danger. Think of those chambers of illness in which you have been confined—and from whence, perhaps, you once thought you should go forth no more but said, with Hezekiah, in the cutting off of your days, "I shall go to the gates of the grave: I am deprived of the residue of my years" (Isaiah 38:10). God has, it may be, since that time, added many years to your life; and you know not how many are in reserve, or how much usefulness and happiness may attend each. Survey your circumstances in relative life: how many kind friends are surrounding you daily and studying how they may contribute to your comfort. Reflect on those remarkable circumstances of providence, which occasioned the knitting of some bonds of this kind, which, next to those which join your soul to God, you number among the happiest. And forget not in how many instances when these dear lives have been threatened, lives perhaps more palpably dear than your own, God has given them back from the borders of the grave, and so added new reasons for love, arising from that tender circumstance, to all your subsequent conversation with them. Nor forget in how gracious a manner He has supported some others in their last moments, and enabled them to leave behind a sweet odor of piety, which has embalmed their memories, revived you when ready to faint under the sorrows of the last separation and, on the whole, made even the recollection of their death delightful.

But it is more than time that I lead on your thoughts to the many spiritual mercies which God has bestowed upon you. Look back, as it were, to the "rock from whence you were hewn, and to the hole of the pit from whence you were digged" (Isaiah 1:1). Reflect seriously on the state wherein divine grace found you, under how much guilt, under how much pollution, in what danger, in what ruin! Think what was and O, think with yet deeper reflection, what would have been the case! The eye of God which penetrates into eternity saw what your mind, amused with the trifles of the present time and sensual gratification, was utterly ignorant and regardless of. It saw you on the borders of eternity, and pitied you. . . . This God saw, and He pitied you. And being merciful to you, He provided, in the counsel of his eternal love and grace, a Redeemer for you, and purchased you to Himself through the blood of his Son. This price, if you will pause and think seriously what it was, must surely affect you to such a degree as to make you to fall down before God in wonder and shame, to think it should ever have been given for you.

To accomplish these blessed purposes, He sent his grace into your heart, so that, though "you were once darkness, you are now light in the Lord" (Ephesians 5:8). He made that happy change which you now feel in your soul, and "by his Holy Spirit, which is given to you," He shed abroad that principle of love (Romans 5:5) which is enkindled by this remembrance, and now flames with greater ardor than before. Thus far He has supported you in your Christian course, and "having obtained help from Him" you continue even to this day. He has not only blessed you, but "made you a blessing" (Genesis 12:2) and though you have not been so useful as that holy generosity of heart which He has excited would have engaged you to desire, yet some good you have done in the station in which He has fixed you. Some of your brethren of mankind have been relieved, and perhaps some thoughtless creature reclaimed to virtue and happiness by his blessing on your endeavors. Some in the way to heaven are praising God for you; and some, perhaps, already there, are longing for your arrival that they may thank you . . . for benefits the importance of which they now sufficiently understand, though while here, they could never conceive it.

Christian, look around on the numberless blessings of one kind and another with which you are already encompassed, and advance your prospect still further to what faith yet discovers within the veil. Think of those now unknown transports with which you shall drop every burden in the grave, when your immortal spirit will mount light and joyful, holy and happy, to God, its origin, support, and hope; to God, the source of being, of holiness and of pleasure; to Jesus, through whom all these blessings are derived, and who will appoint to you a throne near to his own, to be forever a spectator and partaker of his glory. Think of the rapture with which you shall attend his triumph in the resurrection day, and receive this poor, moldering, corruptible body, transformed into his glorious image, and then think, "These hopes are not mine alone, but the hopes of thousands and millions. Multitudes whom I number among the dearest of my friends upon the earth are rejoicing with me in these things, and God gives me sometimes to see the smiles on their cheeks, the sweet, humble hope that sparkles in their eyes and shines through the tears of tender gratitude, and to hear that little of their inward fullness and joy which language cannot express. Yea, and multitudes more, who were once equally dear to me with these, though I have laid them in the grave, and wept over the dust, are living to God in the possession of inconceivable delights and drinking large draughts of the water of life which flows in perpetual streams at his right hand."

O Christian, you are still intimately united and allied to them! Death cannot break a friendship thus cemented, and it ought not to render you insensitive to the happiness of those friends for whose memory you retain so just an honor. They live to God as his servants; they "serve him and see his face" (Revelation 22:3,4) and they make but a small part of that glorious assembly. . . . And will you not adore that everlasting spring of holiness and happiness from whence each of their joys is derived? Yea, I will add, while the blessed angels are so kindly regarding us, while they are ministering to you, O Christian, and bearing you in their arms "as an heir of salvation" (Hebrews 1:14) will you not rejoice in their blessedness too? And will you not adore that God who gives them all the superior glory of their more exalted nature, and gives them a heaven, which fills them with blessedness even while they seem to withdraw from it that they may attend on you?

This, and infinitely more than this, the blessed God is, and was, and shall ever be. The happiness of the blessed spirits that surround his throne, and your happiness, O Christian, are immortal. These heavenly luminaries shall glow with an undecaying flame, and you shall shine and burn among them when the sun and the stars are gone out. Still shall the unchanging Father of lights pour forth his beams upon them; and the lustre they reflect from Him, and their happiness in Him, shall be everlasting, ever growing.

Bow down, O child of God, thou heir of glory; bow down, and let all that is within thee unite in one act of grateful love; and let all that is around thee, all that is before thee in the prospects of an unbounded eternity, concur to elevate and transport thy soul, that thou mayest, as far as possible, begin the work and blessedness of heaven, in falling down before the God of it, in opening your heart to his gracious influences, and in breathing out before Him that incense of praise which these warm beams of his presence and love have so great a tendency to produce, and to ennoble with a fragrance resembling that of his paradise above.

# Hymns

## Happy Day

Oh, happy day, that fixed my choice
   On thee, my Saviour and my God!
Well may this glowing heart rejoice,
   And tell its raptures all abroad.

Oh, happy bond, that seals my vows
   To him who merits all my love!
Let cheerful anthems fill his house,
   While to that sacred shrine I move.

'Tis done, the great transaction's done;
   I am my Lord's, and he is mine;
He drew me, and I followed on,
   Charmed to confess the voice divine.

Now rest, my long-divided heart!
   Fixed on this blissful centre, rest;
Oh, who with earth would grudge to part,
   When called with angels to be blest?

High Heaven, that heard the solemn vow,
   That vow renewed shall daily hear,
Till in life's latest hour I bow,
   And bless in death a bond so dear.

1755

# Hark, the Glad Sound!

Hark, the glad sound! the Saviour comes,—
  The Saviour promised long;
Let every heart prepare a throne,
  And every voice a song.

On him the Spirit, largely poured,
  Exerts his sacred fire;
Wisdom and might, and zeal and love
  His holy breast inspire.

He comes, the prisoners to release,
  In Satan's bondage held,
The gates of brass before him burst,
  The iron fetters yield.

He comes, from thickest films of vice,
  To clear the mental ray,
And on the eyeballs of the blind
  To pour celestial day.

He comes, the broken heart to bind,
  The bleeding soul to cure;
And with the treasures of his grace
  To enrich the humble poor.

His silver trumpets publish loud
  The Jubilee of the Lord;
Our debts are all remitted now,
  Our heritage restored.

Our glad hosannas, Prince of peace!
  Thy welcome shall proclaim,
And heaven's eternal arches ring
  With thy beloved name.

1735

# Lovest Thou Me? Feed My Lambs

JOHN 21:15

Do not I love thee, O my Lord?
  Behold my heart and see;
And turn each cursed idol out
  That dares to rival thee.

Do not I love thee from my soul?
  Then let me nothing love:
Dead be my heart to every joy,
  When Jesus cannot move.

Is not thy name melodious still
  To mine attentive ear?
Doth not each pulse with pleasure bound
  My Saviour's voice to hear?

Hast thou a lamb in all thy flock,
  I would disdain to feed?
Hast thou a foe, before whose face
  I fear thy cause to plead?

Would not my ardent spirit vie,
  With angels round the throne,
To execute thy sacred will,
  And make thy glory known?

Would not my heart pour forth its blood
  In honor of thy name?
And challenge the cold hand of death
  To damp the immortal flame?

Thou know'st I love thee, dearest Lord;
  But oh, I long to soar
Far from the sphere of mortal joys,
  And learn to love thee more!

# My God, and Is Thy Table Spread

LUKE 14:17

My God, and is thy table spread,
　And doth thy cup with love o'erflow?
Thither be all thy children led,
　And let them all thy sweetness know.

Hail, sacred feast, which Jesus makes,
　Rich banquet of his Flesh and Blood!
Thrice happy he who here partakes
　That sacred Stream, that heavenly Food.

Why are its bounties all in vain
　Before unwilling hearts displayed?
Was not for them the Victim slain?
　Are they forbid the children's bread?

O let thy table honoured be,
　And furnished well with joyful guests;
And may each soul salvation see
　That here its sacred pledges tastes. Amen.

# JOHN WESLEY
## 1703 · 1791

Engraving from the drawing by Henry Edridge, R. A. Wesley here would be in his sixties (c. 1770).

## INTRODUCTION

The life of John Wesley is among the best-known lives of Christian leaders in the English-speaking world. Yet it has also been among those most subject to a kind of "hagiographical" coloring, and a more candid review is desirable especially to set the context for an appreciation of his spirituality.

To begin with, John Wesley was a man of almost ferociously disciplined personality and character. Much of this he came by naturally. His father Samuel was an establishment Anglican clergyman of severe demeanor who once paraded an adulteress through the streets to shame her and who forced an unwanted (and disasterous) marriage upon one of his daughters when she tried to elope with a man not of his own choosing. He was a rigorous scholar, whose major project was a commentary on Job, and a strict disciplinarian of his congregation. His wife, Susannah, daughter of a notable Puritan family, was more than a match for him. Legendary for the rigid rules of order by which she governed the lives of her children through every conceivable hour and aspect of day and night and for her conviction that the path to right child-rearing was to "break their wills" by physical punishments (which would be doubled if they should cry audibly), she also could and did stand up to her husband on a number of issues. One of the most notable of these involved her refusal to join her husband in prayers for the Protestant King William of Orange, since she remained loyal to the exiled Catholic King James and his family—a dispute she carried to the point of temporary separation from her husband. She wielded an enormous influence over the lives of Charles and John long after their father's death, and it is no accident that the various forms of "methodist rules" from the Holy Club onwards derive from models really established by her.

To these imposing parents were born nineteen children in as many years, of whom nine survived to adulthood. John was their second surviving son, born at Epworth Rectory on June 17, 1703. His early education, like that of all his siblings, was at the hands of his mother. At ten years of age he was admitted to the Charterhouse School in London, though not without the imposition of an additional regimen prescribed from home, which included his father's insistence that he should run at top speed three times around the Charterhouse each morning for his "constitution." Away from home, John displayed an early instinct for imperious behavior, and was reprimanded for haranguing the younger students instead of keeping company with those his own age. (His recorded reply to his monitor was "Better to rule in hell than serve in heaven.") But he also did well academically in all his subjects, including the study of Hebrew, and went up to Oxford at sixteen years of age.

Wesley was a bright and diligent student, always short of money to pay his tuition, but undeterred in his study. When he took the B.A. degree four years later, his father pressed him to become a clergyman; his mother agreed with this directive and John complied, beginning studies in divinity in 1720. In this, his earliest influences were spiritual writers rather than theologians. He read Thomas à Kempis, Jeremy Taylor, Blaise Pascal, Don Juan d'Avila, the hermit Gregory Lopez, Miguel de Molinos, François Fenelon, and Jean-Baptiste de Renty. He then turned to the early fathers of the church, among them Ignatius of Antioch, Polycarp, Clement of Rome, and "Macarius the Egyptian," a fourth-century writer whose work owed principally to the great patriarch of Greek orthodoxy, Gregory of Nyssa. In this way, Wesley acquired a strong strain of Catholic asceticism to amplify some of the convictions of his parents, and additional models to fortify the developing *religio* (Latin "order") of his personal life. But in all of these pursuits he was also being drawn, he observed, to writers who inculcated a "religion of the heart."

In September 1725 he was ordained deacon by the bishop of Oxford and preached his first sermon at a nearby village within the month. Yet there was soon another pull on his time and talents. In recognition of his academic achievement, as well as his exemplary behavior, Wesley was elected Fellow of Lincoln College in Oxford in March 1726. This would mean teaching duties in the university and, in due course, the life of an Oxford don. Because such responsibilities did not then conflict with clerical status, and perhaps because he viewed the appointment as temporary, and an honor, his father at first approved. John began lecturing in Greek and took the M.A. in 1727. But by August of that year, he had taken leave to obey his father's request that he come home and act as his assistant (curate) in the Epworth parish. John traveled frequently back to Oxford and was ordained priest there the following year.

About this time, he read William Law's *Christian Perfection* and *Serious Call*, which both clarified still formulating aspects of his own spirituality and provided a higher standard for practical Christian life. He went to visit Law at Putney (the Gibbon estate) and was introduced by him to further mystical writings—mostly of the fourteenth through sixteenth centuries. Although Wesley later broke with Law on the matter of the individual or "solitary" religion endorsed by Law and some of the writers he championed, his idea of Christian perfection derives directly from his spiritual readings of this period.[1]

When the autumn term of 1729 arrived, Wesley failed to appear on campus to meet his students. A letter was sent to him in late October by the university rector, reminding him of the statutory obligations of his fellowship. He returned in late November to take up his duties, and soon discovered the Holy Club, as his brother Charles and two other undergraduates called it, whose members were already tagged as "methodists" for their diligence in academic study and religious observance. John joined, and at once took over leadership. While this was always a small group, it came to include such significant figures as Benjamin Ingham, Thomas Broughton, John Clayton, James Hervey, and later (1735) George Whitefield. In addition to providing mutual reinforcement and fellowship for its own members, the Holy Club ministered to the poor, providing clothing and sometimes education for destitute children. The group also initiated a prison ministry, visiting prisoners in the castle daily, offering morning and evening prayer there three days a week, preaching on Sundays, and administering communion to the inmates once a month.

In this manner Wesley continued at Oxford for five years—teaching, conducting the affairs of the "methodists," and pursuing his own precise and ascetic lifestyle.[2] On June 11, 1734, he preached a sermon before the university, having first obtained permission from the vice-chancellor because of what Charles called its "Jacobite" or Catholic character. All during this period Wesley senior kept urging John home, without success, until when his father was on his death-bed John appears to have been moved to respond. Shortly after the funeral, however, his plans changed, and by September he was ready to leave, with his mother's blessing, for Georgia. Along with the American governor James Oglethorpe, his brother Charles, Benjamin Ingham, Charles Delamotte, and (by coincidence) a group of Moravians, he embarked in December 1735. Wesley spent much of the trip learning German and speaking to the Moravians.

The Georgian venture proved something of a fiasco. Wesley's attempt to minister to the priestless colonists was rejected for its excesses of pastoral intervention in private lives, for Wesley's insistence on primitive Catholic observances, and for the enforcement of certain elements of his own ascetic lifestyle (for example, morning service at 5 A.M.). He also had an abortive romantic attachment to a woman who eventually (apparently in frustration over John's indecisiveness) became engaged to someone else; he behaved so badly after this rejection that he was sued for defamation of character, and then, to make matters worse, he fled a magistrate's restraining order before the sentencing, leaving his friend Delamotte to face the indelicate music when his riddance was discovered.

It was back in England, in February 1738, that John met the Moravian Peter Böhler and attended the Fetter Lane Chapel, from which conversation and experience began to grow his understanding of "saving faith." It is in this context that the famous Aldersgate experience came. On an evening in late May, he attended evening prayer at St. Paul's and was powerfully moved by the singing of the anthem, "Out of the deep have I called unto Thee, O Lord." Later, he went, rather unwillingly, to a small society meeting on Aldersgate Street, where, hearing a reading of Luther's preface to his commentary on Romans, Wesley felt his heart "strangely warmed" and was at once moved to pray for his enemies. Though it is clear that this experience was but part of a process begun much earlier, May 24, 1738, was clearly an important turning point in Wesley's spiritual life, and it was from this time forward that he felt prompted to preach salvation by faith.[3]

Looking now for a focus for his desire to work out the gospel, he traveled to the Moravian communities in Germany, typically finding there much to disapprove. After a session in Marienborn, during which time he was apparently asked to dig Count Zinzendorf's garden, he returned to Oxford, peremptorily drew up an unasked for set of rules for the Moravian societies in England, and almost as suddenly prepared to go in a different direction himself.

George Whitefield, following the example of Howell Harris and others, had begun the practice of open-air preaching in the west country, and Whitefield now pressed Wesley toward the same effort. Although he at first found the idea distasteful, he was finally prevailed upon. Reflecting on Christ's own example in the Sermon on the Mount, John went to the outskirts of Bristol (where presumably Whitefield had gathered a crowd), stood on a little height of ground and spoke to what he reckoned were "about three thousand people." His itinerant evangelical work had begun, and he was never to look back.

In 1739, Wesley bought a derilect foundry in London for preaching purposes in what became Tabernacle Street, Finsbury Square, and began his organization of Methodist "societies" or study groups. His preaching there and elsewhere in the next year was marked by charismatic manifestations, what were then sometimes called "convulsive" phenomena (see the letter to his brother, Samuel, below). Wesley's theology—and spirituality—were more and more characterized by an emphasis on free grace, and his dissociation from Calvinism in this respect precipitated a split with Whitefield. This led to there being "two sorts of Methodists," and notwithstanding that Wesley and Whitefield were personally reconciled in 1742 and held joint services in 1749–50, the division continued to characterize different developments in the movement well into the next century. Wesley's own position had in part to do with his greater emphasis on lay preaching and lay societies. No one recruited anything like so many men into the preaching of the gospel; he inspired others with his vision. Yet it is an irony that many of Wesley's first lay preachers went over to the Calvinist side, and in what is undoubtedly a reflection on the difficulty he had working with men, almost all the others eventually went their own way as well, from Ingham and Maxfield even to his own loyal brother Charles. It was evident from the beginning that the intense and domineering personality of this disciplined little man, as effective an instrument for evangelism and organization as it was to prove, would bear no rivals near the throne. Wesley was a man of unyielding will and forcefulness, and though he characterized his followers as people not to be distinguished for external conformities but for their attitude of heart (see *The Character of a Methodist,* following), he also told them in plain terms what to wear, how to wash and keep their hair, when to rise, how often to eat, what to read, and what, more or less, to think. He allowed himself to be called "the bishop or overseer of all congregations gathered by him as a preacher of the Gospel,"⁴ and by the institution of general conferences both consolidated his movement and maintained personal direction over it.

Wesley's preaching travels from 1739 to the end of his life are a truly prodigious accomplishment. In a time when there was no rail service and when except for a few moderately well-graded coach roads the rest of England's "roads" were little but muddy tracks and mangled ruts, he rode between four and five thousand miles a year on horseback to conduct his preaching missions and visit his societies. Altogether in his lifetime it is estimated that he traveled (by horseback and, later in life, in a small carriage, or "pillion") about 250,000 miles, almost entirely in England, Scotland, and Ireland. Much of the travel was in cold rain, mud, and slush such as would turn many a would-be successor home to the fire. His influence in Ireland and Scotland was very great (he crossed the Irish Sea forty-two times after 1747), and he was several times to the Isle of Man. In all of this, the diminutive (five feet two inches) and fiery-eyed giant among men was gifted with extraordinary health. His vigor he attributed to rising at four, preaching at five, a disciplined disposition of the daytime hours, preaching again in late afternoon and evening, and where possible, eating only one meal a day. In 1742 he gave up tea, though he retained a keen fondness for cider all his life and was happy to make moderate use of wine. At the age of seventy-seven he was recommending fasting on Fridays as a therapy for "nervous disorders." It was only the next year, in 1789, that he contracted the diabetes which hastened his demise.

One is compelled to confess that many of Wesley's sermons are likely to have sounded better than they now read. It is another of the paradoxical qualities of this extraordinary person that he who preached disciplines of the mind as much as of the heart and body has left us with sermon texts that often seem to lack clarity of logic or coherence in their organization. There is, moreover, surprisingly little in the way of pastoral guidance in his voluminous correspondence that has enduring spiritual value; most of the letters are taken up with directives for organization of the societies, the pursuit of theological disputes, or "correcting" opinions. Yet some of the eight volumes of his extant letters, and part of his extensive journals, do offer us valuable insight into his intense and heartfelt convictions and dedication. They also confirm, among other things, that he was at least as much an administrator, organizer, educator, and social reformer as he was an evangelist in the usual sense. He was keenly interested in providing a higher quality of education for Christian lay leadership than could have been imagined for people of the classes in which he found most of his candidates. And whoever followed his direction and mastered the fifty volumes of his translation and edition of classics in the *Christian Library* series (a fair representation of his own formative reading) would certainly acquire a better education in many respects than most ordinands get today.

By 1763, Wesley was desperate to obtain ordination for some of his lay preachers and when bishop after bishop refused, he took the dubious expedient—against the counsel of all his close friends and associates—of asking one Erasmus, who claimed to be bishop of Arcadia in Crete, to do the job. Erasmus knew no English, but agreed. This proved only a stopgap measure, however, and eventually Wesley felt driven to perform ordinations himself; from 1785 through 1789 several Methodist missionaries were "set apart" for ministry in North America and Scotland. These actions constituted the formal break of Wesley's United Societies from the Church of England. They also culminated a drift which had long been basic to the disaffection of Charles and others, who felt their call was to a revitalization of the Established Church.

Wesley's notorious mismanagement of his relationships with women is well treated in various biographies[5] and is not central to our purposes here, except to say that though he was powerfully attracted to women, and they to him, he seems to have been extremely unsuited to marriage. Those close to him, perhaps especially Charles, knew that better than he did, and it was in hiding from them that he contracted his unwise and fateful marriage with the widow of a merchant, Molly Vazeille, in 1751. They separated after a little more than four years, and while her neurotic jealousy and physical abuse of John are often cited as reasons for the dissolution, it must in fairness be added that Wesley's asceticism, his disciplinary rigidity, his almost despotic desire for control, his exhausting itinerary and continuous absences could hardly add up to a responsible commitment on his part to the "vocation," as Fletcher was to call it, of marriage. Mrs. Wesley died in 1781.

Wesley's last years were spent in a much improved state of general reputation and honor. Some of this was won at the political level, by his eventual siding with the Crown against the American Revolution; his published opinions on the matter were warmly greeted by both government officials and men of letters like Samuel Johnson.[6] His many writings were by now in wide circulation. He had, in fact, collected his own *Works* and republished them in Bristol in thirty-two volumes (1771–74).[7] Among these writings were books on household science, electricity, an English dictionary which, *pace* Johnson, he had not hesitated to call "the best in the world," and a treatise on home remedies which had gone through thirty-six editions by 1840. Not all of this diverse work, as may be expected, is equally valuable. Even in the matter of the education of children, for example, where he suggested children be allowed "neither to play or cry," it is well that others such as Hannah More were to supplant his ideas. Yet the achievement of John Wesley even in the volume of his words alone remains remarkable in the extreme, and upon those 120,000 followers in Britain and America by the end of the century, and many millions since, a large proportion of his written work has had an enduring influence.

In a frivolous age—an age of licentiousness and madness more than of reason, of rampant insincerity and hypocrisy in the church—Wesley and his followers in the evangelical movement at large had in fact effected a virtual cultural revolution. The tremendous work of prison reform, begun back in Oxford in the first days of the Holy Club, and the parallel work of ameliorating the conditions in mental institutions and hospitals constitute by themselves one of the greatest practical witnesses to the gospel that has ever been known, and countless thousands have been benefited by the mercy of God which flowed from these efforts. In little coal mining communities, mill towns, and seaports all across the British Isles, people of the poorer classes were given both eternal and temporal benefits of the gospel, acquiring with their conversion, Christian education, and spiritual fellowship a new and immeasurably enhanced sense of human dignity. The image of God was being restored in the downtrodden and oppressed, the fatherless and widows were being comforted, and prisoners and the sick visited with kindness on an unprecedented scale. Wesley's own abiding contribution had been to encourage a submission to the most rigid demands of the gospel in order that the gospel might be seen to be spoken in life, not merely in a show of words, and the fruits of his witness made a rich harvest all over the British Isles. By the end of this period the effects had been felt everywhere, and, as Canon Overton has put it, a substantial body of the populace thought "that to be *serious* and to be *Evangelical* were only different ways of saying the same thing."[8]

Late in February 1791 the weight of years, of 45,000 sermons preached, 230 works written, and the countless efforts of shepherding so large and unwieldy a "congregation" began to take their inevitable toll. Wesley's last sermon was preached on February 23, and he retired home exhausted and in a fever. His last letter—to young William Wilberforce, enthusiastically encouraging him in his efforts to abolish the slave trade—was written on the 24th. His friends were summoned to his bedside two or three days later. The evening before his death he came out of a coma to sing "I'll praise my Maker while I've breath," and to say to all those about the bed, "the best of all is—God is with us!" The next morning he opened his eyes about ten o'clock and, looking at each of the persons round his bed, whispered "Farewell!" Instinctively all fell on their knees, and as Joseph Bradford led in prayer, the ardent emperor of the evangelical revival died peacefully. When the prayer was finished, the assembled group broke into an anthem of praise.[9] According to his instructions his body was laid out in the cheapest wool, the last few pounds he had in his pockets were divided among four poor itinerant preachers; no funeral hearse was hired, but six unemployed laborers were given a pound each to carry his body to the grave. After several days of lying in state at the City Road Chapel, where thousands of mourners filed by to pay their respects, he was buried secretly before dawn on March 9 in a vault at the rear of Methodism's most historic monument. His life had nearly spanned the century, and the transformation of grace which he experienced in his own heart had entered into the very fabric of English identity, creating a spiritual inheritance for many which no one could have imagined would arise from the moral wasteland of that time.[10]

NOTES

1. Cf. *The Letters of the Rev. John Wesley, A.M.*, ed. John Telford (London: Epworth Press, 1931; rpt. 1960), vol. 5, pp. 313, 342. He also wrote a stiff letter to Law, rebuking his quietism, to which Law declined to reply. His own *Plain Account of Christian Perfection* (2nd ed., 1766), like his sermons on the subject, are heavily indebted to Law, though lacking the earlier writer's coherence.

2. The rules of the Oxford Methodists are a reasonable indication of this lifestyle; see below.

3. This is evident not only from his letters but also from his sermons. For example, his Oxford sermon of January 1, 1783, "The Circumcision of the Heart," differs little in content or emphasis from his subsequent preaching. Except in one journal entry, Wesley himself does not stress the Aldersgate experience, and in his *Short History of the*

*People Called Methodists* and *Plain Account of Christian Perfection,* both of which are a form of spiritual autobiography, he traces his spiritual development in steps which led from Oxford to Georgia, then straight to Germany with the Moravians. In his collection entitled *John Wesley* (New York: Oxford University Press, 1964), the leading Methodist historian Albert Outler places the conversion in the period between 1725 and 1728, during the time of his intensive reading of spiritual writers in preparation for ministry (p. 7).

4. From the Bristol Conference Minutes of 1745 (Bristol, 1862), vol 1, pp. 26–27.

5. See, for example, Marjorie Bowen, *Wrestling Jacob: A Study of John Wesley and Some Members of his Family* (London: Religious Book Club, 1938), which, although biased against Wesley, offers useful material of a sort often (understandably) entirely passed over by others such as Leslie Church, *Knight of the Burning Heart* (London: Epworth Press, 1938).

6. The relevant tracts are the "Calm Address to the Inhabitants of England" (1777) and "A Serious Address" (1778); Johnson himself had written a "Calm Address to our American Colonies" (1775) on the same subject.

7. This, of course, excludes his editions and translations in fifty volumes and his many collaborations with Charles and others.

8. J. H. Overton, *Evangelical Revival in the Eighteenth Century* (London: Longmans, Green, 1886), p. 160.

9. J. Wesley Bready, *England Before and After Wesley* (London: Hodder and Stoughton, 1938), gives a fine and moving account of Wesley's last days.

10. The earliest full biography of Wesley, by John Hampson (1791), was not well received by the Methodist societies. Whitehead's *Life* appeared in the same year, followed by a biography by Thomas Coke and Henry Moore in 1792, which had been authorized and issued by the conference as the "official" version of his life. Methodist historians and biographers have been somewhat discomforted with an embarrassingly conspicuous lack of eulogy for Wesley shortly after his death. In one of the earliest responses to news of his passing (1791) the Methodist preacher Samuel Bradburn apologizes for this and offers his own "short account" as "better than none." He then goes on to measure the real extent of Wesley's loss to the movement from the point of view of the preachers and societies themselves:

> The chief point in which the death of Mr. Wesley will affect the Methodist connexion is, the preachers thereby lose their "centre of union." They considered themselves as his sons in the Gospel; and to his direction they freely submitted. But they owe no such submission to any other man. It is therefore impossible that there should ever be another king in our Israel.

See *Select Letters Chiefly on Personal Religion by the Rev. John Wesley, A.M., with a sketch of his character by the Rev. Samuel Bradburn* (London: John Mason, 1837), p. xxvii.

Thomas C. Oden has recently prepared an anthology of some of John Wesley's best discourses in modernized English, *The New Birth* (San Francisco: Harper & Row, 1984). While it came to my attention too late to be used in the preparation of this volume, readers wanting to pursue Wesley further in an accessible version will find Oden's book invaluable.

# from the Sermons

## The Scripture Way of Salvation (1765)

"Ye are saved through faith" (Ephesians 2:8)

NOTHING CAN BE more intricate, complex and hard to understand than "religion" as it has been often described. And this is not only true concerning the religion of the heathens (even many of the wisest of them), but concerning the religion of those also who have been in some sense, Christians—yes, people of great renown in the Christian world, those who seemed to be "pillars" of the faith. Yet how easy to understand, how plain and simple a thing is the genuine faith of Jesus Christ, provided only that we take it in its original form, just as it is described in the oracles of God! It is exactly suited by the wise Creator and Governor of the world to the weak understanding and narrow capacity of mankind in our present state. How obvious this is, both with regard to the end it proposes and the means to attain that end. The end is, in one word, "salvation" and the means to attain it, "faith."

It is easily discerned that these two little words—"faith" and "salvation"—include the substance of all the Bible, the marrow, as it were, of the whole Scripture. So much the more should we take all possible care to avoid all mistake concerning them and to form a true and accurate understanding concerning both. Let us then seriously inquire: (I) What is salvation?; (II) What is that faith whereby we are saved? and (III) How are we saved by it?

## I. The Nature of Salvation

First then, "what is salvation?"

The salvation which is here spoken of is not what is frequently understood by that word—going to heaven, to eternal happiness. It is not the soul's going to paradise (which our Lord termed "Abraham's bosom"). It is not a blessing which lies on the other side of death or (as we usually say) "in the other world." The very words of the text itself put this beyond all question: "Ye *are* saved." It is not something at a distance. It is a present thing, a blessing which through the free mercy of God you are now in possession of. Nay, the words may be rendered with equal propriety: "Ye *have been* saved." So the salvation which is here spoken of might be extended to the entire work of God, from the first dawning of grace in the soul until it is consummated in glory.

If we take this in its fullest extent, it will include all that is wrought in the soul by what is frequently termed "natural conscience," but more properly called "preventing grace."* This means all the "drawings of the Father," the desires after God which, if we yield to them, increase more and more: all that "light" wherewith the Son of God "enlighteneth every one that cometh into the world," showing them to "do justly, love mercy, and walk humbly with his God"; all the "convictions" which his Spirit from time to time, works in every child of man (although, it is true, most people stifle them as soon as possible, and after a while forget or at least deny that ever they had them at all). But we are at present concerned only with that "salvation" which the apostle is directly speaking of. And this consists of two general parts: justification and sanctification.

## 1. Justification

Justification is another word for pardon. It is the forgiveness of all our sins and, what is necessarily implied by this, our acceptance with God. The price by which this has been procured for us (commonly termed the "meritorious cause" of our justification) is the blood and righteousness of Christ, or, to express it a little more clearly, all that Christ has done and suffered for us, until he "poured out his soul for the transgressors." The immediate effects of justification are the *peace* of God, a "peace that passeth all understanding," and a "rejoicing in *hope* of the glory of God" "with *joy* unspeakable and full of glory" (Philippians 4:7; Romans 5:2; 1 Peter 1:8).

## 2. Sanctification

And at the same time that we are justified—yea, in that very moment—sanctification begins. In that instant we are "born again, born from above, born of the Spirit." There is a real as well as a relative change. We are inwardly renewed by the power of God. We feel "the love of God shed abroad in our heart by the Holy Spirit which is given unto us," producing love to all mankind, and more especially to the children of God, expelling the love of the world, the love of pleasure, of ease, of honor, of money, together with pride, anger, self-will and every other evil disposition. In a word, our "earthly, sensual, devilish mind" is changed into "the mind which was in Christ Jesus" (Philippians 2:5).

How naturally do those who experience such a change imagine that all

*Cf. "On Working Out Our Own Salvation," in *Works of the Rev. John Wesley, A.M.*, ed. Thomas Jackson (London, 1829–31), vol. 6, pp. 511–12.

sin is gone, that it is utterly rooted out of their heart and has no longer any place there! How easily do they draw that inference, "I *feel* no sin; therefore I *have* none. It does not *stir*; therefore, it does not *exist*. It has no *motion*; therefore, it has no *being!* But it is seldom long before they are undeceived, finding sin was only suspended, not destroyed. Temptations return and sin revives, showing it was but stunned before, not dead. Such persons now feel two principles in themselves, plainly contrary to each other, "the flesh lusting against the Spirit" (Galatians 5:17), nature opposing the grace of God. They cannot deny that although they still feel power to believe in Christ and love God, and although his Spirit still "witnesses with their spirits that they are children of God," yet they feel in themselves sometimes pride or self-will, sometimes anger or unbelief. They find one or more of these frequently stirring in their heart, though not conquering, perhaps even "thrusting sore at them that they may fall" but "the Lord is their help."

How exactly did Macarius,* fourteen hundred years ago, describe the present experience of the children of God: ". . . The inexperienced, when . . . grace operates, presently imagine they have no more sin, whereas those who have discretion cannot deny that even we who have the grace of God may be molested again. . . . For we have often had instances of some among the brethren who have experienced such . . . grace as to affirm that . . . they had no sin in them, and yet, after all, when they thought themselves entirely freed . . . from it, the corruption that lurked within was stirred up anew and they were well nigh burnt up."**

From the time of our being "born again," the gradual work of sanctification takes place. We are enabled by the Spirit to "mortify the deeds of the body" (Romans 8:11,13) and of our evil nature, and as we are more and more dead to sin, we are more and more alive to God. We go on from grace to grace, while we are careful to "abstain from all appearance of evil" (1 Thessalonians 5:22) and are "zealous of good works (Titus 2:4) as we have opportunity, doing good to all men while we walk "in all his ordinances blameless, therein worshipping him in spirit and in truth" while we take up our cross and deny ourselves every pleasure that does not lead us to God.

It is thus that we wait for *entire* sanctification, for a *full* salvation from all our sins—from pride, self-will, anger, unbelief—or, as the apostle

---

*"Macarius the Egyptian" has proved actually to be a fifth-century Syrian monk whose spirituality was heavily influenced by St. Gregory of Nyssa.

**From Wesley's abridgement of *The Homilies of Macarius,* in his *Christian Library* (Bristol, 1749–55), vol. 1, p. 97. The ellipses are Wesley's.

expresses it, "go on unto perfection" (Hebrews 6:1). But what is "perfection"? The word has various senses: here it means perfect love. It is love excluding sin, love filling the heart, taking up the whole capacity of the soul. It is love "rejoicing ever more, praying without ceasing, in everything giving thanks."

## II.  *The Character of Faith*

But what is that "faith" through which "we are saved"? This is the second point to be considered.

Faith, in general, is defined by the apostle as ἔλεγχος πραγμάτων οὐ βλεπομένων, "an evidence," a divine "evidence and conviction" (the word means both) "of things not seen"* (not visible, not perceivable either by sight or by any other of the external senses). It implies both a supernatural evidence of God and of the things of God—a kind of spiritual "light" exhibited to the soul—and a supernatural "sight" or perception of it. Accordingly, the Scripture speaks of God's giving sometimes light, and sometimes the power of discerning it. Consider St. Paul: "God, who commanded light to shine out of darkness, hath shined in our hearts to give us the light of the knowledge of the glory of God in the face of Jesus Christ" (2 Corinthians 4:6). And elsewhere he speaks of "the eyes of our understanding being opened" (Ephesians 1:18). By this twofold operation of the Holy Spirit, having the eyes of our souls *opened* and *enlightened,* we see the things which the natural "eye hath not seen, neither the ear heard." We have a prospect of the invisible things of God; we see the "spiritual world" which is all round us and yet no more discerned by our natural faculties than if it had no existence. And we see the "eternal world," piercing through the veil which hangs between time and eternity. Clouds and darkness then rest upon it no more, but we already see the glory which shall be revealed.

Taking the word in a more particular sense, faith is a divine evidence and conviction not only that "God was in Christ, reconciling the world unto himself" (2 Corinthians 5:19), but also that "Christ loved *me* and gave himself for *me*." It is by this faith (whether we term it the "essence" or a "property" of it) that we "receive" Christ, that we receive him in all his offices as our prophet, priest and king. It is by this that he is "made . . . unto us wisdom, and righteousness, and sanctification, and redemption" (1 Corinthians 1:30).

But is this the "faith of assurance" or the "faith of adherence," you

---

*Wesley is quoting the Greek text (Hebrews 11:1) from memory and amplifying it, perhaps from the commentary of St. John Chrysostom; all standard texts read πραγμάτων ἔλεγχος.

might ask. The Scripture mentions no such distinction. The apostle says, "There is one faith and one hope of our calling"—one Christian, saving faith—just as there is "one Lord" in whom we believe and "one God and Father of us all." And it is certain that this faith necessarily implies an "assurance" (which is here only another word for "evidence," it being hard to tell the difference between them) that "Christ loved *me,* and gave himself for *me.*" For "he that believeth" with the true living faith "hath the witness in himself" (1 John 5:10). "The Spirit witnesseth with his spirit that he is a child of God." "Because he is a son, God hath sent forth the Spirit of his Son into his heart, crying, Abba, Father," giving him an assurance that he is so and a childlike confidence in Him. But let it be observed that, in the very nature of the thing, the assurance goes before the confidence. For a person cannot have a childlike confidence in God until he knows he is a child of God. Therefore, confidence, trust, reliance, adherence, or whatever else it be called is not the first (as some have supposed) but the second branch or act of faith.

## III. *Salvation "by Faith"*

It is by *this* faith that we are saved, justified and sanctified, taking that word in its highest sense. But how are we justified and sanctified by faith? This is the third part of our study. And since it is the main point in question, and a point of no ordinary importance, it will not be improper to give it a more distinct and particular consideration.

### 1. The only condition of justification

Firstly, then, how are we "justified by faith"? In what sense is this to be understood? I answer that faith is the *condition,* and the *only* condition, of justification.

It is the *condition:* none is justified except he that believes, and without faith, no one is justified. And it is the *only* condition: this alone is sufficient for justification. Everyone who believes is justified, whatever else he has or has not. In other words, no one is justified until he believes; everyone, when he believes, is justified.

But does not God command us to repent also, yes, and to "bring forth fruits meet for repentance," to cease, for instance, from doing evil, and learn to do well? And are not both of these of the utmost necessity, insomuch that if we willingly neglect either, we cannot reasonably expect to be justified at all? And if this be so, how can it be said that faith is the *only condition* of justification?

God does undoubtedly command us both to repent and to bring forth fruits meet for repentance, which if we willingly neglect, we cannot reasonably expect to be justified at all. Therefore, both repentance and fruits meet for repentance are, in some sense, necessary to justification. But they are *not* necessary in the *same sense* with faith, nor in the same *degree*. Not in the same *degree,* for those fruits are only necessary *conditionally* if there be time and opportunity for them. If time and opportunity are not present, a person may be justified without fruits, as was the thief upon the cross. But he cannot be justified without faith. That is impossible. Likewise, let a person have ever so much repentance, or ever so many of the "fruits meet for repentance," yet all of this does not [of itself] at all avail. One is not justified until he believes. But the moment he believes, with or without those fruits, yes, with more or less repentance, he is justified. . . . Repentance and its fruits are only *remotely* necessary—necessary as a consequence of faith—whereas faith is *immediately* and *directly* necessary to justification.

It remains that faith is the only condition which is *immediately* and *proximately* necessary to justification.

2. The only condition of sanctification

"But do you believe we are *sanctified* by faith? We know you believe that we are justified by faith, but do you not believe and accordingly teach that we are sanctified by our works?"

So it has been roundly and vehemently affirmed for these five-and-twenty years. But I have constantly declared just the contrary, and that in all manner of ways. I have continually testified in private and in public that we are sanctified as well as justified by faith. And, indeed, each of these great truths well illustrates the other. Exactly as we are justified by faith, so are we sanctified by faith. Faith is the *condition,* and the *only* condition, of sanctification, exactly as it is of justification. Is is the *condition*: none is sanctified but he that believes; without faith no one is sanctified. And it is the *only* condition: this alone is sufficient for sanctification. Everyone that believes is sanctified, whatever else he has or has not. In other words, no one is sanctified until he believes; everyone, when he believes, is sanctified.

"But is there not a repentance consequent upon, as well as a repentance previous to, justification? And is it not incumbent on all who are justified to be 'zealous of good words'? Yea, are not these so necessary that if a person willingly neglects them he cannot reasonably expect that he shall ever be sanctified in the full sense, that is, 'perfected in love'? Can he grow at all in grace, in the loving knowledge of our Lord Jesus Christ? Can he retain the grace which God has already given him? Can he continue in the faith which he has received, or in the favor of God? Do you not yourself allow all this, and continually assert it? But, if this be so, how can it be said that faith is the *only condition* of sanctification?"

I do allow all this and continually maintain it as the truth of God. I allow there is a repentance consequent upon, as well as a repentance previous to, justification. It is incumbent on all who are justified to be zealous of good works. And these are so necessary that if a person willingly neglect them, he cannot reasonably expect that he shall ever be sanctified. He cannot "grow in grace," in the image of God, [in] the mind which was in Christ Jesus. Indeed, he cannot retain the grace he has received; he cannot continue in faith or in the favor of God.

What is the inference we must draw from this? Why, that both repentance, rightly understood, and the practice of all good works—works of piety as well as works of mercy (now properly so-called, since they spring from faith)—are, in *some sense,* necessary to sanctification. I say "repentance rightly understood" for this must not be confounded with the former repentance. The repentance consequent upon justification is very ✓ different from that which is antecedent to it. It [does not proceed from] guilt, or a sense of condemnation, or a consciousness of the wrath of God. It does not suppose any doubt of the favor of God, or any "fear that hath torment." It is properly a *conviction,* wrought by the Holy Spirit, of the ✓ sin which still "remains" in our heart, of the φρόνημα σαρχος, "the carnal mind," which does still *remain* "even in them that are regenerate," although it does not, any longer, *reign.* It does not now have dominion over them. It is a conviction of our tendency to evil, of an heart bent to backsliding, of the still continuing tendency of the flesh to lust against the spirit. Sometimes, unless we continually watch and pray, it lusts to pride, sometimes to anger, sometimes to love of the world, love of ease, love of honor, or love of pleasure more than of God. It is a conviction of the tendency of our heart to self-will, to atheism or idolatry and, above all, to unbelief, whereby, in a thousand ways and under a thousand pretences, we are ever "departing," more or less, "from the living God."

With this conviction of the sin remaining in our hearts, there is joined a clear conviction of the sin remaining in our lives, still cleaving to all our words and actions. In the best of these we now discern a mixture of evil, either in the spirit, the matter, or the manner of them, something that could not endure the righteous judgement of God, were He "extreme to mark what is done amiss." Where we least suspected it, we find a taint of pride or self-will, of unbelief or idolatry, so that we are now more ashamed of our best duties than formerly of our worst sins. And hence we cannot but feel that these are so far from having anything meritorious in them, indeed, so far from being able to stand in the sight of the divine justice, that for those also we should be guilty before God were it not for the blood of the covenant.

Experience shows that—together with this conviction of sin *remaining* in our hearts, and *cleaving* to all our words and actions, as well as the guilt which on account of them we should incur were we not continually sprinkled with the atoning blood—one thing more is implied in this repentance: namely, a conviction of our helplessness, of our utter inability to think one good thought or to form one good desire and, much more, to speak one word aright, or to perform one good action, except through his free, almighty grace, first going before us and then accompanying us every moment.

"But what good works are those, the practice of which you affirm to be necessary to sanctification?" First, all works of piety such as public prayer, family prayer, and "praying in our closet," receiving the Lord's Supper, searching the Scriptures by hearing, reading, meditating, and using such a measure of fasting or abstinence as our bodily health allows. Secondly, all works of mercy, whether they are related to the bodies or souls of persons, such as feeding the hungry, clothing the naked, entertaining the stranger, visiting those that are in prison or sick or variously afflicted, endeavoring to instruct the ignorant, to awaken the stupid sinner, to quicken the lukewarm, to confirm the wavering, to comfort the feeble-minded, to succour the tempted, or contribute in any manner to the salvation of souls from death. This is the repentance and these the fruits meet for repentance which are necessary to full sanctification. This is the way wherein God has appointed his children to "wait" for complete salvation.

In this context we can see the extreme mischievousness of that seemingly innocent opinion that there is no sin in a believer, that all sin is destroyed, root and branch, the moment a person is justified. By totally preventing [the life of] repentance, it quite blocks up the way to sanctification. There is no place for repentance in one who believes that there is no sin either in his life or heart. Consequently, there is no place for his being "perfected in love," to which that repentance is indispensably necessary.

It may therefore likewise appear that there is no possible danger in expecting full salvation in this way. For suppose we were mistaken, suppose no such blessing ever was or can be attained, yet we lose nothing. Nay, that very expectation quickens us in using all the talents which God has given us, yes, in improving them all, so that when our Lord comes, he will receive his own "with increase."

But to return. Though it be allowed that both this repentance and its fruits are necessary to full salvation, yet they are not necessary either in the same *sense* as faith, or in the same *degree*. Not in the same degree, for these fruits are only necessary *conditionally,* if there be time and opportunity for them. A person may be sanctified without them. But he cannot be sanctified without faith. Likewise, let a man have ever so much of this repentance, or ever so many good works, yet all this does not [of itself] at all avail. He is not sanctified until he believes. But the moment he believes, with or without those fruits—yes, with more or less of this repentance—he is sanctified. . . . For this repentance and these fruits are only *remotely* necessary—necessary as a means to the continuance of his faith, as well as the increase of it—whereas faith is *immediately* and *directly* necessary to sanctification. It remains, that faith is the only condition which is *immediately* and *proximately* necessary to sanctification.

## IV. *The Experience of Faith*

"But what is that faith whereby we are sanctified, saved from sin, and perfected in love?" It is a divine evidence and conviction, first, that God *has promised* it in the Holy Scripture. Until we are thoroughly satisfied about this, there is no moving one step further. And one would imagine there needed not one word more to satisfy a reasonable person of this than the ancient promise, "Then will I circumcise thy heart, and the heart of thy seed, to love the Lord thy God with all thy heart, and with all thy soul" (Deuteronomy 30:6). How clearly do these words express being perfected in love, how strongly do they imply being saved from all sin. For as long as love takes up the whole heart, what room is there for sin?

It is a divine evidence and conviction, secondly, that what God has promised He *is able* to perform. Admitting, therefore, that "with men it is impossible" to "bring a clean thing out of an unclean," to purify the heart from all sin and to fill it with all holiness, we nevertheless affirm that "with God all things are possible." And surely no one ever imagined it was possible to any power less than that of the Almighty! But if God speaks, it shall be done. God says, "Let there be light," and there is light.

It is, thirdly, a divine evidence and conviction that He is able and willing to do it *now*. And why not? Is not a moment to Him the same as a thousand years? He cannot want more time to accomplish whatever is his will. And He cannot want or stay for any more "worthiness" or "fitness" in the persons He is pleased to honor. We may therefore boldly say, at any point of time, "Now is the day of salvation" (2 Corinthians 6:2)! "Today, if ye will hear his voice, harden not your heart" (Hebrews 3:7-8)! "Behold, all things are now ready; come unto the marriage!"

To this confidence, that God is both able and willing to sanctify us *now*, there needs to be added one thing more—a divine evidence and conviction that He *does* it. In that hour it is done. God says to the inmost soul, "According to thy faith be it unto thee" (Matthew 9:29). Then the soul is pure from every spot of sin; it is "clean from all unrighteousness" (1 John 1:9). The believer then experiences the deep meaning of those solemn words, "If we walk in the light as he is in the light, we have fellowship one with another, and the blood of Jesus Christ his Son cleanses us from all sin" (1 John 1:7).

"But does God work this great work in the soul *gradually* or *instantaneously?*" Perhaps it may be gradually wrought in some, in the sense that they do not advert to the particular moment wherein sin ceases to be. But it is infinitely desirable, were it the will of God, that it should be done instantaneously, that the Lord should destroy sin "by the breath of his mouth," in a moment, in the twinkling of an eye. And so He generally does, a plain fact of which there is evidence enough to satisfy any unprejudiced person. You, therefore, look for it every moment! Look for it in the way described above, in all those "good works" whereunto you are "created anew in Christ Jesus." There is then no danger; you can be no worse, if you are no better, for that expectation. For were you to be disappointed of your hope, still you would have lost nothing.

But you shall not be disappointed of your hope. It will come, and will not tarry. Look for it then every day, every hour, every moment! Why not this hour this moment? Certainly you may look for it now, if you believe it is by faith. And by this token you may surely know whether you seek it by faith or by works. If by works, you want something to be done first, before you are sanctified. You think, "I must first *be* or *do* thus or thus." Then you are seeking it by works unto this day. If you seek it by faith, you may expect it as you are, and if as you are, then expect it now.

It is of importance to observe that there is an inseparable connection between these three points—expect it by faith; expect it as you are; and expect it now. To deny one of them is to deny them all. To allow one is to allow them all. Do you believe we are sanctified by faith? Be true then to your principle and look for this blessing just as you are, neither better nor worse, as a poor sinner that has still nothing [with which] to pay, nothing to plead but "Christ died." And if you look for it as you are, then expect it now. Hold back for nothing. Why should you? Christ is ready and He is all you want. He is waiting for you! He is at the door! Let your inmost soul cry out:

> Come in, come in, thou heavenly Guest!
> Nor hence again remove;
> But sup with me and let the feast
> Be everlasting love.*

*From Charles Wesley, *Hymns of God's Everlasting Love* (London, 1741).

# The Marks of the New Birth

("So is every one that is born of the Spirit." John 3:8)

How IS everyone who is "born of the Spirit"—that is, born again—born of God? What is meant by being born again, being born of God, or being born of the Spirit? What is implied in being a son or a child of God, or having the Spirit of adoption? That these privileges, by the free mercy of God, are ordinarily connected to baptism (which is termed by our Lord in a preceding verse as being "born of water and of the Spirit") we know, but we would know what these privileges are. What *is* the new birth?

Perhaps it is not needful to give a definition, since the Scripture gives none. But as the question is of the deepest concern to every child of man—since "except a man be born again," born of the Spirit, "he cannot see the kingdom of God"—I propose to lay down the marks of the new birth in the plainest manner, just as I find them laid down in Scripture.

## I. *Faith*

The first of these, and the foundation of all the rest, is faith. So St. Paul says, "Ye are all the children of God by faith in Christ Jesus" (Galatians 3:26). And St. John says, likewise, "to them gave he power" (ἐξουσίαν, the right or privilege, it might better be translated) "to become the sons of God, even to them that believe on his name; which were born," when they believed "not of blood, nor of the will of the flesh," not by natural generation, "nor of the will of man," like those children adopted by human parents, in whom no inward change is thereby wrought, "but of God" (John 1:12,13). And again, in the Epistle of John, we are told that "whosoever believeth that Jesus is the Christ is born of God" (1 John 5:1).

### 1. Not mere assent

But it is not a barely notional or speculative faith that is here spoken of by the Apostles. It is not a bare assent to this proposition: "Jesus is the Christ," nor, indeed, to all the propositions contained in our creed or in the Old and New Testament. It is not merely an assent to any or all these credible things, as credible. For to say this would be as much as to say (and who could hear it?) that the devils were born of God, for they have this faith. They, trembling, believe both that Jesus is the Christ and that all Scripture, having been given by inspiration of God, is true as God is true. It is not only an assent to divine truth upon the testimony of God or upon the evidence of miracles, for they also heard the words of the mouth of Jesus and knew Him to be a faithful and true witness. They had no choice

219

but to receive the testimony He gave, both of Himself and of the Father who sent Him. They saw likewise the mighty works which He did, and accordingly believed that He "came forth from God." Yet, notwithstanding this faith, they are still "reserved in chains of darkness unto the judgement of the great day."

## 2. Active confidence in God

For all this is no more than a dead faith. The true and living Christian faith, which whoever has is born of God, is not only assent, an act of understanding, but a disposition which God has wrought in the heart— "a sure trust and confidence in God that, through the merits of Christ, his sins are forgiven and he is reconciled to the favor of God." This implies that a person first renounce himself, In order to be "found in Christ," to be accepted through Him, he totally rejects all "confidence in the flesh" that, "having nothing to pay," having no trust in his own works or righteousness of any kind, he comes to God as a lost, miserable, self-destroyed, self-condemned, undone, helpless sinner, as one whose mouth is utterly stopped and who is altogether "guilty before God." Such a sense of sin (commonly called 'despair' by those who speak evil of the things they do not understand), together with a full conviction, such as no words can express, that of Christ alone comes our salvation, as well as an earnest desire for that salvation, must precede a living faith, a trust in Him who "for us paid our ransom by his death, and fulfilled the law in his life." This faith then, whereby we are born of God, is "not only a belief of all the articles of our faith, but also a true confidence in the mercy of God through our Lord Jesus Christ."*

## 3. Power over sin

An immediate and constant fruit of this faith by which we are born of God, a fruit which can in no way be separated from it, no, not for an hour, is power over sin. We have this power over *outward* sin of every kind, over every evil word and work, for wherever the blood of Christ is thus applied, it "purgeth the conscience from dead works," and over *inward* sin, for it purifies the heart from every unholy desire and attitude. This fruit of faith St. Paul has largely described in the sixth chapter of his Epistle to the Romans. "How shall we," he asks, "who [by faith] are dead to sin, live any longer therein?" "Our old man is crucified with Christ, that the body of sin might be destroyed, that henceforth we should not serve sin." "Likewise, reckon ye yourselves to be dead unto sin, but alive

---

*In this paragraph as well as others Wesley is drawing on the Articles of the Church of England to make his point.

unto God through Jesus Christ our Lord. Let not sin therefore reign" even "in your mortal body," but yield yourselves unto God, as those who are alive from the dead. "For sin shall not have dominion over you"—God be thanked, who once "were servants of sin—but being made free. . . ." Now the plain meaning of this text is: God be thanked that though you were, in time past, the servants of sin, yet now being free from sin, you have become the servants of righteousness.

The same priceless privilege of the children of God is as strongly asserted by St. John, particularly with regard to . . . outward sin. After he had been crying out as one astonished at the depth of the riches of the goodness of God ("Behold, what manner of love the Father hath bestowed upon us, that we should be called the sons of God! Beloved, now are we the sons of God; and it doth not yet appear what we shall be: but we know that, when he shall appear, we shall be like him; for we shall see him as he is" [1 John 3:1ff.]), he soon adds, "Whosoever is born of God doth not commit sin; for his seed remaineth in him: and he cannot sin, because he is born of God" (v. 9).

Now some will say, "True. Whoever is born of God does not commit sin *habitually.*" *Habitually!?* Where does it say that? I can't find it there. It is not written in the Book. God plainly says, "he doth not commit sin," and you add "habitually." Who are you to meddle with the oracles of God, adding to the words of this book? Beware, I beg of you, lest God "add to thee all the plagues that are written therein," especially when the comment you add is such that it quite swallows up the text. By this μεθοδεία πλάνης, this artful method of deceiving, the precious promise is utterly lost. Indeed, by this κυβεία ἀνθρώπων, this tricking and shuffling of men, the word of God is made of none effect.

O beware, you who thus take away from the words of this book— who, taking away the whole meaning and spirit from them, leave only what may indeed be termed a dead letter—lest God take away your part out of the book of life!

Let us allow the apostle to interpret his own words, by the whole context of his discourse. In the fifth verse of this chapter he has said: "Ye know that he [Christ] was manifested to take away our sins; and in him is no sin." What is the inference he draws from this? "Whosoever abideth in him sinneth not: whosoever sinneth hath not seen him, neither known him" (v. 6) To enforce this important doctrine, he appends a highly necessary caution: "Little children, let no man deceive you" (for many will endeavour to do so, to persuade you that you may be unrighteous, that you may commit sin and still be children of God); "He that doeth righteousness is righteous, even as he is righteous. He that committeth sin is of the devil; for the devil sinneth from the beginning." *Then* he says:

"Whosoever is born of God doth not commit sin; for his seed remaineth in him: and he cannot sin, because he is born of God." "In this," adds the apostle, "the children of God are manifest, and the children of the devil." By this plain mark (the committing or not committing of sin) they are distinguished from each other. The same point is made in the fifth chapter: "We know that whosoever is born of God sinneth not; but he that is begotten of God keepeth himself, and that wicked one toucheth him not" (v. 18).

## 4. Peace

Another fruit of this living faith is peace. For "being justified by faith," having all our sins blotted out, "we have peace with God through our Lord Jesus Christ" (Romans 5:1). This indeed our Lord Himself, the night before his death, solemnly bequeathed to all his followers: "Peace I leave with you" (you who "believe in God" and "believe also in me"); "my peace I give unto you: not as the world giveth, give I unto you. Let not your heart be troubled, neither let it be afraid" (John 14:27). And again: "These things have I spoken unto you, that in me ye might have peace" (John 16:33). This is that "peace of God which passeth all understanding," that serenity of soul which it has not entered into the heart of a natural man to conceive and which it is not possible for even the spiritual man to utter. And it is a peace which all the powers of earth and hell are unable to take away. Waves and storms beat upon it but they cannot shake it, for it is founded upon a rock. It keeps the hearts and minds of the children of God at all times and in all places. Whether they are in ease or in pain, in sickness or health, in abundance or want, they are happy in God. In every state they have learned to be content—yea, even to give thanks unto God through Christ Jesus—for they are well assured that "whatsoever is, is best," because it is his will concerning them. Even in all the vicissitudes of life their heart stands fast, believing in the Lord.

## II. *Hope*

A second scriptural mark of those who are born of God, is hope. Thus St. Peter, speaking to all the children of God who were then scattered abroad, says: "Blessed be the God and Father of our Lord Jesus Christ, which according to his abundant mercy, hath begotten us again unto a lively hope" (1 Peter 1:3). ἐλπίδα ζῶσαν, a 'lively' or 'living' hope, the apostle calls it, because there is also a 'dead' hope (just as there is a 'dead' faith), a hope which is not from God but from the enemy of God and man. [Such a hope is] also evident by its fruits for, as it is the offspring of pride, it is also the parent of every evil word and work. On the other hand, everyone who has in him this living hope is holy, "as he that calleth him is holy"; everyone who can truly say to his brethren in Christ, "beloved, now are we the sons of God, and we shall see him as he is" purifies himself "even as He is pure."

This hope implies, first, the testimony of our own spirit or conscience, that we walk "in simplicity and godly sincerity," and secondly, the testimony of the Spirit of God, "bearing witness with [or "to"] our spirit, that we are the children of God," and "if children, then heirs, heirs of God, and joint heirs with Christ."

## 1. Assurance of belonging

Let us carefully observe what is here taught us by God Himself concerning this glorious privilege of his children. *Who* is it that is here said to bear witness? Not our spirit only, but another, even the Spirit of God. He it is who "beareth witness with our spirit." *What* is it He bears witness of? "That we are the children of God; and if children, then heirs . . ." (Romans 8:16,17) "if so be that we suffer with him," if we deny ourselves, if we take up our cross daily, if we cheerfully endure persecution or reproach for his sake, "that we may also be glorified together." And *in whom* doth the Spirit of God bear this witness? In all who are the children of God. . . .

The variation of the phrase in the fifteenth verse is worthy of our observation. "Ye have received the spirit of adoption, whereby we cry, Abba, Father!" *You*, as many as are the sons of God, have in virtue of your sonship received that self-same spirit of adoption whereby *we* cry, Abba, Father (*we*, the apostles, prophets, teachers . . . *we*, through whom you have believed, the "ministers of Christ and stewards of the mysteries of God"). As *we* and *you* have one Lord, so we have one Spirit. As we have one faith, so we have one hope also. *We* and *you* are sealed with one "spirit of promise," the earnest of *your* and of *our* inheritance, the same Spirit bearing witness with your spirit and with ours "that we are the children of God."

## 2. Comfort and joy

And thus is the Scripture fulfilled: "Blessed are they that mourn; for they shall be comforted." For it is easy to believe that though sorrow may precede this witness of God's Spirit with our spirit (indeed *must*, in some degree, while we groan under fear and a sense of the wrath of God abiding on us), yet as soon as any person feels it in himself, his sorrow is turned into joy. Whatever his pain may have been before, as soon as that "hour is come, he remembereth the anguish no more, for joy" that he is born of God.

It may be that many of you now have sorrow, because you are "aliens from the commonwealth of Israel," because you are conscious that you have not this Spirit and that you are "without hope and without God in the world." But when the Comforter is come, "then your heart shall rejoice," yea, "your joy shall be full" and "that joy no man taketh from you" (John 10:22). "We joy in God," you say, "through our Lord Jesus Christ, by whom we have now received the atonement," and "by whom we have access into this grace," this state of . . . favor or reconciliation with God "wherein we stand, and rejoice in hope of the glory of God" (Romans 5:2).

You, says St. Peter, whom God has "begotten again unto a lively hope, are kept by the power of God unto salvation: wherein ye greatly rejoice, though now for a season, if need be, ye are in heaviness through manifold temptations; that the trial of your faith may be found unto praise, and honour, and glory at the appearing of Jesus Christ; in whom, though now ye see him not, ye rejoice with joy unspeakable and full of glory" (1 Peter 1:5ff.). Unspeakable indeed! It is not for the human tongue to describe this joy in the Holy Spirit. It is "the hidden manna which no man knoweth save he that receiveth it."

But this we know: such joy not only remains, but overflows in the depth of affliction. Are the consolations of God small when all earthy comforts fail? No so. Rather, when sufferings most abound, the consolations of his Spirit abound still more—so that the sons of God can "laugh at destruction when it cometh," and at need, pain, hell and the grave. For we know Him who "hath the keys of death and hell" and will shortly "cast them into the bottomless pit" and we hear even now the great voice out of heaven saying, "Behold, the tabernacle of God is with men, and he will dwell with them, and they shall be his people, and God himself shall be with them, and be their God. And God shall wipe away all tears from their eyes; and there shall be no more death, neither sorrow, nor crying, neither shall there be any more pain; for the former things are passed away" (Revelation 21:3,4).

## III. *Love*

A third scriptural mark of those who are born of God, and the greatest of all, is love, even "the love of God shed abroad in their hearts by the Holy Ghost which is given unto them" (Romans 5:5). "Because they are sons, God hath sent forth the Spirit of his Son in their hearts, crying, Abba, Father!" (Galatians 4:6). By this Spirit, continually looking up to God as their reconciled and loving Father, they cry to Him for their daily bread, for all things needful whether for their souls or bodies. They continually pour out their hearts before Him, knowing that "they have the petitions which they ask of him" (1 John 5:15). Their delight is in Him. He is the joy of their heart, their shield and their "exceeding great reward." The desire of their soul is toward Him. It is their "meat and drink to do his will" and they are "satisfied as with marrow and fatness, while their mouth praiseth him with joyful lips" (Psalm 63:5).

And, in this sense also, "everyone who loveth him that begat, loveth him that is begotten of him" (1 John 5:1). His spirit rejoices in God his Saviour. He "loveth the Lord Jesus Christ in sincerity." He is so "joined unto the Lord" as to be one spirit with Him. His soul depends upon Him, and chooses Him as altogether lovely, "the chiefest among ten thousand." He knows and feels what it means to say, "My beloved is mine, and I am his" (Canticles 2:16). "Thou art fairer than the children of men; full of grace are thy lips, because God hath anointed thee for ever!" (Psalm 45:2).

1. Firstfruits: Love for our neighbors

The necessary fruit of this love of God is the love our neighbor, of every soul whom God has made—not excepting our enemies, not excepting those who are now "despitefully using" and persecuting us. This is a love through which we love every person as ourselves, as we love our own souls. Indeed, our Lord has expressed it still more strongly, teaching us to "love one another, even as he hath loved us." Accordingly, the commandment written in the hearts of all those who love God is none other than this: "As I have loved you, so love ye one another." Now, says the apostle, "herein perceive we the love of God, in that he laid down his life for us" (1 John 3:16), from which he justly infers that "we ought [likewise] to lay down our lives for the brethren." If we feel ourselves ready to do this, then we truly love our neighbor. Then "we know that we have passed from death unto life, because we [thus] love the brethren" (1 John 3:14). "Hereby know we" that we are born of God, that we "dwell in him, and he in us, because he hath given us of his [loving] Spirit" (1 John 4:13). For "love is of God; and every one that [thus] loveth is born of God, and knoweth God" (1 John 4:7).

But some may possibly ask: "Does not the apostle say, 'This is the love of God, that we keep his commandments'" (1 John 5:3)? Yes, and this *is* the love of our neighbor, just as it is the love of God. But what would you infer from this: that keeping the outward commandments is all that is implied in loving God with all your heart, with all your mind and soul and strength, and in loving your neighbor as yourself? that the love of

God is not an affection of the soul but merely an outward service? that the love of our neighbor is not a disposition of heart but a mere habit of outward works?

To simply state so wild an interpretation of the apostle's words is sufficient to confute it. The plain indisputable meaning of the text is: this is the sign or proof of the love of God, of our keeping of the "first and great commandment," that we keep *all* the rest of his commandments. For true love, if it is shed abroad in our heart, will constrain us to do this, since whoever loves God with all his heart cannot but serve Him with all his strength.

## 2. Obedience

A second fruit, therefore, of the love of God (insofar as it can be distinguished from that love) is universal obedience to Him we love, and conformity to his will: obedience to all the commands of God, internal and external; obedience of the heart and life in every attitude and in all manner of conversation. One of the attitudes most obviously implied here is zeal for good works—a hunger and thirst to do good in every possible way unto all people, rejoicing to "spend and be spent" for them, for every child of man, not looking for any recompense in this world but only in the resurrection of the just.

## IV. *Born of the Spirit*

I have now plainly laid down those marks of the new birth which I find laid down in Scripture. This is the way God Himself answers that weighty question, "What is it to be born of God?" If the appeal is made to the oracles of God, *this* is [how we recognize] "every one that is born of the Spirit." This is what it is, in the judgement of the Spirit of God, to be a son or a child of God: it is so to *believe* in God, through Christ, as not to commit sin, and to enjoy at all times and in all places that "peace of God which passeth all understanding." It is so to *hope* in God through the Son of his love as to have not only the "testimony of a good conscience" but also the Spirit of God "bearing witness with your spirits, that ye are the children of God"—from which cannot but spring rejoicing in Him through whom you have received the atonement. It is also so to *love* God, who hath thus loved you (as you never loved any creature) so that you are constrained to love all people as yourselves, with a love not only ever burning in your hearts but flaming out in all your actions and conversations, and making your whole life one "labor of love," and one continued obedience to the commands: "Be ye merciful, as God is merciful"; "Be ye holy, as I the Lord am holy"; "Be ye perfect, as your Father which is in heaven is perfect."

## 1. Baptism

Who then are you that are thus born of God? You "know the things which are given to you of God." You well know that you are the children of God and "can assure your hearts before him." And everyone of you who has observed these words cannot but feel, and know of a truth, whether at this hour (answer to God and not to man!) you are thus a child of God or not. The question is not "what you were made in baptism?" (do not evade!) but "what are you now?" Is the Spirit of adoption now in your heart? To your own heart let the appeal be made. I ask not whether you were born of water and of the Spirit, but whether you are *now* the temple of the Holy Spirit who dwells in you. I know that you were "circumcised with the circumcision of Christ" (as St. Paul emphatically terms baptism), but does the Spirit of Christ and of glory *now* rest upon you? Otherwise, "your circumcision is become uncircumcision."

Say not then in your heart, "I was once baptized, and therefore am now a child of God." Alas, that argument will not hold. How many are the baptized gluttons and drunkards, the baptized liars and common swearers, the baptized railers and evil-speakers, the baptized whoremongers, thieves, extortioners? What do you think? Are these now the children of God? Verily, I say unto you, whoever you are, unto whom any of these characteristics apply, "Ye are of your father the devil, and the works of your father ye do." Unto you I call, in the name of Him whom you crucify afresh, and in his words to your circumcised predecessors: "Ye serpents, ye generation of vipers, how can ye escape the damnation of hell?"

How, indeed, except you are born again? For you are now dead in trespasses and sins. To say, then, that you cannot be born again, that there is no new birth but in baptism, is to seal you all under damnation, to consign you to hell without help and without hope. And perhaps some may think this is just and right. In their zeal for the Lord of Hosts they may say, "Yea, cut off the sinners, the Amalekites! Let these Gibeonites be utterly destroyed! They deserve no less." True. But neither do you, nor I. My own and your desert, as well as theirs, is hell, and it is mere mercy, free, undeserved mercy, that *we* are not now in unquenchable fire.

You will say, "but we are washed," we are born again "of water and the Spirit." So were they. This, therefore, is no distinction at all, unless you *are now* what they once *were*. Do you not know that "what is highly esteemed of men is an abomination in the sight of God?" Come forth, you saints of the world, you that are honored of men, and see who will cast the first stone at them, at these wretches not fit to live upon the earth, these common harlots, adulterers, murderers. Only learn first what it means [when it says], "He that hateth his brother is a murderer" (1 John 3:15) or "He that looketh on a woman to lust after her hath committed adultery with her already in his heart" (Matthew 5:28). "Ye adulterers and adulteresses, know ye not that the friendship of the world is enmity with God?" (James 4:4).

## 2. Regeneration

"Verily, verily, I say unto you, ye [also] must be born again." "Except ye [also] be born again, ye cannot see the kingdom of God." Lean no more on the staff of that broken reed, that you *were* born again in baptism. Who denies that you were then made children of God, and heirs of the kingdom of heaven? But, notwithstanding this, you are *now* children of the devil. Therefore, you must be born again. And let not Satan put it into your heart to cavil at a word, then the thing itself is clear. You have heard what the marks of the children of God are: all you who have them not in your souls, baptized or unbaptized, must receive them, or without doubt you shall perish everlastingly. And if you have been baptized, your only hope is this—that those who were made the children of God by baptism, but are now the children of the devil, may yet again receive "power to become the sons of God," that they may receive again what they have lost, even the "spirit of adoption, crying in their hearts, Abba, Father!"

Amen, Lord Jesus! May everyone who prepares his heart yet again to seek thy face receive again that spirit of adoption and cry out, "Abba, Father!" Let him now again have power so to believe in thy name that he may become a child of God—to know and feel he hath "redemption in thy blood, even the forgiveness of sins," and that he "cannot commit sin, because he is born of God." Let him be now "begotten again unto a living hope," so as to "purify himself as thou art pure." And "because he is a son," let the spirit of love and glory rest upon him, cleansing him "from all filthiness of flesh and spirit," and teaching him "perfect holiness in the fear of God."

# *from* A Scheme of Self-Examination Used by the First Methodists in Oxford (c. 1730)*

SUNDAY. *Love of God and Simplicity:* means of which are prayer and meditation.

1. Have I been simple and recollected in everything I said or did? Have I been: (a) *simple* in everything, i.e. looked upon God, my Good, my Pattern, my One Desire, my Disposer, Parent of Good; acted wholly for Him; bounded my views with the present action or hour?

(b) *recollected*, i.e., has this simple view been distinct and uninterrupted? Have I, in order to keep it so, used the signs agreed upon with my friends wherever I was? Have I done anything without a previous perception of its being the will of God? Or, without a perception of its being an exercise of a means of the virtue of the day? Have I said anything without [such a perception]?

2. Have I prayed with fevor? At going in and out of church? In the church? Morning and evening in private? Monday, Wednesday, and Friday, with my friends at rising? Before lying down? On Saturday noon? All the time I am engaged in exterior work in private? Before I go into the place of public or private prayer, for help therein? Have I wherever I was, gone to church morning and evening, unless for necessary [deeds of] mercy? And spent from one hour to three in private? Have I in private prayer frequently stopped short and observed [with] what fervor [I have been praying]? Have I repeated it over and over, till I focused on every word? Have I at the beginning of every prayer or paragraph acknowledged I cannot pray? Have I paused before I concluded in his name, and focused on my Saviour now interceding for me at the right hand of God, and offering up these prayers?

3. Have I duly used spontaneous prayer?** That is, have I every hour

---

*The following comprises an extract only from the "Rules," which were organized around a specific daily regime. Each day had its own special "virtue" on which the members particularly focused their energies and prayer; here are included the rules for Sunday (its "virtue of the day" being love of God and simplicity) and Monday (its being love of man). The rules were reprinted by Wesley in the *Arminian Magazine,* 1781, and are available in vol. 11 of the *Works* (1831), pp. 514ff.

**Wesley's word here is "ejaculations," which has the force of a "sudden outburst" of fervent prayer.

prayed for humility, faith, hope, love and the particular virtue of the day? Considered with whom I was the last hour, what I did and how? With regard to recollection, love of man, humility, self-denial, resignation, and thankfulness? Considered the next hour in the same respects, offered up all I do to my Redeemer, begged his assistance in every particular, and commended my soul to his keeping? Have I done this deliberately (not in haste), seriously (not doing anything else the while) and fervently as I could?

4. Have I duly prayed for the virtue of the day? That is, have I prayed for it at going out and coming in? Deliberately, seriously, and fervently?

5. Have I used a Collect at nine, twelve, and three? Grace before and after eating (aloud at my own room)? Deliberately, seriously, fervently?

6. Have I duly meditated? Every day, unless for necessary [deeds of] mercy (a) from six etc. to prayers? (b) from four to five: what was particular in the providence of this day? how ought the virtue of the day to have been exerted upon it? how did it fall short? (here faults); (c) on Sunday from six to seven, with Kempis? From three to four on redemption, or God's attributes? Wednesday and Friday from twelve to one on the Passion? After ending a book, on what I had marked in it?

MONDAY. *Love of Man*

1. Have I been zealous to do, and active in doing good?

(a) Have I embraced every probable opportunity of doing good, and preventing, removing, or lessening evil?

(b) Have I pursued it with my might?

(c) Have I thought anything too dear to part with, to serve my neighbor?

(d) Have I spent an hour at least every day in speaking to someone or other?

(e) Have I given anyone up, till he expressly renounced me?

(f) Have I, before I spoke to any, learned, as far as I could, his temperament, way of thinking, past life, and peculiar hindrances, internal and external?

(g) Have I in speaking, proposed the motives, then the difficulties, then balanced them, then exhorted him to consider both calmly and deeply, and to pray earnestly for help?

(h) Have I, in speaking to a stranger, explained what religion is not (not negative, not external) and what it is (a recovery of the image of God), searched at what step in it he stops, and what makes him stop there? Exhorted and directed him?

(i) Have I persuaded all I could to attend public prayers, sermons and sacraments? And in general, to obey the laws of the Church catholic, the Church of England, the State, the University, and its respective colleges?

(j) Have I, when taxed with any act of obedience, avowed it, and turned the attack with sweetness and firmness?

(k) Have I disputed upon any practical point, unless it was to be practised just then?

(l) Have I in disputing (i) asked him to define the terms of the question, to limit it (what he grants, what denies); (ii) delayed speaking my opinion, let him explain and prove his, then insinuated and pressed objections?

(m) Have I after every visit, asked him who went with me, "Did I say anything wrong?"

(n) Have I, when anyone asked advice, directed and exhorted him with all my power?

2. Have I rejoiced with and for my neighbor in virtue or pleasure? Grieved with him in pain, for him in sin?

3. Have I received his infirmities with pity, not anger?

4. Have I thought or spoken unkindly of or to him? Have I revealed any evil of anyone, unless it was necessary to some particular good I had in view? Have I then done it with all the tenderness of phrase and manner, consistent with that end? Have I in any way appeared to approve those who did otherwise?

5. Has good will been, and appeared to be, the spring of all my actions towards others?

6. Have I duly used intercession (a) before and (b) after speaking to anyone? (c) for my friends on Sunday? (d) for my pupils on Monday? (e) for those who have particularly desired it, on Wednesday and Friday? (f) for the family in which I am, every day?*

---

*This "examination of conscience" may be compared with those of Doddridge (pp. 182–88) and Fletcher (pp. 371–75).

# *from* The Character of a Methodist (1742)

"Not as though I had already attained"

## To the Reader

SINCE THE name first came abroad into the world, many have been at a loss to know what a Methodist is, what are the principles and the practice of those who are commonly called by that name, and what the distinguishing marks of this sect "which is everywhere spoken against."

And it being generally believed that I was able to give the clearest account of these things (as having been one of the first to whom that name was given, and the person by whom the rest were supposed to be directed), I have been called upon, in all manner of ways, and with the utmost earnestness, so to do. I yield at last to the continued urgings both of friends and enemies, and do now give the clearest account I can, in the presence of the Lord and Judge of heaven and earth, of the principles and practice whereby those who are called "Methodists" are distinguished from other people.

I say those who are *called* Methodists, for let it be well observed that this is not a name which they take to themselves, but one fixed upon them by way of reproach, without their approbation or consent. It was first given to three or four young men at Oxford, by a student of Christ Church—either in allusion to the ancient sect of Physicians (so called for their teaching that almost all diseases might be cured by a specific *method* of diet and exercise) or from his observing a more regular *method* of study and behavior than was usual with those of his age and station.

I should rejoice (so little ambitious am I to be at the head of any sect or party) if the very name might never be mentioned more, but be buried in eternal oblivion. But if that cannot be, at least let those who will use it know the meaning of the word they use. Let us not always be fighting in the dark. Come, and let us look one another in the face. And perhaps some of you who hate what I am *called* may love what I am by the grace of God, or rather, what "I follow after, if that I may apprehend that for which also I am apprehended of Christ Jesus."

## I. *What a Methodist is Not*

The distinguishing marks of a Methodist are not opinions of any sort. His assenting to this or that scheme of religion, his embracing any particular set of notions, his espousing the judgement of one man or of another, are all quite beside the point. Whoever, therefore, imagines that a Methodist is a person of such or such an opinion, is grossly ignorant of the whole affair; he mistakes the truth totally. We believe, indeed, that "all Scripture is given by the inspiration of God," and herein we are distinguished from Jews, Turks, and infidels. We believe the written word of God to be the only and sufficient rule both of Christian faith and practice, and herein we are fundamentally distinguished from those of the Roman Church. We believe Christ to be the eternal, supreme God, and herein we are distinguished from the Socinians and Arians. But as to all opinions which do not strike at the root of Christianity, we think and let think. So whatever they are, whether right or wrong, [such opinions] are not distinguishing marks of a Methodist.

Neither are words or phrases of any sort. We do not place our religion, or any part of it, in being attached to any peculiar mode of speaking, any quaint or uncommon set of expressions. The most obvious, easy, common words, wherein our meaning can be conveyed, we prefer before others, both on ordinary occasions, and when we speak of the things of God. We never, therefore, willingly or designedly, deviate from the most usual way of speaking—unless we express scripture truths in scripture words, which, we presume, no Christian will condemn. Neither do we affect to use any particular expressions of Scripture more frequently than others, unless they are such as are more frequently used by the inspired writers themselves. So it is as gross an error to place the marks of a Methodist in his words as in opinions of any sort.

Nor do we desire to be distinguished by actions, customs, or usages of an indifferent nature. Our religion does not lie in doing what God has not required, or abstaining from what He has not forbidden. It does not lie in the form of our apparel, in the posture of our body, or the covering of our heads, nor yet in abstaining from marriage or from meats and drinks, which are all good if received with thanksgiving. Therefore, no one who knows whereof he speaks will fix the mark of a Methodist here—in any actions or customs purely indifferent, undetermined by the word of God.

Nor, lastly, is a Methodist distinguished by laying the whole stress of religion on any single part of it. If you say, "Yes he is, for he thinks we are saved by faith alone," I answer that you do not understand the terms. By salvation he means holiness of heart and life. And this he affirms to spring from true faith alone. Can even a nominal Christian deny this? Is this placing a part of religion for the whole? Do we then make void the law through faith? God forbid! Yea, we establish the law. We do not place the whole of religion (as too many do, God knows) either in doing no harm or in doing good, or in using the ordinance of God. No, not in all of them together, wherein we know by experience a man may labor many years and at the end have no religion at all, nor more than he had at the beginning. Much less in any one of these, or, it may be, in a scrap of one of them, like a woman who fancies herself a virtuous woman only because she is not a prostitute, or a man who dreams he is an honest man merely because he does not rob or steal: may the Lord God of my fathers preserve me from such a poor, starved religion as this! Were this the mark of a Methodist, I would sooner choose to be a sincere Jew, Turk, or pagan.

## II. *The True Mark of a Methodist*

"What then is the mark? Who is a Methodist, according to your own account?" I answer: a Methodist is one who has "the love of God shed abroad in his heart by the Holy Spirit given unto him," one who "loves the Lord his God with all his heart, and with all his soul, and with all his mind, and with all his strength." God is the joy of his heart, and the desire of his soul, which is constantly crying out, "Whom have I in heaven but thee? There is none upon earth that I desire beside thee! My God and my all! Thou art the strength of my heart, and my portion forever!"

He is therefore happy in God, yea, always happy, as having in him "a well of water springing up into everlasting life" and overflowing his soul with peace and joy. Perfect love now having cast out fear, he rejoices evermore. He "rejoices in the Lord always," even in God his Saviour, and in the Father, "through our Lord Jesus Christ, by whom he hath now received the atonement." Having found "redemption through his blood, the forgiveness of his sins," he cannot but rejoice whenever he looks back on the horrible pit out of which he is delivered, when he sees "all his transgressions blotted out as a cloud, and his iniquities as a thick cloud." He cannot but rejoice whenever he looks on the state wherein he now is, "being justified freely, and having peace with God through our Lord Jesus Christ." For "he that believeth hath the witness of this in himself," being now the son of God by faith. "Because he is a son, God hath sent forth the Spirit of his Son into his heart, crying Abba, Father!" And "the Spirit itself beareth witness with his spirit, that he is a child of God." He rejoices also, whenever he looks forward "in hope of the glory that shall be revealed." Yea, his joy is full, and all his bones cry out, "Blessed be the God and Father of our Lord Jesus Christ, who, according to his abundant mercy, has begotten me again to a living hope of an inheritance incorruptible, undefiled, and that fades not away, reserved in heaven for me!"

And he who has this hope, thus "full of immortality, in everything giveth thanks," as knowing that this (whatsoever it is) "is the will of God in Christ Jesus concerning him." From Him, therefore, he cheerfully receives all, saying, "Good is the will of the Lord" and, whether the Lord gives or takes away, [he] blesses the name of the Lord. For he has "learned in whatsoever state he is, therewith to be content." He knows "both how to be abased and how to abound." Everywhere and in all things he is instructed both to be full and to be hungry, both to abound and suffer need. Whether in ease or pain, sickness or health, life or death, he gives thanks from the bottom of his heart to Him who orders it for good—knowing that "every good gift cometh from above," and none but good can come from the Father of Lights, into whose hand he has wholly committed his body and soul as into the hands of a faithful Creator. He is there "careful (anxious or uneasy) for nothing," having "cast all his care on Him that careth for him," and in all things resting on Him after "making his request known with thanksgiving."

For indeed, he "prays without ceasing." It is given him "always to pray, and not to faint." Not that he is always in the house of prayer (though he neglects no opportunity of being there). Neither is he always on his knees (although he often is) or on his face, before the Lord his God. Nor yet is he always crying aloud to God, or calling upon Him in words. For many times, "the Spirit maketh intercession for him with groans that cannot be uttered." But at all times the language of his heart is this: "Thou brightness of the eternal glory, unto thee is my heart, though without a voice, and my silence speaketh unto thee." And this is true prayer, and this alone. But his heart is ever lifted up to God, at all times and in all places. In this he is never hindered, much less interrupted, by any person or thing. In retirement or company, in leisure, business, or conversation, his heart is ever with the Lord. Whether he lie down or rise up, God is in all his thoughts; he walks with God continually, having the loving eye of his mind still fixed upon Him, and everywhere seeing "Him that is invisible."

And while he thus always exercises his love to God, by praying without ceasing, rejoicing evermore, and in everything giving thanks, this commandment is written in his heart, that "he who loveth God should love his brother also." And he accordingly loves his neighbor as himself; he loves every person as his own soul. His heart is full of love to all mankind, to every child of "the Father of the spirits of all flesh." That a person is not personally known to him is no bar to his love; no, nor [the fact] that he is known to be such as he approves not, or that he repays hatred for good will. For he "loves his enemies," yea, and the enemies of God, the "evil and unthankful." And if it is not in his power to "do good to them that hate him," yet he ceases not to pray for them, though they continue to spurn his love, and still "despitefully use him and persecute him."

For he is "pure in heart." The love of God has purified his heart from all vengeful passions, from envy, malice and wrath, from every unkind temper or malign affection. It has cleansed him from pride and haughtiness of spirit, whereof alone comes contention. And he has now "put on bowels of mercies, kindness, humbleness of mind, meekness, longsuffering." So he "forbears and forgives if he has a quarrel against any, even as God in Christ hath forgiven him." And indeed all possible ground for contention, on his part, is utterly cut off. For none can take from him what he desires, seeing he "loves not the world, nor any of the things of the world," being now "crucified to the world, and the world crucified to him," being dead to all that is in the world, the "lust of the flesh, the lust of the eye, and the pride of life." For "all his desire is unto God, and to the remembrance of his name."

Agreeable to this his one desire, is the one design of his life, namely to do not his own will, but the will of Him that sent him. His one intention at all times and in all things is not to please himself, but Him whom his soul loves. He has a single eye. And because "his eye is single, his whole body is full of light." Indeed, where the loving eye of the soul is continually fixed upon God, there can be no darkness at all, "but the whole is light, as when the bright shining of a candle doth enlighten the house." God then reigns alone. All that is in the soul is holiness to the Lord. There is not a motion in his heart but what is according to his will. Every thought that arises points to Him, and is in obedience to the law of Christ.

And the tree is known by its fruits. For as he loves God, so he keeps his commandments—not only some, or most of them, but all, from the least to the greatest. He is not content to "keep the whole law, and offend in one point," but has, in all points, "a conscience void of offence towards God and towards man." Whatever God has forbidden, he avoids; whatever God has enjoined, he does, whether it be little or great, hard or easy, joyous or grievous to the flesh. He "runs the way of God's commandments," now that his heart is set at liberty. It is his glory to do so; it is his daily crown of rejoicing "to do the will of God on earth, as it is done in heaven," knowing it is the highest privilege of the angels of God, of those that excel in strength, to fulfill his commandments, and hearken to the voice of his word.

All the commandments of God he accordingly keeps, and that with all his might. For his obedience is in proportion to his love, the source from whence it flows. And therefore, loving God with all his heart, he serves Him with all his strength. He continually presents his soul and body a living sacrifice, holy, acceptable to God, devoting himself entirely without reserve—all he has, and all he is—to his glory. All the talents he has received, he constantly employs according to his Master's will, every power and faculty of his soul, every member of his body. Once he yielded them unto sin, and the devil "as instruments of unrighteousness," but now, "being alive from the dead, he yields them all as instruments of righteousness unto God."

By consequence, whatsoever he does, it is all to the glory of God. In all his employment of every kind, he not only aims at this (which is implied in having a single eye) but actually attains it. His business and refreshments, as well as his prayers, all serve this great end. Whether he sit in his house or walk by the way, whether he lie down or rise up, he is promoting, in all he speaks or does, the one business of his life. Whether he puts on his apparel, labors, or eats and drinks, or diverts himself from too exhausting labor, it all tends to advance the glory of God, by peace and good will among men. His one invariable rule is this: "Whatsoever ye do, in word or deed, do it all in the name of the Lord Jesus, giving thanks to God and the Father by him."

Nor do the customs of the world at all hinder his "running the race that is set before him." He knows that vice does not lose its nature though it becomes ever so fashionable, and remembers that "every man is to give an account of himself to God." He cannot, therefore, follow even a multitude to do evil. He cannot "fare sumptuously every day," or "make provision for the flesh to fulfill the lusts thereof." He cannot "lay up treasure on earth," any more than he can take fire into his bosom. He cannot "adorn himself" on any pretence "with gold or costly apparel." He cannot join in or countenance any diversion which has the least tendency to vice of any kind. He cannot speak evil of his neighbor, any more than he can lie either for God or man. He cannot utter an unkind word of anyone, for love keeps the door of his lips. He cannot speak idle words; "no corrupt communication" ever comes out of his mouth—nothing which is not good to the use of edifying or fit to minister grace to the hearers. But "whatsoever things are pure, whatsoever things are lovely, whatsoever things are [justly] of good report," he thinks, and speaks, and acts, "adorning the Gospel of our Lord Jesus Christ in all things."

Lastly, as he has time, he does good unto all men, unto neighbors and strangers, friends and enemies, in every possible way. Not only [does he minister] to their bodies—by feeding the hungry, clothing the naked, visiting those who are sick or in prison—but much more does he labor to do good to their souls, according to the ability which God gives—to awaken those who sleep in death, to bring those who are awakened to the atoning blood, that "being justified by faith, they may have peace with God," and to provoke those who have peace with God to abound more in love and good works. And he is willing to "spend and be spent" herein, even "to be offered up on the sacrifice and service of their faith," so that all may "come unto the measure of the stature of the fullness of Christ."

These are the principles and practices of our sect; these are the marks of a true Methodist. By these alone do those who are in derision so called desire to be distinguished from other people. If anyone say, "Why these are only the common fundamental principles of Christianity!"—this is the very truth. I know they are no other, and I would to God both you and all people knew that I, and all who follow my judgement, do vehemently refuse to be distinguished from others by any but the common principles of Christianity—the plain, old Christianity that I am teaching—and renouncing and detesting all other marks of distinction. And whoever is what I preach (let him be called what he will, for names change not the nature of things), he is a Christian not in name only, but in heart and in life. He is inwardly and outwardly conformed to the will of God, as revealed in the written Word. He thinks, speaks, and lives according to the method laid down in the revelation of Jesus Christ. His soul is renewed after the image of God, in righteousness and in all true holiness. And having the mind that was in Christ, he walks as Christ walked.

By these marks, by these fruits of a living faith, do we labor to distinguish ourselves from the unbelieving world, from all those whose minds or lives are not according to the Gospel of Christ. But from real Christians, of whatever denomination they be, we earnestly desire not to be distinguished at all, nor from any who sincerely follow after what they know they have not yet attained. No: "whosoever doeth the will of my Father which is in heaven, the same is my brother, and sister, and mother." And I beseech you, brethren, by the mercies of God, that we be in no way divided among ourselves. Is your heart right, as my heart is with yours? I ask no further question. If it be, give me your hand. For opinions or terms let us not destroy the work of God. Do you love and serve God? It is enough. I give you the right hand of fellowship. If there be any consolation in Christ, if any comfort of love, if any fellowship of the Spirit, if any bowels and mercies, let us strive together for the faith of the Gospel, walking worthy of the vocation wherewith we are called—with all lowliness and meekness, with longsuffering, forbearing one another in love, endeavoring to keep the unity of the Spirit in the bond of peace, remembering that there is one body and one Spirit, even as we are called with one hope of our calling, "one Lord, one faith, one baptism, one God and Father of all, who is above all, and through all, and in you all."

# Jesus, Thy Blood and Righteousness*
## *"Christi Blut und Gerechtigkeit"*

Jesus, thy blood and righteousness
My beauty are, my glorious dress;
Midst flaming worlds, in these arrayed,
With joy shall I lift up my head.

Bold shall I stand in thy great day,
For who aught to my charge shall lay?
Fully absolved through these I am,
From sin and fear, from guilt and shame.

The holy, meek, unspotted Lamb,
Who from the Father's bosom came,
Who died for me, e'en me to atone.
Now for my Lord and God I own.

Lord, I believe thy precious blood,
Which at the mercy-seat of God
Forever doth for sinners plead,
For me—e'en for my soul—was shed.

Lord, I believe were sinners more
Than sands upon the ocean shore,
Thou hast for all a ransom paid,
For all a full atonement made.

When from the dust of death I rise
To claim my mansion in the skies,
E'en then this shall be all my plea:
Jesus hath lived, hath died for me.

Thus Abraham, the Friend of God,
Thus all heaven's armies bought with blood,
Saviour of sinners, thee proclaim;
Sinners of whom the chief I am.

*Translated and abridged by John Wesley, 1740, from Count Nicolaus Ludwig von Zinzendorf, 1739.

Jesus, be endless praise to thee,
Whose boundless mercy hath for me,—
For me, and all thy hands have made,
An everlasting ransom paid.

Ah! give to all thy servants, Lord,
With power to speak thy gracious word;
That all who to thy wounds will flee,
May find eternal life in thee.

Thou, God of power, thou, God of love,
Let the whole world thy mercy prove!
Now let thy word o'er all prevail:
Now take the spoils of death and hell.

# *from the* Letters

## *Charismatic Manifestations*

To His Brother Samuel                    *Bristol, May 10, 1739*

Dear Brother,

The having abundance of work upon my hands is only *a* cause of my not writing sooner. *The* cause was rather my unwillingness to continue an unprofitable dispute.*

The gospel promises to you and me, and our children, and all that are afar off—even as many of those whom the Lord our God shall call as are not disobedient unto the heavenly vision—"the witness of God's Spirit with their spirit that they are the children of God," that they are now at this hour all accepted in the Beloved. But it witnesses not that they shall be. It is an assurance of present salvation only, therefore not necessarily perpetual, or irreversible.

I am one of many witnesses of this matter of fact, that God does now make good this His promise daily, very frequently during a representation (how made I know not, but not to the outward eye) of Christ either hanging on the cross or standing on the right hand of God. And this I know to be of God, because from that hour the person so affected is a new creature both as to his inward dispositions and outward life. "Old things are passed away, and all things become new."

A very recent instance of this I will give you. While we were praying at a Society here, on Tuesday the 1st instant, the power of God (so I call it) came so mightily among us that one, and another, and another fell down as thunder-struck. In that hour many that were in deep anguish of spirit were all filled with peace and joy. Ten persons, till then in sin, doubt, and fear, found such a change that sin had no more dominion over them;

---

*Samuel, schoolmaster at Blundell's School, had been much alarmed at reports of his brother's "enthusiasm," especially at reports of extravagant emotional and physical outbursts in connection with some of his preaching. He has written letters expressing his horror of what he thought excesses, even "downright madness," and had been reproved for his lack of spiritual discernment. John intends this letter, then, as both explanation and vindication of the charismatic phenomena which had been attending his ministry that year. Unhappily, Samuel died at the end of 1739, still estranged from his brothers.

instead of the spirit of fear, they are now filled with that of love and joy and a sound mind. A Quaker who stood by was very angry at them and biting his lips and knitting his brows when the Spirit of God came upon him also, so that he fell down as one dead. We prayed over him, and he soon lifted up his head with joy and joined with us in thanksgiving.

A bystander, one John Haydon, was quite enraged at this, and, being unable to deny something supernatural in it, labored beyond measure to convince all his acquaintance that it was a delusion of the devil. I was met in the street that next day by one who informed me that John Haydon was fallen raving mad. It seems he had sat down to dinner, but wanted first to make an end of a sermon he was reading. At the last page he suddenly changed color, fell off his chair, and began screaming terribly and beating himself against the ground. I found him on the floor, the room being full of people whom his wife would have kept away, but he cried out, "No, let them all come; let all the world see the just judgement of God." Two or three were holding him as well as they could. He immediately fixed his eyes on me, and said, "Aye, this is he I said deceived the people, but God hath overtaken me. I said it was a delusion of the devil, but this is no delusion." Then he roared aloud, "O thou devil, thou cursed devil, yea, thou legion of devils, thou canst not stay in me! Christ will cast thee out. I know his work is begun. Tear me to pieces if thou wilt; but thou canst not hurt me." He then beat himself again, and groaned again, with violent sweats and heaving of the breast. We prayed with him, and God put a new song in his mouth. The words were, which he pronounced with a clear, strong voice: "This is the Lord's doing, and it is marvellous in our eyes. This is the day which the Lord hath made; we will rejoice and be glad in it. Blessed be the Lord God of Israel, from this time forth forevermore." I called again an hour after. We found his body quite worn out and his voice lost. But his soul was full of joy and love, rejoicing in hope of the glory of God.

I am now in as good health (thanks be to God) as I ever was since I remember, and I believe shall be so long as I live; for I do not expect to have a lingering death. The reasons that induce me to think I shall not live long are not such as you would consider to be of any weight.* I am under no concern over this. Let my Master see to it.

Oh may the God of love be with you and my sister more and more! I am, dear brother,

Your ever affectionate Brother

JOHN WESLEY

*John Wesley was given both to drawing lots and to opening the Bible at random to seek direct spiritual guidance. As a result of one of these experiences, he believed that he would be martyred soon, at Bristol, probably in the course of his field preaching there.

# Christian Prudence

TO SIR JAMES LOWTHER, AFTERWARDS EARL OF LONSDALE
*London, May 16, 1759*

DEAR SIR,

Since I received your favor I have had many thoughts on worldly and Christian prudence. What is the nature of each? How do they differ? How may we distinguish one from the other?

It seems worldly prudence either pursues worldly ends—riches, honor, ease, or pleasure—or pursues Christian ends on worldly maxims or by worldly means. The grand maxims which obtain in the world are, "the more power, the more money, the more learning, and the more reputation a man has, the more good he will do." And whenever a Christian, pursuing the noblest ends, forms his behavior by these maxims, he will infallibly (though perhaps by insensible degrees) decline into worldly prudence. He will use more or less of conformity to the world, if not in sin, yet in doing some things that are good in themselves yet (all things considered) are not good for him, and perhaps at length using guile or disguise, simulation or dissimulation, either seeming to be what he is not, or not seeming to be what he is. By any of these marks may worldly prudence be discerned from the wisdom which is from above.

Christian prudence pursues Christian maxims, and by Christian means. The ends it pursues are holiness in every kind and in the highest degree, and usefulness in every kind and degree. And herein it proceeds on the following maxims: the help that is done upon earth, God doeth Himself. It is He that worketh all in all, and that not by human power (generally He uses weak things to confound the strong), not by men of wealth (most of his choicest instruments may say, "Silver and gold have I none"), not by men of reputation, but by the men that were as the filth and offscouring of the world, all of which is for this plain reason, "that no flesh may glory in his sight."

Christian prudence pursues these ends upon these principles, by only Christian means. A truly prudent Christian, while in things purely indifferent he becomes all things to all men, yet wherever duty is concerned, the example of all mankind matters no more than a grain of sand. His word is then:

> *Non me, qui caetera, vincit*
> *Impetus; et rapido contrarius evehor orbi*
>
> ["I steer against their notions; nor am I
> Borne back by all the current of the sky."]

He will not, to gain the favor or shun the hate of all, omit the least point of duty. He cannot prevail upon himself on any account or pretence to use either simulation or dissimulation. There is no guile in his mouth, no evasion or ambiguity. Having one desire, one design, to glorify God with his body and with his spirit; having only one fear

> Lest a motion, or a word,
> Or thought arise to grieve his Lord;

having one rule, the Word of God; one guide, even his Spirit, he goes on in childlike simplicity. Continually seeing Him that is invisible, he walks in open day. Looking unto Jesus, and deriving strength from Him, he goes on in his hope, till he is called up to be ever with the Lord.

Oh that this were in all points your own character! Surely you desire it above all things. But how shall you attain? Difficulties and hindrances surround you on every side! Can you bear with my plainness? I believe you can. Therefore I will speak without any reserve. I fear you have scarce one friend who has not more or less of the prudence which is not from above. And I doubt you have (in or near your own rank) hardly one example of true Christian prudence! Yet I am persuaded your own heart advises you right, or rather God in your heart. Oh that you may hearken to his voice alone, and let all creatures keep silence before Him! Why should they encumber you with Saul's armor? If you essay to go forth thus, it will be in vain. You have no need of this, neither of his sword or spear, for you trust in the Lord of Hosts. O go forth in his strength, and with the stones of the brook you shall overthrow all your enemies.

I am, dear sir,

Your obedient servant for Christ's sake

JOHN WESLEY

# A Plan for Christian Education at Home

To Margaret Lewen*                                          *June 1764*

1. You want to know God, in order to enjoy Him in time and in eternity.

2. All that you want to know of Him is contained in one book, the Bible. Therefore your one point is to understand this. And all you learn is to be referred to this, as either directly or remotely conducive to it.

---

*Miss Lewen was a recent convert, twenty-two years of age, and devoted to Wesley, to whom she made a gift of a chaise and pair of horses. She died at the home of Mary Bosanquet (later Mrs. Fletcher) only two years after this letter was written.

3. Might it not be well, then, to spend at least two hours every day in reading and meditating upon the Bible—reading every morning (if not every evening too) a portion of the Old and then of the New Testament? If you would save yourself the trouble of thinking, add Mr. Henry's *Comment;* if you would only be assisted in thinking, add the *Explanatory Notes.*

4. But I find a difficulty already. Can you help me over it? Have you more candor than almost anyone in the world? Will you not blame me for recommending, as they come in the way, tracts published by myself? I think you will not. So I will set down these (in their place) as freely as other books.

5. Your studying hours (if your constitution will bear it) might be five or six hours a day, perhaps from nine to twelve in the morning, and from two to four or five in the afternoon. And whenever you begin to be tired with books that require a strong and deep attention, relax your mind by interposing history or poetry or something of a lighter nature.

6. The first thing you should understand a little of is Grammar; in order to do so it will suffice to read first the Kingswood *English Grammar* (which is exceedingly short) and then Bishop Lowth's *Introduction.*

7. Next it would be worth your while to acquire a little knowledge in Arithmetic. Dilworth's *Arithmetic* would give you full as much as you want.

8. You might proceed to Geography. But in this I would not advise you to encumber yourself with many books. You need only master one, Randal's *Geographical Grammar,* and then betake yourself to the Globes. I believe those of Mr. Adams are the best, to which you may add his little book of *Instructions.*

9. Logic naturally follows, and I really think it is worth all the rest put together. But here I am at a full stop, for I know no good treatise on the subject in English, except Aldrich's *Logic,** and that I am afraid you cannot understand without an instructor. I shall be glad to give you a little assistance in the short time we have together.

10. As to Ethics (or Moral Philosophy) there is fully as much of it as you want in Langbain's *Compendium.*

11. In Natural Philosophy you have a large field. You may begin with a *Survey of the Wisdom of God in the Creation.* This contains the substance of Ray, Derham, Niewentyt, *Nature Displayed,* and all the other celebrated books on the subject. You may add that fine book, Mr. Jones' *Principles of Natural Philosophy.* Thence you will easily pass to the Glasgow [Edinburgh] abridgement of Mr. Hutchinson's *Works.* The abridgers give not

---

*It is curious that Wesley does not here refer to the work on this subject by Isaac Watts, which was the standard University text of the period.

only all his sense, but all his spirit. You may add to these the beautiful tracts of Lord Forbes, and if you would go a little further, Mr. Baker's ingenious *Treatise on the Microscope*.

12. With any or all of the foregoing studies you may intermix that of History. Geography and Chronology are termed the two eyes of history. Geography has been mentioned before, and I think all you want of Chronology may be learned from Marshall's *Chronological Tables*.

13. You may begin with Rollin's *Ancient History;* afterwards read in order Puffendorf's *Introduction to the History of Europe,* the *Concise Church History,* Burnet's *History of the Reformation,* the *Concise History of England,* Clarendon's *History of the Great Rebellion,* Neal's *History of the Puritans,* his *History of New England,* and Solis's *History of the Conquest of Mexico.*

14. Whitby's *Compendium of Metaphysics* will introduce you to that science. You may go on with Locke's *Essay on Human Understanding,* Bishop Browne on the *Nature, Procedure, and Limits of Human Understanding,* and Malebranche's *Search after Truth.*

15. For Poetry you may read Spenser's *Faery Queen* [sic], Fairfax's or Hoole's *Godfrey of Bulloigne,* select parts of Shakespeare, *Paradise Lost,* the *Night Thoughts,* and *Moral and Sacred Poems.*

16. You are glad to begin and end with Divinity. But I must not expatiate here. I will only recommend to your careful perusal Bishop Pearson *On the Creed,* Mr. Nelson's *Sermons,* and the *Christian Library.*

This course of study, if you have the resolution to go through it, will, I apprehend, take you three, four, or five years, according to the degree of your health and of your application. And you will then have knowledge enough for any reasonable Christian. But remember, before all, in all, and above all, your great point is to know the only true God and Jesus Christ whom He has sent.

I am, dear Miss Lewen,
Your affectionate brother

JOHN WESLEY

## *Against Slavery*

TO WILLIAM WILBERFORCE          *Balam, February 24, 1791*

DEAR SIR,

Unless the divine power has raised you up to be as *Athanasius contra mundum,** I see not how you can go through your glorious enterprise in

*"Athanasius against the world."

opposing this execrable villainy, which is the scandal of religion, of England, and of human nature. Unless God has raised you up for this very thing, you will be worn out by the opposition of men and devils. But if God be for you, who can be against you? Are all of them together stronger than God? O be not weary of well doing! Go on, in the name of God and in the power of his might, till even American slavery (the vilest that ever saw the sun) shall vanish away before it.

Reading this morning a tract written by a poor African, I was particularly struck by that circumstance, that a man who has a black skin, being wronged or outraged by a white man, can have no redress; it being a *law* in all our colonies that the oath of a black against a white goes for nothing. What villainy is this!

That He who has guided you from youth up may continue to strengthen you in this and all things is the prayer of, dear sir,

Your affectionate servant

JOHN WESLEY

# CHARLES WESLEY
## 1707 · 1788

The hymnwriter in his early sixties (1770).

## INTRODUCTION

Better English poets there may be, but there is none so widely known as Charles Wesley, and, as Robert Southey observed, surely none so widely quoted on deathbeds or in times of pressing need. Even ardent critics of Methodism have had little but praise for Charles, who was not only a great composer of hymns but a tireless worker among the poor, arranging for their children to go to school and for the release of those in debtors' prison. He was not only an effective evangelist but, in the ministry he had in London toward the close of his life, he proved a great leader of worship and was widely noted for his spirit of prayer. A contemporary writes:

> Never did I hear such praying. Never did I see or hear such evident marks of fervency in the service of God. At the close of every petition a serious "Amen," like a gentle rushing sound of water, ran through the whole audience . . . indicating a lively fervent devotion I was never witness to before. If there be such a thing as heavenly music upon earth, I heard it there.[1]

Charles was born the eighteenth child to his parents, the third and youngest surviving son and, as a seven-months baby, was reared with difficulty. Like his brother Samuel and William Cowper he was educated at Westminster School. A bright and able student, he was elected King's scholar in 1721, and school captain (head boy)—an office which he used to protect weaker students and those who were abused because of Catholic origins. An Irish nobleman of distant family connection offered to adopt him and so make him heir to his estate, but he refused, going in 1726 to Christ Church College, Oxford. At Westminster he had been tutored by his older brother Samuel; he refused to have John be his tutor in Oxford. It was while John was on leave from Oxford that he "persuaded two or three young scholars to accompany me, and to observe the method of study prescribed by the statutes of the University. This gained me the harmless nickname of methodist."[2]

Whatever else is true about the name (it had been applied to some Puritans in the previous century), it is clear enough that at this time Charles was the first so called, and that he was initially called a "methodist" simply for advocating a system of study, study of any serious kind being an extremely rare thing, and intimidating amidst the profligate indolence of Oxford in that period.[3]

When John returned to Oxford late in 1729, he took over leadership of the study group—predictably. But Charles was keen, and even after his graduation in 1730 and the commencement of his work as a Latin tutor (in which he excelled), he was ardent for the movement's objectives of promoting study and religious observance, such as regular attendance at chapel. When George Whitefield first turned to the group in 1732 he did so through Charles. During all these years he sought only to continue as a tutor and conspicuously avoided any movement toward ordination, though he continued to read deeply in mystical writers and the early spiritual classics of the medieval church.

Strikingly different from John in character, he nevertheless was always loyal to him; against his oldest brother Samuel's opposition and despite his own misgivings he was eventually ordained and left with John on his American voyage in 1735. Acting officially as secretary to the governor of Georgia, he engaged in preaching on the side, with dismal results. Discouraged, he returned to England and to Oxford. There he assisted Count Zinzendorf and the Moravians, worked closely with Bishop Potter, and, still seeking a focus for his spiritual life, consulted William Law (without satisfaction). Then he met Peter Böhler, who studied English with him during a visit to Oxford. Böhler put Luther's commentary on Galatians into his hand. It was a pivotal experience: the same book which had so moved the simple Puritan John Bunyan eighty-five years earlier, now profoundly spoke to the Oxford academic. On Whitsunday (Pentecost) 1738, everything came to a point of solution and release, a similar experience coming to John in London the following Wednesday. Though not yet licenced, Charles resumed preaching with new zeal and immediately encountered various expressions of stiff opposition, culminating in a summons to the archbishop's Lambeth Palace, where he was censured and made to pay a huge fine for trespass (for walking across a private meadow on his way to preach to a crowd on Kensington Common).

With nothing else left to him, he started his itinerant preaching ministry in the summer of 1739 in Bristol, and for the next seventeen years traversed England and Wales, making two visits also to Ireland. A much more restrained preacher than Whitefield, and a less awe-inspiring personality than his brother John, he was nonetheless fluent and effective, and his music added a powerful dimension to his evangelistic meetings that the others most often lacked. Both by conviction and style he was more tolerant than John, and it is indicative of his disposition that he was able to report of his reception in Ireland that "the Presbyterians say I am a Presbyterian; the Anglicans that I am a minister of theirs; and the Catholics are sure that I am a good Catholic in my heart."[4]

In 1749, Charles married Sally Gwynne, of the well-known Welsh family Gwynne, in what was the only evidently happy marriage of the Wesley family, and one of the few to be discovered among the evangelical leaders of the time. Sally's beautiful voice led the singing in Charles's meetings, and she accompanied him on his many journeys.

Altogether in his lifetime Charles Wesley wrote about 6,500 hymns. About 500 of these are in use today by a variety of Christian denominations around the world. Following from his own early attraction to a meditative spirituality, the emphasis of his hymns is on worship, praise, and devotion. His sacramental hymns (1745) teach clearly the pre-Reformation doctrine of the "real presence" of Christ in the Eucharist, and are thus consistent with his general stress on the active presence of the Holy Spirit in rightly engaged worship.

It must be said that Charles entirely opposed any drift of the Methodist movement away from the Established Church. Indeed, when it seemed that this might be the eventuality, he preached against it, calling for renewal within the church rather than another form of dissent. The Anglican establishment, for their own purposes, welcomed this stand, and even offered him a benefice worth the astonishingly large sum of £500 per year. This he declined without hesitation. Yet he used every opportunity to try to obtain for Methodist preachers admission to Anglican orders.

After 1761 his health failed, and he was forced to retire from his saddleback ministry to Bath. Concerned with what seemed to him excesses in his brother's stress on the doctrine of "Christian perfection," he characteristically drew back from extreme formulations, preferring to speak of a gradual process of maturation and deepening of the spiritual life in its growth toward God. Maintaining, despite their differences in these points, his strong personal loyalty to John, he nevertheless turned his own efforts more and more toward prison ministry and other grassroots work. When a wealthy patron of the Methodist movement offered his family a furnished house in London he moved there to continue these labors principally in the capital; after 1778, he took up regular preaching duties at City Road Chapel, in which he continued till his death in 1788. In respect for his own wishes he was buried at the parish church of St. Marylebone (having declined burial at City Road Chapel because the ground was unconsecrated). His coffin was borne to its place of interment by eight Anglican priests.

Charles Wesley was not a commanding person in the flesh. Short, somewhat round-faced, he was apparently near-sighted, abrupt in conversation, and awkward in social manner. He had a remarkable—but probably quite irritating—ability both to read and compose while life and conversation were going on all around him, yet despite these well-developed powers of concentration he was notoriously absent-minded, and clearly depended heavily on his wife Sally for the maintenance of anything like the methodical and disciplined regulation of life to which he aspired. Yet his spiritual character was luminous, and communicated itself immediately to those who came into conversation with him.

William Wilberforce, who considered the more prominent John "a fine old fellow," was captivated by Charles. He met him in 1786 in the house of Hannah More, and his later recollection of that encounter reveals something of the special presence of this unusual man:

> . . . when I came into the room Charles Wesley rose from the table, and coming forward to me, gave me solemnly his blessing. I was scarcely ever more affected. Such was the effect of his manner and appearance that it altogether overset me, and I burst into tears, unable to restrain myself.[5]

John Wesley wrote of his brother that "his least praise was his talent for poetry, although Dr. [Isaac] Watts did not scruple to say that that single poem, 'Wrestling Jacob,' was worth all the verses he himself had written."[6] At our distance it is clear, however, that the greatest debt we owe to Charles Wesley is for the gift of his great hymns of the faith. In his own time, when hymn singing for the working class was essentially a new thing, his verse had a dramatic impact. In the words of the great historian J. Wesley Bready, we need, to appreciate this, to imagine the singing "multitudes, up and down the land, including many who had once been drunkards, prostitutes, wife-beaters, bruisers, gamblers, smugglers, sluggards, and thieves, as they joined in the refrain:

> My chains fell off, my heart was free
> I rose, went forth, and followed Thee.[7]

In such compositions as "Christ the Lord Is Risen Today," "O For a Thousand Tongues to Sing," "And Can It Be that I Should Gain," countless thousands have been blessed, and the outpouring of divine poetry from this one man's pen after Pentecost 1738 must surely be reckoned as one of the great testaments of inspiration in the history of English spiritual literature.

## NOTES

1. Quoted in Marjorie Bowen, *Wrestling Jacob: A Study of the Life of John Wesley* . . . (London: The Religious Book Club, 1938), p. 272.
2. Letter to Thomas B. Chandler, April 28, 1785.
3. "Charles Wesley" entry in the *Dictionary of National Biography,* p. 300.
4. Letter dated Kinsale, September 8, 1748.
5. Quoted in Robert Isaac Wilberforce and Samuel Wilberforce, *The Life of William Wilberforce,* 5 vols. (London: Murray, 1839), vol. 1, p. 248; cf. p. 206.
6. *Conference Minutes,* 1788.
7. J. Wesley Bready, *England Before and After Wesley,* p. 272.

# Hymns and Poems

## Wrestling Jacob

BASED ON GENESIS 32:26–31, AND HOSEA 12:4

Come, O thou Traveller unknown,
    Whom still I hold, but cannot see!
My company before is gone,
    And I am left alone with thee;
With thee all night I mean to stay,
And wrestle till the break of day.

I need not tell thee who I am,
    My misery or sin declare.
Thyself hast called me by my name:
    Look on thy hands, and read it there.
But who, I ask thee, who art thou?
Tell me thy name, and tell me now.

In vain thou strugglest to get free;
    I never will unloose my hold.
Art thou the Man that died for me?
    The secret of thy love unfold:
Wrestling, I will not let thee go,
Till I thy name, thy nature know.

Wilt thou not yet to me reveal
    Thy new, unutterable name?
Tell me, I still beseech thee, tell;
    To know it now resolved I am:
Wrestling, I will not let thee go,
Till I thy name, thy nature know.

'Tis all in vain to hold thy tongue,
    Or touch the hollow of my thigh:
Though every sinew be unstrung,
    Out of my arms thou shalt not fly;
Wrestling, I will not let thee go,
Till I thy name, thy nature know.

What though my shrinking flesh complain,
  And murmur to contend so long?
I rise superior to my pain:
  When I am weak, then I am strong:
And when my all of strength shall fail,
I shall with the God-man prevail.

My strength is gone, my nature dies;
  I sink beneath thy weighty hand;
Faint to revive, and fall to rise:
  I fall, and yet by faith I stand.
I stand, and will not let thee go,
Till I thy name, thy nature know.

Yield to me now, for I am weak,
  But confident in self-despair;
Speak to my heart, in blessings speak;
  Be conquered by my instant prayer:
Speak, or thou never hence shalt move,
And tell me if thy name is Love.

'Tis Love! 'tis Love! thou diedst for me;
  I hear thy whisper in my heart.
The morning breaks, the shadows flee;
  Pure, universal Love thou art:
To me, to all, thy bowels move;
Thy nature and thy name is Love.

My prayer hath power with God; the grace
  Unspeakable I now receive;
Through faith I see thee face to face;
  I see thee face to face, and live.
In vain I have not wept and strove;
Thy nature and thy name is Love.

I know thee, Saviour, who thou art,
  Jesus, the feeble sinner's Friend;
Nor wilt thou with the night depart,
  But stay and love me to the end:
Thy mercies never shall remove;
Thy nature and thy name is Love.

The Sun of Righteousness on me
  Hath rose with healing in his wings:

Withered my nature's strength; from thee
  My soul its life and succor brings.
My help is all laid up above:
Thy nature and thy name is Love.

Contented now, upon my thigh
  I halt, till life's short journey end;
All helplessness, all weakness, I
  On thee alone for strength depend;
Nor have I power from thee to move:
Thy nature and thy name is Love.

Lame as I am, I take the prey;
  Hell, earth, and sin, with ease o'ercome;
I leap for joy, pursue my way,
  And as a bounding hart fly home,
Through all eternity to prove
Thy nature and thy name is Love.

1742

# Love Divine, All Love Excelling

Love divine, all love excelling,
    Joy of heaven, to earth come down;
Fix in us thy humble dwelling;
    All thy faithful mercies crown.
Jesus, thou art all compassion;
    Pure, unbounded love thou art:
Visit us with thy salvation;
    Enter every trembling heart.

Breathe, O breathe thy loving Spirit
    Into every troubled breast;
Let us all in thee inherit,
    Let us find the promised rest:
Take away our power of sinning,
    Alpha and Omega be,—
End of faith, as its beginning,
    Set our hearts at liberty.

Come, almighty to deliver,
    Let us all thy life receive;
Suddenly return, and never,
    Nevermore thy temples leave.
Thee we would be always blessing,
    Serve thee as thy hosts above;
Pray, and praise thee without ceasing;
    Glory in thy precious love.

Finish, then, thy new creation;
    Pure and sinless may we be:
Let us see thy great salvation
    Perfectly restored by thee:
Changed from glory into glory,
    Till in heaven we take our place:
Till we cast our crowns before thee,
    Lost in wonder, love, and praise!

1746

# Oh, for a Heart to Praise My God

Oh, for a heart to praise my God,
  A heart from sin set free!
A heart that always feels thy blood,
  So freely spilt for me!

A heart resigned, submissive, meek,
  My great Redeemer's throne,
Where only Christ is heard to speak,
  Where Jesus reigns alone.

Oh! for a lowly, contrite heart,
  Believing, true, and clean,
Which neither life nor death can part
  From him that dwells within.

A heart in every thought renewed,
  And full of love divine,
Perfect, and right, and pure, and good—
  A copy, Lord, of thine!

Thy tender heart is still the same,
  And melts at human woe;
Jesu, for thee distressed I am—
  I want thy love to know.

My heart, thou know'st, can never rest
  Till thou create my peace
Till, of my Eden repossessed,
  From every sin I cease.

Fruit of thy gracious lips, on me
  Bestow that peace unknown,
The hidden manna, and the tree
  Of life, and the white stone.

Thy nature, gracious Lord, impart;
  Come quickly from above;
Write thy new name upon my heart,
  Thy new, best name of love!

1742

# Come, Thou Almighty King

Come, thou almighty King!
Help us thy name to sing,
　Help us to praise:
Father, all-glorious,
O'er all victorious,
Come, and reign over us,
　Ancient of days!

Jesus, our Lord, arise;
Scatter our enemies,
　And make them fall:
Let Thine almighty aid
Our sure defence be made;
Our souls on thee be stayed
　Lord, hear our call.

Come, thou incarnate Word!
Gird on thy mighty sword;
　Our prayer attend:
Come, and thy people bless,
And give thy word success;
Spirit of holiness,
　On us descend!

Come, holy Comforter!
Thy sacred witness bear,
　In this glad hour:
Thou, who almighty art,
Now rule in every heart,
And ne'er from us depart,
　Spirit of power!

To the great One in Three,
The highest praises be,
　Hence, evermore!
His sovereign majesty
May we in glory see,
And to eternity
　Love and adore!

1757

# Jesu, Lover of My Soul*

Jesu, lover of my soul,
    Let me to thy bosom fly,
While the nearer waters roll,
    While the tempest still is high;
Hide me, O my Saviour, hide,
    Till the storm of life be past;
Safe into the haven guide;
    Oh, receive my soul at last!

Other refuge have I none;
    Hangs my helpless soul on thee;
Leave, ah, leave me not alone,
    Still support and comfort me!
All my trust on thee is stayed,
    All my help from thee I bring;
Cover my defenceless head
    With the shadow of thy wing!

Wilt thou not regard my call?
    Wilt thou not accept my prayer?
Lo! I sink, I faint, I fall!
    Lo! on thee I cast my care!
Reach me out thy gracious hand!
    While I of thy strength receive,
Hoping against hope I stand,
    Dying, and behold I live!

Thou, O Christ, art all I want;
    More than all in thee I find:
Raise the fallen, cheer the faint,
    Heal the sick, and lead the blind!
Just and holy is thy name;
    I am all unrighteousness;
False and full of sin I am,
    Thou art full of truth and grace.

*John expressed displeasure with this hymn for what he felt was its excessive emotionalism, especially in stanza 3, and asked that it be repressed.

Plenteous grace with thee is found,
　Grace to cover all my sin;
Let the healing streams abound;
　Make and keep me pure within!
Thou of life the fountain art;
　Freely let me take of thee;
Spring thou up within my heart!
　Rise to all eternity!

1740

# And Can it be That I Should Gain

And can it be that I should gain
  An interest in the Savior's blood?
Died he for me, who caused his pain?
  For me? Who him to death pursued?
Amazing love! How can it be
That thou, my God, shouldst die for me?

'Tis myst'ry all: th'Immortal dies!
  Who can explore his strange design?
In vain the firstborn seraph tries
  To sound the depths of love divine.
'Tis mercy all! Let earth adore!
Let angel minds inquire no more.

He left his Father's throne above
  (So free, so infinite his grace!),
Emptied himself of all but love,
  And bled for Adam's helpless race.
'Tis mercy all, immense and free,
For, O my God, it found out me!

Long my imprisoned spirit lay,
  Fast bound in sin and nature's night.
Thine eye diffused a quick'ning ray;
  I woke; the dungeon flamed with light.
My chains fell off, my heart was free,
I rose, went forth, and followed thee.

No condemnation now I dread,
  Jesus, and all in him, is mine.
Alive in him, my living head,
  And clothed in righteousness divine,
Bold I approach th'eternal throne,
And claim the crown, through Christ my own.

1739

# Holy Spirit

Jesus, we on the word depend,
    Spoken by thee while present here,
"The Father in my name shall send
    The Holy Ghost, the Comforter."

That promise made to Adam's race,
    Now, Lord, in us, even us, fulfill;
And give the Spirit of thy grace,
    To teach us all thy perfect will.

That heavenly Teacher of mankind,
    That Guide infallible impart,
To bring thy sayings to our mind,
    And write them on our faithful heart.

He only can the words apply
    Through which we endless life possess,
And deal to each his legacy,
    His Lord's unutterable peace.

That peace of God, that peace of thine,
    Oh, might he now to us bring in,
And fill our souls with power divine,
    And make an end of fear and sin;

The length and breadth of love reveal,
    The height and depth of Deity;
And all the sons of glory seal,
    And change, and make us all like thee!

1746

263

# Stay, Thou Insulted Spirit, Stay

Stay, thou insulted Spirit, stay,
  Though I have done thee such despite;
Nor cast the sinner quite away,
  Nor take thine everlasting flight.

Though I have steeled my stubborn heart,
  And still shook off my guilty fears;
And vexed, and urged thee to depart,
  For forty long rebellious years:

Though I have most unfaithful been
  Of all who e'er thy grace received;
Ten thousand times thy goodness seen,
  Ten thousand times thy goodness grieved:

Yet oh, the chief of sinners spare,
  In honor of my great High Priest;
Nor in thy righteous anger swear
  To exclude me from thy people's rest.

This only woe I deprecate,
  This only plague, I pray, remove,
Nor leave me in my lost estate,
  Nor curse me with this want of love.

If yet thou canst my sins forgive,
  From now, O Lord, relieve my woes;
Into the rest of love receive,
  And bless me with the calm repose.

From now, my weary soul release;
  Upraise me with thy gracious hand,
And guide into thy perfect peace,
  And bring me to the promised land.

1749

# The Eucharistic Mystery

Oh the depth of love Divine,
  Th' unfathomable grace!
Who shall say how bread and wine
  God into man conveys!
*How* the bread his flesh imparts,
  *How* the wine transmits his blood,
Fills his faithful people's hearts
  With all the life of God!

Let the wisest mortal show
  How we the grace receive,
Feeble elements bestow
  A power not theirs to give.
Who explains the wondrous way,
  How through these the virtue came?
These the virtue did convey,
  Yet still remain the same.

How can heavenly spirits rise,
  By earthly matter fed,
Drink herewith Divine supplies,
  And eat immortal bread?
Ask the Father's Wisdom *how*;
  Him that did the means ordain!
Angels round our altars bow
  To search it out in vain.

Sure and real is the grace
  The manner be unknown;
Only meet us in thy ways,
  And perfect us in one.
Let us taste the heavenly powers;
  Lord, we ask for nothing more:
Thine to bless, 'tis only ours
  To wonder and adore.

1745

# Communion Hymn

Jesu, my Lord and God bestow
All which thy sacrament doth show,
　　And make the real sign
A sure effectual means of grace,
Then sanctify my heart, and bless,
　　And make it all like thine.

Great is thy faithfulness and love,
Thine ordinance can never prove
　　Of none effect, and vain;
Only do thou my heart prepare
To find thy real presence there,
　　And all thy fulness gain.

1745

# Christ the Lord Is Risen Today

"Christ the Lord is risen to-day,"
Sons of men and angels say!
Raise your joys and triumphs high:
Sing, ye heavens; thou earth reply.

Love's redeeming work is done;
Fought the fight, the battle won:
Lo! the sun's eclipse is o'er,
Lo! he sets in blood no more!

Vain the stone, the watch, the seal,
Christ hath burst the gates of hell:
Death in vain forbids his rise,
Christ hath opened Paradise.

Lives again our glorious King!
Where, O death, is now thy sting!
Once he died our souls to save;
Where's thy victory, boasting grave!

Soar we now where Christ hath led,
Following our exalted Head:
Made like him, like him we rise,
Ours the cross, the grave, the skies.

King of glory! Soul of bliss!
Everlasting life is this,
Thee to know, thy power to prove,
Thus to sing, and thus to love.

1739

# Come, Thou Long-Expected Jesus

Come, thou long-expected Jesus,
    Born to set thy people free,
From our fears and sins release us,
    Let us find our rest in thee.
Israel's strength and consolation,
    Hope of all the earth thou art;
Dear Desire of every nation,
    Joy of every longing heart.

Born thy people to deliver,
    Born a child and yet a king,
Born to reign in us forever,
    Now thy gracious kingdom bring:
By thine own eternal Spirit
    Rule in all our hearts alone;
By thine all-sufficient merit
    Raise us to thy glorious throne.

1746

# Ye Servants of God*

Ye servants of God, Your Master proclaim,
And publish abroad His wonderful name:
The name all-victorious Of Jesus extol;
His kingdom is glorious, And rules over all.

The waves of the sea Have lift up their voice,
Sore troubled that we In Jesus rejoice;
The floods they are roaring, But Jesus is here;
While we are adoring He is always near.

Men, devils engage, The billows arise,
And horrible rage, And threaten the skies;
Their fury shall never Our steadfastness shock,
The weakest believer Is built on a Rock.

God ruleth on high, Almighty to save,
And still he is nigh, His presence we have;
The great congregation His triumph shall sing,
Ascribing salvation To Jesus our King.

Salvation to God Who sits on the throne!
Let all cry aloud, And honor the Son!
Our Jesus praises The angels proclaim,
Fall down on their faces, And worship the Lamb.

Then let us adore, And give Him his right,
All glory, and power, And wisdom and might,
All honor and blessing, With angels above,
And thanks never ceasing, And infinite love.

1745

---

*This hymn is a splendid example of Charles's gift for rhythm and rhyme together, and with its split stanza effect it acquires the extra emphasis of caesura. In this it harks back to the earliest roots of English vernacular hymnody, the verse of Wesley's Anglo-Saxon forebears, who might well have admired this great "storm song" in praise of the Creator.

# Lo! He Comes with Clouds Descending*

Lo! He comes with clouds descending,
    Once for favored sinners slain;
Thousand thousand saints attending,
    Swell the triumph of his train:
        Hallelujah!
    God appears on earth to reign.

Every eye shall now behold him
    Robed in dreadful majesty;
Those who set at nought and sold him,
    Pierced and nailed him to the tree,
        Deeply wailing,
    Shall the true Messiah see.

The dear tokens of his passion
    Still his dazzling body bears;
Cause of endless exultation
    To his ransomed worshipers;
        With what rapture
    Gaze we on those glorious scars!

Yea, Amen! let all adore thee,
    High on thy eternal throne;
Savior, take the power and glory
    Claim the kingdom for thine own;
        Jah, Jehovah,
    Everlasting God, come down!

1758

*As found in most hymn books, this has a fifth and sixth stanza, additions which occurred in adaptations by John Cennick and Martin Madan. Later, it was expanded to nine stanzas by Sir Samuel Brydges. See the General Introduction for further information.

# Pilgrim Song

Come on, my partners in distress,
My comrades through the wilderness,
  Who still your bodies feel;
Awhile forget your griefs and fears,
And look beyond this vale of tears
  To that celestial hill.

Beyond the bounds of time and space
Look forward to that heavenly place,
  The saints' secure abode;
On faith's strong eagle pinions rise,
And force your passage to the skies,
  And scale the mount of God.

Who suffer with our Master here,
We shall before his face appear,
  And by his side sit down;
To patient faith the prize is sure,
And all that to the end endure
  The cross, shall wear the crown.

Thrice blessed bliss-inspiring hope!
It lifts the fainting spirits up,
  It brings to life the dead;
Our conflicts here shall soon be past,
And you and I ascend at last
  Triumphant with our head.

That great mysterious Deity
We soon with open face shall see;
  The beatific sight
Shall fill heaven's sounding courts with praise,
And wide diffuse the golden blaze
  Of everlasting light.

The Father shining on his throne,
The glorious, co-eternal Son,
   The Spirit, one and seven,*
Conspire our rapture to complete,
And lo! we fall before his feet,
   And silence heightens heaven.

In hope of that ecstatic pause,
Jesu, we now sustain the cross,
   And at thy footstool fall,
Till thou our hidden life reveal,
Till thou our ravished spirits fill,
   And God is all in all.

1749

*Referring to the "seven gifts" of the Spirit.

# Soldiers of Christ, Arise

Soldiers of Christ, arise,
   And put your armor on,
Strong in the strength which God supplies
   Through his eternal Son;
Strong in the Lord of Hosts,
   And in his mighty power;
Who in the strength of Jesus trusts,
   Is more than conqueror.

Stand, then, in his great might,
   With all his strength endued;
But take, to arm you for the fight,
   The panoply of God:
That, having all things done,
   And all your conflicts past,
Ye may o'ercome, through Christ alone,
   And stand entire at last.

Stand, then, against your foes,
   In close and firm array:
Legions of wily fiends oppose
   Throughout the evil day:
But meet the sons of night,
   But mock their vain design,
Armed in the arms of heavenly light,
   Of righteousness divine.

Leave no unguarded place,
   No weakness of the soul;
Take every virtue, every grace,
   And fortify the whole:
Indissolubly joined,
   To battle all proceed;
But arm yourselves with all the mind
   That was in Christ your Head.

But above all lay hold
　　On faith's victorious shield;
Armed with that adamant and gold,
　　Be sure to win the field:
If faith surround your heart,
　　Satan shall be subdued;
Repelled his every fiery dart,
　　And quenched with Jesus' blood.

Jesus hath died for you;
　　What can his love withstand?
Believe, hold fast your shield, and who
　　Shall pluck you from his hand?
Believe that Jesus reigns;
　　All power to him is given:
Believe, till freed from sin's remains;
　　Believe yourselves to heaven.

To keep your armor bright,
　　Attend with constant care,
Still walking in your Captain's sight,
　　And watching unto prayer.
Ready for all alarms,
　　Steadfastly set your face,
And always exercise your arms,
　　And use your every grace.

Pray, without ceasing pray,
　　Your Captain gives the word;
His summons cheerfully obey,
　　And call upon the Lord:
To God your every want
　　In instant prayer display;
Pray always; pray, and never faint;
　　Pray, without ceasing pray.

In fellowship alone,
　　To God with faith draw near;
Approach his courts, besiege his throne
　　With all the power of prayer:
His mercy now implore,
　　And now show forth his praise;
In shouts, or silent awe, adore
　　His miracles of grace.

To God your spirits dart;
   Your souls in words declare;
Or groan, to him who reads the heart,
   The unutterable prayer:
His mercy now implore,
   And now show forth his praise;
In shouts, or silent awe, adore
   His miracles of grace.

Pour out your souls to God,
   And bow them with your knees;
And spread your heart and hands abroad,
   And pray for Zion's peace:
Your guides and brethren bear
   Forever on your mind;
Extend the arms of mighty prayer,
   In grasping all mankind.

From strength to strength go on;
   Wrestle and fight and pray;
Tread all the powers of darkness down,
   And win the well-fought day:
Still let the Spirit cry,
   In all his soldiers,—Come,
Till Christ the Lord descend from high,
   And take the conquerors home.

1749

## For Believers Seeking Perfect Love

God of eternal truth and grace,
  Thy faithful promise seal!
Thy word, thy oath to Abraham's race,
  In us, even us fulfill.

Let us, to perfect love restored,
  Thy image here receive;
And in the presence of our Lord
  The life of angels live.

That mighty faith on me bestow
  Which cannot ask in vain,
Which holds, and will not let thee go
  Till I my suit obtain.

Till thou into my soul inspire
  The perfect love unknown,
And tell my infinite desire,
  Whate'er thou wilt, be done.

But is it possible that I
  Should live, and sin no more?
Lord, if on thee I dare rely,
  The faith shall bring the power.

On me that faith divine bestow
  Which doth the mountain move;
And all my spotless life shall show
  Th'omnipotence of love.

1762

# A Charge to Keep

A charge to keep I have,
   A God to glorify;
A never-dying soul to save,
   And fit it for the sky:

To serve the present age,
   My calling to fulfil;
Oh, may it all my powers engage
   To do my Master's will.

Arm me with jealous care,
   As in thy sight to live;
And oh, thy servant, Lord, prepare
   A strict account to give!

Help me to watch and pray,
   And on thyself rely!
Assured if I my trust betray,
   I shall forever die.

1762

# GEORGE WHITEFIELD
## 1714 · 1770

Engraving by F. Halpin. Whitefield as a mature evangelist (c. 1765).

## INTRODUCTION

When it comes to open-air preaching and mass evangelism, the age of Wesley produced no equal to the man whom Methodist history usually accords a secondary status, George Whitefield.[1] In an age of great preachers, he was demonstrably the greatest, and in the spread of the revival in England and Wales to the rest of the English-speaking world, notably Scotland and America, none had so wide or deep an impact upon his hearers. One of his Victorian biographers assures us that "with the doubtful exception of Wyckliffe, no man probably ever excited in this island so profound a sensation in the public mind, by personal addresses . . . on the subject of religion."[2] If this judgment seems at first too generous, it is admirably upheld by the best modern study of Whitefield, that of Arnold Dallimore, and it is increasingly clear to historians that his was the reputation most eminently associated with the success of revival preaching in his own time.[3] With two centuries of hindsight we see that if John Wesley was father to the worldwide spread of the Methodist church, George Whitefield was a crucial forerunner to the evangelical tradition at large. And within the Anglican church itself, to which he remained loyal despite his commitments to reform, he has been inspirational not only to figures like John Newton and William Romaine in the same century, but also to a surviving and increasingly fruitful evangelical Anglicanism in our own time.[4]

Whitefield was born sixth son and youngest child of Thomas and Elizabeth Whitefield at their tavern, the Bell Inn, in Gloucester, on December 16, 1714. His father died two years later, but his mother continued with the inn and made every effort to obtain for her children a good education. In 1724, she remarried, albeit unhappily, and two years after that young George was sent out to school at St. Mary de Crypt nearby. Here he developed a passion for plays, acting in several—though sometimes, to his embarrassment, in "girls' clothes." In later years he rejected the theater, but this experience clearly served to develop his oratorical gifts.[5] Feeling that family circumstances could not permit him to go to university, he gave up Latin before his fifteenth birthday and soon after left school to become his mother's assistant in the inn, for a year and a half drawing pints, mopping floors, and cleaning rooms. Then, through the financial assistance of friends (including a relative of Lady Huntingdon), he was enabled to go to Oxford and entered Pembroke College before his eighteenth birthday in 1732.

His interest in matters of faith began before his arrival at Oxford. Like so many others, he had his spiritual consciousness first quickened by reading Thomas à Kempis, and subsequently William Law's *Devout Call* and *Christian Perfection*. He became a communicant in the Anglican church in 1731, and began to stay up late at night reading the Bible. By the time he reached Oxford he had already heard of the Holy Club and was not long in arranging a contact with Charles Wesley, who talked warmly with him and lent him books, including the Catholic writer Castaniza's *Combat* and the Scots Puritan Henry Scougal's *The Life of God in the Soul of Man* (1627), both of which affected him strongly. This initial reading was followed by other books and a gradual introduction to others of the club, during which time he "began, like them, to live by rule and to pick up the very fragments of his time, that not a moment of it might be lost." Speaking in his *Journals,* Whitefield continues:

> Whether I ate or drank, or whatsoever I did, I endeavored to do all to the glory of God. Like them . . . I received [the sacrament] every Sunday at Christ Church. I joined with them in keeping the stations by fasting Wednesdays and Fridays and left no means unused which I thought would lead me nearer to Jesus Christ.
>
> Regular retirement, morning and evening, at first I found some difficulty in submitting to; but it soon grew profitable and delightful. As I grew ripe for such exercises, I was from time to time engaged to visit the sick and the prisoners, and to read to poor people, till I made it a custom, as most of us did, to spend an hour every day in doing acts of charity.
>
> The course of my studies I soon entirely changed. Whereas before I was busied in studying the dry sciences, and books that went no further than the surface, I now resolved to read only such as entered into the heart of religion, and which led me directly into an experimental knowledge of Jesus Christ, and Him crucified. The lively oracles of God were my soul's delight. The book of the divine laws was seldom out of my hands: I meditated therein day and night.[6]

The content of this account offers us excellent insight into the life of the "despised Methodists," as they were called, and the tone reflects his always transparent desire for faithful stewardship in his own calling. He read his Greek Testament, consulted Henry's *Commentaries* and books of spirituality such as the Puritan Richard Baxter's *Call to the Unconverted* and the Anglican Bishop Hall's *Contemplations*. He was deeply devoted to the sacrament, and powerfully offended by "the miserable delusion of the author of that work called *The Plain Account of the Sacrament* which sinks that holy ordinance into a bare memorial."[7] Whitefield located the climax of his own conversion experience in the year 1735, the same year he became a full member of the Holy Club.

He was ordained deacon at Gloucester on June 20, 1736, preached his first sermon at St. Mary de Crypt a week later, and graduated in July.

With the Wesleys' departure from Oxford he took over leadership of the few remaining Oxford Methodists. These fellow students were an enormous encouragement to each other in their developing walk of faith. Of them Whitefield writes succinct praise:

> Never did persons, I believe, strive more earnestly to enter in at the strait gate. They kept their bodies under even to an extreme. They were dead to the world, and willing to be accounted as the dung and offscouring of all things, so that they might win Christ. Their hearts glowed with the love of God, and they never prospered so much in the inward man as when they had all manner of evil spoken against them falseley without.[8]

Whitefield was soon, however, to be called away from this company. He preached in London, but turned down a profitable curacy there, feeling he was being directed to go out to Georgia. After a year of extremely successful itinerant preaching in the churches of the west of England and in London (during which time his first printed sermon [1737] ran quickly through three editions), and pursuing further prison work, he boarded ship for Georgia at Deal. While the ship lay in harbor awaiting its last provisions and favorable tides and winds, another vessel carrying a defeated and defensive John Wesley sailed into the same port. On disembarking, Wesley learned immediately of Whitefield's presence (he had been preaching in the town to make good use of the time before his departure) but resolved, on the basis of drawing lots, not to see his old colleague; he also drew another lot, and sent the result to Whitefield by letter, directing that he "should go back to London."[9] This by return letter Whitefield respectfully declined to do, being quite sure of his own mission, and set sail on February 2, 1738, for America.

Beginning with a spiritually productive layover at Gibraltar, he then used his three months shipboard to evangelize his captive audience, and with considerable effect. His stay in Georgia, despite the extreme awkwardness created by his predecessor's actions, was also successful. He was far more flexible than Wesley had been, showed himself open to communion with other denominations and parties, and had a genuine sympathy for the colonists. Before leaving he had established schools and laid plans for an orphanage. For the purposes of raising funds for this work, and also obtaining his ordination as priest, he set sail for England on August 28. After a rough return trip, he landed in Ireland, spent two weeks preaching there, then came to England and to Oxford, where on January 14, 1739, he was ordained by Bishop Benson and assigned Savannah, Georgia, as his parish. Lady Huntingdon attended the ordination with some of her friends.

Whitefield attended Moravian meetings at the Fetter Lane society, but unlike Wesley made numerous contacts also with Dissenting congregations and their leadership, including a notably friendly acquaintance with Isaac Watts. Following the successful example of Howell Harris and other Welsh evangelists, he tried open-air preaching first at Kingswood, near Bristol, on February 17, 1739. Among the converts that day was Thomas Maxfield, later an assistant preacher under John Wesley. And though this period had its setbacks—one of which was a widespread negative response to the publication of his *Journals* (the first of which are embarrassingly naive and egotistical), it was also a time of triumph in the field. Whitefield's open-air crowds grew and grew, and when Bishop Butler of Bristol denied him access to local pulpits and forbad him even to preach in prisons, he threw all of his energies into mass evangelism.

Thousands came to hear him. Largely because of the sheer popularity of his preaching and the patent unpopularity of his subject—repentance—he was soon denied pulpits in Oxford and London. It is probably true that his tremendous oratorical powers, coupled with a tendency to regard too highly his press clippings, did lead to excess in these days. A friend of Philip Doddridge heard him on Kennington Common in May 1739 and thought he projected "an assumption of inspiration and infallibility." Isaac Watts, wishing he "had not risen above any pretences to the ordinary influences of the Holy Spirit, unless he could have given some better evidences of it," spoke candidly to Whitefield about his concerns.[10] It is to Whitefield's credit that he could and did receive criticism from such people on occasion (in contrast to Wesley), and within a few years he had won the high esteem of men like Doddridge and Watts, the latter of whom he visited in kindly fellowship a half-hour before his death.

Before that spirit of conciliation matured, however, Whitefield had become England's most widely known "enthusiast," had insubordinately rejected the pastoral counsel of Bishops Gibson and Butler, offending many churchmen with what now seems unnecessary self-assertion, and become the butt of an enormous range of satirical and polemical attacks. It is certain that by 1745 he was widely regarded as the leader of the movement; of the more than 200 pamphlets leveled against the Methodists by mid-century, 154 are directed specifically at Whitefield.[11] It is also clear, however, that he was giving the movement unprecedented visibility and acquiring a huge following. At Stoke Newington on July 31, 1739, he preached to twenty thousand people on the topic "The Serpent Beguiling Eve," and such massive gatherings were far from uncommon.

In August 1739, Whitefield was at sea once more enroute to America with the funds he needed for his work there. Before leaving, he asked

John Wesley to look after his already large band of followers—perhaps as many as ten thousand people in each of the cities of Bristol, London, and Gloucester. This was in some ways remarkable in itself, because of Wesley's already announced contention against the doctrine of predestination widely held by those already won by Howell Harris, Whitefield, and others. Whitefield and Harris both asked Wesley to refrain from raising the issue for fear of creating division and also to avoid preaching the doctrine of perfection, but to focus instead on the preaching of repentance and salvation by faith. Wesley had not agreed to this, yet Whitefield still promoted his influence among his large "congregation" and, with Howell Harris as a witness, committed the care of souls to Wesley until he should return. In one of the sadder chapters of the history of the revival, Wesley set out immediately to undermine Whitefield by preaching perfection and against predestination, and by actually divesting Whitefield of title in the Bristol preaching hall and the school being built at Kingswood, splitting the congregations and setting out to establish his own "United Societies."12

Meanwhile, Whitefield had landed in America, and begun preaching in Philadelphia and New York before moving on through Maryland, Virginia, and Carolina toward Savannah, Georgia. His preaching, mostly in Presbyterian meeting houses and in fields, was enthusiastically received. With a voice that, it was said, on a windless evening carried well for a mile, and with a strong dramatic appeal (including a tendency to be reduced to tears during his own discourse), Whitefield had become an irresistible attraction. In England he had already been noted for the emotional and auricular power of his voice: Lord Chesterfield joked that he had but to pronounce the word "Mesopotamia" to set his audiences to weeping, and the great actor Garrick once said he would give one hundred pounds to be able to pronounce the exclamation "Oh!" as electrically as Whitefield. In America, Benjamin Franklin, among others, was fascinated by the power of his voice and preaching and did experiments on the human voice at his sermons, but also noted with approbation the changes being wrought in the lives of his fellow citizens.13 When Whitefield finally arrived in Savannah he had collected enough money to build the orphanage, was granted land by the colony, and the building of Bethesda House commenced. Much of the money he collected from his subsequent thirty years of preaching in Britain and America went to the support of this orphanage.

All in all Whitefield traveled seven times across the ocean, in a time when a one-way passage could take three months at great hazard, and altogether he spent more than ten years preaching up and down the "thirteen colonies," though rarely enough in his own parish, which was

tended by an assistant, the schoolmaster James Habersham. During his
1739–41 visit especially, when his efforts were combined with those of
Jonathan Edwards, Gilbert Tennent, and others, he became perhaps the
"prime mover" in the American Great Awakening,[14] and thus a formative figure in English spiritual history on both sides of the Atlantic. He
had a significant influence upon the divinity students at Harvard College
and the College of New Haven (though he fell into disfavor with the
faculty and administration of both institutions in the process), and one of
the local schools he founded evolved into the University of Pennsylvania.
By preaching to raise money for Wheelock's Indian Missionary School
and the College of New Jersey, and obtaining contracts and donations for
each in England, he contributed substantially to the founding of what are
now, respectively, Dartmouth College and Princeton University, in both
of which he hoped to see the training of ministers of the gospel.

These extensive travels, combined with responsibilities of preaching,
collecting money for the support of orphanages and schools, and trying
to keep unity in the revival movement were together an almost impossible burden to Whitefield's not very robust constitution. Personal stresses
also took their toll. When he returned to England after his second American sojourn, desperate for money to keep Bethesda afloat, he found that
Wesley had alienated a majority of his followers, that he had neither
congregations nor support, and that almost no one would come to hear
him preach.[15] The split was damaging in many ways, and when Whitefield began to gain back support and his followers built him a preaching
hall called "The Tabernacle" just up the street from Wesley's United
Societies "Foundery" in Moorfield, and then added another rival "tabernacle" in Bristol, the painfulness of this division between two powerful
personalities became evident to all. Whitefield sought diversion from the
stress by going to preach in Scotland, but even there fell into controversy.
Riding away from it all, perhaps, he headed toward Abergavenny in
Wales, and into one of the odder episodes in his generally remarkable
history.

His friend and associate, Howell Harris, had fallen in love with an
intelligent and spiritually minded widow named Elizabeth James, and
they had been mutually drawn toward marriage. Harris, however, hesitated because of his conviction that the kind of ministry to which he had
been called required of him a celibate state. In what may now seem a
disturbing gesture, he wrote to Whitefield, nominating his own intended
as the ideal wife for a man he regarded as his spiritual superior. Whitefield
had expressed the desire for a wife, chiefly for the purpose of caring for
the Georgia orphanage in his absence, and although Mrs. James was ten
years his senior, he was interested. As he had, he noted, no time for

courtship, it suited him to have a woman preselected, as it were, and on the basis of one visit and few letters he was now returning to marry her. Harris, still transparently in love with the bride-to-be, and she with him, was to give her away—and their mutual torment was only increased by the wedding party having to ride three days in frustration from town to town across South Wales before a priest willing to marry the couple could be found. The deed was finally done in Caerphilly, November 14, 1741, and within a week Whitefield had left again on a preaching journey.

Although the marriage seems to have had its moments of happiness, within two months Whitefield was expressing a yearning "for that blessed time when we shall neither marry nor be given in marriage, but be as the angels of God." It is also painfully apparent that Harris and Mrs. Whitefield were troubled by a continuing strong attachment to each other for at least ten years.[16] The Whitefields had one son, born in 1743, who died within months. Elizabeth made only one trip to Savannah with her husband, late in 1744, but while there she spent more than two years dreadfully ill (having a series of four miscarriages in sixteen months), and then almost as long a period of solitude when Whitefield left her behind to go to Bermuda and on to Scotland. She traveled home alone, landing in England in June 1749, and afterward remained in London while her husband was on his preaching journeys.

Whitefield's preaching tours always attracted huge crowds, and almost always won numerous converts. A custom of passing up notes to him during the service (even in the midst of the sermon), by which means individuals would declare repentance or ask for prayer, grew to characterize his meetings. Occasionally, as at the great Cambuslang services in Scotland and on several instances in America, members of the congregation would be seized with hysteria and convulsions, the general confusion of which brought much criticism on Whitefield (as it had on Wesley).

To unify and encourage the collaborative efforts of his colleagues, he pioneered the idea of conferences, the first gathering of Calvinistic Methodists being held in 1743, eighteen months before Wesley was to follow with his own version. It was characteristic of the spirit of Whitefield's conferences (as his sermons) that they declared firmly for staying within the Established Church. Whitefield said that he would leave the organization of "societies" to others and tend instead to mass evangelism. He also invited the cooperation of outsiders. As early as September 1743 Doddridge preached at the Tabernacle, opening his own pulpit shortly after to Whitefield, and this type of cooperation was typical of Whitefield's ministry in America as well. Although the faculty and president of Harvard had published a bitter attack on him in earlier years, by 1763–65 he was putting much effort into acquiring books to refurbish their library after it had burned down. The Presbyterian College of New Jersey (Princeton) awarded him an honorary M.A. in 1754, though he declined ever to put the title after his signature. Uncompromising in his purpose, energetic in his labors, loyal to the church, open to others, refusing to bear a grudge, and capable despite his troublesome ego of curious acts of humility: these are among the admirable qualities of George Whitefield.

He was undeniably a complicated person, however, and behind his smooth, round face and beaming smile, a restless mind and driven spirit were always agitating. Fastidious in the extreme, and rigidly methodical in his habits, he grew actually quite corpulent after the age of forty. Though he argued for evangelism of American negroes, he bought a plantation and slaves in South Carolina to help support his orphanage and defended slavery on numbers of occasions on what he thought of as "biblical grounds."[17] Though his pastoral office required of him a more even perspective, when Lady Huntingdon made him one of her many chaplains in 1748 he often embarrassed her, as well as his own colleagues, by adopting a fawning and adulatory posture in the relationship.

Whitefield became the best known of Lady Huntingdon's chaplains, and the gratitude he expressed for her patronage and protection was unquestionably genuine. Moreover, in many respects she was his single most important mentor. After opening her college at Trevecca (1768) and her chapel at Tunbridge Wells (July 1769), he set out for his last trip to America with renewed intentions of building a college himself beside the orphanage at Bethesda. Sensing he might not live to see this project completed, he bequeathed all his American holdings to the countess before embarking on his preaching and fundraising mission.

Between April 24 and September 29, 1770, he traveled throughout Pennsylvania and New England, preaching nearly every day. On the evening of the 29th he was staying at the manse of Jonathan Parsons, the Presbyterian minister of Newburyport, Massachusetts. Scheduled to preach the next morning, he was exhausted and wanted to go to bed, but a crowd had already gathered in front of the manse. He was prevailed upon to preach to them from the staircase, and as he began to speak the occasion overtook him; he continued in his exhaustion until finally the bedcandle in his hand burned out in its socket. Whitefield went upstairs a sick man, spent the night fitfully turning pages of his Bible and a copy of Isaac Watt's *Hymns,* gasping for each breath. Gripped by what he thought were attacks of asthma (but which were more like angina pectoris), he died about six o'clock on Sunday morning, September 30, and was buried at his own request in a vault beneath the publit of the Presbyterian meeting house in the same town.

The orphanage at Savannah, Bethesda, burned down in June 1773 and was never rebuilt; indeed, Lady Huntingdon was unable to cover its huge debts, and the whole complex, plantations included, were forfeited to the state in 1791.

The tributes to Whitefield were many and magnificent. John Wesley preached a funeral sermon, Charles composed a poetic eulogy. William Cowper's tribute to the great evangelist includes these lines:

> He loved the world that hated him; the tear
> that dropped upon his Bible was sincere.
> Assailed by scandal and the tongue of strife,
> his only answer was a blameless life.[18]

If poetic licence here omits some of the facts, these words indicate none-theless some measure of the man's impact upon his contemporaries. His role in the revival is perhaps best summed up by John Newton, however, in a memorial sermon preached at Olney:

> I have not read or heard of any person, since the apostles' days, of whom it may be more emphatically said, "He was a burning and a shining light" than the late Mr. Whitefield, whether we consider the warmth of his zeal, the greatness of his ministerial talents, or the extensive usefulness with which the Lord honored him. I do not mean to praise the man, but the Lord who furnished him, and made him what he was. He was raised up to shine in a dark place. The state of religion when he first appeared in public was very low in our established church. I speak the truth, though to some it may be an offensive truth. The doctrines of grace were seldom heard from the pulpit and the life and power of godliness were little known. Many of the most spiritual among the dissenters were mourning under a sense of a great spreading declension on their side. What a change has taken place throughout the land within a little more than thirty years, that is, since the time when the first set of despised ministers came to Oxford! And how much of this change has been owing to God's blessing on Mr. Whitefield's labors, is well known to many who have lived through this period, and can hardly be denied by those who are least willing to allow it. . . . His zeal was not like wildfire, but directed by sound principles, and a sound judgement. . . . The Lord gave him a manner of preaching which was peculiarly his own. He copied from none, and I never met with anyone who could imitate him with success.[19]

## NOTES

1. In fact, many great figures of this period have commonly been overlooked because of the center stage occupied by John Wesley himself. These include, among others not treated in this volume, Daniel Rowland, John Cennick, John Berridge, and

especially the Welsh evangelist Howell Harris (1714–1773), whose open-air preaching was enormously successful before Whitefield and Wesley came into the field, and whose lifelong work was enormously fruitful.

2. John Foster, in an essay reprinted along with *George Whitefield's Journals* (1737–41) in the 1909 William Wale edition brought out again by William Davis (Gainesville: Scholars' Facsimiles and Reprints, 1969), p. 15.

3. I am deeply indebted to this magnificent work, ably written and a mine of careful research: Arnold Dallimore, *George Whitefield: The Life and Times of the Great Evangelist of the Eighteenth Century Revival*, 2 vols. (Westchester, Ill: Cornerstone, 1969, 1980).

4. Canon Hay Aitken at the turn of the century suggested that "the existence and growing influence of the Evangelical party in the Church of England is indirectly due, to a very large extent, to the labours of George Whitefield" (quoted in Davis's edition of the *Journals*, p. 12).

5. *Journals*, pp. 29–30.

6. Ibid., p. 38.

7. Ibid., p. 46.

8. Ibid., p. 39.

9. Dallimore, *George Whitefield*, vol. 1, p. 150.

10. Ibid., vol. 1, p. 345.

11. Ibid., vol. 1, pp. 340, 381.

12. Ibid., vol. 2, pp. 21–30.

13. Franklin became friendly with Whitefield, and it is clear that the two men had compatibly pioneering spirits. Franklin went so far as to propose that they team up to found a new community on the Ohio River (this project died on the vine) and was the first publisher of Whitefield's *Journals* and later his *Works*. See Dallimore, vol. 2, pp. 440–53.

14. Edwin S. Gaustad, *A Religious History of America* (New York: Harper & Row, 1966), p. 44.

15. Dallimore, vol. 2, pp. 47ff.

16. Dallimore (vol. 2, pp. 101–13) gives a full, if understandably apologetic, treatment of the situation.

17. Again, Dallimore treats this difficult aspect of Whitefield's history quite fairly (vol. 2, pp. 367–69; 520). Whitefield was not alone in this, alas; Lady Huntingdon also purchased and owned slaves.

18. William Cowper, "Hope" (lines 574–77), in *The Poetical Works of William Cowper*, ed. H. S. Milford (London: Oxford University Press, 1905 [1963]), p. 72.

19. Quoted from Joseph Belcher, *George Whitefield, A Biography* (New York: American Tract Society, 1857), p. 450.

# from the Sermons

## The Nature and Necessity of Self-Denial (1737)*

> "And he said unto them all, If any man will come after me, let him deny himself." (Luke 9:23)

WHOEVER READS the Gospel with a single eye and sincere intention will find that our blessed Lord took all opportunities of reminding his disciples that his kingdom was not of this world, that his doctrine was a doctrine of the cross, and that their professing themselves to be his followers would call them to a constant state of voluntary suffering and self-denial.

The words of the text afford us one instance, among many, of our Saviour's own behavior in this respect. For having in the preceding verses revealed Himself to Peter and the other apostles to be the Christ of God, He tells them in the twenty-second verse—lest they should be too much elated with such a privileged discovery of his deity, or think that their relationship to so great a person would be attended with nothing but pomp and grandeur—that the Son of Man was to suffer many things in this world, though He was to be crowned with eternal glory and honor in the next. Moreover, if any of them or their posterity would share in the same honor, they must take their share with Him in his self-denial and sufferings. For He said unto them all, "If any man will come after me, let him deny himself. . . ."

From these words, I shall consider these three things: first, the nature of the self-denial recommended in the text, and in how many respects we must deny ourselves in order to follow after Jesus Christ; secondly, the universality and reasonableness of this duty of self-denial; and thirdly, I shall offer some considerations which may serve as incentives to reconcile us to, and quicken us in, the practice of this doctrine of self-denial.

## I. What Self-Denial Means

First, then, I am to show the nature of the self-denial recommended in the text, and in how many respects we must deny ourselves in order to follow Jesus Christ.

*This sermon reveals the strong emphasis of Oxford Methodist spirituality on Whitefield's preaching. Like almost all of his fifty-six published sermons, it comes from his first years as a preacher, and is therefore all the more remarkable for its strength of

290

## 1. Denying our own understanding

Now as the faculties of the soul are distinguished by the understanding, will, and affections, so in all these must each of us deny himself. We must not "lean to our own understanding," being "wise in our own eyes and prudent in our own sight," but we must submit our short-sighted reason to the light of divine revelation. For there are spiritual mysteries which are above (though not contrary to) our natural reason. And therefore we shall never become Christians unless we "cast down imaginations, and every high thing that exalteth itself against the knowledge of God, and bring into captivity every thought to the obedience of Christ" (2 Corinthians 10:5). It is in this respect, as well as others, that we must become "fools for Christ's sake," and acknowledge we know nothing as we ought to know it without revelation. We must then, with all humility and reverence, embrace the mysterious truths revealed to us in the Holy Scriptures, for thus only can we become truly wise, even wise unto salvation. It was part of our blessed Lord's thanksgiving to his heavenly Father that He had "hid these things from the wise and prudent, and had revealed them unto babes." And in this respect also we must be converted and become as little children, teachable and willing to follow the Lamb into whatsoever mysteries He shall be pleased to lead us, and believe and practise all divine truths—not because we can demonstrate their value in ourselves but because God, who cannot lie, has revealed them to us.

In this light we may trace infidelity to its fountainhead. For it is nothing else but a pride of the understanding, an unwillingness to submit to the truth of God, that makes so many, professing themselves wise, to become such fools as to deny the Lord who has so dearly bought them, and dispute the divinity of that eternal Word in whom they "live and move and have their being." Whereby, it is justly to be feared that they will bring upon themselves sure, if not swift, destruction.

## 2. Denying our self-will

To continue: as we must deny ourselves in our understanding, so also must we deny or (as it might be more properly rendered) renounce our wills. That is, we must make our own wills no standard for action, but "whether we eat or drink, or whatsoever we do, we must do all" not merely to please ourselves, but "to the glory of God." Not that we are therefore to imagine we are to have no pleasure in anything we do

---

composition. Whitefield preached on fewer occasions than John Wesley, partly owing to his shorter life, but still managed eighteen thousand deliveries of what were, typically, longer sermons.

(wisdom's ways are ways of pleasantness) but pleasing ourselves must not be the principle but rather only the byproduct of our actions.

And I cannot lay too much emphasis upon this doctrine because it is the grand secret of our holy religion. It is this, my brethren, that distinguishes the true Christian from the mere moralist and nominal Christian, and which alone can render any of our actions acceptable in God's sight. "For if thine eye be single," says our blessed Lord (Matthew 6:22)—that is, if you aim simply to please God without any regard to your own will— then "thy whole body," that is, all your actions, "will be full of light," agreeable to the gospel which is called light. But "if thine eye be evil," if your intention be diverted any other way, "thy whole body," all your actions, "will be full darkness," unprofitable and capable of no reward. For we must not only do the will of God, but do it because it is his will; since we pray that God's will may be done on earth as it is in heaven. And, no doubt, the blessed angels not only do everything that God wills but do it cheerfully on this principle, because God wills it. And if we live as we pray we must go and do likewise.

Furthermore, as we must renounce our own wills in *doing,* so likewise must we renounce them in reconciling ourselves to the will of God. Whatsoever befalls us, we must say with good old Eli, "It is the Lord, let him do what seemeth him good," or with one that was infinitely greater than Eli, "Father, not my will, but thine be done." O Jesu, thine was an innocent will, and yet Thou renounced it. Teach us also, O our Saviour, to submit our wills to thine, in all the evils which shall be brought upon us, and in everything enable us to give thanks, since it is thy blessed will concerning us!

### 3. Denying our creature comforts

Thirdly and lastly, we must deny ourselves, as in our understanding and wills, likewise in our affections. Most particularly we must deny ourselves the pleasurable indulgence and self-enjoyment of riches. "If any man will come after me," says our blessed Lord, "he must forsake all and follow me." And again (to show the inconsistency of the love of the things of this world with the love of the Father) He tells us that "unless a man forsake all that he hath, he cannot be my disciple."

Far be it from me to think that these texts are to be taken in a literal sense, as though they obliged rich persons to go sell all that they have and give to the poor (for that would put it out of their power to be serviceable to the poor for the future) but they certainly imply that we are to set loose, sell, and forsake all in affection, and be willing to part with everything when God shall require it at our hands. That is, as the apostle observes, we must use the world as though we used it not, and though we are *in* the world we must not be *of* it. We must look upon ourselves as stewards and not proprietors of the manifold gifts of God, providing first what is *necessary* for ourselves and our households and expending the rest not in indulgences and superfluous ornaments forbidden by the apostle but in clothing, feeding, and relieving the naked, hungry or distressed disciples of Jesus Christ. This is what our blessed Lord would have us understand ✓ by forsaking all, and in this sense must each of us deny himself.

I am aware that this will seem a 'hard saying' to many, who will be offended because they are covetous and "lovers of pleasure more than lovers of God." But if I yet pleased such persons, I should not be the servant of Christ. No, we must not, like Ahab's false prophets, have a lying spirit in our mouths (cf. 1 Kings 22:22), nor fail to declare (with Saint Paul) the whole will of God. Rather, like honest Micaiah, out of pity and compassion, we must tell the truth, even though some may falsely think we prophecy not good, but evil concerning them.

But to proceed: as we must renounce our affection for riches, so likewise our affections for relationships, when they stand in opposition to our love of and duty to God. For thus saith the Saviour of the world: "If any man will come after me, and hateth not his father and mother, his children and brethren and sisters, yea and his own life also, he cannot be my disciple" (Luke 14:26). Strange doctrine, this! How can these things be? Can God contradict Himself? Has He not bid us honor our father and mother? And yet we are here commanded to hate them. How must these truths be reconciled? Why, by interpreting the word "hate," not in a rigorous and absolute sense, but comparatively—not as implying a total alienation but a lesser degree of affection. For thus our blessed Saviour Himself (the best and surest expositor of his own meaning) explains it in a parallel text (Matthew 10:37): "He that loveth father or mother more than me is not worthy of me: he that loveth son or daughter more than me is not worthy of me." So that when the persuasions of such of our friends (as for our trial they may be permitted to be) are contrary to the will of God, we must say with Levi, "we have not known them," or, in agreement with our blessed Lord's rebuke of Peter, "Get you behind me," my adversaries, "for you savour not the things that be of God, but the things that be of men."

To conclude this point: we must deny ourselves in incidental things. For it might easily be shown that as many, if not more, perish by an immoderate use of things in themselves insignificant as by any gross sin whatever. A prudent Christian therefore will consider not only what is lawful, but what is expedient also—not so much what degrees of self-denial best suit his inclinations here, as what will most effectually break his will, and fit him for greater degrees of glory hereafter.

But is this the [present] teaching of Christianity? And is not the Christian world then asleep? If not, whence the self-indulgence, whence the reigning love of riches which we meet with everywhere? Above all, whence that predominant greediness of sensual pleasure which has so overrun this sinful nation that if a pious stranger was to come amongst us, he would be tempted to think some heathen Venus was worshipped here, and that many indeed were the temples dedicated to her service? But we have the authority of an inspired apostle to affirm that they who live in such a round of pleasure are dead while they live.

Therefore, as the Holy Spirit says, "Awake thou that sleepest, and Christ shall give thee light" (Ephesians 5:14). But the power of raising the spiritually dead belongs only unto God. Do Thou therefore, O Holy Jesus, who by thy almighty Word commanded Lazarus to come forth, though he had lain in the grave many days, speak also as effectually to these spiritually dead souls, whom Satan for many years has so fast bound by sensual pleasures that they are not so much as able to lift up their eyes or hearts to heaven.

## II. *Why Self-Denial is Necessary*

I pass on now to the second general point proposed, to consider the universal obligation and reasonableness of this doctrine of self-denial.

### 1. Christ's command

When our blessed Master had been discoursing publicly concerning the watchfulness of the faithful and wise steward, his disciples asked him, "Speakest thou this parable to all, or only to us?" The same question I am aware has been, and will be, put concerning the foregoing doctrine. For too many, unwilling to take Christ's easy yoke upon them and in order to evade the force of the Gospel precepts, would pretend that all those commands concerning self-denial, renouncing themselves and the world, were intended only for our Lord's first and immediate followers, and not for us or our children. But such persons greatly err, not knowing the Scriptures, nor the power of godliness in their hearts. For the doctrine of Jesus Christ, like his blessed self, is the same yesterday, today and forever. What He said unto one, He said unto all, even unto the ends of the world: "If any man will come after me, let him deny himself."

And in the text it is particularly mentioned that "he said [this] unto them all." And lest we should still absurdly imagine that this word "all" was to be confined to his apostles, with whom He was then discoursing, it is said in another place that Jesus turned unto the multitude and said, "If any man will come after me, and hateth not his father and mother, yea and his own life also, he cannot be my disciple" (Luke 14:26). [As William Law puts it:]

> When our blessed Lord had spoken a certain parable, it is said, the scribes and pharisees were offended, for they knew the parable was spoken against them. And if Christians can now read these plain and positive texts of Scripture, and at the same time not think they are spoken of them, they are more hardened than Jews, and more insincere than Pharisees.*

In the first part of this discourse I observed that the precepts concerning forsaking and selling all did not oblige us in a literal sense, because the condition of the church does not demand it of us as it did of the primitive Christians. Even so, the same deadness to the world, the same abstemious use of and readiness to part with our goods for Christ's sake, is as absolutely necessary and obligatory for us as it was for them. For although the church may differ in its outward condition in different ages, yet with respect to the purity of its inward state it was, is, and always will be invariably the same. And all the commands which we meet with in the Epistles—about "mortifying our members which are upon the earth," of "setting our affections on things above," and of not being conformed to this world—are incontestable proofs that the same holiness, heavenly-mindedness and deadness to the world is as necessary for us as for our Lord's immediate followers.

2. Making Space in our Hearts

But further, just as such an objection reveals an ignorance of the Scriptures, so it is a manifest proof that such as make it are strangers to the power of godliness in their hearts. For since the sum and substance of religion consists in our recovery from our fallen estate in Adam, by a new birth in Christ Jesus, there is an absolute necessity for us to embrace and practise self-denial. Since we have not only a new house to build but an old one first to pull down, we must necessarily therefore be dead to the world before we can live unto God. In short, all things belonging to the old man must die in us before the things belonging to the Spirit can live and grow there.

When Jesus Christ was about to make his public appearance and to preach the glad tidings of salvation to a benighted world, his harbinger John the Baptist was sent to prepare his way before Him. In like manner, when this same Jesus is about to take possession of a converted sinner's heart, self-denial, like John the Baptist, must prepare the way before

*Whitefield is quoting here from Law's *Christian Perfection*.

Him. For we must mourn before we are capable of being comforted; we must undergo the spirit of bondage, in order to be made meet to receive the spirit of adoption.

### 3. Medicine for our Condition

Were we indeed in a state of innocence, and had we, like Adam before his fall, the divine image fully stamped upon our souls, we would have no need of self-denial. But since we are fallen, sickly, disordered creatures, and this self-suffering and self-renunciation is the indispensable means of recovering our primitive glory, methinks that to endeavor to shake off and reject such a salutary practice on account of the difficulty attending it at first, is too much like the obstinacy of a perverse sick child, who nauseates and refuses the medicine held out to it by a skillful physician or tender parent because it is a little ungrateful to the taste.

Had any of us seen Lazarus when he lay full of sores at the rich man's gate, or Job, when he was smitten with ulcers from the crown of his head to the sole of his foot, and had we at the same time prescribed to them some healing medicines which, because they involved a little pain, these would not apply to their wounds, should we not with justice think that they were either fond of a diseased body or unaware of their sicknesses? But our souls, by nature, are in an infinitely more deplorable condition than the bodies of Job and Lazarus when full of ulcers and boils. For alas, our "whole head is sick," and "our whole heart faint; from the crown of the head to the sole of the foot, we are full of wounds and bruises and putrifying sores, and there is no health in us" (cf. Isaiah 1:5–6). Jesus Christ, like a good physician, in the Gospel doctrine of self-denial, presents us with a spiritual medicine to heal our sickness. But if we will neither receive nor apply it, 'tis a sign that we are not aware of the wretchedness of our state or else that we are unwilling to be made whole.

Even Naaman's servants could say, when he refused Elijah's orders to wash in the river Jordon that he might cure his leprosy: "Father, if the prophet had bid thee do some great things would'st thou not have done it? How much rather then, when he saith to thee, Wash and be clean?" And may not I very properly address myself to you in the same manner, my brethren? If Jesus Christ, our great Prophet, had bid you do some great and very difficult thing, would you not have done it? Much more then should you do it when He only bids you deny yourselves what would certainly hurt you if enjoyed. And behold, you shall be made perfectly whole.

But to illustrate this by another comparison: in the twelfth chapter of the Acts, we read that Saint Peter was kept in prison, and "was sleeping between two soldiers, bound with two chains. And behold an angel of the

Lord came upon him, and smote Peter on the side, saying, arise up quickly. And his chains fell off from his hands." But had this great apostle, instead of rising up quickly and doing as the blessed angel commended him, hugged his chains and begged that they might not be let fall from his hands, would not anyone think that he was in love with slavery and deserved to be executed next morning? And does not the person who refuses to deny himself act as inconsistently as this apostle would have done if he had neglected the means of his deliverance? For our souls are, by nature, in a spiritual dungeon, sleeping and fast bound between the world, the flesh and the devil, not with two but ten thousand chains of lusts and corruptions. Now Jesus Christ, like Saint Peter's good angel, by his Gospel comes and opens the prison door, prescribes self-denial, mortification, and renunciation of ourselves and the world as so many spiritual keys which will unlock our shackles, make them fall off from our hearts and so restore us to the glorious liberty of the sons of God. But if we will not arise quickly, gird up the loins of our mind and deny ourselves, as He has commanded, are we not in love with bondage, deserving never to be delivered from it?

Indeed I will not affirm that this doctrine of self-denial appears in this favorable light to everyone. No, I am well aware that to the natural man it is foolishness and to the young convert a hard saying. But what says our Saviour? "If any man will do my will, he shall know of the doctrine whether it be of God, or whether I speak of myself" (John 7:17). This, my dear friends, is the best, the only way of conviction. Let us up and be doing! Let us arise quickly and deny ourselves and the Lord Jesus will remove those scales from the eyes of our minds which now like so many veils hinder us from seeing clearly the reasonableness, necessity and inexpressible advantage of the doctrine that has been now delivered. Let us but once thus show ourselves men, and then the Spirit of God will move on the face of our souls as He did once upon the face of the great deep, and cause them to emerge out of that confused chaos in which they are most certainly now involved as long as we are strangers and enemies to self-denial and the cross of Christ.

Notwithstanding that this doctrine of self-denial is, when rightly understood, so reasonable and beneficial, yet many, it is to be feared, like the young man in the Gospel, are ready to go away sorrowful.

## III. *Incentives to Self-Denial*

We therefore proceed now to the third and last general point, offering some considerations which may serve as incentives to reconcile us to, and quicken us in, the practice of this duty of self-denial.

### 1. Meditation on the life of Christ

The first means I shall recommend to you is to meditate frequently on the life of our blessed Lord and Master Jesus Christ. Oh, may we often think on Him, our grand Exemplar, follow Him from his cradle to his cross, and see what a self-denying life He leads! And shall not we drink of the cup that He drank of, and be baptized with the baptism that He was baptized with? Or think we that Jesus Christ did and suffered everything in order to have us excused and exempted from sufferings? No, far be it from any sincere Christian to judge after this manner! For Saint Peter tells us, "He suffered for us, leaving us an example, that we should follow his steps" (cf. 1 Peter 4:1). Had Christ, indeed, like those that sat in Moses's chair, laid heavy burdens of self-denial upon us (supposing they were heavy, which they are not) while refusing to touch them Himself with one of his fingers, we might have had some excuse to complain. But since He has asked us to do nothing but what He has first put into practice Himself, you are inexcusable, O disciple, whoever you are, who would be above your persecuted, self-denying Master. And you are no good and faithful servant if you are unwilling to suffer and sympathize with your mortified, heavenly-minded Lord.

### 2. Examples of the apostles, prophets and martyrs

Next to the pattern of our blessed Master, think often on the lives of the glorious company of the apostles, the goodly fellowship of the prophets, and the noble army of martyrs, who by a constant looking to the author and finisher of our faith, have fought the good fight and are gone before us to inherit the promises. See, again and again, how holy, self-denying and unblameable were their lives. If self-denial were necessary for them, why not for us also? Are we not men of like passions with them? Do we not live in the same wicked world as they did? Have we not the same good Spirit to assist, support and purify us as they had? And is not the same eternal inheritance held out as a reward of our self-denial and renunciation of the world as was offered to them? And if we have the same nature to change, the same wicked world to withstand, the same good Spirit to help, and the same eternal crown to reward our obedience, why should we not lead the same lives as they did? . . . Why don't we do as they did? Or why does the church set apart festivals to commemorate the deaths and sufferings of the saints except to encourage us to follow them as they did Christ?

### 3. The pains of hell

Thirdly, think often of the pains of hell. Consider whether it is not better to cut off a right hand or foot and pluck out a right eye, if they offend us (or cause us to sin) rather than "to be cast into hell, into the fire that never shall be quenched; where the worm dieth not, and the fire is not quenched" (cf. Mark 9:43–44). Think how many thousands there are now imprisoned with damned spirits in chains of darkness unto the judgement of the Great Day, for not complying with the commandment in our text. And think withal that this, this must be our own fate shortly, unless we are wise in time and submit to those easy conditions our Saviour has prescribed us in order to avoid it. Do you think they now imagine Jesus Christ to be a hard Master, or rather do you not think that they would give ten thousand times ten thousand worlds could they but return to life again and take Christ's easy yoke upon them?

Can we dwell with everlasting burnings more than they? No. If we cannot endure this commandment—"Come, deny yourselves, take up your crosses"—how shall we endure that irrevocable sentence—"Depart from me, ye cursed, into everlasting fire prepared for the devil and his angels"? Yet I hope those amongst whom I am now preaching the kingdom of God are not so insincere as to need to be driven to their duty by the terrors of the Lord, but rather desire to be drawn by the cords of love.

## 4. The joys of heaven

Lastly, therefore, often meditate on the joys of heaven. Think, think with what unspeakable glory those happy souls are now encircled who when on earth were called to deny themselves as well as we, and were not disobedient to that call. Lift up your hearts frequently toward the mansions of eternal bliss and, with an eye of faith like the great Saint Stephen, see the heavens opened and the Son of Man with his glorious retinue of departed saints sitting and solacing themselves in eternal joys, and with unspeakable comfort looking back on their past sufferings and self-denials as so many glorious means which exalted them to such a crown.

Hark! Methinks I hear them chanting forth their everlasting hallelujahs, and spending an eternal day in echoing forth triumphant songs of joy. And do you not long, my brethren, to join this heavenly choir? Do not your hearts burn within you? "As the hart panteth after the water-brooks," do not your souls "so long after the blessed company of these sons of God?" Behold then a heavenly ladder reached down to you by which you may climb to this holy hill. If any man will come after them, let him deny himself and follow them. It was this, my brethren, exalted the Holy Jesus Himself, as man, to sit at the right hand of his worshipful Father. By this alone every saint who ever lived ascended into the joy of their Lord: and by this we, even we also, may be lifted up into the same most blissful regions, there to enjoy an eternal rest with the people of

God, and join with them in singing doxologies and songs of praise to the everlasting, blessed, all-glorious, most worshipful Trinity, for ever and ever.

Which God of his infinite mercy grant, &c.

# The Almost Christian (1738)*

"Almost thou persuadest me to be a Christian" (Acts 26:28)

THESE WORDS contain the candid confession of King Agrippa which, since it has some reference to what went before, it may not be improper to relate to you the substance of the preceding verses to which these words are so closely connected.

The chapter out of which the text is taken contains an admirable account the great Saint Paul gave of his wonderful conversion from Judaism to Christianity, when he was called to make his defense before Festus and another gentile governor. Our blessed Lord had long since foretold that "when the Son of Man should be lifted up, his disciples should be brought before kings, for his name's sake, for a testimony unto them" (cf. Matthew 10:18). And very good was the design of infinite wisdom in thus ordaining it. For Christianity being from the very beginning a doctrine of the cross, the princes and rulers of the earth thought themselves too high to be instructed by such lowly teachers, or too comfortable to be disturbed by such unwelcome truths. They therefore would have always continued strangers to Jesus Christ and Him crucified had not the apostles, by being arraigned as criminals before them, gained opportunities of preaching to them Jesus and the resurrection.

Saint Paul knew full well that this was the main reason his blessed Master permitted his enemies at this time to arraign him at a public bar. Therefore, in compliance with the divine will, he thought it not sufficient merely to make his defence, but endeavored at the same time to convert his judges. And this he did with such demonstration of the Spirit and of power that Festus, unwilling to be convinced by the strongest evidence, cried out with a loud voice: "Paul, much learning doth make thee mad." To which the brave apostle (like a true follower of the holy Jesus) meekly

---

*This sermon was preached at the parish church of St. John, Wapping, early in 1738 and published the same year by James Hutton at the Bible and Sun booksellers in London. John Wesley also preached and published a sermon with this text and title three years later (July 25, 1741) before the members of the University at St. Mary's Church, Oxford.

replied: "I am not mad, most noble Festus, but speak forth the words of truth and soberness." But in all probability seeing that King Agrippa was affected by his words, and observing in him an inclination to know the truth, he applied himself more particularly to him. "The king," he said, "knoweth of these things; before whom also I speak freely; for I am persuaded that none of these things are hidden from him." And then, that if possible he might complete his wished-for conversion, he, with an inimitable strain of oratory, addressed himself still more closely: "King Agrippa, believest thou the prophets? I know that thou believest them." At which the emotions of the king began to work so strongly that he was obliged in open court to admit himself affected by the prisoner's preaching, and in sincerity to cry out: "Paul, almost thou persuadest me to be a Christian."

These words, taken in their context, afford us a lively representation of the different reception the doctrine of Christ's ministers, who come in the power and spirit of Saint Paul, meet with nowadays in the minds of men. For notwithstanding they, like this great apostle, "speak forth the words of truth and soberness"—and with such energy and power that all their adversaries cannot gainsay or resist—yet too many, like the most noble Festus, are either too proud to be taught or too sensual, too careless, or too worldly-minded to live up to their doctrine. In order to excuse themselves they cry out that "much learning," much study, or, what is more unaccountable, much piety "hath made thee mad." And though, blessed be God, all do not thus disbelieve our report, yet amongst those many others who gladly receive the Word and confess that we speak the words of truth and soberness, there are so few who arrive at any higher degree of piety than that of Agrippa, or are any further persuaded than to be "almost Christians," that I cannot but think it highly necessary to warn my dear hearers of the danger of such a state.

Therefore, from the words of the text, I shall endeavor to consider these three things: first, what is meant by an "almost Christian"; secondly, what are the chief reasons why so few arrive no higher than to be "almost Christians"; and thirdly, the ineffectuality, danger, absurdity and uneasiness that attend those who are "almost Christians." Finally, I shall conclude with a general exhortation, to set all upon striving not only to be *almost* but *altogether* Christians.

## I. *Characteristics of the Almost Christian*

First, then, I am to consider what is meant by an *almost* Christian. An *almost Christian,* if we consider him with respect to his duty to God, is one who halts between two opinions. He wavers between Christ and the world. He wants to reconcile God and Mammon, that is, light and darkness, Christ and Belial. It is true that he has an inclination to religion, but then he is very cautious about going too far in it. His false heart is always crying out, "Spare thyself. Do thyself no harm." He prays indeed that God's will may be done on earth as it is in heaven but then, notwithstanding, is very partial in his own obedience, and fondly hopes that God will not be so extreme as to mark everything that he wilfully does amiss, even though an inspired apostle has told him that whoever offends in one point is guilty of all. Above all, this person is one who depends much on outward ordinances and upon that account looks upon himself as righteous (and despises others) although at the same time he may be as great a stranger to spiritual life as any other person whatsoever. In short, he is fond of the *form,* but never experiences the *power* of godliness in his heart. He goes on year after year, feeding and attending on the means of grace, but then, like Pharoah's lean kine, is never the better, but rather the worse for them.

If you consider such a person with respect to his neighbor, he is strictly just to all. But this does not proceed from any love to God or regard to man, but only out of a principle of self-love—because he knows dishonesty will spoil his reputation and consequently hinder his prosperity in the world.

Such a person depends much on being 'negatively' good, contenting himself with the consciousness of having done no one any harm—though he reads in the Gospel that the unprofitable servant was cast into outer darkness, and the barren fig-tree cursed and dried up from the roots, not for bearing *bad* fruit, but *no* fruit.

He is no enemy to charitable contributions, if not too frequently requested. But then he is quite unacquainted with the kind offices of "visiting the sick and inprisoned, clothing the naked, and relieving the hungry." He thinks that these things are appropriate only to the clergy, though his own false heart tells him that nothing but pride keeps him from exercising these acts of humility and that Jesus Christ, in the twenty-fifth chapter of Matthew, condemns persons to everlasting punishment not for being fornicators, drunkards or extortioners but merely for neglecting these charitable offices. "When the Son of Man," says our blessed Lord Himself, "shall come in his glory, he shall set the sheep on his right hand, and the goats on his left. And then shall he say unto them on his left hand, depart from me, ye cursed, into everlasting fire prepared for the devil and his angels. For I was an hungered, and ye gave me no meat; I was thirsty, and ye gave me no drink; I was a stranger, and ye took me not in; naked, and ye clothed me not; sick and in prison, and ye visited me not. Then shall they also say, Lord, when saw we thee an hungered, or athirst, or a stranger, or naked, or sick, or in prison, and did not minister unto thee? Then shall he answer them, Verily I say unto you, inasmuch as ye have not done it unto one of the least of these my brethren, ye did it not unto me. And these shall go away into everlasting punishment" (Matthew 25:31–46).

I thought it proper to give you this whole passage of Scripture entire, because our Saviour lays such a particular stress upon it. And yet despite that, it is so little regarded that, were we to judge by the practice of Christians, one should be tempted to think there were no such verses in the Bible.

Now, to proceed in our characterization of an *almost Christian*. If we consider such a person with respect to himself, we may say that he is strictly sober in himself (just as before we said he was strictly honest with his neighbor). But both his honesty and sobriety proceed from the same principle of a false self-love. It is true that he runs not into the same excess of riot as other men, but then this is not out of obedience to the laws of God but either because his constitution does not well handle intemperance or because he is cautious about forfeiting his reputation or rendering himself unfit for daily business. Yet, although he is so prudent as to avoid intemperance and excess for these reasons, he always goes to the extremity of what is lawful. It is true that he is no drunkard, but this is hardly a matter of Christian self-denial. He cannot think our Saviour to be so austere a master as to deny us to indulge ourselves in some particulars. And so, by this rationalization, he is kept out of a sense of true religion, as much as if he lived in debauchery or any other crime whatever.

As to settling his principles as well as practice, he is guided more by the world than by the Word of God. In his opinion, the way to heaven cannot be as narrow as some would make it. Therefore, he considers not so much what Scripture requires as what such and such a good person does, or what will best suit his own corrupt inclinations. Upon this account, he is not only very restrained himself, but likewise very solicitous of young converts, whose faces are set heavenward, taking the devil's part in bidding them to "spare themselves," although they are doing no more than what the Scripture strictly requires them to do. The consequence of this is that he does not permit himself to enter into the kingdom of God, and those who are entering in, he hinders.

Thus lives the *almost Christian*. Not that I can say I have fully described him to you, but from these outlines and sketches of his character, if your consciences have done their proper duty and made a personal application of what has been said to your own hearts, I cannot but fear that some of you may observe certain features in this picture, odious as it is, too closely resembling your own. Therefore, I cannot but hope at the same time that you will join with the apostle in the words immediately following the text and wish yourselves not only *almost,* but *altogether* Christians.

## II. *Causes of the Condition*

But it is time for me to proceed to consider the reasons why so many are no more than *almost Christians.*

### 1. Ignorance

The first reason is because so many set out with false notions about faith. Though they live in a Christian country, they do not know what Christianity is. This perhaps may be judged a hard saying, but experience sadly confirms the truth of it. Some people imagine that faith consists in being of this or that communion; more think it has to do with morality; most imagine a round of duties and a model of performances. Few (very few) acknowledge it to be what it really is—a thorough, inward change of nature, a spiritual life, a vital participation in Jesus Christ, a union of the soul with God which the apostle expresses by saying, "He that is joined to the Lord is one spirit."

Hence it happens that so many, even of the most knowledgeable of those who profess to be Christians, when you converse with them concerning the essence, the life and soul of faith—I mean our new birth in Jesus Christ—confess themselves quite ignorant of the matter, and cry out with Nicodemus, "How can this thing be?" And no wonder then that so many are only *almost Christians,* when so many do not even know what Christianity is. No marvel so many take up with the form, when they are quite strangers to the power of Godliness, or content themselves with the shadow when they know so little about the substance of it. And this is one cause why so many are *almost,* and so few are *altogether* Christians.

### 2. Embarrassment

A second reason why so many are no more than *almost Christians* is a servile fear of man. Multitudes there are, and have been, who, though awakened to a sense of the divine life and having tasted and felt the powers of the world to come, have—out of a base sinful fear of being counted odd or condemned by others—allowed all those good impressions to wear off again. It is true they have some esteem for Jesus Christ, but then, like Nicodemus, they would come to Him only by night. They are willing to serve Him, but they want to do it secretly for "fear of the Jews." They have a mind to see Jesus, but they cannot come to Him because of the crowd, for fear of being laughed at, and ridiculed by those with whom they used to dine.

But well did our Saviour prophesy of such persons: "How can ye love me which receive honour one of another?" Alas! Have they never read that the friendship of this world is enmity with God, and that our Lord Himself has threatened: "Whosoever shall be ashamed of me or of my words, in this wicked and adulterous generation, of him shall the Son of Man be ashamed, when he cometh in the glory of his Father and of his holy angels" (Mark 8:38). But no wonder that so many are no more than *almost Christians,* since so many love the praise of men more than the honor which comes of God.

### 3. Material prosperity

A third reason why so many are no more than *almost Christians* is a reigning love of money. This was the pitiable case of that forward young man in the Gospel, who came running to our blessed Lord and, kneeling before Him, enquired what he must do to inherit eternal life. Our blessed Master replied: "Thou knowest the commandments, Do not kill, Do not commit adultery, Do not steal," to which the young man replied (oh that every young man here present could do so too!), "All these have I kept from my youth." But when our Lord proceeded to tell him, "Yet lackest thou one thing, Go sell all that thou hast and give to the poor," he was "grieved at that saying, and went away sorrowful," for he had great possessions!

Poor youth! He had a good mind to be a Christian, and to inherit eternal life, but thought it too dear if it could be purchased at no less an expense than of his whole estate! And thus many, both young and old, nowadays come running to worship our blessed Lord in public and kneel before Him in private and enquire of his Gospel what they must do to inherit eternal life. But when they find they must renounce the self-enjoyment of riches, and forsake all in affection to follow Him, they cry, "the Lord pardon us in this thing! We pray thee, have us excused."

But is heaven so small a trifle in such a person's esteem as not to be worth a little gilded earth? Is eternal life so mean a purchase as not to deserve the temporary renunciation of a few transitory riches? Surely it is. But however inconsistent such behavior may be, this inordinate love of money is too evidently the common and fatal reason that so many are no more than *almost Christians.*

### 4. Creature comforts

Nor is the reigning love of pleasure a less uncommon or less fatal reason. . . . Thousands and thousands there are who despise riches and would willingly be true disciples of Jesus Christ if parting with their money would make them so. But when they are told that our blessed Lord has laid it down as an indispensable condition that "whosoever will come after him must deny himself," they, like the pitiable young man mentioned before, go away sorrowful. For they have too great a love for sensual pleasures. They will, like Herod, perhaps send for the ministers of Christ, as he did for John, and hear them gladly. But touch them in their Herodias, tell them they must part with such and such a darling pleasure, and with wicked Ahab they cry out, "Hast thou found us, O our enemy?"

Tell them of the necessity of mortification, fasting and self-denial, and it is as difficult for them to hear as if you were to bid them cut off a right hand or pluck out a right eye. They cannot think our blessed Lord requires so much at their hands, though an inspired apostle has commanded us to "mortify our members which are upon the earth." And he himself, even after he had converted millions and was very near arrived to the end of his race, professed that it was his daily practice to "keep under his body, and bring it into subjection, lest after he had preached to others, he himself should be a castaway" (1 Corinthians 9:27).

But some people think they are wiser than this great apostle, and chalk out to us what they falsely imagine an easier way to happiness. They would flatter us that we may go to heaven without offering violence to our sensual appetites, and enter in at the strait gate without striving against our carnal inclinations. And this is another reason that so many are only *almost* and not *altogether* Christians.

## 5. Fickleness

The fifth and last reason I shall discuss is a fickleness and instability of character.

It has been, no doubt, the misfortune that many a minister and sincere Christian has met with, to weep and wail over numbers of promising converts who seemingly began in the Spirit but after awhile have fallen away and ended in the flesh, not for want of right ideas about faith, nor out of a servile fear of man, nor out of a love of money or sensual pleasure but out of an instability and fickleness of temperament.

They looked upon faith merely as a novelty, as something which pleased them for awhile but after their curiosity was satisfied they have laid it aside again. Like the young man that came to see Jesus with a linen cloth about his naked body (Mark 14:51–52), they have followed him for a season, but when temptations have come to take hold on them, for want of a little more resolution they have been stripped of all their good intentions and "fled away naked." They at first, like a tree planted by the waterside, grew up and flourished, but having no root in themselves, no inward principle of holiness and spirituality, were like Jonah's gourd soon dried up, cut down, and withered. Their good intentions are only too like the violent motions of the animal spirits in a body newly beheaded which, though impetuous, are not lasting.[2] In short, they set out well in their journey to heaven, but finding the way either narrower or longer than they expected . . . they have made an eternal halt, and so returned like the dog to his vomit, or like the sow that was washed to her wallowing in the mire!

But I tremble to pronounce the fate of those so unstable in their profession of faith, who, having put their hands to the plow, for want of a little more resolution shamefully look back. How shall I repeat to them that dreadful threat: "If any man draw back, my soul shall have no pleasure in him!" And again, "It is impossible,"—that is, exceedingly difficult at least, "for those that have been once enlightened, and have tasted the good gift of God's Holy Spirit, and the powers of the world to come, if they should fall away, to be renewed again unto repentance" (cf. Hebrews 6:4–6). But notwithstanding that the Gospel is so severe against apostates, yet many that have begun well, through a fickleness of character (Oh that none of us here present may ever be such) have been by this means made of the "number of those that turn back unto perdition." And this is the fifth and last reason I shall give why so many are only *almost* and not *altogether Christians*.

But you, brethren, have not so learned Christ. God forbid that a fear of a little contempt, a love of a little worldly gain, or a fondness for a little sensual pleasure, or want of a steady resolution, should hinder you from entering into eternal life. . . .

## III. *The Folly of the Almost Christian*

Let us therefore proceed now to consider the folly of being no more than an *almost Christian*.

### 1. "Almost" is useless for salvation

The first proof I shall give of the folly of such a way of life is that it is ineffectual for salvation. It is true that such persons are almost good, but almost to hit the mark is really to miss it. God requires us to love Him with all our hearts, with all our souls, and with all our strength. He loves us too well to admit any rival, because as much as our hearts are empty of God, so much must they be unhappy. The devil indeed, like the false mother who came before Solomon, would have our hearts divided, as she would have had the child cut in two. But God, like the true mother, will have all or none. "My son, give me thy heart," thy whole heart, is the general call to all. And if we do not perform this, we never can expect the divine mercy.

Persons may indeed flatter themselves that a partial obedience will serve them well enough—but God at the great day will strike them dead, as He did Ananias and Sapphira by the mouth of his servant Peter, for pretending to offer Him all their hearts while they are keeping back from Him the greater part. They may perhaps impose upon their fellow creatures for awhile, but He that enabled Ahijah to cry out, "Come in, thou wife of Jeroboam," when she came disguised to enquire about her sick son, will also see through their most artful dissimulations; if their hearts are not whole with Him, He will appoint them their portion with hypocrites and unbelievers.

2. Damage to others

But secondly, what renders a half-way spirituality more inexcusable is that it is not only insufficient for our own salvation but also most prejudicial to the salvation of others.

An *almost Christian* is one of the most hurtful creatures in the world. He is a wolf in sheep's clothing. He is one of those false prophets our blessed Lord bids us beware of in his Sermon on the Mount, who would persuade people that the way to heaven is broader than it really is. Such persons thus "enter not into the kingdom of God themselves, and those that are entering in they hinder." These, these are those who turn the world into a lukewarm Laodicean spirit, who hand out false lights and so shipwreck unthinking benighted souls on their voyage to the haven where they hope to be. These are the ones who are greater enemies to the cross of Christ than infidels themselves, for everyone recognizes the unbeliever, but an *almost Christian*, through his subtle hypocrisy, draws away many after him and must therefore expect to receive the greater damnation.

3. Ingratitude to God

Thirdly, as it is most prejudicial to ourselves and hurtful to others, so it is the greatest form of ingratitude we can express toward our Lord and Master Jesus Christ. Did He come down from heaven and shed his precious blood to purchase these hearts of ours, and shall we only give Him half of them? Oh how can we say we love Him when our hearts are not wholly with Him? How can we call Him our Saviour when we will not endeavor sincerely to offer ourselves to Him and so let Him see the fruit of his love and be satisfied!

Had any of us purchased a slave at a most expensive price, who was earlier subject to the utmost miseries and torments and had no hope of release if we had shut up our heart of compassion from him, and had this slave afterwards grown rebellious or denied giving us more than half his service, how we would exclaim against his base ingratitude! And yet you are such a slave yourself, O man, who can acknowledge yourself to be redeemed from infinite unavoidable misery and punishment by the death of Jesus Christ, and yet you will not give yourself wholly to Him. Shall we deal with God our Maker in a manner we would not be dealt with by a person like ourselves? Shall we mete out a lesser measure of love to our Saviour than we would have dealt to ourselves? God forbid!

## IV. *Conclusion*

No, let us scorn all such base and treacherous treatment of our King and Saviour, even our God. Let us not make half-hearted efforts all our lives to go to heaven, and yet plunge ourselves into hell at last. Let us give God our whole hearts, and no longer halt between two opinions. If the world be God, let us serve it; if pleasure be a god, let us serve that; but if the Lord be God, let us, oh let us serve Him alone.

Alas! Why, why should we be so in love with slavery that we will not wholly renounce the world, the flesh and the devil which, like so many spiritual chains, bind down our souls and hinder them from flying up to God.

Alas! What are we afraid of? Is not God able to reward our complete obedience? If He is, as even the *almost Christian*'s lame way of serving Him seems to admit, why then will we not serve Him entirely? For the same reason we do so much, why do we not do more? Or do you think that being only half-hearted in your faith will make you happy but that going further will render you miserable and uneasy?

Alas! This, my brethren, is delusion all over! For what is it but this half-piety, this wavering between God and the world, that makes so many that are seemingly well disposed still such utter strangers to the comforts of the spiritual life? They choose just as much religion as will disturb them in their pleasures, and follow their pleasures just far enough to deprive themselves of the comforts of [true] religion. Whereas, on the contrary, if they would sincerely leave all impeding affections, and give their hearts wholly to God, they would then (and they cannot until then) experience the unspeakable pleasure of having a mind at unity with itself, and enjoy such a peace of God as even in this life passes all understanding, and to which they were entire strangers before.

It is true. If we want to devote ourselves entirely to God, we are bound to meet with contempt. But this is because contempt is necessary to heal our pride. We must renounce some sensual pleasures. But this is because those make us unfit for spiritual desires, which are infinitely better. We must renounce the love of the world. But this is so that we may be filled with the love of God. And when this experience has enlarged our hearts, we shall, like Jacob when he served for his beloved Rachel, think nothing too difficult to undergo, no hardships too tedious to endure because of the love we shall then have for our dear Redeemer. Easy, thus, and delightful will be the ways of God even in this life. But when once we throw off these bodies, and our souls are filled with all the fullness of God, oh, what heart can conceive, what tongue can express, with what unspeakable joy and consolation we shall then look back on our past sincere and hearty services which have procured us so invaluable a reward!

Do you think, then, my dear hearers, that we shall be sorry we have done so much? Or do you not rather think we shall be ashamed that we did not do more, and blush that we were so hesitant to give up all to God when he intended hereafter to give us Himself?

Let me therefore, to conclude, exhort you my brethren, to have always the unspeakable reward of a full obedience set before you. Consider in this context that every degree of holiness you neglect, every instance of spiritual life you pass by, is a jewel taken out of your crown, a degree of blessedness lost in the eyes of God. Oh! If you always think and act in this way then you will no longer be laboring to confuse matters between God and the world. On the contrary, you will be daily endeavoring to give up yourselves more and more unto Him. Then you will be always watching, always praying, always aspiring after further degrees of purity and love, and so consequently always preparing yourselves for a fuller light and enjoyment of that God in whose presence there is fullness of joy, and at whose right hand there are pleasures forevermore!

Amen! Amen!

# from the Letters

## Exhortation to Seminarians

My Dear Brethren in Christ,

The cordial love I bear you will not suffer me to neglect writing to you; as God has been pleased to bless my ministry to your souls, so I think it my duty to watch over you for the good, and assure you constantly you are all upon my heart.

Your last letter gave me great pleasure—but it was too full of acknowledgements, which I by no means deserve. To Him alone, from whom every good and perfect gift comes, be all the thanks and glory.

I heartily pray God that you may be burning and shining lights in the midst of a crooked and perverse generation. Though you are not of the Church of England, yet if you are persuaded in your own minds of the truth of the way wherein you now walk, I leave it. However, whether Conformists or Nonconformists, our main concern should be to be assured that we are called and taught of God—for none but such are fit to minister in holy things.

Indeed, my dear brethren, it rejoiced me much to see such dawnings of grace in your souls, except that I thought most of you were bowed down too much with a servile fear of man. But as the love of the Creator increases, the fear of the creature will daily decrease in your hearts. Nicodemus, who at first came by night to our Lord, afterwards dared to own Him before the whole council in open day. I pray God make you all thus minded. For unless your hearts are free from worldly hopes and worldly fears, you never will speak boldly as you ought to speak. The good old Puritans, I believe, never preached better than when in danger of being taken to prison as soon as they had finished their sermon. And however the church may be at peace now, I am persuaded [that] unless you go forth with the same attitude you will never preach with the same demonstration of the Spirit, and of power.

Study therefore, my brethren, I beseech you by the mercies of God in Christ Jesus. Study your hearts as well as books; ask yourselves again and again whether you would preach for Christ if you were sure to lay down your lives for doing so. If you fear the displeasure of a man for doing your duty now, assure yourselves you are not yet thus minded.

But enough of this. I love to hope well of you all. I trust, as you are enlightened with some degree of knowledge in the mysteries of godliness, you will henceforth determine not to know anything but Jesus Christ, and Him crucified. This is, and this (the Lord being my helper) shall be the only study of, my dear brethren,

Your affectionate friend, brother, and servant in Christ,

G.W.

# Exhortation to American Students

TO THE STUDENTS, ETC., UNDER CONVICTIONS AT THE COLLEGES OF CAMBRIDGE [Harvard] AND NEW-HAVEN [Yale], IN NEW ENGLAND AND CONNECTICUT

DEAR GENTLEMEN,

With unspeakable pleasure have I heard that there seems to be a general concern among you about the things of God. It was no small grief to me that I was obliged to say of your college that "your light was become darkness"—yet are ye now become light in the Lord.

I heartily thank God, even the Father of our glorious Redeemer, for sending dear Mr. T— among you.* What great things may we not now expect to see in New England, since it has pleased God to work so remarkably among the sons of the prophets? Now we may expect a reformation indeed, since it is beginning at the house of God.

A dead ministry will always make a dead people, whereas if ministers are warmed with the love of God themselves, they cannot but be instruments of diffusing that love among others. This, this is the best preparation for the work whereunto you are to be called. Learning without piety will only make you more capable of promoting the kingdom of Satan. Henceforward, therefore, I hope you will enter into your studies not to get a parish, nor to be polite preachers, but to be great saints.

This, indeed, is the most compendious way to true learning, for an understanding enlightened by the Spirit of God is more open to divine truths and, I am certain, will prove most useful to mankind. The more holy you are, the more will God delight to honor you.

I hope the *good old divinity* will now be precious to your souls, and you

---

*Gilbert Tennent, who was, along with Jonathan Edwards and Whitefield, one of the leaders of the Great Awakening in America.

will think it an honor to tread in the steps of your pious forefathers. They were acquainted with their own hearts. They knew what it was to be tempted themselves, and therefore from their own experience knew how to give help to others. O may you follow them, as they followed Christ. Then great, very great will be your reward in heaven. I am sure you can never serve a better Master than Jesus Christ, or be engaged in a higher employment than in calling home souls to Him.

I trust, dear gentlemen, you will not be offended at me for sending you these few lines. I write out of the fulness of my heart. I make mention of you always in my prayers. Forget me not in yours. I am a poor weak worm. I am the chief of sinners, and yet, O stupendous love!, the Lord's work still prospers in my unworthy hands. Fail not to give thanks, as well as to pray for

Your affectionate brother and servant in our common Lord,

G.W.

## To an Orphan

To Thomas Webb  *On board the* Mary and Ann, *July 27, 1741*

Dear Thomas,

How inconsistent is the devil! How artfully does he strive to keep poor souls from Christ! Sometimes he labors to drive poor souls into despair; sometimes to presumption. These are the two rocks against which he would fain have poor souls to make shipwreck of faith and a good conscience. I pray God to enable you to steer a middle course.

May you see your misery, and at the same time see your remedy in the cross and wounds of Jesus Christ. He calls to all weary, heavy-laden souls; consequently He calls to you. Your coming to Him will be a proof of your election. The devils know nothing of God's decrees. If ever [Satan] should tempt you so again, say, "If I do perish, I will perish at the feet of Christ." He is willing to save, to save to the uttermost. He sees, he feels your anguish. He longs to rejoice over you. Venture therefore upon him.

Thomas, be not faithless, but believing. Christ shall yet show you his hands and his feet. He is the same now as He was yesterday, full of love and graciousness to self-condemned sinners. That you may experience the full power and efficacy of the Redeemer's blood is the ardent prayer of, dear Thomas

Your sincere friend,

G.W.

# Obtaining the Holy Spirit

To the Inhabitants of Savannah *From on board the* Mary, *October 2, 1738*

My Good Friends,

As God has been pleased to place you more especially under my care, so, whether absent or present, I think it my duty to contribute my utmost endeavors towards promoting the salvation of your precious and immortal souls. For this end, and this only, God is my judge, came I amongst you; for this end am I now parted from you for a season; and for this end do I send you this general epistle. I love, I pray for, therefore do I write to you all without exception.

But what shall I write to you about? Why, of our common salvation, of that one thing needful, of that new birth in Christ Jesus, that ineffable change which must pass upon our hearts before we can see God, and of which you have heard me discourse so often. Let this, my dear friends, be the end of all your actions. Have this continually in view, and you will never do amiss. The author of this blessed change is the Holy Ghost, the third person in the ever-blessed Trinity. The Father made, the Son redeemed, and the Holy Spirit is to sanctify, and so apply Christ's redemption to our hearts.

The means to attain this Holy Spirit you know, and the way you know—self-denial and the way of the cross. "If any man will come after me," says Jesus Christ, "let him deny himself, and take up his cross daily, and follow me." And I cannot but think it a particular blessing which you enjoy above others, because you are in a new colony where daily crosses must necessarily fall in your way. Oh then, I beseech you by the mercies of God in Christ Jesus, make a virtue of necessity, and take up your daily crosses with resignation and thanksgiving.

Another means to attain the Holy Spirit is public worship, for Christ has promised [that] where two or three gather together in his name, there will He, by his Spirit, be in the midst of them. For your zeal in this particular, I have often blessed God within myself, and made mention of it to others. O continue likeminded, and as in my presence do not forget the assembling of yourselves together in the house of God, for there you will have the Scriptures read, though not expounded, and the Holy Spirit, if you apply to Him, will open your understandings and guide you into all truth.

Many other means there are of attaining the Holy Ghost, such as reading the Scriptures, secret prayer, self-examination, and receiving the blessed sacrament, all of which I would insist on, could they be comprised in a letter. But this must be deferred till I see you in person, and am qualified to administer unto the sacred symbols of Christ's blessed body and blood.* In the meanwhile think not that I shall forget you in my prayers. No, I remember my promise, and whilst the winds and storms are blowing over me, I make supplication to God on your behalf. Though absent in body, I am present in spirit, and joy in hopes of hearing of your zeal for the Lord. Remember, my dear friends, that for the space of near four months, I ceased not, day and night, warning every one of you to repent and turn to God, and bring forth fruits meet for repentance. Repent you therefore, and walk in all things as becometh the gospel of our Lord Jesus Christ, and then, and then only, shall your sins be blotted out.

Finally, my brethren, be all of one mind. Let there be no divisions among you, for a kingdom divided against itself cannot stand. Be over careful for nothing, but in everything, with supplications and thanksgiving, make your wants known unto God. Speak not evil one of another, brethren, but live at peace among yourselves. And the God of peace shall in all things direct and rule your hearts. Brethren, pray for us, and that God may restore me to you as soon as possible. In about eight months, God willing, I hope to see you. In the meanwhile you shall not be forgotten by

Your affectionate, though unworthy, minister in Christ Jesus,

GEORGE WHITEFIELD

## Open-Air Preaching I

To Mr. L—                                        *London, May 11, 1742*

With this, I send you a few out of the many notes I have received from persons who were convicted, converted, or comforted in Moorfields, during the late holidays. For many weeks, I found my heart much pressed to determine to venture to preach there at this season, when, if ever, Satan's children keep up their annual rendezvous.

I must inform you that Moorfields is a large spacious place, give, as I have been told, by one Madam Moore, on purpose for all sorts of people to divert themselves in. For many years past, from one end to the other,

---

*While with these people, Whitefield, being only a deacon, was not empowered to administer the sacraments; at this writing, he was enroute to England to be ordained as a priest the following January, and to raise further support for the orphanage. In his absence, an unordained assistant was left in charge both of the orphan work and the community worship services.

booths of all kinds have been erected, for mountebanks, players, puppet shows, and such like.

With a heart bleeding with compassion for so many thousands led captive by the devil at his will, on Whit-Monday, at six o'clock in the morning, attended by a large congregation of praying people, I ventured to lift up a standard amongst them in the name of Jesus of Nazareth. Perhaps there were about ten thousand in waiting, not for me, but for Satan's instruments to amuse them.

Glad was I to find that I had for once as it were got the start on the devil. I mounted my field pulpit; almost all flocked immediately around it. I preached on these words, "As Moses lifted up the serpent in the wilderness, so shall the Son of Man be lifted up, &c." They gazed, they listened, they wept; and I believe that many felt themselves stung with deep conviction for their past sins. All was hushed and solemn.

Being thus encouraged, I ventured out again at noon; but what a scene! The fields, the whole fields seemed, in a bad sense of the word, all white, ready not for the Redeemer's, but Beelzebub's harvest.* All his agents were in full motion—drummers, trumpeters, merry andrews, masters of puppet shows, exhibiters of wild beasts, players, &c., &c. all busy in entertaining their respective audiences. I suppose there could not be less than twenty or thirty thousand people.

My pulpit was fixed on the opposite side, and immediately, to their great mortification, they found the number of their attendants sadly lessened. Judging that like Saint Paul, I should now be called as it were to fight with beasts at Ephesus, I preached from these words: "Great is Diana of the Ephesians."** You may easily guess, that there was some noise among the craftsmen, and that I was honored with having a few stones, dirt, rotten eggs, and pieces of dead cats thrown at me, whilst engaged in calling them from their favorite but lying vanities. My soul was indeed among lions, but far the greatest part of my congregation, which was very large, seemed for awhile to be turned into lambs. This encouraged me to give notice that I would preach again at six o'clock in the evening.

I came, I saw, but what—thousands and thousands more than before if

---

*Whitefield is here (typically) rhetorically self-conscious, inviting his reader to associate "fields white unto harvest" (white fields) and even the date, Whit-Monday (the day after Whitsunday, or Pentecost), with his own name; Moorfields (pronounced "Morefields") may also suggest to his imagination more fields to preach in in days to come.

**Whitefield appreciates that what got St. Paul into trouble at Ephesus (Acts 19:23–41) exactly parallels the situation in which he finds himself; he is endangering a brisk trade in dubious goods.

possible, still more deeply engaged in their unhappy diversions, but some thousands amongst them waiting as earnestly to hear the Gospel. This Satan could not brook. One of his choicest servants was exhibiting, trumpeting on a large stage, but as soon as the people saw me in my black robes and my pulpit, I think all to a man left him and ran to me. For a while I was enabled to lift up my voice like a trumpet, and many heard the joyful sound. God's people kept praying, and the enemy's agents made a kind of roaring at some distance from our camp.

At length they approached nearer, and the merry andrew (attended by others, who complained that they had taken many pounds less that day on account of my preaching) got up upon a man's shoulders, and advancing near the pulpit attempted to slash me with a long heavy whip several times, but always with the violence of his motion tumbled down. Soon afterwards, they got a recruiting sergeant with his drum, &c. to pass through the congregation. I gave the word of command, and ordered that way might be made for the king's officer. The ranks opened, while all march'd quietly through, and then closed again.

Finding those efforts to fail, a large body quite on the opposite side assembled together, and having got a large pole for their standard, advanced towards us with steady and formidable steps, till they came very near the skirts of our hearing, praying, and almost undaunted congregation. I saw, gave warning, and prayed to the captain of our salvation for present support and deliverance. He heard and answered; for just as they approached us with looks full of resentment, I know not by what accident, they quarrelled among themselves, threw down their staff and went their way, leaving however many of their company behind, who before we had done, I trust were brought over to join the besieged party.

I think I continued in praying, preaching, and singing (for the noise was too great at times to preach) about three hours. We then retired to the Tabernacle, with my pockets full of notes from persons brought under concern, and read them amidst the praises and spiritual acclamations of thousands, who joined with the holy angels in rejoicing that so many sinners were snatched, in such an unexpected, unlikely place and manner, out of the very jaws of the devil.

This was the beginning of the Tabernacle Society. Three hundred and fifty awakened souls were received in one day, and I believe the number of notes exceeded a thousand. But I must have done, believing you want to retire to join in mutual praise and thanksgiving to God and the Lamb, with

Yours, &c.,

G.W.

# Open-Air Preaching II

My Dear Friend,

Fresh matter of praise; bless ye the Lord, for He hath triumphed glorious-ly. The battle that was begun on Monday was not quite over till Wednes-day evening, though the scene of action was a little shifted. Being strongly invited, and a pulpit being prepared for me by an honest Quaker, a coal merchant, I ventured on Tuesday evening to preach at Mary-le-bon fields, a place almost as much frequented by boxers, gamesters, and such like, as Moorfields. A vast concourse was assembled together, and as soon as I got into the field pulpit, their countenance bespoke the enmity of their hearts against the preacher. I opened with these words: "I am not ashamed of the Gospel of Christ, for it is the power of God unto salvation to every one that believeth."

I preached in great jeopardy, for the pulpit being high, and the sup-ports not well fixed in the ground, it tottered every time I moved, and the numbers of enemies strove to push my friends against the supports in order to throw me down. But the Redeemer stayed my soul on Himself, there I was not much moved, unless with compassion for those to whom I was delivering my master's message, which I had reason to think, by the strong impressions that were made, was welcome to many.

But Satan did not like thus to be attacked in his strongholds, and I narrowly escaped with my life, for as I was passing from the pulpit to the coach, I felt my wig and hat to be almost off. I turned about, and observed a sword just touching my temples. A young rake, as I afterwards found, was determined to stab me, but a gentleman, seeing the sword thrusting near me, struck it up with his cane, and so the destined victim providen-tially escaped. Such an attempt excited abhorrence; the enraged multitude soon seized him, and had it not been for one of my friends, who received him into his house, he might have undergone a severe discipline.

The next day, I renewed my attack in Moorfields, but would you think it? After they found that pelting, noise, and threatenings would not do, one of the merry andrews got up into a tree very near the pulpit, and shamefully exposed his nakedness before all the people. Such a beastly action quite abashed the serious part of my audience; whilst hundreds of another stamp, instead of rising up to pull down the unhappy wretch, expressed their approbation by repeated laughter. I must own at first it gave me a shock—I thought Satan had now almost outdone himself—but recovering my spirits, I appealed to all, since now they had such a spectacle before them, whether I had wronged human nature in saying, after pious Bishop Hall, that "man, when left to himself, is half devil and half a beast," or, as the great Mr. Law expressed himself, "a motley mixture of the beast and devil." Silence and attention being thus gained, I concluded with a warm exhortation, and closed our festival enterprises in reading fresh notes that were put up, praising and blessing God amidst thousands at the Tabernacle, for what He had done for precious souls, and on account of the deliverances He had wrought out for me and his people. I could enlarge, but being about to embark in the *Mary and Ann,* for Scotland, I must hasten to subscribe myself,

Yours, &c.

G.W.

P.S. I cannot help adding that several little boys and girls who were fond of sitting round me on the pulpit while I preached and handing to me people's notes, though they were often pelted with eggs, dirt, &c thrown at me, never once gave way, but on the contrary, every time I was struck, turned up their little weeping eyes and seemed to wish they could receive the blows for me. God make them in their growing years great and living martyrs for Him, who out of the mouth of babes and sucklings perfects praise!

# CHRISTOPHER SMART
## 1722 · 1771

From the portrait in Pembroke College, Oxford. Used by permission of the Master
and Fellows of the College.

## INTRODUCTION

"Poor Kit Smart," as he has often been called, was one of the remarkable geniuses of English poetry. Among nearly one thousand pages of writing, he has left behind not less than five university (Cambridge) prize poems, numerous accomplished examples of high style occasional verse, the librettos for two oratorios (*Hannah*, 1764, and *Abimelech*, 1768), and an undoubted triumph of religious verse, *The Song to David* (1763). Robert Browning and Dante Gabriel Rosetti, among others, have with justice called this last poem one of the masterpieces of the English language. Yet Smart was committed on dubious grounds to a mental hospital in 1759, and almost all of his own contemporaries shrank from even his memory in embarrassment; it was as though the sea had swallowed him up.

During his early years as a London "hack writer," Smart was well known and well liked in literary circles. He was apparently a little person, dark-eyed, handsome, and charming. He had enjoyed a brilliant career at Cambridge. Graduating in 1742, he was elected Fellow of Pembroke in 1745, and made an assistant ("praelector") in philosophy. For some years afterward he was kept on the payroll as a kind of poet-sometimes-in-residence and had thus acquired credentials and connections that could serve him well in London. But he seems never to have been able to take advantage of these opportunities. Always in debt, he had a serious problem with alcohol, and despite many good projects started, far too few were finished or properly successful. He started up a journal in which he had collaborators as distinguished as Samuel Johnson, but the journal failed. He undertook a partial translation of Horace (1750), but this had inadequate success. In 1752, he seems to have suffered the first attack of what we now call "depression" in response to these difficulties. Happily, it did not last long.

Later in the same year, in the midst of "a perfect whirlwind of activity," Smart fell in love with Anna Maria Carnan. She was the daughter of a printer, and now step-daughter to another printer, John Newbery, the bookseller who had so much influence on Smart's later career. Like her mother, Anna had been raised quietly as a Catholic, and still kept (quietly, as was necessary) her form of faith.[1] Her marriage to Smart—for which no precise date is known, since it was apparently a Catholic ceremony and therefore unregistered—began happily. Smart collaborated with his father-in-law on a new three-penny journal called *The Midwife, or The Old Woman's Magazine,* which ran from late 1751 through 1753. He brought out his first volume of poems with Newbery in 1752, and the prestige of the volume is indicated in its list of official "subscribers"—which included Samuel Richardson, Thomas Gray, William Collins, David Garrick, and Voltaire. But it was not a moneymaker, and when news of Smart's marriage forced resignation of his fellowship at Cambridge, financial woes became acute. He was now entirely dependent on his success as a hack writer to maintain a living for himself and his family. Various projects followed, including another abortive journal and a complete prose translation of Horace (1756) by which the bookseller seemed to make money but Smart almost nothing. He now had two small daughters to provide for and pressures upon him were mounting. His wife and children were forced to go to the home of a sister in Ireland in consequence of Smart's inability to pay the bills.

In February 1756, Smart was deeply discouraged and contracted a severe fever. His depression became acute. This time, however, he seems to have experienced in his illness a deep conviction of sin and a genuine process of repentance. We do not know who ministered to him, if anyone, or how. Yet both his physical and spiritual health returned, and he wrote a thankful poem describing his recovery, "Hymn to the Supreme Being," the theme of which is drawn from the story of King Hezekiah, reprieved at the point of death and given a new lease on life so that he might dedicate himself now wholly to God. It expresses for Smart his "second birth . . . a birth of joy," an experience of grace and healing. He returned to work with a new sense of purpose. Whereas once his mercurial temperament had sent him up and down in rapid succession, he now seemed to be simply "up."

And this is where the worst of his troubles began. Feeling a new sense of vocation, Smart announced he would write no longer for the gossipy secular journals by which he had made his living. In fact, he refused to write anything that he felt was not explicitly in praise of God. With his muse now "Christ the Word," he wanted to be, as he said, a "reviver of ADORATION among Englishmen." He plunged himself into reading the Bible. Then taking to heart the injunction of St. Paul to the Thessalonians to "pray without ceasing," he began to pray almost anywhere he found himself, deliberately engaging what he himself called "jeopardy," "confessing God openly." His worldly fellow Londoners (hiding rather stiffly behind a mask of rationalism their antipathy to anything spiritual) reacted as if he was a leper. Johnson comments:

> Madness frequently discovers itself by unnecessary deviation from the usual modes of the world. My poor friend Smart shewed the disturbance of his mind, by falling upon his knees, and saying prayers in the street, or in any other unusual place. Now although, rationally speaking, it is greater madness not to pray at all than to pray as Smart did, I

am afraid there are so many who do not pray, that their understanding is not called into question.[2]

Others thought his case simply one of extremism; many other extremists went unnoticed, and Smart might have as well, except that

> he knelt down in the streets and assembly rooms, and wherever he was when the thought crossed his mind—and this indecorous conduct obliged his friends to place him in a confinement whence many mad as he remain excluded only because their delusion is not known.[3]

Another of his contemporaries writes that

> In every other transaction of life no man's wits could be more regular than those of Smart, for this prevalence of one idea pertinaciously keeping the first place in his head had in no sense, except in what immediately related to itself, perverted his judgement at all; his opinions were unchanged as before, nor did he seem more likely to fall into a state of distraction than any other man; less so, perhaps, as he calmed every violent start of passion by prayer.[4]

But too many took him for plain "mad," seeing his actions as ludicrous and attributing his apparent madness to religious "enthusiasm." It may be that the spread of this opinion proved decisive for his father-in-law who, fearing the exposure of Smart's "enthusiasm" might lead to prosecution of his daughter and her children for their Catholic faith (as we have seen, "Romanists" and "enthusiasts" were lumped together as confederate demons by the Established authorities), acted swiftly. On June 17, 1756, Newbery "turned the key on Christopher Smart with the consent of all his relatives," and he became a prisoner in his own house.

It is difficult for us to imagine the lot of such an unfortunate as Smart. The private institution to which he was finally taken in May 1757 was St. Luke's Asylum, a "new institution" founded in 1750. While much to be preferred to the horrors of Bedlam (in which the inmates were left in chains on dirty straw until they died, and where each Sunday visitors were allowed in to gawk, prod, abuse, and laugh at the frenzy of their victims) it could still be a miserable environment. Patients were prisoners, with the desperately ill and relatively healthy ofen placed together in conditions of cruelty and rituals of degradation. (One thinks here of the terrible story of Alexander Cruden, author of the famous *Concordance* to the Bible, who escaped one midnight in 1739 stark naked and manacled out the window of such a madhouse in Bethnal Green.)

Although Smart was discharged in May of 1758, his family seems to have kept him privately confined again, lest he should pray on the streets. On August 13 Smart was persuaded to sign over all royalties and a small inheritance to his mother; he was placed back in the institution in 1759. Toward the end of this period, he was evidently more fortunate than most. Although it was rumored that his *Song to David* had been scratched with a key on the wall, by the time Samuel Johnson came to visit him in 1762 he had pen and paper and, as we can infer from his poetry, perhaps even a Bible. He was able to take exercise by digging in the hospital garden. Johnson told Charles Burney, with some feeling: "I did not think he ought to be shut up. His infirmities were not noxious to society. He insisted on people praying with him; and I'd as lief pray with Kit Smart as anyone else."[5] (It is worthwhile noting that Johnson was apparently the only one of Smart's literary friends known to have visited him, and that, expecting only a brief confinement, Johnson had at the beginning written numerous articles over Smart's name in an effort to keep up his contractual obligations for him and some badly needed money flowing in.)

By 1763, a House of Commons enquiry into private mental institutions was underway, and an article which appeared in the *Gentleman's Magazine* in January of that year exposed the brutality and absolute denial of rights which were common in such places.[6] It may be that these events helped obtain Smart's release. In any case, on or near the last day of January, a relatively unknown person, one John Sherrat, a London merchant with a reputation for piety, charity, and concern for the sick and imprisoned, simply walked in and "cut him out" under the keeper's nose. It happens that this was the very week in which the chief proprietor of such establishments was being examined before the House Committee.

The great period of Smart's Christian poetry is 1759–63, the years of his confinement for ostensible madness. As his *Jubilate Agno* shows, he never believed himself to be insane and felt that he had been confined by treachery. He used his time well, however, reading his Bible, praying for the other inmates, and using his writing as a form of prayer and praise. His great long poem, the *Song to David*—metrically brilliant, structurally and conceptually intricate, and above all, intelligent—was written before his release.

The last years of the life of Christopher Smart were passed initially in diligence in his work and an attempt to provide for his family by his religious verse. But the taint of "mad enthusiasm" was on his reputation. London critics rejected the brilliance so readily praised in the nineteenth and twentieth centuries, since they thought it intemperate. The poetry sold poorly as a result. Smart wrote two biblical oratorios and metrical versions of the Psalms (1765). He did a versification of the parables of Jesus (1768), which he hoped would be used in Sunday schools. He set out to do a complete body of hymns to revitalize the liturgy of the Anglican church, arguing that "it would be better if the liturgy were musically performed."

We do not know where Christopher Smart attended church, or who, if anyone, was his spiritual adviser or pastor. His spirituality has been compared to that of William Law, with whose theology, at least, his thought seems compatible. But Smart is more exuberant than Law, and writes with a special kind of tenderness that is seldom found except in those who have known much pain and have still been able to rejoice. What has been called a "Franciscan" quality in his spirituality shows up everywhere in his verse after 1754.[7] He was a keen student of nature and certainly knew more names of animals, birds, fish, and flowers than any contemporary poet. In his lines all creation—from the "alcedo, who makes a cradle for its young, which is rock'd by the winds," to "the sword-fish, whose aim is perpetual & strength insuperable"—is made to praise God, catching up the human spirit in adoration of divine goodness.

Smart's last work was a collection of *Hymns for the Amusement of Children,* in which all of these qualities remain evident. He wrote them as a spiritual exercise, and as a spiritual exercise they should be read. The volume went through three editions in five years, but before the first appeared in 1770, Smart was already in debtors' prison; in fact, some of the lines about praying for enemies almost certainly related to his torments there.[8] He penned a note not long before his death to a Rev. Jackson, who seems to have been among the Methodist preachers working in London's prisons and asylums. It offers a terse witness to his helplessness and distress:

> Being upon the recovery from a fit of illness, and having nothing to eat, I beg you to lend me two or three shillings, which (God willing) I will return, with many thanks, in two or three days.[9]

Always lucid to this point, he now began to deteriorate, and on May 20, 1771, died of starvation and fever.

Among all the evidences of grace abounding in this great period, none seems more convincing now, perhaps, than the poetry of Christopher Smart. A persistent note of humility, gratitude, and adoration of God characterizes everything Smart produced through all those terrible years. Destitute, hungry, deprived of family, unable to ward off the wolves of debt no matter how late he burned the midnight oil or how prodigious his literary output, he sang always the new song of a redeemed soul, even from behind bars. What more eloquent witness to the transforming power of God's spirit could a poet provide, who from the misery of an insane asylum wrote these words:

. . . Beauteous the moon full on the lawn;
And beauteous, when the veil's withdrawn,
  The virgin to her spouse:
Beauteous the temple deck'd and fill'd,
When to the heav'n of heav'n's they build
  Their heart-directed vows. . . .

Precious the penitential tear;
And precious is the sigh sincere,
  Acceptable to God:
And precious are the winning flow'rs,
In gladsome Israel's feast of bow'rs,
  Bound on the hallow'd sod.

More precious that diviner part
Of David, ev'n the Lord's own heart,
  Great, beautiful, and new:
In all things where it was intent,
In all extreams, in each event,
  Proof—answ'ring true to true.

Glorious the sun in mid career;
Glorious th' assembled fires appear;
  Glorious the comet's train:
Glorious the trumpet and alarm;
Glorious th' almighty stretch'd-out arm;
  Glorious th' enraptur's main:

Glorious the northern lights astream;
Glorious the song, when God's the theme;
  Glorious the thunder's roar:
Glorious hosanna from the den;
Glorious the catholic amen;
  Glorious the martyr's gore:

Glorious—more glorious is the crown
Of Him that brought salvation down
  By meekness, call'd thy Son;
Thou at stupendous truth believ'd,
And now the matchless deed's achiev'd,
  DETERMINED, DARED, and DONE.

## NOTES

1. Christopher Devlin, *Poor Kit Smart* (London: Rupert Hart-Davis, 1961), p. 66.
2. James Boswell, *Life of Samuel Johnson*, vol. 1, p. 397.
3. Katherine C. Balderston, ed., *Thraliana: The Diary of Mrs. Hester Lynch Thrale*

(Oxford, 1942), vol. 2, p. 728; cf. Sophia B. Blaydes, *Christopher Smart as a Poet of His Time: A Re-appraisal* (The Hague: Mouton, 1966), p. 59.

4. Mrs. Piozzi, writing in *The Gentleman's Magazine* (July 1849), p. 24; cf. Edward G. Ainsworth and Charles E. Noyes, *Christopher Smart: A Biographical and Critical Study* (Columbia: University of Missouri Press, 1943), p. 88.

5. Boswell, *Life of Samuel Johnson*, vol. 1, p. 397.

6. *Gentlemen's Magazine* for January 1763, quoted by Devlin as follows:

> When a person is forcibly taken or artfully decoyed into a private madhouse, he is, without any authority or any further charge, than that of an impatient heir, a mercenary relation, or a pretended friend, instantly seized upon by a set of inhuman ruffians trained up to this barbarous profession, stripped naked, and conveyed to a dark-room. If the patient complains, the attendant brutishly orders him not to rave, calls for assistants, and ties him down to a bed, from which he is not released until he submits to their pleasure. Next morning, a doctor is gravely introduced who, taking the report of the keeper, pronounces the unfortunate person a lunatic, and declares that he must be reduced by physic. If the revolted victim offers to argue against it by alleging any proofs of sanity, a motion is made by the waiter for the doctor to withdraw, and if the patient, or rather the prisoner, persists in vindicating his reason, or refuses to take the dose, he is then deemed raving mad; the banditti of the whole house are called in, the forcing instruments are brought, upon which the sensible patient must submit to take whatever is administered. When the poor patient thus finds himself deprived of all communications with the world, and denied the use of pen and paper, all he can do is to compose himself under the unhappy situation in the hope of a more favourable report. But any composure under such affliction is immediately deemed a melancholy or sulky fit by the waiter who reports it as such to the doctor in the hearing of the despairing prisoner, whose misery is thus redoubled in finding that the doctor prescribed a repetition of the dose, and that from day to day, until the patient is so debilitated in body that in time it impairs his mind.

7. See Devlin, pp. 138–51; J. Middleton Murray, *Discoveries* (London, 1924), p. 186.

8. See Devlin, pp. 188–89:

> One of the worst things about a Debtor's Prison was the mental torture, which the keepers after long practice had reduced to a fine art. The prisoner on arrival would be flung into an unspeakably contaminated cell and left there; on payment of a fee he would be given better quarters; then he was told that he would be sent back to the original cell if the fee was not raised. The screw, having been once fitted, could be tightened or relaxed as seemed most profitable.

9. *Gentleman's Magazine,* July 1779, p. 339, cited in Ainsworth and Noyes, p. 141, Devlin, p. 189.

# Hymn to the Supreme Being

ON RECOVERY FROM A DANGEROUS fiT OF ILLNESS, 1756

When *Israel's* ruler\* on the royal bed
   In anguish and in perturbation lay,
The down reliev'd not his anointed head,
   And rest gave place to horror and dismay.
Fast flow'd the tears, high heav'd each gasping sigh
When God's own prophet thunder'd—MONARCH,
                       THOU MUST DIE.

And must I go, th'illustrious mourner cry'd,
   I who have serv'd thee still in faith and truth,
Whose snow-white conscience no foul crime has died
   From youth to manhood, infancy to youth,
Like *David,* who have still rever'd thy word
The sovereign of myself and servant of the Lord!

The judge Almighty heard his suppliant's moan,
   Repeal'd his sentence, and his health restor'd;
The beams of mercy on his temple shone,
   Shot from that heaven to which his sighs had soar'd;
The sun retreated at his maker's nod
And miracles confirm the genuine work of God.

But, O immortals! What had I to plead
   When death stood o'er me with his threat'ning lance,
When reason left me in the time of need,
   And sense was lost in terror or in trance,
My sick'ning soul was with my blood inflam'd,
And the celestial image sunk, defac'd and maim'd.

I sent back memory, in heedful guise,
   To search the records of preceding years;
Home, like the raven to the ark,\*\* she flies,
   Croaking bad tidings to my trembling ears.
O Sun, again that thy retreat was made,
And threw my follies back into the friendly shade!

But who are they, that bid affliction cease!—
   Redemption and forgiveness, heavenly sounds!

\*Hezekiah, in Isaiah 37–39.
\*\*Genesis 8:7.

328

Behold the dove that brings the branch of peace,
    Behold the balm that heals the gaping wounds—
Vengeance divine's by penitence supprest—
She struggles with the angel, conquers, and is blest.*

Yet hold, presumption, nor too fondly climb,
    And thou too hold, O horrible despair!
In man humility's alone sublime,
    Who diffidently hopes he's *Christ's* own care—
O all-sufficient Lamb! in death's dread hour
Thy merits who shall slight, or who can doubt thy power?

But soul-rejoicing health again returns,
    The blood meanders gently in each vein,
The lamp of life renew'd with vigour burns,
    And exil'd reason takes her seat again—
Brisk leaps the heart, the mind's at large once more,
To love, to praise, to bless, to wonder and adore.

The virtuous partner of my nuptial bands,
    Appear'd a widow to my frantic sight;
My little prattlers lifting up their hands,
    Beckon me back to them, to life, and light;
I come, ye spotless sweets; I come again,
Nor have your tears been shed, nor have ye knelt in vain.

All glory to th'ETERNAL, to th'IMMENSE,
    All glory to th'OMNISCIENT and GOOD,
Whose power's uncircumscrib'd, whose love's intense;
    But yet whose justice ne'er could be withstood,
Except thro' him—thro' him, who stands alone,
Of worth, of weight allow'd for all Mankind t'atone!

He rais'd the lame, the lepers he made whole,
    He fix'd the palsied nerves of weak decay,
He drove out Satan from the tortur'd soul,
    And to the blind gave or restor'd the day,—
Nay more,—far more unequal'd pangs sustain'd,
Till his lost fallen flock his taintless blood regain'd.

My feeble feet refus'd my body's weight,
    Nor wou'd my eyes admit the glorious light,
My nerves convuls'd shook fearful of their fate,
    My mind lay open to the powers of night.

*Genesis 32:24–28.

He pitying did a second birth bestow
A birth of joy—not like the first of tears and woe.

Ye strengthen'd feet, forth to his altar move;
    Quicken, ye new-strung nerves, th'enraptur'd lyre;
Ye heav'n-directed eyes, o'erflow with love;
    Glow, glow, my soul, with pure seraphic fire;
Deeds, thoughts, and words no more his mandates break,
But to his endless glory work, conceive, and speak.

O! penitence, to virtue near allied,
    Thou can'st new joys e'en to the blest impart;
The list'ning angels lay their harps aside
    To hear the music of thy contrite heart;
And heav'n itself wears a more radiant face,
When charity presents thee to the throne of grace.

Chief of metallic forms is regal gold;
    Of elements, the limpid fount that flows;
Give me 'mongst gems the brilliant to behold;
    O'er *Flora's* flock imperial is the rose:
Above all birds the sov'reign eagle soars;
And monarch of the field the lordly lion roars.

What can with great *Leviathan* compare,
    Who takes his pastime in the mighty main?
What, like the *Sun,* shines thro' the realms of air,
    And gilds and glorifies th'ethereal plain—
Yet what are these to man, who bears the sway?
For all was made for him—to serve and to obey.

Thus in high heaven charity is great,
    Faith, hope, devotion hold a lower place;
On her the cherubs and the seraphs wait,
    Her, every virtue courts, and every grace;
See! on the right, close by th'Almighty's throne,
In him she shines confest, who came to make her known.

Deep-rooted in my heart then let her grow,
    That for the past the future may atone;
That I may act what thou hast giv'n to know,
    That I may live for THEE and THEE alone,
And justify those sweetest words from heav'n,
"THAT HE SHALL LOVE THEE MOST* TO WHOM
                        THOU'ST MOST FORGIVEN."

*Luke 7:41–43.

# *from* Jubilate Agno (1759–1763)*

## ("REJOICE IN THE LAMB")

REJOICE in God, O ye Tongues; give the glory to the Lord,
and the Lamb.
Nations, and languages, and every Creature, in which is the
breath of Life.
Let man and beast appear before him, and magnify his name together.
Let Noah and his company approach the throne of Grace,
and do homage to the Ark of their Salvation.
Let Abraham present a Ram, and worship the God of his Redemption.
Let Isaac, the Bridegroom, kneel with his Camels, and bless
the hope of his pilgrimage.
Let Jacob, and his speckled Drove adore the good Shepherd of Israel.
Let Esau offer a scape Goat for his seed, and rejoice in the
blessing of God his father.

\* \* \*

For I am not without authority in my jeopardy, which I
derive inevitably from the glory of the name of the Lord.
For I bless God whose name is Jealous—and there is a zeal
to deliver us from everlasting burnings.
For my estimation is good even amongst the slanderers
and my memory shall arise for a sweet savour unto the Lord.
For I bless the PRINCE of PEACE and pray that all the
guns may be nail'd up, save such as are for the rejoicing days.
For I have abstained from the blood of the grape and that
even at the Lord's table. . . .

*This long, disjunctive sequence was composed on the "Let"/"For" antiphonal
model which Bishop Robert Lowth, in his *Lectures on the Sacred Poetry of the Hebrews*
(*De Sacra Poesi Hebraeorum*), had pointed out was characteristic of Hebrew psalmody. Smart had read this book avidly. His own lines are notes, comprising a kind of
annotation to prayer, which he never intended should be published and which were
not until this century. The style is epigrammatic, even gnomic, in parts recalling the
Proverbs of Solomon as well as the Psalms. Students of English literature will be
familiar with the famous sequence, "For I will consider my cat Jeoffry," not included among the excerpts printed here. I have likewise omitted many of the
"Let . . ." sections. See the edition of *Jubilate Agno* by W. H. Bond (1954), and the
excellent recent study by Karina Williamson, *The Poetical Works of Christopher Smart*
(Oxford: Clarendon, 1980).

For I meditate the peace of Europe amongst family bickerings
and domestic jars. . . .*

For I preach the very GOSPEL of CHRIST without comment
& with this weapon shall I slay envy.

For I bless God in the rising generation, which is on my side.

For I have translated in the charity, which makes things
better & I shall be translated myself at the last.

For he that walked upon the sea, hath prepared the floods
with the Gospel of peace.

For the merciful man is merciful to his beast, and to the trees
that give them shelter.

For he hath turned the shadow of death into the morning,
the Lord is his name.

For I am come home again, but there is nobody to kill the
calf or to play the musick.

* * *

For I am a little fellow, which is intitled to the great
mess by the benevolence of God my father.

For I this day made over my inheritance to my mother
in consideration of her infirmities.

For I this day made over my inheritance to my mother
in consideration of her age.

For I this day made over my inheritance to my mother
in consideration of her poverty.

For I bless the thirteenth of August, in which I had the
grace to obey the voice of Christ in my conscience.

For I bless the thirteenth of August, in which I was
willing to run all hazards for the sake of the name
of the Lord.

For I bless the thirteenth of August, in which I was
willing to be called a fool for the sake of Christ.

For I lent my flocks and my herds and my lands at once unto the Lord.

For nature is more various than observation tho'
observers are innumerable.

* * *

*I.e., quarrels.

For the story of Orpheus is of the truth.*
For there was such a person a cunning player on the harp.
For he was a believer in the true God and assisted in the spirit.
For he playd upon the harp in the spirit by breathing upon the strings.
For this will affect every thing that is sustained by
   the spirit even every thing in nature.
For it is the business of a man gifted in the
   word to prophecy good.
For it will be better for England and all the world
   in a season, as I prophecy this day.
For I prophecy that they will obey the motions of the
   spirit descended upon them as at this day.
For they have seen the glory of God already come down
   upon the trees.
For I prophecy that it will descend upon their heads also.
For I prophecy that the praise of God will be in every
   man's mouth in the Publick streets.
For I prophecy that there will be Publick worship in the
   cross ways and fields.

\* \* \*

FOR I pray the Lord JESUS that cured the LUNATICK to
   be merciful to all my brethren and sisters in these houses.
For they work me with their harping-irons,** which is
   a barbarous instrument, because I am more unguarded than others.
For the blessing of God hath been on my epistles,
   which I have written for the benefit of others.
For I bless God that the CHURCH OF ENGLAND is one
   of the SEVEN even the candlestick of the Lord.
For the ENGLISH TONGUE shall be the language of the WEST.
For I pray Almighty CHRIST to bless the MAGDALEN*** HOUSE
   & to forward a National purification.

---

*Orpheus, the legendary Greek harpist who won back his bride from the dead by his playing, was often associated with David, whose harmonious harp was seen as an instrument of healing (i.e., of Saul), and as an image of the word hidden in the heart and "played" there—meditated upon day and night. See Smart's fine long *Song to David* (1763), and his Cambridge prize poem of 1755.
**Instruments used by asylum orderlies to force drugs down the throats of unwilling patients.
***An institution started in 1758 by the pressure of evangelicals to protect and re-habilitate prostitutes.

For I have the blessing of God in the three POINTS
    of manhood, of the pen, of the sword, & of chivalry.
For I am inquisitive in the Lord, and defend the
    philosophy of the scripture against vain deceit.
For the nets come down from the eyes of the Lord
    to fish up men to their salvation.
For I have a greater compass both of mirth and
    melancholy than another.

* * *

For the Sin against the HOLY GHOST is INGRATITUDE.

* * *

For the SHADOW is of death, which is the Devil, who can
    make false and faint images of the works of Almighty God. . . .
For SHADOW is a fair word from God . . .
For the shadow is his and the penumbra is his and his the
    perplexity of the phenomenon.

* * *

For I am the Lord's News-Writer—the scribe-evangelist . . .
For being desert-ed is to have desert in the sight of God
    and intitles one to the Lord's merit.
For things that are not in the sight of men are thro' God of
    infinite concern. . . .
For TIMES and SEASONS are the Lord's—Man is no
    CHRONOLOGER.

* * *

For the CLAPPING of the hands is naught unless it be to the
    glory of God.
For God will descend in visible glory when men begin to applaud him.

* * *

For the Argument A PRIORI is GOD in every man's
    CONSCIENCE.
For the Argument A POSTERIORI is God before every man's eyes.

* * *

For a NEW SONG also is best, if it be to the glory of God; and
taken with the food like the psalms. . . .
For a good wish is well but a faithful prayer is an eternal benefit.

\* \* \*

For the doubling of flowers is the improvement of the
gardners talent.
For the flowers are great blessings.
For the Lord made a Nosegay in the meadow with his
disciples & preached upon the lily.*
For the angels of God took it out of his hand and
carried it to the Height.
For a man cannot have publick spirit, who is void of
private benevolence.
For there is no Height in which there are not flowers.
For flowers have great virtues for all the senses.
For the flower glorifies God and the root parries the adversary.
For the flowers have their angels even the words of God's Creation.
For the warp & woof of flowers are worked by perpetual
moving spirits.
For flowers are good both for the living and the dead.
For there is a language of flowers.
For there is a sound reasoning upon all flowers.
For elegant phrases are nothing but flowers.
For flowers are peculiarly the poetry of Christ.
For flowers are medicinal.
For flowers are musical in ocular harmony.
For the right names of flowers are yet in heaven. God
make gardners better nomenclators.
For the Poorman's nosegay is an introduction to a Prince.

\* \* \*

For I prophecy that the general salutation will be
The Lord Jesus prosper you I wish you good luck in the
name of the Lord Jesus.
For I prophecy that men will learn the use of their knees.
For every thing that can be done in that posture (upon the
knees) is better so done than otherwise.

*The "nosegay" here relates to an old metaphor for the Beatitudes, found often in
spiritual writers of the Middle Ages (cf. the *fioretti* or "little flowers" of St. Francis,
which correspond to this image).

# *from* Hymns for the Amusement of Children (1772)

## Wisdom

Father of lights, conduct my feet
  Thro' life's dark, dang'rous road;
And, O, let ev'ry step still bring
  Me nearer to my God.

Let heaven-ey'd prudence be my guide,
  And, when I go astray,
Recall my feet from folly's path,
  Into a better way.

Teach me thro' ev'ry various scene
  To keep my end in view,
And whilst I tread life's mazy track
  Let wisdom be my clue.

That wisdom which is from above
  Abundantly impart;
And let it guard, and guide, and warm
  And penetrate my heart;

Till it shall lead me to thyself,
  Fountain of bliss and love;
And all my darkness be dispers'd
  In endless light above.

# Melancholy

O pluck me quick the raven's quill,
  And I will set me down,
My destin'd purpose to fulfil,
But with this interrupted skill,
  Of thought and grief profound.

How to begin, and how depart,
  From this sad fav'rite theme,
The man of sorrow in my heart,
I at my own ideas start,
  As dread as Daniel's dream,

As soon as born the infant cries,
  For well his spirit knows,
A little while, and then he dies,
A little while, and down he lies,
  To take a stern repose.

But man's own death is not th' event,
  For which most tears are due;
Wife, children, to the grave are sent,
Or friends, to make the heart repent
  That it such blessings knew.

O thou, which on the mountain's brow,
  By night didst pray alone;
In the cold night didst pay thy vow,
And in humiliation bow,
  To thrones and pow'rs thine own.

Tell us, for thou the best can tell,
  What Melancholy means?
A guise in them that wear it well,
That goes to music to dispel
  Dark thoughts and gloomier scenes.

Say, didst thou solitude desire,
  Or wert thou driv'n away,
By rank desertion to retire,

Without or bed, or food, or fire,
   For all thy foes to pray.

Yet thou didst preach of future bliss,
   Peace permanent above,
Of truth and mercy's holy kiss,
Those joys, which none that love thee miss,
   O give us grace to love.

# Hymn Against Despair (Old Ralph in the Wood)

A raven once an acorn took
   From Bashan's tallest stoutest tree;
He hid it by a limpid brook,
   And liv'd another oak to see.

Thus Melancholy buries Hope,
   Which Providence keeps still alive,
And bids us with affliction cope,
   And all anxiety survive.

# Obedience

Thee, dearest Lord, my soul adores,
   I would be only thine;
To thee my heart and all its pow'rs
   I willingly resign.

Give me a calm and thankful heart,
   From ev'ry murmur free;
The blessings of thy grace impart,
   That I may live to thee.

Whate'er thy sacred will ordains,
   O give me strength to bear;
And let me know my Father reigns,
   And trust his tender care.

Whate'er thy providence denies
   I calmly would resign;
For thou art just, and good, and wise,
   Lord, bend my will to thine.

Be this the purpose of my soul,
   And my determin'd choice,
To yield to thy supreme control,
   And in thy will rejoice.

O, may I never faint nor tire,
   Nor wander from thy ways;
But (which is all my soul's desire)
   Help me to sing thy praise.

# Humility

Folly builds high upon the sand,
  But lowly let my basis be;
Firm as a rock my hope shall stand,
  Deep founded in humility.

Content, when threat'ning ills obtrude,
  Sweet meek-ey'd patience, arm my soul;
And let a prudent fortitude
  Teach me my passions to control.

My God, I long to know thee still,
  To love, and fear, and trust thee more
To live submissive to thy will,
  And whilst I feel thy grace, adore.

My faith and love, obedient be;
  Dear Saviour! teach me thy commands;
My ardent soul still follows thee,
  And trusts her int'rests in thy hands.

Let love and mercy, all divine,
  Justice, descending from the skies,
Kindness and truth, my heart incline,
  Still to forgive mine enemies.

Thus may I act the Christian part,
  The social, human and divine,
Whilst a wise zeal inspires my heart;
  Then shall I know that heaven is mine.

# Forgiveness of Injuries

And is the Gospel peace and love?
  Such let our conversation be;
The serpent blended with the dove,
  Wisdom and meek simplicity.

Whene'er the angry passions rise,
  And tempt our thoughts and tongues to strife,
To Jesus let us lift our eyes,
  Bright pattern of the Christian life!

O, how benevolent and kind!
  How mild, how ready to forgive!
Be this the temper of our mind,
  And these the rules by which we live!

Dispensing good where'er he came,
  His greatest foes still felt his love!
O, if we love the Saviour's name,
  Let his divine example move!

Their malice rag'd without a cause,
  Yet, with his last expiring breath,
He pray'd for murderers on the cross,
  And bless'd his enemies in death.

Lord, shall thy bright example shine
  So long in vain before mine eyes!
Give me a soul akin to thine,
  To bless and love mine enemies.

# Truth

'Tis thus the holy Scripture ends,
  "Whoever loves or makes a lie,
On heav'n's felicity depends
  In vain, for he shall surely die."

The stars, the firmament, the sun,
  God's glorious work, God's great design,
All, all was finish'd as begun,
  By rule, by compass, and by line.

Hence David unto heav'n appeals,
  "Ye heav'ns his righteousness declare";
His signet their duration seals,
  And bids them be as firm as fair.

Then give me grace, celestial Sire,
  The truth to love, the truth to tell;
Let everlasting sweets aspire,
  And filth and falsehood sink to hell.

# JOHN FLETCHER
### 1729 · 1785

Engraving by T. A. Dean from the painting by J. Jackson, R. A. (c. 1780).

## INTRODUCTION

John William Fletcher (Jean Guillaume de la Fléchère) was born to a noble family in Nyon, Switzerland, in 1729. From his earliest years he showed extraordinary intellectual capacity. After a brilliant performance in classical literature at the University of Geneva, he nevertheless rejected suggestions that he enter academic life or the ministry. For whatever reasons, he wanted instead to become a mercenary soldier. It was not to be. His first venture, which was to take him on a Portuguese man-of-war to Brazil, was prevented when he had an accident before he could embark. He tried once again through an uncle who promised to obtain a commission for him with the Dutch army; this too went unrealized when the uncle died before the arrangements could be completed. Discouraged, Fletcher set out in 1752 on a visit to England, and ended up for a season as tutor to a nobleman's sons in Shropshire. It was here that he was attracted to the preaching of itinerant Methodists, and converted. After having shown himself prepared, he was five years later ordained deacon and priest on two successive Sundays by John Egerton, bishop of Bangor, at the Chapel Royal, St. James in London.

Fletcher's first ministerial assignment was to assist John Wesley at the West Street Chapel, and to preach at various locations to French Huguenot refugees in their native tongue (his own first language). He was, in this connection, later urged to return to Switzerland to minister, but felt called rather to stay in England. He became assistant to the vicar of Madeley, a parish ten miles out of London, which was "remarkable for little else than the ignorance and profaneness of its inhabitants, among whom respect to men was as rarely to be observed as piety toward God."[1] Yet he grew so convinced of his pastoral calling there that he resisted both the encouragement to itinerant evangelism by his friends the Wesleys (especially Charles) and the offer of a parish worth twice the salary, to take up duties as full-time vicar at Madeley in 1760. Extremes of opposition, including threats of physical violence and legal action, did give him pause; he wrote to Charles Wesley, on March 10, 1761, that he had bouts with "the spirit of Jonah." Yet by a wonderful combination of grace and toughness, he stuck with it. He was, in fact, to stay in this one parish all the rest of his life.

Fletcher was not timid about rousing his difficult parishioners from their spiritual torpor. John Wesley observes of his persistence that

> those sinners who endeavored to hide from him he pursued to every corner of his parish, by all sorts of means, public and private, early and late, in season and out of season, entreating and warning them to flee the wrath to come. Some made it an excuse for not attending church on

Sunday morning that they could not awake early enough to get their families ready. He provided for this also. Taking a bell in his hand, he set out every Sunday for some months at five in the morning, [ringing] around the most distant parts of the parish, inviting all the inhabitants to the house of God.[2]

He was in other respects also such an example of ministry as Wesley could only approve. He established lay societies in the Wesleyan manner and gave lavishly to the poor—so much so, in fact, that he actually damaged his own health by an excess of abstinence.

In 1768, Fletcher was taken into the friendship of the countess of Huntingdon, who made him one of her many evangelical chaplains and soon involved him in superintending her college at Trevecca in Wales. In order that he could remain in his parish, he acted as a kind of chancellor, with the man who was later to become his biographer and editor, Joseph Benson, as headmaster. To this school, founded for "pious young men of whatever denomination for the ministry," he came frequently. Benson writes: "It is not possible for me to describe the veneration in which we all held him. Like Elijah in the schools of the prophets, he was revered—almost adored—and that not only by every student, but by every member of the [college] family. And indeed he was worthy."[3]

Fletcher was highly principled. When the controversy over Calvinism broke out in 1771, he resigned his chancellorship at Trevecca rather than contribute to acrimony, Lady Huntingdon holding strongly to the Calvinist side. And, though principled, he was also a peacemaker. To Benson, dismissed for siding with the Arminians, he wrote that he should

> cast the mantle of forgiving love over circumstances that might injure the cause of God, so far as it is put into the hands of that eminent lady [Countess Huntingdon] who hath so well deserved of the church of Christ. Rather suffer in silence than make a noise to cause Philistines to triumph.[4]

He wrote not only his well-known *Checks to Antinomianism* (1771) in response to the controversy—a work revealing acute intellect and a lively sense of humor—but also his *Essay on Truth* (on "salvation by faith"), dedicated to Lady Huntingdon (1773), and then in 1776 a book entitled *The Reconciliation,* which was devoted to healing the divisions on scriptural principles.

In 1776, Fletcher also wrote in opposition to the American Revolution. The booklet somehow found its way into the hands of the king, and he was asked through the lord chancellor to name his "preferment" in the Established Church as a political reward. He declined firmly, saying "I want nothing but more grace."

347

His writings are all of a piece with this character. As John Wesley put it, "He writes as he lives. I cannot say I know such another clergyman in England or Ireland."[5] Yet, like his pastoral work, Fletcher's writing was for the most part directed to his own flock. It consists less of published sermons than of doctrinal and devotional books for the deepening of his parishioners' spiritual life. Like all of his fellow evangelicals, he made the fact of human sinfulness the foundation of his development of the meaning of salvation, but in his many pastoral letters and devotional meditations he emphasizes in compelling prose the joys as well as the challenges of consistent Christian living. The selections which follow are derived from these sources, and constitute some of the very best of Christian devotional writing in the eighteenth century.

Fletcher had been single all his life, but in 1781, at the age of fifty-two, he married Mary Bosanquet. One of John Wesley's friends and steady correspondents, Mary was a woman of considerable acumen and presence. She was Wesley's most notable exception to his observance of the general Pauline injunction about women speaking in church, and indeed she spoke at conferences and churches both, notably to great effect in Bath and Kingswood in December 1777.[6] She also ran what seems to have been an exemplary Christian school in Leytonstone. Evidently attractive, she had resisted other offers of marriage, admirably managed the awkward interest of Wesley himself, and entertained Fletcher's declarations of affection for more than eight years before agreeing to him. She had said of any would-be marriage that "it must be with one I can not only love but highly reverence and esteem, one that is qualified to be my guide, one who is eminent not only in grace but likewise in understanding."[7] In Fletcher it seems she found the man with whom her own mind and heart could be met on an even footing. Fletcher himself, in a lovely passage in one of his letters, describes his marriage as a new vocation:

I have now a new call to pray for a fulness of Christ's holy, gentle, meek, loving Spirit, that I may love my wife as He loved his spouse, the Church. But the emblem is greatly deficient: the Lamb is worthy of his spouse, and more than worthy, whereas I must acknowledge myself unworthy of the yokefellow whom heaven has reserved for me. She is a person after my own heart, and I make no doubt we shall increase the number of the happy marriages in the Church Militant. Indeed they are not so many, but it may be worth a Christian's while to add one more to their number. . . . Had I searched the three kingdoms, I could not have found one brother willing to share gratis my weal, woe and labors, and complacent enough to unite his fortunes to mine; but God has found me a partner, a sister, a wife, to use St. Paul's language, who is not afraid to face with me the colliers and bargemen of my parish, until death part us. Buried together in our country village, we shall help one another to trim our lamps, and wait . . . for the coming of the heavenly Bridegroom.[8]

In a time hardly notable for strong marriages, it is evident that he and Mary were extremely happy together, and that she was a great support and encouragement to him in his few remaining years. She traveled with him on a unique preaching mission to Dublin, joined in his active ministry of teaching, and attended closely to his physical needs as his health became more fragile; already, the persistent respiratory disease which severely undercut his health at the age of forty-five was slowly but certainly overtaking him.

Fletcher died in Madeley on August 14, 1787, recognized by saint and sinner alike for an exemplary life. It is said that when the atheist philosopher Voltaire was asked who was the most Christlike person in the modern world he replied without hesitation, "John Fletcher of Madeley."[9] John Wesley's text for the funeral sermon was "Mark the perfect man, and behold the upright, for the end of that man is peace" (Psalm 37:37). He said that he had never met so holy a man, nor ever expected to this side of eternity. And, as the *Dictionary of National Biography* puts it, "the testimony of others is equally explicit."

Among these many other testimonies, the sketch by his own wife Mary (which forms the actual basis of Wesley's *Life* of Fletcher)[10] is especially valuable. Though he was, by nature, she observes, "a fiery, passionate spirit," God's grace had beautifully subdued that nature, "and he was meek, like his Master, as well as lowly in heart." It is only fitting that Mary Bosanquet Fletcher's words should themselves conclude this brief introduction, for they capture most intimately the Spirit which breathes through all of his life and work:

It was his constant endeavor to maintain an uninterrupted sense of the presence of God. In order to [do] this, he was slow of speech, and had the greatest government of his words. Indeed he both acted, and spoke, and thought, as under the eye of God. And thus setting God always before him, he remained unmoved in all occurrences, at all times and on every occasion possessing inward recollection. Nor did I ever see him diverted therefrom on any occasion whatever, either going out or coming in, whether by ourselves or in company. Sometimes he took his journeys alone, but above a thousand miles I have travelled with him, during which neither change of company, place, nor the variety of circumstances which naturally occur in travelling ever seemed to make the least difference in his firm attention to the presence of God. To preserve that uniform habit of soul, he was so watchful and recollected that, to such as were inexperienced in these things it might appear like distractedness. Although no one could converse in a more lively and acute manner, even on natural things, when he saw it was to the glory of God, he was always striving to raise his own and every other spirit to a close and immediate intercourse with God. And I can say with truth, all his union with me was so intermingled with prayer and praise that every activity and every meal was, as it were, perfumed therewith.[11]

NOTES

1. *Dictionary of National Biography,* p. 312. The description is from Joseph Benson's biography of Fletcher, now long out of print. But Fletcher's early letters, some of which were collected by Benson, describe in vivid detail mob scenes, violence, and rabble rousing led by local "gentlemen" who opposed reform of any kind. See especially Fletcher's letters to Charles Wesley dated August 19, 1761, and October 12, 1761, in *Posthumous Pieces of the Late Reverend John William de la Fletchere* (Dublin: Robert Napper, 1802), pp. 92–94:

> . . . discouragements follow one after another with very little intermission. Those which are of an inward nature are sufficiently known to you; but some are peculiar to myself, especially those I have had for eight days past, during Madeley wake. Seeing that I could not suppress these Bacchanals, I did all in my power to moderate their madness; but my endeavors have had little or no effect: the impotent dike I opposed only made the torrent swell and foam, without stopping its course. You cannot well imagine how much the animosity of my parishioners is heightened, and with what boldness it discovers itself against me, because I preached against drunkenness, shows, and bull baiting. The publicans and malt-men will not forgive me; they think that to preach against drunkenness and to cut their purse is the same thing. . . .

2. *Dictionary of National Biography,* p. 312.
3. Ibid., p. 313.
4. Ibid.
5. *The Letters of the Rev. John Wesley,* ed. John Telford (London: Epworth Press, 1931; rpt. 1960), vol. 5, p. 304. Fletcher's style, too, is graceful, to a degree remarkable for one not writing in his native tongue.
6. Wesley, *Letters,* vol. 5, p. 257; vol. 6, pp. 290–91.
7. Ibid., vol. 5, p. 70.
8. Fletcher, *Posthumous Pieces,* p. 232.
9. C. J. Abbey and J. H. Overton, *The English Church in the Eighteenth Century* (London: Longmans and Green, 1887), p. 343. John Fletcher's brother-in-law, M. de Bottens, was an intimate friend of Voltaire. (Indeed, much to the surprise of his friend James Ireland when they traveled to Switzerland in 1778, and to all who knew him in England, Fletcher proved to be from a prominent Swiss family.)
10. Despite the fact that Fletcher's friend and colleague Joseph Benson was writing a *Life of Fletcher,* John Wesley quickly requested his papers from Mrs. Fletcher so that

he might undertake such a work himself. This is understandable, perhaps, in light of Wesley's evident view of Fletcher as an exemplar of "Christian perfection" (he had actually wanted Fletcher to succeed him as leader of the Methodist movement); it is apparently in this connection that selections from the *Life* are included by Frank Whaling in his *John and Charles Wesley: Selected Writings and Hymns,* in the Classics of Western Spirituality series (New York: Paulist Press, 1981), pp. 146–61. Much of Wesley's biography of Fletcher consists of direct quotation or paraphrase of Mary Bosanquet Fletcher's reminiscences and her husband's correspondence, and it is thus indispensable for a fuller appreciation of this remarkable pastoral life.

11. The Wesley *Life* may be found in the *Works of John Wesley* (Grand Rapids: Zondervan, 1958–59 [a photo offset of the authorized ed. published in 1872]), vol. 11. The passage here quoted may also be consulted in the edition by Whaling, pp. 155–56.

# *from* Meditations

## I

## "The Kingdom of Heaven Suffereth Violence, And the Violent Take it by Force" (Matthew 11:12)

THE GRAND device of Satan is to prevent us from seeing the necessity of this holy violence, or from putting it in execution. To prevent the effect of this stratagem, our blessed Lord gives us the plainest directions in these words: "Strive to enter in at the strait gate"; "Labour for the meat that endureth to eternal life" etc., etc. But in no Scripture is the direction more plain than in that of the text before us: *"The kingdom of heaven suffereth violence, and the violent take it by force."* Let us consider, first, the nature of this kingdom; secondly, how the violent take it by force; and thirdly, let us respond to an objection to the doctrine of the text.

First, then, the kingdom is that of grace, which brings down a heavenly nature and felicity into the believing soul. The kingdom within us is righteousness and peace, and joy. It is Jesus, apprehended by faith as *given for us,* and felt by love as *living for us.* In a word, it is the image of God lost in Adam and restored by Christ: pardon, holiness, and happiness issuing in eternal glory.

This kingdom permits certain kinds of 'violence'. One kind is toward those lords who reign over us—the world, the flesh and the devil. These rebels must be turned out. Our own wills must be overcome, and ourselves surrendered up to God as to our lawful and chosen sovereign. Further, a humble, holy, sacred 'violence' must be used in prayer: with Jesus—that He would open in our hearts the power of faith, apply the efficacy of his blood and bestow upon us the spirit of prayer or, in other words, the prayer of faith; with the Father—that He would look through the pillar of fire and discomfit all our enemies; and with the Holy Spirit—that He would take up his abode with us.

Of this violence we have an example in Jacob wrestling with the angel, who said, "I will not let thee go, till thou bless me" (Genesis 32:26). Here Jacob, being left alone, takes advantage of his solitude; danger and trouble move him in the right way. He prays, prays earnestly, and that against much discouragement. God and man seem to oppose him, for the angel of the covenant wrestled as if to get loose from his hold. It was a spiritual wrestling. He wept and made supplication, but before he could prevail the angel touched the hollow of Jacob's thigh, and hindered him from wrestling in his own strength. Then the Spirit alone made intercession; nature failed and grace was conqueror: "When I am weak, then am I strong."

The angel said, "Let me go," as God once said to Moses, "Let me alone" (Exodus 32:10). Thus does the Lord sometimes try our faith. This was the case of the woman of Canaan when Jesus at first did not answer her, and afterwards said, "It is not meet to take the children's bread, and cast it to the dogs" (Mark 7:27). But when she still worshipped, prayed and waited, she obtained these words of approbation: "O woman, great is thy faith!" as well as the answer of her prayer. So the angel says, "Let me go, for the day breaketh"—your affairs need you; you must have rest—but Jacob foregoes all for the blessing—rest, family, weariness, pain—and answers, "I will not let thee go, unless thou bless me."

So must it be with us; none prevail but those "who take the kingdom by violence". . . . And so it is with faithful wrestlers: God resists only to increase our desires, and we must be resolved to hearken to nothing that would hinder. Weariness, care, friends, fear and unbelief must all be thrown aside when we seek to see God face to face and to be brought into the light of life.

Those who are weary of the Egyptian yoke of outward and inward sin, who cannot rest without the love of Jesus, the life of God, at last become violent. They forcibly turn away from the world. By force they attack the devil. They bring themselves by force before God and drag out by strong confession the evils that lurk within. Against these they fight, by detesting and denying them. Their strength is in crying mightily to the Lord, and expecting continually that fire which God will rain from heaven on them. All this must be done by force, and with great conflicts, but it is against our nature, which has the utmost resistance in it.

The words of the text allude to the taking of a fortified town by storming it. This is of all military expeditions the most dangerous. The enemy is covered and hidden, and those who scale the walls have nothing but their arms and courage. But can the wrestling soul overcome, can he take this kingdom? Ah no, not by his own strength. But his Joshua will take it for him. God only requires that we should entreat Him to do this. The prayer of repentance, the prayer of faith, storm Mount Sion, the city of God. He that is violent shall receive the kingdom of God—justification and sanctification. But remember, the violent bear it away *by force.* There shall be many hard struggles with God's enemies and, it may be, many with the Lord Himself, before He declares us conqueror.

353

Some will object: "We have no might, and to endeavor to take the kingdom by violence is taking the matter out of God's hand! Is it not better to wait for the promise, stand still and see the salvation of God?"

If you mean by standing still not agonizing to enter in at the strait gate, not wrestling in prayer and fighting the good fight of faith—may God save you from *this* stillness! You err, not knowing the Scriptures. The standing still there recommended is to possess your soul in patience, without dejection, fear and murmuring. Stand still as the apostles did, who watched together in prayer, ran with patience the race set before them, and fought manfully as faithful soldiers under the banner of the cross. Any other stillness is of the devil and leads to his kingdom.

Search the New Testament, and show me one person standing still after he had been convinced of his need. Did the Centurion, did the woman of Canaan, did blind Bartimaeus stand still? Did St. Paul, did the woman with the bloody issue stand still? Did not all of them use the strength they had?

I do not desire you to use what you do not have, but merely to be faithful stewards of the manifold grace entrusted to you. A kingdom, a kingdom of heaven is before you, and power to reign with Jesus as his priests and kings. Stir up then your faith! Reach forward to the things which are before you. Become a wrestling Jacob, and you shall shortly be a prevailing Israel. Be not discouraged for, as a good man observes, "God frequently gives in one moment what He has apparently withheld for many years."

# II
# On Pleasure

DYING TO pleasure, even the most innocent of pleasure, we shall live to God.

Of pleasures, there are four sorts: *sensual* pleasures—pleasures of the eye, ear, taste and smell, ease, indulgence, etc.; pleasures of the *heart*—attachments, entanglements, creature love, unmortified friendships; pleasures of the *mind*—curious books, deep researches, speculations, hankerings after news, wit, fine language; and pleasures of the *imagination*—schemes, fantasies, and suppositions.

God requires that we should deny ourselves in all these respects for several reasons. (1) God insists on having the heart, which He cannot have if pleasure has it; God is a jealous God. (2) There is no solid union with God until, in a Christian sense, we are dead to creature comforts; pleasure is the gordian knot. (3) God is purity. Hankering after pleasure—the bait of temptation—is the cause of almost all our sins. (4) God calls us to show our faith and love by a spirit of sacrifice; pleasure is Isaac. (5) Denying ourselves, hating our life, dying daily, crucifying the flesh, putting off the old man are Gospel precepts. So is cutting off the right hand, plucking out the right eye, and forsaking all to follow Christ. (6) God makes no exceptions. All the offending members must be cut off, every leak must be stopped, or the corrupting pleasure which we have spared will become more aggressive. (7) Pleasures render the soul incapable of the operations of the Spirit, and obstruct divine consolations.

Now nature is all for pleasure, and lives upon sensuality. The senses, heart, mind and imagination pursue always objects that may gratify them. We love pleasure enough to deprive ourselves of everything to enjoy it in some kind or other, and we undergo hardships to procure it. Nature frets horribly if disappointed in this favorite pursuit, and yet if nature is pampered, grace must be starved.

Earthly pleasures have a corrupting nature. For example, that of taste, if indulged, spreads through, corrupts and dissipates all the powers of the soul and body. It is so much the more dangerous as it hides itself under the mask of necessity or color of lawfulness where it does all the mischief of a concealed traitor. It betrays with a kiss, poisons with honey, wounds in its smiles, and kills while it promises happiness.

Indulgence enervates and renders us incapable of suffering from God, men, devils or self, and stands continually in the way of our doing, as well as allowing, the will of God. It is much easier, therefore, to fly from pleasure than to remain within due bounds in its enjoyment. The greatest saints find nothing so difficult. Nothing makes them tremble so much as the use of pleasure, for it requires the strictest watchfulness and the most vigorous attention. One must walk steadily if he would walk safely on the brink of the precipice.

The absolute necessity of dying to pleasure will be apparent from the following considerations. The earthly senses must be made spiritual; the sensual heart purified; the wandering mind fixed; the foolish imagination made sober. Worldly pleasures are all little, low and transitory, and a hindrance to our chief good. Much moderation, however, is to be used in the choice and degree of our mortification. Through pride, nature often prompts us to great extremes, which hurt the body and sometimes lead the mind into sourness and obstinacy. But to know and walk in the right path of self-denial, we have need of much recollection.

# III
## On Lukewarmness

THE LUKEWARM are of two sorts. The first will speak against enormities but plead for little sins—will go to church and sacrament but also to plays, races and shows; will read the Bible and also romances and trifling books. They will have family prayer, at least on Sundays, but after it [indulge in] unprofitable talk, evil speaking and worldly conversation. They plead for the church, yet leave it for a card party, a drinking companion or the fireside. They think they are *almost* good enough and that those who aim at being better are surely hypocrites. They are under the power of anger, evil desire and anxious care, but suppose all people are the same; they talk much of being saved by true repentance and doing *all* they can. They undervalue Christ, extol morality and good works, yet do next to none themselves. They plead for old customs; they want to do things as their fathers did (though ever so contrary to the word of God) and whatever has not custom to recommend it (however much it is recommended in Scripture) is accounted by them a heresy. They are greatly afraid of being thought 'too good' and of making too much ado about their souls and eternity. They want to be *sober,* but not *enthusiasts.* The Scriptures they quote most and understand least are "Be not righteous over much"; "God's mercies are over all his works"; "There is a time for all things," etc. They call themselves by the name of Christ but worship Baal.

The second sort of lukewarm persons assent to all the whole Bible, talk of repentance, faith and the new birth, commend holiness, plead for religion, attend the sacrament and profess to be and to do more than others. But they yield to carelessness, self-indulgence, fear of man, dread of reproach and of loss, hatred of the cross, love of ease, and the false pleasures of a vain imagination. These say, do and really suffer many things, but remain short of the true change of heart, the one thing needful being still lacking. They are as the foolish virgins, without oil, or as the man without his wedding garment.

Of these the Lord has said that He "will spew them out of his mouth." But why so severe a sentence? For several reasons. (1) Christ will have a person hearty and true to his principles; He looks for truth in the inward parts (commending even the unjust steward as a *consistent* character!). (2) True faith admits of no lukewarmness, and it is by persons of this character that his name is blasphemed. (3) A bad servant is worse than a careless neighbor, and a traitor in the guise of a friend is more hateful and more dangerous than an open enemy (Judas was more infamous than

Pilate). (4) The cold have nothing to trust to, and harlots and publicans enter into the kingdom of heaven before *moral* or *evangelical* pharisees who, in different degrees, know their Master's will and do it not: "They shall be beaten with many stripes."

# IV
# On Hypocrisy

MANY PRETEND to a share of the holy Child, but we want all the wisdom of the true Solomon to know the mother from the harlot. A hypocrite hides wickedness under a cloak of goodness: clouds without rain, wells without water, trees without fruit, the ape of piety, the mask of sin, glorious without and carrion within. They do not put off [evil] but throw a cloak over it.

## I. *Satan an Arch-Hypocrite*

Having rebelled against God Himself, Satan endeavored to vent his malice and envy on God's favorite, man. He disguised himself as a serpent, showed much love and friendship, and by that appearance deceived Eve. Though God has prepared an antidote, yet he goes about murdering the children of men with increasing craft (for he is now the old serpent). And he is still opposing Christ, picking up the seed of the word, hindering the sowers, sowing tares. He is the strong man, armed with the force of an angel, the subtlety of a fallen angel, as able to insinuate himself into souls as into serpents. His baits are pleasure for the sensual, wealth for the muckworm, honor for the ambitious, and science for the curious. In each he transforms himself into an angel of light, gilding all with heavenly appearances, but his light is darkness, and how great is that darkness!

He works admirably on predispositions. In the case of ignorance or evil or forgetfulness of the sword of the Spirit, he finds us blind or blinds our eyes to make us turn better in his mill. In the case of security, he puts far from us the thoughts of death: "Ye shall not surely die." In the case of idleness, [we should recall that] when David was idle at home and Joab in the field, Satan took that opportunity to draw him into the snare of lust. In the case of unreasonable scruples of conscience, he causes discouragement or encourages extremes. If he can't put out the fire of zeal he will make it break out at the chimney, and drive fasting into starving.

He suits his temptations to his subjects, drives the nail that will go, and

357

causes the stream of natural propensities to flow. He does not, in general, tempt the old to pleasure, the young to covetousness, or the sick to drunkenness—but he tempts each to impatience.

## II. *The Moral Hypocrite*

Many mistake nature for grace, and so rest short of a true change. Good health, keen wit, lively character and a good natural temperament puff up many. The tempering makes a vast difference in many blades, all made of the same metal. Some will bend before they break, others break before they bend. Good nature, without grace, makes a fairer show than grace with an evil nature: a cur outruns a greyhound with a clog.*

The hypocrite derives his honor from his birth, the child of God from his new birth. The hypocrite has his perfections from the body (from his complexion and constitution, which are not praiseworthy) but the Christian has them from his better part, the soul. . . .

The hypocrite serves God with what costs him nothing, only going down the stream.** But the Christian works with effort and industry, wrestles, and keeps his body under.

The hypocrite is disposed to some virtues, and refrains from those vices which are contrary to his taste and disposition, as an elephant abhors a mouse. But the Christian shuts every door against sin and is thoroughly furnished to every good work.

The hypocrite puts reason in the place of religion. On the contrary, the Christian brings reason under the command of religion, his understanding bowing to faith and his free will to God's free grace.

The hypocrite spins his virtues from himself, spiderlike. . . . The Christian has his virtues from above. The one is like marshy ground, the other is watered from heaven. Again, the hypocrite curses himself by allotting to reason the control of appetites, not knowing that his reason is crooked. But the Christian puts everything under the strict rule of grace. Grace is Sarah, reason Hagar. The one talks of right reason, the other rectifies it.

The hypocrite puts honesty in the place of piety. But the Christian is honest and kind from a principle of genuine piety. . . . The hypocrite has for virtues only shining vices, virtues proceeding from unsanctified reason and spoiled by the intention. Thus a covetous, indolent man avoids and hates law suits; he is sober and temperate through love of money or of

*I.e., with a fetter or hobble.
**I.e., taking the route of least resistance.

health and reputation; he is diligent and industrious to maximize profit. But the Christian has the truth even if he lacks the perfection of virtue. The one shines as rotten wood, the other as gold in the ore.

The hypocrite talks up virtue and exclaims against vice rather by speech than practice. But the king's daughter is "glorious *within*." The one speaks, the other lives, great things.

The hypocrite keeps himself from gross sins but harbors spiritual corruptions. Does he subdue his passions? They get in the way of his self-glory and his complacency. Does he do good? It is merely in order to be more in love with himself. The Christian cleanses himself from all spiritual vices. The one lives on an overflow of self-love, while the other is emptied of self and filled with Christ.

The hypocrite compares himself favorably with the child of God when the Christian is at a disadvantage—such as, for example, when he is fallen or overtaken in an infirmity—but the whitest devil shall not stand in the judgement with the most tawny child of God. The meteor may blaze, but the star stands in its place.

## III. *The Hearing Hypocrite*

The hearing hypocrite hears Christ's word without benefit. He assembles with the pious, whom he deceives just as he hopes to deceive Christ (Luke 13:26). He goes to meet Christ not as the bride but only as the bride's friend. He is the stony ground: he is sermon-proof, repels conviction, takes nothing to himself or shakes it off as sheep do the rain. He has the forehead of a whore (Jeremiah 3:3) and refuses to be ashamed. Christ condemns him both as a worker of iniquity and a builder upon the sand. The Christian hears in such a way that his profiting appears unto all. He hears Christ Himself through the minister and the word is able to save his soul as a savor of life unto life. Nor is he a forgetful hearer, but a doer also of the word.

The hypocrite will hear only such ministers as suit his prejudices: Balaam suits Balak, a lying prophet Ahab. He will neglect or slight others. The Christian hears God's voice through every messenger of his; the plainer the message the better he receives the message—as from "an angel of God, even as Christ Jesus" (Galatians 4:14). He judges not of the word by the preacher, but of the preacher by the word. He, like Jehosaphat, would rather hear Micaiah preach than the four hundred prophets of Baal (1 Kings 22).

The hypocrite listens in hopes of hearing something new; therefore, when he has heard something a few times he grows weary and longs for a new preacher. An unsanctified heart, like a sick stomach, loathes its daily bread. But the Christian is never tired of the sincere milk of the word; he desires no new wine. He still likes manna after forty years, saying "evermore give us this bread."

The hypocrite hearkens more after eloquence than substance. He likes Apollos better than Christ's messenger. He does not listen for life; he sports with the infirmities of Samson while death is at the door. The Christian looks most to the power of the word. He comes not as to a show but as to the courts of justice. He weighs the matter rather than the manner, and regards the message more than the messenger. The one falls down before man, the other before God.

The hypocrite will not hear all. Comforts, promises and general truths he loves; the doctrine of the cross he hates. A foil, a wooden sword that draws no blood suits him. The Christian hears all God's word, loves to be smitten, and does not say "Hast thou found me, O mine enemy?" but "Search me and try my heart."

The hypocrite looks on the word as if it were a story or a landscape. He loves to hear of Christ's miracles, of the prodigal son, etc., but he draws a curtain before his own picture. The Christian looks on the word as a mirror in which to see himself. The one uses the word as children their books, looking more at the pictures than the lesson; the other sees himself and changes his life.

Typically the hypocrite hears without preparing his heart to listen. He pay more attention to his outward than his inward man. He uses no exercise to get an appetite; it is enough for him if he hears, even if he digests nothing. He sows among thorns, having never ploughed, and they choke everything. The Christian has been at his labors, comes hungry to the house of God, longing to be fed, and is not willing to go without his portion.

The hypocrite hears only for the present time, as he would hear a concert of music. The Christian hears both for the time present and that to come. He studies what he hears to the end that he may turn it into practice. He remembers that word, "Take heed how you hear. . ."

. . . Sometime the hypocrite shudders under the word, but he shifts this feeling off before it has taken hold of his heart. As a tree shaken by the wind takes deeper root, so he grows more rooted in his sins. Fearfulness surprises the hypocrite before he is aware; he is ashamed of himself, angry at the preacher and, Cain-like, he runs from God rather than going to Him. But the Christian trembles at the word and is afraid to sin against it. One is like Pharaoh, the other like Jonah.

The hypocrite is a seeming friend but a secret foe to the Gospel. When the word is a hammer, he is an anvil; when it is a fire, he is clay. But the Christian is both reconciled to and transformed into the word, receiving it as the word of God in the love of God. If the word is a nail, it nails him to Christ. . . .

## IV. *The Praying Hypocrite*

The praying hypocrite prays with his tongue, but not with his heart. The heart of the Christian starts first in prayer.

The hypocrite asks according to his wishes, looking no further, like Israel for quails. . . . He is wavering, and double-minded, thinking "Can God furnish a table in the wilderness?" The Christian asks in faith, nothing wavering, as Moses at the Red Sea, while all Israel cried and expected death.

The hypocrite is sometimes presumptuous, asking "How is that I have fasted, and you did not see?" The Christian always comes as a poor beggar, crying with the Centurion, "I am not worthy." The other quarrels with God if not answered: "This evil is of the Lord." But the Christian waits patiently, saying, "It is the Lord, let Him do as He pleases."

The hypocrite prays without repentance for the iniquity in his heart. The Christian confesses and forsakes his sin.

The hypocrite prays without faith, without expecting an answer. Therefore he often cuts short his prayer, especially in secret. The Christian pours out his soul in prayer, giving good measure pressed down, running over, assured that "If ye, being evil, know how to give good gifts unto your children, how much more shall my heavenly Father give his holy Spirit to them that ask it?"

At other times the hypocrite will exceed measure—but only in company. . . . The true Christian measures his prayers by his affections and by works of charity and duty.

The hypocrite prays in adversity, not in prosperity. He comes like the leper or beaten child. The Christian, as the loving son, prays in prosperity, without the compulsion of the rod. Or perhaps the other *will* pray in prosperity, but in adversity his heart sinks, like Nabal's; he murmurs, complains and cries out, "Why does the Lord do this to me?" The Christian remembers those words of St. James, "Is any afflicted, let him pray." The one, as a bastard, runs away. The other kisses the rod, and sees everything as the answer of prayer, submitting himself wholly to the will of God.

## V. *The Preaching Hypocrite—Worse than All*

Listened to by men, not called of God, the <u>preaching hypocrite preaches Christ, but not for Christ.</u> "Put me," he says, "into the priest's office, that I may eat a morsel of bread." He is, perhaps, a preacher of righteousness, but also a worker of iniquity. But the true Christian preacher only spends and is spent upon Christ and his kingdom. He is careful not only of his gifts but of his grace, seeking not merely to be sent of men but of God. The one preaches himself and for himself, while the other preaches Christ and for Christ.

· The hypocrite is ambitious to show his learning, to be admired rather than to be useful. No so St. Paul (1 Corinthians 2). A scribe well instructed brings out of his own treasures things new and old.

The hypocrite brings in learning, but not divine learning; his artificial fire has no warmth in it. But the Christian minister, though perhaps learned in Egyptian wisdom as was Moses, and in Greek literature as was St. Paul (who quoted Aratus to the Athenians, Menander to the Corinthians, Epimenides to Titus [Acts 17:28; 1 Corinthians 15:33; Titus 1:12]) never uses it but as the handmaiden, Christ crucified being his chief knowledge.

The hypocrite uses divine learning to human and carnal ends, to get preferment or fame, to support opinions or parties. The minister of Christ does not handle the word of God deceitfully but by manifestation of the truth. He glories not in his preaching but sees it as a necessity being laid upon him by Christ.

The hypocrite chooses subjects on which he may shine and please. The Christian minister chooses those which may awaken and edify, disclaiming men-pleasing. The one shoots over the heads, the other aims at the hearts of his hearers, suiting himself to the humblest capacity.

The hypocrite puts on a face of zeal without zeal and trying to move others he is himself unmoved. He cannot say with Christ, "The zeal of thine house has eaten me up." His zeal is an *ignis-fatuus,* or perhaps a heathenish fire lighted at Seneca's torch—not a burning as well as a shining light. He may have some feelings, but they end when his sermon or prayer does; he may show some warmth for the church, like Jehu, simply because it serves his party interests (cf. 2 Kings 9:1–10:31). But the true Christian minister has more zeal in his bosom than on his tongue. Elijah-like, he has the word of the Lord as a fire in his bones. His soul mourns in secret places for the sins he reproves openly (Jeremiah 13:17). He can put the stamp of experience on what he preaches, and his zeal has a very large measure of Gospel love; it saves others while it consumes himself.

The hypocrite is perhaps strict in his rules, but he is loose in practice, laying heavy burdens that he will not touch himself. He is like a signpost which shows the way but never walks in it. He promises liberty while he is himself the slave of sin. The true preacher is afraid to preach what he does not practice; he lives his sermons over. As a brave captain, he says, "Follow me," and he aims at perfection as well as light.

The one makes the way to heaven as broad as he can, at least to himself, and often indulges others in order to screen himself. The other makes the way to heaven narrower for himself than for his hearers, and never gives up the least of the word, lest his own foot should be pinched.

# V
# *"Thou Wilt Keep Him in Perfect Peace . . ."*

*"Thou wilt keep him in perfect peace, whose mind is stayed on thee, because he trusteth in thee"* (Isaiah 26:3).

THE VERY center of Christian religion is union with Christ and the receiving of Him as our all. This is in other words called "faith" or "staying our minds on Him." To the doing of this there are many hindrances but the two greatest and most general are the following.

The first of these is a lack of self-knowledge. This keeps ninety-nine out of one hundred from Christ. They know not (or rather, feel not) that they are blind, naked, leprous, helpless and condemned—that all their works can make no atonement, and that nothing they can do will fit them for heaven. When this is truly known, the first great hindrance to our union with Christ is removed.

The second is a lack of understanding of the gospel of Christ. This is a failure to see in Scripture the firm foundation given us for this pure and simple faith, the only solid ground of focussing our souls on God. We must remember that the gospel is *good* news, and not be slow of heart to believe it. Christ receives sinners. He undertakes all of their concerns. He gives not only repentance but remission of sins and the gift of the Holy Spirit. He creates them anew; his love first makes the bride and then delights in her. Not viewing Christ in this light, as the Author and Finisher of our salvation, hinders the poor humble penitent from casting himself wholly on the Lord, even though He has said, "Cast thy burden on the Lord, and he shall sustain thee" (Psalm 55:22).

I do not mention sin, for sin is the very thing which renders man the object of Christ's pity. Our sins will never turn away the heart of Christ

363

from us, for they brought Him down from heaven to die in our place. The reason that iniquity causes separation between God and our souls is because it turns our eyes from Him and shuts up in us the capacity of receiving those light-beams of love which are ever descending upon and offering themselves to us. But sin sincerely lamented and brought by a constant act of faith and prayer before the Lord shall soon be consumed like thorns laid close to a fire. Only let us live in this expectation and the Lord will pass through them and burn them up together.

When the soul feels its own helplessness and receives the glad tidings of the gospel, it turns toward Christ. And though the world, the flesh and the devil pursue, so that the soul seems often to be on the brink of ruin, it has still only to listen to the gospel and turn toward Christ like a drowning man to a single plank with the words, "I can only perish," and then remembering that "thou wilt keep him in perfect peace, whose mind is stayed on thee, because he trusteth in thee."

The consequence of thus trusting is that God keeps the soul from its threefold enemy, defends it in temptation, in persecution, and in depression. Through all, it finds power to repose itself on Christ, to say "God shall choose my inheritance for me." Here the Christian finds peace with God, peace with himself, and peace with all around him. This is the peace of pardon and the peace of holiness; both are obtained by focussing the mind on Christ. Such a person walks in the perpetual recollection of a present God, and is not disturbed by anything. If he feels sin, he carries it to the Saviour, and if [he is] in heaviness, through manifold temptations, he still holds firm his confidence; he is above the region of the clouds.

The careless sinner is not to be exhorted to trust in Christ. It would be to cast pearls before swine. Before an act of faith there must be an act of self-despair; before filling, there must be emptiness. Is this your condition? Then permit me to take away your false props. Upon what do you prop up your soul? Upon your honesty, morality, humility, doing good, church-going, business, friends, or confused thoughts of God's mercy? This will never do. You must be brought to say, "What shall I do to be saved?" Without trembling at God's word, you cannot receive Christ. Nothing short of *love* will do.

The penitent needs and, blessed be God, has every encouragement. You have nothing but sin; it is time you should understand the gospel. You see yourself sinking; Christ is with you. You despair of yourself; hope in Christ. You are overcome; Christ conquers. Self-condemned; He absolves. Why do you not believe? Is not the messenger, the word, the Spirit of God, sufficient? You want a joy unspeakable; the way to it is by thus waiting patiently upon God. Look to Jesus. He speaks peace. Keep looking, and your peace shall flow as a river.

# *from* Letters on the Manifestation of Christ (c. 1775)*

SIR,

Having proved, in my first letter, the existence of the spiritual senses to which the Lord manifests himself, I shall now enter upon that subject, by letting you know, as far as my pen can do it, what is the nature of that manifestation which makes the believer more than conqueror over sin and death.

Do not gratify yourself, Sir, by dismissing me as an "enthusiast." I do not insist, as you may imagine, upon a manifestation of the voice, body or blood of our Lord to our external senses. Pilate heard Christ's voice, the Jews saw his body, the soldiers handled it, and some of them were literally sprinkled with his blood. But this served no spiritual purpose; they knew not God manifest in the flesh.

Nor do I understand by the term "manifestation" such a knowledge of our Redeemer's doctrine, offices, promises and performances as the natural man can attain by the force of his understanding and memory. All nominal believers, all foolish virgins, by conversing with true Christians, hearing gospel sermons and reading evangelical books acquire historical and doctrinal knowledge of Jesus Christ. Their understandings are informed but, alas, their hearts remain unchanged. Acquainted with the letter, they continue ignorant of the Spirit. Boasting, perhaps, of the greatness of Christ's salvation, they remain altogether unsaved; full of talk about what He has done for them, they know nothing of Christ in them, the hope of glory.

Much less do I mean by "manifestation" such a representation of our Lord's person and sufferings as the natural man can form for himself by the force of a warm imagination. Many, by seeing a striking picture of Jesus bleeding on the cross or hearing a sentimental discourse on his agony in the garden are deeply affected and melted into tears. They raise in themselves a lively idea of a great and good man unjustly tortured to death; their soft passions are appealed to, and pity fills their heaving breasts. But alas, they remain strangers to the revelation of the Son of God by the Holy Spirit. The murder of Julius Caesar, emotionally de-

*This is the second of six letters which, taken together, offer a full discussion of the question of manifestations of Christ in contemporary experience.

scribed, would have the same effect upon them as the crucifixion of Jesus Christ. A profound play would touch them as easily as a profound sermon, and much to the same purpose, for in either case their impressions and their tears are generally wiped away together.

Nor yet do I understand by this word good desires, meltings of heart, victories over particular corruptions, a confidence that the Lord can and will save us, power to stay ourselves on some promises, gleams of joy, rays of comfort, enlivening hopes, touches of love—not even foretastes of Christian liberty and of the good Word of God. These are rather the delightful drawings of the Father than the powerful revelation of the Son. These, like the star that led the wise men for a time and then disappeared and appeared again, are helps and encouragements to come to Christ and not a divine union with Him by the revelation of Himself.

I can more easily tell you, Sir, what this revelation is *not* than what it is. The tongues of men and angels lack proper words to express the sweetness and glory with which the Son of God visits the souls that cannot rest without Him. This blessing is not to be described, but enjoyed. It is to be written not with ink, but with the spirit of the living God, not on paper or tables of stone but in the fleshly tables of the heart. May the Lord Himself explain the mystery by giving you to eat of the hidden manna, and bestowing upon you the new name which no man knows save he that receives it. In the meantime, consider the following rough draft of this mercy and, if it is agreeable to the letter of the word, pray that it may be engraved on your heart by the power of the Spirit.

The revelation of Christ by which a nominal believer becomes a holy and happy possessor of the faith is a supernatural, spiritual, experimental manifestation of the Spirit, power and love—and sometimes of the person—of God manifest in the flesh, whereby He is known and enjoyed in a manner altogether new. It is as new as the knowledge that a person who had never tasted anything but bread and water would have of honey and wine if, being dissatisfied with the best descriptions of those rich products of nature, he actually tasted them for himself.

This manifestation is, sooner or later, in a higher or lower degree vouchsafed to every sincere seeker through the medium of one or more of the spiritual senses opened in his soul, in a gradual or instantaneous manner as it pleases God. No sooner is the veil of unbelief which covers the heart rent through the agency of the Spirit, and the efforts of the soul struggling into a living belief of the word; no sooner, I say, is the door of faith opened than Christ who stood at the door and knocked comes in and reveals Himself full of grace and truth. Then the tabernacle of God is with man. His kingdom comes with power. Righteousness, peace and joy in the Holy Spirit spread through the newborn soul. Eternal life begins, heaven is open on earth, the conscious heir of glory cries "Abba, Father," and from blessed experience can witness that he is come to Mount Sion, to the city of the living God, the heavenly Jerusalem, and to an innumerable company of angels, to the general assembly and church of the first-born which are written in heaven, and to God the Judge of all, and to the spirits of just men made perfect, and to Jesus the mediator of the new covenant, and to the blood of sprinkling, which speaks better things than the blood of Abel.

If this experience of Christ is allowed to have its effect, the results will be admirable. The believer's heart, now set at liberty from the guilt and dominion of sin and drawn by the love of Jesus, pants after greater conformity to his holy will, and mounts up to Him in prayer and praise. His life is a course of cheerful evangelical obedience, and his most common actions become good works done to the glory of God. If he lives up to his blessings, outward objects entangle him no more. Having found the great I AM, the eternal substance, he looks upon all created things as shadows. Man, the most excellent of all, appears to him altogether lighter than vanity. Yea, doubtless he counts all things but loss for the excellency of the knowledge of Christ Jesus his Lord, esteeming them but dung that he may win Christ and, to the last, be found in Him, not having his own righteousness but that which is through the faith of Christ—so that by new revelations of Himself he may know Him and the power of his resurrection every day more clearly.

In the meantime, he casts his sins and miseries upon Jesus, and Jesus bestows his righteousness and happiness upon him. . . . Thus, they are mutually related with one another and, to use St. Paul's endearing expressions, they are espoused and married. Joined by the double band of redeeming love and saving faith, they are one spirit, just as Adam and Eve were, by matrimony, one flesh. "This is a great mystery," says the apostle, but thanks be to God, it is made manifest to his saints" (Ephesians 5:32).

If you ask, sir, "how can these things be? Describe to me the particular *manner* of these manifestations," I reply in our Lord's words to Nicodemus, "art thou a master in Israel," indeed even more, a Christian, "and knowest not these things?" Verily I say unto you, though we cannot fix the exact mode and precise manner of the breathing of the Spirit, yet we speak what we do know and testify what we have seen, but you receive not our witness. Marvell not, however, if we find it impossible to tell you all the particulars of a divine manifestation. You yourself, though you feel the wind, see its amazing effects and hear the sound of it, cannot tell whence it comes and whither it goes. Much less could you describe it to the satisfaction of one who had never heard or felt it himself. Many earthly things cannot be conceived by earthly men. The blind, for example, can never conceive the difference of colors. What wonder then if natural men do not understand us, when we tell them of heavenly things.

Nevertheless, I would in general observe that the manner in which the manifestation of the Son of God is vouchsafed is not the same in all persons nor in the same person at all times. The wind blows where it will and much more the Spirit of the living God. His thoughts are not as our thoughts. He dispenses his blessings not as we expect them but as it pleases Him. Most commonly, however, the sinner, driven out of all his refuges of lies, feels an aching void in his soul. Unable to satisfy himself any longer with the husks of empty vanity, dry morality and speculative Christianity, and tired with the best form of godliness which is not attended with the power of it, he is brought to a spiritual famine and hungers after heavenly food. Convinced of unbelief, he feels a lack of faith in God's operation. He sees that nothing short of an immediate display of the Lord's arm can bring his soul into the kingdom of God, and fill it with righteousness, peace and joy in the Holy Spirit. Sometimes, encouraged by lively hopes, he struggles into liberty of heart, and prays with groanings which cannot be uttered. At other times, almost sinking under a burden of guilty fear or stupid unbelief, he is violently tempted to throw away his hope and go back to Egypt. But an invisible hand supports him and, far from yielding to this low suggestion, he resumes courage and determines to follow on to know the Lord or to die seeking Him. Thus he continues wandering up and down in a spiritual wilderness until the Lord gives him the rest of faith, the substance of things hoped for, the evidence of things not seen.

This evidence comes in various ways. Sometimes, the spiritual *eye* is first opened. . . . Then the believer, in a divine transforming light, discovers God in the man Christ, perceives unspeakable glories in his despised person, and admires infinite wisdom, power, justice, and mercy in the blood of the cross. He reads the Scripture with new eyes. The mysterious book is unsealed, and everywhere testifies of Him whom his soul loves. He views experientially as well as doctrinally his need of the Redeemer, the firmness of his promises, the sufficiency of his righteousness, the preciousness of his atonement, and the completeness of his salvation. He sees and feels Christ's involvement in everything. Thus he beholds, believes, wonders and adores. Sight being the noblest sense, this sort of manifestation is generally the brightest.

Perhaps his spiritual *ear* is first opened, and that voice which raises the dead, "Go in peace, thy sins are forgiven thee," passes with power through his waiting soul. He knows by the gracious effect [that] it is the voice of Him who said once, "Let there be light and there was light." He is aware of a new creation, and can say, by the testimony of God's Spirit bearing witness with his spirit, "This is my beloved's voice; He is mine, and I am his. I have redemption through his blood, even the forgiveness of my sins"—and, having much forgiven, he loves much and obeys in proportion.

Frequently also Christ manifests Himself first and chiefly to the spiritual *feeling*. He takes the burden of guilt, dejection and sin from the heavy-laden soul, and in its place imparts a strong sense of liberty, peace, love and joy in the Holy Spirit. The ransomed sinner, enabled to overcome racking doubts or dull insensibility, believes now with the heart unto righteousness and makes confession with the mouth unto salvation. Surely, says he, "In the Lord, I have righteousness and strength. This is the finger of God. This day is salvation come to my soul. None but Jesus could do this for me. The Lord He is God; He is my Lord and my God."

This manifestation is generally the lowest, being made to a lower sense. Therefore great care ought to be taken not to confound it with the strong drawings of the Father, on which it borders. Some babes in Christ who, like young Samuel, have not yet their senses properly exercised to know the things freely given to them from God, are often made uneasy on this very account. Nor can they be fully satisfied until they find the effects of this manifestation as lasting, or they obtain clearer ones by means of the nobler senses—the sight or hearing of the heart.

Though I contend only for those discoveries of Christ which are made by the *internal* senses, because these only are promised to *all*, yet I cannot without contradicting Scripture deny that the external senses have been involved in some manifestations. When Abraham saw his Saviour in his day, he was, it seems, allowed to wash his feet with water (Genesis 18:3), as the penitent harlot did with her tears at a later time. And Saul, on his way to Damascus, saw Jesus' glory and heard his voice both externally and internally, for they that journeyed with him "saw the light and heard a voice," although they could not distinguish the words which were spoken.

Sometimes also manifestations, though merely internal, have appeared externally to those who were favored with them. When the Lord called Samuel in Shiloh, the pious youth supposed the call was outward, and ran to Eli saying, "Thou callest me." But it seems the voice had struck his spiritual ear only; otherwise the high priest who was within hearing would have heard it as well as the young prophet. And although Stephen steadfastly looked up to heaven as if he really saw Christ there with his bodily eyes, it is plain he discovered Him only with those eyes of his faith, for the roof of the house where the court was held bounded his outward sight and if Christ appeared in the room so as to be visible to common eyes the council of the Jews would have seen Him as well as the pious prisoner at the bar.

Hence we learn: (1) that the knowledge of spiritual things, received by spiritual sense, is as clear as the knowledge of natural things obtained by bodily sense; (2) that it is sometimes possible to be doubtful whether the outward eye or ear is not involved in particular revelations, since this was not only the case of Samuel but of St. Paul himself, who could not tell whether the unspeakable words he heard in paradise struck his bodily ears or only those of his soul; (3) that no stress is to be laid upon the external circumstances which have sometimes accompanied the revelation of Christ. If aged Simeon had been as blind as old Isaac, and as much disabled from taking the child Jesus in his arms as the paralytic, the internal revelation he had of Christ could have made him say with the same assurance, "Now Lord, let thy servant depart in peace, for mine eyes have seen thy salvation." If the apostle Paul had not been struck to the ground, and his eyes dazzled by outward light, his conversion would not have been less real, provided he had been inwardly humbled and enlightened. And, if Thomas, waiving the carnal demonstration he insisted upon, had experienced only in his inner man that Christ is the resurrection and the life, he could have confessed Him with as great a consciousness that he was not mistaken as when he cried out, "my Lord, and my God!"

I am, Sir, Yours,

J. F.

# *from* The Test of a New Creature:

## Points of Self-Examination for Adult Christians (c. 1774)

*"Examine yourselves, whether ye be in the faith"*  (2 Corinthians 13:5).

WHATEVER IS THE state of any person wholly renewed must be to some degree the state of all who are born from above, and whatever is the fruit of perfect holiness, to walk according to the same standard must be the way to obtain the same salvation. The image of God is one, grace is the same, and to be in Christ is to believe and have the fellowship of his Spirit.

Regeneration differs only in degrees of strength and soundness. In our early experience of justification the divine life in us is comparatively small, and mixed with sin. But when perfectly renewed, we are strong and every part pure, holding by faith that salvation which makes us one with the Son of God.

The law given in our first state and the law required by the Gospel— the covenant of works and the covenant of faith—are different. Whatever we see in the example of Jesus and whatever He promises to bestow on his followers are unquestionable privileges of Gospel salvation. Neither is the whole of this salvation, of our justification or of our renewal after the image of God, finished until the resurrection, when we shall see Him as He is, and beholding Him face to face, his name shall be written in our foreheads. Nor can we ever have so much of the likeness of God as to be incapable of more. Rather, the more we obtain of his image and favor, the more we are enabled to receive forever and ever.

### Questions for Self-Examination

1. Do I feel any pride, or am I a partaker of the meek and lowly mind that was in Jesus? Am I dead to all desire of praise? If any despise me, do I like them the worse for it? Or if they love and approve me, do I love them more on that account? Am I willing to be accounted useless, and of no consequence, glad to be made of no reputation? Do humiliations give me real pleasure, and is it the language of my heart to say: "Make me little, and unknown,/Lov'd and prize'd by God alone"?

2. Does God bear witness in my heart that it is purified—that in all things I please Him?

3. Is the life I live "by the faith of the Son of God," so that "Christ lives in me"? Is Christ the life of all my affections and designs, as my soul is the life of my body? Is my eye single, and my soul full of light—all eye within and without—always watchful?

4. Do I have the presence of God? Does no cloud come between God and the eye of my faith? Can I "rejoice evermore, pray without ceasing, and in everything give thanks"?

5. Am I saved from the fear of man? Do I speak plainly to all, neither fearing their frowns nor seeking their favors? Have I no shame of my faith, and am I always ready to confess Christ, to suffer with his people, and to die for his sake?

6. Do I deny myself at all times, and take up my cross as the Spirit of God leads me? Do I embrace the cross in every form it presents itself to me, being willing to give up my ease and convenience to oblige others? Or do I expect them to conform to my hours, ways and customs? Does the cross sit light upon me, and am I willing to suffer all the will of God? Can I trample on pleasure and pain? Have I

> A soul inur'd to pain,
> To hardship, grief and loss;
> Bold to take up, firm to sustain,
> The consecrated cross?

7. Are my bodily senses and outward things all sanctified to me? Do I not seek my own things, to please myself? Do I seek grace more for God than myself—preferring the glory of God to all in earth or heaven, preferring the Giver to the gift?

8. Am I poor in spirit? Do I take pleasure in infirmities, necessities, distresses, reproaches, so that out of weakness, want and danger I may cast myself on the Lord? Have I no false shame in approaching God? Do I seek to be saved as a poor sinner, by *grace alone*?

9. Do I lean not on my own understanding? Am I ready to give up the point when contradicted, unless conscience forbid, and am I easy to be persuaded? Do I esteem everyone better than myself? Am I as willing to be a cypher as to be useful and does my zeal burn bright notwithstanding this willingness to be nothing?

10. Have I no false wisdom, goodness, strength, as if the grace I feel were my own? Do I never take that glory to myself which belongs to Christ? Do I feel my need of Christ as much as ever, to be my all? Do I draw near to God, as poor and needy, only presenting before Him his well beloved Son? Can I say:

> Every moment Lord I need
> The merit of thy death.
> Still I'll hang upon my God,

> Till I thy perfect glory see,
> Till the sprinkling of thy blood
> Shall speak me up to thee?

Do I find joy in being thus nothing, empty, undeserving, giving all the glory to Christ? Or do I wish that grace made me *something,* instead of God all?

11. Have I meekness? Does it bear rule over all my impulses, affections and desires, so that my hopes, fears, joy, zeal, love and hatred are duly balanced? Do I feel no disturbance from others, and do I desire to give none? If any offend me, do I still love them, and make it an occasion to pray for them? If condemned by the world, do I entreat? If condemned by the godly, am I one in whose mouth there is no reproof, replying only as conscience, and not as impatient nature, dictates? If in the wrong, do I confess it? If in the right, do I submit (being content) to do well and suffer for it? It is the sin of superiors to be overbearing and of inferiors to be stubborn; if, then, I am a servant, do I yield not only to gentle persons but to the brash and pushy as well, commiting my cause in silence to God. Or when a master, do I show all long suffering? The Lord of all was as one who serves. If I am the greatest, do I make myself least and the servant of all? If a teacher am I lowly, meek and patient, not conceited, self-willed or dogmatic? Am I ready to give up the claims of respect due to age, station, parent, master, etc., or do I rigidly exact those demands?

12. Do I possess resignation? Am I content with whatever is, or may be, feeling that God, the Author of all events, does and will do all for my good? Do I desire nothing but God, willing to part with all if the Lord manifests his will for my so doing? Do I know how to abound and yet not gratify unnecessary appetites, but being content with things needful do I faithfully and freely dispose of all the rest for the assistance of others? Do I know how to suffer need? Is my confidence in God unshaken even while I feel the distress of poverty and have the prospect of future need while, humanly speaking, strangling would seem better than life? And, in these circumstances, do I pity those who, having plenty, waste it in excess instead of helping me?

13. Am I just, doing in all things as I would others should do unto me? Do I render due homage to those above me, not presuming on their leniency and graciousness? As a superior do I exercise no undue authority, taking no advantage of the timidity, respect or dependency of any person. Do I consider the great obligation superiority lays me under of being lowly and kind, and of setting a good example?

14. Am I temperate, using the world and not abusing it? Do I receive outward things in the order of God, making earth a ladder to heaven? Is the satisfaction I take in creation consistent with my being dead to every-thing below, and a means of leading me more to God? Is the turn of my

mind and general disposition in due subjection, not leading me to any extreme either of too much silence or of too much talkativeness, of reserve or freedom?

15. Am I courteous, not severe, adapting myself to all with sweetness, striving to give no one pain, but to gain and win all for their good?

16. Am I vigilant—redeeming time, taking every opportunity of doing good—or do I spare myself, being careless about the souls and bodies to which I might do good? Can I do no more than I do? Do I perform the most servile offices, such as require labor and humiliation, with cheerfulness? Is my conversation always seasoned with salt, at every time administering some kind of favor to those I am with?

17. Do I love God with all my heart? Do I constantly present myself, my time, substance, talents, and all that I have, a living sacrifice? Is every thought brought into subjection to Christ? Do I like or dislike only such things as are pleasing or displeasing to God?

18. Do I love God with all my strength and are my spiritual faculties always vigorous? Do I give way to no sinful laziness? Am I always on my watch? Do business, worldly care, or conversation never dampen my fervor and zeal for God?

19. Do I love my neighbor as myself—every person for Christ's sake—and honor all persons as the image of God? Do I think no evil, listen to no groundless surmises, nor judge from appearances? Can I bridle my tongue, never speaking of the fault of another except with a view to do good, and when I am obliged to do this, have I the testimony that I sin not? Have I that love which hopes, believes and endures all things?

20. How am I in my sleep? If Satan presents an evil imagination, does my will immediately resist, or give way to it?

21. Do I bear the infirmities of age or sickness without seeking to repair the decays of nature by strong sedatives, and do I make Christ my sole support, casting the burden of a feeble body into the arms of his mercy?

Many consider that perfect love which casts out fear as instantaneous. All grace is so, but what is given in a moment is enlarged and established by diligence and fidelity. That which is instantaneous in its coming is made perfect in its increase.

This is certain. Too much grace cannot be desired or looked for, and to believe and obey with all the power we have is the highway to receive all we have not. There is a day of Pentecost for believers, a time when the Holy Spirit descends abundantly. Happy they who receive most of this perfect love, and of that establishing grace which may preserve them from such falls and decays as they were before liable to.

Jesus, Lord of all, grant your pure gifts to every waiting disciple. Enlighten us with the knowledge of your will and show us the mark of the prize of our high calling. Let us die to everything which is not you, and seek you with our whole heart, until we enjoy the fulness of the purchased possession. Amen.

# *from* Pastoral Letters

## *On Two Controversies*

To the Rev. Charles Wesley          *Madeley, September 20th, 1762*

My Dear Sir,

It is well for me, I have not an implicit faith in your half promises of coming to see me. I am sorry that my delay has furnished you with an excuse, but comfort myself still with the idea that you will not wholly deprive me of the pleasure of embracing you, and that your visit is only postponed for a little season.

The creed "*quod habes et habes*" ["Believe that you have it, and you have it"] is not very different from those words of Christ, "What things soever ye desire, when ye pray, believe that ye receive them, and ye shall have them" (Mark 11:24). The humble reason of the believer, and the irrational presumption of the enthusiast, draw this doctrine to the right hand and the left. But to split the hair—here lies the difficulty. I have told you that I am no party man; I am neither for nor against the witness of Christian perfection, *without examination*. I complain of those who deceive themselves; I honor those who do honor to their profession; and I wish we could find out the right way of reconciling the most profound humility with the most lively hopes of grace. I think you insist on the one, and Madan on the other, and I believe you both sincere in your views. God bless you both and, if either of you goes too far, may the Lord bring him back.

Truly, you are a pleasant casuist. What! "It hath pleased thee to regenerate this infant with thy Holy Spirit, to receive him for thine own child by adoption, and to incorporate him into thy holy church": does all this signify nothing more than being taken into the *visible* church?

How came you to think of my going to leave Madeley? I have, indeed, had my scruples about the above passage and some in the burial service; but you may dismiss your fears and be assured I will neither marry nor leave my church without advising with you. *Adieu.*

Your affectionate brother,

J. F.

# A Pastoral Commendation

To the Congregation at Madeley        *Bath, October 30, 1765*

To those who love the Lord Jesus Christ, in and about Madeley: Peace be multiplied to you from God the Father, and from the Lord Jesus Christ, through the operations of the Holy Spirit. Amen.

By the help of divine providence and the assistance of your prayers, I came here safe. I was, and am still, a good deal weighed down under the sense of my own insufficiency to preach the unsearchable riches of Christ to poor, dying souls.

This place is the seat of Satan's gaudy throne. The Lord has, nevertheless, a few names here who are not ashamed of Him, and of whom He is not ashamed, both among the poor and among the rich. There are not many of the last, though blessed be God for anyone. It is a great miracle if *one* camel passes through the eye of a needle. . . . I thank God that none of you are rich in the things of the world. You are freed from a double snare, even from Dives' portion in this life.* May you know the happiness attending your state. It is a mercy to be driven to the throne of grace, even by physical need, and to live in dependence on divine mercy for a morsel of bread.

I have been sowing the seed the Lord has given me both in Bath and Bristol, and I hope your prayers have not been lost upon me as a minister. For though I have not been enabled to discharge my office as I would, the Lord has still in some measure stood by me and overruled my foolishness and helplessness. I am much supported by the thought that you bear me on your hearts, and when you come to the throne of grace to ask a blessing for me in the name of Jesus, the Lord in no wise casts you out.

In regard to the state of my soul, I find, blessed be God, that as my day is so is my strength to travel on—through either good or bad report. My absence from you serves two good purposes for me. I feel more my insufficiency, and the need of being daily ordained by Christ to preach his gospel; and I shall value the more my privileges among you, please God I return safely to you.

I had yesterday a most advantageous offer of going, free of charge, to visit my mother, brothers and sisters in the flesh, whom I have not seen for eighteen years. But I find my relations in the spirit are nearer and

---

*Dives is the traditional name for the condemned person in the biblical story of the rich man and Lazarus (Luke 16:20–31).

dearer to me than my relations in the flesh. I have, therefore, rejected the kind offer, so that I may return among you and be comforted by our mutual faith.

I hope, dear brethren, that you improve much under the ministry of that faithful servant of God, Mr. Brown, whom providence blessed you with. Make haste to gather the honey of knowledge and grace as it drops from his lips, and may I find the hive of your hearts so full of it on my return that I may share with you in the heavenly store. In order that this may happen, beseech the Lord to excite your hunger and thirst for Jesus' flesh and blood and to increase your desire for the sincere milk of the word. When people are hungry, they will find time for their meals, and a good appetite does not think a meal a day too much. As you go to your spiritual meals, do not forget to pray all the way, and to feast your souls in hopes of hearing some good news from heaven and from Jesus, the faithful, loving friend whom you have there. And when you return, be sure to carry the unsearchable riches of Jesus' dying and rising love home to your houses in the vessel of a believing heart.

Let your light be attended with the warmth of love. Be not satisfied merely to know the way to heaven, but walk in it immediately, constantly, and joyfully. In all things be truly in earnest. You may, indeed, impress your brethren by a formal attendance on the means of grace, but you cannot deceive the Searcher of hearts. Let Him always see your hearts struggling towards Him; and if you fall through heaviness, sloth, or unbelief, do not make a bad matter worse by continuing helpless in the ditch of sin and guilt. Up and away to the fountain of Jesus' blood. It will not only wash away the guilt of past sins but strengthen you to tread all iniquity under your feet for the time to come. Never forget that the soul of the diligent shall be made fat, and that the Lord will spew the lukewarm out of his mouth unless He gets that love which makes one fervent in spirit, diligent in business, serving the Lord.

You know the way to get this love is:

1. to consider the free mercy of God, and to believe in the pardoning love of Jesus, who died—the just for the unjust—to bring us to God;

2. to be frequently if not constantly applying this faith, with all the attention of your mind and all the fervor of your heart: "Lord, I am lost, but Christ hath died";

3. to try actually to love, as you can, by setting your affections on Christ whom you see not and, for his sake, on your brethren, whom you do see;

4. to be much in private prayer for yourselves and others, and to try to keep up that communion with God and your absent brethren.

I beg you, in order to do this, not to forsake the assembling of yourselves together, as the manner of some is. And when you meet as a society, be neither backward nor forward to speak. Esteem yourselves, everyone, as the least in the company, and be glad to sit at the feet of the lowest. If you are irritated with anyone, yield not to the temptation. Pray much for that love which hopes all things, and puts the best construction even upon the worst of failings. I beg, for Christ's sake, that I may find no divisions nor offences among you on my return: "If there be any consolation in Christ, if any comfort of love, if any fellowship of the Spirit, if any bowels and mercies, fulfil ye my joy, that ye be like-minded, having the same love, being of one accord, and of one mind. Let nothing be done through strife and vain glory; but in lowliness of mind, let each esteem [the] other better than themselves."

I earnestly request the continuance of your prayers for me, both as a minister and as your companion in tribulation. Ask particularly that the Lord would keep me from hurting his cause in these parts, and that when providence shall bring me back among you I may be more thoroughly furnished for every good work. Pardon me if I do not salute you all by name; my heart does so, if my pen does not. That the blessing of God in Jesus Christ may crown all your hearts and all your meetings is the earnest prayer, my beloved brethren, of . . . Yours,

J. F.

## To One Approaching Death

To Miss Hatton                              *Madeley, January 9th, 1767*

My Dear Friend,

The alteration for the worst I discovered in your health the last time I had the pleasure of seeing you makes me sit down to take a survey with you of our approaching dissolution. The dream of life will soon be over; the morning of eternity will soon succeed. Away then with all the shadows of time. Away from them to the eternal substance—to Jesus, the first and the last, by whom, and for whom, all things consist.

We stand on the shore of a boundless ocean: death, like a lion, comes to break our bones. Let us quietly strip ourselves of our mortal robes that He may do with us as the Lord shall permit. . . . My dear friend, believe in Jesus: believe that your sins, red as crimson, are made white as snow by the superior tincture of his blood.

Believe yourself into Christ. By simple faith, believe that He is your everlasting head. Nor can you believe a lie, for God has given that dear Saviour to the worst of sinners to be received by a lively faith, and has declared that it shall be done unto us "according to our faith." If you simply take Jesus to be your head, by the mystery of faith, you will be united to the resurrection and the life.

The bitterness of death is past, my dear friend. Only look to Jesus: He died for you—died in your place—died under the frowns of heaven that we might die under its smiles. The head was struck off that the members might be spared. Stand then in Him. Be found in Him. Plead that He has wrought a sinless righteousness for you and has more than sufficiently atoned for you by his cruel sufferings and ignominious death.

Pay attention to neither unbelief nor doubt; fear neither sin nor hell; choose neither life nor death. All these are swallowed up in the immensity of Christ and triumphed over in his cross. Believe that He has made an end of sin, that you are made beautiful in Him, pardoned, accepted, and beloved of God in the one Mediator, Jesus Christ. Reason not with the law, but only with Him who says, "Come and let us reason together; though your sins be as scarlet, they shall be as white as snow" (Isaiah 1:18).

Fight the good fight of faith. Hold fast your confidence in the atoning, sanctifying blood of the Lamb of God. Through his blood the accuser of the brethren is cast out. Confer no more with flesh and blood. Hunger and thirst after righteousness; eat the flesh and drink the blood of the Redeemer, and live in Christ that you may die in Him.

Up, and be doing the work of God! Believe in Him whom He has sent. Kiss the Son lest He be angry. Grasp Him as one who has fallen into deep waters grasps the branch that hangs over him.

O slumber no more! Go meet the Bridegroom. Behold, He comes! Trim your lamp; hold up the vessel of your heart to the streaming wounds of Jesus, and it shall be filled with the oil of peace and gladness. Quit yourself like a soldier of Jesus. Look back to the world—the things and friends about you—no more. I entreat you as a companion in tribulation and charge you as a minister: go, at every breath you draw, according to the grace and power given you, to the Physician who gives up on no patient, who says: "Him that cometh unto me, I will in no wise cast out" and "He that believeth in me, though he were dead, yet shall he live."

E'er long there will be time no more. O my friend! Stir up yourself to lay hold on Him by faith and prayer; and let not those few sands that remain in your glass flow without the blood of Jesus. They are too precious to be offered up to slothful flesh, which is going to turn out its immortal inhabitant. Gladly resign your dust to the dust whence it was taken, and your spirit to Him who gave and redeemed it. Look to Him, in spite of flesh and blood, of Satan and unbelief, and joyfully sing the believer's song: "O death, where is thy sting? O grave, where is thy victory? Thanks be to God, who giveth us the victory, through our Lord Jesus Christ!" Let your surviving friends rejoice over you as one faithful unto death—as one triumphing in death itself.

I am just informed of dear Miss Fragena's death. She caught a fever in visiting the poor who were sick of that distemper, and lived a week to withstand and rejoice in dying pains. As she lived, she died—a burning and a shining light. E'er long you will meet her in Abraham's bosom, whence she beckons you to follow her as she followed Christ. Be of good cheer! Be not afraid: the same God who helped her will carry you through. Your business is to commend yourself to Him, and to keep safe that which you commit to Him unto that day.

To his faithfulness and love I commend you; and am, my dear friend, yours in Him,

J. F.

## Of Philosophers and Children

To James Ireland                    *Nyon, Switzerland, July 15, 1778*

My Dear Friend,

I have ventured to preach once, and to expound once in the church. Our [Calvinist] ministers here are very kind and preach to the purpose; a young one of this town gave us lately a very excellent Gospel sermon. Yet grown up people stand fast in their stupidity, or in their self-righteousness.

The day I preached, I met with some children in my wood, walking or gathering strawberries. I spoke to them about our Father, our common Father. We felt a touch of brotherly affection. They said they would sing to their Father as well as the birds, and followed me attempting to make such melody as you know is commonly made in these parts. I outrode them, but some of them had the patience to follow me home, and said they would speak with me, but the people of the house stopped them, saying I would not be troubled with children. They cried and said they were sure I would not say so, "for I was their good brother."

The next day when I heard this, I enquired after them, and invited them to come to me, which they have done every day since. I make them little hymns which they sing. Some of them are [transcribed] under sweet drawings. Yesterday I wept for joy on hearing one speak of conviction of sin, and joy unspeakable in Christ which had followed, as would do [credit to] an experienced believer in Bristol.

Last Sunday I met them in the wood; there were one hundred of them, and as many adults. Our first pastor has since desired me to desist from preaching in the wood (for I had indeed exhorted them) for fear of giving umbrage, and I have complied from a concurrence of circumstances which are not worth mentioning. I therefore meet them in my father's yard.

In one of my letters, I promised you some anecdotes concerning the death of our two great philosophers, Voltaire and Rousseau. Mr. Tronchin, the physician of the Duke of Orleans being sent for to attend Voltaire in his illness at Paris, Voltaire said to him, "Sir, I desire you would save my life. I will give you half of my fortune if you lengthen out my days only for six months. If not, I shall go to the Devil, and shall carry you away along with me."

Mr. Rousseau died more decently, as full of himself as Voltaire was of the wicked one. He paid that attention to nature and the natural sun which the Christian pays to grace and the Sun of righteousness. These are some of his last words to his wife, which I copy from a printed letter circulating in these parts: "Open the window, that I may see the green fields once more. How beautiful is nature! How wonderful is the sun! See that glorious light it sends forth! It is God, who calls me. How pleasing is death to a man who is not conscious of any sin! O God, my soul is now as pure as when it first came out of thy hands; crown it with thy heavenly bliss!"

God deliver us from self and Satan, the internal and external fiend! The Lord forbid we should fall into the snare of the Sadducees, with the former of those two famous men, or into that of the Pharisees with the latter.

Farewell in Jesus.

J. F.

# Of "Putting on Christ"

To the Masters and Students of Lady Huntingdon's College
*Madeley, July 23, 1770*

Grace, mercy and peace attend you, my dear brethren, from God our Father and from our Lord and Brother Jesus Christ.

*Brother,* do I say? But should I not rather have written *all?* Is not He all and in all? *All* to believers, for He is their God or the λογος (the word), and their friend, brother, father, spouse, etc., etc., as He is λογος γενομενος σαρξ (the word made flesh). From Him, through Him, and in Him, I salute you in the Spirit. I believe He is here with me and in me; I believe He is yonder with you and in you; for "in Him we live, and move, and have" not only our animal, but our rational and spiritual "being." I believe it, I say, therefore I write.

May the powerful grain of faith remove the mountain of remaining unbelief that you and I may see things as God sees them, that we may no more judge by appearances, but judge [with] righteous judgement—that we may no more walk by carnal sight, but by faith, the sight of God's children below! When this is the case, we shall discover that the Creator is all indeed, and that creatures (which we are wont to put in his place since the fall) are mere nothings, passing clouds that our Sun of Righteousness hath thought fit to clothe Himself with, and paint some of his glory upon. In an instant He could scatter them into their original nothing, or reabsorb them forever, and stand without competitor, וחרה, the Being.

But suppose that all creatures should stand forever, little signatures of God; what are they even in their most glorious estate but as tapers kindled by his light, as well as formed by his power? Now conceive a sun, a spiritual sun, whose center is everywhere, whose circumference can be found nowhere, a sun whose lustre as much surpasses the brightness of the luminary that rules the day as the Creator surpasses the creature. And say, "what are the twinkling tapers of good men on earth; what is the smoking flax of wicked creatures; what the glittering stars of saints in heaven?" Why they are all lost in his transcendent glory—and if any one of these would set himself up as an object of esteem, regard or admiration, he must indeed be made with self and pride; he must be (as dear Mr. Howell Harris hath told us) a foolish apostate, a devil.

Understand this, believe this, and you will sink to unknown depths of self-horror for having aspired at being *somebody,* self-humiliation for seeing yourself *nobody,* or, what is worse, an *evil-body.* But I would not have you dwell even upon this evil so as to lose sight of your sun, unless it be to see Him covered on this account with your flesh and blood, and wrapped in the cloud of our nature. Then you will cry out with St. Paul, "O the depth!" Then finding his manhood is again reabsorbed into the Godhead, you will gladly renounce all selfish separate existence in Adam and from Adam. You will take Christ to be your life, you will become his members by eating his flesh and drinking his blood, you will consider his flesh as your flesh, his bone as your bone, his spirit as your spirit, his righteousness as your righteousness, his cross as your cross, and his crown (whether of thorns or glory) as your crown. You will reckon yourselves to be dead indeed unto sin, but alive unto God, through his dear Redeemer. You will renounce propriety, you will heartily and gladly say, "Not I, but Christ liveth, and only because He lives I do, and shall live also." When it is so with us, then are we creatures in our Creator, and redeemed creatures in our Redeemer. Then we understand and feel what He says . . . , "Without me, the Creator, ye are nothing; without me, the Saviour, ye can do nothing."

"The moment I consider Christ and myself as two, I am gone," says Luther, and I say so too. I am gone into self and into antichrist for that which will be *something* will not let Christ be *all,* and what will not let Christ be *all,* must certainly be antichrist. What a poor jejune dry thing is doctrinal Christianity compared with the clear and heartfelt assent that the believer gives to these fundamental truths! What life, what strength, what comfort, flow out from them! O, my friends, let us believe, and we shall see, taste, and handle the word of life. When I stand in unbelief I am like a drop of muddy water drying up in the sun of temptation; I can neither comfort, nor help, nor preserve myself. When I do believe and close in with Christ, I am like that same drop losing itself in a boundless, bottomless sea of purity, light, life, power and love. There my good and my evil are equally nothing, equally swallowed up, and grace reigns through righteousness unto eternal life. There I wish you all to be; there I beg you and I may meet with all God's children. I long to see you, that I may impart unto you (should God make use of such a worm) some spiritual gift, and that I may be comforted by the mutual faith both of you and me, and by your growth in grace and in divine as well as human wisdom, during my long absence.

I hope matters will be arranged so that I may be with you to behold your order before the anniversary. Meanwhile I remain your affectionate fellow laborer, and servant in the Gospel of Christ.

J. Fletcher

# Seeking God's Image

To Henry Brooke                    *Madeley, February 29th, 1785*

My Dear Brother,

We are all shadows. Your mortal parent has passed away; and we pass away after him. Blessed be the author of every good and perfect gift for the shadow of his eternal paternity displayed to us in our deceased parents. What was good, loving and lovely in them is hid with Christ in God, where we may still enjoy it *implicitly,* and where we shall *explicitly* enjoy it when He shall appear.

A lesson I learn daily is to see things and persons in their invisible root, and in their eternal principle, where they are not subject to change, decay and death, but where they blossom and shine in the primeval excellence allotted them by their gracious Creator. By this means, I learn to walk by faith and not by sight. Yet, like a child, instead of walking straight and firm in this good spiritual way I am still apt to cling here or there. This makes me cry, "Lord, let me see all things more clearly, that I may never mistake a shadow for the substance nor put any creature, no not for a moment, in the place of the Creator who deserves to be loved, admired and sought after with all the powers of our souls."

Tracing his image in all the footsteps of nature or looking for the divine signature on every creature as we should look for the king's image on an old rusty medal, is true philosophy. And to find out that which is of God in ourselves is the true wisdom—genuine godliness. I hope you will never be afraid nor ashamed of it. I see no danger in these studies and meditations, provided we still keep the end in view—the all of God, and the shadowy nothingness of all that is visible.

With respect to the great pentecostal display of the Spirit's glory, I still look for it within and without; to look for it aright is the lesson I am learning. I am now led to be afraid of that in my nature which would choose pomp, show and visible glory. I am afraid of falling by such an expectation into what I call a spiritual judaizing—into a looking for Christ's coming in my own pompous conceit, which might make me reject Him if his wisdom (to crucify mine) chose to come in a more ordinary way, if, instead of coming in his Father's glory He chose to come meek, riding not on the cherubim but on the foal of an ass.

Our Saviour said, with respect to his going to the feast, "My time is not yet come." Whether his time to come and turn the thieves and buyers out of the outward church is yet come, I know not. I doubt Jerusalem and the holy place are ready yet to be trodden underfoot by the gentiles. But my Jerusalem! Why it is not swallowed up in the glory of that which comes down from heaven is a question which I wait to be solved by the teaching of the great Prophet who alone is possessed of urim and thummin. The almighty power to wrestle with Him is all divine, and I often pray:

> That mighty faith on me bestow,
> Which cannot ask in vain,
> Which holds, and will not let thee go,
> Till I my suit obtain:

Till thou into my soul inspire,
That perfect love unknown,
And tell my infinite desire,
Whate'er thou wilt be done.*

In short, the Lord crucifies my wisdom and my will every way. But I must be crucified as the thieves. All my bones must be broken, for there is still in me that impatience with wisdom which would stir when the tempter says, "Come down from the cross." It is not for us to know the times and seasons, the manner and mystical means of God's working, but only to hunger and thirst and lie passive before the great Potter. In short, I begin to be content to be a vessel of clay or of wood, so I may be emptied of self and filled with my God, my all. Don't give up your confident hope: it saves still secretly, and has a present and, by and by will have a great recompence of reward.

I am glad, exceeding glad, that your dear partner goes on simply and believingly. Such a companionship is a great blessing, if you know how to make use of it. For when two of you shall agree touching one thing in prayer, it shall be done. My wife and I endeavor to fathom the meaning of that deep promise. Join your line to ours, and let us search what, after all, exceeds knowledge—I mean the wisdom and the power, the love and faithfulness of God.

My wife and I embrace you both, and pray you would help one another and us by your prayers. *Adieu.* Be God's, as the French say, and see God yours in Christ, for you, and for all our dear brethren. We are your obliged friends,

J. AND M. F.

*See the hymn of Charles Wesley, "For Believers Seeking Perfect Love," above.

# JOHN NEWTON
## 1725 · 1807

Newton at about the age of sixty-five, from an engraving by J. Sartain.

## INTRODUCTION

The life of John Newton offers some of the most interesting reading in eighteenth-century biography.[1] He was born in 1725 of an independent Protestant mother and a mariner father who had been educated by Spanish Jesuits. He was taught by his mother to read before the age of four, and to know the Shorter Catechism and the hymns of Isaac Watts. When she died in 1731, Newton was only six.

His father remarried, sent his son to a boarding school until he was ten, then commenced his own part in young Newton's education by bringing him aboard his ship. Young John made five voyages to the Mediterranean, spent a number of difficult months with a paternal friend in Alicante, Spain, then returned to England where his father obtained him a trading position in the West Indies. Before he left, he went to visit relatives of his mother in Kent, and, at the age of seventeen fell deeply in love with fourteen-year-old Mary Catlett (who was, seven years later, to become his wife), and returned too late to catch his ship. He signed on a ship to Venice, yet managed once again to arrive at the dock too late. When the same offense was repeated still again, his father was understandably irate.

With the outbreak of war with France, Newton was press-ganged into the navy and soon made a midshipman. Once again he overstayed shore leave, was arrested as a deserter, publicly flogged and demoted to the rank of a common sailor. He contemplated suicide, but because of Mary Catlett thought better of it. When one day later he saw a shipmate leaving ship for a vessel bound for Guinea, he joined him, and in Africa took up work with a slave dealer, at the hands of whose African wife (ironically enough) he suffered brutal abuse and ill treatment, only to be rescued in the nick of time by a friend of his father's.

In all of these events and many others he was persuaded to record in his autobiographical *Authentic Narrative* (1764), Newton was receiving his primary education in what is now sometimes referred to as "the school of hard knocks." But Newton, like many such people before and after him, was made by these educational experiences a fitter instrument than many of his contemporaries for the subtler arts and sciences. While in Africa he studied Euclid, doing his propositions on the sand. At sea he taught himself Latin by means of a copy of Horace and a Latin Bible. He learned likewise French, Spanish, and—later—Greek and Hebrew. His father, who died in 1750 as governor of Fort York in Hudson's Bay, would have been surprised.

In the midst of all, through the combined impressions of a near final shipwreck on the one hand and a reading of Thomas à Kempis' *Imitation of*

*Christ* on the other, the most significant milestone in his education—his conversion—was, as he was later to write, effected by "amazing grace." His character and fortunes improved, and he became master of a slave ship. At first he was no more troubled by his profession than the vast majority of his mid-eighteenth-century countrymen or the Americans to whom their cruel trade was directed. Then, as his reading of the Bible began to stir his conscience, he began to pray that God would "fix" him in "a more humane calling." In 1754, while he was having tea with Mary (now his wife) two days before he was to set sail, he had a stroke. He was only twenty-nine years of age. Though he recovered fairly quickly, never to succumb again, he took the experience as a divine directive and soon resettled in Liverpool, where he was conveniently provided with the position of tide surveyor. But his heart had been stirred up to a less comfortable calling. While continuing his work he studied Scripture and scriptural commentaries diligently.

Newton was especially inspired by George Whitefield, whom he went to hear at Moorfields, with others of the open-air preachers. He applied for ordination himself in the Church of England, but was repeatedly turned down.[2] When he confided his disappointment to John Wesley, with whom he talked often during this period, Wesley lamented, in his *Journal* (March 20, 1760), the obstacles placed in his way:

> Our Church requires that clergymen should be men of learning, and, to this end, have an University education. But how many have an University education, and yet no learning at all! Yet these men are ordained! Meantime, one of eminent learning, as well as unblameable behaviour, cannot be ordained *because he was not at the University!* What a mere farce is this!

Finally, through the influence of Lord Dartmouth (an evangelical) Newton was ordained by the bishop of Lincoln, Dr. Green, and, again through the influence of Dartmouth, installed in 1764 in his first parish at Olney, ten years after his fateful stroke.

He spent sixteen successful years at the little village of Olney. After his first three years he published his first volume of sermons, dedicating them to the congregation which had heard them in their full length—probably about twice as long as the printed versions he published. In his Preface something of Newton's forthright character is displayed. He says that he had two motives for publishing the sermons. The first of these was to give a clear exposition of evangelical doctrine both to inform and, if possible, to correct "the mouth of slander"—that is, critics from the ecclesiastical establishment who were habitually intolerant of Newton's kind of preaching. The second was to a similar purpose aimed at his own flock:

My other motive is a desire of promoting your edification. It is my comfort that many of you live by the truths of the gospel, and highly prize them. You will not therefore be unwilling to view the substance of what you once heard with acceptance. But it is to be feared that the far greater part of the congregation have need to have the things pertaining to their peace pressed upon them again and again for a different reason, not because they know them and therefore love to have them brought to their remembrance, but because they have hitherto heard them without effect. For the sake of both therefore I am willing to leave an abiding testimony amongst you. I hereby take each of your consciences to witness, that I am clear of your blood, and that, to the best of my knowledge and ability, I have not shunned to declare the whole counsel of God.

With his quiet voice and unshowy manner, Newton might seem an understated preacher. But he pandered to no one.

In the same year (1767) the talented and troubled poet, William Cowper, came to Olney. Newton was to become a major influence in Cowper's life, and a friend; together they collaborated in writing the famous *Olney Hymns* (1779), several of the most familiar of which are included in this volume. His counseling of Cowper was typical of the real center of his ministry. People came to him from far and wide for help and guidance. They included lords and ladies, bankers and rich merchants, simple cottagers, even a Mohawk Indian chief converted under Whitefield in America and suffering culture shock in Britain. They came to talk, and to be encouraged; afterward, many of them were to receive the continuing pastoral correspondence for which Newton is justly famous. These letters, some of which were collected in his *Cardiphonia* (1787), reveal just how much the struggle of eighteenth-century spirituality was in what we should call now the area of psychological conflict and its remedy, what Newton (like Watts before him) calls

> the study of the human heart with its workings and counter-workings as it is differently affected in a state of nature or a state of grace, in the different seasons of prosperity, adversity, conviction, temptation, sickness, and the approach of death.[3]

Such counseling, in its Christian distinction between psyches needing to be understood in their "state of nature" and those needing to be understood in a "state of grace," was remarkably astute and, on the evidence, wonderfully effective. Compared to an approach we might take today, Newton is far less indulgent with respect to personal analysis; such analysis he manages deftly, indicatively, and succinctly, often in only a few lines. What he chooses to concentrate on is the art of healing and of consolation. In this aspect of his pastoral role, he was able to be of crucial help to such people as Hannah More, William Wilberforce (in the crisis of ✓ his conversion in 1785, and subsequently), and young Charles Simeon, when he visited at Cambridge.

For all of his remarkable learning, Newton never forgot that humility before God is the most valuable of all lessons, that "the fear of the Lord is the beginning of wisdom." As Gilbert Thomas has so admirably put it:

> It is Newton's glory that, though he became a considerable scholar and public character in the City of London, surrounded by the perils of affluence and flattery, he retained unimpaired the wisdom and simplicity of one who had seen God's wonders in the deep.[4]

Newton's greatest collection of sermons, perhaps, is the series he preached at his second and last charge, St. Mary, Woolnoth, in the heart of London, during 1784 and 1785, while Handel's *Messiah* was enjoying a spectacularly successful rerun at Westminster Abbey. This series of fifty sermons treats the scriptural passages of Handel's oratorio in a lucid evangelical exposition. *Messiah,* itself a series of contemplations on the plan of salvation, and musically the talk of London, offered Newton a magnificent opportunity for preaching both timely and eternal. The sermons are rich with the fruits of his own lifelong education, even as they are consistent with the themes which had characterized some of his best early preaching: the last of the *Messiah* sermons included here is substantially a revision of Sermon 10 from Olney, which itself had been part of a series of five on Matthew 11:26–30. But one sees in this later version both how much Newton was attuned to his now urban and educated audience, and how consistently he held to the central character of his constant text. He knew the Scriptures intimately; they formed the very language that he spoke, and as St. Augustine once said was true of all those who are scholars of the Word, its wisdom became his wisdom.

## NOTES

1. Cf. Josiah Bull, *John Newton* (London, 1868); Richard Cecil, *Memoirs of the Rev. John Newton* (London, 1808), for early assessments; also the excellent chapter in Gilbert Thomas's *William Cowper and the Eighteenth Century* (London: Ivor Nicholson and Watson, 1935), pp. 193–224. A modern edition of Newton's autobiography, *Out of the Depths: An Autobiography,* has been printed by Moody Press, Chicago.

2. During this period he made many excursions as a lay preacher into Yorkshire, where his zeal sometimes outran his maturity. It is typical of him that he tells the following story on himself in *Omricon's Letters* (1774), no. 5: he was asked to preach at White Chapel, and went to a tea beforehand. When asked if he desired to withdraw an hour or so before preaching he declined in a cavalier fashion, saying he thought he was

well enough prepared, and went on with his tea and conversation. When the time to preach came he began fluently, but in a few minutes lost all sense of what he wanted to say. He tried in his confusion to begin again, with no success, finally prevailing upon his host, Mr. Edwards, to take his place and conclude. He was so embarrassed by this incident that he could hardly face people in the street, but as he says, the mortification was the means of his learning an important lesson.

3. From the Preface to *Cardiphonia* (1787).

4. Thomas, *William Cowper,* pp. 201–2.

*from* Sermons at Olney (1767)

## The Small Success
## of the Gospel Ministry

At that time Jesus answered and said, I thank thee, O Father, Lord of
heaven and earth, because thou hast hid these things from the wise and
prudent, and hast revealed them unto babes.   Matthew 11:25

OUR BLESSED Lord perfectly knew beforehand the persons who would
profit by his ministry, but his observations, conduct and discourses were
intended as a pattern and instruction to his followers. He is said to have
marvelled at the unbelief of some and at the faith of others—not as though
either was strange to Him, who was acquainted with all hearts and always
knew what He Himself would do—but it is spoken of Him as a man, and
to show how his ministers and people should be affected upon similar
occasions.

In the preceding verses He had been speaking of Capernaum and other
places where his mighty works had been performed in vain. He had
pronounced a sentence against them, and foretold that their punishment
would be heavier in proportion to the greatness of the privileges they had
abused. But this was not a pleasing task for Him. Mercy and grace were
his delight, and He usually expressed sorrow and pain for the obstinacy of
sinners. He wept for his avowed enemies and prayed for the murderers
who nailed Him to the cross. It was not without grief that He declared the
approaching doom of these cities. Yet raising his thoughts from earth to
heaven, He acquiesced to the will of his heavenly Father and expressed the
highest satisfaction in his direction. He knew that however some would
harden themselves, there was a remnant who would receive the truth, and
that the riches and glory of the divine sovereignty and grace would be
magnified.

Before I enter upon the particulars, this connection of the words will
afford us ground for several observations.

I

[We see, first,] that the small success and efficacy of the preached gospel
upon multitudes who hear it is a subject of wonder and grief to the

ministers and people of God. It was so to our Lord Jesus, considered as a preacher and messenger, and they, so far as they have received his Spirit, judge and act as He did.

1. Those who have indeed tasted that the Lord is gracious have had such a powerful experience in their own souls of the necessity and value of the gospel that, in their first warmth, and till painful experience has convinced them of the contrary, they can hardly think it possible that sinners should stand out against its evidence. They are ready to say: "Surely it is because they are ignorant. They have not had opportunity of considering the evil of sin, the curse of the law, and the immense goodness of God manifested in his Son. But when these things shall be plainly and faithfully set before them, surely they will submit and thankfully receive the glad tidings."

With such sanguine hopes Melancthon entered the ministry at the dawn of the Reformation. He thought he had only to speak and to be heard in order to convince. But he soon found himself mistaken, and that the love of sin, the power of prejudice and the devices of Satan were such obstacles in his way that nothing less than the mighty operations of the Spirit of God could break through. And all who preach upon his principles and with his views have known something of his disappointment. Speaking from the feelings of a full heart, they are ready to expect that others should be no less affected than themselves. But when they find that they are heard with indifference—perhaps with contempt—that those whose salvation they longed for are enraged against them for their labour of love, and that they cannot prevail upon their dearest friends and nearest relatives, this grieves and wounds them to the heart.

2. They have been convinced themselves that unbelief was the worst of all their sins. Therefore, though they pity all who live in the practice of sin, yet they have a double grief to see them reject the only means of salvation and [feel] that this contempt will lie more heavily upon them than any thing they can be charged with besides. It gladdens the heart of a minister to see a large and attentive assembly, but how this joy is dampened by a just fear lest any, lest many, should receive this grace of God in vain and have cause at last to bewail the day when the name of Jesus was first sounded in their ears.

It seems plain then that those who are indifferent about the event of the gospel, who satisfy themselves with this thought that the elect shall be saved and feel no concern for unawakened sinners, make a wrong inference from a true doctrine and know not what spirit they are of. Jesus wept for those who perished in their sins. St. Paul had great grief and sorrow of heart for the Jews, though he gives them this description: "They please not God, and are contrary to all men." It well becomes us while we marvel at the gift of grace to ourselves to mourn also over others. And inasmuch as secret things belong to the Lord and we cannot be sure that some for whom we have at present but little hopes may at last be brought to the knowledge of the truth, we should be patient and forbearing after the pattern of our heavenly Father, and endeavour by every probable and prudent means to stir them up to repentance, remembering that they cannot be more distant from God than by nature we were ourselves.

## II

The best relief against those discouragements we meet with from men is to raise our thoughts to God and heaven. For this the Lord Jesus offers a precedent. He said, "I thank thee, O Father." The word here signifies to confess, to promise or consent, and to praise.* [It is] as if it had been said: "I glorify thy wisdom in this respect, I acknowledge and declare it is thy will, and I express my own consent and approbation." Our Lord's views of the divine counsels were perfect and therefore his satisfaction was complete. It is said that He rejoiced in spirit when He uttered these words. And the more we increase in faith and in the knowledge of God, the more we shall be satisfied in his direction and shall see and say, "He hath done all things well." It is needful for our comfort to be well established in the truth suggested in my text, that the Lord hath provided for the accomplishment of his own purposes and that his counsels shall surely stand. From this doctrine we may infer:

1. That where the faithful labours and endeavours of ministers and others to promote the knowledge of grace and the practice of holiness fail of success, they shall still be accepted. The servants of Christ may in their humble measure adopt the words of their Lord and Master by the prophet: "Though Israel be not gathered, yet shall I be glorious in the Lord, and my God shall be my strength" (Isaiah 49:5). When He sent forth his first disciples, He directed them wherever they entered to say, "Peace be to this house! And if a son of peace be there" (if there be any who thankfully accept your salutation and message) "your peace shall rest upon it; if not it shall return to you again" (Luke 10:6). That is, your good wishes and endeavours shall not be lost for want of proper objects, but when they seem without effect on others shall be productive of the happiest consequences to yourselves. You shall receive all you were desirous to communicate. Thus his ministers are to declare his whole will, whether men will hear or whether they shall refuse. And if they do this with a single eye to

*The Greek word is ἐξομολογέω; cf. Matthew 3:6; Luke 22:2; and Romans 15:9. [Newton's note]

his glory and in humble dependence upon his blessing, they are not answerable for the event; they shall in no wise lose their reward.

2. Faithful endeavours in the service of the gospel shall not wholly fail. Though all will not hear, some certainly shall both hear and obey. Though all are by nature equally averse and incapable, yet there shall be a "willing people, in the day of God's power" (Psalm 110:3). If the wise and prudent turn away from the truth, there are babes to whom it shall be revealed. The Lord renews unto us a pledge of his faithfulness in this concern every time the rain descends. For thus He has promised: "As the rain cometh down and the snow from heaven, and returneth not thither but watereth the earth, and maketh it bring forth and bud, that it may give seed to the sower, and food to the eater: So shall my word be that goeth forth out of my mouth; it shall not return unto me void, but it shall accomplish that which I please; and it shall prosper in the thing whereto I send it" (Isaiah 55:10).

3. The divine sovereignty is the best thought we can retreat to for composing and strengthening our minds under the difficulties, discouragements and disappointments which attend the publication of the gospel. The more we give way to reasonings and curious inquiries, the more we shall be perplexed and baffled. When Jeremiah had been complaining of some things which were too hard for him, the Lord sent him to the potter's house and taught him to infer from the potter's power over the clay the just right which the Lord of all hath to do what He will with his own (Jeremiah 18:6). It is only the pride of our own hearts that prevents this consideration from being perfectly conclusive and satisfactory. How many schemes derogatory to the free grace of God, tending to darken the glory of the gospel and to depreciate the righteousness of the Redeemer, have taken their rise from vain and unnecessary attempts to vindicate the ways of God—or rather to limit the actings of infinite wisdom to the bounds of our narrow understanding, to sound the depths of the divine counsels with our feeble plummets, and to say to Omnipotence, Hitherto shalt thou go, and no further. But upon the ground of the divine sovereignty we may rest satisfied and stable. For if God appoints and overrules all according to the purpose of his own will, we have sufficient security both for the present and the future.

With respect to the present: we may firmly expect what Scripture and reason concur to assure us, that the Judge of all the earth will do right. Whatever to us appears otherwise in his proceedings should be charged to the darkness and weakness of our minds. We know that in every point of science difficulties and objections occur to young beginners which at first glance may seem almost unanswerable; but as knowledge increases the difficulties gradually subside, and at last we perceive they were chiefly owing to the defects of our apprehension. In divinity it is wholly so: "God is light, and in him is no darkness at all": his revealed will is like Himself, just, holy, perfectly pure and perfectly consistent in every part. We may safely rest upon this general maxim, that the Judge of all the earth shall do right. Though He does not give us a particular account of his dealings, and we are not fully able to comprehend them, yet we ought— against all appearances and proud reasonings—to settle it firmly in our minds that everything is conducted in a manner worthy of the views which God has given us of Himself in his holy word, as a Being of infinite justice, wisdom, goodness and truth. And further,

With respect to the future: [we may know that] He has appointed a day when He will make it apparent that He has done right. Though clouds and darkness are now upon his proceedings, they shall ere long be removed. When all his designs in providence and grace are completed, when the present imperfect state of things shall be finished, when the dead, small and great, are summoned to stand before Him, then the great Judge will condescend to unfold the whole train of his dispensations and will justify his proceedings before angels and men. Then every presumptuous cavil shall be silenced, every difficulty solved. His people shall admire his wisdom, his enemies shall confess his justice. The destruction of those who perish shall be acknowledged deserved, and of themselves; and the redeemed of the Lord shall ascribe all the glory of their salvation to Him alone. What we shall then see it is now our duty and our comfort assuredly to believe.

## III

The great subject of our Saviour's joy, and which, so far as it is apprehended, will bear up his servants above all their difficulties and disappointments—I mean the consideration of the sovereign hand of God directing the success of his word when and where He pleases—we must defer speaking of till the next opportunity. And we shall close at present with a few inferences from what has been said thus far by way of introduction.

1. Take heed how you hear. The gospel of salvation which is sent to you will be either a savour of life unto life, or of death unto death, to every soul of you. There is no middle ground. Though in a common and familiar way of speaking we sometimes complain that the gospel is preached without effect, there is in reality no possibility that it can be without effect. An effect it must and will have upon all who hear it.

397

Happy they who receive and embrace it as a joyful sound, the unspeakable gift of God's love. To these it will be a savour of life unto life. It will communicate life to the soul at first and maintain that life in defiance of all opposition till it terminates in glory. But woe, woe to those who receive it not. It will be to them a savour of death unto death. It will leave them under the sentence of death already pronounced against them by the law which they have transgressed, and it will consign them to eternal death under the heaviest aggravations of guilt and misery.

Remember the doom of Capernaum, and why it was denounced. Jesus preached amongst them the words of eternal life, and they rejected Him. This was all. In other things perhaps they were no worse than their neighbours, and they probably disdained to hear themselves judged worthy of a heavier punishment than Sodom and those cities which for their abominations were consumed with fire from heaven. But our Lord assures us, it shall be more tolerable for Sodom and Gomorrah in the day of judgment than for those who slight his word. For this guilt and condemnation is not confined to the Jews who rejected his person, but extended to all who should at any time treat his gospel with contempt. However inconsiderable his ministers are in other respects, if they faithfully deliver his message, He has declared Himself closely interested in the reception they meet with. "He that receiveth you, receiveth me; and he that despiseth you, despiseth both me and him that sent me" (Matthew 10:40). It is therefore at your peril to treat what we say with indifference (if we speak in agreement with the Scriptures); the word of God which we preach will judge you at the last day.

2. Be afraid of being wise in your own eyes, lest you should approach the character of those from whom the righteous God sees fit to hide the knowledge of those truths without which they cannot be saved. The gospel is not proposed to you to ask your opinion of it, that it may stand or fall according to your decision, but it peremptorily demands your submission. If you think yourselves qualified to judge and examine it by that imperfect and depraved light which you call your reason, you will probably find reasons enough to refuse your assent. Reason is properly exercised in the ordinary concerns of life, and has a place in religious inquiries insomuch as none can or do believe the gospel without having sufficient reasons for it. But you need a higher light, the light of God's Spirit, without which the most glorious displays of his wisdom will appear foolishness to you. If you come simply, dependent and teachable, if you pray from your heart with David, "Open thou mine eyes, that I may see wondrous things in thy law" (Psalm 119:18), you will be heard, and answered. You will grow in the knowledge and grace of our Lord

Jesus Christ. But if you neglect this, and trust in yourselves, supposing this promised assistance of the Holy Spirit unnecessary, the glorious light of the gospel will shine upon you in vain, for Satan will maintain such hold of you by this pride of your heart that you will remain in bondage and darkness, that you shall neither see it nor desire to see it.

3. Those of you who have some spiritual apprehension of these things have reason to praise God that you see a little. You were once quite blind; you saw neither your disease nor your remedy. You could discern nothing of the excellence of Christ or the beauties of holiness. But now the eyes of your understanding are in some measure enlightened. It is the grace of God that has made you thus far to differ from what you once were, and from what multitudes around you still are. Be thankful. Accept this as a token for good. Be not discouraged that the beginnings are small, but wait on the Lord, and they shall be increased. Seek Him by prayer. Converse with your Bible. Attend upon the public ordinances. In the humble use of these means (while you endeavour to act faithfully according to the light you have already received) you shall gradually advance in wisdom and comfort. The Christian's growth is not instantaneous, but by degrees, as the early dawn increases in brightness till the perfect day (Proverbs 4:18), and as the corn comes forward surely though unperceived (Matthew 13:31–32). In this manner your views of gospel-truth shall increase in clarity, evidence and influence till you are removed from this land of shadows to the regions of perfect light to behold the truth as it shines in the person of Jesus without a veil and without a cloud forever.

## Guilt Removed, and Peace Restored

> O Lord, open thou my lips, and my mouth shall show forth thy praise.   Psalm 51:15

THE HISTORY OF David is full of instruction. Everything recorded of him affords us either consolation or caution. In his example we see much of the sovereign power and providence of God.

When a youth, though the least of his father's house, he was singled out and called from following sheep to rule a kingdom. We see him supported through a variety of difficulties, and at length established in his throne to the amazement and confusion of his enemies.

In him likewise we have a striking proof of the evil that is in the heart of man. Who would have thought that David, the man so highly favoured, so wonderfully protected—a man after God's own heart, who in the time of his distress could say, "My soul thirsteth for God, even for the living God" (Psalm 42:2)—that he should be in an unguarded hour seduced, surprised, and led captive of the devil? From gazing he proceeds to adultery, from adultery to murder, and at length sinks into such a stupid frame of mind that an express message from God was needful to convince him of his sin.

And in this circumstance we further see the riches of divine grace and mercy, how tenderly the Lord watches over his sheep, how carefully He brings them back when wandering from Him, and with what rich goodness He heals their backslidings and loves them freely. David was fallen, but not lost. "The thing which he had done, displeased the Lord" (2 Samuel 11:27). Yet his loving-kindness and faithfulness were unalterable. He was interested in that covenant "which is well ordered in all things and sure" (2 Samuel 23:5) and therefore when he confessed his sin the Lord assured him by his servant Nathan that "he had put away his sin, and he should not die for it" (2 Samuel 12:13).

However, though the Lord is thus gracious in passing by the iniquity of his children, yet He will let them know by sorrowful experience that "it is an evil and a bitter thing to sin against him" (Jeremiah 2:19). Though He will not cast off, He will chasten; He will withdraw his presence and suspend his gracious influences, and this to a sensitive heart is a heavy punishment. Though David was delivered from the fear of death and hell, he penned this psalm in the bitterness of his soul. He did not consider the Lord as his enemy, but as a friend and father whom he had greatly offended. He longed to be reconciled, but could not as yet recover his former confidence. He hoped indeed that a time of refreshment would come from his presence and therefore he continued waiting; but for the present he made heavy complaint that his bones were broken and his mouth stopped. He had lost his strength and life, and found he could not restore himself. He was struck dumb by his late fall and therefore he breathes out this prayer: "O Lord, open thou my lips, and my mouth shall show forth thy praise."

From these words I propose to consider that mournful situation which too often happens in the Christian life, when the believer's mouth is stopped and his lips closed, so that he cannot show forth the praises of his God. And in this view, I shall first point out to you the persons who have reason to make this complaint, then explain what is implied in their lips being thus shut up, and show you by what means the Lord opens the closed lips; [finally] I shall observe that when a person's lips are thus opened, his mouth and all that is within him will certainly show forth the Lord's praise. May the Holy Spirit apply the word, and command a blessing upon the whole!

# I

This petition especially suits two sorts of persons, [the backsliding believer, and the doubting believer].

1. [Let us first consider] the backsliding believer—one who has formerly known the goodness of God, has rested in his love and rejoiced in his salvation, "has tasted that the Lord is gracious" (1 Peter 2:3) and walked with comfort in the way of his commandments, but at length by an unguarded conduct or by building wood, hay and stubble upon the Lord's foundation (1 Corinthians 3:11–13) has grieved the good Spirit of God, so that He is withdrawn. The comforter and instructor of his soul is far from him, and therefore he sits in darkness and silence. He retains only a sense of his loss, and can do no more than sigh out this prayer: "O Lord, open thou my lips."

2. The doubting believer—or unbelieving believer, if I may be allowed the expression—is one who has been deeply convinced of sin, and taught by the Spirit of God that there is no salvation but in the Lord Jesus Christ. He loves the word and ways and people of God, is careful to the utmost of his power to abstain from the evil that is in the world, and esteems the "loving kindness of the Lord to be better than life" (Psalm 63:3). He is one at whom the enemy has often made deadly thrusts that he might fall (Psalm 118:13), but the Lord has secretly upheld him through many a bitter hour, and he finds that he is not cut off yet though he perhaps expects it every day. Such as these have indeed sufficient ground to say, "If the Lord was not on my side, I had been swallowed up long ago" (Psalm 124:3). They have reason to conclude with David, "By this, if by nothing else, I know that thou favourest me, seeing my enemies, who have assaulted me so continually, have not yet prevailed against me" (Psalm 41:11). But yet through a sense of past guilt, a sight of present corruptions, the prevalence of unbelief, the workings of a legal spirit, the want of a clear apprehension of the Lord's way of justifying the ungodly, and from the force of Satan's temptations (who is exceedingly busy to press all these things upon the heart), the mouths of these are likewise stopped. They cannot believe, and therefore they cannot speak. However, there are seasons and intervals when they obtain a little glimpse of hope and then the whole desire of their souls is expressed in the words of my text: "O Lord, open thou my lips, and my mouth shall show forth thy praise."

# II

I proceed to consider what may be included in this situation—that is, what is it to have the mouth stopped? The persons I have mentioned have the same liberty of speech in common affairs as others, but because they cannot converse freely with Him who, notwithstanding all their doubts and fears and follies, still maintains a secret hold of their souls, they account themselves no better than dumb. They cannot speak to the Lord nor of him, nor for him, as they wish and ought to do. These are the three aspects of their complaint, and therefore they sigh and say: "O Lord, open thou my lips."

1. Alas! says the believer that has sinned and lost his strength, "O that it was with me as in times past" (Job 29:2). I well remember when I had freedom of access and found it good to draw near to my God, when I could pour out all my complaints and cares before Him, and leave them with Him. I remember the time when my heart was overwhelmed within me, and my spirit was burdened (Psalm 142:3). I saw myself a wretched, helpless sinner. Innumerable evils took hold of me. I thought I was marked out for destruction. I found Satan at my right hand, waiting for permission to seize my soul and make me his prey forever (Zechariah 3:1). I looked round but saw no way to escape, and gave up all for lost. But O, I remember when none in heaven or earth could help me, how the Lord drew near to me in the day of my distress and said unto my soul, "Fear not, I am thy salvation" (Lamentations 3:57). He revealed Himself as an almighty and sufficient Saviour. He said, "Deliver him from going down to the pit, I have found a ransom" (Job 33:24) "He brought me out of the horrible pit, and miry clay, and set my feet upon a rock" (Psalm 40:2). "He brought me into his banqueting-house, and his banner over me was Love. I sat down under his shadow with great delight, and his fruit was sweet unto my taste" (Song of Songs 2:3–4).

This was the beginning, but it was not all. Many a gracious visit He favoured me with afterwards. O the sweet hours of secret prayer! O the happy communion in which I walked with Him all the day long! "Then in the multitude of thoughts within me his comforts refreshed my soul" (Psalm 94:19). Then I could smile at Satan's rage and face a frowning world. Every blessing of common providence was doubly welcome, for I could read his name of love written upon it. And every affliction brought resignation and peace because I saw my father's hand in it and found at a throne of grace renewed strength always suited to my need. Happy were those times, but alas! they are gone—

I could hardly then persuade myself that I should be moved any more. I little thought there was such desperate wickedness in my heart that after so much experience of his goodness I should foolishly wander from him again. But O, what a change have I lived to see! I have grieved that good Spirit of God by which I was sealed, and now I find myself in the hands of my enemies. The Lord hides Himself and stands afar off, and I have lost the power of prayer. Those precious promises which once were the joy of my soul, which I could boldly plead at the throne of grace and say "all these are mine," have no longer any power or sweetness. I read them, but I cannot feel them, and my trials and sins—which once I could cast upon my Saviour and thereby find instant relief—are now a heavy burden too great for me to bear. Mercies have lost their relish and afflictions have lost their usefulness since neither the one or the other are of force to stir up my soul to prayer: "O Lord, open thou my lips."

I remember likewise when I had this freedom in speaking with God—how pleasing it was to me to speak of him. My heart was full and running over with a sense of his goodness, so that it was my meat and drink to say: "Come unto me all you that fear God, and I will tell you what he hath done for my soul" (Psalm 66:16). Then the company of his people was delightful indeed. The meanest of his children that would sit and hear me speak of his loving kindness was precious to me. I esteemed them the excellent of the earth (Psalm 16:3; 55:14), in whom was all my delight. We took sweet counsel together, and walked to the house of God in company. And I thank God I love them still, but I can neither help them nor be helped by them as in times past. In vain they say unto me, "Come, sing us one of the songs of Zion. Alas! How can I sing the songs of the Lord in a strange land? My harp is hung upon the willows, my tongue cleaveth to the roof of my mouth" (Psalm 137:3–5). I dwell in darkness and silence as those long dead. "O Lord, open thou my lips."

And when I could thus speak to God, and of him, I had likewise liberty to speak for him. "I was then very jealous for the Lord of hosts" (1 Kings 19:10). It wounded my soul to hear his name profaned, to see his commandments broken and his gospel slighted. I had a tender concern for poor sinners. I could not but wish that, if possible, every person I met might know what I knew and feel what I felt. And especially where I had friendship and influence I was ready to use it to the best purpose. "The love of Christ constraineth me to lay myself out for his service" (2 Corinthians 5:14). I could not but oppose sin and self-righteousness, and plead the cause of my Saviour upon every occasion. I was not ashamed of the gospel of Christ, for I felt it the power of God unto salvation in my own soul (Romans 1:16) and durst recommend it to everyone as the only balm for sin and sorrow. But now, "the crown is fallen from my head; woe unto me, for I have sinned" (Lamentations 5:16). I am shut out from the fountain and all my streams are dried up. My comforts and my usefulness are declined together:

> O Lord, open thou my lips, and my mouth shall show
> forth thy praise.

Such is the complaint of the backslider in heart, when he is filled with his own ways. And the same, with little variation, is true of the doubting tempted soul too. These will confess that the experience I have described is the desire of their hearts. Such communication with God, such a freedom in his ways, such a zeal for his service is the very thing they mean when they intreat the Lord to open their lips. And indeed they cannot, they dare not deny but they have at times had some little taste of them; otherwise they would not know what I mean. For those things are to the natural man the merest folly imaginable. He understands them not, and therefore he despises them; nay, he hates them with a perfect hatred and opposes them with all his heart.

But still they complain under a present burden. One dark hour of temptation blots out all the traces of comfort they have known, and they refuse consolation. They will insist on it: "I have no chance in the matter; I cannot get near Him and I fear I never shall. When I attempt to pray a sense of my sins and sinfulness stops my mouth. I see the Lord not upon the golden mercy seat but upon the fiery throne of justice, and I am ready to call upon the rocks and mountains to hide me from his presence. When I would commune with his people I am silenced by that dreadful word "What hast thou to do, to declare my statutes, or to take my covenant into thy mouth" (Psalm 50:16). When I would bear my feeble testimony for Him in the world, conscience alarms me and says "Thou that teachest others, teachest thou not thyself?" (Romans 2:21). And then "the enemy comes in like a flood" (Isaiah 59:19), saying "God has forsaken him; persecute and take him, for there is none to deliver him" (Psalm 71:11). Thus "I spend my days in groaning and water my couch with tears" (Psalm 6:6).

This is a heavy burden indeed and would be insupportable except that the faithful Shepherd in a secret unseen way affords timely succour and sets bounds to the raging enemy beyond which he cannot pass: "Hitherto thou shalt come" (Job 38:11), thus far thou art permitted to vex and wound and tear, but no farther. The Lord knows our limits and has promised with every temptation to provide either strength to endure or a way to escape (1 Corinthians 10:13). Two things are proper to be mentioned for the encouragement of such souls to wait on and expect deliverance.

The first of these is the example of the saints. Think not your lot strange, as though some new and unheard of thing had befallen you. Thousands and ten thousands now in glory have tasted, yea drunk deeply of this cup before you. And many yet upon earth who are now rejoicing in the light of God's countenance have said in times past, as you say now, "I shall one day perish by the hand of these enemies; the Lord hath cast me quite off, and I shall never live to see his goodness in the land of the living" (1 Samuel 27:1; Psalm 74:1). Or, if you choose Scripture-proofs, you need only read the book of Job, the Psalms and the Lamentations of Jeremiah to be convinced that some whom you number amongst the Lord's most eminent and highly favoured servants have been reduced to use such expressions as suit your situation no less than if they had been written for you alone. Do not they say that they were broken with breach upon breach; that the arrows of God stuck fast in them; that the Lord wrote bitter things against them and counted them his enemies; that He had shut them up within stone walls and covered Himself with a cloud that they might not see Him (Job 16:14)? These are but a small part of their complaints, and what can you say more than this?

Again, consider the precious promises of the Word. Are they not expressly directed to you? Do you account yourself a backslider? "Return unto me, ye backsliding children, and I will receive you, saith the Lord" (Jeremiah 3:14,22). Do you think yourself a sinner of uncommon magnitude? Still the Lord saith, "Though your sins be as scarlet, they shall be white as snow; though they be red like crimson, they shall be as wool" (Isaiah 1:18). Do you say your neck is as an iron sinew, and your brow brass? Yet hear the word of the Lord: "Hearken unto me, ye stouthearted, that are far from righteousness. I bring near my righteousness, it shall not be far off" (Isaiah 46:13). Is there something peculiarly dreadful in your case, something that you could hardly be prevailed on to entrust to your dearest friend? Yet be not afraid, for truth has said "All manner of sin and blasphemy shall be forgiven unto men. Let the wicked forsake his way, and the unrighteous man his thoughts and let him return unto the Lord, and he will have mercy upon him; and to our God, for he will abundantly pardon" (Matthew 12:31).

But still, when we have said all, we are but miserable comforters. Even with the word of God in our mouths we speak too often in vain. It is the Lord alone that can open the lips. And O that this may be the happy opportunity of gracious appearance in favour of all here present, that our wounds may be healed and our tongues loosened to proclaim his praise! Lift up your hearts to Him, while I endeavour to show you by what means or in what manner the Lord is pleased to open the lips that have long been closed. This is the third particular which I propose to consider from my text.

## III

I say then, that when the Lord is about to open the lips He proceeds by the following steps.

1. He opens the eyes. We are often in a similar situation as Hagar in the wilderness. The water was spent in the bottle and she sat down in despair.

There was a well or fountain close to her sufficient to have supplied her with water to her life's end, but she saw it not till God opened her eyes. (Genesis 21:15–19). Just so many a poor soul is distressed and says, "My stock is spent; I had but little grace at the best and, alas! that little is gone." And now if the Lord should ask some hard thing, would you not do it to obtain a supply? You would willingly take a long journey, or part with all your wealth to have grace abounding in your hearts, but you know you cannot expect help in this way. It is true, all contrivances of our own will have no effect. But blessed be God, they are as needless as they would be useless. We need not dig in the earth nor climb the skies nor cross the seas: our remedy is near (Romans 10:6–8). We need no costly offerings of silver or gold; our remedy is inexpensive. Come, gaze no longer upon your empty bottle but look to the fountain, the river, the ocean of all grace.

May the Lord open your eyes (as He did the eyes of Elisha's servant in 2 Kings 6:17) and I will undertake to point you to an object that shall answer all your wants. Look unto the Lord Jesus Christ. Look unto Him as He hangs naked, wounded, bleeding, dead and forsaken on the cross. Look unto Him again as He now reigns in glory, possessed of all power in heaven and in earth, with thousands of thousands of saints and angels worshipping before Him, and ten thousand times ten thousand ministering unto Him. Then compare your sins with his blood, your wants with his fulness, your unbelief with his faithfulness, your weakness with his strength, your inconstancy with his everlasting love. If the Lord opens the eyes of your understanding you will be astonished at the comparison.

Would you compare a small grain of sand upon the shore with the massive mountains which hide their heads in the clouds and spread their roots from sea to sea? Or the spark of a glow-worm with the noonday sun? Yet there is less disproportion between these than between the utmost capacity of your desires and wants and the immense resources provided for you in the righteousness, compassion and power of our dear Redeemer. "He is able to save to the uttermost" (Hebrews 7:25). And all our trouble arises chiefly from this, that our eyes are holden so that we do not know him (Luke 24:16). Therefore the first step towards opening the lips is to open our eyes that we may see Him, and look upon Him by such a sight as loosened the tongue of unbelieving Thomas and constrained him to cry out, "My Lord and my God" (John 20:28).

2. When the eyes are thus opened, the Lord in the next place, and by that as a means, opens the ear. When Christ is out of sight we are deaf to all the calls, invitations and promises of the Scripture. But a believing view of Him who died that we might live rouses the attention and makes us willing and able to hear what the Lord will speak to his people (Psalm 85:8). And what does He say from the cross? "Look unto me, and be ye

saved. If I be lifted up I will draw all men to me. Behold my hands, my feet, my pierced side; all this I bore for you. Be not afraid, only believe. O thou of little faith, wherefore dost thou doubt? See, sinner, how I have loved thee. I have trodden the wine press alone. I have destroyed death and him that has the power of death. There is henceforth no condemnation to them that believe in me." And what does He say from his kingdom? "I have prayed for thee, that thy faith fail not. For a season you have sorrow but I will see you again and your heart shall rejoice. Him that cometh to me I will in no wise cast out. I am the first and the last that was dead and am alive. I keep the keys of death and hell, and save whom I will. Cast thy burden upon me, I will sustain thee. I will take away thy iniquity. Be of good cheer, thy sins are forgiven thee. Go in peace, and sin no more."* My sacrifice, my God, what words are these!

3. By opening the eye to see his excellence and power and the ear to hear his gracious words, He in the next place opens the heart. He breaks the prison doors, forces Himself an entrance and sets the prisoner at liberty. He touches the rock, and the waters flow (Psalm 78:20). Now a true and filial repentance takes place; now sin appears exceedingly sinful indeed. There was a sorrow before but it was fruitless and ineffectual. Now the sight of Him who was pierced for our sins and the welcome sound of pardon proclaimed in the conscience produce a sorrow after a godly sort, a repentance never to be repented of.

Thus it was with the woman who washed our Lord's feet (Luke 7:38–47). She had been a great sinner; much was forgiven her and therefore she loved much. Thus it was with Peter; he had been a grievous backslider, he had been with Jesus upon the mount and seen the excellent glory and he was stout in his protestation, "Though all men deny thee, yet will not I." But he shrank at the voice of a girl and said, "I know not the man." When the servants spoke to him he cursed and swore. But when Jesus looked upon him, he wept (Luke 22:61–62). Do you think our Lord looked upon him with disdain and indignation? No, rather with a look of love, a look that at once convinced him of his sin and gave him to understand that the Lord pitied and forgave him. This look broke his heart in pieces. He went out and wept bitterly. And afterwards, though greatly humbled as to confidence in himself, yet when asked the question he could boldly appeal to the searcher of hearts, "Lord, thou knowest all things, thou knowest that I love thee" (John 21:17).

And when the eyes, the ears, the heart are thus opened, when the understanding is enlightened, the will engaged, and the affections in-

---

*Isaiah 45:22; John 12:22; John 20:27; Mark 5:36; Matthew 14:31; Isaiah 63:3; Hebrews 2:14; Romans 8:1; Luke 22:32; John 16:22; John 6:37; Revelation 1:17,18; Psalm 55:22; Micah 7:19; Matthew 9:2; John 8:11.

flamed, the cure is wrought. Then the lips will open naturally and the mouth be filled with thanksgiving and praise. O that it would please the Lord to give to me and to each of you a clearer knowledge of this blessed change from heartfelt experience than is in the power of words (of my poor words especially) to describe! Come, my friends, "let us return unto the Lord, for he hath wounded, and he will heal us; he hath smitten, and he will bind us up" (Hosea 6:1).

Verily, we are all guilty in this matter. We have all provoked him by unbelief and wandering from his good way, and therefore we live so far below our privileges and are so often heavy and sorrowful when we have in Him the grounds of continual joy. Now let us unite in this prayer, "O Lord, open thou our lips, display thy power in the midst of us, heal all our breaches, rend the veil of our unbelief, blot out the thick clouds of our sins, cleanse us from all our iniquities and idols, and teach our stammering tongues and barren hearts to show forth the praise of thy abundant goodness."

## IV

I proceed now to my final observation, that if the Lord is pleased to answer our desire and to open your lips in this manner then you will surely praise Him. You will praise Him with your mouths and in your lives; you will thankfully acknowledge his mercy, his power, and his wisdom.

1. You will praise his mercy. Is the cooling stream welcome to the thirsty soul? Is a reprieve acceptable to a poor condemned criminal? Still more welcome is a sense of pardoning love to a soul that has felt the evil and effects of sin. What, to be taken from the dunghill (1 Samuel 2:8) and made a companion with princes! To have all our guilt and complaints removed at once! To be snatched as it were from the brink of hell and placed in the very suburbs of heaven! To be able to say, "O Lord, thou wast justly angry with me, and I went mourning under a sense of thy displeasure; but now thine anger is turned away, and thou comfortest me" (Isaiah 12:1). Is not this a mercy, especially considering how undeserving we are of the smallest favour? And further, the way in which it was conveyed, that the pardon, though free to us, is a pardon bought with blood—that it cost the Lord Jesus his life, his soul, to effect that blessed reconciliation in which we are beginning to rejoice. Still more, that all we can now receive of his love is but a taste, a small thing, in comparison of what He has reserved for us! O what mercy is here! O what thanks does it call for! "O Lord, open thou our lips, and our mouth shall show forth thy praise."

2. You will praise his power. "I thought," says the poor soul at such a

time, "I was fallen so low that there was no help. The more I toiled and laboured in my own strength, the further the blessing seemed from me. I know by experience that none but an almighty arm could relieve me. Creatures, means and contrivances I had tried, and tried again, but found them all physicians of no value. But now, the "right hand of the Lord has done wonderfully, the right hand of the Lord has brought mighty things to pass" (Psalm 118:15,16; Isaiah 38:15). What shall I say? He hath both spoken himself, and also hath done it. The work is his; to Him be the glory. I got not this victory by my own bow (Psalm 44:6), neither did my own arm save me, "but the Lord himself has been pleased to show the exceeding greatness of his mighty power in my behalf" (Ephesians 1:19). Therefore, "not unto us, but unto thy name, O Lord, be the glory and the praise" (Psalm 115:1).

3. You will praise his wisdom. "What I do," said our Lord to Peter, "thou knowest not now, but thou shalt know hereafter" (John 13:7). The mourning soul often asks the question with David, "I will say unto God, my rock, why hast thou forsaken me? Why go I mourning because of the enemy?" (Psalm 42:9). When the Lord turns your mourning into joy, you shall know why. You will then see that there was a need of all these things (1 Peter 1:6). It is to show you what is in your hearts, to mortify the spirit of self-righteousness, "to teach you that without him you can do nothing" (John 15:5), to make you wise and experienced against Satan's devices, to give you a tender sympathy and fellow feeling in the sufferings and infirmities of your brethren, and to enable you to encourage and comfort others (2 Corinthians 1:4) who shall be hereafter in your situation, by relating what you have seen and known yourself in your various conflicts and strivings against sin. These are some of the reasons why the Lord suffers his dear children to groan, being burdened, and sometimes permits their enemies to gain a short advantage over them, that He may humble and prove them (Deuteronomy 8:2–16) in order to do them good in their latter end. And O, with what wisdom is all this appointed! A little of it we may see at present, but we shall not have a complete view till we get safe home. Then to look back upon the way by which He led us through this wilderness will furnish matter for eternal praise.

Furthermore, not only your mouths but your lives also shall praise Him. What is the language of a believing heart when the Lord pardons his sins and binds up his wounds? It is this: "Now Lord, I am thine, thy vows are upon me, for thou hast redeemed me, O Lord God of truth. Shall I continue in sin because grace has abounded? God forbid! I am crucified with Christ, crucified to the world, and the world to me. The love of Christ constrains me. The time past is sufficient to have lived in vanity; henceforth I am the Lord's. He has bound me by his tender mercies to present myself, body and soul, to his service. Here, O Lord, I offer my whole self, all that I am, and all that I have, a living sacrifice, holy and acceptable to thee. O let me never, never wander from thee again, but walk in the light as thou art in the light and have communion with thee here below till thou shall remove me out of the reach of sin and sorrow forever."*

If there are any here who have neither known the loving kindness of the Lord, nor mourned under the sense of his displeasure, I am sure your lips are closed to this hour. And should you die thus incapable of praising the God who made you and the grace which has brought the sound of the gospel to your ears, it were better for you that you had never been born (Matthew 26:24). You have much reason to cry out, "O Lord, open thou my lips." Open my eyes to see my danger, to see the evil of my nature and life. Open my lips to confess my wickedness. Open my heart to receive thy word, that I likewise may bear a part in the praises thy people pay thee, and not perish (as without thy mercy I must do) with a lie in my right hand (Isaiah 46:20). Consider: the time is short (1 Corinthians 7:29); death is near and may be sudden. May the Lord enable you to consider the things belonging to your peace (Luke 19:42) before they are hid from your eyes!

And you, my friends, who at present enjoy the light of God's countenance, who know your sins are forgive for his name's sake (1 John 2:12), and have a happy freedom of access at the throne of grace, O be mindful of your privileges. Beware of sin, beware of self, beware of Satan. Your enemy envies you your liberty, he watches you with subtlety and malice, he spreads snares for your feet; he desires to have advantage of you that he may sift you as wheat (Luke 22:3). Therefore be upon your guard, be humble, make much of secret prayer, keep close to the Scriptures of God; by the words of his lips you shall be preserved from the paths of the destroyer (Psalm 17:4). Attend diligently upon the ordinances, and speak often one to another (Malachi 3:16) in love and faithfulness of what the Lord has done and prepared for you, and of what manner of persons you ought to be in all holy conversation and godliness (2 Peter 3:11). Thus you shall be kept safe from evil. Jesus has prayed for you that your faith may not fail (Luke 22:32). Fix your eye and your heart upon him (Hebrews 12:2), as He that must do all for you, all in you, all by you. And He has said, "Yet a little while, and surely I come quickly" (Revelation 3:11). Hold fast that which thou hast. Be thou "faithful unto death, and I will give thee a crown of life. Amen. Even so, come Lord Jesus" (Revelation 2:10; 22:20).

*Psalm 116:14,16; 31:5; Romans 6:1; Galatians 2:20; 6:14; 2 Corinthians 5:14; 1 Peter 4:3; Romans 12:1; 1 John 1:7. [Newton's note]

# *from* Messiah: Or, the Scriptural Passages which Form the Subject of the Celebrated Oratorio of Handel (1786)

## *The Consolation*

Comfort ye, comfort ye my people, saith your God. Speak ye comfortably to Jerusalem, and cry unto her, that her warfare is accomplished, that her iniquity is pardoned: for she hath received at the Lord's hand double for all her sins.   Isaiah 40:1,2

THE PARTICULARS OF the great mystery of godliness as enumerated by the Apostle Paul constitute the grand and inexhaustible theme of the gospel ministry: "God manifest in the flesh, justified in the Spirit, seen of angels, preached unto the Gentiles, believed on in that world, received up into glory" (1 Timothy 3:16). It is my wish and purpose to know nothing among you but this subject, to preach nothing to you but what has a real connection with the doctrine of Jesus Christ and Him crucified, and with the causes and the effects of his obedience unto death, even the death of the cross. But a regard to the satisfaction and advantage of my regular hearers has often made me desirous of adopting some plan which might lead me to exhibit the principal outlines of the Saviour's character and mediation in a regular series of discourses, so as to form, if not a picture, at least a slight sketch of those features of his glory and of his grace which endear Him to the hearts of his people. Such a plan has lately, and rather unexpectedly, occurred to me. Conversation in almost every company, for some time past, has much turned upon the commemoration of Handel, the grand musical entertainments and particularly his Oratorio of the *Messiah,* which has been repeatedly performed on that occasion in Westminster Abbey. If it could be reasonably hoped that the performers and the company assembled to hear the music, or the greater part, or even a very considerable part of them, were capable of entering into the spirit of the subject, I will readily allow that the *Messiah*—executed in so masterly a manner, by persons whose hearts as well as their voices and instruments were tuned to the Redeemer's praise, accompanied with the grateful emotions of an audience duly affected with a sense of their obligations to his love—might afford one of the highest and noblest gratifications of which we are capable in the present life. But they who love the Redeemer, and therefore delight to join in his praise, if they did not find it convenient or think it expedient to hear the *Messiah* at Westminster may comfort themselves with the thought that, in a little time, they shall be still more abundantly gratified. Ere long death shall rend the veil which hides eternal things from their view and introduce them to that unceasing song and universal chorus which are even now performing before the throne of God and the Lamb. Till then, I apprehend that true Christians, without the assistance of either vocal or instrumental music, may find greater pleasure in a humble contemplation on the words of the *Messiah* than they can derive from the utmost efforts of musical genius.

This therefore is the plan I spoke of. I mean to lead your meditations to the language of the Oratorio, and to consider in their order (if the Lord on whom our breath depends shall be pleased to afford life, ability and opportunity) the several sublime and interesting passage of Scripture which are the basis of that admired composition.

If He shall condescend to smile upon the attempt, pleasure and profit will go hand in hand. There is no harmony to a heaven-born soul like that which is the result of the combination and coincidence of all the divine attributes and perfections manifested in the work of redemption; mercy and truth meeting together, inflexible righteousness corresponding with the peace of offenders, God glorious and sinners saved. There is no melody upon earth to be compared with the voice of the blood of Jesus speaking peace to a guilty conscience, or with the voice of the Holy Spirit applying the promises to the heart and sweetly inspiring a disposition of confidence and adoption. These are joys which the world can neither give nor take away, which never pall upon the mind by continuance or repetition; the sense of them is always new, the recollection of them is always pleasant. Nor do they only satisfy but [they also] sanctify the soul. They strengthen faith, animate hope, add fervency to love, and both dispose and enable the Christian to run in all the paths of holy obedience with an enlarged heart.

## I. *Division of Handel's Oratorio*

The *Messiah* of Handel consists of three parts. The first contains prophecies of his advent and the happy consequences, together with the angel's message to the shepherds informing them of his birth, as related by St. Luke. The second part describes his passion, death, resurrection and ascension, his taking possession of his kingdom of glory, the commencement of his kingdom of grace upon the earth, and the certain disappointment and ruin of all who persist in opposition to his will. The third part expresses the blessed fruits and consummation of his undertaking in the deliverance of his people from sin, sorrow and death, and in making them finally victorious over all their enemies. The triumphant song of the redeemed to the praise of the Lamb who bought them with his own blood closes the whole. The arrangement or series of these passages is so judiciously disposed, so well connected and so fully comprehends all the principal truths of the gospel that I shall not attempt either to alter or to enlarge it. The exordium or introduction which I have read to you from the prophecy of Isaiah is very happily chosen.

## II. *The Introductory Text: Isaiah 40:1,2*

If, as some eminent commentators suppose, the prophet had any reference in this passage to the return of Israel from Babylon into their own land, his principal object was undoubtedly of much greater importance. Indeed their deliverance from captivity and their state afterwards as a nation do not appear to correspond with the magnificent images employed in the following verses. For though they rebuilt their city and temple, they met with many insults and much opposition and continued to be a tributary and dependent people. I shall therefore waive the consideration of this sense.

The eye of the prophet's mind seems to be chiefly fixed upon one august personage who was approaching to enlighten and bless a miserable world; and before he describes the circumstances of his appearance he is directed to comfort the mourners in Zion with an assurance that this great event would fully compensate for all their sorrows. The state of Jerusalem, the representative name of the people of God, was very low in Isaiah's time. The people who in the days of Solomon were attached to the service of God, honoured with signal tokens of his presence and favor and raised to the highest pitch of temporal prosperity, were now degenerated: the gold was become dim, and the fine gold changed. Iniquity abounded, judgments were impending, yet insensibility and security prevailed, and the words of many were stout against the Lord. But there were a few who feared the Lord, whose eyes affected their hearts, and who mourned for the evils which they could not prevent. These and these only were in strictness of speech the people of the Lord, and to these the message of comfort is addressed. Speak to Jerusalem comfortably, speak to her heart (as the Hebrew word is), to her true condition, and tell her that there is balm for all her wounds, a cordial for all her griefs in this one consideration: Messiah is at hand.

In the prophetic style things future are described as present, and that which the mouth of the Lord has spoken of as sure to take place is considered as already done. Thus the prophet rapt into future times contemplates the manifestation of Messiah, the accomplishment of his great undertaking, and all the happy consequences of his obedience unto death for men, as though he stood upon the spot and, with John the harbinger of our Lord (whose appearance he immediately describes) was pointing with his finger to the Lamb of God that taketh away the sin of the world.

This comfortable message consists of two parts. First, the removal of evil: her warfare is accomplished, her iniquity is pardoned. Secondly, promise of good more than equivalent to all her afflictions: she hath received at the Lord's hand double for all her sins.

Two ideas are included in the original term translated "warfare": (1) a state of service connected with hardship, like that of the military life (Numbers 1:3); (2) an appointed time, as it is rendered in Job (Job 7:3; 14:14).

These ideas apply equally to the mosaic dispensation. The spirit of that institution was comparatively a spirit of bondage, distance and fear; and the state of the church while under the law is likened by the apostle to that of a minor who, though he be an heir, is under tutors and governors and differeth but little from a servant until the time appointed of the Father (Galatians 4:1–4). The ceremonial law with respect to its inefficacy is styled "weak" and, with respect to the long train of its multiplied, expensive, difficult and repeated conditions, a "yoke" and "burden." But it was only for a prescribed time. The gospel was designed to supercede it, and to introduce a state of life, power, liberty and confidence. The blackness and darkness, the fire and tempest, and other circumstances of terror attendant on the promulgation of the law at Mount Sinai (Hebrews 12:18–22), which not only struck the people with dismay but caused even Moses himself to say, "I exceedingly fear and quake," were expressive of its design. This was not to lead the people of Israel to expect peace and hope from their best obedience to that covenant, but rather to convince them of the necessity of a better covenant established upon better promises, and to direct their hopes to Messiah, who was prefigured by all their sacrifices, and who in the fulness of time was to make a complete atonement for sin by the sacrifice of Himself. Then their legal [and] figurative constitution would cease, shadows give place to substance, and true worshippers of God would be instructed, enabled and encouraged to worship Him in spirit and in truth; no more as servants, but in the temper of adoption, as the children of God by faith in the Son of his love.

There is a considerable analogy to this difference between the law and the gospel, as contradistinct from each other, in the previous distress of the sinner when he is made aware of his guilt and danger as a transgressor of the law of God, and the subsequent peace which he obtains by believing the gospel. The good seed of the word of grace can only take root and flourish in a soil duly prepared. And this preparation of the heart (Proverbs 16:1), without which all that is read or heard concerning Messiah produces no permanent good effect, is wholly from the Lord. The first good work of the Holy Spirit upon the heart of fallen man is to convince of sin (John 16:9). He gives some due impressions of the majesty and holiness of the God with whom we have to do, of our dependence upon Him, of our obligations to Him as our creator, lawgiver and benefactor. Then we begin to form our estimate of duty, of sin and its desert, not from the prevalent maxims and judgment of mankind around us, but from the unerring standard of Scripture. Thence new and painful apprehensions arise—the lofty looks of man are humbled, his haughtiness is brought low, his mouth stopped, or only opened to confess his guilt and vileness and to cry for mercy.

He now feels himself under the law: it condemns him and he cannot reply, it commands him and he cannot obey. He has neither righteousness nor strength, and must sink into despair, were it not that he is now qualified to hearken to the gospel with other ears, and to read the Scriptures with other eyes (if I may so speak) than he once did. He now knows he is sick and therefore knows his need of a physician. This state of anxiety, conflict and fear, which keeps comfort from his heart and perhaps slumber from his eyes, is often of long continuance. There is no common standard whereby to determine either the degree or the duration. Both differ in different persons; and as the body and the mind have a strong and reciprocal influence upon each other, it is probable the difference observable in such cases may in part depend upon constitutional causes. However, the time is a prescribed time and, though not subject to any rules or reasonings of ours, is limited and regulated by the wisdom of God. He wounds and He heals in his own appointed moment. None that continue waiting upon Him, and seeking salvation in the means which He has directed shall be finally disappointed. Sooner or later He gives them, according to his promise, beauty for ashes, the oil of joy for mourning, and the garment of praise for the spirit of heaviness (Isaiah 41:3). This warfare is accomplished when they rightly understand and cordially believe the following clause: "Her iniquity is pardoned."

Though the sacrifices under the law had an immediate and direct effect—to restore the offender for whom they were offered to the privileges pertaining to the people of Israel considered as a nation or commonwealth—they could not of themselves cleanse the conscience from guilt. It is a dictate of right reason no less than of revelation that it is not possible that the blood of bulls and of goats should take away sin (Hebrews 10:4). For this purpose the blood of Christ had a retrospective efficacy and was the only ground of consolation for a convinced sinner from the beginning of the world. He was proposed to our first parents as the seed of the woman who should break the serpent's head (Genesis 3:15). In this seed Abraham believed and was justified, and all of every age who were justified were partakers of Abraham's faith.

Therefore the apostle teaches us that when God set Him forth as a propitiation through faith in his blood, He declared his righteousness in the remission of sins that were past (Romans 3:25). For though we may suppose God would have declared his mercy in forgiving sin upon any terms, no consideration but the death of his Son could have exhibited his righteousness—that is his holiness, justice and truth—in the pardon of sin. True penitents and believers were pardoned and saved under the law, but not by the law. Their faith looked through all the legal institutions toward Him who was represented and typified by them. But the types which revealed Him in a sense concealed Him likewise. So that though Abraham saw his day and rejoiced, and a succession of the servants of God foresaw his glory and his sufferings and spoke of Him, yet in general the church of the Old Testament rather desired and longed for than actually possessed that fulness of light and knowledge concerning the person, offices, love and victory of Messiah, which is the privilege of those who enjoy and believe the gospel (Hebrews 11:39, 40).

Yet great discoveries of these things were vouchsafed to some of the prophets, particularly to Isaiah, who on account of the clarity of his vision of the Redeemer and his kingdom has been sometimes styled a fifth evangelist. The most evangelical part of his prophecy, or at least that part in which he prosecutes the subject with the least interruption, begins with this chapter and with this verse (40:1). And he proposes it for the comfort of the mourners in Zion in his day.

We know that the Son of God, of whom Moses and the prophets spoke, is actually come (1 John 5:20), that the atonement for sin is made, the ransom for sinners paid and accepted. Now the shadows are past, the veil removed, the night ended, the dawn and the day is arrived, yea the Sun of Righteousness is arisen with healing in his beams (Malachi 4:2).* God is reconciled in his Son, and the ministers of the gospel are now authorized to preach comfort to all who mourn under a consciousness of sin, to tell them all manner of sin is forgiven for the Redeemer's sake and that the iniquity of those who believe in Him is freely and abundantly pardoned.

Though the last clause of the verse does not belong to the passage as

*The KJV has "healing in his wings"; this may be perhaps a silent extension of the metaphor on either Newton's or the printer's part.

selected for the Oratorio,* it is so closely connected with the subject that I am not willing to omit it: "She has received at the Lord's hand double for all her sins."

The meaning here cannot be that her afflictions had already been more and greater than her sins had deserved. The just desert of sin cannot be received in the present life, for the wages of sin is death and the curse of the law—or, in the apostle's words, "everlasting destruction from the presence of the Lord and the glory of his power" (2 Thessalonians 1:9). Therefore a living man can have no reason to complain under the heaviest sufferings. If we acknowledge ourselves to be sinners, we have likewise cause to acknowledge that He hath not dealt with us according to our iniquities. (Nor can the words be so applied to Messiah as to intimate that even his sufferings were more than necessary or greater than the exigency of the case required. The efficacy of his atonement is indeed greater than the actual application and sufficient to save the whole race of mankind if they truly believed in the Son of God. [Yet] we read that He groaned and bled upon the cross till He could say, "It is finished," but not longer. It becomes us to refer to infinite wisdom the reasons why his sufferings were prolonged for such a precise time, but I think we may take it for granted that they did not endure an hour or a minute longer than was strictly necessary.) The expression [in Isaiah] seems to be elliptical, and I apprehend the true sense is that Jerusalem should receive blessings, double, much greater, than all the afflictions which sin had brought upon her, and in general [application] to us, to every believing sinner, that the blessings of the gospel are an unspeakably great compensation and over balance for all afflictions of every kind with which we have been or can be exercised. Afflictions are the fruit of sin, and because our sins have been many, our afflictions may be many. "But where sin has abounded, grace has much more abounded" (Romans 5:20).

Before our Lord healed the paralytic man who was brought to Him, he said, "Be of good cheer, thy sins are forgiven thee" (Mark 2:5). His outward malady rendered him an object of compassion to those who brought him, but he appears to have been aware of an inward malady which only Jesus could discern or pity or relieve. I doubt not but his conscience was burdened with guilt. An assurance therefore that his sins were forgiven was sufficient to make him of good cheer, whether his palsy were removed or not. To this purpose the Psalmist speaks absolutely and without exception: "Blessed is the man," however circumstanced, "whose transgression is forgiven, whose iniquity is covered"

---

*Handel's libretto goes immediately to v. 3: "The voice of him that crieth in the wilderness, Prepare ye the way of the Lord . . ."

(Psalm 32:1). Though he be poor, afflicted, diseased, neglected or despised, if the Lord imputeth not his iniquity to him, he is a blessed man.

There is no situation in human life so deplorable that a recognition of the pardoning love of God cannot support and comfort the sufferer under it, compose his spirit, yea make him exceedingly joyful in all his tribulations. For he who feels the power of the blood of Jesus cleansing his conscience from guilt and giving him access by faith to the throne of grace with liberty to say Abba, Father, he knows that all his trials are under the direction of wisdom and love, are all working together for his good, and that the heaviest of them are light and the longest momentary in comparison with that far more exceeding and eternal weight of glory which is reserved for him in a better world (2 Corinthians 4:16, 17). Even at present in the midst of his sufferings, having communion with God and a gracious submission to his will, he possesses a peace that passeth understanding and which the world can neither give nor take away.

## III. *Conclusion*

I shall close this preliminary discourse with a few observations, by way of edification.

1. How justly may we adopt the prophet's words, "Who is a God like unto thee" (Micah 7:18)! Behold and admire his goodness! Infinitely happy and glorious in Himself, He has provided for the comfort of those who were rebels against his government and transgressors of his holy law. What was degenerate Israel, and what are we, that He should thus anticipate us with his mercy, remember us in our low estate and redeem us from misery in such a way and at such a price! Salvation is wholly of grace (Ephesians 2:5), not only undeserved but undesired by us until He is pleased to awaken us to a sense of our need of it. And then we find every thing prepared that our wants require or our wishes can conceive: yea, that He has done exceedingly beyond what we could either ask or think.

Salvation is wholly of the Lord (Psalm 3:8), and bears those signatures of infinite wisdom, power and goodness which distinguish all his works from the puny imitations of men. It is every way worthy of Himself—a great, a free, a full, a sure salvation. It is great, whether we consider the objects, miserable and hell-deserving sinners; the end, the restoration of such alienated creatures to his image and favor, to immortal life and happiness; or the means, the incarnation, humiliation, sufferings and death of his beloved Son. It is free, without exception of persons or situations, without any conditions or qualifications, but such as He Himself performs in them and bestows upon them. It is full, including every desirable blessing: pardon, peace, adoption, protection and guidance through this world, and in the world to come eternal life and happiness in the unclouded, uninterrupted enjoyment of the favor and love of God, with the perfect and perpetual exclusion of every will.

2. When the Lord God who knows the human heart would speak comfort to it, He proposes one object, and only one, as the necessary and all-sufficient source of consolation. This is Messiah. Jesus in his person and offices, known and received by faith, affords a balm for every wound, a cordial for every care.

If we admit that they who live in the spirit of the world can make a poor shift to amuse themselves and be tolerably satisfied in a state of prosperity while everything goes on according to their wish, while we make this concession (which, however, is more than we need allow them, for we know that no state of life is free from anxiety, disappointment, weariness and disgust), yet we must still consider them as objects of compassion. It is a proof of the weakness and disorder of their minds that they are capable of being satisfied with such trifles. Thus if a lunatic conceives his cell to be a palace, that his chains are ornaments of gold, if he calls a wreath of his straw a crown, puts it on his head and affects the language of majesty, we do not suppose the poor creature to be happy simply because he tells us that he is so. Rather, we consider his complacency in his situation as an effect and proof of his malady. We pity him, and if we were able, would gladly restore him to his senses, though we know a cure would immediately put an end to his pleasing delusions.

But, I say, supposing or admitting the world could make its votaries happy in a state of prosperity, it will, it must, leave them without resource in the day of trouble. And they are to be pitied indeed who, when their gourds are withered, when the desire of their eyes is taken from them with a stroke, or the evil which they most feared touches them, or when death looks them closely in the face, have no acquaintance with God, no access to the throne of grace, but being without Christ are without a solid hope of good hereafter, though they are forced to feel the vanity and inconstancy of everything here.

But they who know Messiah, who believe in Him and partake of his Spirit, cannot be comfortless. They recollect what He suffered for them. They know that every circumstance and event of life is under his direction, and designed to work for their good—that though they sow in tears, they shall soon reap in joy. Therefore they possess their souls in patience and are cheerful, yea comfortable, under those trying dispensations of providence which, when they affect the lovers of pleasure, too often either excite in them a spirit of presumptuous murmuring against the will of God or sink them into despondency and all the melancholy train of evils attendant on those who languish and pine away under that depression of spirits appropriately called a broken heart.

3. To be capable of the comfort my text proposes, the mind must be in

a suitable disposition. A free pardon is a comfort to a malefactor, but it implies guilt. Therefore, they who have no apprehension that they have broken the laws would be rather offended than comforted by an offer of pardon. This is one principal cause of that neglect, yea contempt, which the gospel of the grace of God meets with from the world. If we could suppose that a company of people who were all trembling under an apprehension of his displeasure—constrained to confess the justice of the sentence but not as yet informed of any way to escape—were to hear this message for the first time and to be fully assured of its truth and authority, they would receive it as life from the dead. But it is to be feared that for want of knowing themselves and their real state in the sight of Him with whom we have to do, many persons who have received pleasure from the music of the *Messiah* have neither found, nor expected, nor desired to find any comfort from the words.

## Messiah's Easy Yoke

Take my yoke upon you, and learn of me, for I am meek and lowly in heart; and ye shall find rest to your souls. For my yoke is easy, and my burden is light.   Matthew 11:29,30

THOUGH THE influence of education and example may dispose us to acknowledge the gospel to be a revelation from God, it can only be rightly understood or duly prized by those persons who feel themselves in the circumstances of distress which it is designed to relieve. No Israelite would think of fleeing to a city of refuge (Joshua 20:2–3) till, by having unwittingly slain a man, he was exposed to the resentment of the next of kin, the legal avenger of blood. But then a sense of his danger would induce him readily to avail himself of the appointed method of safety.

The skill of a physician may be acknowledged in general terms by many, but he is applied to only by the sick (Matthew 9:12). Thus our Saviour's gracious invitation to come to Him for rest will be little regarded till we really feel ourselves weary and heavy laden. This is a principal reason why the gospel is heard with so much indifference. For though sin be a grievous illness and a hard bondage, yet one effect of it is a strange stupidity and infatuation which renders us (like a person in a delirium) oblivious to our true state. It is a happy time when the Holy Spirit, by his convincing power, removes that stupor which, while it prevents us from fully perceiving our misery, renders us likewise indifferent to the only means of deliverance.

Such a conviction of the guilt and desert of sin is the first hopeful symptom in a sinner's situation—but it is necessarily painful and distressing. It is not pleasant to be weary and heavy laden, but it awakens our attention to Him who says, "Come unto me, and I will give you rest," and makes us willing to take his yoke upon us.

Oxen are yoked to labour. From hence the yoke is a figurative expression to denote servitude. Our Lord seems to use it here both to suggest our natural prejudices against his service and to obviate them. Though He submitted to sufferings, reproach and death for our sakes, though He invites us not because He has need of us but because we have need of Him and cannot be happy without Him, yet our ungrateful hearts think unkindly of Him. We conceive of Him as a hard master, and suppose that if we engage ourselves to Him we must bid farewell to pleasure and live under a continual restraint. His rule is deemed too strict, his laws too severe, and we imagine that we could be more happy following our own plans than by acceding to his. Such unjust, unfriendly and dishonourable thoughts of Him whose heart is full of tenderness, whose spirit melts with love, are strong proofs of our baseness, blindness and depravity. Yet still He continues his invitation, "Come unto me"—as if He had said, 'Be not afraid of me. Only make the experiment and you shall find that what you have accounted my yoke is true liberty, and that in my service, which you have avoided as burdensom, there is no burden at all, for my ways are ways of pleasantness, and all my paths are peace.' I have a good hope that many of my hearers can verify from their own happy experience that (according to the beautiful expression in our liturgy) his service is perfect freedom.

If we are really Christians, Jesus is our Master—our Lord—and we are his servants. It is vain to call him "Lord, Lord" (Luke 6:46) unless we keep his commandments. They who know Him will love Him, and they who love Him will desire to please Him not by a course of service of their own devising but by accepting his revealed will as the standard and rule to every part of which they endeavour to conform in their temperament and their conduct. He is likewise our Master in another sense—that is, He is our great Teacher. If we submit to Him as such, we are his disciples or scholars.* We cannot serve him acceptably unless we are taught by Him.

The philosophers of old had their disciples who imbibed their convictions and were therefore called after their names, [such] as the Pythagoreans and Platonists, from Pythagoras and Plato. The general name of Christians, which was first assumed by the believers at Antioch (possibly

---

*I.e., in the sense of "students." A good proportion of the St. Mary, Woolnoth, congregation would have been among the best-educated people of the day. William Wilberforce was in regular attendance at this time.

by divine direction) signifies that they are the professed disciples of Christ.

If we wish to be truly wise—to be wise unto salvation—we must apply to Him. For in this sense the disciple or scholar cannot be above his Master (Luke 6:40). We can learn of men no more than they can teach us. But He says, "Learn of me," and He cautions us against calling anyone "master" upon earth. He does, indeed, instruct his people by ministers and instruments, but unless He is pleased to superadd his influence, what we seem to learn from them alone will profit us but little. Nor are the best of them so thoroughly furnished—nor so free from mistake—as to deserve our implicit confidence. But they whom He condescends to teach shall learn what no merely human instruction can impart. Let us consider the peculiar and unspeakable advantages of being his scholars.

1. In the first place, this great Teacher can give the capacity requisite to the reception of his sublime instructions. There is no prospect of excelling in human arts and sciences without a previous natural ability suited to the subject. For instance, if a person has not an ear and taste for music, he will make but small proficiency under the best masters. It will be the same with respect to the mathematics or any branch of science. A skilfull master may improve and inform the scholar if he be rightly disposed to learn, but he cannot communicate the disposition. But Jesus can open and enliven the dullest mind; He teaches the blind to see and the deaf to hear. By nature we are intractable and incapable of relishing divine truth, however advantageously proposed to us by men like ourselves. But happy are his scholars! He enables them to surmount all difficulties. He takes away the heart of stone, subdues the most obstinate prejudices, enlightens the dark understanding and inspires a genius and a taste for the sublime and interesting lessons he proposes to them. In this respect, as in every other, there is none teacheth like Him (Job 36:26).

2. He teacheth the most important things. The subjects of human science are, comparatively, trivial and insignificant. We may be safely ignorant of them all. And we may acquire the knowledge of them all without being wiser or better with respect to the proper concerns of our true happiness. Experience and observation abundantly confirm the remark of Solomon, that "He who increaseth knowledge increaseth sorrow. The eye is not satisfied with seeing, nor the ear with hearing" (Ecclesiastes 1:3, 18). Unless the heart be seasoned and sanctified by grace, the sum total of all other acquisitions is but "vanity and vexation of spirit" (Ecclesiastes 2:17). Human learning will neither support the mind under trouble nor weaken its attachment to worldly things, nor control its impetuous passions, nor overcome the fear of death. The confession of the learned Grotius, towards the end of a life spent in literary pursuits, is

much more generally known than properly attended to. He had deservedly a great name and reputation as a scholar, but his own reflection upon the result of his labours expresses what he learned, not from books and ordinary course of studies, but from the Teacher I am commending to you. He lived to leave this testimony for the admonition of the learned, or to this effect: *"Ah, vitam prorsus perdidi nihil agendo laboriose"* ("Alas! I have wasted my whole life in taking much pains to no purpose.")* But Jesus makes his scholars wise unto eternal life, and reveals that knowledge to babes—to persons of weak and limited abilities—of which the wisdom of the world can form no idea.

3. Other teachers, as I have already hinted, can only inform the head, but his instructions influence the heart. Moral philosophers, as they are called, abound in fine words and plausible speeches concerning the beauty of virtue, the fitness of things, temperance, benevolence, and equity. And their scholars learn to talk like them. But their fine and admired sentiments are mere empty notions, destitute of life and efficacy, and frequently leave them as much under the tyranny of pride, passion, sensuality, envy and malice as any of the vulgar whom they despise for their ignorance. It is well known, to the disgrace of the morality which the world applauds, that some of their most admired sentimental writers and teachers have deserved to be numbered among the most wanton and despicable of mankind. They have been slaves to the basest and most degrading appetites and the tenor of their lives has been a marked contradiction to their fine-spun theories.** But Jesus Christ effectually teaches his disciples to forsake and abhor whatever is contrary to rectitude or purity, and inspires them with love, power and a sound mind. And if they do not talk of great things, they are enabled to perform them. Their lives are exemplary and useful, their deaths peaceful, and their memory precious.

4. The disciples of Jesus are, or may be, always learning. His providence and wisdom have so disposed things in subserviency to the purposes of his grace that the whole world around them is as a great school,

---

*Hugo Grotius, the great seventeenth-century scholar, author of *Adamus Exul* (1601) and *Observations Concerning the Original of Government* (1652), among other works.

**Among the most notable objects of this kind of criticism in Newton's time were included famous writers such as Samuel Johnson's biographer, James Boswell, and Laurence Sterne. Sterne, author of *A Sentimental Journey* and the sensational *Tristram Shandy,* was an Anglican clergyman; his apparent contradictions in profession earned him direct attack by many of his fellow clergymen of evangelical persuasion, notably among them William Law. Boswell's scandalous lifestyle was a reproach to Samuel Johnson. But a list of their fellow travelers in this period would be a long one indeed.

and the events of every day with which they are connected have a tendency and suitableness, if rightly considered, to promote their instruction. Heavenly lessons are taught and illustrated by earthly objects, yet we are incapable of understanding them at present unless the mode of instruction be thus accommodated to our situation and weakness.

The Scripture points out to us a wonderful and beautiful analogy between the outward visible world of nature and that spiritual state which is called the kingdom of God. The former is like a book written in cypher, to which the Scripture is the key which, when we obtain [it], we have the other opened to us. Thus, wherever they look, some object presents itself which is adapted either to lead their thoughts directly to Jesus or to explain or confirm some passage in his word. So, likewise, the incidents of human life, the characters we know, the conversation we hear, the vicissitudes which take place in families, cities and nations—in a word, the occurrences which furnish the history of every day—afford a perpetual commentary on what the Scriptures teach concerning the heart of man and the state of the world as subject to vanity and lying in wickedness. And thereby the great truths, which it behooves us to understand and remember, are more repeatedly and forcibly exhibited before our eyes and brought home to our hearts. It is the peculiar advantage of the disciples of Christ that their lessons are always before them, and their Master always with them.

5. Men who are otherwise competently qualified for teaching in the branches of science they profess often discourage and intimidate their students by the impatience, austerity and distance of their manner. They fail in that condescension and gentleness which are necessary to engage the attention and affection of the timid and the volatile, or gradually to soften and to shame the perverse. Even Moses, though eminent for his forbearance towards the obstinate people committed to his care, and though he loved them and longed for their welfare, was at times almost wearied by them (Numbers 11:11,12). But Jesus, who knows beforehand the weakness, the dullness and the obstinacy of those whom He deigns to teach, to prevent their fears is pleased to say: "Learn of me, for I am meek and lowly." With what meekness did He converse among his disciples, while He was with them upon earth. He allowed them at all times a gracious freedom of access. He bore with their mistakes, reproved and corrected them with the greatest mildness, and taught them as they were able to bear, with a kind accommodation to their prejuduces, leading them on, step by step, and waiting for the proper season of unfolding to them those more difficult points which for a time appeared to them to be hard sayings.

And though He be now exalted upon his glorious throne and clothed with majesty, still his heart is full of tenderness and his compassions still abound. We are still directed to think of Him not as one who cannot be touched with a feeling of our infirmities but as exercising the same patience and sympathy towards his disciples now which so signally marked his character during his state of humiliation. The compliment of the orator to a Roman emperor, though excessive and absurd when addressed to a sinful worm—that they who dared speak to him were ignorant of his greatness, and they who dared not were equally ignorant of his goodness—is a just and literal truth if applied to our meek and gracious Saviour. If we duly consider his greatness alone, it seems almost presumption in such creatures as we are to dare to take his holy name upon our polluted lips; but then, if we have a proportionate sense of his unbounded goodness and grace, every difficulty is overruled, and we feel a liberty of drawing near to him, though with reverence yet with the confidence of children when they speak to an affectionate parent.

A person may be meek, though in an elevated situation of life, but Jesus was also lowly. There was nothing in his external appearance to intimidate the poor and the miserable from coming to him. He was lowly or humble. Custom, which fixes the force and acceptance of words, will not readily allow us to speak of humility as applicable to the great God. Yet it is said: "He humbleth himself to behold the things that are in heaven, and in earth" (Psalm 113:6). Humility, in strictness of speech, is an attribute of magnanimity, an indifference to the little distinctions by which weak and vulgar minds are affected. In the view of the "high and holy One who inhabiteth eternity" (Isaiah 57:15), all distinctions that can obtain among creatures vanish, and He humbles Himself no less to notice the worship of an angel than [to see] the fall of a sparrow to the ground.

But we more usually express this idea by the term "condescension." Such was the mind that was in Christ (Philippians 2:5). It belonged to his dignity, as Lord of all, to look with an equal eye upon all his creatures. None could recommend themselves to Him by their rank, wealth or abilities [which are all] gifts of his own bounty. None were excluded from his regard by the want of those things which are in estimation among men. And to stain the pride of human glory He was pleased to assume a humble state. "Though he was rich, he made himself poor" (2 Corinthians 8:9) for the sake of those whom He came into the world to save. In this respect He teaches us by his example. "He took upon him the form of a servant" (Philippians 2:7), a poor and obscure man, to abase our pride, to cure us of selfishness, and to reconcile us to the cross.

The happy effect of his instructions upon those who receive them is rest to their souls. This has been spoken to before, but as it is repeated in the text I shall not entirely pass it over here. He gives rest to our souls by restoring us to our proper state of dependance upon God. [This is] a state of reconciliation and peace, and deliverance from guilt and fear. [It is] a state of subjection, for until our wills are duly subjected to the will of God we can have no rest. He accomplishes this by showing us the vanity of the world and thereby putting an end to our wearisome desires and pursuits after things uncertain, frequently unattainable [and] always unsatisfying, by a communication of sublimer pleasures and hopes than the present state of things can possibly afford, and lastly, by furnishing us with those aids, motives and encouragements which make our duty desirable, practicable and pleasant.

How truly then may it be said that "His yoke is easy and his burden light"!—such a burden, as wings are to a bird, raising the soul above the low and grovelling attachments to which it was once confined. They alone can rightly judge of the value of this rest who are capable of contrasting it with the distractions and miseries, remorse and forebodings of those who live without God in the world.

But we are all, by profession, his scholars. Ought we not seriously to enquire what we have actually learned from Him? Surely the proud, the haughty, the voluptuous and the worldly, though they have heard of his name and may have attended on his institutions, have not hitherto sat at his feet or drunk of his Spirit. It requires no long train of examination to determine whether you have entered into his rest or not or, if you have not yet attained it, whether you are seeking it in the ways of his appointment. It is a rest for the soul. It is a spiritual blessing, and therefore does not necessarily depend upon external circumstances. Without this rest, you would be restless and comfortless in a palace. If you have it, you may be at least comparatively happy in a dungeon. Today, if not before today, while it is called today, hear his voice. And while He says to you by his word, "Come unto me, and learn of me," let your hearts answer: "Behold we come unto thee, for thou art the Lord our God" (Jeremiah 3:22).

# *from the* Letters (1787)

## *Christian Character*

My Lord,

Without any preamble, I purpose now to wait on your lordship with a few thoughts on the meaning of that name which first obtained at Antioch—in other words, what it is to be a Christian. What are the effects which (making allowance for the unavoidable infirmities attending upon the present state of mortality) may be expected from a real experimental knowledge of the Gospel? I would not insinuate that none are Christians who do not come up to the character I would describe, for then I fear I should unchristian myself, but only to consider what the Scripture encourages us to aim at as the prize of our high calling in this life. It is generally allowed and lamented that we are too apt to live below our privileges, and to stop short of what the spirit and the promises of the Gospel point out to us as attainable.

Mr. Pope's admired line, "An honest man's the noblest work of God,"* may be admitted as a truth when rightly explained. A Christian is the noblest work of God in this visible world, and bears a much brighter impression of his glory and goodness than the sun in the firmament. And none but a Christian can be strictly and properly honest: all others are too much under the power of self to do universally to others as they would others should do unto them, and nothing but a uniform conduct upon this principle deserves the name of honesty.

The Christian is a new creature, born and taught from above. He has been convinced of his guilt and misery as a sinner, has fled for refuge to the hope set before him, has seen the Son and believed on Him. His natural prejudices against the glory and grace of God's salvation have been subdued and silenced by almighty power; he has accepted the Beloved and is made acceptable in Him. He now knows the Lord, has renounced the confused, distant, uncomfortable notions he once formed of God, and beholds Him in Christ, who is the way, the truth, and the

---

*From Alexander Pope (1688–1744), the great poet of Newton's day, in his *Essay on Man,* Epistle IV, line 248. For Pope, the "honest man" is essentially an enlightened latitudinarian. Newton's comment is a gentle but firm critique of "polite" humanism which was too optimistically and uncritically maintained by many of his contemporaries.

427

life—the only door by which we can enter to any true satisfying knowledge of God or communion with Him. But he sees God in Christ reconciled, a Father, Saviour and Friend who has freely forgiven him all his sins and given him the spirit of adoption. He is now no longer a servant—much less a stranger—but a son, and because a son, an heir already vested with all the promises, admitted to the throne of grace, and an assured expectant of eternal glory.

The Gospel is designed to give us not merely a possibility or a probability, but a certainty both of our acceptance and our perseverance, till death shall be swallowed up in life. And though many are sadly fluctuating and perplexed on this point (and perhaps all are so for a season) yet there are those who can say: "We know that we are of God." Therefore they are steadfast and unmoveable in his way, because they are confident that their labour shall not be in vain but that when they shall be absent from the body they shall be present with their Lord. This is the state of the advanced, experienced Christian who, being enabled to make his profession the chief business of his life, is strong in the Lord and in the power of his might. Everyone who has this hope in Christ "purifieth himself, even as He is pure."

I would now attempt a sketch of the Christian's temper, formed upon these principles and hopes, under the leading branches of its exercise respecting God, himself, and his fellow creatures.

The Christian's temper God-ward is evidenced by *humility*. He has received from Gethsemane and Golgotha such a sense of the evil of sin and of the holiness of God, combined with his matchless love to sinners, as has deeply penetrated his heart. He has an affecting remembrance of the state of rebellion and enmity in which he once lived against this holy and good God, and he has a quick perception of the defilements and defects which still debase his best services. His mouth is therefore stopped as to boasting: he is vile in his own eyes and is filled with wonder that the Lord should visit such a sinner with such a salvation. He sees so vast a disproportion between the obligations he is under to grace and the returns he makes that he is disposed—yea, constrained—to adopt the apostle's words without affectation, and to account himself less than the least of all saints. And knowing his own heart, while he sees only the outside of others he is not easily persuaded there can be a believer upon earth so faint, so unfruitful, so unworthy as himself.

Yet, though abased, he is not discouraged, for he enjoys peace. The dignity, offices, blood, righteousness, faithfulness and compassion of the Redeemer (in whom he rests, trusts, and lives) for wisdom, righteousness, sanctification and redemption are adequate to all his wants and wishes. They provide him with an answer to every objection, and give him no less confidence in God than if he were sinless as an angel, for he sees that though sin has abounded in him, grace has much more abounded in Jesus. With respect to the past, all things are become new; with respect to the present and future, he leans upon an almighty arm and relies upon the word and power which made and upholds the heavens and the earth. Though he feels himself unworthy of the smallest mercies, he claims and expects the greatest blessings that God can bestow; and being rooted and grounded in the knowledge and love of Christ, his peace abides and is not greatly affected either by the variation of his own experience or the changes of God's dispensations towards him while here.

With such a sense of himself—such a heartfelt peace and heavenly hope—how can his spirit but breathe love to his God and Saviour? It is indeed the perfection of his character and happiness that his soul is united by love to the chief good. The love of Christ is the joy of his heart and the spring of his obedience. With his Saviour's presence he finds a heaven begun upon earth, and without it all the other glories of the heavenly state would not content him. The excellence of Christ; his love to sinners, especially his dying love; the love shown toward himself in seeking and saving him when lost, saving him to the uttermost . . . but I must stop! Your lordship can better conceive than I can describe how and why Jesus is dear to the heart that knows Him.

That part of the Christian's life which is not employed in the active service of his Lord is chiefly spent in seeking and maintaining communion with him. For this he plies the throne, studies the word of grace, and frequents the ordinances where the Lord has promised to meet with his people. These are his golden hours, and when thus employed how poor and trivial does all that the world calls great and important appear in his eyes! Yea, he is solicitous to keep up an intercourse of heart with his Beloved in his busiest hours, and so far as he can succeed, it alleviates all his labours and sweetens all his troubles. And when he is neither communing with his Lord nor acting for Him, he accounts his time lost and is ashamed and grieved.

The truth of his love is manifested by submission. This is twofold and absolute, and without reserve in each. He submits to his revealed will as made known to him by precept and by his own example. He aims to tread in his Saviour's footsteps, and internalizes* all of his commandments, without exception and without hesitation. Again, he submits to his providential will: he yields to his sovereignty, acquiesces to his wisdom. He knows he has no right to complain of anything, because he is a sinner, and

---

*Newton's original phrase here, now unfortunately archaic, is "makes conscience of all his commandments"—which is much stronger than our equivalent.

he has no reason, because he is sure the Lord does all things well. There-fore his submission is not forced, but is an act of trust. He knows he is not more unworthy than he is unable to choose for himself, and therefore rejoices that the Lord has undertaken to manage for him. And were he compelled to make his own choice he could only choose that all his concerns should remain in that hand to which he has already committed them.

And thus he judges of public as well as of his personal affairs. He cannot be an unaffected spectator of national sins, nor without apprehen-sion of their deserved consequences. He feels and almost trembles for others, but he himself dwells under the shadow of the Almighty in a sanctuary that cannot be forced. Therefore, should he see the earth shaken and the mountains cast into the midst of the sea his heart would not be greatly moved, for God is his refuge. The Lord reigns. He sees his Sav-iour's hand directing every dark appearance and over-ruling all to the accomplishment of his own great purposes: this satisfies him, and though the winds and waves should be high he can venture his own little bark in the storm, for he has an infallible and almighty Pilot on board with him. And indeed, why should he fear when he has nothing to lose? His best concerns are safe, and other things he holds as gifts from the Lord, to whose call he is ready to resign them in whatever way He pleases, well knowing that creatures and instruments cannot of themselves touch a hair of his head without the Lord's permission, and that if He does permit them it must be for the best.

I might enlarge farther . . . but I shall proceed to consider the Chris-tian's attitude respecting himself. He lives in a godly and sober way. By sobriety we mean more than that he is not a drunkard. His attitude toward God, of course, shapes him to a moderation in all temporal things. He is not overly scrupulous or superstitious. He understands the liberty of the Gospel, that every creature of God is good if it be received with thanksgiving. He does not aim at being needlessly narrow nor practise self-devised austerities. The Christian is neither a stoic nor a cynic, yet he finds daily cause for watchfulness and restraint. Satan will not often tempt a believer to gross crimes; our greatest snares and sorest conflicts are usually found in things lawful in themselves but hurtful to us by their abuse, engrossing too much of our time or of our hearts, or somehow indisposing us for communion with the Lord. The Christian will be jealous of anything that might entangle his affections, dampen his zeal, or restrict him in his opportunities of serving his Saviour.

He is likewise content with his situation because the Lord chooses it for him; his spirit is not eager for additions and alterations in his circum-stances. If Divine Providence points out and leads to a change, he is ready to follow, though it should be what the world would call from better to worse, for he is a pilgrim and a stranger here, and a citizen of heaven. As people of fortune sometimes in travelling submit cheerfully to inconvenient accommodations very different from their homes, comforting themselves with thinking that they are not always to live so, so the Christian is not greatly solicitous about externals. If he has them, he will use them moderately. If he has but few of them, he can manage well enough without them: he is but upon a journey, and will soon be at home. If he be rich, experience confirms our Lord's words (Luke 12:15), and satisfies him that a large room, a crowd of servants and twenty dishes upon his table add nothing to the real happiness of life. Therefore he will not have his heart set upon such things. If he be in a humbler state, he is more disposed to pity than to envy those above him, for he judges they must have many encumbrances from which he is free. However, the will of God and the light of his countenance are the chief things the Christian, whether rich or poor, regards; and therefore his moderation is made known unto all men.

A third branch of the Christian's temperament respects his fellow creatures. And here, methinks, if I had not filled a sheet already, I could enlarge with pleasure. We have, in this degenerate day, among those who claim and are allowed the name of Christian, too many of a narrow, selfish, mercenary spirit. But in the beginning it was not so. The Gospel is designed to cure such a spirit, but gives no indulgence to it. A Christian has the mind of Christ, who went about doing good, who makes his sun to shine upon the good and the evil, and sendeth rain on the just and the unjust. His Lord's example forms him to the habit of diffusive benevolence; he breathes a spirit of good will to mankind and rejoices in every opportunity of being useful to the souls and bodies of others, without respect to parties or interests. He commiserates, and would, if possible, alleviate the miseries of all around him. If his actual services are restrained by want of ability, still all share in his sympathy and prayers. Acting in the spirit of his Master, he frequently meets with a measure of the like treatment, but if his good is requited with evil, he labours to overcome evil with good. He feels himself a sinner, and needs much forgiveness: this makes him ready to forgive. He is not haughty, captious, easily offended, or hard to be reconciled with, for at the feet of Jesus he has learned meekness. And when he meets with unkindness or injustice he considers that, though he has not deserved such things from men, they are instruments employed by his heavenly Father (from whom he has deserved to suffer much more) for his humiliation and chastisement, and he is therefore more concerned for their sins than for his own sufferings, and prays after the pattern of his Saviour: "Father, forgive them, for they know not what they do!" He knows he is fallible; therefore he cannot be self-assured. He knows he is frail, and therefore dares not be judgemental. As a member of society, he is just, punctual in the discharge of every relative duty, faithful to his engagements and promises, rendering to all their dues, obedient to lawful authority, and acting to all men according to the golden rule of doing as he would be done by. His conduct is simple, devoid of artifice, and consistent, attending to every branch of duty. In the closet, the family, the church, and in the transactions of common life, he is the same man, for in every circumstance he serves the Lord and aims to maintain a conscience void of offence in his sight. No small part of the beauty of his profession in the sight of men consists in the due government of his tongue. The law of truth and kindness and purity is upon his lips. He abhors lying and is so far from inventing a slander that he will not repeat a report to the disadvantage of his neighbour, however true, without evident necessity. He conversation is cheerful but inoffensive, and he will no more wound another with his wit (if he has a talent that way) than with a knife. His speech is with grace, seasoned with salt, and suited to promote the peace and edification of all around him.

Such is the Christian in civil life. But though he loves all mankind, he stands in nearer relation and bears an especial brotherly love to all who are partakers of the faith and hope of the Gospel. This regard is not confined within the pale of a denomination, but extended to all who love the Lord Jesus Christ in sincerity. He calls no man master himself, nor does he wish to impose a shibboleth of his own upon others. He rejoices in the image of God wherever he sees it, and in the work of God wherever it is carried on. Though tenacious of the truths which the Lord has taught him, his heart is open to those who differ from him in less essential points, and he allows to others that right of private judgement which he claims for himself. He is disposed to hold communion in love with all who acknowledge the Head. He cannot indeed countenance those who set aside the one foundation which God has laid in Zion and maintain errors derogatory to the honour of the Saviour or subversive of the faith and experience of his people, yet he wishes well to their persons, pities and prays for them, and is ready in meekness to instruct them that oppose. But there is no bitterness in his zeal, for he is aware that raillery and invective are dishonourable to the cause of truth and quite unsuitable in the mouth of a sinner, who owes all that distinguishes him from the vilest of men to the free grace of God. In a word, he is influenced by the wisdom from above which, as it is pure, is likewise peaceable, gentle and easy to be entreated, full of mercy and good works, without partiality and without hypocrisy.

I must just recur to my first point, and observe that with this spirit and deportment the Christian, while he is enabled to maintain a conscience void of offence towards God and man, is still aware and mindful of indwelling sin. He has his eye more upon this fact than upon his attainments, and therefore finds and confesses that in everything he comes exceedingly short, and that his best services are not only defective but defiled. He accounts himself an unprofitable servant, is abased in his own eyes, and derives all his hope and comfort as well as his strength from Jesus, whom he has known, received, and trusted, to whom he has committed his soul, in whom he rejoices and worships God in the spirit, renouncing all confidence in the flesh, and esteeming all things as loss for the excellency of the knowledge of Christ Jesus his Lord.

If I have lately been rather tardy in making my payments to his lordship, I have proportionately increased the quantity.* It is high time I should now relieve your patience. I hope I long to be a Christian indeed, and I hope this hasty exemplification of my wishes will answer to your lordship's experience better than I fear it does to my own. May I beg a remembrance in your prayers, that He who has given me to will and desire may work in me to be and to do according to his own good pleasure.

I am &c.

## God's Will and Our Ambitions

IT IS INDEED natural for us to wish and to plan, and it is merciful of the Lord to disappoint our plans and to cross our wishes. For we cannot be safe, much less happy, except in proportion as we are weaned from our own wills and made simply desirous of being directed by his guidance. This truth (when we are enlightened by his word) is sufficiently familiar to the judgement, but we seldom learn to reduce it into practice without being trained awhile in the school of disappointment. The schemes we form look so plausible and convenient that when they are broken we are ready to say: "What a pity!" We try again, and with no better success. We are grieved, and perhaps angry and plan out another, and so on. At length, in the course of time, experience and observation begin to con-

*Newton refers not to money, but rather to self-imposed "debts" of correspondence. This letter was written in September 1772 while he was still at Olney but being visited by all manner of people seeking spiritual counsel, among whom this nobleman was one, and with whom he then corresponded to continue this aspect of his pastoral work.

vince us that we are not more able than we are worthy to choose aright for ourselves. Then the Lord's invitation to cast our cares upon him and his promise to take care of us appear valuable; and when we have finished with planning, his plan in our favour gradually opens, and He does more and better for us than we could either ask or think.

I can hardly recollect a single plan of mine of which I have not since seen reason to be satisfied that had it taken place in season and circumstance just as I proposed it would, humanly speaking, have proved my ruin. Or at least it would have deprived me of the greater good the Lord had designed for me. We judge of things by their present appearances, but the Lord sees them in their consequences. If we could do so likewise, we should be perfectly of his mind, but as we cannot, it is an unspeakable mercy that He will manage for us, whether we are pleased with his management or not. And it is spoken of as one of his heaviest judgements when He gives any person or people up to the way of their own hearts and to walk after their own counsels.

Indeed, we may admire his patience towards us. If we were blind, and reduced to desire a person to lead us, and should yet pretend to dispute with him and direct him at every step, we should probably soon weary him, and provoke him to leave us to find the way by ourselves if we could. But our gracious Lord is long-suffering and full of compassion; He bears with our impertinence, yet He will take methods both to shame and to humble us, and to bring us to a confession that He is wiser than we. The great and unexpected benefit He intends us by all the discipline we meet with is to tread down our wills and bring them into subjection to his. So far as we attain to this we are out of the reach of disappointment, for when the will of God can please us we shall be pleased every day and from morning to night—I mean with respect to his dispensations.

O the happiness of such a life! I have an idea of it; I hope I am aiming at it, but surely I have not attained it. Self is active in my heart, if it does not absolutely reign there. I profess to believe that one thing is needful and sufficient, and yet my thoughts are prone to wander after a hundred more. If it be true that the light of his countenance is better than life, why am I solicitous about anything else? If He be all-sufficient and gives me more liberty to call Him mine, why do I go a-begging to creatures for help? If the smallest as well as the greatest events in which I am concerned are under his immediate direction, if the very hairs of my head are numbered, then my care (any further than a care to walk in the paths of his precepts and to follow the openings of his providence) must be useless and needless—yea indeed sinful and heathenish, burdensome to myself and dishonourable to my profession. Let us cast down the load we are unable to carry, and if the Lord be our shepherd, refer all and trust to

Him. Let us endeavour to live to Him and for Him today and be glad that tomorrow, with all that is behind it, is in his hands.

It is storied of Pompey that when his friends would have dissuaded him from putting to sea in a storm he answered, "It is necessary for me to sail, but it is not necessary for me to live."* O pompous speech, in Pompey's sense! He was full of the idea of his own importance, and would rather have died than have taken a step beneath his supposed dignity. But it may be accommodated with propriety to a believer's case. It becomes us to say: It is not necessary for me to be rich, or what the world accounts wise; to be healthy, or admired by my fellow worms; to pass through life in a state of prosperity and outward comfort. These things may be, or they may be otherwise, as the Lord in his wisdom shall appoint. But it is necessary for me to be humble and spiritual, to seek communion with God, to adorn my profession of the Gospel, and to yield submissively to his disposal in whatever way, whether of service or suffering, He shall be pleased to call me to glorify Him in the world. It is not necessary for me to live long, but highly expedient that whilst I do live I should live to Him. Here then I would find my desires, and here, having his word both for my rule and my warrant, I am secured from asking amiss. Let me have his presence and his Spirit, wisdom to know my calling, and opportunities and faithfulness to improve them; and as to the rest, Lord, help me to say: "What thou wilt, when thou wilt, and how thou wilt."

## The Sovereignty of God

MY LORD,
The first line of Horace's epistle to Augustus, when rightly applied, suggests a grand and cheering idea. As addressed by the poet, nothing can be more blasphemous, idolatrous, and absurd; but with what comfort and propriety may a Christian look up to Him to whom all power is committed in heaven and earth and say: *Cum tot sustineas et tanta negotia solus.*** Surely a more weighty and comprehensive sentence never dropped from an uninspired pen. And how beautifully and expressively is it closed by the word *solus!* The government is upon his shoulders; and though He is concealed by a veil of second causes from common eyes, so

---

*The life of Pompey, Roman consul and great enemy of Caesar, is thirty-second in the series written by Plutarch in his *Lives,* which was very popular in seventeenth- and eighteenth-century England and appeared in several translations.
**You alone uphold so many and great labors.

that they can perceive only the means, instruments, and contingencies, by which He works—and therefore think He does nothing—yet in reality He does *all,* according to his own counsel and pleasure, in the armies of heaven and among the inhabitants of the earth.

Who can enumerate the *tot et tanta negotia,** which are incessantly before his eye, adjusted by his wisdom, dependent on his will, and regulated by his power in his kingdoms of providence and grace? If we consider the heavens, the work of his fingers, the moon and the stars which He has ordained; if we call in the assistance of astronomers and glasses to help us in forming a conception of the number, distances, magnitudes, and motions of the heavenly bodies; the more we search, the more we shall be confirmed that these are but a portion of his ways. But He calls them all by their names, upholds them by his power, and without his continual energy they would rush into confusion, or sink into nothing.

If we speak of intelligences, He is the life, the joy, the sun of all that are capable of happiness. Whatever may be signified by the thrones, principalities, and powers in the world of light, they are all dependent upon his power and obedient to his command. It is equally true of angels as of men that without Him they can do nothing. The powers of darkness are likewise under his subjection and control. Though but little is said of them in Scripture, we read enough to assure us that their number must be immensely great, and that their strength, subtlety, and malice are such that we may tremble to think of them as our enemies, and probably should, but for our strange insensibility to whatever does not fall under the cognisance of our outward senses. But He holds them all in a chain, so that they can do or attempt nothing but by his permission; and whatever He permits them to do (though they mean nothing less) has its appointed subservience in accomplishing his designs.

But to come nearer home, and to speak of what seems more suited to our scanty apprehensions—still we may be lost in wonder. Before this blessed and only Potentate all the nations of the earth are but as the dust upon the balance and the small drop of a bucket, and might be thought (if compared with the immensity of his works) scarcely worthy of his notice. Yet here He presides, pervades, provides, protects, and rules. In Him his creatures live, move, and have their being. From Him is their food and preservation. The eyes of all are upon Him: what He gives they gather, and can gather no more; and at his word they sink into the dust. There is not a worm that crawls upon the ground, or a flower that grows in the pathless wilderness, or a shell upon the sea shore, but bears the impress of his wisdom, power, and goodness.

*So many and great labors.

With respect to men, He reigns with uncontrolled dominion over every kingdom, family, and individual. Here we may be astonished at his wisdom in employing free agents, the greater part of whom are his enemies, to accomplish his purposes. But however reluctant, they all serve Him. His patience likewise is wonderful. Multitudes, yea nearly our whole species, spend the life and strength which He affords them and abuse all the bounties He heaps upon them in the ways of sin. His commands are disregarded, his name blasphemed, his mercy disdained, his power defied, yet still He spares. It is an eminent part of his government to restrain the depravity of human nature and in various ways to check its effects which, if left to itself without his providential control, would presently make earth the very image of hell. For the vilest men are not suffered to perpetrate a thousandth part of the evil which their hearts would prompt them to. The earth, though lying in the [domain of the] Wicked One, is filled with the goodness of the Lord. He preserveth man and beast, sustains the young lion in the forest, feeds the birds of the air which have neither storehouse nor barn, and adorns the insects and the flowers of the field with a beauty and elegance beyond all that can be found in the courts of kings.

Still more wonderful is his administration in his kingdom of grace. He is present with all his creatures, but in a peculiar manner with his own people. All of these are monuments of a more illustrious display of power than that which spread abroad the heavens like a curtain and laid the foundations of the earth. For He finds them all in a state of rebellion and enmity, and makes them a willing people, and from the moment He reveals his love to them He espouses their cause and takes all their concerns into his own hands. He is near and attentive to every one of them, as if there was only that one. This high and lofty One who inhabits eternity, before whom the angels veil their faces condescends to hold communion with those whom men despise. . . .* He comforts them when in trouble, strengthens them when weak, makes their beds in sickness, revives them when fainting, upholds them when falling, and so seasonably and effectually manages for them that though they are persecuted and tempted, though their enemies are many and mighty, nothing that they feel or fear is able to separate them from his love.

And all this He does *solus*. All the abilities, powers, and instincts that are found amongst creatures are emanations from his fullness. All changes, successes, disappointments—all that is memorable in the annals

---

*The text here has a confused or misprinted sentence, which seems to be making the point that God is no respecter of persons—or, as we might say, no respecter of public image—and that he will readily bypass a sultan or czar on his way "to manifest Himself to a humble soul in a mud-walled cottage."

of history, all the risings and falls of empires, all the turns in human life—take place according to his plan. In vain men contrive and combine to accomplish their own counsels. Unless they are parts of his counsel likewise, the efforts of their utmost strength and wisdom are crossed and reversed by the feeblest and most unthought-of circumstances. But when He has a work to accomplish and his time is come, however inadequate and weak the means He employs may seem to a carnal eye, the success is infallibly secured: for all things serve Him, and are in his hands as clay in the hands of the potter. Great and marvellous are thy works, Lord God Almighty! Just and true are thy ways, thou King of saints!

This is the God whom we adore. This is He who invites us to lean upon his almighty arm, and promises to guide us with his unerring eye. He says to you, my lord, and even to me: "Fear not, I am with thee; be not dismayed, I am thy God; I will strengthen thee, yea I will help thee, yea I will uphold thee with the right hand of my righteousness." Therefore, while in the path of duty and following his call, we may cheerfully pass on regardless of apparent difficulties, for the Lord, whose we are, and who has taught us to make his glory our highest end, will go before us. And at his word crooked things become straight, light shines out of darkness, and mountains sink into plains. Faith may and must be exercised, experience must and will confirm what his word declares, that the heart is deceitful and that man in his best estate is vanity. But his promises to them that fear Him shall be confirmed likewise, and they shall find him in all situations a sun, a shield, and an exceeding great reward.

I have lost another of my people: a mother in our Israel—a person of much experience, eminent grace, wisdom and usefulness. She walked with God forty years. She was one of the Lord's poor, but her poverty was decent, sanctified, and honourable. She lived respected, and her death is considered as a public loss. It is a great loss to me. I shall miss her advice and example, by which I have been often edified and animated. But Jesus still lives. Almost her last words were, "The Lord is my portion, saith my soul."

I am, &c.

## Discerning Pastoral Vocation

DEAR SIR,
Your favour of the 19th February came to my hand yesterday. I have read it with attention, and very willingly sit down to offer you my thoughts. Your case reminds me of my own: my first desires towards the ministry

were attended with great uncertainties and difficulties, and the perplexity of my own mind was heightened by the various and opposite judgments of my friends. The advice I have to offer is the result of painful experience and exercise, and for this reason perhaps may not be unacceptable to you. I pray our gracious Lord to make it useful.

I was long distressed, as you are, about what was or was not a proper call to the ministry; it now seems to me an easy point to solve, but perhaps will not be so to you till the Lord shall make it clear to yourself in your own case. I have not room to say so much as I could. In brief, I think [a true call] principally includes three things.

1. [The first of these is] a warm and earnest desire to be employed in this service. I apprehend [that] the man who is once moved by the Spirit of God to this work will prefer it, if attainable, to hoards of gold and silver, so that, though at times intimidated by a sense of its importance and difficulty compared with his own great insufficiency (for it is to be presumed a call of this sort, if indeed from God, will be accompanied with humility and self-abasement), yet he cannot give it up. I hold it a good rule to inquire on this point whether the desire to preach is most fervent in our most lively and spiritual moments and [also] when we are most laid in the dust before the Lord. If so, it is a good sign. But if, as is sometimes the case, a person is very earnest to be a preacher to others when he finds but little hungerings and thirstings after grace in his own soul, it is then to be feared his zeal springs rather from a selfish principle than from the Spirit of God.

2. Besides this affectionate desire and readiness to preach, there must in due season appear some competent sufficiency as to gifts, knowledge and utterance. Surely, if the Lord sends a man to teach others He will furnish him with the means. I believe many have intended well in setting up to be preachers yet went beyond or before their call in so doing. The main difference between a minister and a private Christian seems to consist in these ministerial gifts which are imparted to him, not for his own sake, but for the edification of others. But then I say, these are to appear in due season; they are not to be expected instantaneously, but gradually, in the use of proper means. They are necessary for the discharge of the ministry, but not necessary as a prerequisite to legitimize our desire after it. In your case, you are young and have time before you; therefore I think you need not as yet perplex yourself with inquiring if you have these gifts already. It is sufficient if your desire is fixed, and you are willing in the way of prayer and diligence to wait upon the Lord for them. As yet you need them not.

3. That which finally evidences a proper call is a correspondent opening in providence by a gradual train of circumstances pointing out the

means, the times, [and] the place of actually entering upon the work. And till this coincidence arrives you must not expect to be always clear from hesitation in your own mind. The principal caution on this point is not to be too hasty in catching at first appearances. If it be the Lord's will to bring you into his ministry, He has already appointed your place and service; and though you know it not at present, you shall at a proper time. If you had the talents of an angel, you could do no good with them till his hour is come and till He leads you to the people whom He has determined to bless by your means.

It is very difficult to restrain ourselves within the bounds of prudence here, when our zeal is warm, a sense of the love of Christ upon our hearts, and a tender compassion for poor sinners is ready to prompt us to break out too soon. But he that believeth shall not make haste. I was about five years under this constraint: sometimes I thought I *must* preach, though it was in the streets. I listened to everything that seemed plausible and to many things that were not so. But the Lord graciously—as if oblivious [to my own wishes]—hedged up my way with thorns. Otherwise, if I had been left to my own spirit, I would have put it quite out of my power to have been brought into such a sphere of usefulness as He in his good time has been pleased to lead me to. And I can now see clearly that at the time I would first have gone out, though my intention was, I hope, good in the main, yet I over-rated myself and had not that spiritual judgment and experience which are requisite for so great a service.

I wish you therefore to take time; and if you have a desire to enter into the Established Church, endeavour to keep your zeal within moderate bounds and avoid everything that might unnecessarily clog your admission with difficulties. I would not have you hide your profession or to be backward to speak for God—but avoid what looks like 'preaching' and be content with being a learner in the school of Christ for some years. The delay will not be lost time; you will be so much the more acquainted with the gospel, with your own heart, and with human nature. This last is a necessary branch of a minister's knowledge, and can only be acquired by comparing what passes within us and around us with what we read in the word of God.

I am glad to find you have a distaste for Arminian and Antinomian doctrines—but let not the mistakes of others sit too heavy upon you. Be thankful for the grace that has made you to differ; be ready to give a reason of the hope that is in you with meekness and fear. But beware of engaging in disputes without evident necessity and some probable hope of usefulness. They tend to eat out the life and savour of religion and to make the soul lean and dry. Where God has begun a real work of grace, incidental mistakes will be lessened by time and experience; where He has not, it is of little signification what sentiments people hold, or whether they call themselves Arminians or Calvinists.

I agree with you, it is time enough for you to think of Oxford yet, and that if your purpose is fixed and all circumstances render it prudent and proper to devote yourself to the ministry you will do well to spend a year or two in private studies. It would be further helpful in this view to place yourself where there is gospel preaching and a lively people. If your favourable opinion of this place should induce you to come here, I shall be very ready to give you every assistance in my power. As I have trod exactly the path you seem to be setting out in, I might so far perhaps be more serviceable than those who are in other respects much better qualified to assist you. I doubt not but in this and every other step you will entreat the Lord's direction, and I hope you will not forget to pray for,

Sir, your affectionate friend, &c.

## On Spiritual Growth

The following letter, from Newton to Hannah More, was occasioned by her writing to him in 1787 of frustration in her attempt to advance spiritual growth by adopting a more meditative style of life. An excerpt from her own letter is here printed to provide a context:

. . . In this pretty quiet cottage, which I built myself two years ago, I have spent the summer. It is about ten miles from Bristol, on the Exeter road, has a great deal of very picturesque scenery about it, and is the most perfect little hermitage that can be conceived. The care of my garden gives me employment, health and spirits.

I want to know, dear sir, if it is peculiar to myself to form ideal plans of perfect virtue, and to dream all manner of imaginary goodness in untried circumstances, while one neglects the immediate duties of one's actual situation. Do I make myself understood? I have always fancied that if I could secure to myself such a quiet retreat as I have now really accomplished that I should be wonderfully good; that I should have leisure to store my mind with such and such maxims of wisdom; that I should be safe from such and such temptations; that, in short, my whole summers would be smooth periods of peace and goodness.

Now the misfortune is, I have actually found a great deal of the comfort I expected, but without any of the concomitant virtues. I am certainly happier here than in the agitation of the world, but I do not find that I am one bit better: with full leisure to rectify my heart and affections, the disposition unluckily does not come. I have the mortification to find that petty and (as they are called) innocent employments can detain my heart from heaven as much as tumultuous pleasures.

If to the pure all things are pure, the reverse must be also true when I can contrive to make so harmless an employment as the cultivation of flowers stand in the room of a vice, by the great portion of time I give up to it, and by the entire dominion it has over my mind. You will tell me that if the affections be estranged from their proper object it signifies not much whether a bunch of roses or a pack of cards effects it. I pass my life in intending to get the better of this, but life is passing away, and the reform never begins. It is a very significant saying, though a very old one, of one of the Puritans, that "hell is paved with good intentions." I sometimes tremble to think how large a square my procrastination alone may furnish to this tesselated pavement. . . .

I heartily commend myself to your prayers, and am, with the most cordial esteem, dear sir, your much obliged and faithful

H. MORE

MY DEAR MADAM,

It is high time to thank you for your favor of the first of November. Indeed I have been thinking so for two or three weeks past, and perhaps it is well for you that my engagements will not permit me to write when I please.

Your hermitage—my imagination went to work at that, and presently built one. I will not say positively as pretty as yours, but very pretty. It stood (indeed without a foundation) upon a southern declivity, fronting a woodland prospect, with an infant river, that is a brook, running between. Little thought was spent upon the house, but if I could describe the garden, the sequestred walks, and the beautiful colors with which the soil, the shrubs, and the thickets were painted, I think you would like the spot. But I awoke, and behold it was a dream! My dear friend William Cowper has hardly a stronger enthusiasm for rural scenery than myself, and my favorite turn was amply indulged during the sixteen years I lived at Olney. The noises which surround me in my present situation, of carriages and carts, and London cries, form a strong contrast to the sound of falling waters and the notes of thrushes and nightingales. But London, noisy and dirty as it is, is my post, and if not directly my choice, has a much more powerful recommendation; it was chosen for me by the wisdom and goodness of Him whose I trust I am, and whom it is my desire to serve. And therefore I am well satisfied with it. And if this busy imagination (always upon the wing) would go to sleep, I would not awaken her to build me hermitages; I want none.

The prospect of a numerous and attentive congregation, with which I am favored from the pulpit, exceeds all that the mountains and lakes of Westmoreland can afford; and their singing, when their eyes tell me their voices come from the heart, is more melodious in my ear than the sweet-est music of the woods. But were I not a servant, who has neither right nor reason to wish for himself, yet has the noblest wish he is capable of forming gratified, I say, were it not for my public services, and I were compelled to choose for myself, I would wish to live near your her-mitage, that I might sometimes have the pleasure of conversing with you and admiring your flowers and garden, provided I could likewise, at proper seasons, hear from others that joyful sound, which it is now the business, the happiness, and the honor of my life to proclaim myself.

What you are pleased to say, my dear Madam, of the state of your mind, I understand perfectly well; I praise God on your behalf, and I hope I shall earnestly pray for you. I have stood upon that ground myself. I see what you yet want to set you quite at ease, and though I cannot give it to you, I trust that He who has already taught you what to desire will, in his own best time, do everything for you, and in you, which is necessary to make you as happy as is compatible with the present state of infirmity and warfare. But He must be waited on, and waited for, to do this; and for our encouragement it is written as in golden letters over the gate of his mercy, "Ask, and ye shall receive; knock, and it shall be opened unto you."

We are apt to wonder that when what we accounted hindrances are removed, and the things which we conceived would be great advantages are put within our power, still there is a secret something in the way which proves itself to be independent of all external changes, because it is not affected by them. The disorder we complain of is internal, and in allusion to our Lord's words upon another occasion, I may say that it is not that which surrounds us, it is not anything in our outward situation (provided it is not actually unlawful) that can prevent or even retard our advances in spiritual life. We are defiled and impeded by that which is within. So far as our hearts are right, all places and circumstances which his wise and good providence allots us are nearly equal; their hindrances will prove helps, their losses gains, and their crosses will ripen into com-forts. But till we are so far apprised of the nature of our disease as to put ourselves into the hands of the great and only Physician, we shall find, like the woman in Luke 8:43, that every other effort for relief will leave us as it found us.

Our first thought, when we begin to be displeased with ourselves and aware that we have been wrong, is to attempt to reform, to be sorry for what is amiss, and to endeavor to amend. It seems reasonable to ask, what more can we do? But while we think we can do so much as this, we do not fully understand the design of the Gospel. This gracious message from God who knows our condition speaks home to our case. It treats us as sinners—as those who have already broken the original law of our nature, in departing from God our creator, supreme lawgiver and benefactor, and in having lived to ourselves instead of devoting all our time, talents and influence to his glory.

As sinners, the first things we need are pardon, reconciliation, and a principle of life and conduct entirely new. Till then we can have no more success or comfort from our endeavors than a man who should attempt to walk while his ankle was dislocated; the bone must be set before he can take a single step with safety, or attempt it without increasing his pain. For these purposes we are directed to Jesus Christ, as the wounded Israelites were to look at the brazen serpent (John 3:14, 15). When we understand what the Scripture teaches of the person, love and offices of Christ, the necessity and final causes of his humiliation unto death, and feel our own need of such a Saviour, we then know Him to be the light, the sun of the world, and of the soul, the source of all spiritual light, life, comfort, and influence, having access to God by Him, and receiving out of his fulness grace for grace.

Our perceptions of these things are for a time faint and indistinct, like the peep of dawn, but the dawning light, though faint, is the sure harbinger of approaching day (Proverbs 4:18). The full-grown oak that overtops the wood, spreads its branches wide, and has struck its roots to a proportionable depth and extent into the soil, arises from a little acorn; its daily growth, had it been daily watched from its appearance aboveground, would have been imperceptible, yet it was always upon the increase. It has known a variety of seasons, it has sustained many a storm, but in time it attained to maturity, and now is likely to stand for ages. The beginnings of spiritual life are small likewise in the true Christian; he likewise passes through a succession of various dispensations, but he advances, though silently and slowly, yet surely—and will stand forever.

At the same time it must be admitted that the Christian life is a warfare. Much within us and much without us must be resisted. In such a world as this, and with such a nature as ours, there will be a call for habitual self-denial. We must learn to cease from depending upon our own supposed wisdom, power, goodness, and from self-complacence and self-seeking, that we may rely upon Him whose wisdom and power are infinite.

It is time to relieve you. I shall therefore only add Mrs. Newton's affectionate respects. Commending you to the care and blessing of the Almighty, I remain, my dear Madam, with great sincerity, your affectionate and obliged servant,

JOHN NEWTON

# *from* Olney Hymns (1779)

## Zion, City of Our God

### Isa. xxxiii. 20, 21.

Glorious things of thee are spoken,
   Zion, city of our God!
He, whose word cannot be broken,
   Formed thee for his own abode:
On the Rock of Ages founded,
   What can shake thy sure repose?
With salvation's wall surrounded,
   Thou may'st smile at all thy foes.

See, the streams of living waters,
   Springing from eternal love,
Well supply thy sons and daughters,
   And all fears of want remove:
Who can faint while such a river
   Ever flows their thirst t'assuage?
Grace, which like the Lord, the giver,
   Never fails from age to age.

Round each habitation hovering,
   See the cloud and fire appear,
For a glory and a covering,
   Showing that the Lord is near.
Thus deriving from their banner
   Light by night, and shade by day,
Safe they feed upon the manna
   Which he gives them when they pray.

Blest inhabitants of Zion,
   Washed in the Redeemer's blood!
Jesus, whom their souls rely on,
   Makes them kings and priests to God.
'Tis his love his people raises
   Over self to reign as kings,
And as priests, his solemn praises
   Each for a thank-offering brings.

Saviour, if of Zion's city
  I through grace a member am,
Let the world deride or pity,
  I will glory in thy name.
Fading is the worldling's pleasure,
  All his boasted pomp and show;
Solid joys and lasting treasure
  None but Zion's children know.

# Looking at the Cross

In evil long I took delight,
  Unawed by shame or fear,
Till a new object struck my sight,
  And stopped my wild career.
I saw one hanging on a tree,
  In agonies and blood,
Who fixed his languid eyes on me,
  As near his cross I stood.

Sure, never till my latest breath
  Can I forget that look;
It seemed to charge me with his death,
  Though not a word he spoke.
My conscience felt and owned the guilt,
  And plunged me in despair;
I saw my sins his blood had spilt,
  And helped to nail him there.

Alas! I knew not what I did:
  But now my tears are vain;
Where shall my trembling soul be hid?
  For I the Lord have slain.
A second look he gave, which said,
  "I freely all forgive;
This blood is for thy ransom paid,
  I die that thou mayst live."

Thus while his death my sin displays
  In all its blackest hue;
Such is the mystery of grace,
  It seals my pardon too.
With pleasing grief and mournful joy
  My spirit now is filled,
That I should such a life destroy,
  Yet live by him I killed.

# Come, My Soul, thy Suit Prepare

"Ask what I shall give thee."
I Kings iii. 5.

Come, my soul, thy suit prepare;
Jesus loves to answer prayer;
He himself has bid thee pray,
Therefore will not say thee nay.

Thou art coming to a King,
Large petitions with thee bring;
For his grace and power are such
None can never ask too much.

With my burden I begin,
Lord, remove this load of sin!
Let thy blood, for sinners spilt,
Set my conscience free from guilt.

Lord! I come to thee for rest;
Take possession of my breast:
There thy blood-bought right maintain,
And without a rival reign.

As the image in the glass
Answers the beholder's face;
Thus unto my heart appear;
Print thine own resemblance there.

While I am a pilgrim here,
Let thy love my spirit cheer!
As my Guide, my Guard, my Friend,
Lead me to my journey's end.

Show me what I have to do,
Every hour my strength renew;
Let me live a life of faith,
Let me die thy people's death!

# The Effort

Approach, my soul, the mercy-seat,
  Where Jesus answers prayer;
There humbly fall before his feet,
  For none can perish there.

Thy promise is my only plea,
  With this I venture nigh;
Thou callest burdened souls to thee,
  And such, O Lord, am I.

Bowed down beneath a load of sin,
  By Satan sorely pressed;
By war without, and fears within,
  I come to thee for rest.

Be thou my shield and hiding-place!
  That, sheltered near thy side,
I may my fierce accuser face,
  And tell him thou hast died.

O wondrous love! to bleed and die,
  To bear the cross and shame,
That guilty sinners, such as I,
  Might plead thy gracious name.

"Poor tempest-tossed soul, be still,
  My promised grace receive":
'Tis Jesus speaks—I must, I will,
  I can, I do believe.

# The Name of Jesus

### CANT. i. 3.

How sweet the name of Jesus sounds
   In a believer's ear!
It soothes his sorrows, heals his wounds,
   And drives away his fear.

It makes the wounded spirit whole,
   And calms the troubled breast;
'Tis manna to the hungry soul,
   And to the weary, rest.

Dear name! the rock on which I build,
   My shield and hiding-place;
My never-failing treasury, filled
   With boundless stores of grace.

By thee my prayers acceptance gain,
   Although with sin defiled;
Satan accuses me in vain,
   And I am owned a child.

Jesus, my Shepherd, Husband, Friend,
   My Prophet, Priest, and King,
My Lord, my Life, my Way, my End,
   Accept the praise I bring.

Weak is the effort of my heart,
   And cold my warmest thought;
But when I see thee as thou art,
   I'll praise thee as I ought.

Till then, I would thy love proclaim
   With every fleeting breath;
And may the music of thy name
   Refresh my soul in death!

# Amazing Grace

Amazing grace! how sweet the sound
  That saved a wretch like me!
I once was lost, but now am found,
  Was blind, but now I see.

'Twas grace that taught my heart to fear,
  And grace my fears relieved;
How precious did that grace appear,
  The hour I first believed!

Through many dangers, toils and snares,
  I have already come;
'Tis grace has brought me safe thus far,
  And grace will lead me home.

The Lord has promised good to me,
  His word my hope secures;
He will my Shield and Portion be,
  As long as life endures.

Yes, when this flesh and heart shall fail,
  And mortal life shall cease;
I shall possess within the veil,
  A life of joy and peace.

There, joys unseen by mortal eyes,
  Or reason's feeble ray,
In ever-blooming prospects rise,
  Unconscious of decay.

Then now, on faith's sublimest wing,
  Let ardent wishes rise,
To those bright scenes, where pleasures spring
  Immortal in the skies.

# WILLIAM COWPER
1731 · 1800

From an engraving by H. B. Hall and Sons, representing Cowper as the recluse of
Olney.

## INTRODUCTION

William Cowper has sometimes been described as "the great poet of the evangelical revival." While strictly speaking, the judgment is extreme (Charles Wesley would seem to have for the movement a greater claim), it is certainly true that Cowper was the most famous and respected of evangelical poets in the latter part of the century. With the emergence of his second major collection of secular poetry in 1785, he was in fact regarded by his critical contemporaries as perhaps the greatest poet of his generation. His place in a volume of eighteenth-century spirituality owes, however, to work written well before this general fame was achieved; the story of how it came to be written offers, indeed, a fascinating insight into the spiritual history of the age.

Cowper's father was a priest in the Anglican church, himself the son of a notable judge, and a nephew of Earl Cowper, sometime lord chancellor of England. His mother, Ann Donne, who died in childbirth when Cowper was only six years of age, was a descendent of the family of John Donne, the seventeenth-century poet and dean of St. Paul's. William was the eldest of the only two children (of seven) to survive infancy. His family's position allowed him to be sent to Westminster School, where he was contemporary with Charles Churchill, the later to be impeached Warren Hastings, and Sir William Russell. In short, he had considerable early advantages. Yet these were not very well employed.

One of Cowper's early tutors was one Vincent Bourne, an easy-going layabout of whom Cowper writes:

> I love the memory of Vinny Bourne. He was so good natured, and so indolent, that I lost more than I got by him; for he made me as idle as himself. He was such a sloven, as if he had trusted to his genius as a cloak for everything that could disgust you in his person.[1]

The comment presages what was to become Cowper's besetting disposition—the idleness so common to the "advantaged" class of the period. He went on to study law at the Inner Temple, but there too he found birds of a feather with whom to flock, whiling away hours in the pubs, chop houses, and coffee houses instead of pursuing his preparation in law. As one of his biographers summarizes, "Cowper, throughout life, lacked personal initiative. He moved only in response to pressure from the outside."[2] This pattern, established so early, finally made him unable to respond well to *any* pressure. Perpetually aware as he was of unpreparedness, and haunted by guilt, he increasingly fled from any kind of responsibility. Thus, when a well-placed cousin offered him a political patronage appointment, he panicked at the prospect of the normal civil service examination. This precipitated three attempts at suicide, and a general nervous breakdown so severe that he was prevented from continuing in even the more modest position which he presently held. Just before Christmas of 1763, he was taken to a private madhouse supervised by Dr. Nathaniel Cotton at St. Albans.

As has often been pointed out, "Cowper's religious terrors were obviously the effect and not the cause of his madness."[3] Nevertheless, the form of his particular despair—an unshakeable conviction that he was eternally damned—made such a deep impression upon his agonized brain during the next five months that he was always in danger of relapsing toward its abyss, even after his conversion and return to the marginal emotional health he enjoyed thereafter. The conversion experience itself, influenced by his cousin, the Methodist preacher Martin Madan, is recorded in his own narrative printed here. What followed—a sheltered life very near the edge but surrounded by the care of Christian "neighbors"—deserves at least a brief outline.

Cowper's brother John, a teaching fellow of what is now Corpus Christi College, Cambridge, undertook to find him permanent lodgings "post-recovery" and settled him in Huntingdon, nearby. Unable to live within his income (a small allowance from his family), he was forced to become a boarder with the priest of a local parish, Morley Unwin, and his wife Mary, who had offered to relieve him. This for a time entailed taking in also the servant Cowper had insisted on bringing with him from Dr. Cotton's. Much of his time with the Unwins was devoted to attending church services (twice daily), singing hymns, and participating in family prayers and the reading and discussion of spiritual writers. He gave the story of his conversion to one of his relatives in 1766 (though it was not published until 1816) and talked loosely about becoming, himself, a priest—much to the alarm of some of those who had been supporting him.

When in the early summer of 1767 Rev. Unwin died after a fall from his horse, Cowper stayed on with Mrs. Unwin, who had become to him something of a second mother. Shortly thereafter both came under the pastoral eye of John Newton. They became friends, and Newton moved them to a house near his parish church in Olney, even employing Cowper as a kind of lay curate in his parish work. Cowper attended services constantly and took part in prayer meetings and in visiting the sick and dying. This was in some sense the first real "work" he had been exposed to, and he seems in the beginning to have responded to it very well, becoming much respected in the parish. When his own brother lay dying at Cambridge, he went off to spend the last months with him, and during this time the brother himself was converted. (Cowper wrote a pamphlet called "Adelphi" about this experience, though it was not to be published until Newton released it in 1802.)

There was no greater influence on the life of Cowper from this point than that of John Newton. He became Cowper's spiritual director and, though sometimes subsequently maligned as an excessively Calvinistic influence upon the poet, Newton was actually a gentle instrument of grace to him in a diversity of ways. After Cowper's abortive engagement to Mary Unwin in 1773, and another relapse into depression, he was persuaded to spend a night in the Newton house—and then could not be talked into leaving for more than a year. Besides giving him employment which brought him into amiable and useful contact with others, Newton also encouraged Cowper's first interest in expressing his faith in the composition of poems and hymns. One of the first of these, on the verge of another serious attack of depression, was the well-known "God Moves in a Mysterious Way." Almost all of Cowper's 68 *Olney Hymns* (published in 1779 with Newton's own 280) were composed between 1771 and 1773, during which time he was working closely with Newton. This was the real beginning of his poetic career; virtually everything that Cowper wrote of significance was composed after this time. Much of the work was read and editorially improved by Newton, and though Newton moved away to his London parish in 1780, he kept in regular contact with Cowper, always concerned for his emotional and spiritual health. In this sense, at least, the mature poetry of William Cowper was actually a foster child of John Newton's pastoral care.

After recovering from his depression, Cowper turned, in 1773, to gardening, small carpentry, and a much more systematic address to his writing as the necessary occupation he lacked. He was still supported by money from various relatives, and living still with Mrs. Unwin. A volume of his poems finally appeared in 1782. Though not well received in London (the *Critical Review* called it a "dull sermon in very indifferent verse"), Benjamin Franklin wrote from France to say that he liked it very much, and it was happily received by Hannah More, who was delighted to discover, as she put it, "a poet . . . [she] could read on Sunday."[4] A curious acquaintance of this period, Lady Austen, encouraged him to experiment in blank verse, which he did in his long poem, "The Task." This appeared with the humorous and very successful "John Gilpin" in 1785. One bookseller alone sold six thousand copies, and immediately Cowper was catapulted into fame. Almost as immediately, he was being asked about how soon his next book would appear. He undertook a translation of Homer—a conservative project and one that promised financial success. But the pressures on him were again too much; following a move to a "better house" in 1787, he had another bout of depression

456

lasting six months, during which time he tried to hang himself again. Mrs. Unwin accidentally entered his room and cut him down. Although his recovery was rapid, he lived from this time forward in relative emotional fragility. His *Homer* did not appear until 1791. He began but did not finish an edition of Milton, and much of the balance of his life was consumed in the mere management of necessity. His last original poem, written two years before his death, was "The Castaway"—a work which expresses as much spiritual uncertainty as his Olney Hymns express an experience of grace. Cowper thus remains an enigmatic and troubling figure in this period, at once a witness to the healing spirit of Christ in those who ministered to him and an example of the destructive psychological forces at work in the society in which he lived. In an age which looked for the well-wrought urn, he was in truth a broken vessel, yet it was given to him to compose some of the most telling spiritual poetry of the period and so become an instrument of grace—grace beyond the reach of art, and speaking a peace he was not himself fully able to know.

## NOTES

1. Quoted in Gilbert Thomas, *William Cowper and the Eighteenth Century* (London: Nicholson and Watson, 1935), p. 75. The eighteenth-century "disease" of idleness is well described by Samuel Johnson in his essay on that subject in the *Idler*, no. 31.

2. Thomas, p. 82.

3. See, for example, the *Dictionary of National Biography* article on Cowper, p. 396.

4. From the *Letters*, quoted in M. G. Jones, *Hannah More* (New York: Greenwood, 1968), p. 90. Cowper developed a comparably strong appreciation for More's writing, and a literary friendship of considerable mutual significance ensued.

# *from* Memoir of the Early Life of William Cowper, Esq. Written by Himself

In this vivid narrative, of which only an excerpt can be included here, Cowper describes his earliest memories, his unhappy, bullied years at Westminster School, his indolence during several years of unproductive study of law at the Inner Temple, and his resulting insecurity at being called to the bar in 1754. He then relates, in painful detail, the fits of depression which overtook him upon his conviction that he was not in fact qualified for the government position he had acquired by family influence and party patronage. The depression culminated in three unsuccessful attempts at suicide—one by an overdose of the drug laudanum, another a thwarted attempt to throw himself from a London bridge, and the third an attempted hanging in his room—followed in turn by loss of his job and a complete breakdown requiring his removal to a private hospital for the mentally ill. We pick up Cowper's story at a point just after his efforts at suicide.

MY SINS were now set in array against me and I began to see and feel that I had lived without God in the world. As I walked to an fro in my chamber, I said within myself, "There never was so abandoned a wretch, so great a sinner." All my worldly sorrows seemed as though they had never been, the terrors which succeeded them seeming so great and so much more afflicting. One moment I thought myself shut out from mercy by one chapter; the next, by another. The sword of the Spirit seemed to guard the tree of life from my touch, and to flame against me in every avenue by which I attempted to approach it. I particularly remember that the parable of the barren fig-tree was to me an inconceivable source of anguish; I applied it to myself with a strong persuasion in my mind that when the Saviour pronounced a curse upon it, He had me in his eye and pointed that curse directly at me.

I turned over all Archbishop Tillotson's sermons in hopes of finding one upon the subject, and consulted my brother upon the true meaning of it—desirous, if possible, to obtain a different interpretation of the matter than my evil conscience would suffer me to fasten on it. "O Lord, thou didst vex me with all thy storms, all thy billows went over me; thou didst run upon me like a giant in the night season, thou didst scare me with visions in the night season."

In every book I opened, I found something that struck me to the heart.

I remember taking up a volume of Beaumont and Fletcher,* which lay upon the table in my kinsman's lodgings, and the first sentence which I saw was this: "The justice of the gods is in it." My heart instantly replied, "It is a truth," and I cannot but observe that as I found something in every author to condemn me, so it was the first sentence, in general, I pitched upon. Everything preached to me, and everything preached the curse of the law.

I was now strongly tempted to use laudanum not as a poison but as an opiate to compose my spirits, to stupify my awakened and feeling mind which was harassed with sleepless nights and days of uninterrupted misery. But God forbad it, who would have nothing to interfere with the quickening work He had begun in me. Neither the lack of rest nor continued agony of mind could bring me to the use of it; I hated and abhorred the very smell of it.

I never went into the street but I thought the people stood and laughed at me and held me in contempt, and I could hardly persuade myself other than that the voice of my conscience was loud enough for everyone to hear it. They who knew me seemed to avoid me, and if they spoke to me seemed to do it in scorn. I bought a ballad of one who was singing it in the street because I thought it was written about me.

I dined alone, either at the tavern where I went in the dark or at the chop-house where I always took care to hide myself in the darkest corner of the room. I slept generally an hour in the evening, but it was only to be terrified in dreams. When I awoke it was some time before I could walk steadily through the passage into the dining room. I reeled and staggered like a drunk man. The eyes of man I could not bear, but when I thought that the eyes of God were upon me (which I felt assured of) it gave me the most intolerable anguish. If, for a moment, a book or a companion stole away my attention from myself, a flash from hell seemed to be thrown into my mind immediately, and I said within myself, "What are these things to me, who am damned?" In a word, I saw myself a sinner altogether, and every way a sinner, but I saw not yet a glimpse of the mercy of God in Jesus Christ.

The capital engine in all the artillery of Satan had not yet been employed against me; already overwhelmed with despair, I was not yet sunk into the bottom of the gulf. This was a fit season for the use of it, and accordingly I was set to inquire whether I had not been guilty of the unpardonable sin, and was presently persuaded that I had.

*Francis Beaumont and John Fletcher, late Elizabethan dramatists, whose plays had been revived and republished during the Restoration period.

A failure to respond to the mercies of God at Southampton, on the occasion above mentioned,* was represented to me as the sin against the Holy Ghost. No favorable construction of my conduct in that instance, no argument of my brother (who was now with me), nothing he could suggest in extenuation of my offences, could gain a moment's admission. Satan furnished me so readily with weapons against myself that neither scripture nor reason could undeceive me. Life appeared to me now preferable to death only because it was a barrier between me and everlasting burnings.

My thoughts in the day became still more gloomy, and my night visions more dreadful. One morning, as I lay between sleeping and waking, I seemed to myself to be walking in Westminster Abbey, waiting till prayers should begin. Presently I thought I heard the minister's voice, and hastened towards the choir. But just as I was upon the point of entering, the iron gate under the organ was flung in my face with a jar that made the Abbey ring; the noise awoke me, and a sentence of excommunication from all the churches upon earth could not have been so dreadful to me as the interpretation which I could not avoid putting upon this dream.

Another time I seemed to pronounce to myself, "Evil be thou my good." I verily thought that I had adopted that hellish sentiment, it seemed to come so directly from my heart. I rose from bed to look for my prayer book and having found it endeavored to pray, but immediately experienced the impossibility of drawing nigh to God unless He first drew nigh to us. I made many passionate attempts towards prayer, but failed in all.

Having an obscure notion about the efficacy of faith, I resolved upon an experiment to prove whether I had faith or not. For this purpose I resolved to repeat the Creed. When I came to the second statement of it** all traces of the former were struck out of my memory, nor could I recollect one syllable of the matter. While I endeavored to recover it, and when just upon the point, I perceived a sensation in my brain like a tremulous vibration in all the fibres of it. By this means, I lost the words in the very instant when I thought to have laid hold of them. This threw me into an agony, but growing a little calmer I made an attempt for the third time; here again I failed in the same manner as before.

---

*Earlier in the narrative, Cowper records that standing on a beach, weighted down with depression, he had been transformed in spirit by the sun suddenly breaking through, which he took at once to be a sign of God's mercy toward him. Later, however, he passed off this incident as nothing more than coincidence. Now he has begun to fear that this rejection of his initial response may have amounted to a deliberate refusal of grace.

**I.e., the section beginning, "And in one Lord Jesus Christ. . . ."

I considered it as a supernatural interposition to inform me that, having sinned against the Holy Ghost, I had no longer any interest in Christ or in the gifts of the Spirit. Being assured of this with the most rooted conviction, I gave myself up to despair. I felt a sense of burning in my heart like that of real fire, and concluded it was an earnest of those eternal flames which would soon receive me. I laid myself down howling with horror while my knees smote against each other.

In this condition my brother found me, and the first words I spoke to him were, "Oh, brother, I am damned! Think of eternity, and then think what it is to be damned!" I had, indeed, a sense of eternity impressed upon my mind, which seemed almost to amount to a full comprehension of it.

My brother, pierced to the heart with the sight of my misery, tried to comfort me, but all to no purpose. I refused comfort, and my mind appeared to me in such colors that to administer comfort to me was only to exasperate me and to mock my fears.

At length, I remembered my friend Martin Madan, and sent for him. I used to think him an enthusiast, but now seemed convinced that if there was any balm in Gilead, he must administer it to me. On former occasions, when my spiritual concerns had at any time occurred to me, I thought likewise on the necessity of repentance. I knew that many persons had spoken of shedding tears for sin, but when I asked myself whether the time would ever come when I should weep for mine, it seemed to me that a stone might sooner do it.

Not knowing that Christ was exalted to give repentance, I despaired of ever attaining it. My friend came to me; we sat on the bedside together and he began to declare to me the Gospel. He spoke of original sin, and the corruption of every man born into the world, whereby everyone is a child of wrath. I perceived something like hope dawning in my heart. This doctrine set me more on a level with the rest of mankind, and made my condition appear less desperate.

Next he insisted on the all-atoning efficacy of the blood of Jesus and his righteousness for our justification. While I heard this part of his discourse, and the scriptures upon which he founded it, my heart began to burn within me; my soul was pierced with a sense of my bitter ingratitude to so merciful a Saviour—and those tears which I thought impossible burst forth freely. I saw clearly that my case required such a remedy, and had not the least doubt within me but that this was the Gospel of salvation.

Lastly, he urged the necessity of a lively faith in Jesus Christ, not an assent only of the understanding but a faith of application, an actual laying hold of it and embracing it as a salvation wrought out for me personally. Here I failed, and deplored my want of such a faith. He told me it was the gift of God which he trusted He would bestow upon me. I could only

461

reply, "I wish He would"—a very irreverent petition, but a very sincere one, and such as the blessed God in his due time was pleased to answer.

My brother, finding that I had received consolation from Mr. Madan, was very anxious that I should take the earliest opportunity of conversing with him again, and for this purpose pressed me to go to him immediately. I was for putting it off, but my brother seemed impatient of delay and at length prevailed on me to set out. I mention this, to the honor of his candor and humanity, which would suffer no difference of sentiments to interfere with them. My welfare was his only object, and all prejudices fled before his zeal to procure it. May he receive, for his recompence, all that happiness the Gospel which I then first became acquainted with is alone able to impart.

Easier, indeed, I was, but far from easy. The wounded spirit within me was less in pain, but by no means healed. What I had experienced was but the beginning of sorrows, and a long train of still greater terrors was at hand. I slept my three hours well and then awoke with ten times a stronger alienation from God than ever. Satan plied me closely with horrible visions and more horrible voices. My ears rang with the sound of torments that seemed to await me. Then did the pains of hell get hold on me, and before daybreak the very sorrows of death encompassed me. A numbness seized upon the extremities of my body, and life seemed to retreat before it; my hands and feet became cold and stiff, a cold sweat stood upon my forehead, my heart seemed at every pulse to beat its last, and my soul to cling to my lips as if on the very brink of departure. No convicted criminal ever feared death more, or was more assured of dying.

At eleven o'clock, my brother called upon me, and in about an hour after his arrival that distemper of mind which I had so ardently wished for actually seized me.

While I traversed the apartment in the most horrible dismay of soul, expecting every moment that the earth would open her mouth and swallow me, my conscience scaring me, the avenger of blood pursuing me, and the city of refuge out of reach and out of sight, a strange and horrible darkness fell upon me. If it were possible that a heavy blow could light on the brain without touching the skull, such was the sensation I felt. I clapped my hand to my forehead and cried aloud through the pain it gave me. At every stroke, my thoughts and expressions became more wild and incoherent; all that remained clear was the sense of sin and the expectation of punishment. These kept undisturbed possession all through my illness without interruption or abatement.

My brother instantly observed the change, and consulted with my friends on the best manner to dispose of me. It was agreed among them that I should be carried to St. Alban's, where Dr. Cotton kept a house for the reception of such patients and with whom I was known to have a slight acquaintance. Not only his skill as a physician recommended him to their choice but his well-known humanity and sweetness of temperament. It will be proper to draw a veil over the secrets of my prison-house; let it suffice to say that the low state of body and mind to which I was reduced was perfectly well calculated to humble the natural vainglory and pride of my heart.

These are the efficacious means which Infinite Wisdom thought meet to make use of for that purpose. A sense of self-loathing and abhorrence ran through all my insanity. Conviction of sin, and expectation of instant judgement never left me from the 7th of December, 1763, until the middle of the July following. The accuser of the brethren was ever busy with me night and day, bringing to my recollection in dreams the commission of long-forgotten sins and charging upon my conscience things of an indifferent nature as atrocious crimes.

All that passed in this long interval of eight months may be classed under two headings, conviction of sin and despair of mercy. But, blessed be the God of my salvation for every sigh I drew, for every tear I shed, since it pleased Him thus to judge me here that I might not be judged hereafter.

After five months of continual expectation that the divine vengeance would plunge me into the bottomless pit, I became so familiar with despair as to have contracted a sort of hardiness and indifference as to the event. I began to persuade myself that while the execution of the sentence was suspended, it would be in my interest to indulge a less horrible train of ideas than I had been accustomed to muse upon. "Eat and drink, for tomorrow thou shalt be in hell" was the maxim on which I proceeded. By this means, I entered into conversation with the Doctor, laughed at his stories and told him some of my own to match them, still, however, carrying a sentence of irrevocable doom in my heart.

He observed the seeming alteration with pleasure. Believing, as well he might, that my smiles were sincere, he thought my recovery well nigh completed. But these were, in reality, like the green surface of a morass, pleasant to the eye but a cover for nothing but rottenness and filth. The only thing that could promote and effectuate my cure was yet wanting— an experimental knowledge of the redemption which is in Christ Jesus.

I remember, about this time, a diabolical species of regret that found harbor in my wretched heart. I was sincerely sorry that I had not seized every opportunity of giving scope to my wicked appetites, and even envied those who, being departed to their own place before me, had the consolation to reflect that they had well earned their miserable inheritance by indulging their sensuality without restraint. Oh, merciful God! What a tophet of pollution is the human soul and wherein do we differ from the devils, unless thy grace prevent us!

In about three months more (July 25, 1764), my brother came from Cambridge to visit me. Dr. C. having told him that he thought me greatly amended, he was rather disappointed at finding me almost as silent and reserved as ever, for the first sight of him struck me with many painful sensations both of sorrow for my own remediless condition and envy of his happiness.

As soon as we were left alone, he asked me how I found myself. I answered, "as much better as despair can make me." We went together into the garden. Here, on expressing a settled assurance of sudden judgement, he protested to me that it was all a delusion, and protested so strongly that I could not help giving some attention to him. I burst into tears and cried out, "if it be a delusion, then am I the happiest of beings." Something like a ray of hope was shot into my heart, but still I was afraid to indulge it. We dined together and I spent the afternoon in a more cheerful manner. Something seemed to whisper to me every moment, "still there is mercy."

Even after he left me, this change of sentiment gathered ground continually, yet my mind was in such a fluctuating state that I can only call it a vague presage of better things at hand, without being able to assign a reason for it. The servant observed a sudden alteration in me for the better, and the man, whom I have ever since retained in my service, expressed great joy on the occasion.

I went to bed and slept well. In the morning, I dreamed that the sweetest boy I ever saw came dancing up to my bedside; he seemed just out of leading-strings, yet I took particular notice of the firmness and steadiness of his tread. The sight affected me with pleasure, and served at least to harmonize my spirits so that I awoke for the first time with a sensation of delight on my mind. Still, however, I knew not where to look for the establishment of the comfort I felt; my joy was as much a mystery to myself as to those about me. The blessed God was preparing me for the clearer light of his countenance by this first dawning of that light upon me.

Within a few days of my first arrival at St. Alban's, I had thrown aside the Word of God, as a book in which I had no longer any interest or portion. The only instance in which I can recollect reading a single chapter was about two months before my recovery. Having found a Bible on the bench in the garden,* I opened upon the 11th of St. John, where

---

*This passage evokes the powerful parallel of St. Augustine's conversion, described in Book 8 of his *Confessions,* where he too comes upon a Bible on a bench in a garden, picks it up and recognizes that the work of redemption in Christ applies to him.

Lazarus is raised from the dead, and saw so much benevolence, mercy, goodness and sympathy with miserable man in our Saviour's conduct that I almost shed tears even after the relation, little thinking that it was an exact type of the mercy which Jesus was on the point of extending towards myself. I sighed, and said, "Oh that I had not rejected so good a Redeemer, that I had not forfeited all his favors!" Thus was my heart softened, though not yet enlightened. I closed the book, without intending to open it again.

Having risen with somewhat of a more cheerful feeling, I repaired to my room, where breakfast waited for me. While I sat at table, I found the cloud of horror which had so long hung over me was every moment passing away, and every moment came fraught with hope. I was continually more and more persuaded that I was not utterly doomed to destruction. The way of salvation was still, however, hid from my eyes, nor did I see it at all clearer than before my illness. I only thought that if it would please God to spare me, I would lead a better life, and that I would yet escape hell if a religious observance of my duty would secure me from it.

Thus may the terror of the Lord make a Pharisee, but only the sweet voice of mercy in the Gospel can make a Christian.

But the happy period which was to shake off my fetters and afford me a clear opening of the free mercy of God in Christ Jesus was now arrived. I flung myself into a chair near the window and, seeing a Bible there, ventured once more to apply to it for comfort and instruction. The first verse I saw was the 25th of the third chapter of Romans: "Whom God hath set forth to be a propitiation through faith in his blood, to declare his righteousness for the remission of sins that are past, through the forbearance of God."

Immediately I received strength to believe it, and the full beams of the Sun of Righteousness shone upon me. I saw the sufficiency of the atonement He had made, my pardon sealed in his blood, and all the fullness and completeness of his justification. In a moment I believed, and received the Gospel. Whatever my friend Madan had said to me long before revived in all its clearness, with demonstration of the Spirit and with power. Unless the Almighty arm had been under me, I think I should have died with gratitude and joy. My eyes filled with tears, and my voice choked with transport, I could only look up to heaven in silent fear, overwhelmed with love and wonder. But the work of the Holy Ghost is best described in his own words; it is "joy unspeakable, and full of glory." Thus was my heavenly Father in Christ Jesus pleased to give me the full assurance of faith, and out of a strong, stony, unbelieving heart, to raise up a child unto Abraham. How glad should I now have been to have spent every moment in prayer and thanksgiving!

I lost no opportunity of repairing to a throne of grace, but flew to it with an earnestness irresistible and never to be satisfied. Could I help it? Could I do otherwise than love and rejoice in my reconciled Father in Christ Jesus? The Lord had enlarged my heart, and I ran in the way of his commandments. For many succeeding weeks, tears were ready to flow if I did but speak of the Gospel or mention the name of Jesus. To rejoice day and night was all my employment. Too happy to sleep much, I thought it was but lost time that was spent in slumber. Oh that the ardor of my first love had continued! But I have known many a lifeless and unhallowed hour since, long intervals of darkness interrupted by short returns of peace and joy in believing.

My physician, ever watchful and apprehensive for my welfare, was now alarmed lest the sudden transition from despair to joy should terminate in a fatal frenzy. But "the Lord was my strength and my song, and was become my salvation." I said, "I shall not die, but live, and declare the works of the Lord; he has chastened me sore, but not given me over unto death. O give thanks unto the Lord, for his mercy endureth forever."

In a short time, Dr. C. became satisfied, and acquiesced in the soundness of my cure, and much sweet communion I had with him concerning the things of our salvation. He visited me every morning while I stayed with him, which was nearly twelve months after my recovery, and the Gospel was the delightful theme of our conversation.

No trial has befallen me since except what might be expected in a state of warfare. Satan, indeed, has changed his battery. Before my conversion, sensual gratification was the weapon with which he sought to destroy me. Being naturally of an easy, quiet disposition, I was seldom tempted to anger; yet it is that passion which now gives me the most disturbance, and occasions the sharpest conflicts. But Jesus being my strength, I fight against it, and if I am not conqueror, yet I am not overcome. . . .

# *from* Olney Hymns (1779)

## Praise for the Fountain Opened

ZECHARIAH 13:1

There is a fountain fill'd with blood
   Drawn from EMMANUEL's veins;
And sinners, plung'd beneath that flood,
   Lose all their guilty stains.

The dying thief rejoic'd to see
   That fountain in his day;
And there have I, as vile as he,
   Wash'd all my sins away.

Dear dying Lamb, thy precious blood
   Shall never lose its pow'r;
Till all the ransom'd church of GOD
   Be sav'd, to sin no more.

E'er since, by faith, I saw the stream
   Thy flowing wounds supply;
Redeeming love has been my theme,
   And shall be till I die.

Then in a nobler sweeter song
   I'll sing thy power to save;
When this poor lisping stammering tongue
   Lies silent in the grave.

LORD, I believe thou hast prepar'd
   (Unworthy tho' I be)
For me a blood-bought free reward,
   A golden harp for me!

'Tis strung, and tun'd, for endless years,
   And form'd by pow'r divine;
To sound in GOD the Father's ears,
   No other name but thine.

# Walking with God

GENESIS 5:24

Oh! for a closer walk with GOD,
    A calm and heav'nly frame;
A light to shine upon the road
    That leads me to the Lamb!

Where is the blessedness I knew
    When first I saw the LORD?
Where is the soul-refreshing view
    Of JESUS, and his word?

What peaceful hours I once enjoy'd!
    How sweet their mem'ry still!
But they have left an aching void,
    The world can never fill.

Return, O holy Dove, return,
    Sweet messenger of rest;
I hate the sins that made thee mourn,
    And drove thee from my breast.

The dearest idol I have known,
    Whate'er that idol be;
Help me to tear it from thy throne,
    And worship only thee.

So shall my walk be close with GOD,
    Calm and serene my frame;
So purer light shall mark the road
    That leads me to the Lamb.

# The Covenant

EZEKIEL 36:25–28

The LORD proclaims his grace abroad!
Behold, I change your hearts of stone;
Each shall renounce his idol god,
And serve, henceforth, the LORD alone.

My grace, a flowing stream, proceeds
To wash your filthiness away;
Ye shall abhor your former deeds,
And learn my statutes to obey.

My truth the great design insures,
I give myself away to you;
You shall be mine, I will be yours,
Your GOD unalterably true.

Yet not unsought, or unimplor'd,
The plenteous grace shall I confer;
No—your whole hearts shall seek the LORD,
I'll put a praying spirit there.

From the first breath of life divine,
Down to the last expiring hour;
The gracious work shall all be mine,
Begun and ended in my pow'r.

# The Sower

MATTHEW 13:3

Ye sons of earth prepare the plough,
    Break up your fallow ground!
The Sower is gone forth to sow,
    And scatter blessings round.

The seed that finds a stony soil,
    Shoots forth a hasty blade;
But ill repays the sower's toil,
    Soon wither'd, scorch'd, and dead.

The thorny ground is sure to baulk
    All hopes of harvest there;
We find a tall and sickly stalk,
    But not the fruitful ear.

The beaten path and high-way side
    Receive the trust in vain;
The watchful birds the spoil divide,
    And pick up all the grain.

But where the LORD of grace and pow'r
    Has bless'd the happy field;
How plenteous is the golden store
    The deep-wrought furrows yield!

Father of mercies, we have need
    Of thy preparing grace;
Let the same hand that gives the seed,
    Provide a fruitful place!

# The Light and Glory of the Word

The Spirit breathes upon the word,
    And brings the truth to sight;
Precepts and promises afford
    A sanctifying light.

A glory gilds the sacred page,
    Majestic like the sun;
It gives a light to ev'ry age,
    It gives, but borrows none.

The hand that gave it, still supplies
    The gracious light and heat;
His truths upon the nations rise,
    They rise, but never set.

Let everlasting thanks be thine!
    For such a bright display,
As makes a world of darkness shine
    With beams of heav'nly day.

My soul rejoices to pursue
    The steps of him I love;
Till glory breaks upon my view
    In brighter worlds above.

# Jehovah-Rophi: I Am the Lord that Healeth Thee

EXODUS 15

Heal us, EMMANUEL, here we are,
    Waiting to feel thy touch;
Deep-wounded souls to thee repair,
    And, Saviour, we are such.

Our faith is feeble, we confess,
    We faintly trust thy word;
But wilt thou pity us the less?
    Be that far from thee, LORD!

Remember him who once apply'd
    With trembling for relief;
"Lord, I believe," with tears he cry'd,
    "O help my unbelief."

She too, who touch'd thee in the press,
    And healing virtue stole,
Was answer'd, "Daughter, go in peace,
    Thy faith hath made thee whole."

Conceal'd amid the gath'ring throng,
    She would have shunn'd thy view;
And if her faith was firm and strong,
    Had strong misgivings too.

Like her, with hopes and fears, we come,
    To touch thee if we may;
Oh! send us not despairing home,
    Send none unheal'd away.

# Jehovah-Nissi: The Lord My Banner

EXODUS 17:15

By whom was David taught,
    To aim the deadly blow,
When he Goliath fought,
    And laid the Gittite low?
Nor sword nor spear the stripling took,
But chose a pebble from the brook.

'Twas Israel's GOD and King,
    Who sent him to the fight;
Who gave him strength to sling,
    And skill to aim aright.
Ye feeble saints, your strength endures,
Because young David's GOD is yours.

Who order'd Gideon forth,
    To storm th' invaders' camp,
With arms of little worth,
    A pitcher and a lamp?
The trumpets made his coming known,
And all the host was overthrown.

Oh! I have seen the day,
    When with a single word,
GOD helping me to say,
    My trust is in the LORD;
My soul has quell'd a thousand foes,
Fearless of all that could oppose.

But unbelief, self-will,
    Self-righteousness and pride,
How often do they steal,
    My weapon from my side?
Yet David's LORD, and Gideon's friend,
Will help his servant to the end.

# Jehovah Our Righteousness

JEREMIAH 23:6

My GOD, how perfect are thy ways!
　　But mine polluted are;
Sin twines itself about my praise,
　　And slides into my pray'r.

When I would speak what thou hast done
　　To save me from my sin,
I cannot make thy mercies known
　　But self-applause creeps in.

Divine desire, that holy flame
　　Thy grace creates in me;
Alas! impatience is its name,
　　When it returns to thee.

This heart, a fountain of vile thoughts,
　　How does it overflow?
While self upon the surface floats
　　Still bubbling from below.

Let others in the gaudy dress
　　Of fancied merit shine;
The LORD shall be my righteousness;
　　The LORD for ever mine.

# Jehovah-Jesus

My song shall bless the LORD of all,
My praise shall climb to his abode;
Thee, Saviour, by that name I call,
The great Supreme, the mighty GOD.

Without beginning, or decline,
Object of faith, and not of sense;
Eternal ages saw him shine,
He shines eternal ages hence.

As much, when in the manger laid,
Almighty ruler of the sky;
As when the six days' works he made
Fill'd all the morning-stars with joy.

Of all the crowns JEHOVAH bears,
Salvation is his dearest claim;
That gracious sound well-pleas'd he hears,
And owns EMMANUEL for his name.

A cheerful confidence I feel,
My well-plac'd hopes with joy I see;
My bosom glows with heav'nly zeal,
To worship him who died for me.

As man, he pities my complaint,
His pow'r and truth are all divine;
He will not fail, he cannot faint,
Salvation's sure, and must be mine.

# Jehovah-Shalom: The Lord Send Peace

JUDGES 6:24

JESUS, whose blood so freely stream'd
To satisfy the law's demand;
By thee from guilt and wrath redeem'd,
Before the Father's face I stand.

To reconcile offending man,
Make Justice drop her angry rod;
What creature could have form'd the plan,
Or who fulfil it but a GOD?

No drop remains of all the curse,
For wretches who deserv'd the whole;
No arrows dipt in wrath to pierce
The guilty, but returning soul.

Peace by such means so dearly bought,
What rebel could have hop'd to see?
Peace, by his injur'd sovereign wrought,
His Sov'reign fast'ned to a tree.

Now, LORD, thy feeble worm prepare!
For strife with earth and hell begins;
Confirm and gird me for the war;
They hate the soul that hates his sins.

Let them in horrid league agree!
They may assault, they may distress;
But cannot quench thy love to me,
Nor rob me of the LORD my peace.

# Wisdom

### PROVERBS 8:22–31

Ere GOD had built the mountains,
  Or rais'd the fruitful hills;
Before he fill'd the fountains
  That feed the running rills;
In me, from everlasting,
  The wonderful I AM
Found pleasures never wasting,
  And Wisdom is my name.

When, like a tent to dwell in,
  He spread the skies abroad;
And swath'd about the swelling
  Of ocean's mighty flood;
He wrought by weight and measure,
  And I was with him then;
Myself the Father's pleasure,
  And mine, the sons of men.

Thus wisdom's words discover
  Thy glory and thy grace,
Thou everlasting lover
  Of our unworthy race!
Thy gracious eye survey'd us
  Ere stars were seen above;
In wisdom thou hast made us,
  And died for us in love.

And couldst thou be delighted
  With creatures such as we!
Who when we saw thee, slighted
  And nail'd thee to a tree?
Unfathomable wonder,
  And mystery divine!
The Voice that speaks in thunder,
  Says, "Sinner I am thine!"

# God Moves in a Mysterious Way

GOD moves in a mysterious way,
   His wonders to perform;
He plants his footsteps in the sea,
   And rides upon the storm.

Deep in unfathomable mines
   Of never failing skill;
He treasures up his bright designs,
   And works his sovereign will.

Ye fearful saints fresh courage take,
   The clouds ye so much dread
Are big with mercy, and shall break
   In blessings on your head.

Judge not the LORD by feeble sense,
   But trust him for his grace;
Behind a frowning providence,
   He hides a smiling face.

His purposes will ripen fast,
   Unfolding ev'ry hour;
The bud may have a bitter taste,
   But sweet will be the flow'r.

Blind unbelief is sure to err,
   And scan his work in vain;
GOD is his own interpreter,
   And he will make it plain.

# Joy and Peace in Believing

Sometimes a light surprizes
  The Christian while he sings;
It is the LORD who rises
  With healing in his wings:
When comforts are declining,
  He grants the soul again
A season of clear shining
  To cheer it after rain.

In holy contemplation,
  We sweetly then pursue
The theme of GOD's salvation,
  And find it ever new:
Set free from present sorrow,
  We cheerfully can say,
E'en let th' unknown to-morrow*,
  Bring with it what it may.

It can bring with it nothing
  But he will bear us thro';
Who gives the lilies clothing
  Will clothe his people too:
Beneath the spreading heavens,
  No creature but is fed;
And he who feeds the ravens,
  Will give his children bread.

Though vine, nor fig-tree neither**,
  Their wonted fruit should bear,
Tho' all the fields should wither,
  Nor flocks, nor herds, be there:
Yet GOD the same abiding,
  His praise shall tune my voice;
For while in him confiding,
  I cannot but rejoice.

*Matt. 6:34.
**Hab. 3:17, 18

# HANNAH MORE
## 1745 · 1833

From an engraving by Heath of the painting done by John Opie for Mrs. Boscawen (1786).

# INTRODUCTION

Hannah More would have been remarkable in any century. She was, in late eighteenth-century England, an outstanding woman of her time. A close friend of Dr. Johnson, the great literary man and lexicographer, Sir Edmund Burke the philosopher, Sir Joshua Reynolds the painter, and David Garrick the Shakespearean actor, she was a part of London's artistic elite during the decade of the American Revolution. In the next decade, following a personal deepening of spiritual interest, she came to know John Newton, Bishops Horne and Porteous, and became a friend and coworker with William Wilberforce. She also worked with Zachary Macaulay and other well-known leaders of the Clapham Society—an evangelical group dedicated to social and political reform. Especially through these later associations—which lasted the remainder of her life—she became a leading educational reformer.

More was born near Bristol, the fourth of five daughters, to a schoolteacher, Jacob More, and his wife Mary.[1] A precocious child, she had before the age of four taught herself to read by listening in on her older sister's lessons. Her nanny had been nurse to the poet laureate John Dryden in his last illness, and Hannah acquired contemporary literary stories from her even as she was having her father read her classical history and biographies from Plutarch. She learned Latin and mathematics from her father, French by conversation with French officers on parole in the neighborhood, and by the age of twelve or thirteen had acquired Italian and Spanish also. About 1757, her oldest sister, then not quite twenty-one, set up a boarding school in Trinity Street, Bristol, where all the sisters came to study, assist, and live. It was so successful that after a few years they were able to build another and better house for themselves in Park Street, as well as one for their (probably dazed but undoubtedly grateful) father at Stony Hill, a little ways off.

From her earliest childhood, Hannah More wrote short fiction and plays. One of these works, a drama called "A Search for Happiness," was published in 1762 (when she was seventeen). She also wrote poems, in one of which she praised the beauty of a neighboring estate. The owner was so entranced with the compliment that he painted excerpts on boards and hung them from trees on his "spacious lawns," and proceeded, he fancied, to fall in love with the poet. It was thus that at the age of twenty-two, Hannah unexpectedly received a proposal of marriage from a man more than twenty years her senior. She accepted. But the gentleman in question, a William Turner, then apparently began to have qualms. He dithered, postponed, broke the engagement twice, and finally after six years literally left her at the altar, sending a note by his groomsman. Since Hannah had long since relinquished her share in the Bristol school in anticipation of the marriage, the blow was devastating in more ways than one. Turner offered an indemnity of £200 per year, which she adamantly refused to accept. Nonetheless, a friendly minister who was also a neighbor, James Stonehouse, arranged to receive the money and invest it until some years later, when Hannah was persuaded to accept it. The old suitor apparently continued to admire her, visited frequently, and even left her an additional £1,000 at his death.

Although there were other offers of marriage, including one from the poet John Langhorne, Hannah resolved never to entertain another suitor, but immediately set out upon a literary career.

She sent off, first, one of her teenage plays to a publisher. "The Inflexible Captive" appeared in 1774, and was successfully performed the next year at Exeter and Bath. She herself, meanwhile, was off to London with two of her sisters. Within a few months she had become an important figure among London's literary elite. She made an immediate impression upon the great actor Garrick and became one of Dr. Johnson's favorites. She circulated, to great acclaim, her clever poem *"Bas Bleu,"* which describes the famous "bluestocking clubs," an answer of literary women to the exclusively masculine preserve of the London coffee houses. She had already become a popular member, and out of this new base she published a long poem, "Sir Eldred of the Bower" (1776), for which she was able to obtain from the publisher the rather handsome sum of forty guineas (more than the annual salary of most English parsons) on the basis of equal pay for equal work; Oliver Goldsmith had received that amount for his extremely popular "Deserted Village," and she would take not a penny less, thank you very much. By this time she was living with her closest friends, Mr. and Mrs. Garrick, and writing her tragedy "Percy," which opened at Covent Garden on December 10, 1777, and ran for twenty-one nights. Four thousand copies of the text were sold in two weeks: she was a major success.

The next major turning point in her life came when Garrick died. Hannah stayed on more or less permanently with Mrs. Garrick (for "twenty winters"), but became increasingly doubtful about literary London and the theatrical world. It seems evident that at some point between Garrick's death (1779) and 1780 she experienced a spiritual quickening which was to galvanize her literary energies as well, focusing them in a new direction. One major influence on her in this period was the writing of William Law. Another was a book of pastoral letters, the *Cardiphonia* of John Newton. She heard Newton preach in 1787, met him, came home with a bundle of sermons and began with him a correspondence that lasted many years, through which he became her spiritual adviser. She also met young William Wilberforce in 1787, and they became fast friends. With the stimulus of these relationships and continued friendship with Mrs. Garrick and Elizabeth Montague, Hannah undertook the serious writing which was to mark her as a major social reformer.

The first of these works, once erroneously attributed to Wilberforce, was concerned with the influence of public lives on private morality (1788). It went rapidly through several editions, and was followed by a host of similar books of Christian cultural criticism and educational reform, including *Strictures on the Modern System of Female Education, With a View of the Principles and Conduct Prevalent among Women of Rank and Fortune* (2 volumes, 1799), a brisk but thoroughgoing criticism of current education and what were then very *avante garde* proposals for its improvement. Her most successful book was *Coelebs in Search of a Wife* (1806), a novel which had eleven editions in its first nine months. But almost all of her two dozen works went through multiple editions in her lifetime, including specifically spiritual writings such as *Practical Piety, or the Influence of the Religion of the Heart on Life and Manners* (2 volumes, 1811), *The Character and Practical Writings of St. Paul* (1815), and her best-known work of this kind, *The Spirit of Prayer* (1825)—which is actually a collection of earlier published observations. She became wealthy enough through her literary successes that she was able to leave large legacies to various Christian societies and charities, having already, in her own lifetime, expended large sums in the cause of charitable work—especially the establishment of Christian schools for the poor.

A tireless translator of gospel precepts into practical action, More offers a rigorous standard for Christian witness: "She who administers reproof with bad manners," she says, "defeats the effect of her remedy. On the other hand, there is a dishonest way of laboring to please everybody . . . [and] she who, with a half-earnestness, sails between the truth and what is fashionable—who, while she thinks it creditable to defend the cause of faith nevertheless does it in faint tones, a studied ambiguity of phrase, and with a certain expression in her face which proves she is not really displeased with what she seems to censure—injures the cause more than he who attacked it."[2] That she practiced what she preached is nowhere more evident than in her *Strictures on the Modern System . . .* , from which the following two excerpts on practical spirituality are drawn.

NOTES
1. This and other essential biographical details are amplified in the excellent biography, *Hannah More,* by M. G. Jones (Cambridge: Cambridge University Press, 1952; New York: Greenwood Press, 1968).
2. From More's *Strictures on the Modern System of Female Education, With a View of the Principles and Conduct Prevalent among Women of Rank and Fortune,* 2 vols. (London: 1799; rpt. Garland Publishing Co., 1974), vol. 1, pp. 8–9. These volumes offer a critique of society and contemporary education, followed by principles and a general plan of education for women in which cultural and intellectual history, along with great literature, are the chief subjects. More's standards are high; few today would dare to imitate her. The sections which follow are her chapters 18 and 19; they are followed in turn by a final chapter on "The Efficacy of Prayer."

# *from* Strictures on the Modern System of Female Education

## *Fashionable Christianity*

I T IS HUMOROUS to hear complaints against the strictness of a life of faith coming from persons who voluntarily pursue a life made infinitely more laborious by attempts to be always fashionable. How really burdensome would Christianity be if it required such careful attention to style, such unremitting labors, such a succession of efforts! If a spiritual life required such hardships and self-denial, such days of hurrying about, such evenings of exertion, such sleepless nights, such perpetual sacrifices of quiet and exile from family as fashion imposes, then indeed the service of Christianity would no longer merit its present description of being "a reasonable service." Then, in fact, the name of perfect *slavery* might be justly applied to that which we are told in the beautiful language of our church is "a service of perfect freedom"—a service, the great object of which is "to deliver us from the bondage of corruption into the glorious liberty of the children of God."

## I. *A Worldly Spirit*

A worldly spirit—by which I mean simply a disposition to prefer worldly pleasures, worldly satisfactions, and worldly advantages to the immortal interests of the soul, letting worldly considerations motivate us instead of spiritual principles in the concerns of ordinary life—a worldly spirit, I say, is not (like almost any other fault) the effect of passion or the consequence of surprise when the heart is off its guard. It is not excited incidentally by the operation of external circumstances on the infirmity of nature. Rather it is itself the spirit, soul and living principle of evil. It is not so much an act as a state of being, not so much an occasional complaint as a tainted constitution of mind. It does not always show itself in extraordinary excess. Even when it is not immediately tempted to break out into overt and specific acts, it is at work within, stirring up the heart to disaffection against holiness, and infusing a kind of moral disability into whatever is intrinsically good. It infects and depraves all the powers and faculties of the soul, for it blinds the understanding to whatever is spiritually good. It operates on the will, making it averse to God, and on the affections, disordering and sensualizing them, so that one may almost say to those who are under the supreme dominion of this spirit of the age what was said to the hosts of Joshua: "Ye *cannot* serve the Lord."

This worldliness of mind is not at all commonly understood, and for the following reason. People suppose that in this world our chief business is with the things of this world, and that to conduct the business of this world well—that is, conformably to moral principles—is the chief substance of moral and true goodness. Religion, if introduced at all into the system, only makes an occasional and, if I may say so, a 'holiday' appearance. To bring religion into everything is thought incompatible with a balanced attention to the things of this life. And so it would be, if by 'religion' is meant 'talking about religion'. It is often said: "One cannot always be praying; we must mind our business and social responsibilities as well as our devotion." When worldly business is thus subjected to worldly maxims, the mind during the conduct of business grows worldly; a continuously increasing worldly spirit dims the sight and relaxes the [real] moral principle on which the affairs of the world ought to be conducted, even as it indisposes the mind for all the exercises of worship and devotion.

But this spirit with respect to business life passes itself off for virtue, so that those who do not think about it are apt to mistake carrying on the affairs of life in a tolerably moral way for 'religion'. They do not see that the evil lies not in their managing business in this way, but in their *not* managing the things of this life in submission to those of eternity, and in *not* managing them with the unremitting consciousness of their own responsibility. The evil does not lie in their not being always on their knees, but in their not bringing their faith from the closet into the world, in their not bringing the spirit of Sunday's devotions into the transactions of the week, and in failing to transform their faith from a dry, speculative and inoperative system into a lively, practical and unceasing principle of action. . . .

## II. *A Worldly Faith*

But as to the faith of worldly persons, however strong it may be in speculation, however orthodox the creed, one cannot help fearing that it is a little defective in sincerity. For if there were in the mind a full persuasion of the truth of revelation and of the eternal bliss it promises, would there not be more obvious diligence to acquire it? We have great ardor in carrying on our worldly projects, because we believe the good which we are pursuing is real and will reward the trouble of the pursuit. We believe

485

[the goal] to be attainable by diligence, and prudently proportion our earnestness to this conviction. But where we see persons professing a lively faith in a better world, yet laboring little to obtain an interest in it, can we avoid suspecting that their belief (not only in *their* title to eternal happiness, but in eternal happiness itself) is not very well grounded, and that, if they were to examine themselves truly, the faith would be found to be much of a piece with the practice?

Even that very taste for enjoyment which leads the persons in question to . . . acquire talents which may enable them to relish the pleasures of a stylish life should induce those who are really looking for a *future* state of happiness to acquire something of the taste, disposition and talents which may prepare them for *its* enjoyment. A neglect to do this must proceed from one of these two causes: either they must think their present course a safe and proper course, or they must think that death will produce some sudden and surprising alteration in their human character.

But the office of death is to transport us to a new state, not to transform us to a new nature. The stroke of death is intended to effect our deliverance out of this world and our introduction into another, but it is not likely to effect any sudden and surprising or total change in our hearts or our tastes. In fact we are assured in Scripture that "he that is filthy will be filthy still, and he that is holy will be holy still." Though we believe that death will completely cleanse the holy soul from its remaining pollutions—that it will exchange defiling corruptions into perfect purity, entangling temptation into complete freedom, want and pain into health and fruition, doubts and fears into perfect security, and oppressive weariness into everlasting rest—yet there is no magic in the wand of death which will convert an unholy soul into a holy one.

It is awful to reflect that such a spirit as we have allowed predominance here will be maintained forever, that just as the will is when we close our eyes upon the things of time, so also will it be when we open them on those of eternity. The mere act of death no more fits us for heaven than the mere act of the mason who pulls down our old house fits us for a new one. If we die with our hearts running over with love of the world, there is no promise to lead us to expect that we shall rise with hearts full of the love of God. Death indeed will expose us to ourselves such as we are, but it will not make us such as we are not. And it will be too late to be acquiring self-knowledge when we can no longer turn it to any account but that of tormenting ourselves. . . .

When the curtain is drawn up at the theatre, though it serves to introduce us to the entertainment behind it, it does not create in us any new faculties to understand or enjoy the entertainment. These must have been already long in the acquiring; they must have been provided beforehand

486

and brought with us to the theatre if we are to appreciate the pleasures of the place, for entertainment can only operate on that taste we bring to it. It is too late to be acquiring when we ought to be enjoying.

That spirit of prayer and praise, those dispositions of love, meekness, peace, quietness and assurance, that indifference to the fashion of a world which is passing away, that longing after deliverance from sin, that desire for holiness together with all the specific marks of the Spirit here must surely constitute some part of our preparation for the enjoyment of a world whose pleasures are all spiritual. . . . Who can imagine any surprise equal to that of a soul that shuts its eyes on a world of sense in which all the objects and delights were so congenial to its nature, and then opens them on a world of the spirit, in which every enjoyment has a new nature—unknown, surprising and completely different? Here pleasures will be as inconceivable to its apprehension and unsuitable to its taste as the pleasures of one sense are to the organs of another, or as the most exquisite works of genius are to absolute imbecility of mind.

While we would with deep humility confess that we cannot purchase heaven by any works or qualifications of our own, and gratefully acknowledge that it must be purchased for us by "Him who loved us and washed us from our sins in his blood," yet let us remember that we have no reason to expect we could be capable of enjoying the pleasures of a heaven thus purchased without first being heavenly-minded. . . .

## III. *Self-Examination*

All 'fashionable' Christians should be reminded that there was no half engagement made for them at their baptism, that they are not partly their own and partly their Redeemer's. He that is "bought with a price" is the sole property of the purchaser. Faith does not consist merely in submitting the opinions of the understanding, but the dispositions of the heart. It is not a sacrifice of mere sentiments but of affections. It is not the tribute of fear extorted from a slave but the voluntary homage of love paid by a child.

Neither does a Christian's piety consist in living in retreat and railing at the practices of the world while perhaps her heart is full of the spirit of that world at which she is railing. It consists in *subduing* the spirit of the world and opposing its practices even while her duty obliges her to live in it.

Now the spirit of the love of the world is not confined only to those who are making their way in high society, nor are its operations restricted to the city limit of the capital or the limited circles of eminence and official splendor. She who inveighs against the luxury and excesses of London, and solaces herself in her own comparative sobriety because her more limited means compel her to take up only the second-hand pleasures of successive watering-places* (which pleasures she pursues avidly) is governed by the same spirit. And she whose still narrower opportunities restrict her to the petty diversions of her provincial town, if she is busy in swelling and enlarging her own smaller sphere of vanity and idleness—however she may comfort herself with her own comparative goodness by railing at the unattainable pleasures of the watering-places or the capital—she too is governed by the same spirit. For she who is as vain, as dissipated and as extravagant as existing circumstances allow would surely be as vain, dissipated and extravagant as the most flamboyant objects of her invective if she could change places with them. It is not merely by what we do that we can be sure the spirit of the world has no dominion over us, but by fairly considering what we would probably do if more were in our power.

The worldly Christian, if I may be allowed such a contradiction in terms, must not imagine that she acquits herself of her religious obligations by her merely weekly attendance at church. There is no covenant by which communion with God is restricted to an hour or two on Sunday. She does not fulfil her obligations by setting apart a few particular days in the year for a devotional retreat, and then flying back to the world as eagerly as if she were resolved to make up for her short fit of self-denial, the stream of her self-indulgence running with a more rapid current from having been interrupted by this forced obstruction. The avidness with which one has seen certain persons of a still less admirable character return to a whole year's carnival after the self-imposed penance of a Passion week gives a shrewd intimation that they considered the temporary abstinence less an act of penitence for the past than as a purchase of indemnity for the future. Such light-weight Protestants are in effect arguing for retaining the old Catholic doctrine of indulgences, which they buy not from the late spiritual court of Rome but from that secret, self-acquitting judge which, ignorant of its own turpitude and of the strict requirements of God's law, has established itself supreme in the tribunal of every unrenewed heart.

But the practice of self-examination is impeded with one clog which renders it peculiarly inconvenient to the stylish and worldly. The royal prophet King David—himself as likely as anyone to be acquainted with the difficulties peculiar to greatness—has annexed as an indispensable concomitant to "communing with your own heart" that we should "be

---

*More is thinking here of the fashionable resorts of the English wealthy classes, such as nearby Bath.

488

still" (Psalm 4:4). Now this part of the injunction renders the other more than a little inconsistent with the present habits of fashionable life; stillness is clearly not one of its obvious constituents. . . . How many things that now work themselves into the habit and pass as acceptable behavior would shock us [if analyzed properly] by their palpable inconsistency! Who, for instance, could stand the sight of such a debtor and creditor account as this—item: so many card-parties, balls and operas due to me in the following year, to balance so many manuals and meditations paid beforehand during the last six days in Lent? However much indignation this suggestion may be treated with, whatever offence may be caused by such a combination of the serious and the ludicrous, and however we may revolt at the idea of such a cheap transaction with our Maker as is suggested by these words, does not the habitual course of some of us closely resemble such an accounting?

Am I then ridiculing particular pious abstinences of contrite sinners? Am I jesting at that "troubled spirit" which God has declared is his "acceptable sacrifice"? God forbid! Such reasonable acts of self-denial have been the practice and continue to be the comfort of some of the most sincere Christians and will continue to be resorted to as long as Christianity and the world shall last. It is good, for example, to turn our thoughts even for a short time not only away from sin and vanity but even from the lawful pursuits of business and the praiseworthy cares of life and, at times, to annihilate as it were the space which divides us from eternity. . . .

Yet to those who seek a short annual retreat as a mere form, or who dignify with the idea of a religious self-denial a week in which it is rather unfashionable to be seen in town—who give something up with an unabated resolution to return later to the same pleasures and the spirit of that world which they intend mechanically to renounce—is it not to be feared that such a short-lived change, which does not even pretend to subdue the principle but only to suspend the act, may only serve to set a keener edge on the appetite for the pleasures one is giving up? Is it not to be feared that the bow may fly back with redoubled violence from having been unnaturally bent? That by varnishing over a life of vanity with the externals of a formal and temporary piety they may not more dangerously mask the troublesome soreness of a tender conscience? For is it not among the delusions of a worldly piety to consider Christianity as a thing which cannot, indeed, safely be omitted but which is to *be got over,* a certain quantity of which is, as it were, to be taken in the lump, with long intervals between repetitions? To consider faith as imposing a set of hardships which must be occasionally encountered in order to procure a peaceable enjoyment of the life hereafter? . . .

## IV. *Faith and Practice*

I am far from suggesting that retreats ought to be prolonged throughout the year, or that all the days of business are to be made equally days of solemnity and continued meditation. This earth is a place in which a much larger portion of ordinary Christians' time must be assigned to action than to contemplation. Women of the higher class were not sent into the world to shun society but to make it better. They were not designed for the cold and visionary virtues of solitudes and monasteries but for the amiable and endearing offices of social life. They are responsible to a faith which does not impose idle austerities but calls for active duties, a faith of which the most benevolent actions need to be sanctified by the purest motives, a faith which does not condemn its followers to the comparatively easy task of seclusion from the world but assigns them the more difficult responsibility of living uncorrupted from it. Moreover, while it forbids them to "follow a multitude to do evil," this faith includes in that prohibition the sin of doing nothing. . . .

Though a contemplative closeting up is not required, the same spirit and attitude of self-denial and humility must by every real Christian be extended throughout all the year. Once this spirit governs the heart, it will not only animate a woman's religious activities but will gradually extend itself to the chastising of her conversation. It will discipline her thought, influence her common business and sanctify her very pleasures. . . .

There is indeed scarcely a more pitiable person than one who, instead of making her faith the informing principle of all she does, has only just enough to keep her in continual fear, who drudges through her stinted exercises with a superstitious kind of terror while her general life shows that the love of God is not the governing principle in her heart. This sort of person seems to suffer all the pains and penalties of Christianity, but is a stranger to "that liberty wherewith Christ has made us free." Let the author offer an illustration of this point in the instance of a lady of this stamp who, returning from church on a very cold day and remarking with a good deal of complacency how much she had suffered in the performance of her 'duty', comforted herself with adding that "she hoped, however, it would *answer*."*

But there is no comfort in any religion short of that by which the diligent Christian strives that all his actions shall have the love of God for their motive, and the glory of God for their purpose. To go about balancing one's good and bad actions against each other, and taking comfort in

*I.e., "fill the bill" or "balance the account."

the occasional predominance of the former, while the cultivation of the principle from which they both spring is neglected, is not the road to all those peaceful fruits of the Spirit to which true Christianity conducts the humble and penitent believer. . . .

## V. *Conclusion*

All our most dangerous mistakes arise from our constantly referring our practices not to the standard of Scripture but to the mutable standard of human opinion, by which it is impossible to fix their real value. For this latter standard in some cases calls those good who do not go to the lengths the notoriously bad allow themselves. The Gospel has a universal, the world a merely local standard of goodness. In some societies only certain vices are dishonourable—such as covetousness and cowardice—while other sins of which our Saviour has said that they which commit them "shall not inherit the kingdom of God" detract nothing from the respect persons receive. Nay, those very characteristics which the Almighty has expressly declared He will judge are received, are caressed, in that which calls itself 'the best company'.

But to weigh our actions by one standard now when we know they will be judged by another hereafter ought to be reckoned the height of absurdity. . . . "How readest thou?" is a more specific direction than any comparison of our own habits with the habits of others. At the Final Judgement it will be of little avail that our actions have risen above those of bad men, if our views and principles shall be found to have been in opposition to the Gospel of Christ.

# *Faithful Christianity*

THE AUTHOR having in this little work given consideration to some of the false notions often imbibed in early life from a bad education, and of their pernicious effects, and having attempted to point out respective remedies for these,* she would now draw all that has been said to a conclusion and declare plainly what she humbly conceives to be the source from which all these false notions and wrong conduct have proceeded.

---

*More is referring here to the main body of her *Strictures* . . . , of which the first volume is largely criticism of contemporary education and the second a series of proposals for a better system.

The prophet Jeremiah gives us the answer: "It is because they have forsaken the fountain of living waters, and have hewn out to themselves cisterns, broken cisterns that can hold no water" (Jeremiah 2:13). Simply put, it is an ignorance past belief of what Christianity really is. The remedy, therefore, and the only remedy that can be applied with any prospect of success, is . . . the Gospel of Jesus Christ.

I have already suggested that religion should be taught at an early period of life, that children should be brought up "in the nurture and admonition of the Lord." The manner in which they should be taught has likewise with great plainness been suggested—that it should be done in so lively and familiar a manner as to make faith attractive and its ways to appear as they really are, "ways of pleasantness." And a slight sketch has been given of the genius of Christianity, by which its attractiveness would more clearly appear. But this being a subject of such vast importance compared with which every other subject sinks into nothing, it seems not sufficient to speak of the doctrines and duties of Christianity in detached parts. Rather it is of importance to point out briefly the mutual dependence of one doctrine upon another, and the influence which these doctrines have upon the heart and life, so that the *duties* of Christianity may be seen to grow out of its *doctrines*. Here it will appear that Christian virtue differs essentially from pagan virtue; it is of a quite different kind. The plant itself is different; it comes from a different root and grows in a different soil.

By this it will be seen how the humbling doctrine of the disobedience of our first parents and the consequent corruption of human nature make way for the bright display of redeeming love. It is from the abasing thought that "we are all as sheep going astray, every one in his own way," that none *can* return to the shepherd of our souls "except the Father draw him," that "the natural man *cannot* receive the things of the spirit because they are spiritually discerned," from this humiliating view of the *helplessness* as well as the guilt and corruption of human nature that we are to turn to the offer of divine assistance. Though human nature will appear from this view in a deeply degraded state, and consequently *all* have cause for humility, yet not one has cause for despair. The disease indeed is dreadful, but a physician is at hand, both able and willing to save us. . . .

We should observe then that the doctrines of our Saviour are, if I may say so, like his coat, all woven into one piece. We should get such a view of their reciprocal dependence as to be persuaded that without a deep sense of our corruption we can never seriously believe in a Saviour, because the substantial and acceptable belief in Him must always arise from the conviction of our need of Him. Without a firm persuasion that the Holy Spirit can alone restore our fallen nature, repair the ruins of sin and renew the image of God upon our heart, we never shall be brought to serious, humble prayer for repentance and restoration. And without this repentance there is no salvation. For although Christ has died for us and consequently to Him alone we must look as a Saviour, yet He has Himself declared that He will save none but those who are truly penitent.

## I. *On the Doctrine of Human Corruption*

When an important edifice is about to be erected, a wise builder will dig deep and look well to the foundations, knowing that without this the fabric will not be likely to stand. The foundation of the Christian faith, out of which the whole structure may be said to arise, appears to be the doctrine of the fall of man from his original state of righteousness, and the corruption, guilt and helplessness of human nature—all of which are consequences of this fall and the natural state of everyone born into the world. It is especially important to acquaint the minds of young persons with this doctrine. They are peculiarly disposed to turn away from it as a morose, unattractive and gloomy idea, and are apt to accuse those who believe it of unnecessary severity, and to suspect them of thinking unjustly ill of mankind. Some reasons which prejudice the inexperienced against the doctrine in question appear to be the following.

Young persons themselves have seen little of the world. In pleasurable society the world puts on its most attractive appearance, and that softness and urbanity which prevail, particularly among persons of fashion, are liable to be mistaken for more than they are really worth. The opposition to this doctrine in the young [therefore] arises partly from a generosity of heart, partly from indulging themselves in optimistic suppositions respecting the world, and partly from the general popularity of the notion that everybody is really wonderfully good.

Now the predisposition to this error in youth arises from their not having a right standard of moral good and evil themselves. . . . Moreover, young people are apt not to know themselves. Not having yet been much exposed to temptation, owing to the prudent restraints in which they have been kept, they little suspect to what lengths in vice they themselves are liable to be carried, nor how far others actually are carried who are set free from those restraints.

Having laid down these as some of the causes of error on this point, I proceed to observe on what strong grounds the doctrine itself stands.

### 1. Empirical evidence

Secular history abundantly confirms this truth [of human corruption], the history of the world being in fact little else than the history of the

493

crimes of the human race. Even though the annals of remote ages lie so involved in obscurity that some degree of uncertainty attaches itself to many of the events recorded, yet this one truth is always clear, that most of the miseries which have been brought upon mankind have proceeded from this innate depravity.

The world we live in furnishes abundant proof of this truth. In a world formed on the deceitful theory of those who assert the innocence and dignity of man, almost all the professions would have been rendered useless by such a state of innocence; they simply would not have existed. Without sin there would have been no sickness; every medical practitioner is a standing evidence of this sad truth. Sin not only brought sickness but death into the world; consequently every funeral presents a more irrefragable argument than a thousand sermons. Had man persevered in his original integrity, there could have been no litigation, for there would be no contests about property in a world where none would be inclined to attack it. Practitioners of law, therefore, from the attorney who prosecutes for a crime to the barrister who defends a criminal or the judge who condemns him, loudly confirm this doctrine. Every military victory by sea or land should teach us to rejoice with humiliation, for conquest itself brings a terrible, though splendid, attestation to the truth of the fall of man.

Even those who deny the doctrine act universally on the principle. Why do we all secure our houses with bolts and bars and locks? Do we take these steps to defend our lives or property from any *particular* fear? From any suspicion of this neighbor or that servant or the other invader? No. It is from a practical conviction of human depravity, from a constant, pervading, but undefined dread of impending evil arising from an inbred sense of general corruption. Are not prisons built and laws enacted on the same practical principle?

But we need not descend to the more degraded members of our species. Why in the fairest transaction of business is nothing executed without bonds, receipts and contracts? Why does not a perfect confidence in the 'dignity of human nature' abolish all these insecurities—if not between enemies, or people indifferent to each other, yet at least between friends and kindred and the most honorable connections? Why? Because of the universal, inborn suspicion of person to person which, from all we see, hear and feel, is interwoven with our very flesh. Though we do not entertain any *individual* suspicion, though we may in fact have the strongest *personal* confidence, yet the acknowledged principle of conduct has this doctrine for its basis. "I will take a receipt, though it were from my brother," is the established voice of mankind. Or, as I have heard it more artfully put, by a fallacy of which the very disguise discovers the principle, "Think every man honest, but deal with him as if you knew him to be otherwise." Just as in a state of innocence the beasts would not have bled for the sustenance of mankind, so their skins would not have been wanted as parchments, as instruments of his security against his fellow man.

## 2. Scriptural evidence

But the grand arguments for this doctrine must be drawn from the Holy Scriptures which, besides implying it almost continually, expressly assert it in instances too numerous to mention. Of these may I be allowed to produce a few? "God saw that the wickedness of man was great, and that every imagination of the thoughts of his heart was only evil continually"; "God looked upon the earth, and behold, it was corrupt; for all flesh had corrupted his way upon the earth. And it repented the Lord that he had made man on the earth, and it grieved him at his heart" (Genesis 6:5,6,12). This is a picture of mankind before the flood, and the portrait does not present more favorable lineaments after that tremendous judgement had taken place. The Psalms abound in lamentations on this depravity: "They are all gone aside; there is none that doeth good, no not one." (Psalm 14:3). "In thy sight," says David, addressing the Most High, "shall no man living be justified" (Psalm 143:2). Job, in his usual lofty strain of interrogation, asks "What is man that he should be clean, and he that is born of a woman that he should be righteous? Behold the heavens are not clean in his sight, how much more abominable and filthy is man, who drinketh iniquity like water?" (Job 15:14–16).

But the Scriptures do not leave us to infer this as a consequence; they state the matter plainly. The wise man tells us that "foolishness is bound up in the heart of a child"; the prophet Jeremiah assures us that "the heart is deceitful above all things, and desperately wicked" (Jeremiah 17:9), and David plainly states the doctrine: "Behold I was shapen in iniquity, and in sin did my mother conceive me" (Psalm 51:5). Can language be more explicit?

The New Testament corroborates the Old. Our Lord's reproof of Peter seems to take the doctrine for granted: "Thou savourest not the things that be of God, but those that be of man" (Matthew 16:23), clearly intimating that the ways of man are opposed to the ways of God. And our Saviour, in that moving discourse to his disciples, tells them plainly that, as they were by his grace made different from others, therefore they must expect to be hated by those who were so unlike them. And it should be

495

particularly observed that our Lord calls those in whom no change of heart has taken place "the world." "If ye were of the world, the world would love its own; but I have chosen you out of the world, therefore the world hateth you" (John 15:19). St. John, writing to his Christian church, states the same truth: "We know that we are of God, and the whole world lieth in wickedness" (1 John 5:19).

Man in his natural state is likewise represented as in a state of guilt, and under the displeasure of Almighty God. "He that believeth not the Son shall not see life; but the wrath of God abideth on him" (John 3:36)— evidently implying that all are *naturally* under the wrath of God.

Our natural state is likewise described as a *helpless* state. "The carnal mind is enmity against God"—awful thought!—"for it is not subject to the law of God, neither indeed can be. So then they that are in the flesh cannot please God" (Romans 8:7–8). What the apostle means by "being in the flesh" is evident by what follows, for speaking of those whose hearts were changed by divine grace, he says, "But ye are not in the flesh, but in the spirit, if so be that the Spirit of God dwell in you"—that is, you are now not in your natural state. The change that has occurred in your minds by the influence of the Spirit of God is so great that your state may properly be called being in the Spirit. Yet the same apostle, writing to the churches of Galatia, tells them that the natural corruption of the human heart is continually opposing the spirit of holiness which influences the regenerate. "The flesh lusteth against the spirit, and the spirit against the flesh, and these are contrary the one to the other" (Galatians 5:17). (This passage, by the way, at the same time it proves the corruption of the heart, proves the necessity of divine influences.)* And the apostle, with respect to himself, freely confesses and deeply laments the workings of this corrupt principle: "O wretched man that I am!" etc.

It has been objected by some who have opposed this doctrine that the same Scriptures which speak of mankind as sinners, speak of some [individuals] as being *righteous*. From this they would argue that though this depravity of human nature may be *general,* it cannot be *universal.* This objection, when examined, serves only, like all other objections against the truth, to establish that which it was intended to destroy. For what do the Scriptures assert respecting the righteous? That there are some whose principles, ideas and conduct are so different from the rest of the world, and from what theirs themselves once were, that while the latter are called the "sons of men," the former are honored with the title of the "sons of God." But nowhere do the Scriptures assert that they are sinless. On the

*I.e., the operation of the Holy Spirit.

contrary, their faults are frequently mentioned; they are moreover represented as those in whom a great change has come about, as ones who have been formerly "dead in trespasses and sins," who have "been called out of darkness into light," who have been "translated into the kingdom of God's dear Son," who have "passed from death to life." And St. Paul puts this matter past all doubt by expressly asserting that "they were all by nature the children of wrath even as others" (Ephesians 2:3). . . .

## 3. Self-deluding objections

It is often urged that the belief in this doctrine [of our corrupt nature] produces many ill effects, and therefore it should be discouraged. That it does *not* produce those ill effects, when not misunderstood or partially represented, we shall attempt to show. At the same time let it be observed that if it be really *true* we must not reject it on account of any of these supposed ill-consequences. Truth may often be attended with disagreeable effects, but if it is truth it must still be pursued. If, for instance, treason should exist in a country, everyone knows the disagreeable effects which will follow such a conviction. But our not believing such treason to exist will not prevent such effect following it; on the contrary, our believing in it may itself prevent the consequences.

Some object, further, that this doctrine debases human nature, and that finding fault with the building is only another way of finding fault with the architect. To the first part of this objection it may be remarked that if man is really a corrupt fallen being, it is proper to represent him as such. The fault then lies in man, not in the representation, which only states the truth. As to the inference which is supposed to follow, namely that it throws the fault upon the Creator, this proceeds upon the false supposition that man's present state is the state in which he was originally created. On the contrary, the Scriptures assert that "God made man upright, but he hath found out many inventions."

It is likewise objected that since this doctrine presents us with such a bad opinion of mankind, it must, consequently, produce ill-will, hatred and suspicion. But it should be remembered that it gives us no worse an opinion of mankind in general than it gives us of ourselves, and such views of ourselves have a very salutary effect, inasmuch as they have a tendency to produce humility. Now humility is not likely to produce ill-will toward others, "for only from pride cometh contention." And as to the views it gives us of mankind, it represents us as fellow-sufferers; surely the consideration that we are companions in misery is not calculated to produce hatred. The truth is, these [negative attitudes toward mankind] have actually followed from a false and partial idea of the subject.

Old persons who have seen much of the world and who have little religion are apt to be strong in their belief in man's corruption. But not holding this view on Christian grounds, their belief shows itself in a narrow and malignant spirit—in uncharitable judgement and harsh opinions.

[Such] suspicion and hatred are also the uses to which Rochefoucault and the other French philosophers have converted this doctrine. Their acute minds intuitively found the corruption of man, but they saw it without its corresponding and correcting doctrine. They allowed man to be a depraved creature, but disallowed his original perfection. They found him in a low state but did not conceive of him as having fallen from a better one. They represent him rather as a brute than an apostate, not taking into account that his present degraded nature and depraved faculties are not his original condition—that he is not as he came out of the hands of his Creator but as he made himself by sin. Nor do they know that he has not even now lost all remnants of his primitive dignity, but is still capable of a restoration more glorious "than is dreamt of in their philosophy."

Perhaps, too, they know from what they themselves *feel,* all the evil to which man is inclined. But they do not know, for they have not felt, all the good of which he is capable by the superinduction of the divine principle. Thus they cast aspersions on human nature instead of fairly representing it, and in so doing it is *they* who denigrate the great Creator.

The doctrine of the fall is likewise accused of being a gloomy, discouraging doctrine, and an enemy to joy and comfort. Now suppose this objection were true in its fullest extent. Is it in any way unreasonable that a being fallen into a state of sin, and come under the displeasure of Almighty God, should feel seriously alarmed at being in such a state? Is the condemned criminal blamed because he is not merry? And would it be thought a kind action to persuade him that he is *not* condemned in order to make him so?

But this charge is *not* true in the sense intended by those who bring it forward. Those who believe this doctrine are *not* the most gloomy people. When, indeed, anyone by the influence of the Holy Spirit is brought to view his state as it really is, a state of guilt and danger, it is natural that fear should be excited in his mind, but it is such a fear as impels him "to flee from the wrath to come." It is such a fear as moved Noah to "prepare an ark to the saving of his house." Such a person will likewise feel sorrow, but not "the sorrow of the world" which "worketh death"; rather it is that godly sorrow which "worketh repentance." This person is in a proper state to receive the glorious doctrine we are next about to contemplate, namely,

II. *That God so Loved the World that He Gave his Only Begotten Son, that Whosoever Believed on Him should not Perish but have Everlasting Life* (John 3:16).

Of this doctrine it is of the utmost importance to form sound ideas, for while it is the only doctrine which can keep the humble penitent from despair, great care must nevertheless be taken that false views of it do not lead us to presumption. In order to understand it rightly, we must not fill our minds with our own reasonings upon it, which have misled some good people, but we must direct ourselves to the Scriptures wherein we shall find it so plainly stated that [we shall see] the mistakes have not arisen from a lack of clarity in the Scriptures but from a desire to make them bend to some favorite notion. By this mode of proceeding it has been rejected by some and so mutilated by others that it hardly retains any resemblance to the Scripture doctrine of redemption.

We are told in this beautiful passage of the *source* of our redemption—the love of God for a lost world; *who* the Redeemer is—the Son of God; and the *purpose* for which this plan was formed and executed—"That whosoever believed in him should not perish but have everlasting life." There is nothing surely in all this to promote gloominess. If kindness and mercy have a tendency to win and warm the heart, here is every incentive to joy and cheerfulness. Christianity looks kindly upon everyone, and with peculiar tenderness on those who, from humbling views of their own unworthiness, might be led to imagine themselves excluded. We are expressly told that "Christ died for *all*"; that "He tasted death for *every* man"; that "He died for the sins of the *whole* world." Accordingly, He has commanded that his Gospel should be preached "to *every* creature," which is, in effect, declaring that not a single human being is excluded. To preach the Gospel is to offer a Saviour, and the Saviour in the plainest language offers Himself to all, declaring "to all the ends of the earth": "Look unto me and be saved." It is therefore an undeniable truth that no one will perish for lack of a Saviour, but by rejecting Him.

But to suppose that because Christ has died for the sins of the whole world the whole world will therefore be saved is a most fatal mistake. The same book which tells us that "Christ died for all," tells us likewise the awful truth that but "few will be saved"! And while it declares that "there is no other name whereby we must be saved" but the name of Jesus, it likewise declares that

### III. *Without Holiness No One shall See the Lord.*

It is much to be feared that some, in their zeal to defend the Gospel doctrines of free grace, have materially injured the Gospel doctrine of holiness, by stating that Christ has done everything in such a way as to mean that there is nothing left for us to do.

But do the Scriptures really speak in this way? "Come, for all things are ready" is the Gospel call, in which we may observe that at the same time that it tells us that all things are ready, it nevertheless tells us that we must "come." Food being provided for us will not benefit us except we partake of it. It will not avail us that "Christ our passover is sacrificed for us," unless we "keep the feast." We must make use of the "fountain which is opened for sin and uncleanness" if we are to be purified. All, indeed, who are thirsty are invited to take of the waters of life freely, but if we feel no thirst, and we do not drink, their saving qualities are of no use to us.

It is all the more necessary to insist on this in the present day, as there is a worldly and fashionable, as well as a low and sectarian antinomianism abroad.* This is an unwarranted assurance of salvation founded on a slight, vague and general confidence in what Christ has done and suffered for us, as if the great object of his life and suffering had been to emancipate us from all duty and obedience. It is assumed that because He died for sinners, we might therefore safely and comfortably go on living in sin, contenting ourselves with now and then a transient, formal and meaningless declaration of our unworthiness and obligation, and the all-sufficiency of his atonement. By this 'quit-rent', of which the cost consists in the mere acknowledgement, the sensual, worldly and vain imagine they shall find a refuge in heaven when driven from the enjoyments of this world.

But this indolent Christianity is nowhere taught in the Bible. The faith inculcated *there* is not lazy, nominal faith, but that faith which "worketh by love," that faith of which the practical language is: "strive that you may enter in"; "so run that ye may obtain"; "so fight that you may lay hold on eternal life." This is the faith which directs us not to be weary in well-doing, but which says, "work out your own salvation," never for-

---

*Those who "maintain that the moral law is not binding on Christians under the law of grace" may obviously do so formally as a point of doctrine; More is here concerned with those who do so tacitly, as a matter of spiritual lassitude.

getting at the same time that "it is God which worketh in us both to will and to do."

Are those rich supplies of grace which the Gospel offers—those abundant aids of the Spirit which it promises—tendered to the slothful? No. God will have all his gifts put to use. Grace must be used, or it will be withdrawn. Nor does the Almighty think it derogatory to his free grace to declare that "those only who do his commandments have right to the tree of life." Nor do the Scriptures represent it as derogatory to the sacrifice of Christ to follow his example in well-doing. The only caution is that we must not work in our own strength, nor try to bring along our contribution of works as if in aid of a supposed deficiency of his merits.

But we must not in our over-caution fancy that because Christ has "redeemed us from the curse of the law" that we are therefore without a law. In acknowledging Christ as a deliverer we must not forget that He is a lawgiver too, and that we are expressly commanded to fulfil the law of Christ. If we wish to know what his laws are, we must "search the Scriptures," especially the New Testament, and there we shall find him declaring

## IV. *The Absolute Necessity of a Change of Heart and Life.*

"Except a man be born again he cannot see the kingdom of God." No mere acknowledgement of his authority, calling him "Lord, Lord," will avail anything unless we do what He commands. Anything short of this is like a man building his house upon the sands, which, when the storms come on, will certainly fall. In the same manner the apostles are continually enforcing the necessity of this change, which they describe under the various names of "the new man" (Ephesians 4:24), "the new creature" (Galatians 6:15), a "transformation into the image of God" (2 Corinthians 12), and a "participation of the divine nature" (2 Peter 1:4). Nor is this change represented as consisting merely in a change of religious opinions, or in exchanging gross sins for those which are more sober and reputable, or in renouncing the sins of youth and assuming those of a quieter period of life, or in leaving off evil practices because we are grown tired of them or find them injurious to our reputation, health or fortune. Nor does it consist in inoffensive and obliging manners or, indeed, in any outward reformation.

But the change consists in "being renewed in the spirit of our minds," in being "conformed to the image of the Son of God," in being "called out of darkness into his marvellous light." And the whole of this great change, its beginning, progress and final accomplishment (for it is represented as a gradual change) is ascribed to

## V. The Influence of the Holy Spirit.

We are perpetually reminded of our utter inability to help ourselves in order that we may set a higher value on those gracious aids which are held out to us. We are told that "we are not sufficient to think anything as of ourselves, but our sufficiency is of God." And when we are told that "if we live after the flesh we shall die," we are at the same time reminded that it is "through the spirit that we must mortify the deeds of the body." We are likewise cautioned that we "grieve not the Holy Spirit of God," and that we "quench not the Spirit." On the contrary, we are exhorted to "stir up the gift of God which is in us."

By all these expressions and many others of like significance, we are taught that while we are to ascribe with humble gratitude every good thought, word and work to the influence of the Holy Spirit, we are not to look on the fact of the Spirit as a source or an excuse for spiritual laziness. It is all too plain that we may reject his gracious offers of assistance; otherwise there would be no occasion to caution us not to do it. Our Lord Himself has illustrated this in the most accommodating and endearing manner: "Behold," says He, "I stand at the door and knock. If any man hear my voice, and open the door, I will come in to him, and will sup with him, and he with me" (Revelation 3:20). Observe, it is not said "if any man will not listen to me, I will force open the door." But if we refuse admittance to such a guest, we must abide by the consequences.

## VI. Our Spiritual Enemy.

This sublime doctrine of the assistance of the Spirit is the more to be prized not only on account of our helplessness, but from the additional consideration of the powerful adversary with whom the Christian has to contend. Here is an article of our faith, by the way, which is growing into general disrepute among the 'politer' classes of society. In fact, there is a kind of ridicule attached to the very suggestion [of the devil], as if it were exploded on full proof of being an absolute absurdity, and utterly repugnant to the 'liberal' spirit of an 'enlightened' age. And it requires no small amount of cleverness of expression and periphrastic ingenuity to get the very mention [of Satan] tolerated. The Scripture doctrine of the existence and power of our great spiritual enemy is considered by the fashionable sceptic as a vulgar invention which ought to be banished with the belief in dreams and witchcraft, by the fashionable Christian as an ingenious allegory but not as a literal truth, and by almost everyone as a doctrine which, when it happens to be introduced at church has at least nothing to do with the *pews* but is by common consent relegated to the *aisles* (if indeed it must be retained at all).

May I, with great humility and respect, presume to suggest to our men of the cloth that they would do well not to participate in these modish curtailments of the Christian faith, nor to shun speaking of this doctrine when it is consistent with their subject to bring it forward. A truth which is seldom brought before the eye imperceptibly grows less and less important. And if it is an unpleasant truth, we grow more and more reconciled to its absence, until at length its intrusion becomes offensive and we learn in the end to renounce what we at first only neglected. Because some coarse and ranting enthusiasts have been fond of using tremendous terms with violence and frequency—as if it were a gratification to them to pronounce judgements and anticipate torments—can *their* coarseness or vulgarity make a true doctrine false or an important one trifling? If such preachers have given offence by their uncouth manner of handling an awful chastening doctrine, that indeed should prompt our treating the subject in a more responsible way, but it is no just reason for avoiding the doctrine altogether. For to keep a truth out of sight because it has been absurdly treated or ill defended might in time be assigned as a reason for keeping back, one by one, every doctrine of our holy church; for which of them has not had imprudent advocates or weak champions?

Let it be remembered that the doctrine in question is not only inter-woven by allusion, implication or direct assertion throughout the whole Scripture, but that it stands prominently personified at the opening of the New as well as the Old Testament. The devil's temptation of our Lord, in which he is not represented figuratively but visibly and palpably, stands on the same ground of authority with other events recorded in Scripture. And it may not be an unuseful observation to remark that the very refusal to believe in an evil spirit is one of his own suggestions—for there is not a more dangerous illusion than to believe ourselves out of the reach of illusions, nor a more alarming temptation than to fancy that we are not liable to be tempted.

But the dark cloud raised by this doctrine will be dispelled by the cheerful certainty that our blessed Saviour having Himself "been tempted like as we are," is "able to deliver those who are tempted."

## VII. *Conclusion.*

From this imperfect sketch we may see how suitable is redemption in Christ to a fallen man! How exactly it meets every need! No one needs now perish because he is a sinner, provided he is willing to forsake his sin, for "Jesus Christ came into the world to save sinners" and "He is now exalted to be a prince and a Saviour, to give repentance and forgiveness of sin." This passage, let us observe, points out to us the order in which He bestows his blessings: he *first* gives repentance, and *then* forgiveness.

We may likewise see how much the character of a true Christian rises above every other approach to life. There is a wholeness, integrity, and completeness in the Christian character. Beside it, a few natural, pleasing qualities not cast in the mould of the Gospel are but as beautiful fragments or well-turned single limbs which, for want of that beauty which arises from the proportion of parts—for want of that connection of the members with the living head—are of little comparative excellence. There may be attractive qualities which are not Christian graces, but the apostle, after enumerating every separate article of attack or defence with which a Christian warrior is to be accoutered, sums up the matter by directing that we put on "the *whole armour* of God." And this completeness is insisted on by all the apostles. One prays that his converts may "stand *perfect* and *complete* in the whole will of God." Another enjoins that they be "*perfect* and *entire,* wanting nothing."

Now we are not to suppose that they expected any convert to be without fault. They knew too well the construction of the human heart. But Christians must have no fault in their principles, their ideas must be straight, their scheme must be faultless, their intention must be single, their standard must be holy, their object must be right, their mark must be "the high calling of God in Christ Jesus." There must be no *allowed* evil, no *warranted* defection, no *tolerated* impunity. Though they do not rise as high as they ought or as they wish in the scale of perfection, yet the scale itself must be correct, and the desire of ascending perpetual, counting the degrees they have already attained as nothing. Every grace must be kept in exercise; victories once achieved over any evil tendency must be not only maintained but extended.

Finally, Christianity so comprises contrary (and, as it may be thought, irreconcilable) excellences, that those which seem so incompatible as to be incapable by nature of being inmates of the same breast, are almost necessarily involved in the Christian character. For instance, Christianity requires that our faith be at once fervent and sober, that our love be both ardent and lasting, that our patience be not only heroic but gentle. It demands dauntless zeal and genuine humility, active service and complete self-renunciation, high attainments in goodness with deep consciousness of our defects. It requires courage in reproving and meekness in bearing reproof, a quick perception of what is sinful with a willingness to forgive the offender, active virtue ready to do everything and passive virtue ready to bear everything. We must stretch every faculty in the service of our Lord, and yet bring every thought into obedience to Him. While we aim to live in the exercise of every Christian grace, we must account ourselves unprofitable servants. We must strive for the crown and yet receive it as a gift and then lay it at our Master's feet. While we are busily trading in the world with our Lord's talents, we must "commune with our heart, and be still." While we strive to practice charity without self-interest, we must be contented to meet with selfishness in return. And while we should be laying out our lives for the good of mankind, we must submit to reproach without murmuring and to ingratitude without resentment. And to render us equal to all these services, the Spirit of Christ bestows not only the precept but the power. He does what the great poet of ethics lamented that Reason could not do: "He lends us arms as well as rules."

Here, if not only the worldly and the timid, but the humble and the well-disposed should demand with fear and trembling, "Who is sufficient for these things?" revelation makes its own reviving answer: "My grace is sufficient for thee." . . .

# WILLIAM WILBERFORCE
## 1759 · 1833

From the engraving by John Murray, showing Wilberforce at age twenty-nine (1788).

INTRODUCTION

William Wilberforce was one of the greatest political reformers the English-speaking peoples have ever produced. A man of intense personal piety, the vigorous practical outworking of his faith was the foundation for everything that characterized his extraordinary contribution to public life. And while it may seem surprising to conclude an historical anthology of spiritual writers with (of all possible choices) a politician, no one who has read the whole, or even a large part, of his *Real Christianity* will doubt that Wilberforce is of signal value as a spiritual writer.[1] Indeed, in the context of this volume, he is in many ways an ideal exemplar of eighteenth-century evangelical spirituality.

Wilberforce was born at his family home on the High Street of Hull, Yorkshire, on August 24, 1759. At grammar school he excelled and used to be set upon a table to read aloud as a model for the other boys. For a time he went to school in London, till he was recalled by his mother for fear he was being "perverted to Methodism" by his aunt, a sister of the evangelical business leader John Thornton.[2] He had always a fine singing voice, and this along with his academic acumen, his personal charm, and conspicuous hospitality made him a popular figure during his college days at St. John's, Cambridge. Although he inherited great family wealth and might have pursued the interest of his estate more closely, he laid it all aside to take up political life and was elected as member for Hull in September 1780.

In London he was again very popular. His singing was praised by the Prince of Wales, and he was famous as a mimic—especially of the prime minister, Lord North (notorious for his role at the time of the American Revolution). He seems at first to have entered naturally into the normal social pleasures and diversions of London's opulent society. Reelected for Hull in 1784, and chosen member for Yorkshire, he was rapidly becoming a noteworthy political success when, on a tour of the Continent, there came a fundamental turning point in his life. It was the summer of 1785, and he and his old grammar school teacher, Isaac Milner, were traveling in Switzerland with Wilberforce's mother and sister. Together with Milner, Wilberforce was reading Philip Doddridge's *Rise and Progress* and studying the Greek New Testament. The result was his conversion, and when he returned to England he immediately told his friends about his decision. William Pitt, with whom he was especially close, and to whom he confided in detail his resolution to dedicate himself to growth in the Christian life, was gracious in acknowledging the change of direction, though reluctant to follow his friend. Wilberforce found his way to St. Mary, Woolnoth, Church and its vicar, John Newton, who from that point became his spiritual adviser.

During the 1786 session of the House, Wilberforce tried unsuccessfully to push through a bill for humane reform of the criminal law. After a retreat in the country for prayer and meditation about the future character of his stewardship, he returned to London and organized a number of bishops to form with him a "society for the reformation of 'manners'" (i.e., lifestyle), obtaining a royal proclamation for it on June 1, 1787. Generally known as the "Proclamation Society," its concern was to oppose the marketing of vice; it instituted proceedings against the producers and purveyors of blasphemous and pornographic publications. Wilberforce also became interested in Christian education and, after meeting Hannah More the same year, he joined with her and Henry Thornton, another evangelical philanthropist, in providing a program of funding for Christian schools for the poor.

Wilberforce had been concerned about the issue of slavery since his youth and when interest in the abolition cause began to grow in this period he was naturally attracted to it. His friend and pastor John Newton, himself a former slave trader, lent extra strength to his concerns, and when the struggling coalition of abolitionists came to him, it was in appreciation of his already established Christian witness as a fit instrument to "represent and stimulate the national conscience"[3] that he was asked to assume leadership of the movement. Pitt also encouraged him, and after a prayerful struggle under a tree in Pitt's own garden, he made the decision which was to shape his own public life and the political history of Britain ever after.

The battle was long and arduous, and it exacted a heavy toll on Wilberforce's fragile health. Yet he had repeated assurances that it was God's work given for him to do. In March 1791, he received from a dying John Wesley that great Methodist leader's last letter, encouraging him on. When things went badly in Parliament, he organized out-of-doors agitation by county meetings. He joined Henry Thornton, Granville Sharp, and Zachary Macauley in the Sierra Leone Company, and from this period forward, with other brothers in faith who were eventually to be known as the "Clapham sect," he found supportive fellowship. In the midst of all of his parliamentary work, he finished his book, *A Practical View of the Prevailing Religious System of Professed Christians in the Higher and Middle Classes of this Country contrasted with Real Christianity* (1797).[4]

In May of the same year, he married Barbara Ann Spooner, of Elmdon Hall, Warwickshire, and moved out of his apartment in Henry Thornton's house to a home nearby on Clapham Common. He and his wife's first social engagement as a married couple was a visit to the home of Hannah More, at Cowslip Green. Support for More's charities was only a small part of Wilberforce's philanthropy; during this period he took part in the foundation of the Church Missionary Society (first discussed at his house, in 1798) and the Bible Society (1803) and also helped to found another "Society for Bettering the Condition of the Poor."

Meanwhile, the struggle for abolition went on, with temporary triumphs, many reverses, and great difficulties. The bill against slave *trade* finally passed on February 23, 1807. But it took another twenty-six years of laborious fighting to get the bill for abolition itself passed. By the time that bill was at second reading, Wilberforce was a very sick man, with only months to live. In the interval, however, he had become regarded as the hero and moral leader of his nation.

Wilberforce's Christian principles were continually being molded by scriptural values rather than conventional party lines. At the expense of offending some of his religious friends and exposing himself to much abuse in the press, he had come out strongly in 1813 for Catholic emancipation—the right of Catholics to hold seats in Parliament. He opposed the influence of wealth and power in promoting social evils of all kinds and poured his own wealth and all his energies and influence into founding and supporting organizations which were to have a signal role in the proclamation of the gospel at home and abroad throughout the nineteenth and into the twentieth century.

How does someone in public life—especially in a self-indulgent and complacent culture—maintain "real Christianity" as a personal calling? Wilberforce escaped contamination by standing apart from all corrupt and self-serving concerns, devoting himself instead to pressing moral issues. He was consistent in his rebuke of social vice, but this was more than balanced by his active personal involvement in procuring practical remedies. Throughout his life, the winsomeness of his character was in being morally upright without ever being morose, and "though profoundly convinced of the corruption of human nature in general, he loved almost every particular human being."[5] His family life was everywhere commended, and in his letters and private papers there is rich testimony to a warmth and quality of friendship with his children for which there is no equal among notable men of the eighteenth century. In one of these letters, he writes to one of his sons:

> In short, my dear Samuel, the best preparation for being a good politician, as well as a superior man in every other line, is to be a truly religious man. For this includes in it all those qualities which fit men to pass through life with benefit to others and with reputation to ourselves. Whatever is to be the effect produced by the subordinate machinery, the main-spring must be the desire to please God, which in a Christian implies faith in Christ and a grateful sense of the mercies of God through a Redeemer, and an aspiration after increasing holiness of heart and life.[6]

Wilberforce evidently modeled these virtues himself with utmost consistency. As the *Dictionary of National Biography* puts it, "it may be safely said that there are few heroes of philanthropy whose careers will better stand an impartial investigation."[7]

The substance of *Real Christianity* involves Wilberforce's concern to extend the evangelical revival from the working class, among whom the Methodists had been so successful, to the class from which came the economic and political initiatives of the day—his own. Like William Law, Philip Doddridge, and others before him, he shows that "nominal Christianity" is utterly ineffectual as.a means for either personal or public salvation. Drawing on the resources of his own active spirituality he creates in this work a compelling invitation to repentance, spiritual renewal, and the deepening work of God's grace in his readers' hearts and lives. The following pages come from the conclusion to the book, and it seems fitting that they should provide a conclusion for this anthology of witnesses to the life of the Spirit in the age of Wesley. They may also serve, I take it, as an appropriate challenge to Christians of the present age.

## NOTES

1. A modernized edition has been prepared by James Houston, with an introduction by U.S. Senator Mark O. Hatfield, for the Classics of Faith and Devotion series (Portland: Multnomah Press, 1983).

2. John Thornton, along with his son Henry, was a key supporter of the evangelical revival through his provision of funds for the purchase of "advowsons"—the titular right to appoint parish priests—normally held from parish to parish all over England by members of the landed gentry. Among those placed in parishes through his efforts was John Newton. See Mary Seely, *The Later Evangelical Fathers: John Thornton, John Newton, William Cowper*, 2nd ed., with a preface by H. C. G. Moule, Bishop of Durham (London, 1914).

3. *Dictionary of National Biography* article on Wilberforce, p. 210.

4. Wilberforce wrote also a second book, *Appeal to the Religion, Justice and Humanity of the Inhabitants of the British Empire on Behalf of the Negro Slaves in the West Indies* (1823) which is entirely devoted to the issue of slavery.

5. *Dictionary of National Biography*, p. 216.

6. See the collection of A. M. Wilberforce, *Private Papers of William Wilberforce* (New York: Burt Franklin, 1968), p. 206.

7. See, for a further account, Oliver Warner's *William Wilberforce and His Times* (London: S. T. Batsford, 1962); also the five-volume biography by his sons, Robert, Isaac, and Samuel Wilberforce (1838).

# from A Practical View . . . of . . . Real Christianity (1797)

## I

## *Advice to Some Who Profess Their Full Assent to the Fundamental Doctrines of the Gospel*

[IN THIS BOOK] we have largely insisted on what may be termed the fundamental practical error of the bulk of professed Christians in our day—their either overlooking or misconceiving the peculiar method which the Gospel has provided for the renovation of our corrupted nature, and the attainment of every Christian grace.

But there are mistakes on the right hand and on the left, and our general proneness when we are flying from one extreme to run into an opposite error renders it necessary to add yet another admonition. The generally prevailing error of the present day, indeed, is that fundamental one which has been already pointed out [i.e., of mistaking nominal Christianity for a real experience of inward grace]. But while we are concerned in the first place with this and, on the warrant of both Scripture and experience, prescribe hearty repentance and lively faith as the only foundation of all true holiness, we must at the same time guard against a practical mistake of another kind. Those who, with penitent hearts have humbled themselves before the cross of Christ, and who, pleading his merits as their only ground of pardon and acceptance with God, have resolved henceforth through the help of his Spirit to bring forth the fruits of righteousness, are sometimes apt to conduct themselves as if they considered their work were now done—or at least as if this were everything they had to do (except, of course, when by periodically falling afresh into sin, another act of repentance and faith may seem to be necessary).

There are not a few in our relaxed age who thus satisfy themselves with what may be termed *general* Christianity, who feel *general* penitence and humiliation from a sense of their sinfulness in *general,* and *general* desires of universal holiness, but who neglect that vigilant and jealous care with which they should labor to extirpate every *particular* corruption, by studying its nature, its root, its ramifications, and thus becoming acquainted with its secret movements, with the means whereby it gains strength, and with the most effectual methods of resisting it. In like manner, they are far from striving with persevering zeal for the acquisition and improvement of every Christian grace. Nor is it unusual for ministers who preach the truths of the Gospel with fidelity, ability, and success, to be themselves also liable to the charge of dwelling altogether in their instructions on this *general* religion, instead of tracing and laying open all the secret motions of inward corruption, and instructing their hearers how best to conduct themselves in every distinct part of the Christian warfare—how best to strive against each particular vice and to cultivate each grace of the Christian character.

Hence it is that in too many persons, concerning the sincerity of whose general professions of Christian faith we should be sorry to entertain a doubt, we yet see little progress made in the ordering of their personal attitudes, in the improvement of their time, in the reform of their plan of life, or in their ability to resist the temptation to which they are particularly exposed. They will confess themselves, in general terms, to be "miserable sinners": this is a tenet of their creed and they feel even proud in proclaiming it. They will occasionally also lament particular failings. But this confession is sometimes obviously made in order to draw forth a compliment for the very opposite virtue, and where this is not the case, it is often not difficult to detect, under this false guise of contrition, a secret self-complacency arising from the demonstration they have afforded of their acuteness or candor in discovering the infirmity in question, or of their frankness or humility in acknowledging it. This will scarcely seem an ungenerous suspicion to anyone who either watches the workings of his own heart or who observes that the faults confessed in these instances are very seldom those with which the person is most clearly and strongly chargeable.

We must plainly warn such persons, and the consideration is seriously pressed on their instructors also, that they are in danger of deceiving themselves. Let them beware lest they simply be nominal Christians of another sort. These persons need to be reminded that there is no short compendious method of holiness, but that it must be the business of their whole lives to grow in grace and, continually adding one virtue to another as far as may be, "to go on towards perfection" (Hebrews 6:1). "He only that doeth righteousness is righteous" (1 John 3:7). Unless "they bring forth the fruits of the Spirit," they can have no sufficient evidence that they have received that "Spirit of Christ," "without which they are none of his" (Romans 8:9). But where, on the whole, our unwillingness to pass an unfavorable judgement may lead us to indulge a hope that "the root of the matter is found in them," yet we must at least declare to [these general Christians] that instead of adorning the doctrine of Christ, they disparage and discredit it. The world sees not their secret humiliation, nor the exercises of their closets, but it is acute in discerning practical weaknesses. And if the world observes that they have the same eagerness in the pursuit of wealth or ambition, the same vain taste for ostentation and display, the same ungoverned moods and dispositions which are found in the generality of mankind, it will treat with contempt their pretences to superior sanctity and indifference to worldly things, and merely be hardened in its prejudices against the only means which God has provided for our escaping the wrath to come and obtaining eternal happiness.

Let him then who would be *indeed* a Christian watch over his ways and over his heart with unceasing circumspection. Let him endeavor to learn both from men and books, particularly from the lives of eminent Christians,* what methods have been actually found most effectual for the conquest of every particular vice, and for improvement in every branch of holiness. Thus studying his own character and observing the most secret workings of his own mind and of our common nature, the knowledge which he will acquire of the human heart in general, and especially of his own, will be of the highest usefulness in enabling him to avoid or to guard against the occasions of evil. And it will also tend, above all things, to the growth of humility, and to the maintenance of that sobriety of spirit and tenderness of conscience which are eminently characteristic of the true Christian. It is by this unceasing diligence, as the apostle declares, that the servants of Christ must make their calling sure. Their labor will not be thrown away, for "an entrance shall" at length "be ministered unto them abundantly into the everlasting kingdom of our Lord and Saviour Jesus Christ" (2 Peter 1:11).

# II
# Advice Suggested by the State of the Times to True Christians

To THOSE who really deserve the name of true Christians, much has been said incidentally in the course of the present work. It has been maintained (and the proposition will not be disputed by any sound or experienced politician) that they are always the most important members of the com-

---

*Wilberforce has a note here citing an extensive list of books, notably Christian biographies of the sort represented by Walton's *Life of Watts*, Orton's *Life of Doddridge*, Mather's *Life of Matthew Henry*, Whitehead's *Life of Wesley*, and Richard Baxter's autobiography.

munity. But we may boldly assert that there never was a period wherein this could more justly be affirmed than in the present—whether we consider the situation, in all its circumstances, of our own country or the general state of society in Europe. Let [real Christians] for their part seriously weigh the important station which they fill, and the various duties which it now peculiarly enforces on them. If we consult the most intelligent accounts of foreign countries which have been recently published and compare them with the reports of former travellers, we must be convinced that religion and the standard of morality are everywhere declining, abroad even more rapidly than in our own country. But still, the progress of irreligion and the decay of morality at home are such as to alarm every thoughtful mind, and to portend the worst consequences, unless some remedy can be applied to the growing evil. We can depend only upon true Christians for effecting, in any degree, this important service. Their sphere of influence is that of our national Church.* In proportion, therefore, as their influence prevails, or as it increases in respect and estimation, from the manifest good conduct of its followers, in that very proportion the church is strengthened in the foundations on which alone it can be much longer supported—the esteem and attachment of its members and of the nation at large. Zeal is required in the cause of religion; they alone can feel it. The charge of eccentricity is bound to be incurred; they alone will dare to encounter it. Uniformity of conduct and perseverance in exertion will be requisite; among no others can we look for those qualities.

Let true Christians then, with becoming earnestness, strive in all things to recommend their profession, and to put to silence the vain scoffs of ignorant objectors. Let them boldly assert the cause of Christ in an age when so many who bear the name of Christians are ashamed of Him. And let them consider that the important duty of suspending for awhile the fall of their country and, perhaps, of performing a still more extensive service to society at large, may devolve upon them. [I do not mean] by busy interference in politics, in which it cannot but be confessed there is much uncertainty, but rather by that sure and radical benefit of restoring the influence of spiritual life and of raising the standard of morality.

Let [true Christians] then be active, useful, generous towards others, and manifestly moderate and self-denying in themselves. Let them be ashamed of idleness as they would be of the most acknowledged sin. When Providence blesses them with affluence, let them withdraw from the competition of vanity and, without sordidness or absurdity, show by

---

*I.e., the Church of England, whose official doctrines were quoted as foundational formulations of biblical Christianity by the Wesleys, Whitefield, Newton, and others in this period.

their modest demeanor and by their retiring from display, that (without affecting oddity) they are not slaves to fashion, and that they consider it their duty to set an example of moderation and sobriety, and to reserve for nobler and more disinterested purposes that money which others selfishly waste in parade, dress and material possessions. Let them evince, in short, a manifest moderation in all temporal things, as becomes those whose affections are set on higher objects than any which this world affords, and who possess within their own hearts a fund of satisfaction and comfort which the world tries to find in vanity and dissipation. Let them cultivate a catholic spirit of universal good will and amicable fellowship towards all those of whatever sect or denomination who, differing from them in nonessentials, agree with them in the grand fundamentals of Christian faith. Let them countenance men of real piety wherever they are found, and encourage in others every attempt to repress the progress of vice, and to revive and diffuse the influence of spirituality and virtue. Let their earnest prayers be constantly offered that such endeavors may be successful, and that the abused longsuffering of God may still extend toward us the invaluable privilege of vital Christianity.

Let true Christians pray continually for their country in this season of national difficulty. We bear upon us but too plainly the marks of a declining empire. Who can say but that the Governor of the universe, who declares Himself to be a God who hears the prayers of his servants may, in answer to their intercessions, for a while avert our ruin and continue [to extend] to us the fulness of those temporal blessings which in such abundant measure we have hitherto enjoyed.* Men of the world, who think only in terms of the natural operation of natural causes—and may only in this light acknowledge the effects of religion and morality in promoting the well-being of the community—may still, according to their humor (with a condescending smile or a sneer of supercilious contempt) read of the service which real Christians may render to their country by conciliating the favor and calling down the blessing of Providence. It may appear in their eyes merely an instance of the same superstitious weakness as that which prompts the terrified inhabitant of Sicily to bring forth the image of his tutelar saint in order to stop the destructive ravages of Ætna. We, however, are sure if we believe the Scripture, that God will be disposed to favor the nation to which his servants belong, and that, in fact, such as they have been the unknown and unhonored instruments by which were drawn down on their country the blessings of safety and prosperity.

*Wilberforce's own note here recommends the reader to "some exquisitely beautiful lines in the last book of Cowper's *Task,* wherein this sentiment is introduced."

But it would be an instance in myself of that very false shame which I have condemned in others if I were not boldly to avow my firm persuasion that to the decline of religion and morality our national difficulties must both directly and indirectly be chiefly ascribed; and that my only solid hopes for the well-being of my country depend not so much on her fleets and armies, not so much on the wisdom of her rulers, or the courage of her people, as on the persuasion that she still contains many who, in a degenerate age, love and obey the Gospel of Christ, and on the humble trust that the intercession of these may still prevail and that for the sake of these, heaven may still look upon us with an eye of favor.